INTELLIGENCE CO-OPERATION
BETWEEN
POLAND AND GREAT BRITAIN
DURING
WORLD WAR II

Vol. I:

The Report of the Anglo-Polish

Historical Committee

INTELLIGENCE CO-OPERATION
BETWEEN
POLAND AND GREAT BRITAIN
DURING
WORLD WAR II

Vol. I:
The Report of the Anglo-Polish
Historical Committee

Editors

TESSA STIRLING
DARIA NAŁĘCZ
TADEUSZ DUBICKI

Co-ordinator of the English Language version of
the Polish papers in this report
PROFESSOR JAN CIECHANOWSKI

VALLENTINE MITCHELL
LONDON • PORTLAND, OR

First published in 2005 in Great Britain by
Vallentine Mitchell
Suite 314, Premier House Station Road
Edgware, Middlesex HA8 7BJ

and in the United States of America by
VALLENTINE MITCHELL
920 NE 58th Avenue, Suite 300,
Portland, OR, 97213-3786, USA

Website: www.info@vmbooks.com

© Crown Copyright 2005

British Library Cataloguing in Publication Data

A catalogue record for this book is available from the British Library

ISBN 0-85303-656-X (cloth)

Library of Congress Cataloging-in-Publication Data

A catalog record for this book is available from the Library of Congress

Typeset in 10.5 on 11.5pt Garamond by FiSH Books, London
Printed in Great Britain by CPI, Bath

Contents

List of Illustrations

1. 'Enigma' – a German coding machine.
2. Marian Rejewski (1905–1980), a Polish cryptologist, co-author of the discovery in 1933, of the theoretical basis for the operation of 'Enigma' and a method allowing for the identification of keys to wires ciphered with the use of 'Enigma'.
3. Henryk Zygalski (1907–1978), a Polish cryptologist, co-author of the discovery, in 1933, of the theoretical basis for the operation of the 'Enigma' and a method allowing for the operation of 'Enigma'.
4. Jerzy Różycki (1909–1942), Polish cryptologist, co-author of the discovery, in 1933, of the theoretical basis for the operation of 'Enigma'.
5. London, 10 Downing Street. Left to right: Lord Halifax Secretary of State for Foreign Affairs, Polish Prime Minister W. Sikorski, Prime Minister W. Churchill, A. Zaleski Polish Foreign Minister.
6. Gen. Stewart Menzies (1890–1968), the Chief of Secret Intelligence Service SIS (1939–1952).
7. Gen. Colin Gubbins (1896–1976), Director of SOE (1943-1946).
8. Col. Harold Perkins (1905–1965), the Chief of Polish Section SOE (1941–1945).
9. Cmdr. Wilfred Dunderdale (1899–1990), 'Wilski', Head of SIS Special Liaison Control (SLC) with the II Bureau of the Polish General Staff.
10. Col. Peter Wilkinson (1914–2000), Head of South-East European SOE Sections.
11. Col. Stanisław Gano (1895–1968), the Chief of the II Bureau (Intelligence) Bureau of the Polish General Staff (1941–1946).
12. Col. Leon Mitkiewicz (1896–1972), Chief of the II Bureau of the Polish General Staff (1940–1941), Head of the Polish Mission at the Combined Chiefs of Staff in Washington.
13. Lt-Col. Leon Bortnowski (1899–1976), the Chief of the Records and Studies Department II Bureau Polish General Staff (1942–1945).

14. Lt-Col. Władysław Gaweł (1897–1978), Head of Radio-Intelligence of the Polish General Staff.
15. Col. Tadeusz Skinder (1897–1952), Deputy Chief of the II Bureau of the Polish General Staff (1943–1945).
16. Lt-Col. Jan Leśniak (1898–1976), in the years 1944–1945 – Assistant to the Chief of the II Bureau of the Polish General Staff.
17. Lt-Col. Stefan Antoni Mayer (1895–1981), Commandant of the Polish Intelligence Officers School 1941–1945.
18. Maj. Jan Henryk Żychoń (1902–1944), the Chief of the Intelligence Department of the II Bureau of the Polish General Staff (1940–1944).
19. Maj. Maksymilian Ciężki (1898–1951) – participated in the deciphering of 'Enigma'; Chief of the German Codes Department at P.C. Bruno (1939–1940), Deputy Chief of Intelligence Station '300' (1940–1943).
20. Lt-Col. Marian Romeyko (1897–1970), Chief of Polish Intelligence Station 'F' in France from January 1942 to January 1943.
21. Lt-Col. Wincenty Zarembski (1897–1966), Chief of Polish Intelligence Station F (1940–1942), Chief of Russian Section of Records and Studies Department of the Polish II Bureau (1942–1945).
22. Maj. Roman Czerniawski (1910–1985), 'Walenty', Chief of the Intelligence Station Interallié Station in France. 'Brutus' in the Double Cross System.
23. Maj. Jan Józef Graliński (1895–1942), an expert in Soviet codes, worked in the Intelligence Station 'Z' and '300' in France.
24. Maj./Lt-Col. Mieczysław Słowikowski (1896–1989), 'Rygor', Chief of Polish Intelligence Station 'Afr.' in Algiers (1941–1944).
25. Capt. Wacław Gilewicz (1902–1992), Chief of the Intelligence Station 'Płn'. ('North') in Stockholm (1940–1941).
26. Capt. Tadeusz Szefer (1896–NN), intelligence officer of the 'A' Intelligence Station in Athens (1940–1941), and of the 'T' Agency in Jerusalem (1941–1945).
27. Capt. Bronisław Eliaszewicz (1897–1958?), Chief of the Intell. Cell 'Tandara' No. 1 in Bucharest.
28. Maj. Edmund Piechowiak (born in 1896), Chief of the 'Bałk.' Intelligence Station in Istanbul from 1943.
29. Lt. Mikołaj Rostworowski (born in 1914), officer of the Intelligence Station 'M' in Madrid.
30. Maj. Mieczysław Jaworski (1897–1949), in the years 1942–1944 Chief of the Central Section of the Intelligence Department of the II Bureau of the Polish General Staff in London.
31. Lt-Col. Stanisław Kara (1893–1955), Chief of the Intelligence Station 'P' in Lisbon and a liaison officer with the Home Army (1940–1944).
32. Maj. Bolesław Ziemiański (1900–1976), Chief of the 'Tusla' Intelligence Cell No. 2 in Bucharest of '"T"' Station' (1941–1943).
33. Maj. Michał Rybikowski (1900–1991), Chief of Intelligence Station 'L' and SKN in Stockholm.
34. Lt. Stefan Ignaszak (1911–2005), 'Cichociemny' an officer of the Home Army Intelligence Service, organizer of systematic reconnaissance of

THE PRIME MINISTER

The Polish Intelligence Services made a unique contribution to Allied victory in the Second World War. This Report brings to light for the first time the true extent of that contribution. This is about a part of history that is not usually told. By its very nature, intelligence is not something that can be immediately made public. The Anglo Polish Historical Committee has had unprecedented access to British Intelligence archives. As a result of the Committee's work, large amounts of new and significant information have been uncovered. This information shows the collective determination and personal sacrifice of the Polish people to fight oppression. The wartime intelligence cooperation was extensive. It covered a wide array of activities from surveillance and counter-espionage to signals and operations.

The publication of this Joint Report, a collaborative effort by British and Polish experts, fills an important gap in the Allies' wartime history. It serves as a reminder of the Europe that we have been able to leave behind, when the United Kingdom and Poland were united in a common effort to defeat totalitarianism. It also allows us to look to our future and our common aim to work together for peace, democracy and prosperity in our continent.

This report is particularly timely on the eve of a new era in Anglo-Polish relationships, as Poland joins the European Union. Britain and Poland are old allies in the new Europe. As we look forward together to a new era in Europe, it is right that we reflect on the crucial period which these war years represent in the friendship between our countries.

Tony Blair

PREZES RADY MINISTRÓW
RZECZYPOSPOLITEJ POLSKIEJ

Current, extremely close relations between Poland and Great Britain have solid historical backing. History joined our nations together in a special way during the Second World War. On 1 September 1939, Poland was the first to stand up to Nazi aggression. Within three days' time Great Britain declared war on the Hitler's Third Reich. The Polish-British alliance functioned until the last day of the war, significantly contributing to ultimate victory.

Up till now, one of the least known pages of the common struggle against Nazism was the activity of Polish intelligence, closely working with British intelligence. Today it can be said that, without the advantage achieved by Poles and Britons on this invisible front, the struggle against Hitler's Germany would have lasted longer and claimed even more victims than it did. Wresting from the enemy his top secrets and keeping his day-to-day activities under constant surveillance dealt a painful blow to the Third Reich. It also made the more effective defence of Great Britain possible.

Those significant events are widely known neither to Poles nor Britons. It would therefore be difficult to underestimate the importance of a publication revealing some of the most secret operations of World War Two.

I wish to express my deep gratitude to the Polish-British Historical Commission, without which such a significant work could not have been published. The large-scale archival research they conducted has led to the discovery and pioneering use of numerous documents confirming the importance of Polish intelligence activities not only in Europe, but also at the remotest corners of the globe. Those efforts should be intensively continued so that no act of heroism might be forgotten. We owe that especially to the Polish ex-servicemen who in their lifetimes have had more than their share of painful experiences.

For all of us, the magnificent heritage of common Polish-British history is a commitment to draw our nations ever closer together. We can achieve more by working together, both in difficult moments, of which there is no lack in today's turbulent world, and amid the ongoing, optimism-fostering drive towards European integration.

Glossary

AAN	Archiwum Akt Nowych – Central Archives of Modern Records (Warsaw)
AG MAE	Archivo General del Ministerio de Asuntos Exteriores – General Archives of the Foreign Ministry (Madrid)
AH-D MNE	Arquivo Histórico-Diplomático do Ministério dos Negócios Éstrangeiros – Historical and Diplomatic Archives of the Foreign Ministry (Portugal)
AHN	Archivo Histórico Nacional – National Historical Archives (Madrid)
AK	Armia Krajowa – The Home Army
AMSWIA	Archiwum Ministerstwa Spraw Wewnętrznych i Administracji Archives of the Ministry of Internal Affairs and Administration
APW	Armia Polska na Zachodzie – Polish Army in the West
AS	Archives of Antonio de Oliveiry Salazar
AWIH	Archiwum Wojskowego Instytutu Historycznego – Archives of Military Historical Institute
AZHRL	Archiwum Zakładu Historii Ruchu Ludowego Archives of Peasants Movement Study Trust
CA MSW	Centralne Archiwum Ministerstwa Spraw Wewnętrznych Central Archives of the Ministry of Internal Affairs
CAW	Centralne Archiwum Wojskowe Central Military Archive (Warsaw)
CCS	Combined Chiefs of Staff
CIGS	Chief of the Imperial General Staff
COS	Chiefs of Staff (British)
CSS	Chief of the Secret Service also known as 'C'
DDG	Deputy Director General
DF	Direction Finding
DGS	Dirección General de Seguridad – Directorate General Security Service, Spain

DMI	Directorate of Military Intelligence
DOK	Dowództwo Okręgu Korpusu – Corps' District Command
EU/P	European Poles – SOE Section Poles abroad
FEA	Foreign Economic Administration (USA)
FO	Foreign Office
GC&CS	Government Code and Cipher School (Bletchley Park)
GCHQ	Government Communications Headquarters
GG	Generalne Gubernatorstwo – General-gouvernement
GS(R)	General Staff (Research)
HIA	Hoover Institute Archives
IAN/TT	Instituto dos Arquivos Nacionais/Torre do Tombo – Institute of National Archives Tombo Tower Lisbon
IH PAN	Institute of History of the Polish Academy of Sciences
IJPA	Józef Piłsudski Institute in America (New York)
IJPL	Józef Piłsudski Institute (London)
IPMS	Polish Institute and Gen. Sikorski Museum (London)
JIC	Joint Intelligence Sub-Committee of the COS
JIS	Joint Intelligence Staff
KOP	Korpus Ochrony Pogranicza – Frontier Defence Corps
MEW	Ministry of Economic Warfare
MI	Military Intelligence
MI 5	British Security Service (Formerly Section 5 of MI)
MI 6	British Secret Intelligence Service – SIS (Formerly Section 6 of MI)
MI 19	Military Intelligence Enemy P/W (Prisoners of War) Interrogation Section
MI(R)	Military Intelligence (Research)
MID (G-2)	Military Intelligence Division (USA)
MON	Polish Ministry of National Defence
MSW	Polish Ministry of Internal Affairs
NARA	National Archives and Records Administration (USA)
NID	Naval Intelligence Directorate
NKWD	'Narodnyj Kommissariat Vnutrennyth Dyel' – National Commissariat of Internal Affairs (A forerunner of the Soviet Security Service KGB)
O de B	Ordre de Bataille – Order of the Battle
OKH	Oberkommando des Heeres – High Command of the German Army (Land Forces)
OSS	Office of Strategic Services (USA)
POWN	Polska Organizacja Walki o Niepodległość – Polish Organisation on War for Independence (in France)
PRO	Public Record Office – The National Archives London
PSZ	Polskie Siły Zbrojne – Polish Armed Forces (in the West)
P&TC	Postal and Telegraphic Censorship
PVDE	Policia de Vigilância e Defesa do Estado – Portuguese Security Police
PW	Placówka Wywiadowcza – Intelligence Station

PWB	Psychological Warfare Branch (Anglo-American)
RGWA	'Rossijskij Gosudarstweiennyj Wojennyj Arkhiv' – Russian National Military Archives Moscow
RSS	Radio Security Service
Schupo	Schutzpolitzei – German Protection Police
SIGINT	Signals Intelligence (general term for interception, & decryption)
SIM	Servicio de Informacion Militar – Military Information Service Spain
SIS	Secret Intelligence Service (later MI 6)
SLC	Special Liaison Control (SIS code for French and Polish intelligence liaison headed by Wilfred Dunderdale)
SO2	Special Operations (later SOE)
SOE	Special Operations Executive
SPP	Studium Polski Podziemnej – Polish Underground Movement Study Trust (London)
SWS	Special Wireless Section
SZP	Służba Zwycięstwu Polski – Service for the Victory of Poland
TNA	The National Archives, London (Formerly, until 2003 PRO)
WIH	Wojskowy Instytut Historyczny – Institute of Military History
WO	War Office
WOPD	Wojskowa Organizacja Propagandy Dywersyjnej – Military Organisation for Diversionary Propaganda
Y service	The interception, analysis and decryption of radio traffic
ZPP	Związek Patriotów Polskich – The Union of Polish Patriots (communists)
ZWZ	Związek Walki Zbrojnej – Union of Armed Struggle

Preface
Genesis of the Committee

Tessa Stirling and Daria Nałęcz

The origin of the Anglo-Polish Historical Committee goes back to an exchange of letters in October and November 1999 between the then Polish Prime Minister, Jerzy Buzek, and the British Prime Minister, Tony Blair. This initiative was greatly welcomed by Polish scholars and veterans who had long hoped that access to the historical sources would enable the preparation of an authoritative and accurate history of the extensive links between the Poles and the British during the Second World War. Prime Minister Buzek pointed out that the close co-operation between the British and the Poles during the Second World War was an important reason why the British enjoyed 'deep respect and sympathy among Poles'.[1] He said that for Poland, the wartime experiences still provided a point of reference and signalled the way towards a free and democratic Europe and he asked for Britain's help in furthering the process of searching for new sources and relevant historical materials. He also pointed to the fact that the Polish resistance movement (the Home Army), through the mediation of the London Headquarters of the Commander-in-Chief, had delivered extremely valuable intelligence reports to the British intelligence service, as well as the deposited archives of the II Bureau; and he asked for assistance in locating these archives.

Prime Minister Tony Blair responded[2] by acknowledging the importance of British-Polish World War II co-operation saying that 'Every Briton remembers with great admiration the Polish contribution to the fight against Nazi oppression, and the strength and resilience of the Polish people during the war years and thereafter'. Prime Minister Tony Blair pledged support in helping to locate surviving records but acknowledged, with regret, that a large number of Polish records were destroyed after the war. This positive exchange of correspondence led directly to the setting up of the Anglo-Polish Historical Committee.

---

1 Polish Prime Minister Jerzy Buzek's letter of 18 October 1999 to Tony Blair.
2 British Prime Minister Tony Blair's letter of 17 November 1999 to Jerzy Buzek.

Anglo-Polish Historical Committee: Membership and Terms of Reference

Tessa Stirling and Daria Nałęcz

The Committee held its inaugural meeting in the Cabinet Office in London on 19 June 2000. The terms of reference[3] as agreed by the Committee at that meeting were as follows:

> To direct and oversee the programme of work of the British and Polish groups of the Anglo-Polish Historical Steering Committee. To identify and evaluate surviving documents illustrating the importance of the contribution of Polish intelligence to the outcome of the Second World War.

The membership of the Committee comprised:

Mrs Tessa Stirling	Joint Chairman
Professor Daria Nałęcz	Joint Chairman
Mr Jan Nowak-Jeziorański	Honorary Chairman
Professor Jan Ciechanowski	Vice-Chairman
Mr Richard Ponman	Secretary
Miss Sally Falk	Secretary
Mr Jan Stanisław Ciechanowski	Secretary
Mrs Heather Yasamee	
Mrs Gill Bennett	
Miss Alison Kerr	
Professor Andrzej Bartnicki	
Dr Andrzej Chmielarz	
Mr Adam Dąbrowski	
Mrs Eugenia Maresch	
Mr Andrzej Przewoźnik	
Dr Andrzej Suchcitz	
Professor Christopher Andrew	
Dr Joanna Hanson	
Mr Bruce Bucknell	

---

3 The terms of reference were agreeed at the 1st meeting of the Committee on 19 June 2000.

The full Committee met on five occasions, three times in London, twice in Warsaw, in the two year period from June 2000. In addition there were numerous informal meetings of sub-committees as well as bilateral planning meetings in London and in Warsaw between the co-Chairmen. Each of the meetings was important in planning and driving forward the work of the committee, and in building good collegiate relationships. However, it was the vast amount of work by Committee members outside of the formal meetings that has formed the basis of this report.

In addition to each of the Committee members, we would like to express our particularly heartfelt thanks to Professor Andrzej Pepłoński, Professor Tadeusz Dubicki, Dr Rafał Wnuk and Dr Jacek Krochmal for their active support of the Committee and their involvement as authors in the preparation of the joint publication.

Methodology

Tessa Stirling and Daria Nałęcz

It was agreed from the outset that the Polish members of the Committee would concentrate on finding information from publicly available sources in the UK and Poland as well as in other countries, notably the USA. The UK members of the Committee would focus on researching the closed archives of British Intelligence agencies.

Historians on the Polish side therefore spent their time combing though publicly available archives to find as much source material from wartime Polish intelligence operatives and any other relevant sources that would add to the existing weight of evidence, to illustrate the contribution of Polish intelligence to the war effort. In so doing, the Polish Committee members discovered numerous unknown and previously unused documents. In the Public Record Office in London (now The National Archives) and National Archives and Records Administration at College Park near Washington, DV (NARA), and in other publicly available archives, Polish Committee members found a large number of relevant papers. This information has informed the chapters in this report prepared by the Polish side of the Committee.

The contribution of the UK side of the committee had a different but complementary focus in that they were exceptionally granted access to the closed archives of the British Secret Intelligence Service through Gill Bennett, the Chief Historian of the Foreign Office. This was a particularly valuable concession to the Committee, and a recognition of the importance of the Committee's work, as none of the records of the Secret Intelligence Service has ever been open to the public either within or outside of Britain. This gave the Committee the substantial benefit of a unique insight of the Polish intelligence contribution from the British Secret Intelligence Service's viewpoint.

The Shape and Structure of the Report

Tessa Stirling and Daria Nałęcz

The report consists of a Preface, Introduction, Historical Background and eight main headings, within which there are 59 separate papers. Together these cover the most important aspects of the Polish intelligence activity during the Second World War. The Committee had to be selective and, inevitably, had to omit some material. Under each heading there are papers by Polish historians and most also have a contribution by a UK historian. We have not attempted to exercise close editorial control over individual chapters. The historians concerned have produced papers based on the sources available to them and have reached their own conclusions and presented their findings in their own way. This is the reason why each paper is accompanied by the name and surname of the given author.

Acknowledgements

Tessa Stirling and Daria Nałęcz

As the Joint Chairmen of the Committee, we wish to express our sincere gratitude to all those who worked so hard on the preparation of this report, in particular, to each of the Committee members. Furthermore, we would like to express our great appreciation to all those who provided assistance and support during the implementation of the project, in particular, to our Prime Ministers Mr Tony Blair and Mr Jerzy Buzek, and to Mr Leszek Miller who supported the final stage of the Committee; to the Ministers of Foreign Affairs, to Mr Robin Cook, Mr Jack Straw, Mr Bronisław Geremek, Mr Władysław Bartoszewski and Mr Włodzimierz Cimoszewicz, who, in the course of mutual discussions, were repeatedly raising issues related to the work of the Committee; to our two Ambassadors – in Warsaw and in London – the Honourable Sir Michael Pakenham, HM Ambassador to Poland and Dr Stanisław Komorowski, Ambassador of the Republic of Poland to the United Kingdom, who expressed constant interest in the work of the Committee and supported its activities, participating in meetings and providing lots of valuable advice and information. They also extended great hospitality to the Committee on the occasions of meetings in London and in Warsaw. We also wish to thank our colleagues from the British National Archives for allowing free access to their files; the Polish Institute and General Sikorski Museum; the Polish Underground Movement Study Trust (1939–1945) in London; the National Archives and Records Administration in Washington at College Park near Washington; the Archive of Modern Records (Archiwum Akt Nowych); the Central Military Archive (Centralne Archiwum Wojskowe); and Józef Piłsudski Institute in London and New York for their help in making documents available to the Committee members. We also wish to express our warm appreciation to Mr Christopher R. Hill, US Ambassador to Poland, the Fulbright Foundation and the authorities of the National Archives and Records Administration at College Park near Washington for granting scholarships and providing assistance in conducting research on extensive American archives.

We wish to acknowledge the State Committee for Scientific Research, the Prime Minister's Office, the Office of the Sejm of the Republic of Poland, and the Ministry of Foreign Affairs for financing of archival queries and the allocation of funds allowing us to publish the report.

The chapters written by Polish authors have been translated by Ms Aleksandra Rodzińska-Chojnowska, Mr Krzysztof Pszenicki and Mr Zbigniew Szlęk and are reproduced here with the permission of the Head Office of State Archives, Poland. The chapters written by British authors are either Crown copyright or have been reproduced here with permission.

Photographs included in the book are in the custody of the Archives of Audio Visual Records (photographs No. 1–4, 27, 31, 34–35, 38, The Central Military Archive in Warsaw (photographs No. 16–19, 23, 25–26, 29–30, 32–33, 37) The Polish Institute and Sikorski Museum (photographs No. 5, 11–14, 20–22, 28, 36) and private collectors (photographs No. 6–10, 15, 24, 39).

This report is the outcome of much hard work by many individuals. Despite its significant size, it should be regarded not as the completion of the work on explaining the complexity of this important period of history but as providing an opportunity for others to continue studies in this area. Indeed, it is our fervent hope that this publication, which so rightly recognises the role played by many courageous and heroic Poles, who put their lives at risk to gather the intelligence information of such vital importance to Great Britain and her Allies, will inspire others to take forward further research.

INTRODUCTION

1
Existing Archival Sources

Daria Nałęcz

During the search for sources stretching over two years, the archival material in Polish, British and American archives was thoroughly examined. Additional searches were conducted in selected Russian, Spanish and Portuguese archives. For the purpose of this report, but also with future research in mind, some 7 thousand copies of documents were taken. These will be deposited in the Archiwum Akt Nowych/Central Archives of Modern Records, further 'AAN', thus enriching the Polish collections.

As far as any description of the activities of Polish intelligence during World War II is concerned, the basic material available at AAN consists of documents created by ZWZ–AK (the Union of Armed Struggle – the Home Army) in the 1939–1945 period. Among the preserved 20 shelf-metres of material, there are documents of the central intelligence network, working directly to its General Headquarters (further 'GHQ'), of intelligence structures of districts and documents of the Research Bureau of the II Bureau (Intelligence) of ZWZ–AK (the Union of Armed Struggle – the Home Army – further as the Home Army) General Headquarters. These consist of reports from the years 1940–1944, analyses and statements of both military and economic intelligence. Some are still accompanied by their appendices, such as drawings, maps or photographs. A large proportion of these documents did not survive. In addition there are various studies, specifications, memoranda, registers and descriptions of industrial plants, the majority prepared for the Records and Studies Department of the II Bureau of the Home Army GHQ. Interestingly, these are complemented by factory plans, technical drawings or photographs of production lines, machines and their parts. Where original documents are missing, on the basis of existing files of agents operating in the Generalgouvernement (GG) and in the Third Reich, it is possible to recreate their working methods and the results achieved. An analysis of financial accounts allows the recreation of organizational structures of intelligence.

These archives are supplemented by 13 volumes with copies of coded messages and correspondence, reports identifying German units, periodic and monthly reports for the period from June 1941 to November 1943.

While the Anglo-Polish Historical Committee was already at work, the AAN archives were enriched by extremely valuable material, which so far had been in private hands. It would be difficult to exaggerate the value of the generous gift of Mrs Hanna Mickiewicz, widow of Adam Mickiewicz, the Chief of the Industrial Research Bureau of the II Bureau of the Home Army GHQ.

This is a complete set of monthly reports of industrial intelligence from October 1941 to June 1944. This set is complemented by material found during building works in Warsaw, (conducted by Irena Eris's Cosmetic Laboratory). In seven glass containers buried in the earth there were typescripts of monthly reports for the period December 1943 to July 1944, as well as the special report no. 1/R of 12 July 1944 concerning the V-2. Valuable archives left by Wincenty Jordan-Rozwadowski, 'Pascal', one of the heads of the F2 intelligence network in France, were donated by his son, Franciszek.

The Home Army GHQ documents are also held by the Wojskowy Instytut Historyczny (Institute of Military History – further 'WIH'). Their collection includes a set of radio reports exchanged between Warsaw and London in the period 1940–1944. These include the British periodical assessments and also intelligence tasks and guidelines. In the 100 folders concerning the Second Bureau there are radio reports for January to July 1944, instructions and intelligence questionnaires, periodic and one-off intelligence assessments and financial accounts. Much valuable information is contained in the written deposition of Tadeusz Nowiński, Marian Rejewski, Tadeusz Szumowski and Marian Utnik.

Among the material held at the Central Military Archive important documents include primarily the folders of the VI Bureau of the Polish General Staff (further PGS), taken from London by Gen. Stanisław Tatar and Col. Marian Utnik. The internal organizational documents and reports are of crucial importance. The 194 folders of decoded reports and radio messages are also important. Among the partially preserved documents of the II Bureau there are, among others, the directives of the Chief of Staff of the PGS, internal orders, organizational reports from June 1944, tasks for individual stations, notes on conversations with the British (Cmdr. W. Dunderdale, Maj-Gen. S. Menzies) and with the Americans, W. Donovan.

In 2000 the Institute of National Remembrance became the depository of the archives so far held by the State Protection Office. These are dominated by the documents originating with the Ministry of Public Security, pertaining mainly to the personnel of intelligence and other services subordinated to the government-in-exile, and include lists of staff and associates of the II and VI Bureaux of the PGS.

Other relevant archives include the Ossoliński National Collection in Wrocław, where some of the papers left by Gen. Kazimierz Sosnkowski are to be found and the Archive of the History of the Peasants Movement, with its papers left by Stanisław Kot.

Polish archives outside Poland also hold documents originating with the government-in-exile and its structures. The largest collection is to be found in London, at the Polish Institute and Sikorski Museum (IPMS) the Polish Underground Movement Study Trust (Studium Polski Podziemnej (SPP)) and the Józef Piłsudski Institute in London.

The Polish Institute and Sikorski Museum holds a set of files from the II Bureau of the PGS reports, sets of reports passed on to the Allies, personnel lists, studies, analyses and information, notes from staff meetings, organizational and training materials, papers of military attachés and numerous personal papers, including those of Col. Wincenty Bąkiewicz, Col. Jan Leśniak, Col. Leon Mitkiewicz, Lt-Col. Władysław Gaweł, Col. Michał Protasewicz, Navy Capt. Brunon Jabłoński, Maj. Wacław Gilewicz. The Institute also holds the archives of Station F2, active in France. Many documents confirm the direct and close contacts with British military intelligence. A large part of the correspondence consists of replies to questions, tasks and requirements of the British side and of additional explanations. There are also the incomplete documents concerning the conversations between the Commander-in-Chief and the representatives of other Allied staffs for 1940–1943, for example on the subject of the 'Bardsea-Monika Plan', Continental Action in Europe, some sabotage and intelligence operations of the Special Department of the Polish Ministry of National Defence, conducted in response to a request by the British side. The Institute also has some documents on the running of the Polish Section of SOE and on the organization of intelligence networks, courier routes and radio intelligence.

As for the Polish Underground Movement Study Trust, this contains primarily the files of the VI Bureau of the PGS and its correspondence with the II Bureau, instructions and guidelines for the the Home Army GHQ and materials sent from Poland to London. Of significant value, and unique in Polish archives, are the original British assessments of reports obtained from Polish intelligence in 1943-1945. Some reports or abbreviated reports sent from Poland survive. A major part of this collection, too, consists of correspondence with the British authorities. Of special importance are the documents left by Gen. Tadeusz Pełczyński, Col. Kazimierz Iranek-Osmecki and Lt-Col. Narcyz Giedronowicz.

The Józef Piłsudski Institute in London holds the papers of Col. Stefan Mayer, Col. Gwidon Langer and Col. Maksymilian Ciężki.

Valuable collections are also to be found in institutions and archives in New York: the Józef Piłsudski Institute and the Polski Instytut Naukowy/The Polish Institute of Arts & Sciences of America.

The first holds the best-preserved documentation of a field station, and one operating on the largest territory, of both Americas. The 'Estezet' files were hidden, saved and later passed on to the Institute by its last chief, Maj. Marian S. Chodacki. This set of documents contains both internal correspondence and that with the Allies and also assessments of field reports, the reports themselves, information on the internal structure of the station and on its personnel. Most of the documents date from the period from mid-1943 to mid-1945.

In addition the Institute has the papers of Witold Langenfeld, who was Deputy Chief and later Chief of the Intelligence Department in the II Bureau of the PGS; the papers of Jan Librach, who directed the Central Bureau of the Continental Action, and the 'Archives of Gen. K.Sosnkowski'.

The Polish Institute of Arts & Sciences of America has some papers of Col. Leon Śliwiński, one of the commanders of intelligence Station F2 in France and those of Maj. Zygmunt Tebinka, who exchanged numerous letters with a person active in the Continental Action in Italy.

Our researches in foreign archives were concentrated mainly on looking for documents testifying to the groundwork, directions, principles, scope and results of Polish intelligence co-operation with Allied intelligence services. Attempts were made to find Allied assessments of the results of work undertaken by Polish intelligence.

Research lasting many months was undertaken primarily in the British Public Record Office (now The National Archives). We were searching for documents illustrating the political side of Polish-British co-operation – which concentrated our attention on the archives of the Foreign Office, the Cabinet Office and those of Prime Minister Winston Churchill himself – and on the proofs of intelligence co-operation. Most surviving documents are to be found in the Special Operations Executive (SOE) files, especially in the files marked HS 4, covering Eastern Europe and the USSR. This is where the documents of the Polish Section of SOE are to be found, as well as documents on the co-operation between SOE and the VI Bureau. The existing documents concerning Polish activity relate to its full scope: in addition to the Polish territory, the Third Reich and the USSR, they cover the Baltic states, France, Italy, Switzerland, North Africa, the Balkan and Iberian Peninsulas and the Middle East. The files marked HS 4/326 reveal the secret agreement on the financing of the Polish intelligence by the British government, dated 19th November 1940. Files marked HS 4/177 contain the agreement on co-operation between the PGS and SOE in radio monitoring. The same set of files holds many reports, intelligence data and assessments of Polish intelligence, especially for the period 1944–1945. Among intelligence reports attention is drawn to information on V-2 rockets, on German preparations for their attack on the USSR and later information on the situation at the Eastern Front and at its rear, reports from concentration camps, stalags, oflags and places of forced labour, and intelligence on the outcomes of Allied bombing of German cities and factories. Information was also found on the fate of Polish reports after 1946 and on the closure of the Polish Section of SOE.

Much interesting information is to be found in other parts of the SOE archive: HS 3, HS 7 especially on the V-2 rockets, HS 8 which includes Peter A. Wilkinson's report to the head of SIS on the successes of Polish intelligence, dated 30th July 1942.

The HW set, among the papers of the Government Code and Cypher School of Bletchley Park, contains documents on the work of Polish cryptographers on Enigma, as well as material on the Polish radio communication and intelligence services in Stanmore. Some documents on radio intelligence were found in the archives of the War Office.

The most significant expectations of finding documents not hitherto utilized in research were invested in the searches carried out by Gill Bennett among the Secret Intelligence Service archives. The material made available to her became the source for the British part of the joint publication. It would therefore be difficult to accept the thesis that such documents have not survived. Without them any academic exploration would not have been possible. Moreover some of the documents which have been made available, as for example the final report of Cmdr. Dunderdale, were not known about beforehand. But the general state of archive preservation, and in particular the absence of the material passed to the British side by the Polish General Staff in 1945 and 1946 which is discussed in more detail by J. Ciechanowski and A. Suchcitz creates a feeling of insufficiency. Attempts to find the Polish-British agreement on intelligence co-operation also failed.

From this perspective the collections of the National Archives and Records Administration (NARA), researched by Polish historians thanks to grants from the Fulbright Foundation, proved surprisingly rewarding. The American archives proved to be a veritable Aladdin's cave. It would appear that the Americans preserved all, or almost all, of the war reports obtained from outside sources, as well as their own, both in summary form and those containing assessments. The value of these documents rests not only on the fact that they permit an assessment of the Polish-American co-operation. But, since Polish intelligence was simultaneously circulating its reports to both Allies, we may assume, with high probability, that many – though certainly not all – such reports which did not survive in the British archives, can be located in NARA. They were, however, subject to a different valuation and there might have been a different intent concerning their usage. In the light of existing sources it is permissible to maintain that for the Americans Polish intelligence was the most significant partner, in terms of both quality and quantity of reports obtained.

The materials of interest here are kept in two archival units: Records of the Office of Strategic Services (OSS) and Records of the War Department General and Special Staffs (WDGSS) Military Intelligence Division (MID). Within the latter a separate sub-unit, entitled Regional Files, was created, consisting of some 3335 boxes. These contain intelligence-type material divided by geographical criteria: by country name in relation to Europe, Latin America and partially Asia – and by the name of the region for the rest of the world as for example 'Far East'. These reports were usually labelled as 'Polish Intelligence', 'Government-in-Exile', 'Polish Source'. In length, they varied from one to 200 pages. Such reports were regularly passed on to the Americans following the meeting of the heads of the two intelligence agencies, which took place on 30th March 1942 in Washington.

Outside NARA an interesting collection is to be found at the Hoover

Institution on War, Revolution and Peace Archives in Stanford, California, where among numerous Polish archival documents two sets of papers important to any research into intelligence activities can be found: those of Col. Leon Mitkiewicz, which include reports from his time as Chief of the II Bureau and of the head of the intelligence Station 'Rygor', Gen. Mieczysław Słowikowski. Due to the kindness of the management of the Hoover Institution, members of the Commission received copies of these papers.

In Portugal research was carried out at the Instituto dos Arquivos Nacionais/Torre do Tombo in Lisbon, with special attention paid to the papers of the Portuguese dictator António de Oliveira Salazar – the so-called Arquivo Salazar. A part of it, namely the archives of the PIDE political police, has been placed fully in the public domain. Searches were also conducted of the materials of the Arquivo Histórico-Diplomático do Ministério dos Negócios Éstrangeiros. In Spain attention was concentrated on the Archivo General del Ministerio de Asuntos Exteriores and Archivo Histórico Nacional in Madrid. There, in the set number 1222, traces were found concerning the Spanish counter-intelligence activities and the German intelligence efforts directed against Polish intelligence endeavours.

Interesting material was also discovered in the Russian State Military Archives, which took over the collections of the former so-called Special Archive, itself created on the basis of documents 'liberated' during World War II. There, in unit number 308, are some files of the 'East' Section of the II Bureau of the PGS, including some personnel files of officers working in that section.

The survey of available sources demonstrates that in spite of numerous major upheavals a part of the archives documenting the war effort of Polish intelligence agencies and their co-operation with Allied intelligence services survived – and what survived may be sufficient for academic study. Thousands of pages of photocopies of original documents, collected by members of the Committee, will facilitate further research, though the need to trawl through documents dispersed around the world will not be fully eliminated. It is hoped that further study may be made easier thanks to the selection of what are in our opinion, the most important source documents which will be presented in the 2nd volume of this Polish-British publication.

2
Note on sources for the UK contribution to the Report of the Anglo-Polish Historical Committee

Gill Bennett

As agreed when the Anglo-Polish Historical Committee was established in June 2000, the UK contribution to the Report is based almost entirely on Intelligence-related records that are not in the public domain or available to external researchers. Research has been carried out for the Committee in the archives of the three principal British Intelligence bodies: the Security Service (MI5), Government Communications Headquarters (GCHQ) and the Secret Intelligence Service (SIS, often referred to as MI6). The main source for the Report is SIS records, since SIS, as the agency concerned with foreign intelligence, was most closely involved with the wartime Polish Intelligence services. The majority of relevant records originating in the Security Service and GCHQ are already in the public domain, but where they are not they have been included in the research.

The records of the Secret Intelligence Service are not released to The National Archives (TNA). This policy was endorsed in February 1998 by the then Foreign Secretary, Robin Cook, who told the House of Commons that he recognised the overwhelmingly strong reasons for continued secrecy, adding that when individuals or organizations co-operate with SIS they do so because an unshakeable commitment is given never to reveal their identities.[1] This essential trust would be undermined by a perception that undertakings of confidentiality were honoured for a limited duration: in many cases, the risk of retribution against individuals can extend beyond a single generation. Since SIS records remain closed, no file references have been given in the text of the Report.

The UK side of the Anglo-Polish Historical Committee has, exceptionally, had full and unrestricted access to SIS records through the Chief Historian of the Foreign and Commonwealth Office. Only a small amount of wartime documentation remains in the SIS archive, and it contains very few reports received from SIS stations overseas or from

---

1 Hansard, *Official Report* (12 February 1998), col. 324.

Allied Intelligence Services. Where these have survived, they are on scattered and often unrelated files. There is no extant body of wartime reports from any particular source, including Polish Intelligence. A thorough search has been made of the archive to try and trace material from or referring to Polish sources. The material contained in the UK contribution to the Report is based on the results of that search.

During the Second World War, it was imperative that information received by SIS reached, as quickly as possible, those departments who could make the best and most timely use of it. On receipt, reports were translated if necessary, stripped of identifying marks to mask their origin, and sent immediately to customers in other departments such as the War Office, Foreign Office and Ministry of Economic Warfare. The originals, their value exploited, were usually destroyed, either during or shortly after the war. SIS was merely a collection agency, and information received by them was never intended for permanent preservation. Such information consisted of secret documents acquired by secret means that should only be known to SIS itself.

Although SIS does not release its own records, some of its wartime material has been transferred to TNA on the files of other government departments, including the files of the Security Service and GCHQ, both of whom have been systematically transferring their wartime holdings to TNA. Intelligence information from SIS was circulated under a 'CX' number or from a 'CX' source, and 'CX' material from Polish liaison was circulated bearing the symbol 'JX'. Although these designations would normally have been deleted from documents in the Public Record Office, researchers for the Polish side of the Anglo-Polish Historical Committee have been successful in finding some SIS material relating to Poland's wartime Intelligence contribution in this way. In some instances this has enabled the UK side of the Committee to track down references in the closed archives.

3
Polish II Bureau Documents Passed to the British Government after 1945

Tessa Stirling

One topic that has been of importance to the Committee from its inception is the fate of the records of the Polish II Bureau which, according to Polish documentary sources, were handed to the British Government's Secret Intelligence Service at the end of the Second World War.

A distinction has to be made between intelligence traffic that was continually being received by the British Secret Intelligence Service from many sources, including Poland, and the 'collection' of intelligence documents that were handed over to the British after July 1945. In the case of the former, the British Secret Intelligence Service acted as a 'post box' when handling the continual intelligence traffic. Once they had ensured that it had been transmitted on to those who needed to receive and, where appropriate, act upon the information, they did not retain this material. The originals from whatever source were destroyed once they had been used. This was the normal practice, and was not confined to Polish intelligence input.

The collection of Polish II Bureau documents that was handed over to the British Secret Intelligence Service after July 1945 was in a different category. These documents were passed to the Secret Intelligence Service for their safekeeping; possibly to avoid the identities of Polish agents being compromised. Polish documentary evidence indicates that the Poles handed over a collection of documents to Cmdr. Dunderdale, their liaison contact with the Secret Intelligence Service, in July 1945. There is also a reference in a minute of 2 March 1946 to the handling of the II Bureau's archive. This referred to a liquidation committee that was to put in order the archives of the II Bureau and to deposit documents with the British authorities.

Since the establishment of the Anglo-Polish Historical Committee in June 2000, British officials have attempted to find these documents, or some indication as to their fate. They have had unprecedented access to intelligence archives, including those of the Secret Intelligence Service.

Despite extensive searches of the Secret Intelligence Service and other intelligence archives, unfortunately no collections of material from the Polish II Bureau dating from the Second World War have been found. Moreover, despite the exhaustive searches of official British archives, no conclusive documentary proof of the destruction of Polish intelligence material has been found. It is, therefore, impossible to be certain at what date destruction may have occurred.

It is possible that documents were destroyed in the late 1940s at a time when large amounts of exploited wartime documentation were disposed of as being of no further use. It is also possible that II Bureau material may have been destroyed during the 1950s when the final remnants of Special Liaison Control (SLC), the section of the Secret Intelligence Service that handled liaison with Polish Intelligence, were being wound up. A letter of 23 May 1959 from the then Special Operations Executive Adviser, Lt-Col. Edward G. Boxshall, to Colonel Iranek-Osmecki of the Polish Liquidation Commission stated that enquiries had been made with Cmdr. Dunderdale, head of SLC. Dunderdale had confirmed that 'all material emanating from the Polish Home Army during the years 1943 and 1944' had been destroyed. Although this letter does not refer to the II Bureau documents (the Home Army had been dealt with by the VI Bureau of Polish Intelligence), the context suggests that *all* material for those years, and indeed for the wider wartime period, had been destroyed.

Administrative correspondence from the late 1950s relating to the winding up of SLC makes no specific mention of the II Bureau documents. There are, however, a number of references to the destruction of SLC's archival material. Minutes dating from May 1957 refer to the running down of SLC and the 'disposal' of all its files. A minute of April 1959 states that Dunderdale was now 'fully embarked on the destruction of his section records'. In June 1959 a minute stated that 'all other papers that still remain may be destroyed'. If any Polish material had survived the post-war destruction programme, it is unlikely to have survived the liquidation of SLC.

The UK side of the Anglo-Polish Historical Committee have, against this background, concluded that the records must, regrettably, have been destroyed. Nor have they found any records or destruction certificates which would clarify what happened to the particular records of the II Bureau. Despite an exhaustive search no such material has been found in the Secret Intelligence Service archives. If any new material about the possible fate of the records should emerge in the future, it will be handed over to the Polish Government.

4

The History of the Polish Intelligence Archives after 1945

Andrzej Suchcitz and Jan Ciechanowski

For almost half a century, the fate of the archive of Polish Intelligence, primarily of the Second Bureau, Polish General Staff, was subject to various conjectures and speculation. Historians specializing in this period were proposing general and unproven statements concerning what happened to this body of documents.

The information available on this subject was put together as late as the end of 1980s.[1] This in turn allowed for more specific research to be undertaken in the search for the missing part of the archives – and finally led to the establishment of the joint Polish-British Historical Committee, with the aim of determining the influence of Polish Intelligence in the victory over the Third Reich in the Second World War. One of the principal objectives of the Committee was to ascertain the fate of that part of II Bureau material, which was passed over to the British authorities during the war, and of the archives deposited with them for safe keeping in 1945–1946.

The commonly held view that the archives of Polish Intelligence were completely destroyed, and consequently that none are to be found in Polish hands, has been proved wrong. A careful trawl through the collections of various Polish institutions, in Poland and abroad, for example in the Central Archives of Modern Records, the Central Military Archive, the Archive of Polish Resistance, the Institute of National Remembrance, the Archive of the Ministry of Internal Affairs and Administration – all in Warsaw – as well as in the Polish Institute and Sikorski Museum, the Polish Underground Movement Study Trust in London, and the Piłsudski Institute in London and New York, established that a significant part of the documents and reports of Polish Intelligence had survived. All material in those Polish institutions is available to researchers without restriction, unlike the documents of the British special services, especially those of the Secret Intelligence Service, also known as MI6. On the other hand a mystery continues to surround the fate of those documents and reports of II Bureau, PGS, which were passed over to SIS during the war and soon after its conclusion. In addition to the many thousands of radio, courier and periodic reports, these materials, often of historic importance, for example the Polish-British intelligence co-operation agreement of September/October 1940, Polish earlier reports on Hitler's new weapons, on the movements of the German army, on U-boats, the production of tanks and airplanes or the results of bombing raids, also contained the records of II Bureau agents, a special library of unique books on intelligence and the archives of Section 'R' – for Russia – which was active in Great Britain in 1940-1945.

For the so-called 'silent service', the approaching end of the war was especially dangerous. By 1944 it was already clear that the dreamt-of peace would not restore independence to Poland. For Poland, the cessation of hostilities meant a substitution of one occupation for another, a Soviet, one. There was no hope of any support from the Western allies, since they themselves agreed to hand over Central and Eastern Europe to Soviet domination. The decision on this was already made in Teheran, in November of 1943. The chiefs of the II Bureau, PGS, had good reason to fear for the future and, in particular, for their archives. In the first instance they had to do everything in their power to prevent the new authorities in Warsaw from obtaining access to these materials, as this would have led to the complete unmasking of the Bureau and its agents. On the other hand, due to the character of their work and the principles governing it, they were reluctant to hand over their archives into the care of one of the emerging Polish émigré institutions in the West. They also doubted whether the Polish State authorities in London would look after the collection with due care. In any case the archives were large, referring as they did to the five and a half years' of the war. Their sheer volume as well as their security became a problem.

As it turned out, the fears of II Bureau Chiefs proved largely unfounded: the vast majority of the archives of both the Polish Government-in-Exile and of PGS remained safe in the care of Polish institutions (IPMS – Polish Institute and Sikorski Museum and SPP – The Polish Underground Movement Study Trust) in London. Half the archive of the VI Bureau, PGS, had survived.

In the hot days of early summer of 1945, the chiefs of the II Bureau had to take a decision on the future of their archives, which contained extremely important historical material testifying to the significant impact of Polish Intelligence on the allied victory in World War II. Available sources indicate that a preliminary selection was made, with the purpose of safekeeping the documents of most historical importance – as well as of material, which could be useful in future operations.[2] A significant proportion of the remainder – though we still do not know how many and what categories of material – was to be burnt. According to the later testimony of Lt-Col. Leon Bortnowski, then Deputy Chief of the II Bureau, on the fate of its personal files, he 'had no idea what (at the time) happened to such documents. I had nothing to do with this issue. I suspect that the Personnel Bureau of PGS, as indeed all the units

quartered in St. Paul's School [in West London, in Hammersmith, where
the PGS was located in 1945] committed an auto-da-fé: their archives
were burnt completely'.[3] Following the recognition of the government in
Warsaw by the British there was panic at PGS, caused by the fear that
the British would order the Poles to transfer everything to the Warsaw
embassy in London. 'Huge bonfires were raging in the school courtyard
and the wind would blow the ashes all over Hammersmith. There were
protests by the locals. The point was that there was nowhere to locate
the archives, with the exception of the private accommodation of the
officers. We – in the II Bureau – were in a better position, as Dunderdale
had an office with cellars, and agreed to take in several truckloads
containing iron chests. Later his office was moved from place to place
and consequently we never saw our archives again [...]'.[4] The
information concerning the burning was also confirmed by (Navy) Lt.
Leon Śliwiński, the former Chief of II Bureau's Station 'F 2' in France. He
added that 'the archives were mainly of secondary importance' and they
were burnt not in the schoolyard, as was the case with other material,
but in its furnaces.[5]

The decision to destroy a large part of the archives is supported by a
contemporary document, which also illustrates the attitudes prevailing at
the time. The letter-instruction to Maj. Stanisław Paprocki of the Liaison
Office of the II Bureau was written by Lt-Col. Bortnowski on 6th July 1945
– that is, on the day the Warsaw government was recognised by the British:

Following your departure to Scotland with your team, certain
developments took place which oblige us to provide you with new
instructions as to the selection criteria with regard to our archives.

1   The documents which earlier had been considered as valuable and
    were to be kept in the Archives in Scotland – are now to be taken
    to London and deposited in the agreed place under special
    protection.

2   Everything else is to be burnt immediately and in situ. This applies
    without exception and in particular to all the documents pertaining
    to:
    • information on the USSR
    • co-operation with the British, Americans, etc.
    • personnel records, accounts, etc.

3   This work is to be carried out as soon as possible, sacrificing
    accuracy if necessary. The point here is not to be overtaken by
    events, which are developing faster than we anticipated. There will
    be no recriminations if you, Major, order the destruction of material
    which individual commanders here would consider necessary. You
    have complete discretion in meeting this objective: to quickly
    secure the documents you consider of value and to destroy
    everything else.

4   As quickly as is possible, please bring the crated documents
    mentioned under 1) above to London and deposit these at the

railway station. Do not bring such documents to Polish General Staff under any circumstances. Later we shall collect the documents ourselves.

We are sending you three officers to speed things up [...]. The new arrivals shall be provided with certain guidelines by their chiefs. When possible, please try to meet the guidelines. Let me stress again: speed is of the essence'.[6]

This instruction is an important source for a number of reasons. First, it is one of the very few contemporary documents with specific guidelines concerning the archives of Polish Intelligence. Second, it provides us with a general idea on what was to be destroyed, including documents of special importance for the history of co-operation between Polish Intelligence and its Allied counterparts. Third, it informs us directly of an earlier transport of a large part of II Bureau's archive to Scotland, with the intention of storing it with some other, unspecified, records (perhaps in the premises of the Archives and Museum Services of the Polish Armed Forces). This would indicate that this part of the archive was thought to be very important. The instruction clearly states that the most important materials were to be brought back to London. Clearly not everything was to be destroyed.

Two weeks later, in a long letter to Col. Wincenty Bąkiewicz, an officer remaining at the disposal of the Commander of Polish 2nd Corps, Gen. Władysław Anders, Bortnowski wrote that:

Intelligence – working under the Foreign Office – received an order to discontinue their co-operation with us. They wrote to us officially that, since the war in Europe had ended, they believed that the co-operation had ended as well. They thanked us profusely and, quoting the agreement of 1940, asked us to immediately hand over to them for the safekeeping all our archives, accounts, radio sets and so on. The very same day and until well into the night Wilfred's [Cmdr. W. Dunderdale – A.S.] representative oversaw the loading of the crates, which were then taken to them. Clearly, they did not control the content (we could have sent them old newspapers!) and to date we can go there and look through the crates, when we need something. Obviously, they gathered only the really important material. As for the rest, we burned it, as we did before, in Warsaw, Paris and Saintes – there were ashes all over Kensington! We had to do the same with our archives in Scotland. We did all this not just because the English asked us to – but also because we feared that the material might land in new hands. Nobody here could have foreseen with any certainty such a turn of events – we could have been ordered to hand the archives over at any time – and it would have been impossible to destroy papers or equipment in an instant. We did not want to expose lots of people who were mentioned, one way or another, in our records and documents, or were listed with Ptak [Maj. Franciszek Ptak – Chief of Finance Section, II Bureau]. Knowing a little about the methods employed by the other side I thought that even the lists of food parcels sent to addresses in Poland might have been used against their recipients. How could we demonstrate that such a parcel was merely to help, and not meant as assistance to persons linked to us'.[7]

These are all the existing testimonies concerning the self-destruction of documents by the II Bureau. We can therefore conclude with certainty that a large part of ill-defined archives of Polish Intelligence was deliberately destroyed by the chiefs of the II Bureau at the end of the war. What remained was two groups of material: those documents handed over to the British, described as 'only the really important', and the documents taken by individual officers of Polish Intelligence and kept in their private accommodation.

We know that throughout most of the war, that is from 1940 until 1945, the II Bureau of the Polish General Staff delivered tens of thousands of reports and messages to the Secret Intelligence Service. In 1944 alone 'the British Staff was provided with, among others, 7,351 intelligence reports, 966 reports on the agents of foreign intelligence services and 29,510 intelligence reports put together on the basis of radio dispatches intercepted and deciphered by Polish signals intelligence'.[8] From the 23rd August 1940 until the 31st December 1944 the II Bureau, PGS, delivered to the British a total of 32,423 intelligence reports, 4097 counter-intelligence reports and 35,288 intelligence reports based on radio dispatches intercepted and deciphered by Polish sigint. In addition, Polish Intelligence provided SIS with 4196 reports based on its special disinformation campaign.[9] Between 1940 and 1944, the II Bureau provided the British with over 76,000 intelligence reports of various kinds. We do not know the number of reports delivered to the British from the 1st January to the 8th May 1945, but it is reasonable to assume that there were several thousand of these. Altogether, the total number of reports provided to the British was certainly higher than 80,000.

We also know from Cmdr. Dunderdale's report (he was the principal British liaison officer and Head of Special Liaison Control of SIS) to Prime Minister Churchill, that of 45,770 reports prepared by Dunderdale's 'P5' Section between the 3rd September 1939 and the 8th May 1945, 22,047, or over 44%, were from Polish sources. (see G. Bennett) Part IV 12. p. XX. It is difficult to accept that all these Polish reports, and those British ones that were based on Polish sources, disappeared almost without trace. It is unlikely that archives containing tens of thousands of documents could have been completely destroyed. At least a proportion of these materials should still be in the SIS archives.

In addition to an explanation as to what happened to the documents handed over during the war, there remains the issue of the fate of the second set of documents. After the conclusion of the war in Europe and a week before the British Government withdrew its recognition from the Polish Government-in-Exile, Commander Dunderdale wrote a significant letter-instruction to the Chief of the II Bureau, PGS, Col. Stanisław Gano. Marked W/4978 and dated 30th June 1945, the letter stated:

> I have to refer to our agreement of 1940, on the basis of which at the end of hostilities in Europe all the records, official documents, radio sets, financial books and correspondence pertaining to our common activities, should be turned over to my representative, who delivers this letter. As you will understand, there is no further need to keep such material, as the closure of our common organisations is approaching its conclusion [...].[10]

This document confirms that the British wished to take over the entire II Bureau archives, and not merely a part. In reality, the majority of such archives were handed over, comprising at least several dozen crates and including the complete records of agents – in other words, these were documents of significant importance. Moreover, this was not the only part of II Bureau archives passed on to the British. The activities of Polish Intelligence were being gradually wound down, especially from the spring of 1946, when the Intelligence Bureau was turned into the Documentary Commission.

On the 7th March 1946 the Chief of Polish General Staff, Gen. Stanisław Kopański, issued two orders, which became the basis of 'the closure of II Bureau, PGS'. This document contains the following on the intelligence archives:

> 6 The archives of Polish Intelligence shall be finally ordered as follows:
> a) documents of importance to the history of the Polish Army or Polish Intelligence shall be passed to the Historical Commission;
> b) documents on the techniques of co-operation of Polish Intelligence with Allied intelligence services, the special reference library and intelligence records shall be deposited as a PGS trust with the British Authorities;
> c) the intelligence materials not valuable within the meaning of points 6a and 6b, and, in particular, such materials which might be used against persons or institutions which co-operated with the II Bureau, shall be destroyed.[11]

The order of the Chief of Staff was consistent with an earlier proposal made by Col. Gano to Brig. C.E.R. Hirsch, Deputy Director of Military Intelligence at the War Office, in which Gano said that:

> Intelligence documents are not within the scope of documentation that will probably be made available, not only for the sake of the safety of persons linked to Intelligence, but also due to the secrecy

resulting from co-operation with the British IS. Moreover, such documentation is our own contribution to the war and constitutes a proof of the reliability of our work.
The classification of archives is one of the main tasks in closing down and is linked to financial controls.[12]

Gano's suggestion was acted upon (in the meantime he become Deputy Chief of General Staff for General Affairs). The II Bureau was formally closed as a unit of the Polish General Staff and the Documentary Commission was established, led by Lt-Col. Bortnowski, formerly Deputy Chief of the II Bureau. When completing its work, the Documentary Commission was required to prepare a detailed report on its activities. The report was to contain a description of what happened to the archives, with 'detailed description of where the [. . .] documents etc. have been deposited on trust, together with the appropriate lists, protocols etc'.[13] Copies of the report were to be 'presented to the Chief of Staff and to one [not named – A.S.] of the Polish institutions abroad, where they were to be kept securely to safeguard against unwarranted access. The third copy was to be kept by the British authorities'.[14] Two final copies were to be included in the material offered for safekeeping within the body of documents of the General Staff.

It is likely that Gano wanted to sanction the earlier actions which in July 1945 passed over to the British the documents on the II Bureau's co-operation techniques with the British, the special reference library and the intelligence records, and destroyed many documents of Polish Intelligence.

Gano maintained that the documents deposited with the British were given in trust by PGS. He also stressed that 'the documents of importance to the history of Polish Army or of Polish Intelligence' were to be handed to the Historical Commission of the PGS as proof 'of our contribution to the war effort and to the reliability of our work'.[15] This shows that Gano attached great importance to the selection of II Bureau archives and, more importantly from the Polish point of view, to the preservation of the most important documents of historical value.

Unfortunately, after half a century, the attempts to find the documents, which were to be passed to the Historical Commission of PGS, and the report on the activities of the Documentary Commission of the II Bureau, have failed.

The fact that we do not have the complete set of documents, especially those relating to the 'techniques of co-operation between Polish Intelligence and SIS, the special reference library and intelligence records including records of agents of the II Bureau makes it impossible to prepare a full history of the Anglo-Polish intelligence co-operation and to assess the Polish contribution to the victory over the Third Reich. However, the work of the Polish-British Historical Committee has enabled the fullest possible account to be prepared.

Our research indicates that not all the materials and equipment were handed over to the British 'for safekeeping' in July of 1945. On the 27th July 1945 Bortnowski wrote to Col. Bąkiewicz as follows:

a) With difficulty I have managed to set up a hide-out in London, a house at the end of the city, where we shall gather the most valuable books, some special equipment etc. Soon there will be a permanent resident there. It will be a kind of club for us, a poste-restante box.

We still do not know where this house, or 'club', was, what was deposited there and what happened to it. Did the British take it over, including the contents? Or did it find its way to some Polish-British 'institution'? Bortnowski wrote also that:

b) We are currently putting together an underground communications centre (out in the country) – in part, of course, with the knowledge of the English, but under the condition that they will not defend us if their top echelons find out. This is drastic, but we decided to do this as there is no other way.[16]

Such a solution was necessary, since until this point in time II Bureau would communicate with Poland only via the intermediary of the VI Bureau – which by then was barred from transmitting intelligence material to Poland, and the supervision of both services ceased to function. In 1944–1945 it was Gen. Stanisław Tatar ('Tabor', 'Turski', 'Erazm') CB, who in the spring of 1944 arrived in Britain by air and became Deputy Chief of Polish General Staff. We do not know what materials of the II Bureau were sent to this 'centre' and what happened to them – indeed, the fate of the centre itself is unknown.

It would seem, then, that the documents and the equipment of the II Bureau were dispersed among a variety of Polish and British archives, institutions, 'clubs' and 'centres', and some found their way to the homes of individual officers.

It is safe to assume that at the time when, officially, II Bureau was being closed, some of its high-ranking officers, with Gen. Anders's knowledge (Anders expected that an armed conflict would soon erupt between East and West), attempted to preserve a nucleus of Polish intelligence 'in case the situation changes, perhaps in a year or two'.

Lt-Col. Bortnowski wanted to secure the essential technical and material resources and the most important records for the future. The contacts with 'the hosts', that is, with the British authorities, were to be maintained at the highest levels only. What Bortnowski hoped to achieve most was to save Section 'R' (for Russia), which was run between 1942 and 1945 by Lt-Col. Wincenty Zarembski ('Tudor'):[17] 'For the time being we have placed it ["Section 'R'" – J.C.] so that, if needed, it could break out and begin independent existence, or rather vegetation'. Bortnowski did not attach such importance to other archival material.[18]

In this case, too, we do not know the fate of the documents of this Section. It may well be that they finally reached SIS and, being 'useful', were not destroyed.

At first, Bortnowski saw Lt-Col. Zarembski as the Head ('the principal person') of the 'kernel' of the Polish Intelligence that was being re-established. He justified it by saying that Col. and Mrs. Zarembski, 'thanks to her industry' (in 1940–1945 she also worked in Intelligence), 'already had a small hotel by the sea, and therefore the means of support and the ability to establish themselves'.[19]

New questions arise in this context: where was this small hotel and what was kept in it? Was it just 'small', though 'valuable' equipment, which, as Bortnowski wrote to Bąkiewicz, 'was stashed away with people' – or also documents?

Regrettably, besides the hotel or rather B&B in Bognor Regis, there are no answers to these questions.

As for the issue of Polish Intelligence documents, which remained in private hands: in the seventies and eighties these have begun to find their way to the Polish archives abroad. There is little doubt that the current state of our holdings outside Poland concerning the war-time the II Bureau owes much to the officers and officials who participated in the closure of the various Bureaux of the former Polish General Staff and of Polish Armed Forces in the West. It is difficult to determine whether, by taking documents with them, they acted on orders or on their own initiative. Among the material deposited at IPMS in the first half of the seventies by Col. Wincenty Bąkiewicz there are numerous official documents, codes of the II Bureau of SBSK, of Polish Army in the East (APW), of Polish Army in the USSR, of Second Corps and of various intelligence Stations. The documents deposited by the descendants of Lt-Col. Władysław Gaweł, Chief of Radio Intelligence Section, are of similar character. This collection reached the IPMS in the eighties, following the death of his widow. The majority of this material consists of official documents of that Section. Somewhat different, though equally valuable, are the collections deposited by the families of Col. Jan Leśniak (held at IPMS), Col. Stefan Mayer and Lt-Col. Gwido Langer (in IJPL), Col. Kazimierz Iranek-Osmecki (in SPP) and Gen. Mieczysław Rygor-Słowikowski (in the Hoover Institution in the US). All these collections are a mixture of original intelligence documents, notes and correspondence. The instruction of the Chief of General Staff, dated March 1946, ordered the transfer of documents 'of importance to the history of the Polish Army or Polish Intelligence' to the Historical Commission. In practice the situation was different. Among the documents relating to the Polish Armed Forces and passed to the IPSM after the war, only a small number related to the II Bureau. These consisted of a separate group of 35 files. This set contained material primarily on the organisation and personnel of the II Bureau and some case documents. This state of affairs continued for several dozen years. From the point of view of Polish Intelligence contribution to Allied victory, much more valuable material was to be found in SPP, which took over the archives of the VI Bureau,

Polish General Staff. These documents survived, because the VI Bureau kept copies of the documents and reports given to the II Bureau, which in turn passed these to the SIS liaison. In the SPP archives there are several dozen files demonstrating the war-time work and achievements of Polish Intelligence, principally the Intelligence of the Home Army General Headquarters. In the 1980s the IPMS in London received an unexpectedly large collection, of some 80 archival units, of II Bureau documents from 1940–1945. The source material concerning Polish Intelligence held in Polish archives in London is quite substantial – over 500 archival units. Some part of II Bureau documents found their way to Poland, taken there by the few returning Bureau officers and their superiors.[20] Among those who went back were Gen. Stanisław Tatar and Lt-Col. Marian Utnik.

When looking for traces of documents originating with Polish Intelligence during the Second World War, it is also necessary to look at the fate of II Bureau archives deposited with the British. The first information on the subject can be traced back to 1948 and indicates that a part of these archives were placed at Ryder Street in Piccadilly, in London, where for a time the offices of Section V – counter-intelligence – were located. The desire to introduce order to these files was mentioned by Lt-Col. Bortnowski in a letter to Col. Stefan Mayer: 'I shall make an appointment with the hosts and at some point we will introduce order there. For the time being I would ask you to place these crates in a corner. We also have there [in Ryder Street – A.S.] several iron cabinets etc., but we have no room to take these to our place'.[21]

At the time the archives were accessible and the Poles had no difficulties in using them. Bortnowski managed to pass some documents from this set to Col. Iranek-Osmecki. These were 'extracts from assessments of reports from Germany, which were passed to the II Bureau, PGS, by the British during the recent war. The extracts were obtained through the efforts of Home Army Intelligence'.[22] Unfortunately this is where the trace ends – apart from the general information that in the fifties Col. Mayer, who was sorting these documents on behalf of the British, had access to them. Later attempts to gain access were not successful. In January 1959 Iranek-Osmecki, working on his memoirs, asked the British Foreign Office for permission to see Home Army Intelligence documents from 1943 and 1944. After two months he received a reply from Lt-Col. Edward G. Boxshall of the Foreign Office saying that 'Commander Dunderdale was consulted and confirmed that all the material from 1943 and 1944 originating with the Home Army has now been destroyed'.[23]

Col. Iranek-Osmecki refused to give up and attempted to reach the Foreign Office again, through the intermediary of Edward Raczyński. Iranek-Osmecki's son, Jerzy, wrote that Raczyński and his father 'went [together] to the Foreign Office and spoke to an official who said that no material like this exists and that due to lack of storage space Polish archives had been destroyed many years ago [...] As luck would have it, very soon afterwards Father saw Stefan Mayer and told him of his unsuccessful visit to the Foreign Office. Mayer responded by saying that it is a great pity that Father did not warn him in advance since he, Mayer, has just seen the documents [...] It would appear that Mayer was indicating that the quest was not hopeless and that perhaps something could be done. But nothing ever happened. I think that the formal refusal given to Raczyński and Father by the Foreign Office closed this particular issue'.[24] Col. Władysław Michniewicz attempted to clarify the fate of the archives in 1963, writing two letters to 'Wiadomości'. There was no response.[25]

Since then, there has been an embarrassed silence for 25 years. In 1979 Gen. Rygor-Słowikowski, working on his memoirs, wanted to gain access to his own reports from the days when he ran the Intelligence Station 'Afryka' of the II Bureau. The answer from the British Defence Ministry was, however, that following assessment and use for various official purposes such material '[...] is almost certain to have been destroyed'.[26]

In the 1970s, and until the present, the legendary courier from Warsaw and well-known Home Army veteran, Jan Nowak-Jeziorański, devoted much of his energy to the search for the missing II Bureau archives.

There can be little doubt that his tireless campaign over many years was instrumental in the establishment of the Polish-British Historical Committee whose aim it is to verify the post-war fate of the missing archives and the preparation of a joint Polish-British publication on the intelligence co-operation during the Second World War.

On 4th July 1978 Nowak-Jeziorański wrote to Jerzy Giedroyc, the Editor of *Kultura* and of *Zeszyty Historyczne* (Historical Files), published in Paris, as follows:

> It is a scandal that Col. Gano, without the authority of his superiors, handed over to the British all of the archives of our II Bureau. Would *Zeszyty Historyczne* be interested in becoming the patron of a campaign to regain these priceless materials and to find somebody to prepare these for publication? [...] It is high time to ascertain who brought to London the drawings and the plans of Peenemünde.[27]

Giedroyc thought that 'an American professor (not a Pole)' would stand a better chance of finding II Bureau archives, 'were he to naively ask questions of the British. Or if Stanford were to ask for photostats for its collection. It is worth trying [...] but I am pessimistic as to the outcome'.[28]

Independently of this initiative, another starting point to the search was an article by Andrzej Suchcitz, entitled *Archiwa wywiadu polskiego po 1945 roku* (*Archives of Polish Intelligence After 1945*), published in the Paris-based *Zeszyty Historyczne* in 1989. An important step in the search for the material handed over to the British was made by the British historian, Dr. Keith Sword, in 1992, when the British Government declared that archives will be easier to access. Sword asked William Waldegrave, then Chancellor of the Duchy of Lancaster, to transfer any Polish documents originally handed over to the British, should they be found, to

IMPS. After several months the answer was that SIS had again trawled through its archives, but had found no Polish materials. Waldegrave only sent Sword a copy of the letter from Lt-Col. Boxshall to Col. Iranek-Osmecki of 1959, already reported above. In a covering note the Private Assistant to Waldegrave's Secretary stated, that the only item found was a copy of a well-known work, *Historique du Réseau F2*, of autumn 1946, which was to be handed over to the Public Record Office.[29] It appeared that the issue was to be closed again. Dr. Sword, who copied the response to Suchcitz, added his postscript: 'Looks like the end of this story. Vandals!'

Two years later another attempt was undertaken by a Polish historian living in London, Prof. Jan Ciechanowski. The opportunity was provided by the forthcoming visit of H.M. Queen Elizabeth II to Poland. Dr. Ciechanowski asked the then Director of the Polish State Archives, Prof. Jerzy Skowronek, for assistance in this matter, and Skowronek prepared an appropriate aide-mémoire.[30] Unfortunately we do not know whether it was delivered to the Queen.

From that point on, the attempts to obtain specific and definitive answers from the British side as to the fate of II Bureau archives were ceaseless. In February 1998 the Chairman of the Polish Institute and Sikorski Museum, Capt. Ryszard Dembiński, and its head of archives, Andrzej Suchcitz, wrote to the Polish Foreign Minister Prof. Bronisław Geremek asking to broach the matter officially with the British Government.[31] A similar inquiry was sent to Robin Cook, the British Foreign Secretary, by Andrzej Morawicz, Chairman of the British-Polish Council.[32]

The fate of the documents was also raised by the Director of Polish State Archives, Dr. Daria Nałęcz, to her British equivalent, Sarah Tyacke, in a conversation at a conference in Stockholm. Nałęcz followed this by a letter, asking 'for action which would explain the fate of these documents, the possibility of finding where they may be kept and how they may be accessed – or for confirmation that they have been destroyed'.[33]

Following the suggestion from the TNA (PRO), in the spring of 1999 Nałęcz approached the Departmental Record Officer at Cabinet Office, asking where the documents are kept, whether bilingual versions are in existence (that is, Polish originals with English translations), how many Polish researchers had access to these documents and what happened to the part of the archive passed on to Cmdr. Dunderdale in 1945.[34]

Ciechanowski approached the Head of Central Europe Department at the Foreign Office, who responded by saying that he would look into this matter and provide an answer later.[35] Ciechanowski then wrote to the Polish Prime Minister, Jerzy Buzek, to officially 'ask the British Government about the fate of reports, documents and archives of the II Bureau (Intelligence) of Polish General Staff'.[36] The letter was accompanied by a list of suggested questions, which could be put to the British Prime Minister, Tony Blair. Jan Nowak-Jeziorański also approached Prime Minister Buzek with a similar suggestion.

Soon after, Dr. Nałęcz received a response to her letter of 21st April from the Head of Histories and Records Unit of the Cabinet Office, Tessa Stirling. The most important sentences were that: 'Having consulted with appropriate Whitehall officials I have to inform you with regrets that all the reports of Polish Intelligence which were in the hands of SIS at the end of the war on the basis of the Agreement of 1940, have been destroyed as being of temporary significance when their utility ceased. A similar fate was shared by the documents handed over to Commander Dunderdale – they have been destroyed [...]. There is no direct evidence to this effect, but it may be that the decision to destroy these documents may have been influenced by worries concerning their sensitive content. In any case and as already explained, in the period under consideration there was a general tendency to reduce the content of archives [...]'.[37]

In her response Nałęcz stated that 'these records, in compliance with the Polish standards of classification of archive materials, would be preserved by the Polish archives as documents worth perpetual preservation. Therefore, we have faced the information about them being destroyed with much sorrow. It will also surely be received with much bitterness by the participants of these events and by historians, who have often addressed the highest political circles in both our States with requests regarding the Records of the Intelligence [...].

Due to the great significance of your information, and also to terminate any further speculation about the history of sets of records related to the activity of the Polish Intelligence, let me address you with a request for some additional information on the liquidation of these materials. Lists of materials liquidated and information about the time of liquidation would be of the greatest importance for us. In particular, we would appreciate receiving copies of applicable protocols'.[38]

The reply, dated 1st July, confirmed the destruction by SIS of the archives of the II Bureau. The World Federation of Home Army Combatants addressed its strong protest to the British Ambassador in Warsaw, John MacGregor, asking him to pass it on to the British Government.[39]

Although Tessa Stirling's response appeared to be final, it was not considered to be necessarily the last word on the matter, especially since an answer was awaited to the State Archives' letter as to the details of the archive's destruction. In October 1999 Prime Minister Buzek wrote to Prime Minister Blair asking 'for the above mentioned documents to be made available to Polish researchers'. Prime Minister Blair responded by saying '[...] the Secret Intelligence Service received a large number of reports during the War which they passed on to their customers, not keeping copies for themselves. Regrettably, it appears that a number of other Polish records, including those handed to the late Commander Dunderdale, were destroyed after the War for reasons explained to Professor Nałęcz.'[40]

In the Polish emigré press Professor Ciechanowski published an article in the outlining the fate of the archives handed over to the British and the Polish-British intelligence co-operation during the Second World War. In conclusion he suggested that 'a Polish-British Historical Commission be set up, to search for the surviving documents and for information on co-operation between the II Bureau and SIS, which could then be published in print'.[41]

On 21st December 1999 at a special joint meeting the Sejm and Senate (the two chambers of Polish Parliament) Foreign Affairs Committees familiarised themselves with the information on the destruction of Polish Intelligence documentation in Great Britain. The Committees suggested that the two Governments 'establish a joint committee of British and Polish archivists and historians to search for any existing documents demonstrating the wartime co-operation of the two allies'.

The Governmental Polish-British Historical Committee for the Documentation of the Activities of Polish Intelligence in the Second World War and its Co-operation with British Intelligence was established in November 2000. In accordance with the Polish Prime Minister's instruction of 15th November 2000, the Commission was to 'research the fate of the intelligence material passed by Polish Intelligence to the British side', among other tasks.[42]

Many facts concerning the fate of the II Bureau archives have been established since the war ended. Further illumination was obtained through the work of the Commission. But at the time of writing, an authoritative and final explanation of the fate of that part of the files, which were passed to SIS from 1940 to 1946, remains an open issue. Among the missing material are the files of the 'Centrala' (Centre), of the headquarters of the II Bureau. There are no documents (agreements) which determined the scope and character of the Polish-British intelligence co-operation, and no Polish operational reports. We do not have the personal files of the agents of the II Bureau, or its special reference library. Many documents on the activities of Section 'R' (for 'Russia') of the II Bureau, Polish General Staff, are missing.

As is clearly seen, a number of issues remain unresolved. This task shall fall to the Polish and British historians of the Second World World War and to its surviving participants – and to Polish and British public opinion.

Notes

1   See: A. Suchcitz, *Archiwa wywiadu polskiego po 1945 roku (Archives of Polish Intelligence after 1945)*, 'Zeszyty Historyczne', Paris 1989, no. 89, pp. 23–24.

2   In February 1945, anticipating the forthcoming end to the war and its impact on Poland, the chiefs of the II Bureau, PGS, and SIS reached an agreement to the effect that a small cell of Polish Intelligence would continue activities once the hostilities ceased to be financed by SIS.

3   As we now know, Col. Bortnowski exaggerated, since a significant proportion of the files of PGS was not destroyed and survived to this day.

4   IPMS, Kol. 79/94, Letter of Col. Bortnowski to Col. Leśniak, 26th April 1975. This information is confirmed in another letter to Leśniak, of 1st December 1975, where Bortnowski adds: 'I myself destroyed everything that was mine and advised or ordered my subordinates to do the same. From September 1939 (Fort Legionów

with the railway wagonload of General Staff papers of the II Bureau taken by the Germans almost in its entirety) via Regina and the cases abandoned in Port Verdon – these were experiences sufficient to know, that the benefits from accumulated paperwork is derived [...] more often by the enemy than by their rightful owners [...]' – in: A. Suchcitz, *Archiwa (Archives)*, op.cit.

5 A. Suchcitz, *Archiwa (Archives)*, op.cit., p. 31.
6 IPMS, Kol. 79/94, Letter-instruction of Lt-Col. Bortnowski to Maj. Paprocki, of 6th July 1945.
7 IPMS, Kol. 138/161, Letter of Lt-Col. Bortnowski to Col. Bąkiewicz of 20th July 1945, p. 2.
8 A. Suchcitz, *Archiwa (Archives)*, op.cit., p. 24.
9 IPMS, A.XII.24/37, Delivered by the II Bureau, Polish General Staff, to the British Staff.
10 IPMS, A.XII.24/57, 'Wilski' [Cmdr. Dunderdale] to Col. Gano, 30th June 1945.
11 IPMS, A.XII.24/58, Closure of the II Bureau, PGS, March 1946, p. 3.
12 Ibid., Letter of Col. Gano to Brig. C.E.R. Hirsch, 2nd March 1946.
13 Ibid., Closure, op.cit., p. 4.
14 A. Suchcitz, *Archiwa (Archives)*, op.cit., pp. 27-28.
15 IPMS,A.XII.24/58, Col. Gano to Brig. C.E.R. Hirsch, 2nd March 1946.
16 IPMS, Kol. 138/161C, letter Lt-Col Bortnowski to Col. W. Bąkiewicz, of 27th July 1945, p. 3.
17 Lt-Col. Zarembski (1897–1966) was one of the most experienced and prominent officers of Polish Intelligence, for years specialising in Russian matters. In the summer of 1939, while still serving in the 64. Infantry Regiment, commanded by Lt-Col. Bolesław Ciechanowski – who was also involved with Polish Intelligence – he travelled on duty to England and France. Immediately before the war he was made the head – 'rezydent' – of the Polish Intelligence in Russia, under the cover of an employee of the Polish Embassy in Moscow. During the war he managed to leave Russia and became Chief of Counter-Intelligence at the Polish Ministry of Military Affairs, which was recreating itself in France. He remained in France, where he led one of the Polish intelligence networks in 1940–1942. From 1942 in England, dealing with Russian affairs. Holder of the highest Polish battle honour: the Order of Virtuti Militari, 5th Class, and the Cross of Valour.
18 IPMS, Kol. 135/161. Lt-Col. Bortnowski to Col. Bąkiewicz, of 26th June 1945.
19 Ibid.
20 A. Kuler, *Dokumenty londyńskiego II Oddziału Sztabu Głównego WP w archiwach Polski Ludowej (Documents of the London-based II Bureau in the Archives of People's Poland)*, 'Zeszyty Literackie WiNu', 2000, no. 14, pp. 165–168.
21 IJPL, Kol. 100/4/3, Lt-Col. Bortnowski to Col. Mayer, 14th September 1948.
22 SPP, vol. 2. 3. 6. 4 doc. 31, Lt-Col. Bortnowski to Col. Iranek-Osmecki, 3rd November 1948.
23 IPMS,A.XII. 24/114 Letter of Jerzy Iranek-Osmecki to Andrzej Suchcitz, 9th September 1989.
24 Ibid.
25 IPMS, Kol. 138/161, Letter of Col. Michniewicz to 'Feluś'(?), 21st February 1965.
26 Letter of the British Defence Ministry to Gen. Słowikowski of 13th July 1979 in: An Afterword by John Herman. *The Importance of Agency Africa: A note on the Historical Evidence and Sources* in: M. Z. Rygor-Słowikowski, *In the Secret Service. The Lighting of the Torch*, London 1988, p. 250.
27 J. Nowak-Jeziorański and J. Giedroyc, *Listy 1952–1998 (Letters 1952–1998)*, Wrocław 2001, p. 454.
28 Ibid., p. 456.
29 IPMS,A.XII.24/114, copies of letters of Dr. K. Sword to Minister W. Waldegrave of 30th June 1992, of Waldegrave to Sword of 22nd July 1992 and letter of Jan Dougal to Sword of 21st October 1992.

30 IPMS, A.XII.24/114, copy of an aide-mémoire of Prof. Jerzy Skowronek, Director of State Archives, to H.M. Queen Elizabeth II, 22nd March 1996.
31 IPMS, A.XII.24/114, copy of letter of R. Dembiński and A. Suchcitz to Minister B. Geremek of 20th February 1998.
32 IPMS, A.XII.24/114, copy of letter of A. Morawicz to R. Cook of 17th March 1998.
33 IPMS, A.XII.24/114, copy of letter of D. Nałęcz to S. Tyacke of 18th September 1998.
34 IPMS, A.XII.24/114, copy of letter of D. Nałęcz to Departmental Record Officer of the Cabinet Office of 21st April 1999.
35 IPMS, A.XII.24/114, copy of letter of J. Ciechanowski to H.T.S. Perce, Head of Central European Department, FCO, of 20th May 1999 and the reply of 25th May 1999.
36 IPMS, A.XII.24/114, copy of letter of J. Ciechanowski to J.Buzek of 8th June 1999.
37 IPMS, A.XII.24/114, copy of letter of T.A. Stirling to D. Nałęcz of 1st July 1999.
38 IPMS, A.XII.24/114, copy of letter of D. Nałęcz to T. A. Stirling of 6th August 1999.
39 IPMS, A.XII.24/114, copy of letter of ŚZŻAK to Amb. J. MacGregor of 27th September 1999.
40 IPMS, A.XII.24/114, copy of letter of T. Blair to J. Buzek of 17th November 1999.
41 Jan Ciechanowski, *Churchill nakazał. Polsko-brytyjska współpraca wywiadowcza w czasie drugiej wojny światowej (On Churchill's Orders. Polish-British Intelligence Co-operation During WW II)*, 'Tydzień Polski' (Polish Weekly), 18th December 1999, 25th December 1999 and 1st January 2000, and Jan Ciechanowski, *Zasługi w popiół obrócone (Valour Turned into Ashes)*, 'Rzeczpospolita', 30th October–1st November 1999.
42 Instruction No.85 of the Chairman of the Council of Ministers J.Buzek of 15th November 2000 in the matter of the Polish part of the Polish-British Historical Committee for the Documentation of the Activities of Polish Intelligence in the Second World War and its co-operation with British Intelligence, par. 2, point 2.

5

Literature on the Activities of Polish Intelligence in World War II

*Jan Stanisław Ciechanowski**

Literature in Polish

The number of publications in Polish on the co-operation between the Polish Armed Forces in the West and the Home Army General Headquarters Intelligence with the special services of the Allies appears quite modest, when compared to the scope and significance of such contacts. In most publications, only a few of the relevant topics, such as Enigma, the V weapons, Home Army Intelligence or the resistance in France, are discussed. The archival material to be found in Polish depositories was used only marginally. For many years the material held in the Central Archive of the Ministry of Internal Affairs in Poland was not accessible, some valuable publications on ZWZ-AK (the Union for Armed Struggle – the Home Army, further as: the Home Army) Intelligence were based mainly on the testimony of individual members of Polish resistance. This was the case, for example, with the book by Michał Wojewódzki, about the information provided by ZWZ-AK Intelligence on the German V weapons.[1] Though his book was aimed at the general, rather than academic reader, it documented the role played by Polish Intelligence in the detection of the Peenemünde centre, as well as the firing range in Blizna. The author described how the information about the weapons was acquired and the knowledge broadened, on the structure of the independent station of Home Army Intelligence 'Lombard', and the role played by the parachutists, who were trained in Great Britain. The publication of this book led to an increase of interest shown in Home Army Intelligence by both the historians and the general reader. It also drew attention to the co-operation with British Intelligence. The role played by the Poles in identifying V weapons is the best-documented achievement of Home Army Intelligence.[2]

---

* Ed. Jan Stanisław Ciechanowski with the help of Andrzej Chmielarz, Eugenia Maresch, Andrzej Pepłoński and Rafał Wnuk.

The publication of Władysław Kozaczuk's book on Enigma proved to be quite a revelation.[3] The author used most extensively the account by Marian Rejewski, a member of the cryptological team set up by the II Bureau of the Polish General Staff, as well as Western publications. His valuable book presented the organization and the work of Polish mathematicians. This publication unquestionably has shown the achievements of Polish Intelligence on the eve of the war and how the Poles exposed the facts to the representatives of British and French Intelligence, how it operates and how to duplicate it. Another important publication on the construction, operation and decoding of this cipher machine was a book by Krzysztof Gaj.[4] Józef Garliński, also wrote about Enigma.[5] References to Polish cryptologists, was mentioned in another book, by Władysław Kozaczuk, on the psychological warfare in the Second World War.[6] How the code was broken and the use made of the product was the subject of several publications by Janusz Piekałkiewicz.[7] His richly illustrated books were first published in the West, and recently were translated and published in Poland. Piekałkiewicz left no doubt as to the decisive role played by Polish Intelligence in the breaking of Enigma. He quoted numerous examples of decoded German reports to demonstrate the importance of them while at war.

Józef Garliński wrote, though only briefly, about the activities of Polish Intelligence in Switzerland.[8] There are several important publications on the Polish resistance in France and in other European countries. The most important of these are by Tadeusz Panecki[9] and Jan E. Zamojski.[10] Tadeusz Dubicki wrote about the Polish intelligence and resistance work in Romania,[11] and Andrzej Przewoźnik[12] covered the same ground in Hungary. Leszek Gondek described some aspects of Polish Intelligence work in Europe.[13] The research for the biography of Maj. Jan Żychoń, Chief of Intelligence Department, the II Bureau, PGS, are of importance.[14] Andrzej Pepłoński wrote the first book and until now the most complete book on the organisation and operations of Polish Military Intelligence in the Second World War.[15] The author described how the II Bureau was recreated, first in France and later in Great Britain; the organization and function of its Centre with field agencies; co-operation with the II Bureau, the Home Army, the activities of the Home Army in the vicinity of the Eastern Front; and co-operation with the British, American, French, Belgian and Soviet Intelligence services. Pepłoński made the most of the archives held at the Polish Institute and Sikorski Museum in London, and made use for the first time the Polish archives in Poland, which shows the role of Polish Intelligence in the Second World War. A major portion of this book deals with the co-operation with British Intelligence. Pepłoński also published several articles on the wartime Polish Intelligence.[16]

Several articles were written by Lt-Col. Marian Utnik, its last head of the VI (Special) Bureau, PGS. He brought out the organizational problems facing the services who were responsible for the training of parachutists and for the transport of equipment, arms and personnel to Poland. Utnik also presented the role of the VI Bureau who acted as intermediary in intelligence communications with the Union of Armed Struggle – the Home Army general Headquarters, (further as: the Home Army GHQ).[17] An important addition to these publications was a series of articles by Leonidas A.B. Kliszewicz, devoted to the operations of the VI Bureau in Europe.[18] Much information on the organization and activities of Polish Intelligence is contained in the memoirs of several couriers, such as Jan Nowak-Jeziorański, Jan Karski and Aleksander Stpiczyński, who maintained communications between London and Warsaw.[19] There were also several valuable publications on the Home Army and Polish Armed Forces in the West and Radio Communication.[20]

By and large the history of the Home Army Intelligence is dealt by Piotr Matusak.[21] Until recently the only substantial analysis was to be found in the unpublished work of the former Home Army GHQ Counter-Intelligence Chief, Bernard Zakrzewski 'Oskar'.[22] Col. Kazimierz Iranek-Osmecki, one of its former Heads, was the author of the first publications on the II Bureau, the Home Army GHQ.[23] A popular book on Home Army Intelligence was prepared in 1987 by Paweł Maria Lisiewicz (*Bezimienni. Z dziejów wywiadu Armii Krajowej* (*Without a Name. On the History of the Home Army Intelligence*, Warsaw, 1987). Its organizational structure was described by M. Ney-Krwawicz in his book entitled *Komenda Główna Armii Krajowej 1939–1945* (*the Home Army GHQ 1939–1945*, Warsaw 1990). Basic information on the organization and operations of Home Army Intelligence in the field can be found in the monographs of individual Districts of the Home Army or of Polish regions.[24]

Among published recollections entitled *Życie na krawędzi. Wspomnienia żołnierzy antyhitlerowskiego wywiadu* (*Life at the Edge. Memoirs of Soldiers of the anti-Hitlerite Intelligence*, ed. by W. Kozaczuk, Warsaw 1980) deserves special attention. One of them was provided by the last Chief of the Records and Studies Department, II Bureau, the Home Army, Bohdan Zieliński (in the Underground Research Department). Interesting reminiscences of the Home Army Intelligence operatives can be found in *Żołnierze Komendy Głównej Armii Krajowej wspominają* (*Memoirs of the Home Army GHQ Soldiers*, ed. by K. Wyczańska, Warsaw 1994). There are also testimonies or retrospective accounts of Aleksander Klotz, who ran one of Home Army intelligence networks in the vicinity of the Eastern Front, and of Halina Zakrzewska, who was responsible for communications with the Eastern intelligence networks.[25] The only published selection of sources on Home Army Industrial Intelligence is *Meldunki miesięczne wywiadu przemysłowego KG ZWZ/AK 1941–1944* (*Monthly Reports of Home Army Industrial Intelligence. 1941–1944*, parts 1–2, Warsaw 2000). A number of documents on the operations and results of II Bureau, the Home Army, can be found in the six-volume *Armia Krajowa w dokumentach 1939–1945* (*Home Army in Documents, 1939–1945*, London 1970–1989).[26]

Literature in Other Languages

The literature published in the West largely does not take into account the activities of Polish Intelligence in the Second World War. There are several reasons for this state of affairs. The most important appears to be the lack of monographs on the Polish secret services in English. It must be recognized here that, as in all other aspects of intelligence work in contemporary times, any disclosure of the details of specific operations or of operational intelligence procedures usually takes place only after a number of years, and even then it is likely to be less than complete. In practical terms, the history of intelligence during the Second World War became the subject of serious study only recently. Another factor is the natural tendency of all the secret services to stress their own successes. This tendency influenced the unwillingness to recognise the disproportionately large contribution of Polish Intelligence to the Allied victory over Germany. The very nature of the policy meant that the authorities of communist Poland were not interested in praising this aspect of Polish contributions. Furthermore, those Poles who did not return to Poland after the war were not in a position to reach the public with the information available to them. The matter was also complicated by the reluctance of the principal players to reveal the secrets of their achievements. Finally, from time to time, there was deliberate disinformation and manipulation, a factor, which played its role in several cases. Deliberate failure to disclose information, or the destruction of some of the documentation, resulted in an almost complete absence of the topic in published sources. To express this in different words: the relevant authorities in several countries were drip-feeding information, which affected the work of historians who wrote about intelligence.

The first important Polish intelligence contribution, which became well-known to public opinion, though even here there were difficulties, concerns Enigma: three talented Polish cryptologists, Marian Rejewski, Jerzy Różycki and Henryk Zygalski, who broke the Enigma code and laid the foundations for the resulting successes in the signals war with the Germans. This, undoubtedly, was the principal Polish contribution to the Allied victory in the Second World War, though for many years it was ignored or belittled.

There are many important academic works, which present the Polish contribution in the light of available documents. These include: Ronald Lewin, *Ultra Goes to War. The First Account of World War II's Greatest Secret Based on Official Documents* (New York, 1978), Peter Calvocoressi, *Top Secret Ultra* (London 1980) and Simon Singh, *The Code Book. The Science of Secrecy from Ancient Egypt to Quantum Cryptography* (New York, 2000, Polish edition as *Księga Szyfrów*, Warsaw 2001). Even before these books were published, there were the memoirs of the retired French general, Gustave Bertrand, who was instrumental in forging the co-operation of Allied intelligence services before and during the war. His book, published three years before Bertrand's death, entitled *Enigma ou la plus grande énigme de la guerre 1939–1945* (Paris, 1973), fully recognized the role of the Polish cryptologists.[27] Bertrand's reminder about the role of the Poles created a huge response, Polish sources on the theme of breaking Enigma and her successes started to be published in English language in the 1980's. In 1980 the Polish émigré historian, Józef Garliński, published *Intercept. The Enigma War* (London, 1980, published in Polish as *Enigma. Tajemnica drugiej wojny światowej*, Warsaw 1980). Four years later Władysław Kozaczuk published *Enigma. How the German Cipher Machine Was Broken and How It Was Read by the Allies in World War Two* (London, 1984). In the 1990s 'The Enigma Bulletin' was published in English, in Kraków, on the initiative and under the editorship of Zdzisław Jan Kapera. Six issues of this periodical have been published to date.[28]

In a number of works, however, the role of the Poles has been ignored. Most authors insisted that without the Poles breaking the secrets of Enigma, the British would have succeeded on their own, and that their success was guaranteed. The former RAF Group Capt. Frederick W. Winterbotham, who headed Air Intelligence in the Second World War, penned one of the most popular publications. This author deliberately ignores the fact that Enigma was broken by the Polish cryptologists.[29] This bestseller, which had a number of editions, was largely responsible for the myth that the secrets of the German coding machine were solved by the British. This laid the foundations for the persistent falsehood – which was sometimes repeated in official statements – on the subject of Enigma.

As for more contemporary works originating in Great Britain, there are examples of the authors who are indifferent, even belittle the Polish contribution, rather than conceal it. An example was the book by Hugh Sebag-Montefiore. The author, a journalist, who gained access to relatively rich source material, concentrated on how the naval version of Enigma was broken.[30] He controversially maintained that the British ability to decipher 'Naval Enigma' was due mainly to the documents provided by a French agent within the German radio intelligence service, Hans Thilo Schmidt ('Asche').[31] In the opinion of this author, who did not have good knowledge of Polish sources, the Poles could not have broken Enigma without these documents. The British journalist stubbornly equates a few documents on the coding machine by this French agent to the solution of the secret itself.[32] Sebag-Montefiore only mentions the Polish achievements in the appendices at the end of his book. It does not mention that Turing's 'bombe' was patterned on Polish invention. In the introduction, which constituted a summary of the research, the Poles are not mentioned at all.[33] Another example of such belittling of the Polish contribution was the classic book by Nigel West (whose real name is Rupert Allason) entitled *MI6. British Secret Intelligence Service Operations 1909–1945* (London, 1983). West maintained that Col. Rivet and Capt. Bertrand carried out the pioneering work on breaking Enigma and that the French discovered the secret in parallel with the Poles. The reconstruction of the German machine was, maintained West, done by the French in conjunction with the Poles. Interestingly, in the Polish edition of this book, the mistakes made by the author had to be corrected by its translator, in the footnotes.[34]

The authors of the official history of British Intelligence in the Second World War, headed by Sir Harry Hinsley, maintained that without the Poles Enigma would have remained unreadable until the fall of France in June 1940. The role of the Poles in this book was presented in a straightforward manner, though there were minor inaccuracies and attempts to demonstrate, without the required evidence, that as far as Enigma was concerned, the British were self-sufficient.[35] The innovation of the British in the making of 'bombs' and 'sheets' in the autumn of 1939 was stressed. No mention was made that both were reconstructed in strict accordance with the suggestions made by the Poles.[36]

There is no proof that the British would have been able to break the Enigma code and to discover how the machine worked, if on the eve of the war the Poles had the same low level of knowledge in these matters, as did their French and British colleagues. But some British authors seem to believe that even without the benefit of Polish experiences and successes, the first time that the machine with its keys was actually captured (which was during the Norwegian campaign in May 1940) would have been sufficient to break the cipher.[37]

The world literature on the various aspects of the German rocket weapons and flying bombs amounts to several hundred titles. These issues have been written about by historians as well as by engineers and physicists. The authors included the father of the German rockets, Walter Dorenberger, the Third Reich's Armaments Minister Albert Speer, and the British Prime Minister Winston Churchill.[38] Most of these books deal with the history of such weapons, their technical parameters, their role in Hitler's war plans, their impact on the conduct of the war – and finally on the influence of German research on the post-war conquest of space. The key role of the Peenemünde centre has been stressed, as were the delays caused by RAF bombing of Peenemünde. Little attention has been paid to the question of how British Intelligence obtained the information on this super-secret facility.

In English-language literature the prevailing view for many years was that the German rockets had been discovered by Constance Babington-Smith, who worked in the RAF's Photographic Analysis Section. Her attention was drawn to the untypical airplane silhouettes (V-1 flying bombs) on what appeared to be launching pads, found on aerial photographs of the Peenemünde area. This view, often presented in books, films and historical programmes, meant that knowledge of other sources of this information remained practically unnoticed. In literature published in the 1970s, information that British Intelligence had some knowledge obtained from 'two forced labourers' employed at the rocket facility began to appear. Both the workers were said to have died during the air raids on Peenemünde. Since nothing in these publications indicated that the two 'workers' were working for Home Army Intelligence, the average reader might have been excused for thinking that they were, in fact, agents of SIS or SOE. Progress has been made, though: for example, in the book by Denis Piszkiewicz, there is a passage noting that the two members of Polish resistance, who 'were informing the British on the rocket research at Peenemünde', were probably killed during the air raid.[39]

By and large, the findings of Polish researchers continued to be absent in English literature. Little has changed following the publication in English, at the end of the 1970s, of Józef Garliński's *Hitler's Last Weapons*.[40] The fact that it was the Poles who obtained the information about the Peenemünde compound is hardly ever mentioned. On the other hand, the observation of the German rocket trials at Blizna by the Poles, and the capture of important V-2 rocket assemblies by Home Army Intelligence had been noticed by some authors. Conversely, for example, Michael Neufeld's *The Rocket and the Reich*, states that there has been 'some impact which was difficult to assess' of 'a small resistance group led by communists' in the rocket production 'Dora' works, hidden underground.[41] While devoting a fair amount of space to the German trials at Blizna, the author did not mention at all the dozens of Polish Intelligence reports which described the details of such trials, the sabotage conducted by Polish workers there, or that the captured V-2 parts were transported by plane to Great Britain (Operation III'). While there is no suspicion of ill will on the part of West European researchers, these omissions can only be explained by the language barrier, which prevented the verification of earlier hypotheses.

Apart from the Enigma issue, undoubtedly the most important success of Polish Intelligence, other achievements and contributions of the Poles were marginally mentioned. Those Polish Intelligence officers who knew the most about intelligence during the war, did not leave much written material. The one book available is the English-language edition of Mieczysław Zygfryd Słowikowski's ('Rygor') *W tajnej służbie* (*In Secret Service*), *Polski wkład do zwycięstwa w drugiej wojnie światowej* (*The Polish Contribution for Victory in the Second World War*), London, 1977).[42] Słowikowski's work is rarely quoted in books in English. One of the very few books in English in which 'Rygor's' work in Algiers is mentioned was Stephen Dorril's *MI6. Fifty Years of Special Operations* (London, 2000),[43] devoted primarily to the post-war intelligence struggle. Dorril refers to the book by the Polish officer. But in most publications whether deliberately or not the role of the Polish Military Intelligence cell in Algiers in the planning of Operation 'Torch' (allied landings in North Africa in November 1942) is not mentioned.

The five-volume, official history of British Intelligence in the Second World War, edited by Professor Hinsley, contains other references to the Polish Intelligence contribution to the Allied victory in the Second World War. But it does not attempt to analyse this contribution in any detail, even though its authors enjoyed unlimited access to all the existing documents, unavailable to other researchers at the time. When describing the relatively low effectiveness of British Intelligence at the outset of the war and its internal conflicts, for example, Hinsley does not mention (except in very general terms) the Polish-British intelligence agreement, which set down the methods of co-operation. The use made of the Polish intelligence networks, which operated without a break in occupied Europe, is hardly mentioned. Volumes two and three did not fully describe the Polish contribution in the matter of V-1 and V-2 weapons. On the other hand the practice of removing any reference as to the origin of information from the SIS reports passed on to its clients made the identification of Polish Intelligence as the source rather difficult.

The British authorities, by denying access to secret intelligence documentation are supplanting it by publishing their own official histories, such as Prof. Michael R. D. Foot's *SOE in France* London (1966), or *SOE in the Low Countries* London (2002), where the activities of its Polish Section were only touched upon. William Mackenzie's *The Secret History of SOE*, written in 1949, was published as recently as 2000. In this book, the Polish contribution to SOE's operations is described very briefly and superficially. The author wrote that 'the Poles were certainly fighting – but no evidence for details will ever be available'. More on the activities of the Poles can be found in the book by the former SOE officer, Brooks Richards, *Secret Flotillas. Clandestine Sea Lines to France & French North Africa 1940–1944* London (1996). In addition to British sources and his own recollections, the author researched Polish documents, kept at the Polish Institute and Sikorski Museum in London.

As for books published by Americans, Richard Harris Smith in his *OSS. The Secret History of America's First Central Intelligence Agency* (Berkeley-Los Angeles-London, 1972) did not mention the importance of the Polish Intelligence reports supplied to Washington.[44] His book was criticized with veracity by Gen. Słowikowski, who wrote an open letter to Smith. The Polish officer pointed out American mistakes concerning Operation 'Torch', as well as avoiding the Polish contribution.[45] True, when Smith wrote his book, access to OSS archives was not yet available,and the reports of American deputy consuls in Algiers, who were OSS officers, deposited in NARA, had no identification that they were sent by 'Rygor'.[46] But after the publication of 'Rygor's' book, Col. John C. Knox, who during the war was American Deputy Consul in Algiers, said in a letter published by *The Daily Telegraph*, that 'The Polish network, under his expert guidance and constant supervision, were by all odds the most efficient and professional in their field, supplying the Allies with a wealth of valuable and proven information'.[47] The successes of 'Rygor's' network remained unreported for many years, though he was awarded the Most Excellent Order of the British Empire by the British and the Legion of Merit by the Americans. The glowing citations for both decorations were easily available. Robert Daniel Murphy, a diplomat and the principal American agent in French North Africa, was another author who did not mention the Polish network in Algiers (*The Diplomat among Warriors*, London, 1964) – though his private letters to 'Rygor' register how grateful the American was for the Pole's excellent work. In one of his letters to the American historian, Słowikowski wrote: 'You seem to attribute a lot of valuable space to the people who matter little, but have no place at all for those who contributed a lot!' In a letter to the Chairman of the Józef Piłsudski

Institute of America, Słowikowski explained his motives for writing his open letter: 'It seems to me, that it would be worthwhile to involve not only the public opinion [among] expatriate Poles, but also among the Americans, since this falsehood had been perpetrated in their country. It feels like a conspiracy to hide the truth, which is unpleasant for those who sold and betrayed Poland'.[48]

Many first-hand witnesses of wartime intelligence seldom reveal the Polish contribution. The role of II Bureau cell in Switzerland or the activities of Halina Szymańska are not mentioned in the memoirs of Allen Dulles, who during the war headed the OSS there.[49] Only the latest biographer of the future Director of CIA, James Srodes, penned some general remarks on the intelligence activities and the role of the wife of a former Polish military attaché in Berlin. These are based on a conversation with an SIS officer.[50] On the other hand we have the testimony of John Colville, who was Private Secretary to Prime Minister Winston Churchill during the war, and who wrote that: 'Probably the best all-round players in the game were the Poles.' Interestingly, Colville mentioned this in his book on William Cavendish-Bentinck, 9th Duke of Portland and his family. It is highly likely that this was the opinion of Cavendish-Bentinck himself, who during the war co-ordinated the various branches of British special services.[51]

Notes

1 M. Wojewódzki, *Akcja V-1, V-2*, Warsaw 1975.
2 See also: M. Wiśniewski, *Polacy w walce z niemiecką bronią V* (*Poles in the Fight Against the German V Weapons*), 'Wojskowy Przegląd Historyczny', 1966, no. 2, pp. 59–87; A. Glass, S. Kordaczuk, D. Stępniewska, *Wywiad Armii Krajowej w walce z V-1 i V-2* (*Home Army Intelligence and the Fight Against V-1 and V-2*), Warsaw 2000; J. Garliński, *Ostatnia broń Hitlera* (*Hitler's Last Weapon*), London 1967.
3 W. Kozaczuk, *W kręgu Enigmy* (*In the Enigma Circle*), Warsaw 1986.
4 K. Gaj, *Szyfr Enigmy. Metody złamania* (*The Enigma Code: How Was It Broken*), Warsaw 1989.
5 J. Garliński, *Enigma*, London 1980.
6 W. Kozaczuk, *Wojna w eterze* (*The Radio War*), Warsaw 1982.
7 J. Piekałkiewicz, *Rommel. Tajna służba w Północnej Afryce 1941–1943* (*Rommel. Secret Service in North Africa 1941–1943*), Warsaw 1996; idem, *Dzieje szpiegostwa* (*History of Espionage*), Warsaw 1999.
8 J. Garliński, *Szwajcarski korytarz* (*The Swiss Corridor*), Paris 1987.
9 T. Panecki, *Polonia zachodnioeuropejska w planach Rządu RP na emigracji (1940–1944). Akcja kontynentalna* (*The Poles in Western Europe in the Plans of Government-in-Exile. Continental Action*), Warsaw 1986.
10 J.E. Zamojski, *Polacy w ruchu oporu we Francji 1940–1945* (*The Poles in the Resistance in France 1940-1945*), Wrocław 1975; idem, *Profesjonaliści i amatorzy. Szkic o dziejach polskiej służby wywiadowczej we Francji w latach 1940–1945* (*Professionals and Amateurs. On Polish Intelligence in France, 1940–1945*), 'Dzieje Najnowsze', 1980, no. 4.
11 T. Dubicki, *Ekspozytura 'R' w Bukareszcie (grudzień 1939–październik 1940)* (*Station 'R' in Bucharest (December 1939–October 1940)*), 'Mars', vol. 1, London-Warsaw 1993, pp. 65–85; idem, *Ewakuacja żołnierzy polskich w Rumunii w latach 1939-1941. Działalność organizacji 'Świt'* (*The Evacuation of Polish Soldiers from*

38 INTELLIGENCE CO-OPERATION BETWEEN POLAND AND GREAT BRITAIN

Romania, 1939–1941. The Activity of the 'Świt' Organisation), 'Przegląd Kawalerii i Broni Pancernej', vol. 9, London 1991, p. 8-38; idem, *Kurier do Lwowa*. *Zbigniew Roman Chaszczyński – 'Kazimierz Polniaczek', 'Kozak' (Courier to Lwów. Zbigniew Roman Chaszczyński – 'Kazimierz Polniaczek', 'Kozak'*), 'Mars', vol. 6, London-Warsaw 1994, pp. 145-164; idem, *Zaginieni kurierzy*. *Antoni Boski 'Strzała' i Bolesław Burkiewicz 'Stały' (The Lost Couriers. Antoni Boski 'Strzała' and Bolesław Burkiewicz 'Stały'*), 'Teki Historyczne', vol. 21, London 1994, pp. 236–249; idem, *Próba ucieczki płk. Józefa Becka z Rumunii (20.10.1940) w świetle archiwaliów rumuńskich (The Attempted Escape of Col. Józef Beck from Romania (20.10.1940) in the Light of Romanian Archives*), 'Zeszyty Historyczne', vol. 117, Paris 1996, pp. 19–45; idem, *Kawalerzysta kurierem. Działalność wachmistrza Jana Kowalskiego 'Józefa Dowbora' w Rumunii 1939–1940 (From Cavalryman to Courier. Sargent Jan Kowalewski 'Józef Dowbór' in Romania, 1939–1940*), 'Mars', vol. 4, London-Warsaw 1997, pp. 77–94; idem, *Łączność kurierska między Bukaresztem a Lwowem 1939–1940 (Courier Communications between Bucharest and Lwów 1939–1940*) [in:] *Z dziejów Wydziału Łączności Zagranicznej Komendy Głównej ZWZ-AK 'Zagroda' (Foreign Communications of the Home Army GHQ 'Zagroda'*), ed. by A. Tomczak, E. Zawacka and others, Toruń 1999, pp. 25–48; idem, *Polska konspiracja na Bukowinie w latach 1939–1944 (Polish Resistance in Bukovina, 1939–1944*), [in:] *Druga wojna światowa na tle stosunków polsko-rumuńskich (WW II in the Light of Polish-Romanian Relations*), Suceava 2000, pp. 43–69; idem, *Bazy wojskowej łączności zagranicznej ZWZ-AK w latach 1939–1945. Studia i materiały (Home Army Military Communications Bases 1939–1945. Studies and Sources), Częstochowa 2000; idem, Rumuńskie aspekty w Akcji Kontynentalnej (1940–1944) (Romanian Aspects of Continental Action, 1940-1944*), [in:] *Kontakty polsko-rumuńskie na przestrzeni wieków (Polish-Romanian Contacts Through the Ages*), Suceava 2001, pp. 11-36; idem, *Konspiracja polska w Rumunii 1939–1945 (Polish Resistance in Romania 1939–1945*), vol. 1, Warsaw 2002; idem, A. Sepkowski, *Afera Starykonia czyli historia agenta gestapo (The Starykoń Affair or a History of a Gestapo Agent*), Warsaw 1998.
12 A. Przewoźnik, *Początki konspiracji polskiej na Węgrzech. Działność Jana Mazurkiewicza na Węgrzech wrzesień 1939–czerwiec 1940 (The Beginnings of Polish Resistance in Hungary. The Activity of Jan Mazurkiewicz in Hungary, September 1939–June 1940*), 'Wojskowy Przegląd Historyczny', vol. 37, 1992, no. 3, idem, *Wojenne losy adwokata Jerzego Kurcyusza (The Fate of Jerzy Kurcjusz, Solicitor, during the War*), 'Palestra', 1997, no. 3–4.
13 L. Gondek, *Na tropach tajemnic III Rzeszy (The Secrets of the Third Reich*), Warsaw 1987.
14 W. Jastrzębski, *Maj. Żychoń i bydgoska ekspozytura wywiadu (Maj. Żychoń and the Bydgoszcz Intelligence Station*), Bydgoszcz 1994; A. Suchcitz, *Major Jan Henryk Żychoń – oficer wywiadu (Maj. Jan Henryk . Żychoń, Intelligence Officer*), 'Teki Historyczne', London 1988–1989, pp. 144–171; idem, *Major Jan Henryk Żychoń – materiały do biografii (Maj. Jan Henryk Żychoń – materials for a biography*), 'Zeszyt Naukowy Muzeum Wojska', Białystok 1990, pp. 102–114.
15 A. Pepłoński, *Wywiad Polskich Sił Zbrojnych na Zachodzie 1939–1945 (The Intelligence Service of Polish Armed Forces in the West 1939–1945*), Warsaw 1995. On Air Intelligence, see also: A. Suchcitz, *Air Intelligence Officer: Wing Commander Ferdynand Bobiński*, 'The Enigma Bulletin', May 1997, no. 2, [Cracow], pp. 87–92.
16 A. Pepłoński, *Współpraca Oddziału II z wywiadem Stanów Zjednoczonych (1941–1942) (II Bureau's Co-operation with American Intelligence, 1941–1942*), 'Wojskowy Przegląd Historyczny', 1991, no. 2; idem, *Udział wywiadu Polskich Sił Zbrojnych na Zachodzie w rozpoznaniu potencjału wojennego III Rzeszy (1939–1945) (Participation of Polish Armed Forces in the West in Intelligence on*

the Third Reich's War Potential, 1939–1945), 'Zeszyty Naukowe WAP', 1988, no. 3; idem, *Dzia łalność wywiadowcza Oddzia łu II Sztabu Naczelnego Wodza w latach 1939–1945 (Intelligence Activity of the II Bureau, PGS, in 1939–1945)*, 'Zeszyty Naukowe ASW', 1990, no. 59.

17 M. Utnik, *Sztab polskiego Naczelnego Wodza w II wojnie światowej (PGS in WW II)*, 'WPH', 1973, no. 4; idem, *Oddzia ł Łącznikowy Komendanta Głównego AK przy Naczelnym Wodzu na emigracji (VI Oddzia ł Sztabu Naczelnego Wodza) (the VI Bureau, PGS)*, 'WPH', 1981, no. 3.

18 L.A.B. Kliszewicz, *Placówka Łączności w Jugos ławii w czasie ostatniej wojny kryptonim 'S ława', 'Drawa' (Communication Post 'S ława', 'Drawa' in Jugoslavia During the Last War)*, 'Zeszyty Historyczne', 1983, no. 65; idem, *'Grzegorz' placówka wojskowej łączno ści w Grecji ('Grzegorz' Military Communications Post in Greece)*, 'Zeszyty Historyczne', 1983, no. 63; idem, *Baza w Sztokholmie (The Stockholm Base)*, 'Zeszyty Historyczne', 1981, no. 58. The above material was published in 6 books in the years 1990 to 2000 by Mars of Warsaw.

19 J. Nowak-Jeziorański, *Kurier z Warszawy (Courier from Warsaw)*, Warsaw-Kraków 1989; J. Karski, *Wielkie mocarstwa wobec Polski (The Main Powers and Poland)*, Warsaw 1992; A. Stpiczyński, *Wbrew wyrokowi losu (Against History's Verdict)*, Warsaw 1988.

20 H. Latkowska-Rudzińska, *Łączno ść zagraniczna Komendy G łównej Armii Krajowej 1939–1944. Odcinek –'Po ludnie' (Foreign Communications of the Home Army GHQ, 1939–1944, Sector South)*, Lublin 1985; H. Czarnocka, *Zasady i organizacja pracy konspiracyjnej w s łużbie łączno ści (Principles and Organisation of Underground Work in Communications), [in:] Łączno ść, sabotaż, dywersja. Kobiety w Armii Krajowej (Communications, Sabotage, Diversion. Women in the Home Army)*, London 1985, pp. 27–52.

21 P. Matusak, *Wywiad Związku Walki zbrojnej-Armii Krajowej 1939–1945 (ZWZ-AK Intelligence 1939–1945)*, Warszawa 2002. See also: idem, *Ruch oporu w przemyśle wojennym okupanta hitlerowskiego na ziemiach polskich w latach 1939–1945 (Resistance in the Arms Industry of the Hitlerite Occupier in Poland 1939–1945)*, Warszawa 1983.

22 B. Zakrzewski, *Formy organizacyjne i relacja o dzia łalności Oddzia łu II Informacyjno-Wywiadowczego KG AK w czasie II wojny światowej (Organisation of Work and an Account on the Activities of the II Bureau, the Home Army GHQ, During WW II)*, Warsaw, IH PAN, A 68/59.

23 *S łużba informacyjno-wywiadowcza Armii Krajowej (the Home Army GHQ Intelligence Service)*, 'Bellona', London, 1949, part 2, pp. 11–22 and idem, *S łużba informacyjno-wywiadowcza Armii Krajowej (the Home Army Intelligence Service)*, [in:] *Polskie Si ły Zbrojne (Polish Armed Forces)*, vol. 3, Armia Krajowa, London 1950.

24 M. Heller, *Ruch oporu na Śląsku Cieszyńskim w latach 1939–1945 (Resistance in the Cieszyn Silesia, 1939–1945)*, Opole 1982; A. Gąsiorowski, *Wywiad i dywersja w Okręgu Pomorskim ZWZ-AK (Intelligence and Diversion in the Pomorze [Pomerania] District of the Home Army GHQ)*, [in:] *Armia Krajowa na Pomorzu (the Home Army in Pomorze [Pomerania]*, red. E. Zawacka, Toruń 1993, pp. 77–110; H. Witkowski, *'Kedyw' Okręgu Warszawskiego Armii Krajowej w latach 1943–1944 ('Kedyw', Warsaw District, the Home Army, 1943–1944)*, Warsaw 1984; J.Z. Sawicki, *VII Obwód Okręgu Warszawskiego Armii Krajowej –'Obroża' ('Obroża': VII Region, Warsaw District, Home Army)*, Warsaw 1990; J. Węgierski, *W lwowskiej Armii Krajowej (the Home Army in Lwów)*, Warsaw 1989; J. Gozdawa-Go łębiowski, *Obszar Warszawski Armii Krajowej (Warsaw District of Home Army)*, Lublin 1992; A. Ropelewski, *W Jędrzejowskim Obwodzie AK (the Home Army Region in Jędrzejów)*, Warsaw 1986.

25 A. Klotz, *Zapiski konspiratora 1939–1945 (Notes of a Conspirator, 1939–1945)*,

Kraków 2001, and H. Zakrzewska, *Niepodległość będzie twoją nagrodą (Independence Shall Be Your Reward)*, Warsaw 1994.

26 K. Leski, *Życie niewłaściwie urozmaicone. Wspomnienia oficera wywiadu i kontrwywiadu AK (A Peculiarly Entertaining Life. Reminiscences of a Polish Intelligence and Counter-intelligence Officer)*, Warsaw 1989; J. Garliński, *Niezapomniane lata). Dzieje Wywiadu Więziennego i Wydziału Bezpieczeństwa Komendy Głównej Armii Krajowej (Remarkable Years. The History of Prison Intelligence and of Security Intelligence of the Home Army GHQ)*, London 1987; S. Jankowski, *Z fałszywym ausweisem w prawdziwej Warszawie (With Fake Ausweis in Real Warsaw)*, vol. 1–2, Warsaw 1984; C. Chlebowski, *Wachlarz. Monografia wydzielonej organizacji dywersyjnej Armii Krajowej, wrzesień 1941–marzec 1943 (Wachlarz. A Monograph of the Special Diversionary Unit of the Home Army, September 1941–March 1943)*, Warsaw 1983; idem, *Cztery z tysiąca (Four in a Thousand)*, Warsaw 1983 (2nd edition, corrected and expanded); J. Tucholski, *Cichociemni (The Parachutists)*, Warsaw 1988 (3rd edition, expanded); A. Ropelewski, *W służbie wywiadu Polski Walczącej (In the Service of Fighting Poland's Intelligence)*, Gdańsk 1994; S. Lewandowska, *Kryptonim 'Legalizacja' 1939–1945 (Cryptonym 'Forged Documents')*, Warsaw 1984; W. Grabowski, *Delegatura Rządu Rzeczypospolitej Polskiej na Kraj 1940–1945 (The Office of the Government Plenipotentiary for Poland)*, Warsaw 1995.

27 Bertrand wrote that all the glory for breaking the cipher belongs to the Poles, who were unrivalled in the world for their knowledge and perseverance (p. 61). The British considered the book to be at least indiscreet (see correspondence at TNA (PRO), HW 25/16, including an assessment of the Frenchman's book by the British cryptographer J. H. Tiltman, 15th May 1974). Bertrand published his book as his reaction to the publication by Michel Garder, *La Guerre Secrète des Services Spéciaux Français 1935–1945*, Paris 1967, which contained numerous mistakes. The first historian who wrote about the success of the Polish cryptologists was Władysław Kozaczuk, who in 1967 published the first edition of his book, *Bitwa o tajemnice. Służby wywiadowcze Polski i Rzeszy Niemieckiej 1922–1939 (A Battle for Secrets. Polish and German Intelligence Services 1922-1939)* (Warsaw 1967), where a short mention is made of the achievement of Polish cryptologists.

28 'The Enigma Bulletin', no. 1, Kraków, December 1990 (includes: G. Bloch, *The French Contribution to the Breaking of 'Enigma'*, pp. 3–13; Z.J. Kapera, *Bericht des Obstlt.i.G., K.G. Langer: Funkaufklärung der Alliierten im Frankreichfeldzug 1940*, pp. 15–32; idem, *Jerzy Witold Różycki (1909–1942)*, pp. 59–62; G. Glünder, *Als Funker und 'Geheimschreiber' im Krieg, 1941–1945*, pp. 33–47; T. Lisiecki, *The Polish Radio Intelligence in the Battle of Monte Cassino*, pp. 49–50; K. Gaj, *The Polish Cipher Machine 'Lacida'*, pp. 51–57); 'The Enigma Bulletin', no. 2, Kraków, May 1997 (includes: J. Rohwer, *International Historiography about Signal Intelligence*, pp. 3-16; C. Boyd, *Anglo-American-Japanese Cryptological Preparations for the Second World War*, pp. 17–52; R. Denniston, *Cicero, Dulles and Philby 1943–1944*, pp. 53–68; R. Erskine, *The Development of Typex*, pp. 69–86; A. Suchcitz, *Air Intelligence Officer: Wing Commander Ferdynand Bobiński*, pp. 87–92; 'The Enigma Bulletin', no. 3, Kraków, May 1998 (includes: A. Stripp, *A British Cryptanalyst Salutes the Polish Cryptanalysts*, pp. 1–3; C. Boyd, *The Role of Cryptologic Intelligence in the Pacific War, 1941–1943*, pp. 5–33); D. Kohnen, *Commanders Winn and Knowles: Winning the U-Boat War with Intelligence, 1939-1943*, Kraków 1999 ('The Enigma Bulletin', no. 4, Kraków 1999); 'The Enigma Bulletin', no 5, Kraków, June 2000 (includes: C. Boyd, *Imperial Japanese Ambassador Oshima Hiroshi: An Extraordinary Source of Allied Intelligence in the Second World War*, pp. 1–24; R.J. Hanyok, *Before Enigma: Jan Kowalewski and the Early Days of the Polish Cipher Bureau, 1919–1922*, pp. 25-33; W. Kozaczuk, *German Clandestine Intelligence in the 1920s*, pp. 35–54; D.J. Sexton, *Thoughts on*

the Poles, Ultra and Communication Intelligence in World War II, pp. 55–62; R.J. Ritter, *Notes on the Early Use of Machine Cipher in Switzerland*, pp. 63–65; H. Ulbricht, *The Enigma-Uhr*, pp. 67–83; Z.J. Kapera, *Mieczysław Zygfryd Słowikowski (1896–1989)*, pp. 84-92); idem, *Before Ultra There Was Gale. Some Contributions to the History of the Polish Enigma, 1932–1942*, Kraków 2002 ('The Enigma Bulletin', no. 6, Kraków 2002).

29 F.W. Winterbotham, *The Ultra Secret*, London 1974. See also: W. Stevenson, *A Man Called Intrepid. The Secret War*, New York–London 1976. Stevenson follows the same trail.

30 H. Sebag-Montefiore, *Enigma. The Battle for the Code*, London 2001. In 1938 the author's family sold Bletchley Park to the British Government. During WW II, Bletchley Park was the Headquarters of British Signals Intelligence.

31 Ibid., pp. 1–2 and 427. See also Simon Singh, *The Code Book*, op.cit, p. 146. Singh is an expert on the technical aspects of signals intelligence.

32 H. Sebag-Montefiore, *Enigma*, op.cit., pp. 304 and 428–429. In this popular book, Schmidt was treated as an almost central character. Writing about the breaking of Enigma, Sebag-Montefiore categorically stated that: 'the formula could not be solved unless Rejewski could somehow get his hands on the settings which the Germans had used'. Sebag-Montefiore mixed up the matter of reconstructing the Enigma machine with the discovery of the system of keys, which was the foundation of the success of the Polish cryptologists. In any case, the author quotes the French, who stated in 1938 that Enigma could not be broken on the basis of information supplied by Schmidt (ibid., p. 34; P. Paillole, *Notre espion chez Hitler*, Paris 1985, p. 163; G. Bertrand, *Enigma*, op.cit., p. 57).

33 Sebag-Montefiore was also very critical of Bertrand's role and depreciated the Frenchman's achievements. Such criticism was not justified by the source material presented in the book. In addition the author noted that the cryptologist Antoni Palluth, who was in a concentration camp under his real name, was not recognized for who he was by the German authorities, aware of some of his activities in Warsaw. Sebag-Montefiore stated: '[...] how close the Germans came to discovering from the Poles everything about the Allies' Enigma secret'. This statement assumed that Palluth would have talked, if recognised. At the same time other Polish officers, Lt-Col. Gwido Langer and Maj. Maksymilian Ciężki, played a deadly game with the Gestapo. Their extensive statements managed to persuade the Germans that during the war Enigma could not be broken. They, and Bertrand, kept the secret of Enigma. The SIS Chief, Stewart Menzies, was also aware of this (H. Sebag-Montefiore, *Enigma*, op.cit., p. 327; also P. Paillole, *Notre espion*, op.cit., p. 244). Sebag-Montefiore provided extensive details on the addictions and private lives of the Poles, and of Schmidt. He devoted no space to the private lives of his own compatriots, with the exception of Turing, though without any drastic details. The caption under Langer's photograph is characteristic: 'Gwido Langer, the head of the Cipher Bureau in Warsaw, told Bertrand in 1931 that Polish cryptographers might be able to use Schmidt's manuals to break the code. After the war was declared, Langer was nicknamed 'Monsieur Beaujolais' because he drank so much wine'. It would be difficult to come up with a more malicious and incorrect description of the head of the Polish Cipher Office of many years' standing. The British journalist also maintained that Langer and Ciężki were guilty of at least 'cheating' Bertrand. With the wrong assumption – that without the documents obtained from Schmidt the success would have been impossible – this would have been permissible. What was typical in this popular book, which had a number of editions and which had mostly excellent press reviews in Great Britain (as demonstrated on its cover), was that the author did not inform the reader at all why on 17th September the Polish cryptologists crossed the Romanian border. In other words, he did not even mention the Soviet invasion of Poland, conducted on the

basis of a treaty with Hitler. Ciężki's decision not to go back to communist Poland, Sebag-Montefiore chose to describe as follows: 'he decided not to live in Poland after the war' (H. Sebag-Montefiore, *Enigma*, op.cit., p. 348).

34 N. West, *MI-6. Operacje*, op.cit., pp. 119–121.

35 *British Intelligence in the Second World War. Its Influence on Strategy and Operations*, by F.H. Hinsley, with E.E. Thomas, C.F.G. Ransom, R.C. Knight, vol. 3, part 2, appendix 30, New York 1988, pp. 945–959. This appendix was a supplement to volume 1. In 1982, Marian Rejewski mentioned a number of factual mistakes made by Hinsley in the first volume (M. Rejewski, *Remarks on Appendix I*, [in:] 'Cryptologia', vol.1, no. 6, January 1982, p. 79; idem, *Mathematical Solution to the Enigma Cipher*, [in:] ibid. pp. 1–18). Most of these mistakes was corrected in volume 3. Hinsley maintained, that the Polish contribution did not affect the breaking of the Naval version of Enigma between August and October 1941 (*British Intelligence*, op.cit., vol. 3, p. 958). According to the opinion of the experts from MI-6 expressed in 1970's, the delays the British would have had to face, if the Poles did not break the code and did not reconstruct the machine, would have been between 9 and 12 months (TNA(PRO), HW 25/16).

36 *British Intelligence*, op.cit., vol. 1, p. 494. Later these were perfected, thanks to the extraordinary abilities of the British cryptographers. The Polish equipment, nevertheless, remained the basic pattern – and this was belittled without any technical analysis or even a straightforward comparison. The authors of the official history of British Intelligence in WW II maintained that the British used the information obtained from the Poles in July 1939 to perfect their own hand operated methods. These amounted to the preparation of a large number of perforated sheets (ibid., op.cit., vol. 1, p. 493). In reality the British made the required number of Polish sheets, as stipulated in the July agreement. In this area, the British did not have any methods of their own.

37 H. Sebag-Montefiore, *Enigma*, op.cit, pp. 428–429, and *British Itelligence*, op.cit., vol. 1, p. 494. There is no factual basis to the statement in the official history of British Intelligence in WW II, that:

'The regular solution of German naval and army Enigma keys began so much later than the beginning of 1941, and was the outcome of so many other developments, that it is unlikely that the Polish contribution made any difference to the dates from which they were mastered', and '(. . .) it is virtually certain that the GC and CS Enigma team would in any case have realised the need to develop analogue machinery for recovering the daily keys as soon as it had discovered the wirings of the Enigma wheels – the more so since the team included Turing, who already had an interest in machine computation' (ibid., pp. 494–495). The methodology employed by the Poles to break the Enigma code shows that knowing the internal arrangement of the rotors was not tantamount to the ability to read the encrypted messages. It is also worth pointing out that the Germans definitely did not assume that the very fact of one machine landing in the hands of their enemies equalled the ability to read the code. The Polish cryptologists had at their disposal certain formerly used keys as early as in the first half of 1930's. Even if an original German Enigma machine was then available, this would have meant little without the use of higher mathematics. In any case the French and the British had the replica of Enigma and sets of keys (possibly more keys than the Poles) from 1939. The British began to read the decrypted messages several months' later, having at their disposal 'Rejewski's bomb' and 'Zygalski's sheets' – and all the other clues, loyally passed on by the Poles.

38 W. Dorenberger, *V-2*, New York, 1954; A. Speer, *Inside the Third Reich Memoirs*, New York 1970; W. Churchill, *The Second World War*, vol. 1-6, *The Invasion of Italy*, London 1948–1953.

39 D. Piszkiewicz, *Przez zbrodnie do Gwiazd*, Warsaw 2000, p. 126. English version published as: *The Nazi Rocketeers. Dreams of Space and Crimes of War* (Westport-London 1995).

40 J. Garlinski, *Hitler's Last Weapons. The Underground War Against the V1 and the V2*, London 1978.

41 M.J. Neufeld, *The Rocket and the Reich. Peenemünde and the Coming of the Ballistic Missile Era*, Harvard 1996.

42 The English edition was published 10 years later: M.Z. Rygor Słowikowski, *In the Secret Service. The Lighting of the Torch*, London 1988. Introduction and foreword by the British historian John Herman, who also wrote *Agency Africa: Rygor's Franco-Polish Network and Operation Torch*, 'The Journal of Contemporary History', no. 4, October 1987.

43 pp. 250 and 826.

44 Regarding Operation 'Torch', on pp. 36–67 Smith said that the Governments-in-Exile of Norway, Belgium, Holland, Czechoslovakia and Poland (in this order) had their own intelligence services, which co-operated with SIS and with OSS (p.166). Smith did not mention that of these services, only Polish Intelligence was autonomous.

45 Józef Piłsudski Institute of America in New York (IJP), M.Z. Słowikowski-Rygor Archive, M.Z. Rygor-Słowikowski to R. H. Smith, London b.d. [1978].

46 See copies of these reports in NARA, College Park, Maryland, Records of the War Department General and Special Staff Entry 77, Military Intelligence Division, 'Regional File' 1922–44, in the collection French North Africa (boxes: 987-1036), and in Algeria (boxes: 68-72).

47 'The Daily Telegraph', London, 27th April 1978.

48 IJP, M.Z. Słowikowski-Rygor Archive, M.Z. Rygor Słowikowski to W. Jędrzejewicz, London 23rd October 1978. Co-operation with Polish Intelligence is also not mentioned in the two biographies of General William J. Donovan, the creator of OSS (R. Dunlop, *Donovan, America's Master Spy*, Chicago-New York-San Francisco 1982; on the other hand, the author mentions the pre-war links between Donovan and Poland, which are little known in Poland – and that for his activity on behalf of the Poles in WW I, Donovan was awarded the Commander's Cross of the Order of Polonia Restituta, p. 107; and A.C. Brown, *The Last Hero. Wild Bill Donovan*, New York 1982).

49 A. Dulles, *The Secret Surrender*, New York-London 1966.

50 J. Srodes, *Allen Dulles. Master of Spies*, Washington 2001. Srodes, quoting a 1992 interview with Nicholas Elliot, SIS Station head in Switzerland towards the end of the war, said that Szymańska was the widow of a Polish officer and a mistress of Admiral Wilhelm Canaris, head of Abwehr – neither of which is true.

51 J. Colville, *Strange Inheritance*, Salisbury 1983, p. 167. Colville also mentions the role of the Poles in the decyphering of the Enigma code, beginning in January 1940 (p. 171).

HISTORICAL BACKGROUND

6
Historical Background

Daria Nałęcz

Twenty short years after regaining its sovereignty, in 1939 the Polish State again faced the possibility of annihilation. The Third Reich, preparing itself for European domination and having subordinated Slovakia and annexed the Czech lands and Moravia, began to raise territorial demands against Poland. The German conquests were accompanied by similar activities by Italy and Japan. Josef Stalin, attempting to regain the influence lost by Russia after World War I and to obtain new advantages, commensurate with his newly acquired aspirations, was formulating equally expansive plans. Stalin, however, did not wish to be the first to make war: he much preferred to be the ultimate playmaker. In the late summer of 1939 Stalin, like Adolf Hitler, was interested in concluding a bilateral non-aggression treaty. The Third Reich and the USSR signed just such a treaty on 23rd August 1939. By so doing, Germany obtained relative security in the proposed war against Poland. For their part the Russians could begin military preparations for the conflict, which they intended to join later. For the moment the Russians were content with lesser gains, provided for in the additional protocols to the treaty.

On 1st September 1939 the German army began to implement their attack on Poland, in preparation since April of the same year. A million and a half well-trained and even better equipped Wehrmacht soldiers, supported by 2,500 tanks and 1,390 aircraft, crossed the eastern borders of Germany. The Polish defence was not fully prepared to face the aggression. The mobilization was incomplete and not all the divisions provided for in the defence plan were formed. The equipment of the Polish army left much to be desired and in any case it had only 610 old-fashioned tanks and as few as 394 warplanes. The defence plan, however, did not assume a victory using just Polish forces. In accordance with the guarantees provided by France and Great Britain, the expectation was that these two states would join the hostilities. It was the combined forces of the three countries together which were to face Hitler's expansionist intentions. The Poles did not know that, in accordance with the assessments of British and French staff officers made as early as spring 1939, these two countries would be unable to render Poland effective assistance in the initial stages of war. It is not surprising that when France and Great Britain declared war on Germany on 3rd September 1939, Polish public opinion reacted enthusiastically, hoping for a swift conclusion of hostilities. Further developments on the fronts, so different from the scenario, which appeared to be correctly implemented, brought only defeats. The heroism of the soldiers, who in numerous places faced the enemy's overwhelming forces for so many days, was insufficient. The lack of an offensive from the West, expected after 3rd September, further sapped the already low public morale, dented by the huge civilian losses caused by air attacks on towns and communication links. On 8th September the Germans began their siege of Warsaw. The progress of their forces was halted by the largest battle of the campaign, the battle of the Bzura River, which was to allow the Polish forces to regroup and to create a new defensive line along the River Dniester. This plan was doomed by the Soviet aggression, started at dawn on 17th September. The assumption that this date was selected by Stalin, who first made certain that the action on the Western front would not proceed beyond a political demonstration, appears to be fully justified.

On the evening of 17th September the Commander-in-Chief, Marshal Edward Rydz-Śmigły, together with the President of the Republic of Poland Ignacy Mościcki and the Prime Minister, Sławoj Felicjan Składkowski, crossed the Polish border and went to Romania, where they were interned. The army, however, continued to fight. Warsaw surrendered on 28th September, Hel – on 2nd October. The battle of Kock raged until 5th October.

In spite of the shock of the defeat in the defensive campaign, despite terror, which included public and secret executions of the civilian population, especially in Pomorze (Pomerania), Wielkopolska and in Śląsk (Silesia), notwithstanding the loss of confidence in the politicians of the ruling camp, the people believed that Germany would be defeated. There was still immense trust in the military might of France and Great Britain and faith in the strength of their alliance with Poland. One manifestation of this faith was the spontaneous emergence, as early as September 1939, of underground structures and cells with the purpose of collecting information about the enemy and the organization of sabotage and diversionary activities. These activities were undertaken both by groups of officers and soldiers who managed to avoid capture and did not evacuate themselves abroad, and by political parties, which began to build their own military structures.

The structures of the State, which as a consequence of the aggression by its two neighbours found itself under occupation, were quickly recreated. In accordance with the Constitution the President, unable to fulfil his office, nominated his successor: Władysław Raczkiewicz, who had reached France. He, in turn, appointed a Government headed by

General Władysław Sikorski, who at the same time became Commander-in-Chief. The Parliament was dissolved. The National Council was set up as a substitute, de facto to advise the President and the Government. The President on the Prime Minister's motion appointed its members. Since the new authorities were constitutionally based, they gained the recognition of France, Great Britain, the United States and the majority of neutral countries. Almost immediately the task of recreating the armed forces was begun. Their foundations consisted of soldiers who managed to avoid captivity. At the beginning of the French campaign these forces counted over 80 thousand soldiers in battle readiness. Some airmen were stationed in France, others in Britain. The Polish Navy made use of British ports. Until June 1940 the main burden of equipping and maintaining these forces rested on the French government, which provided shelter both to the armed forces and to the Polish authorities.

The re-emerging state structures abroad wished to control and to centralize the resistance activities in occupied Poland. The achievement of this aim was not easy. The distance, communication difficulties, lack of trust dating back to the political differences of the inter-war years – but most of all the war itself – these were barriers which required time to overcome. But the goal was finally achieved. The strongest of the military organizations, which emerged in Poland, the Service for Poland's Victory (Służba Zwycięstwu Polski–SZP), which was initiated and set up by General Michał Tokarzewski-Karaszewicz, subordinated itself to the government-in-exile. Replaced by the Związek Walki Zbrojnej (Union of Armed Struggle – the Home Army) in November 1939 – and renamed Armia Krajowa (the Home Army) in February 1942, this became the base for the Polish Underground State. It was active on the territory taken over by both occupying powers and was divided into Areas and Districts. It also had a number of specialized organizational units. The principal civilian organ of state in occupied Poland was the Office of the Government Plenipotentiary for the Homeland.

However, not all political, cultural, educational or even military activity was subject to the government-in-exile. In the circumstances created by war, with regard to significant political differences and the terror and extermination used by the occupiers, this was impossible. The sheer scale of repression, the mass deportations as forced labour, and to the labour and death camps, the deliberate policy (employed by both occupying powers) of physically destroying the intelligentsia. With their own administration set up in occupied territories – all of this was an impediment to any activity, above all making personal contacts difficult. On the other hand a failure to observe strict requirements of conspiracy often had tragic consequences: in accordance with the doctrine of joint responsibility the numbers of those who were punished were much greater than the immediate circle of conspirators.

His Polish conquests did not satisfy Hitler. But the difficulties of the campaign, and especially the significant Panzer and Luftwaffe losses, slowed down the development of offensive actions. The Third Reich mounted its new offensive in the spring of 1940. On 9th April Denmark was overrun in one day. On the same day war against Norway began, with the seizure of Narvik. A month later an attack resulted in the occupation of Holland, Belgium and Luxemburg. Next, having by-passed the Maginot Line, the German army attacked France. The French defence collapsed. On 14th June the German forces entered Paris.

For the Polish Army, the collapse of France meant the end of French hospitality and quick evacuation. Conditions were agreed between General Sikorski and the new British Prime Minister, Winston Churchill. Some 27 thousand officers and men managed to reach Great Britain. The Carpathian Brigade, later to gain fame in the defence of Tobruk, escaped from Syria to Palestine and also managed to join the British. Every 10th pilot in the Battle of Britain, which started in July 1940, was a Pole. Thus begun a very fruitful period of Polish – British co-operation, encompassing both military affairs, including that in the intelligence field (to which this publication is devoted), as well as in political affairs.

The organizational and operational status of the Polish Armed Forces, the formation of which was begun under the treaty with France, was regulated by the Polish–British agreement of 5th August 1940 (expanded on 22nd August). Polish units joined the common Allied operations. The Army and the Air Force fought in Northern Europe (1940), in Western Europe (1940, 1944–1945), in North Africa, in the Middle East and in Italy. It was in Italy that the Polish 2nd Corps, which emerged from the amalgamation of Polish units in the Middle East with the army evacuated by General Władysław Anders from the Soviet Union, gained fame. The Polish Navy took part in operations in the Atlantic, the North Sea, the Norwegian Sea, the Arctic Sea and the Mediterranean. It also protected the convoys and patrolled the Channel. The 14 Polish squadrons under RAF command participated not only in defensive actions, but also in the raids on Germany and in the Allied landings in Normandy in June 1944. Altogether some 300 thousand troops served in the Polish Armed Forces. In May 1945 their strength was estimated at some 200 thousand.

The Polish war effort, the participation in the war against the Axis powers, was to be an argument in favour of the restitution of the State. The principal foundation of the Polish policy was the return to Poland's pre-war borders. This goal was linked to the tasks given to the ZWZ–AK (the Union of Armed Struggle – the Home Army, further the Home Army) operating on the Polish soil. The Home Army was to prepare an uprising, which was to take place when the regular Polish units crossed the State border. On the basis of this plan staff functions and officer corps were organized, so as to be ready to form full-strength military units. It was not expected that the wait for military victory would be so long and that the balance of political power in Europe and in the world would be so thoroughly transformed. These transformations influenced the modification of the aims of Polish military formations. The diversionary, intelligence, self-defence, informational and propaganda tasks were systematically broadened. In all, some 110 thousand military operations were undertaken throughout Poland, resulting in some 100 thousand underground soldiers losing their lives. The German attack on the USSR, and in particular the overcoming of the German offensive by the Red Army which, from the summer of 1943, started its victorious march Westwards, brought a significant change. The orders transmitted to Poland at the time spoke of fighting against the retreating German units and of the coming out into the open of the underground Polish military and civilian authorities once Soviet units arrived.

With the USSR joining the war against the Third Reich in June 1941, the political balance on which Polish policy rested had changed. After the collapse of France, Great Britain became the most important ally. But for Britain the Soviet partner was much more important than the Polish one. This was the reason for the pressures on the Polish government to re-establish diplomatic relations, to sign a treaty of mutual assistance and co-operation and a military agreement. General Sikorski was prepared to make this move, but first he wanted Soviet guarantees as to the validity of the borders as settled in the Riga peace treaty. He did not, however, obtain such assurances. He was negotiating with the Soviet ambassador to London, Ivan Mayski, who did not address this issue at all. Sikorski was not aware of the Soviet position presented in the talks with the British to the effect that the USSR had no intention of leaving the territories taken by it in 1939. His agreement to sign the treaty with the USSR cost Sikorski a major cabinet crisis.

The Polish Prime Minister hopefully began to look for the goodwill of the Americans, especially after the US joined the war following the Japanese attack on Pearl Harbor. But here, too, he was to be disappointed. The US had its own aims, only to a limited degree linked to the situation in Europe. The situation in the Far East and the war with Japan were more important for them. In this case, too, the Soviet partner counted for more.

Meantime the Polish–Soviet relations were systematically worsening. There was no shortage of tensions surrounding the formation of the Polish army, being recruited from among Polish deportees and prisoners of war. General Sikorski's agreement to evacuate this army out of the USSR to Iran, to fight in the Middle East, was considered a typical example of disloyalty, though de facto Moscow was glad to be rid of a problematic ally. Moreover the absence of Poles on the Eastern front was treated as a convenient excuse to disregard Polish arguments. Finally the Polish–Soviet relations collapsed following the German communiqué of 13th April 1943 on the discovery of the mass graves of Polish officers at Katyń. Soviet diplomacy considered the content of this communiqué to be a provocation and an attempt to shift the blame for a crime committed by the Third Reich. The Germans responded with an appeal to the International Red Cross asking it to dispatch experts. The Polish government submitted a similar appeal. This was sufficient for the USSR authorities to break relations with the Polish government and constituted a convenient argument for open support for the Polish communists, who wanted to create their own political structures on the Soviet territory. By then Stalin was determined to conduct his own active policy concerning Polish territory and to introduce there an administration which would do his bidding. These desires were supported by the fact that the Red Army no longer was on the defensive and was soon to win the largest armoured battle of the war, at Kursk. This meant that the initiative at the front was now with Moscow. The swift advance of the Soviet armies westwards indicated that it was they who would be the first to reach Polish soil, and not the other Allies.

Observing the developments in the East, President Roosevelt began discussing with Prime Minister Churchill about the possibility of invading Europe, to fulfil the obligation made almost a year earlier to open up a 'second front' against the armies of the Third Reich. Both leaders had also commenced a debate concerning the future world order. They concluded that the decisive voice should belong to the victorious powers, that is the US, Great Britain and the USSR. They also considered the possibility of including a fourth partner: China. There was no room in this scenario for small and middle-sized countries. Their fate was to be decided by the largest coalition partners. The first decisions were made at the Tehran conference at the end of November and early December 1943. Though attempts were made to keep these confidential, the Big Three reached an understanding concerning, among other issues, Polish borders. In the East these were to be identical with those specified in the Soviet–German treaty; in the West – the Oder river.

With time, the Polish leaders began to understand the gravity of the situation and the strength of their argument weakened as General Sikorski was no longer among them, having died at Gibraltar on 4th July 1943. His successor, Stanisław Mikołajczyk, was prepared for a far-reaching compromise, which however did not find the approval of even his immediate entourage. He agreed to territorial concessions believing that the sovereignty of the state was more important. To guarantee sovereignty, he accepted the principle of a coalition government to include the communists. These concessions, however, proved insufficient.

The Polski Komitet Wyzwolenia Narodowego (Polish Committee of National Liberation, further 'PKWN'), set up at the end of July 1944 under Soviet tutelage, in effect a government in competition with the government-in-exile, began to enter into international agreements on their own terms. One of the first was the border agreement with the Council of People's Commissars. On 31st December 1944 the PKWN was replaced by the Provisional Government.

The major offensive started by the Red Army in January 1945 in as little as a month and a half led to the dislodgement of the German forces from almost the whole of the Polish territory. NKVD units, supported by the Polish security forces linked to the Provisional Government, started mass arrests of armed resistance members and of people linked to the administration subject to the government-in-exile. In March 1945 the Government Plenipotentiary and members of the Home Council of Ministers were arrested.

By agreeing in Tehran and confirmed in Yalta to the division of influence in Europe corresponding to the current areas of military presence of specific armies, the Allies hoped that the political future would be decided in free elections. These were to take place as soon as hostilities ceased. In relation to Central and Eastern Europe these expectations have failed. The emergence of the Provisional Government of National Unity on 28th June 1945, which incorporated a few members of the government-in-exile, and the withdrawal of recognition from the government-in-exile began a new period in the history of Poland. This brought about the change of the political and economic system and the reversal of alliances.

The Polish State lost 20% of its territory and 30% of its population. During the war every fifth citizen perished – which meant that Poland led in the terrible league table of deaths per one thousand inhabitants. In Poland the death toll was 220 per thousand population; in the USSR – 116; in France – 15, in Great Britain – 8. On the other hand the number of émigrés who did not want to or could not return to Poland increased by 500 thousand. Almost 40% of the national wealth was destroyed.

Border changes, population movements, the break-up of social relationships, the extermination of the major part of the intelligentsia during the war – all this, combined with the strength of the new apparatus of repression, facilitated the introduction of a new ideology, a new vision of the future and of the past. It led to changes in the pantheon of national heroes and prevented any assessment of Polish policies during the war. Another half century had to pass to enable others to return to these issues – to pay homage and testimony of their deeds.

7

British-Polish Intelligence Collaboration during the Second World War in Historical Perspective

Christopher Andrew

The Second World War was, to a greater extent than any previous conflict, an intelligence war. At a series of critical points in both the Western and Pacific theatres, intelligence demonstrated a remarkable capacity to operate as a force multiplier and, in so doing, hastened the defeat of both Germany and Japan. Largely for that reason, the war produced an unprecedented degree of allied intelligence collaboration. Britain's most extensive intelligence collaboration of the war was ultimately with her most powerful ally, the United States. The founding of the 'special relationship' with the Polish intelligence community, however, preceded that with the United States.

Intelligence collaboration was the product of a much broader British-Polish special relationship. If the Battle of Britain was, as Churchill famously described it, Britain's 'finest hour', it was also the finest hour of British-Polish airforce collaboration. Of the 1,733 German aircraft destroyed during the Battle of Britain, 203 were shot down by Polish squadrons. Polish land forces also fought with distinction alongside their British allies in a great variety of theatres: among them the Western Desert, Italy, Norway, the ill-fated Arnhem operation and the victorious Normandy landings. The smaller Polish naval units took part in combined operations ranging from the successful pursuit of the German battleship, *Bismarck*, in May 1941 to convoy escort duties during the Battle of the Atlantic, the longest drawn-out battle in the history of naval warfare, during which German U-boats came close to breaking the vital lifeline between Britain and North America. Despite the moments of tension which inevitably occur in even the closest of alliances, the intelligence communities of Britain and Poland, like their armed services, had the common conviction that they were jointly engaged in one of the most decisive conflicts in the history of the world.

Neither the range nor the intimacy of the British-Polish intelligence collaboration established early in the Second World War had any historical precedent. No foreign signals intelligence (SIGINT) agency had ever provided British codebreakers with assistance as important as that provided by Polish cryptanalysts in the attack on the German Enigma machine cipher. Much of the story of the Polish contribution to ULTRA, the best intelligence in the history of warfare, is now well known. It is often forgotten, however, that Polish cryptanalysis improved the morale as well as the working methods of British codebreakers. At the outbreak of war there was widespread pessimism within the Government Code and Cypher School (GC&CS), the British SIGINT agency, about the prospects for breaking Enigma. Frank Birch, who became head of the naval section at Bletchley Park, later wrote to its director, A. G. Denniston, 'Defeatism at the beginning of the war, to my mind, played a large part in delaying the breaking of codes.'[1] Until the now celebrated visit in July 1939 of British and French cryptanalysts to the Cipher Bureau at Pyry, outside Warsaw, GC&CS had no idea of the progress made by the Poles. After a meeting in Paris in January 1939 with two senior members of the Cipher Office, who were under orders not to reveal the extent of their success, a GC&CS representative wrote dismissively – and inaccurately – about the Poles: 'Practical knowledge of enigma nil'. When Dillwyn 'Dilly' Knox, the GC&CS chief cryptanalyst, was shown the Polish clone of Enigma at Pyry, he was initially stunned and probably annoyed at the discovery that GC&CS had been so successfully deceived six months earlier. After initially maintaining 'a stony silence', however, Knox, according to Denniston, became 'his own bright self & won the hearts & admiration of the young men with whom he was in touch'.[2] Though Polish assistance was of great importance, Knox subsequently improved on Polish cryptanalytic methods and the 'bombe' devised by Alan Turing, the basis of most British successes against the variants of Enigma, was radically different in design from the Polish 'bomba'.[3]

The closest and most extensive British-Polish collaboration was in human intelligence (HUMINT) rather than in SIGINT. In June 1940 Polish intelligence became the first foreign agency in British history to be permitted to run from London a full range of HUMINT operations with its own training establishments, codes, communications base and clandestine networks operating in a wide swathe of German-occupied and neutral Europe as well as parts of North Africa, the Middle East, the Far East and the Americas. The Polish government-in-exile agreed to pass to SIS all the intelligence it received, except for that dealing with Poland's internal affairs. In August, Commander Wilfred 'Biffy' Dunderdale, the SIS officer responsible for liaison with the Poles, reported that 'Liaison with all sections of the Polish I[ntelligence] S[ervice] is now working smoothly and satisfactorily'.[4]

Probably the most important Polish intelligence passed to SIS over the next year concerned German preparations for Operation BARBAROSSA, the invasion of the Soviet Union which began on 22 June 1941. On 5 February 1941 British military intelligence referred to a report (probably from a Polish source, though the report itself does not survive in British archives) that the movement of German troops and armour to the east was so large that it was causing congestion on the railways between Berlin and Warsaw. During May Polish intelligence provided details of a series of German troop movements by rail to the east, only one of which was mentioned in Enigma decrypts. Along with other intelligence from non-Polish sources which pointed to BARBAROSSA, however, the significance of these reports was largely misunderstood. Whitehall wrongly believed that Hitler was deferring a decision on whether to attack the Soviet Union pending the outcome of negotiations with Moscow. The Joint Intelligence Committee (JIC), which bore the main responsibility for intelligence assessment, reported on 23 May that the advantages to Germany of reaching agreement with Russia were 'overwhelming'. Not till 12 June, ten days before the beginning of BARBAROSSA, did the JIC report that Hitler had definitely decided to attack. That it had finally grasped this important truth was due chiefly to the fact that, with the establishment of the Joint Intelligence Staff (JIS) to assist it, the JIC had at last the machinery required to collate and assess all available information on enemy strategy.[5] Britain's ability to interpret the intelligence it received from the Poles, as from all other sources, was thus crucially dependent on the development of its own assessment system.

Thanks in large part to Churchill's staunch support, the JIC became, for all its faults, the best intelligence assessment system in the history of warfare. Probably the Polish intelligence valued most highly by the JIC in the final stages of the war concerned the development of Germany's V-weapons, which would have posed an even greater threat had war in Europe continued after May 1945. Polish intelligence provided reports from both the research station at Peenemünde and the test-site at Blizna. Remarkably, in July 1944, one month after V-1 'flying bombs' were launched against Britain for the first time, one of the Poles who had been monitoring the tests at Blizna succeeded in cycling 200 miles to a secret airstrip and flying to London with fragments of the even more dangerous V-2 rocket (used against British targets from September) and important documents on V-weapons development.[6]

There was also unprecedentedly close British-Polish collaboration in special operations. As chief of staff of the British military mission to Poland in the summer of 1939, Colin Gubbins (later Major-General and, from September 1943, executive director of SOE) brought back to London a device known as a time-pencil, capable of detonating plastic explosive after pre-set periods from ten minutes to thirty hours. Originally invented by the Germans during the First World War, improved by the Poles and perfected by the SOE's secret research establishment, Section X,[7] the time-pencil became a key part of SOE's sabotage armoury. More than twelve million of them were manufactured during the Second World War. The first SOE airlift of military supplies to any resistance group in occupied Europe was to Poland on 15 February 1941. Assisted by SOE supplies and training, Polish saboteurs played a major part in disrupting Nazi railway traffic on the Eastern Front, destroying or seriously damaging an estimated 6,000 locomotives. In the autumn of 1941 they came close to assassinating Hitler while he was travelling on his personal train, the Führerzug, to his headquarters in East Prussia, the Wolfschanze ('Wolf's Lair'). Polish resistance fighters succeeded in laying several kilograms of explosive on a railway line over which the Führerzug was due to travel. Hitler had a narrow escape as the result of an unscheduled stop. A German train which overtook the Führerzug detonated the explosive, killing 430 of those on board. This episode later provided part of the inspiration for Operation FOXLEY, SOE's own never-implemented plan to assassinate Hitler.[8]

The destruction of important Polish and British intelligence records in the years following the Second World War has, unhappily, produced serious gaps in the historical record of wartime intelligence collaboration. The failure of SIS to preserve Polish intelligence records entrusted to it at the end of the war has caused understandable surprise in Poland – sometimes even the misguided suspicion that SIS or the British government still has these documents but for bizarrely machiavellian reasons refuses to release them. The root cause of Polish surprise derives from unfamiliarity with SIS's record-keeping policy half a century or more ago. Sadly, the idea that the intelligence files in its keeping were an important part of the national archives which had to be preserved for future historical research did not occur to SIS. Once files had ceased to have current or potential operational significance, SIS often saw no reason to preserve them. At the end of the Second World War SIS confidently expected all the records which it preserved to remain secret indefinitely. To argue that Polish intelligence files could not have been destroyed by SIS half a century ago because of what we *now* recognise as their historical importance is anachronistic. Until 1992 successive British governments refused to admit officially that Britain had ever possessed a foreign intelligence service. Even today no SIS files, going right back to its foundations in 1909, have been declassified – though, happily, SIS documents are sometimes to be found in the files of other government departments. There is, however, one significant (though not adequate) compensation for the serious gaps in wartime intelligence archives. The destruction of documents in British files has forced Polish historians to cast their net widely in archives outside both Britain and Poland. Some of the chapters in this volume are a tribute to the imagination and ingenuity of their search for source material on British-Polish intelligence collaboration.

Apart from the gaps in the archives, the main obstacle to understanding the achievements of British-Polish wartime intelligence collaboration are the conspiracy theories which pollute much popular intelligence history. Few academic historians take seriously claims that Roosevelt (or Churchill) had intelligence which gave advance warning of the Japanese attack on Pearl Harbor but allowed the attack to go ahead as a way of bringing the United States into the war. This and other intelligence myths of the Second World War, however, are still widely believed. Sadly, these myths include the claim that the tragic death of Sikorski when his Liberator crashed on take-off from Gibraltar in 1943 was an assassination ordered by Churchill and carried out by British intelligence, which sabotaged the aircraft. In reality, Churchill's papers, as well as Foreign Office and Cabinet Office files, demonstrate that he regarded Sikorski as the best possible Polish leader. A detailed investigation carried out in 1969 by the Co-ordinator of Intelligence, Sir Dick White (a distinguished former head of both MI5 and SIS), which was endorsed by the Cabinet Secretary, Sir Burke Trend, concluded that there was no evidence that the crash of the Liberator was anything other than a tragic accident. The report on the investigation is available in the National Archives.[9] Research for this volume has uncovered no evidence which casts doubt on it.

But for the forcible inclusion of post-war Poland in the Soviet Bloc, wartime British-Polish intelligence co-operation would undoubtedly have continued into peacetime. Harold Perkins, head of SOE's Polish section, wrote in October 1944 that he knew of 'very few Englishmen' who could compare with Polish intelligence's 'first-hand knowledge of Russia, of Russian mentality, and of Russian methods'. This represented, he declared, 'an asset which should not lightly be discarded'.[10] The Soviet construction of a new Polish security and intelligence service, in its own Stalinist image was, of course, to make that asset unavailable to Cold War British intelligence. It is, however, the precedent of the wartime special relationship rather than the experience of the Cold War which now influences British-Polish relations at the beginning of the twenty-first century.

The relations between the intelligence communities of different states remain one of the least studied aspects of twentieth-century relations. The study of the wartime British-Polish special relationship is an essential stage in filling that important lacuna. It also remains relevant today at a time when the twin threats of fanatical trans-national terrorism and the proliferation of weapons of mass destruction make necessary international intelligence collaboration on an even larger scale than during the Second World War.

Notes

1   Birch to Denniston, 27 December 1940: copy in the possession of the Bletchley Park cryptanalyst, the late Christopher Morris. Christopher Andrew, *Secret Service: The Making of the British Intelligence Community*, 3rd edition (London: Sceptre, 1992), p. 631.

2   GC&CS minute, 13 January 1939; Denniston, 'How the News was brought from Warsaw at the end of July 1939', n.d., PRO HW 25/12. Ralph Erskine, 'Breaking Air Force and Army Enigma', in Michael Smith and Ralph Erskine (eds), *Action This Day* (London: Bantam, 2001), p.52. The articles in *Action This Day* provide the most up-to-date one-volume account of the work of Bletchley Park.

3   R. Erskine, 'Breaking Air Force and Army Enigma', pp. 53–7.

4   See chapter 2.

5   F.H.Hinsley et al., *British Intelligence in the Second World War* (London: HMSO, 1979-90), vol. 1, ch. 14.

6   Hinsley et al., *British Intelligence in the Second World War*, vol.3, part 2, chs. 41–2.

7   Section X is not to be confused with 'Station X', a codename for Bletchley Park.

8 M. R. D. Foot, *SOE: An Outline History of the Special Operations Executive, 1940–46* (London: Pimlico, 1999), pp. 264–5. Denis Rigden, *Kill the Führer: Section X and Operation Foxley* (Thrupp, Gloucestershire: Sutton Publishing, 1999), pp. 10–11.

9 The National Archives (TNA): (PRO) PREM 13/2644.

10 TNA: PRO, CAB 81/132-3. Michael Smith, *New Cloak, Old Dagger: How Britain's Spies Came in from the Cold* (London: Victor Gollancz, 1996), p. 110.

8

Consideration of the situation of Poland and the Poles during the Second World War

Jan Ciechanowski

I. Poland in Defeat, September 1939–June 1941

Poland was the first country to resist German aggression. The German attack on Poland, which precipitated the outbreak of the Second World War and finally led to the destruction of the Third Reich, began on 1 September 1939. The bulk of the German army and air force was thrown into the struggle. The Germans were aware that they were taking a serious risk, but, though Britain and France declared war on 3 September, it was Poland which bore the main brunt of Nazi aggression. Only massive and immediate support from Britain and France on the Western Front could have saved her from destruction, but no offensive was forthcoming despite Polish expectations and demands. The British and French declaration of war were for the time being merely diplomatic gestures. Britain did not expect to save Polish independence at the beginning of the war. Indeed, it was believed that nothing could be done to assist Poland. France for her part did nothing more than launch a probing attack upon the German Siegfried line which was little more than a token gesture and gave no relief to Poland. Gen. Alfred Jodl, the head of the Wehrmacht-führrungsstall, stated after the war: 'If we did not collapse in 1939, that was only because the approximately 110 French and English divisions in the West, which during the campaign remained completely inactive.'

The situation in Poland was catastrophic. The Polish army badly deployed, only partially mobilised and desperately short of modern equipment, was no match for the formidable German military machine. Hitler engaged in Poland 65 divisions, including all his armoured and motorised large formations, altogether around 1,500,000 men with 10,000 guns and mortars, 2,500 tanks and over 1,500 aeroplanes. Fifteen panzer and motorised divisions with powerful air support were the spearhead of the German advance. With the mobility, fire power and air support the Germans could conduct a war of movement and for the first, but not the last time, display their mastery of Blitzkrieg tactics.

As one German general put it quite recently: 'We Germans know how to start wars but we do not know how to finish them'. Hitler's plan was simple. Assuming that Britain and France would remain inactive, he concentrated his efforts upon destroying Poland as soon as possible. [Two army groups, the southern group in Silesia and Slovakia under Gen. Gerd von Rundstedt and the northern group under Gen. Fedor von Bock in Pomerania and East Prussia, were to launch simultaneous attacks enveloping Warsaw and the area a little to its east, with the intention of encircling and destroying the Polish armies deployed in the bend of the Vistula before they could retreat behind the lines of the rivers Vistula, Narew and San. They planned a second wider encircling movement east of those formations which might evade the jaws of the inner trap.] The geography of the German-Polish frontiers favoured this strategy, allowing the Germans to deploy their forces from the outset in such a way as to make encirclement possible. The Polish army could not hope to defend itself successfully in such a situation. The Polish plan was based on the assumption that the Germans would deploy against Poland the bulk of their forces and that the Poles would have to adopt a defensive position, preventing their troops from being destroyed until the Anglo-French offensive in the west, which they expected would begin on the fifteenth day of French mobilisation. The aim was to inflict heavy losses on the Germans in the hope of holding a defensive position and preventing undue loss of territory and, above all, of the important industrial areas west of the Vistula. The chances of this plan succeeding were slender. The Polish Commander-in-Chief, Marshal Rydz-Śmigły, realised that the Germans had a numerical and material superiority, but he failed to recognise its true extent. He failed also to envisage the possibility of Soviet intervention in Poland, although some Polish commanders considered it a foregone conclusion after the signing of the German-Soviet pact and were fully aware that Poland would be the loser in her first encounter with Germany. Rydz-Śmigły trusted in the Anglo-French offensive in the west, believing that the war would be long and arduous but would end with a final victory for Poland and her allies. The German plan in fact succeeded beyond all expectations.

The Polish army was defeated in a piecemeal fashion by the Germans, despite the customary heroism of the Polish soldiers and the tactical skill of their officers in the field. Most Polish front-line units fought well, but bravery and tenacity could not avert disaster.

On 17 September the Red Army entered Poland and the Polish government and high command left Poland for Romania. The Soviet invasion occurred when the campaign was already effectively lost, but it did hasten the collapse of Polish resistance and prevented many Polish units from escaping abroad. Warsaw fell on 28 September, though some Polish units did continue to resist until 5 October, when they finally capitulated. The entire campaign had lasted thirty-five days. For the Poles it was a shattering and bitter defeat, leading to the *de facto* disappearance of Poland from the map of Europe. The overwhelming German superiority meant that the outcome of the campaign was never in doubt.

However, the campaign bought time for the Western Allies to prepare themselves for their own encounter with Germany. Further, it provided the Western Allies with a splendid, if brief, chance of launching a successful offensive against Germany in the west, a chance which they failed to exploit. Abandoned by her allies, Poland could not hope to withstand the German onslaught for long.

The bulk of the German forces had to be committed to overcome the Poles, and the expenditure in ammunition, petrol and material was such as to preclude concurrent major operations in the West or elsewhere. If the French and the British attacked at the time in the west the Germans would have had nothing with which to resist. The Germans lost about 45,000 men, about half of the losses they were to sustain from the outbreak of the war to the attack on Russia in June 1941. In material they lost 241 aeroplanes, 236 tanks (and 419 were partly damaged) and armoured cars, about 370 guns and mortars and 11,000 military vehicles. Polish losses were very much higher, amounting to 200,000 killed and wounded and 420,000 taken prisoner. Only some 90,000 Polish soldiers managed to escape abroad to Romania, Hungary and Lithuania. The Red Army captured about 200,000 officers and men. For the Poles, Soviet intervention in 1939 was an act of treachery, a stab in the back.

Probably Stalin's basic motives for entering into an Agreement with Hitler were his desire to regain the territories Russia had lost in the years 1917 to 1921, and a wish to keep her out of the war, which he knew would break out in Europe, for as long as possible. It is also probable that only after the fall of France in 1940 he realised that the USSR faced a situation of immense gravity. The USSR was faced by a victorious Germany in control of almost all Western and Central Europe with their economic and industrial resources.

Hitler, for his part, had to review German strategy after the Battle of Britain and the failure to bring about a British submission. The logic of the situation was to attempt to knock out the USSR before the USA intervened actively in the European war, since it obviously favoured Britain, having provided war materials in the crisis 1940-41.

Meanwhile, at the end of September 1939 Poland found herself once again under foreign domination; partitioned by Germany and Russia. Poland was divided by the German-Soviet agreement of 28 September 1939 into two parts or 'zones of interest'. The territory west of the line of the rivers Pisa, Narew, Bug and San was occupied by Germany, while the areas to the east were allocated to the USSR. The demarcation line known as the Ribbentrop-Molotov Line approximated roughly to the Curzon Line of 1919–20. Germany acquired territory amounting to almost 189,000 square kilometres, which were primarily ethnically Polish with a population of 21.8 million, while the Soviet Union occupied about 200,000 square kilometres inhabited by about 13.2 million people. Berlin and Moscow agreed not to tolerate 'Polish agitation' in their occupation zones. By the end of October 1939 it became clear that they had no intention of establishing a rump state in any form or shape. Their policy was to be one of partition and annexation pure and simple. From the outset both parties set about strengthening their hold in Poland by establishing an administrative structure to control their zones. For the Poles there could be no question of collaborating with the occupying powers. Poland was the one country under German domination which did not produce a figure of the character of Quisling or Pétain.

The German security forces considered all Poles to be members of the resistance. Indeed, the Gestapo believed that by May 1941 there was not a single Pole who would come forward and really work for Germany. The Germans were to complain that it was impossible to subdue the Poles because of their 'fanatical faith' in the resurrection of Poland.

Moscow was anxious to 'justify' and 'legalise' its annexation policies in Eastern Poland. Soviet entry into Poland was represented as the result of the virtual collapse of the Polish State and the government and arising out of a need to protect Ukrainian and Byelorussian 'blood brothers'. In November 1939 the occupied territories were incorporated into the USSR. It was claimed that this step was based on the right of the 'Western Ukrainians' and 'Western Byelorussians' to self-determination. They constituted the majority of the population and demanded through 'democratically' elected assemblies assimilation with the Soviet Union.

The Polish government refused to accept this disposition of the eastern provinces, which it continued to regard as an integral part of Poland, questioning the legality of annexation and dismissing as fraudulent the elections which preceded it. From 29 November 1939, the Soviet authorities considered all Polish citizens domiciled in the annexed provinces now to be Soviet subjects. Politically and socially dangerous elements were 'liquidated' or deported to Siberia and Asiatic Russia.

About 23,000 people branded by Beria as staunch enemies of the Soviet authorities and system were shot on Stalin's orders in the Spring of 1940. They included army and police officers, civil servants, judges, politicians, industrialists and landowners. Well over 400,000 people suffered deportation, including not only prominent citizens and officials, but even peasants, poor shopkeepers, foresters and artisans, together with their families.

Further, it was declared that Polish rule would never return. Molotov declared that 'nothing was left of Poland, the ugly offspring of the Versailles Treaty'.

As relations with Germany started to deteriorate, the attitude of the Soviet authorities began to change but the first encounter of Poles with Stalin and Stalinism was far from pleasant, even for Polish communists and their sympathisers. When Germany attacked the Soviet Union in June 1941, Poles and Russians were united by their having a common enemy, but the experience of Poles at the hands of the German and Soviet authorities confirmed the Polish belief that independence could best be achieved by reliance on the Western powers.

In brief, the defeat of Poland began for the Polish nation a period of oppression, terror and destruction, which lasted almost six years and in its magnitude and ferocity surpassed anything that the Poles, in their eventful and often tragic history, had had to endure. But it was also a period of great Polish military, political and diplomatic activity.

The total Polish losses during the last war amounted to 4,500,000 people, most of them deliberately done to death by the Germans. Only 664,000 people were killed in the course of military operations. It is estimated that during the war Poland lost 45 per cent of her doctors, 57 per cent of her lawyers, 15 per cent of her teachers, 40 per cent of university professors, almost 50 per cent of qualified engineers, 30 per cent of technologists and technicians and 18 per cent of the clergy. This dismal catalogue of losses among the educated classes and professional elite and the terrorisation of ordinary workers and peasants show that the Poles were indeed involved in a struggle for survival. The Jews were assigned to total extermination. The Germans liquidated almost the entire Jewish population, murdering about 2.5 million Polish citizens of Jewish origin. Only about 50,000 survived, of whom 5,000 were children. Those who escaped owed their lives to the help of the Poles. As Lucjan Blit has emphasised, 'every Jew who survived in Nazi-occupied Poland did so only because Gentile Poles risked their lives to hide them'. Poles who sheltered or helped Jews risked their lives, being liable for summary execution.

Meanwhile, on 30 September, while the remnants of the Polish army were still resisting the Germans in Poland, a new Polish Government was formed in Paris under the premiership of Gen. Władysław Sikorski, the old government having been interned in Romania.

In this way the continuation and constitutional legality of the highest Polish authorities – the President, Cabinet and Supreme Command – were safeguarded, and occupied Poland acquired a new leadership uncompromised by the autocratic tendencies of the pre-war regime, or the stigma of military defeat.

Sikorski had, since 1908, been connected with the Polish struggle for independence. He was a 'staunch and resolute democrat' and opponent of the pre-war regime. On 30 September he was requested by Władysław Raczkiewicz, the new President of Poland, to form a Polish government-in-exile, in which the pre-war opposition parties were represented. On 7 November he was appointed Commander-in-Chief of the Polish Armed Forces. By combining these two offices – of both political and military head of the government – Sikorski became the dominant figure of the Cabinet. In Poland also he was regarded as the country's war-time leader.

Sikorski's Government of National Unity was recognised by France, Britain and the USA as well as most neutral countries. It was situated first in Paris and, after a short stay in Angers from November 1939, moved to London with the fall of France. A Parliament-in-Exile, composed of the four main political parties – the Peasant Party, the Polish Socialist Party, the National Democrats and the Party of Labour, together with the Jewish national minority – was established in the form of the National Council, the members of which were appointed by the President on the recommendation of the Prime Minister. Paderewski was appointed chairman but, owing to his ill-health, the deputy chairman, the leader of the Peasant Party, Stanisław Mikołajczyk, presided over its proceedings. Sikorski tried to deal with France and Britain on equal terms, but his position was weak when his government depended upon them for support not only for itself, but also for the equipment of the Polish army-in-exile. Polish troops raised up in France in the winter of 1939–40 were short of uniforms and equipment, which were to be supplied by the French government. In June 1940 the Polish forces of all arms amounted to 84,000 in the west, composed largely of men from the Polish forces who had escaped from Poland, and the Polish citizens living in France. The army consisted of four infantry divisions, two infantry brigades and one armoured brigade. The air force stationed partly in France and partly in Britain, consisted of 9,170 men and the navy operating from the British ports 1,400. The Western Allies were willing to help the Poles to reorganise their forces and were pledged to restore an independent Poland, but they were not prepared to antagonise Moscow to support Polish claims. It was doubtful whether they would be able to restore Poland within her pre-1939 frontiers. Britain believed that Poland's claim to territories east of the Curzon Line was questionable. Indeed, in October 1939, Lord Halifax, the British Foreign Minister, stated that the Russians had advanced their boundary to what was substantially the frontier recommended by Britain in 1919–21.

To improve relations with Moscow the British were trying to persuade the Poles that the loss of the eastern provinces were the necessary price for Russo-Polish rapprochement. The question of the Soviet-Polish frontiers was to be one of the most acute problem which the Allies had to face in the years 1939–45. The Poles were reluctant to relinquish their rights, but Sikorski himself had doubts of Poland's ability to recover the areas annexed by the USSR and believed that Poland should be compensated at the expense of Germany. In his messages to Poland Sikorski called for national solidarity in the face of the German and Soviet threat and assured the Poles at home that the post-war Poland would be a democracy in which social justice would prevail. Sikorski's ideal Poland would be a liberal democracy with a primarily free-market economy, but the frontiers of the new Poland remained to be defined.

The nucleus of a Polish resistance leading to the creation of the Home Army (Armia Krajowa – AK) and the Polish Underground State was created in Warsaw in September 1939, when Gen. Michał Karaszewicz-Tokarzewski established a clandestine military organisation. The leaders of the resistance tried to organise a force capable of day-to-day resistance to both Germany and the USSR in preparation for a national insurrection in the last stages of the war in Poland.

From the outset one of the essential aims of the resistance was to assist in restoring an independent Poland. All the main efforts of the resistance were to be directed towards preparation of a rising and organisation of cadres for the future administrative organs of the state. This demanded achievement of national unity and close co-operation between the government and the resistance.

The link between the government and the Home Army and the Underground State had serious repercussions for the future of the resistance and of Poland herself. In brief, the émigré government's policies, activities and standing among Poland's allies affected the fortunes of the resistance in Poland and vice versa.

On 10 May Germany attacked the Netherlands, Belgium and France. With the beginning of the Battle of France, Winston Churchill became Prime Minister in Britain, upon which the Polish government would have to depend for support after the collapse of France in June 1940. The fall of France was a severe blow to all Poles but no one thought of capitulation. The Polish troops in France had fought well and hard, but suffered heavy losses. Most of the front-line units were destroyed or interned in Switzerland. After the French capitulation an Anglo-Polish agreement provided for the evacuation of the government and the remnants of the army, about 25,000 men, to Britain.

In June 1940 Britain assumed a special responsibility for the fate of Poland and became her main ally and protector. On 19 June 1940 Churchill assured Gen. Sikorski that: 'We are comrades in life and death. We shall conquer together or we shall die together.' The two Prime Ministers shook hands. That handshake, Sikorski said later, 'meant more to me than any signed treaty or alliance or any pledged word'. In this manner the Anglo-Polish alliance was reaffirmed and cemented. Churchill assured Sikorski that he could count on him 'for ever' and that Britain, 'will keep faith with the Poles'. Thus a very close political and military co-operation started to develop between Great Britain and Poland at a time when both countries were fighting for their very survival and when Germany seemed to be invincible.

Anglo-Polish co-operation was to last for the rest of the war and, although it finished after Yalta in a flurry of mutual recriminations, it left a deep imprint on the histories and psyches of both nations.

Poland and Great Britain were the only two countries which fought against Hitler's Germany from the very beginning of the last war to its – for the majority of Poles – bitter end.

In the summer of 1940 under Churchill's leadership, Britain fought alone against the Axis Powers and kept the faltering anti-German alliance alive. At that time defeated Poland was her main ally, which testifies to the seriousness of the situation. While helping Britain in many ways, the United States was still non-combatant and the Soviet Union was still trying to cultivate good relations with Nazi Germany.

The actions of the Poles in 1940 were not insignificant. Polish fighter pilots played an honourable role in August–September 1940 in the Battle of Britain, constituting the largest single element in Fighter Command, with the Polish 303 Squadron in particular distinguishing itself by its outstanding success in shooting down German aircraft.

It was not on Britain alone that Sikorski tried to rely upon. In March 1941 he visited the USA to secure American support for Poland's war effort and obtain permission to enlist volunteers among Americans of Polish descent. He drew American attention to the atrocities committed by the Germans and plight of Polish Jews. Sikorski informed Roosevelt of his efforts to promote the establishment of federal unions in Central Europe, especially the Czech-Polish plans for post-war co-operation. A Polish union with the Czechs, it was hoped, would make these countries independent of both Berlin and Moscow. Sikorski's plans for the Polish-Czech co-operation were very far-reaching, but the Czechs, wary of any plans for the future which might not find approval with the USSR upon which they intended to base their security, were to dissociate themselves from the Polish venture.

Sikorski, a few days before the German invasion of Russia, came to the conclusion that an improvement in Soviet-Polish relations was essential. He was compelled, however, to move with care in the light of the distrust of the USSR entertained by Poles at home and abroad. Further, to reach a satisfactory understanding with Moscow, he would have to solve the thorny problems of the Soviet-Polish frontiers and the citizenship of Poles deported to Russia. The restoration of diplomatic relations was therefore fraught with difficulty. On the Soviet side there existed a traditional distrust of the Poles nurtured by memories of earlier national conflicts in the disputed borderlands. If at times the diplomacy of Sikorski was to appear equivocal, he had many unpleasant alternatives with which to contend.

On 22 June 1941 Germany invaded the Soviet Union. The entire course of the war in Europe was changed. As Jan Karski rightly put it: 'Overnight the USSR found itself on the side of Britain. Overnight the problem of Soviet-Polish relations acquired a new significance. The role of the Soviet Union was the single most important issue affecting the relations between the Polish, British and American Governments. In Churchill's own words, 'the attitude of Russia to Poland lay at the root of our early relations with the Soviets'.

II The ill-fated alliance, July 1941 – April 1943

The outbreak of German-Soviet hostilities brought Britain reprieve from an apparently near hopeless situation and inspired most people in German-occupied Europe with a new hope of victory. The German attack on the USSR opened new possibilities in regard to Polish-Soviet relations. The fact that both the Soviets and Poles were fighting against the common enemy made for temporary Polish-Soviet rapprochement. From the very beginning of the German-Soviet war Churchill made great efforts to establish and cultivate good relations with Stalin, and to convince the Soviet leader of his sincerity, goodwill and support.

On 30 July a Soviet-Polish pact was signed in London. The treaty provided for the restoration of Russo-Polish diplomatic relations, military co-operation, the creation of the Polish Army in the USSR, and an amnesty for all Polish citizens detained in the Soviet Union. It failed to settle the question of the future frontiers between the two countries, although Moscow recognised that the Nazi-Soviet agreements of 1939 lost their validity. During the negotiations leading to the Soviet-Polish treaty both sides laid claims to pre-war eastern Poland.

Sikorski's failure to settle the frontier problem in 1941 left open the whole question of the future of Polish-Soviet relations, especially in the event of a decisive Soviet victory. This lack of Russo-Polish understanding with regard to the territorial question made co-operation between the Russians and Poles difficult and led to a split in the Polish Cabinet.

A number of important problems bedevilled Russo-Polish co-operation. First, there were arguments connected with the size, equipment and deployment of the Polish Army in Russia, commanded by Gen. Władysław Anders, which finally led to its withdrawal to the Middle East in the summer of 1942, in an atmosphere of mutual recrimination. Secondly, there was a question of about 14,000 missing Polish army officers and policemen captured by the Russians, whose disappearance Stalin could not explain satisfactorily. In fact they had been murdered on his orders in the Spring of 1940. Finally, there were constant Russo-Polish disputes about the citizenship of all persons who resided in the Polish territories annexed by the Soviet Union.

The main bone of contention was, however, the unresolved frontier dispute, which intensified at the beginning of 1943, when the Red Army started to regain the initiative on, the Eastern Front, after the battle of Stalingrad, and its eventual return to Poland appeared likely.

At the end of February 1943, the Polish government again stated that they stood by the pre-war frontiers. In reply Moscow accused the Poles of refusing to recognise the 'historic rights' of the Ukrainians and Byelorussians to its nationhood and national unity.

Further, Stalin informed Churchill that he was ready to agree to the Curzon Line, with some adjustments, as a new frontier with Poland, and that Russo-Polish relations 'would depend on the character of the Polish government'. This prompted London to try to bring about, with the help of Washington, a general settlement of the Russo-Polish frontier in spite of insuperable difficulties involved in such an understanding.

It became obvious that Russo-Polish relations were again entering a new and dangerous stage; they were reaching a breaking point.

The final break occurred on 25 April 1943 soon after the German announcement of the discovery at Katyń Woods, near Smolensk, Soviet territory occupied by the Germans, of the mass graves of thousands of Polish officers captured by the Red Army in September 1939. The discovery was followed by Polish and German requests to the International Red Cross in Geneva for an investigation of the whole affair. In response to this tactically unfortunate Polish move, Moscow accused the Polish government of co-operating with the Nazis in slandering them and of putting pressure upon them in order to gain territorial concessions. The Russians argued that this made relations between Moscow and the Polish government impossible.

Thus a wide chasm opened between the Soviet and Polish authorities, at a time when close understanding was needed. Churchill tried to prevent this but to no avail. He was determined, however, to heal the breach between Russia and Poland, in the interest of Allied unity.

The British felt that the Katyń atrocity had been committed by the Russians, however, they urged the Poles to say as little as possible about it. Churchill believed that the Katyń affair was an embarrassment and 'not one of these affairs where absolute certainty was either urgent or desirable'. He also argued that: 'There is no use prowling around the three year old graves of Smolensk.'

Meanwhile, on 6 December 1941 Japan attacked Pearl Harbor. On 11 December 1941 Germany declared war on the USA. As a result of these developments the war assumed global dimensions and the Grand Alliance was finally formed. The outbreak of the conflict in the Far East and Anglo-American involvement in it strengthened the role of Russia within the Alliance, and diminished that of Poland even further. Throughout the war the Red Army bore the main brunt of the struggle against Germany by engaging the bulk of Nazi land forces on the Eastern Front. America's entry into the war placed her enormous economic, financial and military resources at the disposal of the allies. But the war in the Pacific was likely to make the US administration cautious of offending Moscow, upon whose aid it might wish ultimately to call to bring the conflict in Asia to an end.

Further, the repulse of the German offensive at Kursk in July 1943 meant that the Red Army would eventually drive back the Germans into Central Europe. The Polish diplomatic position could not be strong in the light of the global policies of the great powers.

The crisis in Soviet-Polish relations was a turning point. Moscow by breaking off diplomatic relations with the Polish government obtained a free hand in dealing with the Polish territorial and political affairs.

Already on 1 March 1943 the Polish communists in the USSR established a Union of Polish Patriots (Związek Patriotów Polskich – ZPP) in Moscow, which soon became a nucleus of the future Soviet-sponsored government of Poland. In June 1943 the ZPP stated that the pre-war Russo-Polish frontiers were inconsistent with the rights of the Ukrainians and Byelorussians. The basis of Polish security was to be an alliance of the Soviet Union, Poland and Czechoslovakia. The reforms it proposed were common to those of the Polish parties in Poland. In May 1943 the ZPP started to organise a new Polish Army in Russia. This army was commanded by Gen. Zygmunt Berling and among its cadre were Soviet officers of Polish descent. The Polish army raised in Russia would serve as a nucleus for a much larger army when the Soviet forces entered Poland and recruits from the liberated areas were embodied in it.

The formation of the ZPP was a warning to the government-in-exile that unless it changed its policy towards the Soviet Union, Stalin might refuse to negotiate with them, having at his disposal a native Polish authority ready to take over the administration of the country, with Soviet help.

As the war went on the Polish armed forces in the west and the east, which, by the end of hostilities, were to be about 700,000 strong, took part in some of the most important battles of the war. The Poles fought at Narvik, Tobruk, Monte Cassino, the Falaise Gap, Arnhem, in France, the Low Countries and Germany. They also took part in the Battle of Britain and the Battle of the Atlantic. Further, the Polish Intelligence Service and the resistance at home provided London with a constant flow of information concerning German military and naval deployment, industrial production and new weapons. I have recently seen newly opened Polish archives which show that the Polish Army had agents collecting and reporting information in almost every German armaments factory and port, in Germany as well as in Poland. It was the Poles, we should remember, who supplied the British with a V-2 rocket engine in the summer of 1944.

However, as Prof. M. R. D. Foot has stressed: 'Probably the most important service the Poles ever rendered to the anti-Nazi cause was something they did before the war had even begun.' On 25 July 1939, in Warsaw, they handed over to the astonished MI6 decipher experts a copy of the modified 'Enigma' machine on which the Germans conducted all their most secret cipher traffic. This had enormous consequences as it allowed the code-breakers at Bletchley Park to 'read' some of the most secret and important German orders and dispositions and distribute them under the code-name 'Ultra' to some of the most senior British – and later on, American and indirectly even Soviet – commanders.

To quote Prof. Foot again: 'Some "Ultra" was of almost unbelievably high quality: operation instructions from Hitler personally to his supreme commanders, which now and again were read by his enemies even before they had been got in the hands of their momentarily absent addressees (...) It all originated with the pre-war Polish Secret Service.'

Further, there were times, as Sir David Hunt, the war-time Chief of Intelligence to Field Marshal Alexander, told me, when the British commanders got a clearer idea of the situation at the front from the information received from 'Ultra' than from the reports of their subordinates.

Recently, the 'Ultra' materials were made available to researchers in The National Archives and they are their own best proof of their vital importance. In fact, it could be said that 'Ultra' introduced an 'extra dimension' into the conduct of the last war. From reading these documents one gets the impression that, during the Battle for Normandy and the closing stages of the Battle for the Atlantic, British and American commanders knew almost every German move and order. The British passed on to the Russians the German plans and dispositions for the Battle of Kursk, which finally decided the outcome of the war on the Eastern Front.

The Polish Government also tried to alert the British and American authorities to the fact that the Germans were consistently destroying Polish and European Jewry in Poland but according to William Cavendish-Bentinck, the war-time head of the Joint Intelligence Committee, the British Government considered the reports to be exaggerated.

III The Years of Tempest, May 1943 – December 1944

In 1943 the war entered a new phase. The Allies went over to the offensive in Russia, Italy and the Far East it was no longer a question of whether the war would be won by the Allies, but when it would end. As the end approached the situation of the Polish government was gradually worsened. Nevertheless, Gen. Sikorski still believed that, with the help of Churchill and Roosevelt, he would be able to come to terms with Stalin. He continued to believe that the Western Allies would sooner or later bring their influence to bear upon the side of Poland.

On 4 July 1943, however, Władysław Sikorski died when the aircraft carrying him crashed at the moment of take-off at Gibraltar. Many condolences carried admiration and respect towards Sikorski but it did not change the fact that he left the Polish Government in a difficult predicament, which was not made any easier by the appointment of his successor. On 14 July a new government was formed under Stanisław Mikołajczyk, the leader of the Peasant Party. On the other hand Gen. Kazimierz Sosnkowski was appointed Commander-in-Chief. In this way the two functions exercised by Sikorski were separated. Mikołajczyk continued to hold to the policy of Sikorski in foreign affairs, hoping to reach an understanding with Stalin which would allow his government to assume power in Poland, with the help of the Polish resistance movement, at the end of hostilities.

Mikołajczyk aimed to establish cordial relations with Moscow and abandon the 'demagogy of intransigence', considering that the calculations in some Polish circles, based on a possible conflict between the Western Powers and Soviet Union were 'illusory and dangerous'. He was aware that the Western Powers were not prepared to fight for the Polish eastern frontiers and that in the event of a crisis they would not support Poland. He hoped nevertheless that, in the event of a Russo-Polish understanding, Britain and the USA would be ready to guarantee Poland's independence. There was an element of exaggeration in his thinking, which made light of the difficulties of conciliating the USSR and inducing the Western Powers to take Poland's side. Sosnkowski on his part, was convinced that the government must defend the territorial and political integrity of Poland 'in spite of all and against all'. He was opposed to making concessions because, in his opinion, they would merely lead to the gradual 'Sovietisation of Poland'. He was convinced that the Western Powers sooner or later 'might be compelled to face a showdown with Russian imperialism', for which reason there was no need to adopt a conciliatory attitude towards Moscow. He maintained that the London Poles could influence neither Soviet policy nor outcome of military operations and were therefore left with no alternative except to defend their rights and 'demand the same from the Western Powers'. He wished to turn the Polish Question into a 'problem for the conscience of the world', a test case for the future of European nations. As Commander-in-Chief he believed that he was entitled to play an important role in politics. His relations with Mikołajczyk were strained and unhappy.

On 30 June 1943 the Commander-in-Chief of the Home Army, Gen. Grot-Rowecki, was arrested in Warsaw by the Gestapo, to be executed on Himmler's orders in 1944. In his place Sosnkowski appointed General Tadeusz Bór-Komorowski, a cavalry officer. So far his career and his professional upbringing did not indicate that he was fit to carry such a high command. As Commander-in-Chief of the Home Army he would hold a responsible position and upon him, rather than the authorities in London, might rest the power of decision at a crucial moment of war.

In October 1943 the government issued the resistance with new directives to guide its activities during the approaching German defeat. The government stated that it might at some future date order the resistance to stage an anti-German 'insurrection', or alternatively to promote an 'intensified sabotage diversion' operation according to the strategic and political situation. The aim of the rising was to free Poland from the Germans and assume political power on behalf of the government. The uprising was meant to be supported by Western Allies. The government, however, was in a quandary because it was unable to inform the resistance what form, if any, such support would take.

From 1941 onwards the British supported intelligence work but most of all air-supplying the Polish resistance movement with highly-trained personnel, money, arms and equipment for sabotage and diversionary activities.

Towards the end of 1943 the British authorities refused, however, to provide the Home Army with weapons and equipment for its planned 'insurrection'. The responsibility for launching such an insurrection was left by the British Cabinet in the hands of the Polish government. On 5 October 1943 Anthony Eden, the British Foreign Secretary, told the British War Cabinet that the question of supplying the Home Army with arms was difficult and such an action, undertaken without consultations with the Russians, might antagonise them.

In fact, from 1941 to 1945 the Home Army received only some 600 tons of supplies from Anglo-American sources.

In accordance with the government's instructions the policy to be adopted towards the advancing Soviet forces was complicated. The directives laid down the principle that, if Soviet-Polish relations were still not restored at the time of the Soviet entry into Poland, the Home Army should act only behind the German lines and remain underground in the areas under Soviet control until further orders from the underground. The decision to conceal the Home Army was a dangerous proposition because, in all probability, it would have led to an open clash with the Soviet security forces with tragic consequences. The instruction contained a contradiction of which its authors appeared unaware. The 'intensified sabotage-diversion' was intended to be a political demonstration, but if the Soviet Union entered Poland, it would have to be carried out as a clandestine action, with units which had been involved in fighting the Germans going underground again. The government was demanding that the Home Army first perform an active role and then disappear, a course which invited the hostility of both the German and Soviet forces.

Bór-Komorowski received these unrealistic orders with dissatisfaction and decided to ignore them. He ordered his men engaged in action with the Germans to reveal themselves to the incoming Soviet forces to 'manifest the existence of Poland' He believed that otherwise all the Home Army operations against the Germans would be credited to the communists.

The Home Army was to stage either 'general and simultaneous insurrection' or an 'intensified diversionary operation', which received the code name of 'Tempest' ('Burza'). The state of the German forces was to determine which of these alternatives was to be adopted. The insurrection was to be undertaken at the imminent collapse of Germany, whereas Tempest was to be launched during a German general retreat from Poland. Tempest was to begin in the east and move westwards as military operations moved into Poland. The essence of the Tempest plan was a number of consecutive uprisings initiated in each area as the German retreat began, rather than a synchronised operation beginning in all areas simultaneously. No operations were to be taken against the Soviet forces or the Polish army raised in the USSR. The Home Army was to conduct its operations independently of the Red Army in view of the suspension of diplomatic relations. The success of Tempest depended above all on timing. Premature engagement with the German forces unassisted by the Red Army could turn Polish attack into disaster. The Home Army had to wait for the last hours of German retreat. Tempest was a simple plan fraught with hazards and dangers in execution. Its chances of success would have been greater if it could have been co-ordinated with Soviet military operations but, in the nature of the situation, this was not possible. Initially large towns were excluded from the Tempest in order to spare their populations suffering and loss of property but, in July 1944, Bór-Komorowski reversed his decision, ordering his men to occupy large towns before the arrival of the Soviet troops, because he had finally realised that the capture of towns was essential to the policy of acting as hosts to the Soviet authorities.

The political intent of Bór-Komorowski's decision was clear: 'By giving the Soviets minimal military help, we are creating political difficulties for them.'

In February 1944 Bór-Komorowski's decision to reveal the Home Army to the Soviet forces was approved by the government. From this moment the die was cast. The government believed that the Home Army operations would result either in securing political power for itself in Poland, or the intervention of the Western Powers on its behalf, and would defend the cause of Poland against the USSR. This view contained a strong element of wishful thinking.

Tempest began first in February in Volhynia and then was extended to the Wilno, Lwów and Lublin areas.

During Tempest in Volhynia a certain pattern of events had emerged which was soon to reappear in other parts of Poland; it became apparent to all concerned, Russians, Germans and Poles alike, that immediately before the arrival of the Red Army into a particular area of the country, some of the local Home Army units would be mobilised, concentrated and thrown into the battle against the Germans. During the fighting temporary contact and co-operation with the Russians would be established. Initially relations between both sides would be cordial and friendly. After the fighting those of the Home Army units which found themselves in Russian-held territory would be disarmed, incorporated into the Berling army, or deported into Russia. As Tempest proceeded, it became clear that Stalin was not prepared to co-operate militarily and politically with the Home Army.

On 19 July Stalin told the Polish communists that as soon as a Polish executive was established he would recognise it as a 'temporary organ of executive power in Poland'. On 22 July the formation was announced of the Polish Committee of National Liberation (Polski Komitet Wyzwolenia Narodowego – PKWN) under the chairmanship of Edward Osóbka-Morawski. From that moment onwards there were two rival organisations, the PKWN which established itself in Lublin backed by the USSR, representing provisional government in embryo, and the Polish Government in London, supported by the Western Powers, competing one with another for control of Poland.

On 1 August 1944 the Home Army rose in revolt against the Germans in Warsaw in a battle which was to last until 3 October. The political motives were those which had been apparent in Volhynia, Wilno and Lwów. Bór-Komorowski wished to prevent the communists from establishing themselves in Warsaw and compel Stalin to recognise the Polish government in London. In the diplomatic sense he hoped to assist Mikołajczyk in his talks in Moscow with Stalin and induce Britain and the USA to support the London Poles. In fact no serious diplomatic preparations for the insurrection had been made, either in London or in Washington, let alone Moscow. Ideologically the authors of the rising were guided by the doctrine of two enemies, the Germans and the Russians, as well as a burning desire to defend Polish independence. The rising was directed militarily against the Germans and politically against the USSR and the PKWN. The decision to fight was based on the belief that the Germans were defeated decisively on the Eastern Front and that the Red Army was about to enter the capital. Bór-Komorowski and the Government Delegate in Poland, Jan Stanisław Jankowski, issued their final order for the insurrection when it was erroneously reported to them that the Soviet tanks were entering the suburb of Praga on the right bank of the Vistula. They assumed that the battle for Warsaw was approaching its climax and presented them with an opportunity to capture the capital shortly before the Soviet forces entered it.

In fact, the decision to stage the rising coincided with the German counter-attack against the Soviet forces on the right bank of the Vistula. The Germans regained the initiative and held it for some days.

There is no doubt that the Soviet failure to take Warsaw in early August was due mainly to military obstacles. This does not, however, explain why Stalin did not act upon Marshal Konstantin Rokossovsky's suggestion that he should renew the offensive on Warsaw after 25 August. It is probable that Stalin decided to abandon Warsaw to its fate and thereby avoid a confrontation with the London Poles, leaving to the Germans the task of crushing his political opponents. His refusal at first to allow planes of the Western Allies carrying supplies to Warsaw to land on Soviet airfields seems to support this suggestion.

In January 1945 the Soviet forces entered a city of ruins and graves. The only allied capital city to become a battleground during the Second World War. Nearly 200,000 Poles were killed during the fighting. The Germans deported the 800,000 survivors from the capital to other parts of Poland or to Germany.

The insurrection and its aftermath helped rather than frustrated the communist assumption of power in Poland. On 6 September 1944 the leaders of the insurrection warned Mikołajczyk: 'It is obvious that with the fall of the insurrection in Warsaw control of the entire country will pass into the hands of the communists.'

Churchill tried to save Warsaw from the utter defeat and destruction by pressing Stalin and Roosevelt to give help to the stricken city.

In fact, only the Russians could have saved Warsaw from complete destruction at the hands of the Germans by launching an immediate offensive aimed at capturing the Polish capital. Stalin refused to do this, claiming that military obstacles and supply difficulties prevented it. The evidence suggests, however, that his refusal was rather a political than a military decision.

Roosevelt was also reluctant to give decisive help to the unfortunate Poles, as he feared that this might upset his relations with Moscow. At this time Roosevelt was pursuing what some people now call a 'Russia first' policy and his interest in Polish affairs was minimal. Roosevelt believed that the Big Three should agree at the 'appropriate time' on a solution to the Polish problem and impose it on the Poles. In 1944 Roosevelt already regarded the Soviet Union and Stalin as the main ally, with whom he wished to establish lasting co-operation including post-war co-operation. Rather naively, Roosevelt believed that, if Stalin were well treated by his Western Allies – kept satisfied by them – he would respond in kind and become 'amenable'. At this time there was a feeling in the west, which Churchill to some extent shared, that after all Stalin was not so bad, and that it was only his 'entourage' which was stopping him from wholehearted co-operation with Washington and London. The idea was to make Stalin a useful and worthwhile member of the Anglo-American club presided over by the United States, which during the war had risen to the rank of a political, economic and military superpower. But Stalin wished to become sole chairman of his own 'progressive' club, in which there was no place for what he called 'imperialists and reactionaries' such as the London Poles. He was determined, after the Red Army's victories at Stalingrad and Kursk, to include Poland and other newly freed East European countries in his won 'club', regardless of their wishes and aspirations, and there was no question that he would join any club run by the United States, even as a co-chairman.

By the end of 1943, there were two clubs in the making, although this fact was obscured by the tug-of-war and the need to defeat the common enemy.

British war-time diplomacy believed that one of its main tasks was to try to improve relations between Poland and the Soviet Union for the sake of allied unity. As he once wrote, Churchill saw Russian treatment of Poland as a touchstone of Anglo-Soviet relations. Both he and Eden devoted a great deal of their time and effort to trying to heal the rift between Poland and the Soviet Union, unfortunately without much success.

Nevertheless, it can be argued with hindsight that Churchill was one of the three main architects, not only of the allied victory – without which the continued existence of Poland as a State and nation would have been impossible – but also of the present-day frontiers and ethnic composition of post-war Poland. This should not be forgotten.

In fact Churchill was the first of the Big Three leaders to make the official suggestions, at the Tehran Conference in 1943, that the frontiers of post-war Poland should be shifted 150 miles to the west at the expense of Germany, that the Poles should cede eastern Poland to the Soviet Union, and that the Germans might be expelled from this newly-drawn Polish State.

Thus, and at a stroke, Churchill proposed to move Poland westward into the very heart of Europe, in order to resolve once and for all the centuries-old territorial dispute between Russia and Poland over eastern Poland with its large Ukrainian and Byelorussian minorities, and by ejecting the German minority to consolidate the prospects for the durability of the newly-proposed Polish frontier in the west.

Although acceptable to Stalin and Roosevelt, this proposal was too radical for the Poles as no Polish leader at the time – neither General Władysław Sikorski, the Polish Prime Minister from 1939 until 1943, nor his successor, Stanisław Mikołajczyk (and these were the two Polish leaders who understood that some territorial concessions were inevitable) was prepared to accept such a drastic solution. The Polish government was not prepared to accept the loss of Wilno and Lwów, two ancient centres of Polish culture and learning in the eastern provinces of Poland. They argued that by resisting such a drastic solution they were in reality defending Poland's independence. They also feared that if they accepted Churchill's proposals they would be abandoned by their compatriots at home and abroad, to whom such ideas were an anathema. Sir Alexander Cadogan, the Permanent Under Secretary at the Foreign Office, felt at the time that 'the Polish Government certainly had a terrible choice before them. They look like choosing to safeguard their own honour at the expense of their country. Whether this is right morally, I don't pretend to say...What are we going to do?'

Thus, in the closing stages of the war, in spite of a vicious circle of proposal and counter proposal, like a Greek tragedy Polish politics moved towards the inevitable. While accepting that it was his duty to restore a strong, independent and democratic Poland, Churchill felt that it would have to be a Poland politically and territorially acceptable to the Soviet Union and this was the line he pursued in both Tehran and Yalta. He hoped that Stalin, for whom he felt some respect and even sympathy, would allow the Polish Government and armed forces to return home. Churchill tried to persuade the Poles that the Russians would in fact keep their pledges to them. His 'heart bled' for Poland. The Soviet advance was a 'brutal fact' which could no more be stopped than the tide from coming in.

In reality the fate of Poland and the rest of Eastern Europe was sealed not so much in Yalta as in Tehran in 1943 when the Big Three decided that the main Anglo-American invasion of Europe would take place in northern France. This meant in practice that the Red Army would be the first to enter Poland and that the Home Army could therefore be ultimately successful against the Germans only in co-operation with it. Today we know that – as recently available documents testify – far from envisaging the possibility of such co-operation, Stalin was determined to destroy the Home Army, an obstacle to the establishment of a pro-Soviet Polish Government in Warsaw.

Churchill's idea that Stalin would be prepared to deal with an independent, non-communist Poland, provided that the latter would accept Russian territorial demands, was unrealistic. His attitude to Russia was not yet fully crystallised. In fact, there were occasions when he seemed to be well aware that, with the Red Army in full control over most of Eastern Europe, Great Britain would not be able to discharge her obligations to Poland. On 13 November 1944 the British Prime Minister told Gen. de Gaulle that 'At present Russia is a great beast which has been starved for a long time. It is not possible to stop her from eating, especially since she now lies in the middle of the herd of her victims. The question is whether she can be kept from devouring all of them. I am trying to restrain Stalin who, if he has an enormous appetite, also has a great deal of good sense. After the meal comes the digestion period. When it is time to digest, the surfeited Russians will have their difficult moments. Then perhaps Saint Nicholas can bring back to life the poor children the ogre has put into the salting tub. Meanwhile I attend every meeting, yield nothing for nothing, and manage to secure a few dividends.'

Churchill's prophetic words were fulfilled over forty years later, in the second half of the eighties, when 'Father Christmas' appeared on the international scene in the shape of Mikhail Gorbachev, who for the sake of rapprochement with the West decided finally to dispense with the Brezhnev Doctrine and allow the Warsaw Pact countries to go their own way. However, the 'digestive problems' had started much earlier, and plagued the Soviet block throughout its entire existence, first in Tito's Yugoslavia, in 1948, and later, after Stalin's death, in Poland, Hungary and Czechoslovakia.

Gorbachev's perestroika and glasnost proved to be fatal cures for gluttony; in the late 1980s the Soviet empire began to disintegrate. Poland was the first country to recover her independence during the heady unforgettable summer of 1989. This time she did so without firing a single shot or breaking a single pane of glass. Once again it had been demonstrated that, while it is possible to swallow Poland, it is impossible to digest her.

Moreover, now, in post-Cold War Europe, we can clearly see the true dimensions of Churchill's solution of the problem of the Polish frontiers. The fact that frontiers of Poland run so close to Berlin which is again the official capital of a reunited Germany is a powerful argument for Polish-German reconciliation and close political, economic and military co-operation. Relations which Russia are also improving. Present day Poland – a fully fledged member of NATO and member of the European Union is a much stronger country with much more secure frontiers than for a long time in history. For many Poles the Second World War in reality ended in 1989 when Poland once again regained her independence. It ended in a victory which eluded us, through no fault of ours, in May 1945.

PART I

THE STRUCTURE AND OPERATION
OF THE INTELLIGENCE OF THE
POLISH HIGH COMMAND

9

Organisation and Operations of the II Bureau, of the Polish General Staff

Andrzej Pepłoński and Andrzej Suchcitz

Despite the complications caused by the defeat in September 1939 and due to the organisational work undertaken in France, Switzerland and Romania just before and in the first days of hostilities, Polish military intelligence preserved the continuity of its activities. Working from Romania and towards the end of September 1939, it undertook offensive activities against both occupying powers.[1]

The emergence of the Polish Government-in-Exile and the rebuilding of the armed forces required the creation of an intelligence structure able to function in the new political and military environment. In mid-November 1939 the so-called Intelligence Department,[2] already in existence in Paris under the command of Maj. Tadeusz Nowiński, was reorganised into the II Bureau of the Polish General Staff (PGS),[3] with Lt-Col. Tadeusz Wasilewski[4] as its Chief and with Lt-Col. Stanisław Gano[5] as the Chief of the Intelligence Department. Since the II Bureau of PGS was being accused of allegedly not recognising the threat of war emanating from Germany and the USSR[6] and as its staff was seen as clearly linked to Sanacja (the name of the ruling political option pre-war, from Latin 'sanatio'), Gen. Władysław Sikorski selected intelligence officers from among those arriving in France by using his political criteria.

Although the II Bureau had to adapt its structures and networks of agents to the tasks allocated by PGS and French intelligence, it soon managed to deliver positive results. This was noted by a group of its officers attached to the French Admiralty. Networks operating in Central Europe and in the Balkans delivered much valuable information on German preparations for the aggression in the West. An important role in the discovery of the aggressive intentions of the German High Command was played by the team of Polish cryptographers working in the 'P.C. Bruno' centre in Gretz-Armainvilliers near Paris.[7] Some mistakes were made at the beginning and the detached attitude of the French authorities – which, doubting the abilities of the Polish forces, considered that they gave way to the Germans too quickly[8] – was not helpful. During the barely more than half year activities of Polish military intelligence on French territory, they nevertheless managed to provide their leaders with many new experiences in terms of work organisation in war conditions, and on foreign territory.

Following the fall of France and the transfer of Polish civilian and military authorities to Great Britain, Polish intelligence was forced to operate in even more complex circumstances. In addition its tasks had significantly broadened while the courier trails became longer – which complicated communications with Poland. Further, it was obvious that in co-operating with British intelligence, II Bureau would have to decide on its main activities in accordance with the requests and directives of allied staffs. What lay behind this was that British Intelligence on the Continent was ineffective, especially in the second half of 1940, when it depended on Polish intelligence.[9]

The structures of the principal military authorities were also adjusted to these requirements. On the basis of an Order of 30th August 1940, the Polish General Staff,[10] the Polish Naval Command and the Air Force Inspectorate[11] were subjected directly to the Commander-in-Chief. II Bureau (Intelligence) itself, without its IV Department (that is, Counter-intelligence, under Lt.-Col. Tadeusz Tokarz) which was incorporated into the Military Affairs Ministry,[12] was responsible directly to the Chief of Polish General Staff.[13] At the same time it was decided that it should consist of the Chief, Deputy Chief and the following Departments: I – General, II – Intelligence, III – Records and Studies and IV – Finance. In addition and in service (professional) terms the Chief of the II Bureau was also responsible for the intelligence units of the Polish Navy and Air Force, the Intelligence Officers School and the offices of military attachés. In time he was also responsible for the Assistant Chief of the Department and Missions 'A' and 'B' attached to the British War Office.[14]

In accordance to the approved organisational principles, the basic task of the II Bureau (Intelligence) was to obtain information on the armed forces and war potential of enemy states and third party states and to analyse their political and military situation while considering also their economic circumstances. To fulfil this mission the II Bureau undertook multi-directional activities. Among the most important were planning and organisation of offensive intelligence, disposing of tasks of military attachés (including Naval and Air attachés), collation of information whether obtained by itself or provided by other sources, as well as research on the armed forces and war potential of third party states. In terms of intelligence gathering the II Bureau co-operated with the other Bureaux of PGS and in particular with the VI Bureau, but also with the Ministries of National Defence, Foreign Affairs and Internal Affairs, as well as with the other ministries. It also conducted its financial and material affairs to meet the needs of information and intelligence gathering.[15]

The detailed organisational instructions on the operations of the PGS indicate that the II Bureau was also entrusted with several other tasks, such as training of information and intelligence personnel, the provision of such training for the operational staffs within the Polish Armed Forces and also intelligence co-operation with the Navy and Air Force Commands.[16]

On the arrival of Polish General Staff in London Col. Leon Mitkiewicz became the Chief of the II Bureau. A pre-war military attaché in Kaunas (from 1st April 1938 to 10th October 1939), he did not have much experience in organising intelligence work, and most importantly, he was never previously employed in intelligence headquarters. This is why when taking over his new duties on 2nd July 1940,[17] he authorised his Deputy, Lt-Col. Stanisław Gano, to undertake the organisation of the intelligence headquarters, trusting his significant experience of intelligence work at staff level, obtained before the war and later in France.

Despite this development it was the Chief of the II Bureau (Col. Mitkiewicz, and from December 1941 Lt-Col. Gano) who was responsible for the operations of the whole information and intelligence service. His duties encompassed, among others, the running of the various organisational units of the II Bureau and the formulation of standards of work, the presentation of the general assessments of the political and military situation to his superiors, the development of co-operation principles with the other allied intelligence services, the regulation of information co-operation with the other agencies of the Polish government, tasking of military attachés, running the Bureau's budget, the planning of the organisational structures of information and intelligence service within the framework of general planning and the preparation of co-operation policies with other information services for the post-war period.[18]

In the second half of January 1944 the steady increase in duties persuaded Lt-Col. Gano to create the additional post of an Assistant to the Chief of the II Bureau, which he entrusted to Lt-Col. Jan Leśniak. The latter's duties were to conduct the affairs of the military attachés, to plan and report on the activities of the totality of information and intelligence activities and to maintain contacts with the British and American middle-ranking records units. In addition he was charged with the running and organisation of lectures on intelligence at the General Staff Academy and at the Intelligence Officers School and – in conjunction with the Deputy Chief of the II Bureau – the supervision of control of information and intelligence departments within the operational staffs of large Polish military formations. As was: Col. Gano, his Deputy, Col. Skinder[19] and the Assistant, Lt-Col. Jan Leśniak, were directly supported by Capt. Stefan Konarski, Capt. Stanisław Bedryjowski and a female civilian official, Ludwika Truszkowska.

The Deputy Chief of the II Bureau Lt-Col. Stanisław Gano until December 1941, from December 1941 to autumn 1942 Lt-Col. Ignacy Kazimierz Banach, from December 1943 to February 1945 Col. Tadeusz Skinder and from February 1945 Lt-Col. Leon Bortnowski) directed the work of the General and Intelligence Departments and supervised the financial management of these Departments. He also co-operated with the Assistant Chief in the matter of organising the work of military attachés and military missions and in the training of the intelligence personnel.[20]

Department I, General, consisted of a Personnel Section and of a registry. It was headed successively, by Lt.-Col. Leon Bortnowski (up to 1940) and Lt-Col. Seweryn Kotarba (from November 1942). The staff consisted of 9 persons (3 officers, 5 civilian personnel and 1 lower-grade official). Among the many detailed tasks of this Department it is worth mentioning those relating to the record keeping of the headquarters personnel of the II Bureau and of field staff (of intelligence stations and cells), military attachés and also of graduates of courses for intelligence officers. The records included information on all former employees of the II Bureau from inter-war years and also of those employed then in the Independent Information Sections at Military District level, in field stations and in external cells. They constituted the staff reserve for the future needs of the II Bureau in Poland. In mid-1944 there were altogether 97 officers of various ranks at the disposal of Department I. Most were junior officers, earlier employed in intelligence stations or cells or in counter-intelligence and also a part of the staff of the Ciphers Office.[21]

The Intelligence Department played a key role in the organisation and activities of the II Bureau of PGS. Its duties involved organisation of work of the intelligence stations and outposts, determining the guidelines of intelligence service operations, co-operation with Polish military and civilian institutions and the maintenance of direct contacts with the intelligence services of the Allies.

The Intelligence Department was sub-divided into the following sections: General with its Translation Subsection, Central, East, Overseas, Intelligence Communications, Offensive Counter-Intelligence and Technical. The chiefs of the II Bureau attached much importance to the correct selection of personnel to work for the Intelligence Department. Leading positions were therefore staffed by experienced officers of whom most were young, with no complexes, not wedded to routines and with none of the political attachments so characteristic of some elder II Bureau PGS officers.[22]

As the Department was so central to all the main tasks of the II Bureau, the operations of the intelligence service of the Polish Armed Forces depended heavily on the selection of its heads. From June 1940 to mid-February 1944 the Chief of the Intelligence Department was Maj. Jan Henryk Żychoń, who was then replaced by his deputy of many years, Maj. Witold Langenfeld. Before the war both worked together in No. 3 Station in Bydgoszcz. Though Maj. Żychoń was a controversial figure, he was also a long-serving intelligence officer with many successes under his belt and was highly rated by American intelligence.

The detailed scope of duties of the Department Chief included the following tasks:[23]

- planning and organising of intelligence 'in all areas of operation' of the II Bureau;
- planning and preparation of elements for the post-war period, in accordance with 'special' directives provided by the Deputy Chief of the II Bureau;
- managing the work of all the constituent units within the Intelligence Department and tasking these with due regard paid to the directives of Polish General Staff, Naval Command, Command of the Polish Air Force and of the Ministry of Defence;
- on the basis of authority delegated by the Deputy Chief of the II Bureau, leading the work of intelligence stations and cells;
- determination of the size of the intelligence fund, presentation of budgetary proposals and assessment of the effectiveness of expenditure by intelligence stations and cells;
- maintenance of contacts with representatives of British intelligence and intelligence of Allied armies, and the exchange of intelligence material;
- co-operation with all Departments of the II Bureau and with the Counterintelligence Department of the Ministry of National Defence;
- management of co-operation between the Intelligence Department and the Organisational and Special Bureau of PGS.

Another task of the Chief of the Intelligence Department was to maintain official contacts with the Ministries of Foreign Affairs and of Internal Affairs and with other State institutions. His Deputy, Maj. Langenfeld, carried out duties as entrusted to him from time to time by his Chief and on a permanent basis was responsible for the following:

- maintenance of contacts with other intelligence services (as, for example, Japanese and Finnish) and of disinformation actions;
- on behalf of the II Bureau, co-operation with British and Polish authorities on sabotage and diversion (Continental Action);
- dealing with co-operation with the VI Bureau of PGS, Ministry of National Defence and Intelligence School;
- management of all military and civilian personnel issues for those employed in the headquarters of the II Bureau and in the field;
- supervision of General Section, Translation Subsection and Technical Section of the Intelligence Department.

These lists of duties indicate a heavy load on the Department leadership. This was necessary, however, as both officers, Żychoń and Langenfeld had to have precise knowledge of the workings of the whole intelligence apparatus when making organisational decisions, tasking or co-operating with the Allies.

The principal intelligence tasks were carried out by several Sections within the Intelligence Department, and especially the Central Section, led by an experienced officer, Capt. Mieczysław Jaworski, a pre-war employee of Section 'Z', responsible for Germany. The staff consisted of Lt. Wiktor Pragłowski, Lt. Bolesław Łaszewski, Lt. Michał Łappa and Hanna Rόżańska, a female civilian employee.

The Chief of the Central Section was responsible for the organisation and management of the stations and cells gathering intelligence in Scandinavia, Czechoslovakia, Germany, Switzerland, Austria, Italy, Belgium, Holland, Denmark, France, Spain, Portugal and North Africa (French, Spanish and Italian), in accordance with the guidelines laid down by the Chief of the Intelligence Department. He was further responsible for tasking stations and outposts, for assessing the work of agents within the networks of the Central Section and for passing these assessments to the field, in accordance with the instructions of Department Chief managed specific intelligence actions (called 'affairs' in the internal language of Department II) and, co-ordinating with British intelligence, organised various transfers to and from stations and cells.[24]

From July 1940 to mid 1944, the number of stations and agents working for the II Bureau in the field grew substantially. At the beginning it was responsible for only 8 stations employing some 30 persons and with barely 30 registered agents. By mid-1944 there were 8 stations, 2 independent intelligence stations and 33 cells, with 1,666 agents.

Events at the front led to numerous changes in the structure of field forces.[25] British intelligence often made suggestions concerning the closure or opening of intelligence stations and cells. Another factor, which determined the positioning of stations, was the exposure of intelligence agents by enemy counter-intelligence.

In early 1941 in France the Central Section ran the following networks: 'F', '300' and 'Int'. There were also Station 'M' in Madrid, 'P' in Lisbon, 'S' in Bern and, 'Płn' and 'L' in Stockholm. In 1942 intelligence stations 'Płn' and 'L' were closed and replaced by Station 'SKN'. These codename changes were related to the changes in leaders and a part of staff. Following the arrest of its Head and staff, in 1941 Intelligence Station 'Int' in Paris was closed. On the other hand a new Intelligence Station, 'Afr.', was established in North Africa. In mid-February 1944 the Central Section was running 5 stations, 2 independent intelligence stations and 20 cells, employing 34 officers, 1 NCO, 2 Officer Cadets, 23 civilians and 1 Private. In mid-1944 the field force working to the Section had 378 agents at its disposal.[26]

In May 1944 there were Intelligence Stations 'F-2', 'P', 'S', 'SKN' and 'Afr.'. The most complicated situation at the time was in France, as this was the period preceding the Normandy landings. The heightened activity of German counter-intelligence led to the exposure of some elements of Intelligence Station 'F' and to numerous arrests among its personnel. The structures not threatened by the Germans were reorganised.[27]

The leadership of the II Bureau attached equal importance to the work of the East Section (Capt. Mieczysław Susicki, then Maj. Jan Billewicz from June 1944), since it dealt with the territories immediately adjacent to Poland, of significant importance for the fulfilment of the post-war foreign policy and for any assessment of the current political and military situation. The East Section dealt also with the Baltic states, the USSR, Hungary, Romania, the Balkan states, Turkey and all the countries of the Middle and Far East. The position of the Intelligence stations and cells run by this Section was also subject to changes.

In July 1940 the East Section had the following stations: 'R' in Bucharest, 'W' in Budapest, 'J' in Belgrade – and single-person cells in Zagreb and Istanbul. At the end of 1940 station 'R' was closed and moved to Istanbul. In 1941 station 'Wudal', and later station 'Russia', were established (in Moscow). In addition in the second half of 1942, the II Bureau of the Polish Army in the USSR established contact with the II Bureau of Polish General Staff. In 1942 further stations were established, 'Zadar' and 'Nora'. Three months later Station 'Ba łk.' in Istanbul encountered some serious organisational problems, and at the same time communications were lost with two intelligence cells, 'Tusla' and 'Tandara', in Romania.[28] Another station, 'Tatar', was closed on the orders of the Chief of the II Bureau of PGS, and part of its staff was transferred to 'Ba łk.' and to 'T' in Jerusalem. Station 'W' in Budapest operated with no changes, but the Chief of the Intelligence Department suggested that it be run again from the London headquarters as its subordination to the the II Bureau of Home Army General Headquarters made it more difficult for it to work against the Germans and their allies. In mid-February 1944 there were 3 stations and 3 cells in the field, staffed by 16 officers, 2 NCOs and 14 civilians. At the time the East Section had 23 agents and 40 informants, despite the fact that the Section staff consisted of only the Head and two employees: Lt. Józef Piękosz and a civilian employee, Halina Bobińska.

Most tasks of the East Section were similar to those of the Central Section, since their general aims were similar. The differences lay in the territories on which activities were conducted. In addition the East Section was of interest to British intelligence, as indicated by some of its specific tasks. The Chief of the Section entrusted 'one-off' tasks to the east intelligence stations and cells – 'in accordance with the tasks proposed by the War Office'.[29] There were also tasks stemming from the Section's search plan, produced by the II Bureau, again related to British guidelines. Its Chief was obliged to quickly pass on to British intelligence all information on organisational changes. An additional duty was to prepare the material gathered by radio monitoring run by station 'T' in Jerusalem.[30]

The Overseas Section's field staff (the Section was run by Capt. Władysław Lach), had different duties and a different organisation. On the basis of an agreement with American intelligence (OSS), in the autumn of 1941 II Bureau established Station 'Estezet' in New York. Soon it had a network of some dozen intelligence cells in both North and South America. By mid-1943 it was raised to the rank of an independent intelligence station.[31] In mid-February 1944 the Overseas Section had 2 independent stations located in the America's a field staff of 6 officers and 6 civilians, who had at their disposal a network of 19 agents and 21 informants. After the Soviet victory at Stalingrad the size of the Overseas

Section was reduced due to military and political developments in Europe – and because both allied intelligence services were by then increasingly interested in the regions of future military operations linked to the creation of the second front.

By mid-February 1944 the Intelligence Department had at its disposal 420 registered and active agents and 91 informants. In the final year of the war the numbers of agents and informers of the II Bureau fell substantially. In early February 1945 the intelligence stations and cells run by the Central Section had only 120 agents (this included 46 in 'SKN' in Stockholm, 28 in 'P' in Lisbon, 46 in 'S' in Bern) and 48 informants (37 in 'SKN', 9 in 'P' and 2 in 'S'). At the same time the networks in North and South America, run by the Overseas Section, co-operated with 16 agents and 26 informants. The relatively low numbers of agents and informants shown in the reports of the Intelligence Department testify to the fast turnover among them. This was standard practice in intelligence services. The reports contained information on active agents only, with whom regular communication was maintained. Agents and informants were dropped for various reasons, most frequently due to their inability to provide information, their being exposed or because they joined the regular Polish Armed Forces. It is worth stressing that those registered with the Headquarters in London were not the sole source of information. Both agents and informants often used information obtained from third parties, whether accidental or permanent, who were not always aware that they were working for Polish intelligence. This was provided for in the instructions issued by the II Bureau. The instructions divided agents into those who were paid, those who co-operated for principled reasons ('ideological agents') and those who were unaware of the purpose. The highest ranking was given to principled agents. Intelligence networks created by intelligence stations and cells co-operated with many resistance movement participants, who passed on information gathered by Polish and other underground organisations. This is why in practice it is not possible to say who was the author of any particular material. Intelligence Station 'F-2' in France had the largest number of members – there were 2,561, both Poles and French. In 1940–1941 the intelligence part of this network numbered 250 agents, and by the end of 1944 there were as many as 2,800 (including 739 permanent ones). On the other hand the lists kept by the II Bureau contained only a small number of the most active members.[32]

The whole of the field force working with the II Bureau functioned in a broadly similar manner. The heads of intelligence stations maintained direct communications with the II Bureau of Polish General Staff. Couriers ensured contacts between stations. Heads of stations ran the agents, the agents in turn ran their informants and other persons who provided information or assistance. Since most of those who co-operated did not have proper training, heads of intelligence stations or cells often carried out the most difficult tasks required by the II Bureau themselves.

In the area of radio communications of the II Bureau, in order to maintain a degree of independence from the British who offered to 'improve' links with Polish stations in Lisbon, Bern and Stockholm, it was striven to use Polish means. Col. Tadeusz Skinder, Deputy Chief of the II Bureau, who in the spring of 1944 stood in for Col. Gano in the latter's absence, agreed to British help, while secretly ordering the stations in Lisbon, Bern and Stockholm to use British assistance as a last resort and to maintain normal communications with headquarters using their underground sets which would be masked by the II Bureau.[33] Communications were dealt with by the Polish Ciphers Section, Correspondence Central, Radio Intelligence (monitoring only) and the Foreign Ciphers Office. On 1st January 1942 all these units were transferred to the Chief of Communications for Polish General staff, with the exception of the Polish Ciphers Section, which became independent. As a consequence the codes prepared for the II and VI Bureaux were not checked for 'robustness and security'. The experience of several years showed that the II Bureau's Ciphers Section did not manage to meet the requirements, which slowed down the transmission of intelligence reports from the field and had caused disorder in the guidelines issued by headquarters and aimed at intelligence stations.[34] Expert assessment of the most important codes, used among others for communicating with the II Bureau's agents in Germany,[35] was undertaken only following the arrival in Great Britain in August 1943 of the leading cryptographers Marian Rejewski and Henryk Zygalski. It was also difficult to accept the policy undertaken by Communication Control, situated in Stanmore near London. The communication requirements of the II Bureau were systematically reduced. In early February 1944 it had at its disposal only 2 radio sets, while VI Bureau, which maintained communications with the Home Army GHQ, had 12. This was due to greater interest being paid by the British to information on the situation around the Eastern Front and in the Reich, submitted by the Home Army's intelligence.[36] Other support units, too, did not ensure that the II Bureau could function correctly. Maj. Gaweł was worried by the organisation of work within the telex network, radio intelligence and Foreign Ciphers Office, all by then a part of the Radio Intelligence Company subordinated to the Signals Department of Polish General Staff. Intelligence gathered by this Company was passed on to British intelligence, to the II Bureau's Records Department and to the Offensive Counter-Intelligence Section at the Intelligence Department. Swedish, German and Soviet stations were monitored regularly. Communication shortages limited, for example, the co-operation with and the management of radio intelligence by the II Bureau.[37] The Bureau's fieldwork suffered also because its stations and networks were poorly equipped with Polish-made radio equipment (the so-called agency radios).

There were problems, too, in training radio specialists. The only place where radiotelegraphy was taught was at the Intelligence Officers School in Glasgow. This threatened the II Bureau's ability to meet new requirements to maintain radio communications. The issues mentioned here do not support the thesis concerning the privileged position of intelligence as against other branches of the Polish Armed Forces.

The various intelligence stations and cells run by the Intelligence Department delivered different results. A comparison of traffic intensity between the sections of the Intelligence Department and their subordinated stations and cells shows that the Central Section was delivering by far the most information. In 1942, when all Sections worked with the highest efficiency, there were 9,168 items of correspondence within the Central Section, 1,767 in the East Section and 1,587 in the Overseas Section. Making allowances for the strategic importance of the territory served by the Central Section, the conclusion is that the importance of information delivered by its subordinated field force was also the highest. Just in the period from 1st November 1941 to 1st May 1942, the various Stations delivered 3,605 intelligence reports: 'F' (France) – 1,227, '300' (France) – 34, 'M' (Madrid) – 156, 'P' (Lisbon) – 299, 'SKN' (Sweden) – 93, 'S' (Switzerland) – 309, 'W' (Hungary) – 70, 'Russia' – 128, 'Afr.' – 936, 'Estezet' – 200, 'Wudal' – 16, 'T' (Jerusalem) – 137. In the same period allied intelligence services received: British intelligence – 4,014 intelligence reports and 321 reports with information on agents, on the organisation of foreign intelligence services and on political, nationalities and security matters,[38] American intelligence – 49 sets of information and 610 intelligence reports; Soviet intelligence – 53 sets and 404 reports; French intelligence – 12 sets and 55 reports; and Belgian intelligence – 3 sets and 15 reports.[39] Of the total number of 9241 reports of various types obtained between 1st July 1942 and 30th June 1943, 4,289 were sent to the Americans, 4,133 – to the British, 637 – to the Soviets and 182 – to the French. Thanks to this the Deputy Chief of American military intelligence, Brig-Gen. Hayes A. Kroner, told General Władysław Sikorski that: 'The Polish Army has the best intelligence in the world. Its value for us is beyond compare. Regretfully there is little we can offer in return'.[40] In 1944, which was the hottest period for intelligence work, the War Office was provided with 37,894 reports, the Americans with 12,068 and the French with 793.[41] All together the number of reports passed on to the British from August 1940 to December 1944 amounted to 71,314 – which included 28,410 with intelligence information. According to British ranking, 25% of reports were assessed as extremely valuable, 60% of very valuable, 12% were considered valuable, 2% of little value and 1% of no value.

Within the Intelligence Department there was the Section of Offensive Counter-Intelligence under Capt. Rudolf Plocek and staffed by 2nd Lt. Wincenty Tarnawski, Corp. Tadeusz Filip and two female civilian employees, Zofia Sarnowska and Bridget Todd. Plocek's duties were:[42] to prepare instructions on offensive counter-intelligence for all intelligence stations and cells, work on offensive counter-intelligence material received by foreign intelligence and their transmission to the Polish authorities and to allied special services, to pass intelligence information received from British and allied intelligence to the field, to study and make intelligence assessments on the intelligence activity and methods of foreign intelligence services, to keep records of hostile intelligence cells and of persons suspected of working for offensive counter-intelligence of the allies. The Section was also tasked to work on issues pertaining to national minorities, to keep dossiers on 'disloyal actions of foreign states in relation to Poland and Polish affairs', to interrogate 'burned' persons returning from the field and to investigate the reasons for any compromise in the operations of Polish intelligence cells.[43] Finally, the Offensive Counter-Intelligence Section was to work out the organisational tasks and working methods employed by the security services of foreign powers and to co-operate with the Counterintelligence Department of the Polish Ministry of National Defence, with British offensive intelligence and, when the need arose, with Allied counter-intelligence.

In early 1944 the Offensive Counter-Intelligence Section had dossiers on 342 persons and organisations. Most had little to do with persons suspected of spying. The majority of dossiers were on the most prominent representatives of the Sanacja, on officers of the II Bureau, on left-wing activists and on persons sympathetic to the Communist movement.[44]

The Counterintelligence Department (CID) of the Polish Ministry of National Defence, that is a separate service which however employed former officers of the II Bureau, carried out the main counter-intelligence activity. CID had the following Sections: General, Counter-Intelligence, Security and Anti-subversives. It co-operated with similar units attached to all the major units of the Polish Armed Forces. In the centre of CID's activities was the Counter-Intelligence Section whose job it was to invigilate the persons arriving in Great Britain as evacuees. This Section had the assistance of the II Bureau both when checking the loyalty of specific individuals and when gathering information on the working methods and organisation of foreign intelligence services, but concentrating on the German ones. Information collected was used to study foreign intelligence services and in training. The Section also gathered information on the situation under the German occupation, which was then passed to the Polish Ministry of Information and Documentation. On the basis of a report on counter-intelligence operations for the period 1st June 1942 to 30th June 1945, prepared by the Chief of CID, Lt-Col. Miniewski, it would transpire that the largest espionage threat was to be found within 2nd Corps (1,259 cases, of which 90 were closed). This threat was clearly linked to the fate of the soldiers arriving from Soviet captivity: there were cases of them being persuaded to work for the NKVD. Among the suspects there were also soldiers allegedly maintaining links with German intelligence. Altogether the records of counter-intelligence contained 3,595 cases of suspected espionage within the Polish Armed Forces.[45] An important activity for the Section was co-operation with the British security services, with which information was exchanged on suspects and on those on UK territory. Between 1942 and 1945, 138 items of information on persons suspected of spying and 278 items on persons newly arrived in Great Britain were passed on to the British.

The activities of the Anti-subversive Section were of a different character: it dealt with the forces' morale, with anti-State activity of national minorities and with subversive activity of communists and their sympathisers. These matters were also of interest to the British security services. Between 1943 and 1945 the British side was provided with 145 various items of information. 63 were to do with minorities issues (Polish, Ukrainian and Jewish), 63 with communism and the remaining 19 were various reports and studies. As for attitudes in the Forces, most of the materials prepared by the Counterintelligence Department expressed optimism since, as these documents stated, in 1944 the morale of the soldiers was boosted by the battles fought by Polish units in Italy, France, Belgium and Holland. On the other hand the fate of the Warsaw Uprising most often caused troops to wonder 'what are we fighting for and whether the blood sacrifice will positively influence the fate of Poland'. However, in mid-1945 the assessment of troop morale by Polish counter-intelligence was still good. It was observed, for example, that many soldiers were still prepared to return to Poland – not because of their recognition for the new authorities, but because they wished to see their families and return to the country.[46]

The Intelligence Department of the II Bureau had a Technical Section set up on 30th June 1943, run by Lt. Konstanty Szałowski and staffed by Second Lt. Kazimierz Zieliński, Staff Sergeant Julian Stefankiewicz, Staff Sergeant Józef Binek, Corp. Stanisław Zalewski and a civilian employee, Wacław Jarmułowicz.[47] The section worked on intelligence technology and photography. It dealt with intelligence chemistry (secret writing, preparation of invisible inks, document security and so on), with forging documents and stamps for intelligence purposes in the field and with the training of candidates for II Bureau's fieldwork in technology and photography. Most of its time was spend on the preparation of material received by the Intelligence Department on film. Just within the 6-month period from 30th June to 31st December 1943 this section fulfilled 450 orders for 81,083 photographic enlargements and 10,890 reproductions. The British who supplied it with equipment and photographic materials aided the section. Some of these supplies were passed on to field stations. The active and multi-faceted co-operation with the British side created the need for the Translation Subsection, which formed a part of the General Section. Its was staffed by Lt. Stefan Kucharski (Head), Capt. Antoni Otrębski, a female civilian employee, Maria Elżbieta Lachówna, and six female civilian translators: Maria Słomczanka, Eleonora Jachimowicz, Anna Galewska, Wanda Stachniewska, Barbara Jones and Marie Rose Howard. The General Section was responsible for recording intelligence correspondence, for the maintenance of records of correspondence delivered and other books of the Intelligence Department. Its records indicate that the highest number of reports provided was delivered to British intelligence. These included not only correspondence on the daily intelligence co-operation but also on the mis-information of Axis intelligence services by the War Office through the Polish intelligence network (the so-called 'Action D'). On diversionary matters separate correspondence was addressed to Brig-Maj.-Gen. Gubbins (SOE) and to the Chief of Staff SIS ('Capt. Howard'). Correspondence books marked 'S', 'E' and 'P', as well as other records kept by the General Section and

Translation Subsection, well document the fact of providing the British side with intelligence information. The Liaison Officer with British intelligence was Maj. Stanisław Paprocki.[48]

On 14 February 1944 Maj. Żychoń passed on his duties as Chief of Intelligence Department to Maj. Langenfeld.[49] This was a good moment to assess the work of the Department and its field operatives and to set its tasks for the immediate future. What was most important now was to increase co-operation with other intelligence services and to increase the flow of intelligence from the Polish side. The intention was to strengthen the links with the Japanese, Swedish, Hungarian and Finnish intelligence services. Stations 'T' in Jerusalem and 'Bałk.' in Istanbul were to begin preparations for the establishment of radio intelligence in the Middle East, directed against the USSR.

One of the fundamental tasks given to the intelligence stations and cells in this region was to uncover 'the Soviet penetration'. In the first instance the Intelligence Department ordered the observation of the activities of official Soviet institutions abroad, such as diplomatic and consular posts, trade missions, TASS agency etc. The second line of inquiry for the II Bureau's stations was the invigilation of communist parties and of communist sympathisers. An important task was the assessment of the influence wielded by the USSR in Greece where a number of powers were in rivalry.[50] Since the II Bureau suspected that certain institutions representing other countries were also active in support of Soviet interests, Polish networks were asked to investigate the official French, Czechoslovak and Yugoslav representatives.

In early May 1945 the heads of all stations run by the II Bureau were ordered to investigate the prospect of establishing new, fully underground intelligence cells, which would not be linked organisationally to Polish diplomatic missions. In June 1945 the stations in existence so far were to begin a process of 'decoupling' from Polish diplomatic posts, having burned their archives, codes and records and having hidden their photographic laboratories and radio transmitters in clandestine premises prepared in advance. The supernumerary station personnel were let go. The II Bureau intended to begin its post-war intelligence activities at the end of July 1945.

In service (professional) terms the Airforce Intelligence Department[51] was responsible to the Chief of the II Bureau PGS. The principal task of this Department was to 'study and work on materials relating to the Axis air forces, for the purposes of the British Air Ministry and our own'.[52] In other matters this Department was run by the GOC-in-C of the Polish Air Force. The Department consisted of four sections 'L-1 West' (Maj., later Lt-Col. Ferdynand Bobiński), 'L-2 South' (Maj. Józef Kiecoń), 'L-3 East' (Maj. Olgierd Cumft) and 'L-4 Technical/Industrial' (Maj. Stefan Szumiel), which conducted intelligence activities using the intelligence stations and cells run by the II Bureau of Polish General Staff and Air attachés. The duties of the Chief of the Department (Lt-Col. Felicjan Sterba and from January 1944 Lt-Col. Adam Kowalczyk) were to lead air intelligence, to maintain records and documentation and conduct general studies and to maintain contacts and co-operation with allied air intelligence. Between July 1940 and July 1945 the Department passed on to the British Air Ministry 4,242 documents (1,388 in 1944 alone). Some consisted of a single page, others were dozens of pages long. The British side considered 309 as very valuable, 2,192 – as valuable, 301 – as useful. The Department's staff consisted of 7 persons (5 officers, 1 NCO, 1 civilian official).[53]

The Intelligence Department of the Polish Naval Headquarters, run by Cmdr. Brunon Jabłoński (Cmdr. Karol Trzasko-Durski from October 1944)[54] worked along similar lines. Having arrived in Paris, Cmdr. Jabłoński, as the only representative of naval intelligence, was delegated to the Detached Group of the II Bureau (Maj. Żychoń), which was attached to the French Admiralty's Intelligence. Jabłoński was made Żychoń's deputy. The Polish group was tasked with establishing contacts 'with our former and surviving agents and to organise new intelligence networks. The first goal is to establish the position of our stations in the countries not at war but next to the ones which are, and on this basis to begin to penetrate Poland and Germany'.[55] This work went slowly and there were difficulties. On reaching Great Britain, this group was again incorporated into the headquarters of the II Bureau. Cmdr. Jabłoński again became the sole personnel of naval intelligence within the Naval Command, co-operating with the II Bureau of Polish General Staff and the British via Lt. R.N. Childsen, the British liaison officer with the Polish Naval Command. It soon transpired that there was no possibility of creating two parallel intelligence organisations, especially since the main objective of the Commander of the Polish Navy was to create as large a fleet as was possible. In any case Rear Adm. Jerzy Świrski, writing to the Commander-in-Chief in the autumn of 1940, stated: 'At this time our Navy does not require Cmdr. Jabłoński's organisation. Its preservation will be needed, however, for post-war work. In Great Britain Polish naval intelligence was reconstructed to aid the Admiralty and for this reason, that is to increase the Polish war effort, was approved by you, General. Naval intelligence deals only with naval matters and passes (information) to the Intelligence Service, who in turn gives it to the Intelligence Division of Admiralty. It is therefore truly a Polish-English naval intelligence. It does not deal with Polish matters and is not in competition with the II Bureau or with any similar activity of other Polish institutions'.[56]

Cmdr. Jabłoński was charged with establishing a naval intelligence unit, which organisationally would be a part of Naval Command, but which in service terms would be subordinated to the II Bureau of Polish General Staff. In April 1942, after a break lasting over a year, Jabłoński returned to the PGS as Chief of Naval Intelligence at Naval Command at the disposal of Chief of the II Bureau of PGS. In June 1943 he additionally became the liaison officer of Naval Command to the VI Bureau of Polish General Staff. The Intelligence Office of Naval Command worked closely with the Intelligence Department of the II Bureau. Part of his duties were to inform the Commander of Naval Command on all matters relating to naval intelligence, to discuss and consult all the needs of naval intelligence with the Chief of the Intelligence Department; to plan and organise naval intelligence at individual intelligence stations and cells through the Central, East and Overseas Sections; to prepare and pass on to Chiefs of Sections in the Intelligence Department tasks of interest to naval intelligence in accordance with the requirements of the British Admiralty, the Chief of Naval Command and the Records and Studies Department of the II Bureau of Polish General Staff; to maintain current records on intelligence matters concerning naval issues; to continue contacts with allied intelligence services with whom co-operation was maintained, to propose candidates for naval intelligence work.

Intelligence issues relating to Poland were the province of the VI Bureau of PGS. This Bureau opposed any attempts on the part of naval intelligence to use its own codes or to gain operational independence in the field.[57] The delays in passing information gathered in Poland to headquarters were a permanent issue, as was the need for expert and critical assessment of information transmitted by radio. The Deputy Chief of the Navy's Intelligence Department, Comdr. Czesław Janicki, was complaining, 'using their own intelligence network, the Norwegians obtain much more and more current information from Gdynia and Gdańsk'.[58]

The Naval Intelligence Department was 'something akin to a research bureau [...] It looks at naval material, segregates it, when necessary has it translated from other languages into Polish or from Polish into English [...] In practical terms all of it worked almost exclusively for the British; it is they who instructed it [...] and it is they, and later the Americans, too, who had the benefit of our efforts'.[59]

According to the organisational chart of the II Bureau presented in June 1944, the Department was divided into:

- Section 1: Germany, occupied countries on the Atlantic coast and the Baltic;
- Section 2: The Mediterranean Basin;
- Section 3: Other countries.

In addition one of the Section Chiefs was also in charge of records and naval studies. The Department had a staff of 11: Chief, 3 Section Chiefs, one of whom was also the Deputy Chief of the Department, 3 officials, and each section with one employee and 4 records staff.[60]

The policy concerning the staff of the II Bureau, conducted until mid-1943, led to the elimination of many experienced officers. Their places were taken by graduates of pre-war intelligence courses without the required experience or by officers who had been trained in the Intelligence Officers School established in London (in Bayswater). In early 1942 it was moved to Glasgow. The School's Commandant and Director was Lt-Col. Stefan Mayer, one of the most experienced intelligence officers, who served for many years before the war as Chief of the Intelligence Department. His Deputy was an equally experienced intelligence officer, Lt-Col. Wilhelm Heinrich. Since demand for new intelligence officers was high, the course programme was substantially curtailed in relation to the pre-war training. Later this was to impact negatively on the quality of work of individual stations and on the work of the Home Army in Poland. Training inadequacies were compensated by bravery and sacrifice. Nevertheless there were many unnecessary cases of security breaches caused by lack of experience among graduates. In his assessment prepared in mid-1944 the Chief of the II Bureau, Col. Gano, stated that: 'The human material at our disposal is varied, even very varied. But in Poland and in stations on enemy territory – it is excellent. People work without any guarantees, ceaselessly and bravely beyond words'.[61]

The lectures at the Intelligence Officers School in Glasgow were divided into three themes: theory, objectives and organisation of intelligence, basic information on the Third Reich and on the situation in occupied Poland. Theoretical lectures were on the principles of gathering information and its verification and on organising one's own intelligence and counter-intelligence. For illustration, the students were asked to solve theoretical case studies. Information on the Third Reich was limited to the basic data on the workings of the armaments industry, on the army, airforce and navy, and also on the organisation of the NSDAP, SS and Gestapo. Information on the situation in Poland was presented at lectures, meetings with emissaries from Poland and through studying of special communiqués and publications prepared by the Polish Government-in-Exile. There were also underground publications as well as newspapers published by the occupier.

The purpose of practical exercises on intelligence techniques was to familiarise the students with the principles of using photography and micro-photography, both for transmitting intelligence reports and for producing false documents and stamps. Chemistry exercises taught, among others, how to prepare poisons and antidotes, how to make invisible inks and developers and how to use various preparations helpful in falsifying documents and transmitting reports. There were also exercises in radio communications, codes, opening locks and making keys and also in how to drive various means of transport. The staff of the School was small: in addition to the commandant and his deputy, there were 10 permanent lecturers and instructors, 1 quartermaster, 1 finance officer and 1 materiel officer, and 8 supporting personnel. They would come to the School individually, for specific lectures. Intelligence photography was taught by Warrant Officer Kazimierz Ćwirko-Godycki; Warrant Officer Bolesław Ziembiewicz, for many years employed by the 'West' Section, prepared the students in intelligence techniques. Among the lecturers were Lt-Col. Wilhelm Heinrich, Maj. Tadeusz Nowiński and the former Chief of 'East' Section, Capt. Jerzy Niezbrzycki. SIS officers conducted specialist lectures on intelligence, diversion and sabotage.

Since the School's task was to prepare officers for intelligence work abroad, in the Polish Armed Forces units in the West, in the II and VI Bureaux of Polish General Staff and in part also in the II Bureau of the Home Army GHQ, both its programmes and the principles of candidate selection were decided individually, before the beginning of each course.[62] The Commandant of the School was responsible to the GOC (Polish Forces in the UK) in terms of administration and finance, but in service and training terms to the Chief of the II Bureau of the Polish General Staff.[63]

Prior to their transmission to the Allies, the materials and information obtained by the Intelligence Department were passed on to the Records and Studies Department for processing and evaluation. The successive Chiefs of this Department were Lt-Col. Ignacy Kazimierz Banach (November 1939 to December 1941) and Lt-Col. Leon Bortnowski (December 1942 to February 1945). The Records and Studies Department had four sections, 'Germany', 'Russia', 'West' and 'General', and dealt primarily with 'obtaining and processing information on Germany and the USSR so as to obtain a current picture of the war potential and internal and military-political situation of these States', presenting its general assessment when required to do so by its superiors and monitoring the situation in the remaining European countries. These tasks were the principal interest of intelligence and indicated the fundamental importance of information about the situation on the Eastern Front. In addition the Department indicated the precise intelligence tasks, followed the progress of land operations on European fronts and issued information bulletins to inform the authorities of the military situation.[64]

The following information formed the basis of the assessments prepared by the Records and Studies Department: reports of the agents of the II Bureau of Polish General Staff, occasional and periodical reports from the II Bureau of the Home Army GHQ, reports from military attachés, intelligence information and information bulletins received as a part of co-operation with Allied staffs, data from press and radio analysis, records of interrogation of Polish prisoners of war, interviews with escapees etc., information passed on by the Special Affairs Department of Ministry of National Defence, Ministries of Foreign Affairs and Internal Affairs and by civilian offices and institutions. II Bureau's co-operation with the Foreign Ministry was of importance. The scope of this co-operation was similar to the situation from the inter-war period and involved not only the 'legalisation' of personnel of intelligence stations and cells run by the II Bureau, but also a multifaceted exchange of political, economic and military information.[65] Often information supplied by the Foreign Ministry contained data of importance to the war. In early December 1939 the Ministry of Foreign Affairs informed the Intelligence Department that all German cement works had intensified their work as the Germans were building fortifications on their border with the Soviet Union.[66] It is the Ministry's foreign missions which most often had information on members of the Polish Diaspora and wartime émigrés suspected of co-operation with German intelligence. Sometimes this was detailed information on people recruited by the Abwehr and directed to places where Poles congregated and even to military units in France and subsequently to Great Britain.[67] The II Bureau was frequently asked to provide an opinion on persons indicated by the Foreign Ministry, especially when such persons claimed that before the war they had co-operated with Polish intelligence.[68]

As the war went on, the co-operation between the II Bureau and the Ministry became closer. And when the Minister, August Zaleski, ordered his diplomatic missions to reveal the sources of such information, the II Bureau obtained additional means to enlarge its own intelligence networks.[69] On the other hand the II Bureau was providing all Legations, Consulates-General and Consulates with information on persons suspected of collaboration with foreign intelligence services and who might apply for a Polish passport, and also on what it found out about the new intelligence techniques used by the Axis countries.[70]

In view of the large influx of information, the personnel of the Records and Studies Department was expanded. At the end of October 1943 its staff of 20 was as follows: Department's Chief, Section 'Germany' – 7 officers, Section 'Russia'– 3 officers, Section 'West' – 2 officers, General Section – 1 officer. The secretariat of the Department employed 1 NCO and 5 civilians. Just over 6 months later the personnel was increased again. And on 1st June 1944 it employed 24 persons (of whom 17 were officers).[71]

Its internal organisation and division of labour indicated the prevalence of German matters. The prime task of the chief of 'Germany' Section was to prepare studies on the political and military situation in the Third Reich and on German forces on Polish soil. The first Subsection (German forces) gathered and analysed information on the organisation of military units, Order of Battle, and the operational use of German forces. This subsection recorded, assessed and prepared for passing on to other intelligence services information on the distribution of German forces, fortification works, operational intentions, troop and materiel transports and conduct of front-line operations. It also analysed the state of human resources, organisation, equipment and morale of German forces. Since there were gaps in available information, these were compensated for by introducing estimates, as was the practice between the wars. Thanks to this detailed analysis of German strength on the Eastern Front at the end of 1941 and in early 1942 and having made allowances for the estimated number of people capable of military service in the Reich, the size of the reserves was assessed at 4 million. Factoring in further data on the call-up of German citizens born between 1886 and 1923 but living outside the Third Reich and the need to ensure the smooth workings of industry, other economic needs and the requirements of the state administration, as early as 1942 the Subsection formed the opinion that the human resources in the Third Reich were steadily getting worse.

The task of the second subsection was to deal with economic and political matters. Information on the morale of the German population, the state of agriculture, coal and steel production was analysed and records were maintained on industrial plants working on war production in

Germany. Internal and foreign policies of Germany, occupied and neutral countries (Sweden, Turkey, Switzerland) were also looked at.

The third subsection dealt with the analysis of intelligence reports arriving from Poland (the II Bureau of the Home Army GHQ) through the intermediary of the VI Bureau of Polish General Staff and the setting of tasks for the Home Army intelligence. In addition maps of German units stationed in Poland were updated, records of industrial plants contributing to the war effort were kept and war production recorded. Since the Records and Studies Department was also charged with co-operation with civilian ministries on the utilisation of information on economic situation in Poland, the Department collected all information received from a multitude of sources.

The 'Russia' Section was to prepare syntheses on the military and economic conditions in the USSR, to evaluate intelligence reports received by the II Bureau, to control the means by which such information was being disseminated, to analyse the Soviet press and to inform persons cleared for access to such information. In addition the Head of the Section participated in conferences organised by the Chief of the II Bureau and by civilian Polish authorities.

The first subsection of the 'Russia' Section kept records on large units of the Red Army, maintained the Soviet order of battle and the distribution of units up to date and followed the situation at the fronts. Information on Soviet human resources and on the organisation and equipment of the military was collated. Records were kept on senior commands, and all this information was distributed to other intelligence services.

The task of the second subsection was to collate and analyse information on the social and political situation of the USSR and on its internal and foreign policies. This included the analysis of the activities of the Soviet government, seen as contrary to the Polish-Soviet agreement of 30th July 1941. The II Bureau had at its disposal numerous documents and items of information from 1942–1944, kept in a special dossier entitled 'False Soviet Game'. One issue under investigation was the murder of Polish officers at Katyń. The II Bureau also had some documents originating with the Soviet security forces, which organised the deportations of the Polish population inhabiting the eastern districts of Poland, including an order entitled 'Instruction on the resettlement of population considered hostile to the Soviet Union from the occupied territories of Lithuania, Latvia and Estonia'[72]

The results of the unit's analytical work were communiqués published every 10 days. These contained the most important information obtained by the II Bureau on various subjects. Most of such information pertained to the changes in the distribution of German forces, data on the production of military equipment in Germany and the size of losses on the Eastern Front. There was also condensed information on German military transports crossing Poland and other countries and on new types of weapons, the preparations for the use of gas weapons etc.

Among the most important issues was German tank production and the losses on the Eastern Front. The comparisons of German and Soviet communiqués testified to the huge numbers of destroyed and damaged enemy tanks. By comparing such information with intelligence reports, the II Bureau was able to opine that though there was a tendency to exaggerate the enemy losses in particular battles, as far as the totality of the front was concerned the losses as stated were close to reality. This conclusion was further supported by the information on tank production in the Reich, on rail transports carrying armoured units to the Eastern front, by information from the front itself and by communiqués of the German Oberkommando des Heeres. The II Bureau did not have full information on the production of tanks in Germany. Its records contained information on 80 larger and smaller factories in the Reich whose annual production was estimated at some 20 thousand tanks. Assuming that this data was not complete, the total annual production was thought to be some 30 thousand units. Similar extrapolations were made on the basis of the II Bureau's information from other sources.

The Studies Department carried out research into the use of the Luftwaffe on the various fronts. Both the tactics employed and the losses were presented. As with tanks, information from protagonists was compared with information collected by Polish intelligence.

Assessments of developments at sea were of a more general character, since these were of less interest and as the II Bureau had only limited ability to gather such intelligence. Nevertheless a systematic effort was made to consider the most important activities in this field.

By the spring of 1944 information on the German preparations for the invasion of France dominated intelligence reports. There were numerous indications that the Germans were seriously considering the possibility of an attack on the Channel coast and in the Mediterranean. Comments by senior German commanders on this were also considered. In early March 1944, for example, there was a remark by Gen. Dittmar, who was certain that any invasion would lead to the Allies' defeat, which in his opinion would turn the tide of the war and lead to German victory.

In relation to the Parisian period, the staff of the II Bureau's headquarters had been significantly reduced. The number of posts in the General Office was cut down from 22 to 9, in the Intelligence Department from 34 to 24. On the other hand the personnel of the Records and Studies Department was increased from 12 to 20. As Counter-Intelligence, which in France had 58 posts, was on 11 March 1940 transferred to the Ministry of National Defence, this significantly reduced the cadres of the II Bureau. In 1941 the headquarters staff consisted of 43 persons: 19 staff officers, 8 junior officers, 1 NCO and 15 civilian employees. By the end of October 1943 there were 62 posts in the II Bureau: 31 officers, 6 NCOs, 24 civilians and 1 lower-rank official.[73] This did not include the staff working in intelligence stations and cells. These personnel changes reflected the Bureau's changing tasks. In April 1944 the establishment of the II Bureau was set at 162 officers and 755 other ranks in headquarters, 8 stations, 2 independent stations and 33 cells.[74]

The budget of the II Bureau was clearly not adequate for its tasks. The size of intelligence personnel was comparable with the pre-war establishment. But the pre-war Intelligence had some 1,500,000 dollars at its disposal, which was much more than some £5 thousand per month allocated since the beginning of the war.[75] Once the co-operation with British intelligence started, this fund was substantially increased, but remained below requirements. The sums allocated annually by the Treasury on SIS's motion fluctuated somewhat. In 1943 the II Bureau had £204,000 at its disposal; by 1944 this grew to £328,000 and the allocation for 1945 was £252,000. Independently from these sums, through the II and VI Bureaux of PGS, the British provided separate funding for the Home Army intelligence and for the Counterintelligence Department of the Ministry of National Defence.[76]

Financial problems are well testified to by the entreaties to heads of intelligence stations and cells emanating from Headquarters of the II Bureau, demanding cuts in disposable expenditure. These stressed that 'pay for both network heads and for network employees should be sufficient to ensure a minimal level of existence. On both ethical and security grounds pay should be set towards the lower end of this minimum.' Such an approach to intelligence activity might have been the outcome of pre-war habits and work methods. Before the war and following a series of provocations, there was reluctance to authorise funds for purchasing intelligence. The recommendation then usually was to organize surveillance and to use 'idealistic' agents.

In the final phase of the war the structures of the II Bureau were determined by its tasks and by the guidelines provided by the Commander-in-Chief and by his Chief of Staff, by its own organisational needs stemming from the assessment of its field force, by the political and military situation in the world and in Poland and by the suggestions received from British and American intelligence services. Work was also carried out on the organisation of intelligence for the post-war period.

The indisputable conclusion from an analysis of the organisational structures of Polish Intelligence Headquarters, both for the pre-war period and throughout the war, up to the last battles in May 1945, is that the Polish authorities had at their disposal a unique card: an organisation built on solid foundations, both structurally and professionally. Despite the defeats, in September 1939 and again in June 1940, it was able to quickly reconstruct and expand its intelligence network. It was able to achieve remarkable results. This was possible because throughout the war Polish intelligence was led by its pre-war officers. There was no discontinuity in activities and no violent personnel purges. This is why when, following the defeat of France, the British intelligence services were fully eliminated from the continent, they turned for assistance in re-creating lost sources of information to the II Bureau of the Polish General Staff. This is also the background to the Polish-British intelligence co-operation agreement, signed in the autumn of 1940. Whether the Polish authorities were able to utilise this advantage is a different matter. And it was a considerable advantage, both in terms of the number of intelligence reports provided and of their quality. This is clearly testified to by the American and British quality assessments, which show that these reports were of high value and were very useful for the allied military effort throughout the Second World War.

Notes

1 Among others, as part of the so-called 'Action South' project, outlined in the Order of 13 Oct. 1939 of the Chief of the II Bureau, Col. Marian Józef Smoleński. More on this in: IPMS, A.XII.55/1, Organisation of Communications with Poland, Bucharest 13 Oct. 1939; T. Dubicki, *Konspiracja polska w Rumunii 1939–1940 (Polish Underground in Romania 1939–1940)*, Warsaw 2002, pp. 58–61; T. Dubicki, *Ekspozytura 'R' w Bukareszcie (grudzień 1939 – październik 1940) (Intelligence Station 'R' in Bucharest, (December 1939– October 1940))*, 'Mars', vol. 1, London-Warsaw 1993, pp. 65–74.

2 The Intelligence Department emerged on the basis of a station of the II Bureau, set up by Maj. Tadeusz Nowiński, delegated for this purpose to Paris some time around 6th October 1939 by the Chief of the II Bureau of Polish General Staff, Col. M. J. Smoleński.

3 The II Bureau consisted of five Departments: General (Maj. Leon Bortnowski), Intelligence (Lt-Col. Stanisław Gano), Records and Studies (Lt-Col. Ignacy Banach), Security/Counter-intelligence (Maj. Wincenty Zarembski), Independent Finance Section (Maj. Franciszek Ptak), Military Censorship (Lt-Col. Stanisław Kara) and of two independent groups: of Maj. Jan Żychoń – attached to 5. Bureau (Intelligence) of the French Admiralty and of Lt-Col. Gwido Langer – cryptographers in the 'Bruno' centre. A further four officers were attached to the Japanese staff. The Headquarters of the Bureau had 150 staff (IPMS, A.XII.24/19, Organisation of the II Bureau of Polish General Staff during the French period, 1940).

4 Until then military attaché in Belgrade (1937–1939).

5 In the inter-war period he was the Chief of the East Section of the Intelligence Department, military attaché in Helsinki (1933–1935) and Head of the Independent Technical Section of the II Bureau of Polish General Staff.

6 At a meeting of the Polish National Council in early March 1940 he admitted that the Polish authorities had precise information on the growing German threat (IPMS, A.XII.24/36, Report of Maj. Adam Świtkowski to the Chief of the II Bureau Polish General Staff, l.dz. 3118/P/44/Secret, of 16th July 1944).

7 See chapter 46 – J.S. Ciechanowski and J. Tebinka, *Współpraca kryptologiczna. Enigma (Cryptological co-operation. Enigma)*.

8 For more, see: T. Panecki, *Wojna obronna Polski 1939 r. w opinii francuskiego Sztabu Generalnego (Polish Defensive War in the opinion of the French General Staff)*, 'Wojskowy Przegląd Historyczny', 1989, no. 3, pp. 428–439.

9 On 26 September 1940 the SIS Head, Brig. Stewart Menzies, and Prime Minister Churchill's Security Adviser, Maj. Desmond Morton, came to see the Chief of the II Bureau, Col. Leon Mitkiewicz. They were worried about 'too large a number of independent and not centrally controlled Polish intelligence services'. In relation to this it was decided that SIS should work exclusively with the II Bureau and that 'any demands of any other institutions shall be considered only with the approval of the II Bureau of PGS' (IPMS, A.XII.24/46, Report of the Head of the II Bureau to the Chief of Staff at Polish General Staff of 27 September 1940). Consequently at a conference with the Polish Chief of Staff it was decided that 'Intelligence stations and cells of the II Bureau of PGS shall gather information on Germany and Russia and conduct military counter-intelligence … To improve information gathering and to achieve a better fit with the organisation of British intelligence it is necessary for

other departments of the (Polish) State to pass all intelligence obtained to the II Bureau of PGS for assessment and proper utilisation' (IPMS, A.XII.24/46, official record of conference on 1 October 1940).

10 It had six Bureaux: I Organisational, II Intelligence, III Operations and Training, IV Quartermaster, V Personnel and VI Special. Chief of Staff was Maj-Gen. Tadeusz Klimecki.

11 More in: M. Utnik, *Sztab polskiego naczelnego wodza w II wojnie światowej (The Polish General Staff in World War II)*, 'Wojskowy Przegląd Historyczny', 1973, no. 4, pp. 186–187.

12 Ministry of National Defence from 19 June 1942. IV Department funtioned as a Security Office.

13 In July 1943 the II Bureau was subordinated to the Deputy Chief of General Staff.

14 Both Liaison Missions to the British War Office were established in November 1943. In terms of the scope of their duties both the 8-strong Mission 'A' (Maj. Leopold Szumski) and the 7-strong Mission 'B' (Maj. Adam Świtkowski) were subordinated to the British authorities, but they remained on the strength of the II Bureau. In addition to their Chiefs, both Missions were divided into sections and registries (IPMS, A.XII.24/21, Organizacja i zakres pracy Oddz. Inf.-Wyw. Sztabu NW stan z dnia 1 VI 1944 r. (Organisation and Scope of Activities of the II Bureau of PGS as of 1 June 1944) l.dz. 4281/Org./Tjn./44).

15 Ibid.

16 IPMS,A.XII.24/56, Instrukcja organizacyjna Sztabu Naczelnego Wodza (Organisational Instruction of PGS), l.dz. 1700/ Org./Tjn. 44 of 1 November 1944.

17 At the same time he represented the Commander-in-Chief in the Inter-Allied Committee in London.

18 IPMS,A.XII,24/21, Organizacja i zakres pracy Oddz. Inf.-Wyw. Sztabu NW. Stan z dnia 1 VI 1944 r. (Organisation and Scope of Activities of the II Bureau of PGS as of 1 June 1944), l.dz. 4281/Org./Tjn./44, p. 4.

19 Between the wars Lt-Col. T. Skinder was Chief of Intelligence for the Frontier Defence Corps and later of Department IIa (offensive intelligence) of the II Bureau of Polish General Staff.

20 CA MSW, the VI Bureau of PGS, no. 295/582, Internal Order of Chief of II Bureau no. 3/44, of 22 January 1944, p. 19.

21 Staff reserve list contained for example the name of Maj. Alfons Jakubianiec, arrested by German counter-intelligence in July 1941, when the Germans were looking for a contact with one of the most famous agents of the II Bureau, codenamed 'Wiktor'.

22 IPMS,A.XII.24/64, Protokół zdawczo-odbiorczy Wydziału Wywiadowczego Oddz. Inf.-Wyw. Sztabu NW z 15 II 1944 r. (Hand-over Certificate of the Intelligence Department of the II Bureau of PGS of 15th February 1944), l.dz. 1242/Wyw./44.

23 IPMS,A.XII.24/21, Organizacja i zakres pracy Oddz. Inf.-Wyw. Sztabu NW. Stan z dnia 1 VI 1944 r. (Organisation and Scope of Activities of the II Bureau of Polish General Staff as of 1 June 1944), l.dz. 4281/Org./Tjn./44.

24 On 5 May 1944, for example, a successful operation, 'Made', consisted of dropping arms, ammunition, food supplies and cigarettes for the French networks (IPMS, A.XII.24/37, Sprawozdanie z pracy Wydziału Wywiadowczego za czas od 5 V do 14 V 1944 r. (Report on the Operations of Intelligence Department from 5 May to 14 May 1944)).

25 See: IPMS,A.XII.24/37, Wykaz ekspozytur i samodzielnych placówek wywiadowczych (The List of Stations and Independent Intelligence Cells).

26 IPMS,A.XII.24/64, Protokół zdawczo-odbiorczy Wydziału Wywiadowczego Oddz. Inf.-Wyw. Sztabu NW z 15 II 1944 r. (Hand-over Certificate of the Intelligence Department of the II Bureau PGS of 15 February 1944), l.dz. 1242/Wyw./44.

27 IPMS,A.XII.24/37, Sprawozdanie z pracy Wydziału Wywiadowczego za czas od 5

V do 14 V 1944 r. (Report on the Operations of the Intelligence Department from 5th May to 14th May 1944).

28 More in: chapter IV – T. Dubicki, *Rumunia (Romania)*.

29 CA MSW, O.VI, 295/582, Organizacja i zakres pracy Oddz. Inf.-Wyw., stan z dnia 1 VI 1944 r., l.dz. 428/Org/Tjn./44, p. 107. (Organisation and Scope of Operations of the II Bureau as of 1 June 1944).

30 Ibid., O.VI, 295/577, Report to the Chief of the II Bureau from Maj. Gaweł of 26 January 1944, p. 199.

31 Ibid., Stan organizacyjny i budżet placówek wywiadowczych w Ameryce Północnej i Południowej na dzień 1 VI 1944 r. (Organisational State and Budget of Intelligence Stations in North and South America as of 1 June 1944), p. 8.

32 The report for 1944 speaks of 100 officers, 1666 agents, 51 civilian officials, 26 Privates and 10 female volunteers. Of this total 11 officers and 78 agents have been arrested, 13 agents shot and 28 lost without trace (IPMS, A.XII.24/37, Sprawozdanie z pracy Wydziału Wywiadowczego Oddz. Inf.-Wyw. Sztabu NW za rok 1944) (Report on the Operations of Intelligence Department of the II Bureau of PGS for 1944).

33 IPMS, Kol. 242/62. Official Note for C-in-C on Radio Communications of the II Bureau of PGS, 1 May 1944.

34 CA MSW, O.VI, 295/577, p. 55.

35 M. Rejewski, *Wspomnienia z mojej pracy w Biurze Szyfrów Oddziału II w latach 1930–1945 (Memoirs of my Work at the Cyphers Office of the II Bureau in 1930-1945)*, A WIH, MiD, I/2/44.

36 CA MSW, O.VI, 295/577, p. 56.

37 M. Rejewski, *Wspomnienia (Memoirs)*, op.cit.

38 Reports for the British intelligence were passed through the SIS Liaison Mission run by Cmdr. Wilfred Dunderdale ('Wilski'). Those destined for the Americans went through Col. Dunn. Maj. Jan Żychoń stressed, however, that 'when passing on intelligence information obtained by our networks, caution must be exercised so that only that information which is required by the Allies to further common aims is passed on. Let us be careful not to pass on material, which is not in our interests to do so' (underlined by Żychoń). On co-operation with SOE he warned that 'this organisation is capable of subverting other intelligence services for its own purposes. I suspect that there might be a unit in SOE (perhaps Maj. Truszkowski) which deals with Polish matters, that is which collects materials on Polish activities etc.' (IPMS, A.XII.24/64, Protokół zdawczo-odbiorczy Wydziału Wywiadowczego Oddz. Inf.-Wyw. Sztabu NW, luty 1944 r. (Hand-over Certificate of the Intelligence Department of the II Bureau of Polish General Staff, February 1944), pp. 1–23).

39 Ibid., A.XII.24/37, Zestawienie wyników pracy Wydziału Wywiadowczego za czas od 1 X 1941 do 1 V 1942 r. (Report on results of Intelligence activities of the II Bureau of PGS from 1 October 1941 to 1 May 1942).

40 Ibid., Zestawienie wyników pracy wywiadowczej Oddziału Wywiadowczego Sztabu NW za czas od 1 VII 1942 do 30 VI 1943 r. (Report on results of the Intelligence activities of the II Bureau of PGS from 1 July 1942 to 30 June 1943). In 1944 the Americans were placing Polish intelligence 'in the first place as a source of information provided to American staff' (Ibid., Sprawozdanie z pracy Wydziału Wywiadowczego Oddz. Inf.-Wyw. Sztabu NW za rok 1944.) (Report on the work of the Intelligence Department of the II Bureau of PGS for 1944).

41 Ibid., Sprawozdanie z pracy Wydziału Wywiadowczego Oddz. Inf.-Wyw. Sztabu NW za rok 1944 (Report on the Work of Intelligence Department of the II Bureau of PGS for 1944); ibid. A.XII.24/57, Ogólne zestawienie z pracy Oddz. Inf.-Wyw. Sztabu NW za okres 1 I do 31 XII 1944 r. jako materiał do sprawozdania MON, 23 I 1945 r. (General Report on the Work of the II Bureau of PGS for 1 January to 31 December 1944; for report of Ministry of National Defence, 23 January 1945).

42 Ibid., A.XII.24/64, Protokół zdawczo-odbiorczy Wydziału Wywiadowczego Oddz. Inf.-Wyw. Sztabu NW z 15 II 1944 r. (Hand-over Certificate of the Department of the II Bureau of PGS of 15 February 1944), l.dz. 1242/Wyw./44.

43 A Section worked, for example, on the freeing from Spanish prison of Capt. Koperski (which succeeded in February 1944), of persons linked to the 'F' network detained by the Germans in France or of Maj. Alfons Jakubianiec, arrested in Berlin (CA MSW, 295/82, p. 89).

44 IPMS,A.XII.24/64, Protokół zdawczo-odbiorczy Wydziału Wywiadowczego Oddz. Inf.-Wyw. Sztabu NW z 15 II 1944 r. (Hand-over Certificate of the Department of the II Bureau of PGS of 15 February 1944), l.dz. 1242/Wyw./44, k. 65–68.

45 Ibid.,A.XII.24/36, Sprawozdanie szefa Samodzielnego Wydziału Wywiadu Obronnego MON płk. dypl. Miniewskiego z VII 1945 r. (Report of the Head of the Counterintelligence Department of the Ministry of the National Defence, Col. Miniewski, July 1945), l.dz. 3889/Org./Tjn./45.

46 Ibid.

47 Ibid.,A.XII.24/37, Obsada Wydziału Wywiadowczego z 14 V 1944 r. (The Staff of the Intelligence Department as of 14 May 1944).

48 Ibid.,A.XII.24/64, Protokół zdawczo-odbiorczy Wydziału Wywiadowczego Oddz. Inf.-Wyw. Sztabu NW z 15 II 1944 r., (Hand-over Certificate of the Intelligence Department of the II Bureau of PGS, of 15th February 1944), l.dz. 1242/Wyw./44.

49 More in: CA MSW, O.VI, 295/94-V/36, k. 21-23; A. Pepłoński, *Wywiad Polskich Sił Zbrojnych na Zachodzie 1939–1945 (Intelligence Service of the Polish Armed Forces in the West 1939–1945)*, Warsaw 1995, pp. 95–97; A. Suchcitz, K. Skrzywan, *Archiwum płk. Stefana Mayera i testament mjr. Jana Zychonia, (Col. Stefan Mayer's Archive and the Last Will of Maj. Jan Żychoń)*, 'Teki Historyczne', vol. 19, London 1988–1989, pp. 242–247; A. Suchcitz, *Maj. Jan Żychoń – materiały do biografii (Maj. Jan Żychoń – Towards a Biography)*, 'Zeszyt Naukowy Muzeum Wojska', Białystok 1990, pp. 102-114.

50 CA MSW, O.VI, 295/582, Ogólne zestawienie zadań dla placówki 'Grecja' w odniesieniu do penetracji sowieckiej (General Tasks for Station 'Grecja'), pp. 76–78.

51 In the inter-war period air intelligence was in the hands of specialist officers in the 'Germany' (Capt., later Maj. Ferdynand Bobiński) and 'Russia' Sections (Capt. Olgierd Cumft). After evacuating to France the duties performed by Maj. Bobiński's Section were defined as 'studies on the airforces of foreign states and especially Germany and Russia; in addition, counter-intelligence on the territories of air units in France, England, Romania and Hungary' (IPMS, Lot.A.IV.1/3b, Notatka: Współpraca Oddziału II DSP z Oddziału II Sztabu NW, 7 III 1940 r. (Note: Co-operation of Department II of Air Force Command with the II Bureau of PGS, 7th March 1940)). When in Great Britain, in the summer of 1942, Maj. Bobiński's Section was transformed and at first, the Air Studies Unit, with Bobiński as its temporary head, Lt-Col. Felicjan Sterba, and later, before it started its work, on 23rd November 1942, it became the Air Intelligence Department under Lt-Col. Felicjan Sterba at the II Bureau of PGS (IPMS, A.XII.24/21, Organizacja i zakres pracy Oddz. Inf.-Wyw. Sztabu NW. Stan z dnia 1 VI 1944 r. (Organisation and Scope of Operations of the II Bureau of PGS as of 1st June 1944)., l.dz. 4281/Org./Tjn./44.

52 IPMS, Lot. A.V.1/7B, Col. S. Gano to the Chief of II Bureau of PGS, 9th September 1942.; A. Suchcitz, *Air Intelligence Officer Wing Commander Ferdynand Bobiński*, 'The Enigma Bulletin', May 1997, Kraków, no. 2, pp. 90-91.

53 Ibid., A.XII.24/21, Organizacja i zakres pracy Oddz. Inf.-Wyw. Sztabu NW. Stan z dnia 1 VI 1944 r. (Organisation and Scope of Operations of the II Bureau of PGS as of 1st June 1944), l.dz. 4281/Org./Tjn./44, p. 28; Archiwum Ferdynanda Bobińskiego (dalej: AFB) (Ferdynand Bobiński Archive, (further AFB), ref: AFB/7, Zestawienie działalności Oddziału Wywiadu Lotniczego za czas od 20 VII 1940 do 8 V 1945 r. (Report on the Activities of Air Intelligence Department); ibid.,

Sprawozdanie szefa Lotniczego Wydziału Wywiadowczego z wykonanych prac za rok 1944, 20 I 1945 r. (Report of the Chief of the Air Intelligence Department for 1944, 20th January 1945); A. Suchcitz, *Air Intelligence*, op.cit., p. 91.

54 The beginnings of naval intelligence are to be found in the pre-war Maritime Affairs Section in the Records Department of the II Bureau, commanded by Cmdr. Rafał Czeczott. At the end of April 1939 the Naval Command began to organise the Independent Foreign Navies Section with Cmdr. Brunon Jabłoński, but all work to achieve this, including sending officers for intelligence courses at II Bureau, attempts to start a naval radio monitoring unit (Cmdr. Konrad Namieśnikowski) and attempts to begin co-operation with naval attachés and with the II Bureau itself, were halted by the outbreak of hostilities. This is why first successes were achieved only after evacuating to France, as part of the detached group of Maj. Żychoń (B. Jabłoński, *Wywiad, czyli służba szpiegowska (Intelligence or the Spying Service)*, part 2, 'Nasze Sygnały', 1972, no. 126, p. 30.).

55 B. Jabłoński, *Wywiad (Intelligence)*, op.cit., p. 30.

56 IPMS, A.XII.24/46, Letter of Rear Adm. J. Świrski to Gen. W. Sikorski, 1st October 1940.

57 See SPP, 2.3.6.1., Notatka z konferencji szefa Wyw. Morskiego z szefem Oddz. Spec. w sprawie wywiadu morskiego w 'K', 23 VII 1943 r. (Note on the Conference of Chief of Naval Intelligence with the Chief of the VI Bureau on the matter of naval intelligence in 'K', 23rd July 1943); SPP, 2.3.6.2.2., Oficerowie wywiadu morskiego, notatka szefa Oddziału Spec. Sztabu NW, 20 VIII 1943 r. (Officers of Naval Intelligence. A Note of Chief of the VI Bureau of PGS of 20th August 1943).

58 SPP, 2.3.6.2.2., Pismo kmdr. ppor. Cz. Janickiego do szefa Oddziału VI Sztabu NW, 17 VI 1944 r. (Comdr. Cz. Janicki's letter to the Chief of the VI Bureau of PGS, 17 June 1944.

59 B. Jabłoński, *Wywiad (Intelligence)*, op.cit., pp. 33–34.

60 IPMS, A.XII.24/21, Organizacja i zakres pracy (Organisation and Scope of Activities), op.cit., p. 30.

61 Ibid., A.XII.24/56, Notatka płk. S. Gano z połowy 1944 r. nt. Oceny pracy Oddziału II Sztabu NW (Col. Gano's Note from 2nd half of 1944 on the assessment of work of the II Bureau of Polish General Staff).

62 J. Tucholski, *Cichociemni (The Parachutists [cichociemny, meaning 'silent and unseen', was the term used to describe London's agents dropped over Poland])*, Warsaw 1985, p. 64.

63 IPMS, A.XII.24/28, Obsada imienna personelu Szkoły Wywiadowczej (The Staff of the Intelligence School), l.dz. 476/Tjn. O.I of 24th February 1942.

64 Ibid., A.XII.24/21, Organizacja i zakres pracy Oddz. Inf.-Wyw. Sztabu NW, stan z dnia 10 VI 1944 r. (Organisation and Scope of Operations of the II Bureau of PGS as of 10th June 1944) l.dz. 4281/Org./Tjn./44., pp. 8–9.

65 AAN, Ambasada RP w Waszyngtonie (Polish Embassy in Washington), vol. 3140, pp. 2, 58; T. Piszczkowski, *Między Lizboną a Londynem (Between Lisbon and London)*, London 1979, pp. 13–21.

66 AAN, Ambasada RP w Londynie (Polish Embassy in London), vol. 1855, p. 4. The phrase used was 'on the German-Soviet demarcation line'.

67 Ibid., Poselstwo RP w Tehranie (Polish Legation in Tehran), vol. 197, p. 13.

68 Ibid., Konsulat Honorowy RP w Casablance (Polish Honorary Consulate in Casablanca), vol. 222, p. 3.

69 Ibid., Ambasada RP w Londynie, Instrukcja MSZ z 16 II 1940 r. (Polish Embassy in London, Foreign Ministry's Instruction of 16th February 1940), l.dz., GM 436/40, p.1.

70 Ibid., Poselstwo RP w Tehranie (Polish Legation in Tehran), vol. 87, p. 3.

71 As of 1 June 1944 the Chiefs of Sections were: Lt-Col. Stanisław Kijak ('Germany'), Maj. Wincenty Zarembski ('Russia'), Maj. Marian Zajączkowski ('West'). Other staff

were Maj. Lucjan Mroczkowski, Maj. Teofil Jusiński, Capt. Jan Sochacki, Capt. Włodzimierz Gulin, Capt. Jan Maśliński, Capt. Józef Utnicki, Capt. Zygmunt Wilkoński, Capt. Ludwik Juchniewicz (IPMS, A.XII.24/21, Organizacja i zakres pracy Oddz. Inf.-Wyw. Sztabu NW. Stan z dnia 1 VI 1944 r. (Organisation and Scope of Operations of II Bureau of PGS as of 1 June 1944), l.dz. 4281/Org./Tjn./44).

72 Ibid., pp. 18–21.

73 CA MSW, O.VI, sygn. 295/588, Rozkaz Naczelnego Wodza (Order of Commander-in-Chief), l.dz. 1450/Tjn. of 28th October 1943.

74 IPMS, A.XII.24/37, Zestawienie wyników pracy Wydziału Wywiadowczego za czas od dnia 1 X 1941 do 1 V 1942. (Report on the Results Achieved by the Intelligence Department between 1st October 1941 and 1st May 1942); ibid., A XII.24/56, Notatka płk. S. Gano w sprawie organizacji Oddziału II wg stanu na dzień 30 IV 1944 r.; ibid., Referat zcy szefa Oddz. Inf.-Wyw. Sztabu NW płk. dypl. T. Skindera o pracy wywiadu, maj 1944 r., s. 3-5.

75 L. Mitkiewicz, Z gen. Sikorskim na obczyźnie (In exile with General Sikorski), Paris 1968, p. 84.

76 CA MSW, O.VI, sygn. 295/588, Pismo Ambasady RP w Londynie do ministra skarbu z 29 XI 1944 r. (Letter from Polish Embassy in London to the Minister of the Treasury of 29 November 1944), l.dz. 154/Tjn./44, p. 276.

10

The Role of the II Bureau of the Union of Armed Struggle–Home Army (ZWZ-AK) Headquarters in the Intelligence Structures of the Polish Armed Forces in the West

Andrzej Pepłoński and Jan Ciechanowski

The organisation of military resistance on Polish soil under both occupying powers and ensuring regular communication with the home country dominated the activities of the Polish Government-in-Exile from the outset. The multitude of organizational and political endeavours was an indication of both the high priority assigned to these tasks and to the difficulties involved in them. The Home Affairs Office, led by Gen. Kazimierz Sosnkowski, played the principal part in these activities. Due to internal political issues, in mid-November 1939 a new committee of Council of Ministers was set up, called the Ministerial Committee for Home Affairs. Gen. Sosnkowski became the Commander of the Union of Armed Struggle and in this respect was the Deputy Commander-in-Chief. In parallel, and independently of work being undertaken in France, the resistance organisations emerging in Poland began to set up intelligence services as their first priority. Since the conditions prevailing under both occupations were in many ways different from those in which the II Bureau of Polish General Staff (PGS) operated, both the organization and the working methods employed by the intelligence organisation of SZP-ZWZ-AK (Service for Poland's Victory–Union of Armed Struggle–Home Army, further the Home Army) were also different, as were its aims.

The Homeland intelligence service had to be constructed almost from scratch, though it was built gradually and systematically. In the early stages the organizational work and the tasking process were undertaken on the exclusive authority of the the Home Army GHQ. The aims of the resistance's offensive intelligence were to prepare it militarily for its current tasks, for various armed operations and for diversion and sabotage, that is for tactical activities, which in the early period were not very intensive. But another aim was to prepare the underground organisations operationally and strategically, linked to the planned future uprising and to the war activities of the allied armies.[1] From its very beginning the the Home Army GHQ fully subordinated itself to the Polish authorities in the West and its military intelligence was expected to co-operate closely with the II Bureau. The issues with other resistance organizations, which also conducted intelligence work, were of secondary importance.

There existed a degree of command duplication whilst the Polish authorities were still in France, which complicated organisational work. The central intelligence unit at the SZP (Service for Poland's Victory) HQ was established on 27th September 1939. In this early period the intelligence groups being set up undertook the observation of the German military units in Warsaw, Kraków, Radom and Kielce.[2] When SZP became the ZWZ (Union of Armed Struggle, further, the Home Army), a new structure of the resistance organisation in the field emerged, encompassing the territories under both occupations, and new organisational units were set up. In mid-January 1940 Gen. Sosnkowski announced the preparation of a general plan of activities in Poland and mentioned intelligence-gathering and systematic approach to information in the first place. Two weeks later not only the basic organizational principles of intelligence but also their main tasks and the so-called questionnaires (lists of issues of most interest to the Polish authorities in Paris) were specified.[3] In March 1940 the 'guidelines for the organisation of intelligence in Poland', regulating the working methods, allocating tasks to specific units and questionnaires on specific issues, were passed on to Poland.[4] The tidying up of the organisation of intelligence in Poland and the strengthening of networks in the Third Reich were also important for the II Bureau of the Polish General Staff.[5]

Following the fall of France and the move of the Polish authorities to London the issue of intelligence in general and in Poland in particular acquired new importance, as indicated by the orders carried by successive emissaries arriving from London. In many cases these orders and suggestions were valuable and helped to improve the effectiveness of intelligence gathering in Poland. By mid-October 1940 both the II Bureau of the Polish General Staff and British intelligence saw the need for the Home Army to build-up its offensive activities, to separate a unit dealing with the war industry in the Third Reich and with maritime industry, and to begin the preparations for establishing intelligence networks which would act in the areas adjacent to the future Eastern Front.[6]

The relative position of the II Bureau of the Home Army in relation to the II Bureau PGS was already being settled. Due to the geographical position of Poland, the ability to obtain information of interest to the allied staffs and in view of the anticipated events in the East the importance of intelligence information gathered in the country increased systematically. The growing tempo of German preparations for a war against the USSR caused an increase in instructions and tasks. In early January 1941 Gen. Sosnkowski ordered the separation of intelligence structures in Poland from the stations conducting deep penetration and operating outside

Poland. The II Bureau of PGS was to organise the work of its intelligence stations under both occupiers in such a manner as not to risk any conflict of interests with the Home Army networks. Since the authorities in London concluded that it was much easier to run intelligence operations from Warsaw, several days before war began in the East all the deep intelligence stations operating under both occupiers were subordinated to the Commander-in-Chief of the Home Army.

As the intelligence structures in Poland were built up, their requirements for radio equipment, experts and, especially, funds, grew. Though people engaged in intelligence were mainly 'not so much expert as committed',[7] the financial appetite was the result of technical costs, such as travel needs of agents, the organisation of courier networks, the need to maintain safe accommodation or to pay informants. It was the task of the VI (Special) Bureau of PGS to meet the various requirements of intelligence in Poland.

The establishment of a specialised service participating in the contacts between Poland and the intelligence headquarters was to meet the requirements of secrecy. The setting up of this service was a consequence of the British idea of supporting underground movements in Europe (SOE) and of strategic planning by the Joint Chiefs of Staff Committee.[8] Nevertheless the broad scope of organisational work undertaken by the VI Bureau, encompassing the creation of land communication bases, the training of parachutists, the securing of radio communications and especially its function as an intermediary in intelligence matters, created a false impression as to its role. In reality it was the II Bureau of PGS which performed the fundamental job, that is tasking the intelligence service of the Home Army and the analysis of reports received, followed by their transmission to British intelligence. In practice there were certain departures from this division of labour, caused mainly by the need to immediately provide information to the allies.

Prior to the establishment of the VI Bureau and for a period of several days, its job was performed by the Home Department, which was a transitory structure set up immediately following the arrival of Polish General Staff in Great Britain.[9] At the beginning of August 1940 the Home Department was transformed into the VI Bureau and from this point it continued to evolve. Its internal organization was not based on any tested principles, as Department VI was given a very particular brief in relation both to the Home Army GHQ and to the II Bureau. The VI Bureau's structure was complex and its establishment large. In mid-1944 the Headquarters of the Bureau employed 61 persons. 312 staff participated in training activities in Great Britain. Together with the staff of its bases and support groups (anti-aircraft and anti-armour), the establishment of the VI Bureau numbered 961 persons including 29 staff officers, 267 other officers, 259 NCOs and Privates and 4 civilian officials.[10]

At first the Intelligence Section of the VI Bureau, led by Lt-Col. Kazimierz Iranek-Osmecki, dealt with co-operation with the Home Army GHQ intelligence. After his departure as an emissary to Poland, his duties were taken over by Maj. Stanisław Kijak. On 20th August 1940 the Bureau was joined by Capt. Teodor Cybulski, seconded from the II Bureau of Polish General Staff. In the early stages their duties were to collect and collate intelligence reports and information arriving from Poland and the transmission of tasks for the Home Army intelligence. Immediately on receipt, intelligence material was passed on to the II Bureau of PGS.[11] VI Bureau was reorganized in early January 1941, when the Organisation and Operations Department was set up, which incorporated the Intelligence Section, established earlier. In addition a new Section, S (for Special Operations), was set up. At this juncture the Organisation and Operations Department had three Sections: Organisation (run by Lt-Col. Wincenty Sobociński), Information (Maj. Stanisław Kijak), and Ciphers (2nd Lt. Stefan Jagiełło). The work of all these Sections, as well as that of the Head of Communications (under Maj. Władysław Gaweł) which was also subordinated to the Chief of the Organisation and Operations Department, was, to a large degree, connected with co-operation with the Home Army's intelligence. The tasks of the Organisation Section included the maintenance of records on the personnel of the Home Army GHQ and its district commands (real names, codenames, military ranks), operational security, guidelines and instructions on underground tactics and technology and records of safe houses. The Section also prepared tasks for emissaries and couriers traveling to Poland by land and air and dealt with all matters relating to the military communication bases with Poland.

The role of Home Army's intelligence in the structure of Polish special services was specified in the detailed orders of the principal military authorities. Such orders regulated their organization and authority. The main intelligence co-operation with the II Bureau of the Home Army GHQ was in the hands of the Intelligence Section. In view of the relationships between the VI and II Bureaux of PGS it is instructive to reproduce the list of the main tasks entrusted to the Intelligence Section.[12]

- to work on situation reports concerning Polish territory, that is on the general situation of the enemy (occupying powers). To prepare situation reports for the VI Bureau, copy such reports and other information to the II Bureau and other Polish General Staff Bureaux units and to interested ministries and members of Home Affairs Committee.
- to work on all issues relating to intelligence matters in Poland, and in particular to work out and to transmit to Poland and to the bases (stations) of intelligence tasks as determined by the II Bureau of PGS; to prepare instructions and guidelines on the intelligence work in Poland and in bases (stations). In this respect, to co-operate with the II Bureau of PGS; to maintain the records of intelligence organization and its lead personnel in Poland and in the bases intelligence stations (cells). To formulate recommendations aimed at improving the effectiveness of intelligence work in Poland and in the intelligence stations (cells).
- to ensure the flow of information to Poland and the bases, this to

include: collecting the daily radio communiqués from the Ministry
of Internal Affairs and supervising the daily transmission of such
communiqués to Poland and the bases; to prepare the 10-day
information bulletins for the intelligence stations (cells) and to
secure their regular and timely transmission.
* to prepare ad-hoc information bulletins for Poland; to collate and
prepare for transmission information and propaganda materials
destined for Poland and the intelligence stations (cells) as received
from the relevant governmental and military authorities, to
maintain records of such materials, to collate information for
Poland destined for the Commander-in-Chief of the Home Army.

These tasks indicate the degree to which the VI Bureau and its stations
and cells, as well as the Ministry of Internal Affairs, supported intelligence
gathering within Poland. It is the case that the VI Bureau was the prime
liaison between the Commander-in-Chief of the Home Army and the PGS.
But in reality the role of the VI Bureau in the management of intelligence
within Poland differed from that which is often assumed. According to Col.
Iranek-Osmecki the Information Office, which he commanded, did not
carry out detailed studies of the enemy, nor did it have proper records at
its disposal. Its research work was limited to the listing of the composition
and dislocation of the forces of the occupying powers. Gen. Sosnkowski,
who directed the military resistance in Poland, used such data, collated for
internal consumption.[13]

In mid-November 1942 following a proposal made by Col. Gano, the
staff of the Intelligence Section (Maj. Kijak and Capt. Cybulski) was
transferred to the II Bureau of PGS. The reason was organizational, in
particular the requirement to maintain permanent contacts with the
intelligence headquarters. The principles of co-operation between the two
Bureaux did not change significantly. The units of the VI Bureau (the Home
Ciphers Office and the Organisation Department) were to continue their
co-operation with the Intelligence Section. The only substantive change
was that from that point on Section 'N' in the Records and Studies
Department of the II Bureau, PGS, carried out the work on the German
forces. The VI Bureau retained the right to object to such tasks being
transmitted to Poland which might have caused the exposure of those who
were to carry out such missions.[14] In January 1943 another change in the
way the two Bureaux worked together was made: it was decided that
immediately following the decoding of signals from the Home Army GHQ
in the VI Bureau, these were to be passed on to the II Bureau. Such signals
were then worked on in the II Bureau Records and Studies Department,
and then passed on to the British intelligence and other military
institutions.[15] In the following months the way information obtained by the
Home Army intelligence was distributed was somewhat modified. It was
decided that material brought in by couriers and containing photocopies of
intelligence, political and economic reports, should be passed in according
to new principles: the first copy of a full text would go to the Commander-

in-Chief and the Chief of General Staff, following which this copy would go to the Chief of the II Bureau for analysis, translation and delivery to SIS. In addition extracts of a report would be made, to be delivered to the office of the Polish Prime Minister, to the Polish Ministries of Foreign Affairs, Internal Affairs, National Defence and Information and Documentation, and to SOE.[16]

The adoption of these principles indicates the growing importance of information obtained in this period by the Home Army intelligence, related to the German-Soviet war.

Support for the thesis that both Polish and British military authorities valued the role played by the Home Army intelligence can be found in the organizational work being undertaken by the various services. An important role was performed by the 'A' Office of the VI Bureau, which dealt with the transportation of people and messages, maintained courier routes and supplied the staff of communications bases with funds, equipment and documentation. The opinions and suggestions concerning the training of intelligence officers in Great Britain for duties in Poland, offered by the Home Army GHQ, were also of importance. Lack of knowledge of conditions obtaining under the German occupation was obvious. Intelligence courses graduates attached unwarranted importance to the legal basis of their postings. Such behaviour was counterproductive, especially in the eastern territories of Poland. As part of its counter-intelligence duties, the Office was also clearing the candidates for fieldwork and of couriers arriving in London. The VI Bureau supported the operations of the Home Army GHQ intelligence by transferring to Poland intelligence officers, funds and intelligence equipment. Financial allocations for intelligence gathering, provided by the British side, were significant. In 1944, the expenditure for intelligence in Poland amounted to 2 million dollars. In addition, and in the same period, 4.5 million dollars were allocated for diversionary and sabotage activities carried out by 'Wachlarz' (Eastern Front Special Operations Command). The total budget for Home Army in 1944 was set at 30 million dollars. The transfer of such sums to Poland required air transport. The organization of air support for Poland was the province of Office 'S' in the VI Bureau, led by Capt. Jan Jaźwiński.[17] From August 1944 such air support was in the hands of Lt-Col. Marian Dorotycz-Malewicz, 'Hańcza', who commanded Base 11 of the VI Bureau, located in Brindisi. 'Hańcza' worked closely with Lt-Col. H.M. Threlfall, the commander of special SOE unit, Force 139, in Italy. It was the task of this unit to support the Polish and Czechoslovak resistance movements in 1943–1945.[18] The job of the Communications Office and the Ciphers Office in the VI Bureau was to transmit instructions to Poland and to receive intelligence reports.[19] The Independent Propaganda Office 'N' supported psychological operations undertaken by Home Army, in co-operation with similar British units.[20]

The most complicated task was to ensure the efficient functioning of the stations and cells of the VI Bureau. These issues were dealt with by the 'A' Office, which specialised in courier communications. The dislocation, structures and tasks of the field force were fluid and depended on local conditions and the general situation in Europe. The stations in Romania, Hungary, Sweden, Turkey, France, Switzerland, Portugal, Italy and Egypt played an important role. The prime task of such stations was to maintain land communications with Poland. On the other hand the bases located in Italy since 1943 had their own special duties, related to the maintenance of radio communications and air support for the Home Army.

It is worth stressing here that the position and role of the Home Army intelligence within the structures of the Polish special services were determined not only by the formal orders of the supreme military authorities. The indirect links and reliance on SIS and SOE and the consequences of such links and working methods were also of importance. Col. Gano maintained that though the Home Army intelligence was not subordinated to the II Bureau of PGS in London, it was from London that it received guidelines, funds, materiel, equipment and trained personnel.[21] This, however, was true only in part. The reality was that the II Bureau of the Polish General Staff, through the VI Bureau, was transmitting to Poland guidelines based mainly on the needs and requests of SIS and its clients. Many British ministries and intelligence agencies among such clients were receiving intelligence in its 'raw', and not polished form, since SIS did not have its own research and studies department. To a significant degree SIS operated to meet the requirements of its clients, who themselves analysed and validated received intelligence reports. In the next stage SIS would transmit the assessments and requests of its clients to the intelligence 'producers', including Polish intelligence. This is testified to by the British assessment of the material received from the Home Army intelligence. There were other formal complications and entanglements, which obscure the real picture. As is made clear by Lt-Col. Leon Bortnowski, all the reports obtained through the efforts of the Home Army intelligence and passed on to the British allies, were marked 'O VI', that is the VI Bureau Special of PGS, which was 'the source of such reports in relation to the II Bureau of PGS'.[22]

Furthermore the VI Bureau, as the spokesman and representative of PGS and the Home Army GHQ, worked closely with SOE, or to be precise with its Polish Section, headed by Capt./Maj./Lt-Col. Harold Perkins. As part of this co-operation many reports from ZWZ-Home Army intelligence received from Poland by the VI Bureau found its way to SOE, though this was not in accordance with the Polish-British intelligence agreement of September 1940. According to this agreement all intelligence reports obtained by Polish intelligence other than those related to Polish internal affairs were to be passed on by the II Bureau of PGS solely to SIS, which then was to transmit these further. But in practice SOE's activities often were different from those originally envisaged. SOE undertook intelligence work, which led to SIS raising sharp objections. Consequently the relations between SIS and SOE were tense throughout. Both these organizations were rivals and fought each other, and Polish issues often fell victim to this rivalry. We do know, however, that Col. Gano had close relations with SOE and its Director-General, Colin Gubbins, who valued Gano highly and considered him a friend. Gano kept General Gubbins informed, in particular on the growth of the resistance movement in Poland.[23] Gen. Gubbins considered Col. Gano to be the most intelligent intelligence officer he had ever met.[24] All this indicates that on Polish matters SOE co-operated not only with the VI Bureau of PGS, designated for such liaison, but also with the II Bureau and in particular with its Chief. Though the British allies attempted to keep intelligence matters out of SOE's purview, in practice and in war conditions this was plainly not possible. On the other hand much information transmitted to London by the Home Army intelligence was of value for SOE's work. And yet Lt-Col. Bortnowski maintained that 'all the information obtained by the II Bureau of PGS was passed on to the British exclusively through the intermediary of a special low-level liaison mission, which in turn distributed such reports to higher-level interested institutions, such as the War Office, Admiralty, Air Ministry, Ministry of Economic Warfare and others'.[25] This list of recipients does not mention SOE at all. The SIS clients not only assessed the forthcoming reports, but more importantly passed on their interest in particular matters, that is guidelines and requests, to the II Bureau of the Home Army GHQ. These assessments contained not only praise and criticisms, but also clear instructions to be carried out. As a consequence the Home Army intelligence worked primarily in accordance with the guidelines and instructions of the British authorities, whether such guidelines and instructions were received from the II Bureau or the VI Bureau in London. It is estimated that some 70% of the total of the Home Army intelligence effort was expended on meeting the needs of our allies: British, American, French and Russian – even after Polish-Soviet diplomatic relations were broken off on 25th April 1943 due to the Katyń issue.

The role and significance of the Home Army intelligence within the structures subordinated to the supreme Polish authorities in London was to a large degree determined by its activities conducted in response to direct requests made by the British special services and other institutions.

The operations of the Home Army intelligence were to a large degree dependent on the supply of financial means, communications equipment, arms and trained personnel.

Altogether between 1941-1944, including the period of the Warsaw Uprising, 346 parachutists[26] (316 soldiers including 34 intelligence operatives, 1 woman soldier, 28 political couriers and 1 Hungarian and 5 British persons) were dropped over Poland from bases in Great Britain and Italy. 609 tonnes of arms and other equipment were also dropped. The parachutists delivered 34 million, 823 thousand, 163 dollars in banknotes and gold, 1,775 pounds sterling in gold, 19 million, 89 thousand, 500 German marks, 40 million, 569 thousand, 800 in Polish occupational currency and 10,000 Spanish pesetas. In 1941–1945 there were 868 flights of which 585 succeeded, that is the parachutists or cargo were delivered. 70 planes with 62 crew and 11 parachutists were lost, as were 1,599 containers and 1 million, 763 thousand, 200 dollars.[27] 10 per cent of the equipment was destroyed. Contrary to earlier assurances, the scope of support provided to the resistance in Poland was less generous than that made available to the underground movements in other countries. This was caused by changes in the allied strategic plans and by the British government's policy towards Poland. After the US entered the war some hope was entertained that in the future it might be possible for regular allied units to engage the Germans in battle on the European mainland. But as the invasion plans were being prepared, the idea of causing a popular uprising in Europe became less attractive and the role of the various resistance movements less important. The British desire to maintain good relations with the USSR had a negative impact on the scope of co-operation between SOE and the Polish resistance.[28] On the other hand the position of British military intelligence strengthened, and SIS was interested in the penetration of areas of possible future allied operations in Europe. One consequence of this was that SIS's requirements for long-range aircraft increasingly frequently prevailed over rival requests emanating from SOE's Polish Section.

Both the scale of financial assistance provided by the British allies and the variety of the forms of aid provided to Poland by the VI Bureau of PGS testify to the unique role performed by the Home Army, and especially its intelligence, in the war. It is worth stressing that independently of the idea of assisting the resistance in Poland formulated at the Polish General Staff, it was the VI Bureau, which represented the Commander-in-Chief of the Home Army in the Home Affairs Committee, thus influencing the requirements concerning the activities of SOE.

Notes

1 K. Iranek-Osmecki, *Służba informacyjno-wywiadowcza Armii Krajowej* (*The Intelligence Service of the Home Army*), 'Bellona', 1949, vol. 2, p.11.
2 AAN, Oddział VI (the VI Bureau), sygn. 293/III-48, p. 330.
3 Wytyczne dla służby wywiadowczej w kraju (Guidelines for intelligence services in Poland) [in:] *Armia Krajowa w dokumentach 1939–1945* (*Documents on the Home Army*), London 1989, vol. 6, pp.118–120.
4 *Polskie Siły Zbrojne w drugiej wojnie światowej* (*Polish Armed Forces in WW II*), vol. 3, *Armia Krajowa* (*Home Army*), London 1950, p. 298.
5 At the time in Poland there were intelligence networks run by organisations such as: Tajna Armia Polska (Secret Polish Army – TAP), 'Muszkieterowie' ('The Musketeers'), Narodowa Organizacja Wojskowa (National Military Organisation – NOW).
6 K. Iranek-Osmecki, *Emisariusz 'Antoni'* (*An Emissary Called Antoni*), Paris 1985, pp. 25–29, 65–75.
7 AAN, Oddział VI, KG AK (the VI Bureau, of the Home Army GHQ) 203/III – 48, p. 330.
8 D. Stafford, *Wielka Brytania i ruch oporu w Europie (1940-1945)* (*Great Britain and the Resistance Movements in Europe 1940-1945*), Warsaw 1984, pp. 43–45.
9 Z.S. Siemaszko, *Łączność radiowa Sztabu NW w przededniu powstania warszawskiego* (*Radio Communications of the PGS on the Eve of the Warsaw Uprising*), 'Zeszyty Historyczne', 1964, no 6, p. 64.
10 CA MSW, the VI Bureau, 295/18, Personnel Establishment of the VI Bureau of PGS as of 1 August 1944, p.129

11 WIH, MiD, V/22/38, M. Utnik, *Paryskie i londyńskie ośrodki dyspozycyjne, relacja*, p. 17.
12 Internal Order no. 2 on the reorganisation of the VI Bureau of PGS of 30th January 1941, l.dz. 357/4 [in:] *Armia Krajowa w dokumentach (Documents on the Home Army)*, op. cit., vol. 6, p. 129.
13 K.Iranek-Osmecki, *Emisariusz (An Emissary)*, op.cit., p. 19.
14 SPP, 3.7.4.1.12., Letter of the Chief of the VI Bureau to the Chief of the II Bureau, PGS, of 11th November 1942, l.dz. 4795/Tjn.42.
15 M. Utnik, *Oddział łącznikowy Komendanta Głównego AK przy Naczelnym Wodzu na emigracji (Oddział VI Sztabu NW) (Liaison Department of the Home Army's Commander-in-Chief attached to the Commander-in-Chief in Exile (the VI Bureau, PGS)*, Wojskowy Przegląd Historyczny, 1982, no. 1, p. 201.
16 Ibid.
17 Pan K. (b. pracownik Oddziału Specjalnego) (Mr K, a Former Employee of Special Department), 'Zeszyty Historyczne', 1969, no. 15, p. 245.
18 *Pomoc lotnicza Wielkiej Brytanii dla Powstania Warszawskiego. Raport pułkownika H.M. Threlfalla (British Air Assistance for the Warsaw Uprising. A Report by Col. H.M. Threlfall)*, edited by J. Ciechanowski, Warsaw 1994, p. 19.
19 The successive Heads of the Communications Office were: Capt. Tadeusz Lisicki, Lt-Col. Tadeusz Rola and Maj. Adam Szanser. Lt. Stefan Jagiełło, previously of the II Bureau, was Chief of the Cypher Office.
20 S. Korboński, *Polskie państwo podziemne. Przewodnik po podziemiu z lat 1939–1945 (The Polish Underground State. A Guide to the Underground 1939–1945)*, Paris 1975, pp. 82–84.
21 IPMS, A.XII.24/57, Pismo płk. dypl. S. Gano do zastępcy szefa Sztabu NW do spraw sił zbrojnych (płk. dypl. H. Piątkowskiego) z 23 I 1945 r. (Letter from Col. Gano to Deputy Chief of Staff for Armed Forces, PGS (Col. H. Piątkowski) of 23 January 1945.
22 SPP, file 2.3.6.4, Letter of Col. L. Bortnowski to Col. K. Iranek-Osmecki of 7 June 1949.
23 P. A. Wilkinson, J. Bright Astley, *Gubbins and SOE*, London 1993, pp. 47 and 181.
24 M.R.D. Foot, *SOE: An Outline History of the Special Operations Executive 1940–1946*, London 1984, p. 109.
25 SPP, file 2.3.6.4, Letter of Col. L. Bortnowski to Col. K. Iranek-Osmecki of 7 June 1949.
26 Including two who were dropped twice.
27 J. Garliński, *Żołnierze i politycy (Soldiers and Politicians)*, London 1971, p. 246, TNA (PRO), HS 7/183, Appendix 11.
28 D. Stafford, *Wielka Brytania*, op. cit.

11

The Operation of the Intelligence Services of the Ministry of Internal Affairs (MSW) and of the Ministry of National Defence (MON)

Andrzej Pepłoński

Apart from the structures of the II and VI Bureaux of the General Staff other special services realised tasks entrusted by other authorities, which frequently rivalled each other. Numerous organisational problems stemming from the rivalry between the Ministerial Committee for Home Affairs and the Ministry of Internal Affairs became apparent already in France.[1] On several occasions the Ministry's persistent striving towards assuming control over the courier communications with the Homeland led to numerous violations of the elementary principles of operational security, while the distrust of Minister Stanisław Kot towards certain members of the Union of Armed Struggle (ZWZ) clearly hampered Intelligence activities.[2] Rivalry and the establishing by various organisations of their own unofficial contacts with foreign intelligence services introduced elements of chaos which could have been very dangerous for the people involved in intelligence work. Gen. Władysław Sikorski, having recognised the scale of this problem, decided to separate the political from military courier communications on 15 April 1940.

After the fall of France the role of the Ministry of Internal Affairs assumed a new significance. The decisive factor was the British concept of deploying the Resistance movement in Europe to combat the Third Reich and its allies. Numerous Polish immigrant groups in France spontaneously created clandestine organisations which functioned, however, without indispensable co-ordination or military and technical support. In this situation, in the autumn of 1940 work was initiated in London on the creation of a new structure which would effectively supervise the new Resistance movement. This mission was entrusted to Jan Librach, former secretary at the Polish Embassy in Paris.[3] The organisational outlines of a new structure, called 'Continental Action', were ready by the end of 1940. Following necessary consultations with the British authorities and with the support of the Polish government, work begun on setting up the Central HQ and field stations of the Action subordinated to the Ministry of Internal Affairs. The Ministerial Committee, headed by Minister Kot, was entrusted with control over the Central Bureau. In France Aleksander Kawałkowski, codename 'Hubert', was the commander of the Polish Organisation of Struggle for Independence (Polska Organizacja Walki o Niepodległość – POWN; for simplicity it will be referred to in future as the Polish Secret Army in France) which – in accordance with its guidelines – was to play a crucial role in the Continental Action. Since the co-operation of particular agencies and the exchange of intelligence were the main focus from the very beginning Maj. Jan Żychoń, Chief of the Intelligence Department, was designated as the representative of the II Bureau responsible for collaboration with the new structure.

During the initial stage the range of tasks to be realised exceeded the actual capabilities of Continental Action. It was suggested to the British authorities that the secret organisation created within the Polish immigrant groups could conduct anti-German military and economic intelligence throughout the world, while subversive activities should be developed first of all in France and Belgium. The intelligence created within the framework of Continental Action was to supplement the intelligence carried out by the II Bureau of the General Staff. Such a domain of activity was to be justified by the possibilities for intelligence gathering by numerous workers of Polish origin employed in factories producing for Germany. Much intelligence forwarded from France confirmed the pertinence of such assumptions. The British, however, were not enthusiastic about the suggestion of a mass participation of Polish immigrants in intelligence since they already had a constant information supply provided by the II Bureau and the Home Army Intelligence. For that reason they focused more on the possibility of using Polish communities abroad for sabotage and diversion activities in the German rear areas.

The project prepared by the Ministry of Internal Affairs assumed, therefore, that Continental Action should be conducted in two directions: a) in occupied countries with large concentrations of Polish immigrants (France, Belgium, the Netherlands, Denmark); b) in neutral states where small cells or surveillance posts were established for information and political purposes and to provide communications between London and Poland.[4] The specific tasks, approved by Minister Kot on the basis of the agreements signed with the British, envisaged paralysing the transportation network along the Belgian-French border, creating a diversion centre in the area of Caen (Normandy), directed against the enemy transportation and communications networks and depots, as well as preparing and conducting a general strike in the French coal and industrial basins. Since both the SOE and the Ministry of Economic Warfare determined that the plans of the Polish Ministry of Internal Affairs could be unrealistic, a new division of tasks and competence was conducted. The Ministry of Internal Affairs was obligated to collect political and economic information about the Axis states, to conduct propaganda and political diversion, to start a campaign to rally Polish immigrants to counter foreign diversion as well as prepare strikes, sabotage and passive resistance in works. The Ministry of National Defence was in turn entrusted with directing and expanding secret organisations among Polish communities ready to engage in diversion and guerrilla warfare in the German army rears. As a result, two branches emerged within Continental Action: the civilian and the military. In the meantime, the civilian clandestine organisation produced increasingly better results. From mid-June 1940 till 11 November 1942 the Intelligence Department of the Polish Secret Army in France, headed by Jerzy Jankowski 'Dominik', provided the II Bureau with about 2,000 reports containing intelligence information. Much information was also supplied by intelligence networks in Belgium, where the Polish Secret Army in France engaged approximately 500 persons and had 31 stations at its disposal. Good results in intelligence were achieved by civilian networks in Denmark and Sweden especially since the conducive geographic location of Denmark and the more than 12,000-strong local Polish community made it possible to obtain information of military significance, as shown by the results of the work performed by the information branch, code named 'Felicja Jeden', part of the 'Felicja' intelligence organisation functioning in Denmark. 'Felicja' specialised in domestic and international land and sea transport. Propaganda campaigns were carried out among Polish workers and soldiers serving in the German Army. Intelligence cells established in the Wehrmacht were supposed to carry out sabotage and diversion after the landing of Allied forces in Europe. The intelligence undertakings carried out by 'Felicja', which controlled eight cells functioning in Copenhagen and larger Danish towns, were steered by Bolesław Rediger, a staff member of the Polish Consulate in Malmö.[5] In correspondence with London 'Felicja' used a cipher devised for its own purposes. At the end of 1941 the structure of the organisation totalled about 30 persons, with more than 150 ready in the event of mobilisation. The sworn-in members included a non-commissioned officer of the Danish Army, three Kriegsmarine sailors and three Wehrmacht soldiers. The Poles employed in the construction of military sites provided the information concerning fortifications constructed by the Germans along the western coast of the Jutland peninsula. The more important successes of the leadership of 'Felicja' included the creation of an agent network on a German mine sweeper in June 1943. It was composed of three Poles who passed over valuable information about the positions and morale of German formations stationed in Denmark as well as the situation in Poland, including anti-aircraft defences in the ports of Gdynia and Gdańsk, ships built in local shipyards, and cases of desertion from the German Army. Another clandestine threesome, established in Helsingor, provided information about the local shipyard and important military sites in Zeeland.[6] The 'Felicja' networks successfully organised transfer routes for escapees from the POW camps in the Reich.

At the turn of 1941 representatives of the Ministry of Internal Affairs attempted to set up clandestine networks on the American continent. However, they violated the elementary principles of operational security and because of that military tasks were taken over by the II Bureau, whereas the role of the Ministry of Internal Affairs was limited to monitoring the Polish community in order to reveal cases of espionage and diversion.

Considering the preparations for the invasion in France it was more important to strengthen the reconnaissance of the German forces and to prepare special operations. On 1 January 1943 the Special Affairs Department (WSS) at the Ministry of National Defence, headed by Maj. Tadeusz Szumowski, formally initiated a 'military diversion'. 'The political action' was still carried out by the Ministry of Internal Affairs. Initially, the structure of the Operational Section of the Special Affairs Department included a single-person information sub-section run by 2nd Lt Gdowski.[7-8] The intelligence work of the Department was connected with the cipher section (Lt. Rossowiecki) and the communications section (Capt. Sobecki).[9] Personnel training took place at special courses organised by the British.[10] The graduates were well prepared for intelligence work. The leadership of the Special Affairs Department attached great importance to thoroughly preparing a cover plan that would include a cover biography and a set of cover documents. Initially, about a dozen landing sites were prepared in France in order to facilitate the transfer of people. From July 1943 to August 1944 15 such operations were carried out involving 24 persons. Moreover, supplies of weapons, equipment and money were dropped by parachute.[11]

The agreement concluded with the British envisaged gathering military information in two phases: in the period preceding the invasion on the Continent and in the course of the invasion itself. The realisation of the first task involved organisations already existing in northern France, but the second phase required the creation of a new network, set on obtaining information of significance for the invasion forces. Such a network was to seek information concerning garrisons, fuel and munitions depots, fortifications, airfields and the protection of more important sites (bridges and railway stations, road bridges). The task of organising an intelligence organisation in three months was entrusted to Capt. Władysław Ważny, 'Tygrys' (Tiger), who was sent to France for this specific purpose on 5 March 1944[12] (more in Part VI, 'France'). During the invasion a separate structure of this network was to focus its attention on information of a tactical and operational significance. The remaining organisational components were to undertake combat-sabotage actions. The network created by Capt. Ważny encompassed northern France along the Armentières-Bruay-Arras-Cambrai line. The tasks assigned by the Special Affairs Department were prepared together with Special Forces HQ as part of a general plan of acquiring information by the Supreme Allied Command or the Commands of the Twenty First Army Group. Since the network directed by Capt. Ważny achieved good results its tasks were expanded in the middle of July

1944 and now included obtaining information about V-1 launching sites as well as the storage, assembly and transport of the missiles.[13]

Fifteen Intelligence reports were sent to London during the period preceding the invasion. The 'Tygrys' network started to deliver information on 23 June 1944, after 'D-Day'. In two months (from 28 August 1944) a hundred coded telegrams containing 170 pieces of various information reached Great Britain. Once decrypted this information was handed over to the Special Forces HQ as well as the Minister of National Defence and the II Bureau of the General Staff. The Special Affairs Department analysed data arranged into three thematic groups: a) general information, movements of military units, seats of the German commands, fortifications; b) launch sites of flying bombs and auxiliary equipment; c) weapon, ammunition and petroleum depots. Among the 170 pieces of information, obtained after the invasion, 25 belonged to group 'a', 103 – to group 'b', and 42 – to group 'c'. The information included in the first category contained data concerning stretches with pales driven into the ground which made it impossible for aeroplanes to land, movements of German troops, and the location of the command of Field Marshal Erwin Rommel.[14] The information gathered by the Special Affairs Department network was very highly valued by the Allies. For example, out of a total of 103 pieces of information classified as 'b' as many as 83 were classified as of 'immediate usefulness'. The majority of the remaining pieces of information were evaluated as 'very useful' or 'useful'. The significance of that information was confirmed by the fact that a liaison officer Maj. Chalmers Wright from SOE was assigned to the Special Affairs Department. Brig. Eric E. Mockler-Ferryman in a letter written to Gen. Marian Kukiel on 19 August 1944 expressed his high regard for the work of the networks supervised by the Special Affairs Department.

Notes

1 T. Dubicki, S. J. Rostworowski, *Sanatorzy kontra Sikorszczycy (Supporters of the 'Sanacja' versus Supporters of Sikorski)*, Warszawa 1993, pp. 5–29.
2 AZHRL, Prof. Kot's files, Copy of a note entitled 'Sprawa' (the Case of) the Union of Armed Struggle, leaf 1.
3 J. Librach, *Nota o 'Akcji Kontynentalnej' (Note about 'Continental Action')*, 'Zeszyty Historyczne', 1973, no. 23, p. 160.
4 T. Panecki, *Polonia zachodnioeuropejska w planach Rządu RP na emigracji (1940–1944). Akcja Kontynentalna (The Polish Community in Western Europe in the Plans of the Government in Exile of the Republic of Poland (1940–1944). Continental Action)*, Warszawa 1986, pp. 93–94.
5 E. S. Kruszewski, *Akcja Kontynentalna w Skandynawii 1940–1945 (Continental Action in Scandinavia 1940–1945)*, Copenhagen 1993, pp. 14–18.
6 Ibid., pp. 69–77.
7 CAW, VI Bureau, Letter from General Sikorski to the Ministry of Internal Affairs, Chief of the General Staff and Lt-Col. J. Iliński, dated 2 April 1942, l. dz. 390/GM/42.
8 T. Panecki, Polonia, op. cit., pp. 98–99.
9 CAW, The VI Bureau, call no. 483, Note by Maj. W. Langenfeld of 1 January 1943.
10 The training included courses on security, parachuting and explosives.

11 Members of the organisation dispatched by the Special Affairs Department were supplied with more than 40 W/T stations, 104 sten machine guns, 111 pistols, over 25 thousand rounds of ammunition, about 950 pounds of explosives, approximately 100 hand grenades, 18,850,000 francs, 47,650 dollars and 48 diamonds.

12 AWIH, call no. V/20/11, Report by the Special Affairs Department information division at the Ministry of National Defence, leaf 20–21.

13 Ibid.

14 Section 'b' included, inter alia, 67 pieces of information about flying bomb launching sites, 17 concerning the transport of such bombs and 15 relating to the effects of air attacks on launchers and depots.

PART II
BRITISH INTELLIGENCE SERVICES

12

British Intelligence Services during the
Second World War

Gill Bennett

It should be noted that this chapter, based on both open and closed official primary sources, is the only account of British Intelligence machinery endorsed by the UK side of the Anglo-Polish Historical Committee. Any account based on secondary sources is necessarily unreliable.

The information from closed British Intelligence records contained in this Report originates mainly from the archives of the Secret Intelligence Service (SIS), or MI6. This Agency, however, constituted only a small part of the complex Intelligence machinery that served the British Government during the Second World War. A detailed description of this machinery and its evolution from inter-war arrangements is set out in the official history of British Intelligence in the Second World War,[1] and need not be rehearsed here. This chapter will give a brief account of those various components of British wartime Intelligence machinery involved in liaison with the Polish authorities, and the way in which they made use of information received from Allied – especially Polish – Intelligence services.

As described in *Hinsley,* British Intelligence machinery between 1919 and 1939 was both fragmented and unco-ordinated. Intelligence gathering, analysis and distribution was carried out with varying degrees of efficiency and success, not only by the dedicated Intelligence bodies, but also by the Service departments (Air, Naval and Military) of the Ministry of Defence, by certain government departments such as the Foreign Office, and by various interdepartmental bodies. Although from 1935 onwards increasing international instability and a growing perceived threat from Germany stimulated a certain amount of unco-ordinated effort towards organisational and professional improvement, the outbreak of hostilities in 1939 found the British Government unsupported by the kind of coherent Intelligence operation necessary for the war effort.

There were a number of reasons for this, including resource constraints, rapid organisational run-down of Intelligence bodies after the

First World War, and an ongoing and unresolved tension between the potential benefits of centralised Intelligence machinery and strong practical and political imperatives towards divided authority and control. Although all these factors persisted into wartime, the operational exigencies of the first two years of the conflict, together with the dynamic impetus provided by Winston Churchill as Prime Minister from May 1940, combined to produce by 1942 an Intelligence establishment more tightly focussed, better integrated and more effective than it had been at any time in the previous twenty years. Nevertheless, Intelligence information was still collected, interpreted and distributed by a number of discrete agencies, even if its final destination, collation and application was controlled more centrally.

Information relating to the Intelligence-gathering activities of British government departments, such as the Foreign Office and Ministry of Economic Warfare, and to the Military, Air and Naval Intelligence activities of the Service departments, can be found in the official records of those departments transferred to The National Archives (TNA). It is, indeed, also possible to find a great deal of information concerning the wartime activities of the Intelligence Agencies themselves in TNA. Both the Security Service (MI5) and Government Communications Headquarters (GCHQ) have embarked on a systematic programme of records release and transfer, and the records of the Special Operations Executive (SOE), set up in 1940, have been transferred to TNA. Since, however, the activities of the Intelligence Agencies are by definition more secret and may be less fully documented, it may be helpful to set out briefly the functions and responsibilities of those most closely involved with Polish Intelligence: GC&CS and the Radio Security Service (RSS), SOE and SIS.

The Government Code and Cypher School (GC&CS, later GCHQ) was formed in 1919 from the cryptanalytical sections of the Admiralty and War Office that had been so successful during the First World War. It was concerned primarily with protecting British cypher communications, and with acquiring intelligence about foreign powers by studying their cypher communications and breaking their codes. As explained in *Hinsley*, this intelligence became known as 'Sigint', a generic term covering activities such as Direction Finding (DF), Traffic Analysis (TA), cryptanalysis and interpretation.[2] From August 1939, GC&CS was housed at Bletchley Park, a country house in Buckinghamshire that became the centre for British codebreaking work throughout the war. From 1919 to 1942 GC&CS was headed by A.G. Denniston, with the title of Deputy Director, since GC&CS came under the authority of SIS whose Chief ('C' or CSS) held the title of Director. In February 1942 Denniston was moved out of Bletchley Park to become head of sections dealing with civil traffic. Edward Travis, Denniston's deputy, became head of military services and therefore in charge at Bletchley.[3]

Before 1939 GC&CS had worked closely with its French analogue, the *Section des Examens* (SE) under Col. Gustave Bertrand, who was to play an important part in respect of Polish Intelligence. It was through Bertrand that GC&CS made contact in 1939 with the Polish cryptographers who had cracked the ENIGMA code and gave a copy of the ENIGMA machine to the British codebreakers established at Bletchley Park.

The ensuing close co-operation between British and Polish cryptological services is described in Chapter VI below. There was, however, little direct contact between them and GC&CS. Liaison was carried on through SIS, and through the Radio Security Service (RSS), the intercept service transferred from MI8 via MI5 to SIS control in May 1941 (RSS operators had already been diverted to GC&CS work).[4] A substantial body of RSS records relating to their liaison with Polish Intelligence have been released to TNA by GCHQ, who have also transferred nearly all their wartime records including the ULTRA intercepts that resulted from the breaking of the ENIGMA codes.

The Special Operations Executive (SOE) was set up in July 1940 under the chairmanship of the Minister of Economic Warfare, Hugh Dalton, with the now-famous imperative from Winston Churchill to 'set Europe ablaze'.[5] Based on Section D of SIS, responsible for sabotage activities overseas, and on elements of the War Office, SOE maintained an uneasy relationship with SIS throughout the war, partly because their respective objectives – the covert collection of intelligence, and attempts to disrupt enemy operations and communications – could be in direct conflict; and partly through constant competition for scarce resources. Polish Intelligence Services had a close relationship with both SOE and SIS. Their contacts with SOE, which were focussed particularly on the activities of the Polish Underground, are described in detail in Mackenzie's official history and documented extensively in SOE papers at TNA.

The Secret Intelligence Service (SIS), originally set up to act as intermediary between the Service (military) departments and British agents (or foreign spies) abroad, was in charge of espionage on an 'inter-Service basis', as *Hinsley* puts it, supplying information to all interested government departments as well as the military authorities. Under the control of the Foreign Office and funded by the Secret Vote, during the interwar years SIS had gradually extended its range to political and economic as well as military information. It supplied Intelligence in response to specific requests, and disseminated Intelligence collected by its agents or supplied to it by a range of contacts.

Through its links with the Diplomatic Service, with the Intelligence and diplomatic services of Allied countries and its international network of agents and contacts, SIS was able to solicit, collect and disseminate information on the political, military or economic situation in many countries of the world. A detailed account of the evolution of its organisation, and its interaction with other Agencies and government departments, can be followed in *Hinsley*. Adm. Hugh Sinclair ('Quex') was Chief of SIS from June 1923 until his death in November 1939, when he was succeeded by Col. S.G. Menzies.

As described in *Hinsley*, both the organisation and methods of SIS were subject to considerable criticism both before and after 1939. While

SIS could provide useful political reports, the restrictions imposed upon it by peacetime financial and staffing controls meant that it was less good at military and industrial information and not geared up to providing the intelligence its customers most wanted, for example on military movements and short-term deployment. While, therefore, the outbreak of hostilities and the spread of Axis control through Europe and beyond made SIS activities increasingly important to the successful prosecution of the war, considerable reorganisation and expansion of SIS was required to enable it to meet successfully the demands made upon it.

In particular, new sections of SIS were created to handle liaison with Allied Intelligence Services, including those of the governments in exile who had established their headquarters in London. Comdr. Wilfred Dunderdale, who had served with SIS in Paris until the fall of France, was put in charge of a section to deal with both Polish Intelligence authorities and with SIS operations carried out in France by non-Gaullists. This section, whose main responsibility was for agent-running and intelligence-gathering, was called successively A4 (July 1940–April 1942), P5 (May 1942–December 1943) and SLC (December 1943 onwards).

As described in Part V below, on the outbreak of war the Polish Intelligence Services were already well developed and organised, with well-established networks that supplied information first to the French, and then the British Intelligence services. SIS contact with Polish Intelligence through section A4 was, therefore, more a question of liaison rather than direction, although SIS provided financial support. A list of duties involved in this liaison, compiled by Dunderdale on 24 August 1940, included:

- handling correspondence to and from the naval, military and air sections of the Polish General Staff Intelligence;
- summarising and distributing information from Polish sources to the General Staff for information, comment and subsequent action;
- drafting and distributing requests from the Poles to SIS representatives and their Polish opposite numbers abroad;
- arranging meetings between SIS experts and their Polish opposite numbers in London;
- contacting Polish naval and military liaison officers on matters relating to administration (e.g. facilities for W/T communication) and collaborating with them in operational plans regarding their European network of agents and contacts;
- summarising and distributing questionnaires concerning subjects on which SIS wished action to be taken by Polish Intelligence;
- consulting SIS HQ with regard to special requirements and conveying instructions to the Poles for action.

SIS archives are not released or transferred to the Public Record Office, but in any case there are very few papers extant in SIS archives concerning day to day liaison with the Poles, or containing reports received from Polish sources. The scale of the activity can only be gauged from the few progress reports that survive. For example, a note by a member of A4 on the circulation of reports from JX (i.e. Polish sources) from 1 January to 28 February 1941 stated that numbered papers in that period (including 25% correspondence, mail and telegrams to representatives abroad) exceeded 900, as compared to 1172 for the previous six months, thus representing an increase of nearly 100% taken on an 8-week basis. Of these 900, over 400 – nearly 50% – were circulated to other sections of SIS, while the remainder were used to answer specific enquiries or were considered to require no further action.

The note also stated that in addition to the production of reports, Polish liaison involved A4 section in a great deal of further work including 'correspondence with and from JX, transmission of comments, questionnaires and individual enquiries from the Sections concerned, JX requirements affecting purchase of material, assistance in the selection of appropriate W/T sites... and personal supervision of the station personnel and workshops', together with 'a series of Memos and Appendices containing details of JX stations and sub-sources... all with the assistance of one secretary'.

Dunderdale's section remained the channel through which all Polish Intelligence liaison with SIS was conducted. Other SIS sections seeking information would channel their requests through it, while A4/P5/SLC staff in turn arranged for the distribution of incoming Intelligence to the appropriate customers. Further details about the work of this section can be found in later chapters of this Report.

British wartime Intelligence records

As indicated above, a great many British wartime Intelligence and Intelligence-related records are already in the public domain. The Security Service and GCHQ have transferred nearly all their wartime records to TNA, and SOE records have now also been transferred. In addition to the records of the Intelligence bodies themselves, a great deal of their material has been transferred to TNA on the files of other government departments to which it was circulated during the war. Such material is not often readily identifiable as Intelligence product, as indications of its origin, including numbers and signatures, have been removed, but sometimes its content or context, or a cross-reference enable the reader to make a good guess as to its origin.

Although the records of the Secret Intelligence Service are not themselves released into the public domain, much of their wartime material, too, has been transferred to TNA on the files of other departments. Only a small amount of wartime material remains in the SIS archive, and it contains very few reports received from SIS stations overseas or from Allied Intelligence Agencies. Where these survive, they are on scattered, unrelated files, such as those of a certain agent or station. There is no extant body of wartime reports from any particular source, including Polish Intelligence. SIS was concerned with the collection and dissemination of information, not with building an archive.

During the war, it was imperative that information received by SIS reached, as quickly as possible, those departments who could make the best and most timely use of it. This included information received from SIS stations overseas and from Allied, including Polish, sources. On receipt it was translated if necessary, stripped of identifying marks to mask its origin, and sent immediately to customers in the War Office, Foreign Office, Ministry of Economic Warfare or elsewhere. The original, its value exploited, was usually destroyed. If not destroyed at the time, it would have been destroyed after the war as being ephemeral and of no further use. Such documents had been produced in response to wartime demand that ceased in 1945: where they contained useful material it had been passed on to customer departments and would be preserved on their files.

Notes

1   F.H. Hinsley et al, *British Intelligence in the Second World War*, Volumes I–V (HMSO, 1979–90), referred to hereafter as *Hinsley*.
2   *Hinsley*, Vol. I, pp. 20-21.
3   Apart from *Hinsley*, a number of studies and memoirs have been published giving details of the work done at Bletchley Park. For a comprehensive account of wartime codebreaking see Stephen Budiansky, *Battle of Wits. The Complete Story of Codebreaking in World War II* (London, 2000).
4   See *Hinsley*, Vol. I, p. 277 and Vol. 4, pp. 72–3.
5   'The Secret History of SOE', the official history of the Special Operations Executive, written between 1945 and 1947 by W.J.M. Mackenzie, was published in 2000. A number of official histories of regional SOE activities have also been published by the Cabinet Office (eg. *SOE in France* by M.R.D. Foot, HMSO 1966).

13
British Special Services

Jan Ciechanowski

I. Intelligence, Signals Intelligence and the Joint Intelligence Committee[1]

Officially, the modern British special services were established in 1909, when two separate intelligence organisations were set up. These were the SIS, offensive intelligence, also known as MI6 to underline its military character, and MI5, the defensive intelligence (counter-intelligence), or the Security Service.

The Signals Intelligence ('Sigint'), operating nation-wide at a strategic level, was established in 1919 through the merger of the Army and Navy signals units which served Great Britain so well during World War I – though both Army and Navy retained the right to conduct tactical signals intelligence, the so-called 'Service Y'.

The Joint Intelligence Committee (JIC), operating as a sub-committee of the Chiefs of Staff, was set up only in 1936, when the highest British authorities appreciated the need to co-ordinate the activities of all the intelligence services.[2] Two contradictory and mutually exclusive tendencies were always present within the thinking of the British governmental circles and among the intelligence community. One argued for the creation of a single, unitary and centrally managed intelligence service. The other preferred the retention of their decentralised character, fearing that a centralised service might grow into a state within the state and begin to threaten democracy.

The foundations and traditions of British special services reach, however, into a much more distant past – they go at least as far back as the reign of Elizabeth I and her minister, Sir Francis Walsingham. To serve in these services, as in the Forces,[3] was always considered by the majority of the British to be a great honour and a reward in itself. During World War II almost the whole of the British academic and intellectual elite served in intelligence, signals intelligence or in SOE. In war, these services recruited first of all well-educated people, with linguistic skills and the knowledge of foreign countries; and persons who could count on a recommendation of a former or current agent. The idea was to reduce the risk of employing unsuitable personnel.

These precautions did not, regrettably, eliminate the risk of penetration by Soviet agents, the most outstanding example of which is the notorious 'Cambridge Five', including Kim Philby, Anthony Blunt and John Cairncross.[4] On behalf of MI5, Blunt was to 'mind' the Polish government in London and the diplomatic posts of allied and neutral countries represented in Great Britain. Blunt supplied his Soviet superiors with plentiful information on Polish matters, including on the relations between the heads of British intelligence agencies and important Polish personages.[5] Soviet agents even managed to reach the signals intelligence agency in Bletchley Park, where Cairncross was serving. Prior to joining MI6 in 1943, he managed to provide Moscow with the plans of the German offensive at Kursk – whose failure in July 1943 finally decided the Soviet victory at the Eastern Front.[6]

SIS's main task was to obtain information gathered outside the British Empire, using stations abroad, contacts and agents, and then to pass such intelligence in its raw form to its clients, among whom the Forces were important customers.[7] SIS operated through its agents who collected human intelligence – ('Humint'), that is information obtained from contacts and spies conducting intelligence work abroad. SIS also conducted counter-intelligence activities outside Great Britain and its overseas possessions, that is to say it acted against foreign intelligence services and defended its own stations and networks against penetration by hostile special services.

In September 1939 the organisational structure of SIS was as follows: Chief (CSS) – Adm. Sir Hugh Sinclair, Assistant Chief (ACSS) – Lt-Col. Claude Dansey, CSO – Cmdr. Rex Howard, his Assistants (ACSO) – Lt-Comm. (RN) Cuthbert Bowlby, Lt. Comm. (RN) Frank Slocum. SIS was subdivided into Sections: I – Political (head Malcolm Woollcombe, deputy – David Footman), II – Military (Col. Stewart Menzies, Maj. Hatton Hall), III – Naval (Cmdr. [RN] Russel, Christopher H. Arnold-Foster), IV – Air (Wing Cmdr. Frederick W. Winterbotham, Maj. John S.B. Perkins), V – Counter-Intelligence (Col. Valentine Vivian, Maj. Felix Cowgill), VI – Economic (Vice Adm. C.J. Limpenny, Bruce Ottley, Robert Smith), VII – Financial (Lt. Comm. [RN] Percy Sykes), VIII – Signals (Henry Maine, Brig. Richard Gambier-Perry), IX – Ciphers (Col. W. Jefferys) and X – Press (Raymond Henniker-Heaton).

In 1940 SIS was reorganised for war. Col. Stewart Menzies[8] became Chief (CSS) in 1939, Lt-Col. Valentine Vivian his first Deputy (DCSS), Lt-Col. Claude Dansey and Gen. Sir James Marshall-Cornwall, Assistant Chiefs (ACSS). 'C' had two Personal Assistants, Peter Koch de Gooreynd and David A. Boyle, PSO was Capt. (RN) C.H. Arnold-Forster, Air Commodore Peake was Principal Administration Officer; DCSO was Patrick Reilly (September 1940 – October 1943) and then Robert Cecil (October 1943 – April 1945). Deputy Heads were: for Army – Brig. W.R. Beddington, for RAF – Air Commodore Lionel G. Payne, for Royal Navy – Col. John K. Cordeaux. The structure of the Sections remained unchanged.[9]

SIS's counter-intelligence was in the hands of Section V, with Kim

Philby as one of its officers, serving in 1943-1944[10] as head of counter-intelligence for the Iberian Peninsula, North Africa and Italy. Towards the end of 1944 Philby became head of Section IX, which fought the KGB and communist influences in the West.[11] According to Soviet sources, in1934-1945 Kim Philby, Guy Burgess and Donald Maclean provided the NKWD with more than 20 thousand pages of valuable secret documents and intelligence reports.[12] As for Blunt and Cairncross, in 1941-1945 they provided Moscow with 7603 assorted important documents and reports.[13] Many of the documents supplied by the 'Cambridge Five' were on Polish matters, including Polish-British intelligence co-operation.[14]

Between the wars, SIS maintained a very close co-operation with French and Czechoslovak intelligence, which supplied it with much valuable information concerning German plans and military and economic potential.[15]

In the same time frame, the Polish-British intelligence co-operation was very limited, and picked up only in the months immediately preceding the outbreak of hostilities. Even then, their co-operation was limited mainly to the dislocation of German forces and to the Enigma issue. At the conference in Pyry (outside Warsaw) the heads of Polish radio (signals) intelligence, Lt-Col. Gwido Langer and Maj. Maksymilian Ciężki provided their British and French allies with the technology and secrets of Enigma.[16] As a matter of fact Polish-British intelligence co-operation was developed only following the fall of France, when the Polish government and the remainder of its armed forces – and, importantly, almost all the commanders of the II Bureau of PGS – arrived in Great Britain.[17]

In early September 1939, in the first days of the war, the German Section of the British Military Intelligence (MI3) anticipated that the Germans would conquer Poland within three weeks and would then offer peace to the Western powers. Once such an offer would be rejected, MI3 predicted, Germany would attack the West – still in 1939.[18] Such prognostications were unlikely to encourage SIS to push for closer co-operation with the II Bureau.

Only following the fall of France did the II Bureau became a valuable, and almost irreplaceable, partner for the British side – since at that stage the British lost almost all their sources and assets within German-occupied Europe. The II Bureau, meantime, managed to maintain its networks there, and soon began energetically to build these up. In addition, the opinion among the Western staff officers was that even having conquered Poland, the Germans would be forced to maintain large forces there, possibly as numerous as those required for their victory, to secure Poland and to safeguard it from the East.[19] Poland, whether fighting or conquered, was of equal value for the Western allies – either way it simply tied up significant German forces. This was an argument for mounting Polish-British intelligence co-operation only after Polish defeat since the war, thought Western staffs, was to last for a long time.

In theory SIS held a monopoly on the collection of Humint overseas.

Its job then was to pass such raw information to its clients, who in turn would subject it to analysis and assessment, and then decide on its best use. SIS was, sui generis, a post office box, collecting gathered intelligence, passing it on, and receiving assessments of reports and requests for more. In other words, SIS represented its clients and depended on them,[20] since it was largely the clients who took the decisions on the scope and character of SIS's intelligence operations. SIS did not have its own research and studies bureau or even the right to interpret collected information. In effect SIS constituted a barrier between the agents operating abroad and its clients, especially the military ones, in Great Britain.

Among SIS's clients were the following Departments of State and their respective intelligence agencies: War Office, Air Ministry, Admiralty, Economic Warfare, Foreign Office, Home Office, Colonial Office, India Office.[21] Intelligence gathering, recruitment and the running of agents, as well as the maintenance of useful contacts was in the hands of heads of SIS's foreign stations, usually acting under the cover of Passport Control Officers, which enabled them to operate in all those countries with whom Great Britain maintained diplomatic relations. On the other hand, such cover made them easily recognizable and therefore easy to follow. To preserve and strengthen the ties between SIS and the War Office, Air Ministry and the Admiralty and their respective intelligence services, in 1921 these intelligence organisations each detached to SIS one of their own intelligence sections. The purpose was to strengthen SIS's ability to collect information abroad for the benefit of the Service departments.[22] These sections, called 'circulating sections', provided SIS with further requests for information, and with their departments' assessments of intelligence already received. Regrettably, this created divided loyalties among the heads and personnel of these detached sections. Moreover, the SIS Chief found it more difficult to control his own organization which, from that point on, performed under dual control: that of SIS Chief and of the heads of Service intelligence units. Not surprisingly, this caused one of the wartime Deputies of the SIS Chief, Col. Valentine Vivien, to describe SIS as a loose confederation of units collectively known as SIS. In addition each of the three Services were in turn to appoint SIS's Chief, known as 'C'. This was to prevent any one of the Services from dominating SIS.

SIS, as well as strategic signals intelligence, was subordinated to and financed by the Foreign Office. The signals intelligence, also known as Station X, operated under the cover of Government Code and Cipher School – GC&CS, during the war located in Bletchley Park. Run on Foreign Office's behalf by 'C', the GC&CS was divided into two departments: 'diplomatic' and 'military'. The first specialised in the breaking of political codes; the second of military ones, of enemy, allied and neutral countries. Following the Third Reich's attack on the USSR on 22nd June 1941, GC&CS ceased its attempts to decode Soviet ciphers.[23] That task was given to the Polish monitoring station in Stanmore.

Gen. Menzies, the SIS Chief, was responsible for the secrecy of the source of 'Ultra' products (that is, of decoded Enigma traffic) and for their distribution. This provided him with very high standing in the British government circles, especially since the prime recipient of this material was the Prime Minister and head of the War Cabinet, Winston Churchill, who 'devoured [such] intelligence').[24] Enigma provided the British with hundreds of thousands of secret German documents of extreme strategic and operational value – in the first instance thanks to the Poles.

The principal task of MI5, subordinated to and financed by the Home Office, was to fight against foreign and enemy agents and networks active in Great Britain and her overseas possessions, to safeguard state secrets and to recruit and run double agents. From 1931 MI5 was responsible for the assessments of all the threats to the internal security of the Kingdom, with the exception of Irish terrorists and anarchists. From that point onwards MI5 became a classical security service. During World War II the principal achievement of MI5 was to deprive the Third Reich of the majority of its pre-war agents through the internment, in early 1940, of all German citizens and of persons suspected of pro-fascist sympathies. MI5 also identified and captured some 200 German agents, whom the Germans attempted to place in Great Britain in 1939–1945. Furthermore, as part of the so-called 'double-cross system',[25] MI5 managed to turn many of these agents, to persuade them to work with British intelligence and to use them to feed Berlin with false political, military and economic information. MI5 was headed by the Directors General who had at his disposal a Deputy, a Secretariat and five Sections: A – Administration (Registry, Legal Office, Finances, Transport, Personnel, Room 005), B – Counter-Intelligence (Counter-Intelligence, Sabotage, Subversive Organisations), C – Security (Personnel clearance), D – Liaison (contacts with the War Office, with MI(L), Air Force Security, Naval Security, Ports Security, Military Police MI-11, Director of Military Intelligence), E – Foreigners (country sections) and F – Overseas Territories (security officers in the colonies, anti-smuggling, contacts with security services in the Dominions, political parties). The successive Director-Generals were Brig. Vernon Kell (1909–1940) and Sir A.W.A. Harker (1940–1947), and during the war the Departments were run by: A – Col. Charles Butler, B – Capt. Guy Liddell, C – Maj. Herbert Bacon, D – Brig. Harry Allen, E – Kenneth Younger, F – Maj. Bertram Ede.[26]

In addition to SIS, MI5 and signals intelligence, Great Britain had a multitude of other, smaller intelligence services, which until 1942 operated independently of each other and in fact in an unco-ordinated way. In effect, the structure of British intelligence was highly complex and differed from the organization of the II Bureau of PGS, which supervised the operations of intelligence, counter-intelligence and signals intelligence – and which, unlike SIS, had well-developed research, records and analysis unit.[27]

The job of the II Bureau was to supply the Polish political and military authorities with secret information, data and predictions of the future in an analysed, worked-up format from all the available sources. The II Bureau worked closely with, but was not responsible to, or financed by, the Polish

Ministry of Foreign Affairs. It was subjugated to, and financed by, the military authorities. It also directed the work of military attachés (who were subject to its authority) attached to Polish diplomatic missions. Its commanders and officers were subject to frequent rotation – to gain promotion they were first required to serve in line units. Thanks to this mechanism, their service in intelligence did not reduce their advancement prospects, unlike the situation in the British armed forces. Only the most talented officers, with best references, served in intelligence. Many completed the General Staff Academy, whose graduates were members of the professional and intellectual élite of the Polish officer corps. As an example in 1928, of 59 officers who graduated from the General Staff Academy that year, 11 were selected for intelligence work. They included the then Lt. Leon Bortnowski, who in 1945–1946 played such an important role in the closure of the II Bureau.[28]

In Great Britain, all the three Services, the Army, the Royal Air Force and the Royal Navy, had their own, independent intelligence services. SIS provided them with raw Humint obtained abroad, and GC&CS, via 'C', with material gathered by the strategic signals information. These services were extensive, with their own management, research and analysis bureau and – in the case of the Army and the Royal Navy – signals intelligence of a lower, tactical, character. During the Second World War, Military Intelligence (MI) had some 20 organisational units and was led by the Directorate of Military Intelligence (DMI), commanded by a general.[29]

In the early stages of the war, in 1939–1940, the Director of Military Intelligence was a Guards officer, Gen. Frederik G. Beaumont-Nesbitt. His successor, Gen. F.H.N. Davidson, was very hard working, but tended to get lost in the detail. His main preoccupation was to make certain that the JIC reports corresponded to the opinions of his superior, Gen. Alan Brooke,[30] the Chief of the Imperial General Staff. Brooke had a lively interest in intelligence matters and, coincidentally, was full of praise for the achievements of Polish intelligence.[31] Davidson headed MI from 26th December 1940 until the end of hostilities. In his opinion 'Polish intelligence made a very substantial contribution to the common Allied cause in the war against Germany'.[32] According to Sir Percy Cradock, the Chairman of JIC in 1985-1992, the most distinguished personality in MI was Lt-Col. Kenneth Strong, Head of MI's German Section (MI3), with his extensive knowledge of the Germans and of Germany, and of his craft.[33] Before the war, Strong was the Assistant British Military Attaché in Berlin; by the end of WW II he was Head of Intelligence for Gen. Eisenhower.[34] MI6 (SIS) and MI5 were both placed within the structures of the Directorate of Military Intelligence, though were not run by it and both operated as independent organizations. MI6 worked to the Foreign Office and MI5 to the Home Office.

Military Intelligence (MI), meantime, worked to the War Office, Air Intelligence (AI) to the Air Ministry and Naval Intelligence (NI) to the Admiralty. Both AI and NI had their separate Directors and command structures, which jealously guarded their independence and prerogatives.

There existed also a separate industrial intelligence working to the Ministry of Economic Warfare (MEW). Political intelligence rested with the Foreign Office which, in addition to information from SIS and GC&CS, received reports from foreign missions and military attaches, obliged to communicate with their military superiors through the Foreign Office.

Despite sharp protests from SIS, which claimed to be the only agency empowered to conduct intelligence outside Great Britain and her overseas possessions, SOE also collected intelligence information. SOE was supposed to pass all collected information to SIS. In theory, SOE was expected to limit its activities to sabotage and diversion and to supporting resistance movements and armed struggle at the enemy's rear.[35]

The organisational structure of British intelligence was extremely complex,[36] and the relationships between its various branches and departments complicated and unclear. Furthermore, the activities of the numerous intelligence agencies, answerable to and financed by separate ministries, were almost unco-ordinated. This was the case not only at the time when the Joint Intelligence Committee was established in 1936, but even in the first years of the war. It was only then that the JIC was forced to act efficiently and energetically,[37] under pressure from the new Prime Minister, Churchill, and the head of JIC, William Cavendish-Bentinck.[38] The September 1940 agreement with Gen. Sikorski on closer British-Polish intelligence co-operation exerted pressure in a similar direction. At the time, Great Britain was carrying on its lonely fight for survival and the majority of SIS's intelligence networks on the continent were paralysed and penetrated by the Germans. Moreover, the Enigma product was still scant and limited to Luftwaffe material. Until the first years of the war British intelligence did not enjoy unified leadership and supervision. Consequently the work of the numerous British intelligence agencies suffered. There was insufficient co-ordination and less than perfect flow and utilisation of information already in its possession. One example might be that, since the pre-war assessment of the strategic potential of the Luftwaffe was exaggerated, the strike ability of the German long-range bomber units was overestimated – even though the German Section of the British Air Intelligence knew full well that the German bombers were primarily for close support and not able to play an independent strategic role. In other words, in 1939 the Luftwaffe was unable to carry out the massive and devastating air raids on London and Paris, so feared by our Western allies.[39]

II. Attempts to Unify the British Intelligence Services
The breakthrough in the co-ordination of British intelligence followed the fall of France, and from that point onwards it is reasonable to speak of a national, more or less unified intelligence effort. The first step was taken when, following the outbreak of the war, JIC was given a broader mandate and its personnel was expanded to allow it to better analyse, interpret and utilise collected intelligence information. Perhaps more significantly, JIC was given direct access to 10 Downing Street, that is to the Prime Minister

and Head of the War Cabinet. Soon after his appointment, Churchill ordered JIC to prepare and present to him and to other members of the War Cabinet, as well as to Chiefs of Staff, reports on the changes in the international situation based on intelligence. This was to be done at any time, day or night. In this way JIC, formally merely a sub-committee of the Chiefs of Staff (COS), became also an agency of the War Cabinet, though for the time-being an informal one. This elevated JIC's prestige and significance enormously.[40] In time the Joint Intelligence Committee was turned into the highest organ of British intelligence and its most important research and analysis bureau, operating at national level.

JIC's principal job was, and remains to this day, to inform the main political and military authorities in Great Britain of its situation and of threats from foreign and enemy states, and to offer for consideration the appropriate solutions and counter-measures based on a detailed analysis of all the available and appropriate intelligence information. JIC was also to distribute the available and properly presented intelligence information to all the Services when such information might be of assistance to the Services in the planning and conduct of war operations.

The membership of JIC consisted of the Chief of SIS (MI6), Director of MI5 (both as of May 1940); the heads of MI, AI, NI; the head of economic and industrial intelligence from the Ministry of Economic Warfare and a Foreign Office representative, who was responsible for political intelligence. The main task entrusted to JIC was to lead and co-ordinate all the British intelligence agencies with the exception of 'deception', which was dealt with by the so-called Double Cross Committee.[41]

During the war and to improve the efficiency of JIC's operation, the Joint Intelligence Staff (JIS) was established. This consisted of less senior intelligence officers whose job it was to prepare the reports and data to be considered and discussed by JIC. The Committee presented its analyses and conclusions for approval to the Chiefs of Staff. JIC co-operated also with another sub-committee of the Chiefs of Staff, the Joint Planning Staff, supplying it with the intelligence information required for the conduct of the war.

For a long time JIC was headed by William Cavendish-Bentinck,[42] a civilian and professional diplomat. His main job as the principal co-ordinator of British intelligence, (or as Anthony Eden put it, 'our chief intelligence officer'),[43] was to ensure the harmonious co-operation of the numerous branches of British intelligence and to increase the effectiveness of SIS – a goal he managed to achieve in 1939–1942.[44] SIS 'developed with time', as Cavendish-Bentinck put it. SIS obtained its most important successes in the closing years of WW II and soon afterwards.[45]

JIC, as indeed all of Great Britain, was not well prepared for war. When Cavendish-Bentinck took it over, his office consisted of three persons: 'a Major, a typist [and himself – JMC] and that was all'.[46] This improved only in the second year of the war, when Great Britain itself was threatened with German invasion.

According to Professor F.H. Hinsley, principal author of the official history of British intelligence during the war (and who himself served in Bletchley Park at the time and went on to lecture in International Relations at Cambridge), the shortcomings in the British intelligence preparations for the war were to a significant degree due to the fact that between the wars it was not given sufficient financial resources to conduct its activities and to prepare for the conflict with Germany. At the height of the Abyssinian crisis in 1935 the Chief of SIS, Adm. Hugh Sinclair, complained that shortage of funds forced him to reduce the scope of his anti-Italian operations, since his total budget 'equalled only the normal cost of maintaining one destroyer in Home waters'.[47] Worse than that: this state of affairs persisted practically until the outbreak of the war. Though the budgetary provision was increased in 1936, it was reduced again following the Munich crisis, in the autumn of 1938. As far as information on the Third Reich was concerned, SIS was increasingly forced to rely on the French.[48] Because of this, in the government circles the British intelligence was considered to be very good.[49]

There can be little doubt that the most serious consequences of this rigorous financial policy were felt after the war began, when rapidly and in difficult circumstances SIS had to put together communications systems, networks and agents who were to stay behind and act in German-occupied territories – since this was not done before the war. Similarly, lack of funds hampered the war preparations of GC&CS as well as its operations following the outbreak of hostilities. Until July 1939,[50] when the British-French-Polish conference took place in Pyry,[51] the British Cryptographers had little hope of breaking the German codes, even should the war come.[52]

Lack of signals intelligence increased the pressure on SIS to provide reliable information on the intentions and equipment of the German forces. But SIS also found itself in difficulties,[53] which in turn provoked sharp criticism addressed to it by the War Office and Air Ministry. The Air Ministry, for example, complained that 'normally 80% of SIS reports on Luftwaffe were disappointing'.[54]

The Foreign Office was also disappointed with SIS's work on the political front. This was defended, however, by its Permanent Under Secretary, Sir Alexander Cadogan,[55] who explained that 'our agents' are obliged to supply information subjected to only preliminary selection, even if second-hand or based on gossip, and that the assessment of such reports is in the hands of the clients.[56] As for information on Germany, the Third Reich[57] delivered some painful blows against SIS.

III. British Intelligence Services at the Outbreak of the War and the Venlo Catastrophe

In 1935 the Germans managed to penetrate the SIS network in Holland, which was the base for British intelligence operations throughout North-Western Europe. The British side realized this only in November 1939 after the Venlo[58] incident, when the Germans managed to kidnap the head of the SIS Dutch station, Maj. R. H. Stevens, and the head of network 'Z',

Capt. S. P. Best. Using subterfuge, they were persuaded by the Sicherheitsdienst (SD) to attend some talks, ostensibly with the representatives of the German anti-Hitler opposition.[59] Stevens and Best went to these 'talks' with the knowledge and approval of Prime Minister Neville Chamberlain and of Foreign Secretary Lord Halifax. Fearing torture, the kidnapped SIS officers revealed to the Germans the structure, functions and staff of SIS headquarters.[60] They also provided the Germans with much detailed information on SIS networks in Western Europe, which helped in their unmasking and liquidation.[61] Stevens was caught by the Germans with a complete list of all his agents in Holland. As early as in November 1939 this forced the British to freeze the station in the Hague, which ran intelligence work in Germany.[62]

The Venlo incident constituted not only a discredit to SIS – it also significantly reduced its ability to operate.[63] In the opinion of Professor Foot, one of the most eminent British experts on the history of British special services, from that point Adm. Sinclair and Col. Claude Dansey, one of the officers closest to Sinclair, suspected that the Germans, able to read their codes and hence with access to their radio dispatches, managed to penetrate not only the Dutch network but also several others.[64] Because of this, in the Dansley 'Z' network, established in 1936, radio was banned as a means of communication.[65] The 'Z' network was in reality working for, and subordinated to, SIS. According to Hinsley, the prohibition on the use of radio was in force in all SIS networks – and in order to maintain radio silence networks were not given radio sets. It was feared that the Germans could read British codes. Due to the expanding German influence, even before the war SIS structures in Austria and Czechoslovakia (which was another base from which the British intelligence conducted its German activities) were lost.[66]

Despite these set-backs, in 1936–1939 SIS obtained much reliable and precise information on Hitler's plans and intentions, many from a high-ranking Abwehr officer, Paul Thümmel. He provided the Czechs, and indirectly the British, much first-class information on the condition and disposition of German forces, on the plans and mobilisation potential and on Luftwaffe equipment – and warned of Hitler's intentions with regard to Czechoslovakia and Poland. All this information was provided to SIS from the Czech intelligence with whom Thümmel, code name A-54, worked closely until his arrest by the Gestapo in October 1941.[67] Another agent supplied SIS with a detailed German mobilisation plan with all subsequent alterations.[68] There can be little doubt that SIS reports on Hitler's plans and intentions in 1938–1939 had a profound impact on British policy towards Poland and Czechoslovakia.

On 21st March 1938 the British Chiefs of Staff submitted to their government a report based on SIS information. The report stressed that Great Britain was not ready for war, which might come because of the situation with Czechoslovakia. It also advocated extreme caution. Lord Halifax considered this report to be very worrying. It is on the basis of this report that the British government decided to attempt to persuade Prague to give up the Sudety Mountains to the Germans, especially since on 28th September 1938, at the high point of the crisis, intelligence informed that should Great Britain declare war on Germany, there would be immediate German air strikes on London.[69]

Based on SIS reports, on 14th November 1938 the Foreign Office came to the conclusion that the Germans were prepared for a strike in the West while simultaneously attempting to improve their position in South-Eastern Europe. The Foreign Office held the view that Hitler was prepared to make war because of the 'catastrophic' financial situation in Germany – and because he considered France and Great Britain to be 'decadent' states, moreover with very poor anti-aircraft defences. The thinking in London was that following Munich, Hitler considered Great Britain to be his Number 1 enemy. Hence the Foreign Office's advocacy of a hard, unyielding line on Germany, to discourage it from war. In mid-November 1938 SIS obtained some information indicating that Hitler was again making preparations for an air offensive on London.[70]

On 23rd January 1939 Lord Halifax stated categorically that Hitler's expansion would be directed westwards and not towards the East – contrary to previous thinking – and that Germany was getting ready to attack Great Britain and Holland from the air. At the same time the Chiefs of Staff contended that the conquest of Holland might lead to a direct threat against Great Britain and that counter-action would be needed, even though the country was still not prepared for war. Three days later, on 26th January 1939, the Foreign Office and the Chiefs of Staff suggested that preparations be started to form the British Expeditionary Corps and that staff talks with the French be held. Not quite a month later, on 22nd February, the British government approved these moves. German units entered Prague on 15th March 1939. Three days later the Foreign Office concluded that there was a direct German threat to Romania. On 28th March the British ambassador to Berlin told London that the German attack on Poland was imminent – unless France and Great Britain declare that this would be considered a casus belli. Chiefs of Staff suggested the immediate consultations on military plans with Poland and Romania. The suggestion was approved by the government, which resolved to begin talks immediately with these countries – and with several others, including the USSR, with a view to create an anti-German coalition. Meantime on 30th March Lord Halifax stated that there were powerful arguments for Great Britain to unambiguously declare itself for Poland. The government accepted Halifax's suggestion and on 31st March Chamberlain provided political guarantees to Warsaw and Bucharest. At the same time the Prime Minister said that there was no expectation of an imminent German attack on Poland.[71]

Information supplied by SIS had a fundamental impact on Chamberlain's historic decision to guarantee Polish independence. Regrettably, British guarantees did not deter Hitler from attacking Poland. In fact they helped to persuade him to seek an agreement with the USSR against Poland and her Western allies.

This was the start of Hitler's mad race towards war, which for Poland began on 1st September 1939, and for her allies two days later. And in that war only two countries – Poland and Great Britain – fought the Germans from the very beginning to the last.

Regrettably, SIS did not anticipate the possibility of an agreement between Berlin and Moscow[72] – but neither did Polish intelligence, or the Polish Foreign Ministry led by Józef Beck. Meantime, however, as early as 20th June the *Chicago Daily Tribune* warned, on the basis of warnings by an 'important diplomat in Moscow', that the German ambassador to the USSR, Count Werner von Schulenburg, received from Stalin an offer of a fourth partition of Poland. He immediately passed this on to Berlin. Hitler responded by offering Stalin an alliance, a joint action against Poland, to be followed by its fourth partition – which in fact took place later. This warning was repeated by a Polish publication in the US, the Chicago-based *Dziennik Zjednoczenia* (*United Daily*), and by the *Dziennik Bydgoski* (*Bydgoszcz Daily*) on 4th July 1939.[73] And when the war was already under way, SIS was unable to discover that the main German attack on France in May 1940 would take place through the Ardennes, though a Polish woman, Halina Szymańska, who worked for them from Bern, informed the British of this. She was the wife of the pre-war Polish military attaché in Berlin.[74]

IV. British Intelligence Services following the Fall of France

The fall of France and the collapse of many SIS stations and networks on the European continent created a very difficult, almost critical, situation for British intelligence. 'The ability of SIS to acquire reliable information had not improved and had in some areas markedly declined'.[75] Ralph Bennett maintains that 'when Germany finally invaded France and the Low Countries in May 1940, SIS was left without a single valuable network in occupied Europe. Apart from Sweden, Switzerland and Portugal, SIS was blind to continental events'.[76]

This state of affairs led to SIS's increasing isolation within the British ruling circles. '[...] Reinforcing the continuing remoteness of the SIS, was a growing indifference of SIS's chief customers, the service departments, to the greater parts of its products'.[77]

In parallel, SIS had increasing problems with communications and transport and the authorities were reluctant to meet its demands for airplanes and equipment.[78]

On 3rd August 1940 Churchill, worried by the unexpected dearth of intelligence information, ordered the then Chief of SIS, Col. Menzies, to take steps to improve the flow of product, to begin with from France. According to the British Prime Minister, at the time Great Britain was as badly cut off from France as it was from Germany.[79] This is why on 24th September 1940 Churchill, in the presence of Gen. Sikorski, ordered Maj. Desmond Morton, his intelligence advisor, to arrange as quickly as possible a meeting between Col. Menzies and Col. Leon Mitkiewicz, the Chief of the II Bureau of PGS. This meeting, with the purpose of regulating British-Polish intelligence co-operation, took place on 26th September

1940. Afterwards Maj. Morton reported to Churchill that 'this morning a meeting between Brig. Menzies and Col. Mitkiewicz took place. SIS Chief was fully satisfied both with the meeting and with the decisions taken there'.[80]

Soon, however, in a letter to Hugh Dalton, the head of the Ministry of Economic Warfare, Morton stated that such co-operation would last only for as long as the British side should find it 'desirable' and 'useful'.[81] In fact, the co-operation was very fruitful and lasted until the end of the war.[82] And it developed at a very difficult time for SIS, when its European structures were disorganised and had to be reconstructed almost from scratch. Moreover, at that time SIS's co-operation with the French intelligence, whether of de Gaulle's brand or that of Vichy, and with the Dutch and the Belgians, was less than excellent.[83]

At that point Polish intelligence had at its disposal significant assets and decently developed radio communications on the continent.[84] By mid-1941, during the Battle for the Atlantic, Polish networks in France were able to provide London with reports on German U-boats leaving their Bordeaux, Brest and Le Havre bases for the sea.[85] Home Army intelligence delivered many and detailed reports on the German preparations for war with the USSR. This was information of strategic value.

According to Sir John Colville, Prime Minister Churchill's trusted war-time secretary, Polish intelligence was the best among all the secret services of countries participating in the war against Germany: 'the Poles were possibly the best players in this intelligence game'.[86] The Chairman of the Joint Intelligence Committee during the war, Cavendish-Bentinck, was of a similar opinion.[87]

On their part, the Germans knew a fair amount about Polish intelligence, especially that of the Home Army. Though they fought Polish intelligence with determination and with varying success, sometimes causing painful losses, they did not manage to destroy it. The Germans considered it to be SIS's shock troops in Europe. And they realized that the Polish networks covered not only almost all of German-occupied Europe, from the Eastern front all the way to the Atlantic and the Pyrenees, but also ethnically German territories.[88]

According to Hinsley the reconstruction of SIS's own networks on the continent was difficult and took time[89] and SIS did not have its own agents in Germany.[90] For SIS this increased the importance and the value of co-operation with the II Bureau of PGS, among whose assets were numerous intelligence networks in the Third Reich.[91]

The importance and role of Polish intelligence increased substantially following Hitler's attack on the USSR, since the main communications and transport routes between Germany and the Eastern front crossed Poland. This allowed Polish intelligence to observe and report on the troop, equipment and materiel movements to the front and indeed back to the Third Reich and to ascertain the mood among German soldiers by intercepting their correspondence with families in Germany. Polish intelligence was also very useful when allied air raids persuaded the

Germans to transfer their industrial plants and research centres deep into Poland, largely beyond the reach of Western bombers – and when the Baltic became the main training and experimental centre for U-boats, and Baltic shipyards their producer.

For SIS the British-Polish intelligence co-operation was not only very useful, since throughout the war the II Bureau of PGS provided it with some 44% of all reports from Europe: it was, in reality, a necessity.

Notes

1 In Great Britain this term is used to describe all special services and their staff. By comparison to pre-war Poland, Great Britain did not, and still does not, have a unified intelligence service, such as the II Bureau of the Polish General Staff in 1918–1945.

2 For more, see Sir Percy Cradock, *Know Your Enemy*, London 2002, p. 7 and subsequent pages; N. Annan, *Changing Enemies. The Defeat and Regeneration of Germany*, London 1995, p. 9 and subsequent pages.

3 Between the wars, service in intelligence was considered by British professional officers to be less attractive than in the forces, and intelligence officers were seen as 'eccentrics' or people not suitable for command. Consequently they were unlikely to obtain promotion to high rank (Sir Percy Cradock, *Know*, op. cit, p. 8).

4 More in Y. Modin with J.C. Deniau and A. Ziarek, *My Five Cambridge Friends*, London 1994, p. 17 and subsequent pages.

5 Ibid, pp. 92–93.

6 Ibid, pp. 111–114; *Action This Day*, ed. by M. Smith and R. Erskine, London 2001, pp. 317–318; C. Andrew, O. Gordijewski, *KGB*, Warsaw 1997, p. 270.

7 For a fuller list of SIS 'clients' see below.

8 Stewart Menzies, Sir (1890–1968), Gen., SIS (MI6) Chief, called 'C', in 1939–1952. Eton College and Horse Guards, numerous decorations for WWI, associated with British intelligence from 1915. In July 1939 participated in the Pyry conference where became familiar with Polish methods and the technology of Enigma deciphers. Following the death of Adm. Sinclair, in November 1939 became Chief of SIS. Throughout the war skilfully and fruitfully co-operated with Churchill, Chiefs of Staff and even with SOE, and with allied intelligence services.

9 N. West, *MI-6. Operacje brytyjskie Tajnej Służby Wywiadu 1909–1945* (*Operations of the British Secret Intelligence Service*), Warsaw 2000, p. 114 (personnel of European SIS stations – pp. 15, 16).

10 Y. Modin, *My Five*, op.cit., p. 85.

11 Ibid, pp. 7, 61 and others. According to Modin, during the war Philby passed on a list of British agents operating all over the world.

12 C. Andrew and V. Mitrokhin, *The Mitrokhin Archive: The KGB in Europe and West*, London 1999, p. 209.

13 M. Carter, *Anthony Blunt. His Lives*, London 2001, pp. 268 and 190.

14 Y. Modin, *My Five*, op.cit., pp. 92-93 and 100.

15 *British Intelligence in the Second World War*, F.H. Hinsley, E.E. Thomas, C.F.H. Ransom, R.C. Knight, vol. 1, London 1979, pp. 51 and 58.

16 See Chapter VI.

17 See Chapter I.

18 *British Intelligence*, op.cit., vol. 1, p. 113.

19 See J. Ciechanowski, *O genezie i upadku II Rzeczypospolitej* (*On the Origins and Fall of the Polish 2nd Republic*), London 1981, p. 25.

20 *British Intelligence*, op.cit, vol. 1, p. 4 and others.

21 Ibid, p. 17.

22 Ibid.
23 More in *Action This Day*, op.cit., p. 15 and others; M. Smith, *Station X. The Codebreakers of Bletchley Park*, London 1998, p. 7 and others; S. Budiansky, *Battle of Wits*, London 2000, p. 62 and others.
24 Percy Cradock, *Know*, op.cit., p. 12.
25 More in *The Oxford Companion to the Second World War*, ed. by I.C.B. Dear and M.R.D. Foot, Oxford 1995, under MI5, pp. 742-744 and under XX-Committee, pp. 1289–1290, and in R.M. Bennett, *Espionage: An A–Z of Spies and Secrets*, London 2002, under UK, pp. 200–201.
26 N. West, *MI6*, op.cit., pp. 18–22 (also for details of organisational structure).
27 More in Chapter I.
28 *W 50-lecie powstania Wyższej Szkoły Wojennej w Warszawie* (*On the 50th Anniversary of the Foundation of the Higher Command Academy in Warsaw*), collected and edited by Col. W. Chocianowicz, London 1969, pp. 355–356.
29 *The Oxford Companion*, op.cit., under Intelligence, p. 1154 and Table 7.
30 P. Cradock, *Know*, op.cit., p. 14.
31 *War Diaries 1939–1945*. Field Marshal Lord Alanbrooke, ed. by A. Danchev and D. Todman, London 2001, p. 161.
32 L. Mitkiewicz, Z gen. *Sikorskim na obczyźnie (Abroad with Gen. Sikorski)*, Paris 1968, p. 115.
33 P. Cradock, *Know*, op.cit., p. 14.
34 Ibid., op.cit., p. 15 and K. Strong, *Intelligence at the Top*, London 1968.
35 More in Chapter III and in W.J.M. Mackenzie, *The Secret History of SOE, The Special Operations Executive 1940–45*, London 2000, p. 75 and others.
36 This is what is often called in Great Britain 'British Intelligence Community'.
37 Sir Percy Cradock, *Know*, op.cit., p. 12 and in P. Howarth, *Intelligence Chief Extra Ordinary*, London 1986, p. 114 and others.
38 P. Cradock, *Know*, op.cit., p. 12-13.
39 *British Intelligence*, op.cit., vol. 1, p. 78 and others.
40 P. Cradock, *Know*, op.cit., p. 12 and others.
41 TNA (PRO), CAB 158 (30), JIC (57 and 123) of 29 November 1957, A Short History of the Joint Intelligence Organisation, compiled by JIC Secretariat in November 1957; P. Cradock, *Know*, op.cit., p. 4 and others. N. Annan, *Changing Enemies*, op.cit., p. 9 and others; P. Howarth, *Intelligence*, op.cit., pp. 114 and 200.
42 William Cavendish-Bentinck (1897–1990), 9th Duke of Portland, diplomat, he had a good knowledge of Poland and the Poles. In 1919–1922 was 3rd Secretary to the British mission in Warsaw, and after the war, in 1945–1947, ambassador to Warsaw. Chairman of JIC from October 1939 to the end of hostilities. It was mainly due to his efforts that in 1940–1941 JIC presented the British authorities with three fundamental and very perceptive strategic and political assessments: immediately following the Battle of Britain, in October 1940, that Great Britain was not threatened with German invasion; at the end of 1940, that there would be no German attack on Gibraltar (as Franco would not permit this); and in February 1941, based mainly on reports from Polish sources on the enlargement by Germans of airfields in Poland, that a German attack on the USSR was unavoidable.
43 P. Howarth, *Intelligence*, op.cit., p. 180.
44 Ibid., pp. 22 and 180.
45 Ibid., p. 188.
46 Ibid., p. 113.
47 *British Intelligence*, op.cit., vol. 1, p. 51.
48 Ibid.
49 P. Howarth, *Intelligence*, op.cit., p. 119.
50 *British Intelligence*. op.cit., vol. 1, p. 56 and others.
51 More in Part V.

52 Ibid, op.cit., vol. 1, pp. 54–55.
53 Ibid., p. 55.
54 Ibid.
55 Ibid., p. 56.
56 Ibid.
57 Ibid., pp. 56-57.
58 *British Intelligence*, op.cit., vol. 1, pp. 14-16.
59 M.R.D. Foot, *SOE in the Low Countries*, London 2001, pp. 14-16.
60 Ibid., p. 15.
61 D. Stafford, *Churchill and Secret Service*, London 2000, p. 192. *The Oxford Companion*, under Venlo incident, p. 1245.
62 Ibid.
63 *British Intelligence*, op.cit., vol. 1, p. 57.
64 *The Oxford Companion*, under Spies, p. 141.
65 Ibid. 'Dansey reckoned that the Germans had penetrated most of MI6's spy networks in Europe through their radio traffic, it was a cast-iron rule of his 'Z' network that they were never to use radio at all'.
66 *British Intelligence*, op.cit., vol. 1, p. 58.
67 *The Oxford Companion*, under Thümmel Paul, p. 1108.
68 *British Intelligence*, op.cit., vol. 1, p. 82.
69 *British Intelligence*, op.cit., vol. 1, pp. 81-82
70 Ibid., p. 82.
71 Ibid., p. 83–84.
72 Ibid., p. 48.
73 *Chicago Daily Tribune* of 20th June 1939, *Dziennik Bydgoski* of 4th July 1939.
74 N. Annan, *Changing Enemies*, op. cit., p. 10; and P. Howarth, *Intelligence*, op.cit., pp. 126–127 and J. Garliński, *The Swiss Corridor*, London 1981, pp. 89–97.
75 *British Intelligence*, op.cit., vol. 1, p. 273.
76 R.M. Bennett, *Espionage*, op.cit., p. 290.
77 *British Intelligence*, op.cit., vol. 1, p. 273.
78 Ibid.,pp. 275–276.
79 A.C. Brown, *The Secret Servant. The Life of Sir Stewart Menzies, Churchill's Spymaster*, London 1988, p. 292.
80 TNA (PRO), PREM 7/6, D. Morton's note to W. Churchill of 26th September 1940. The note carries Churchill's initials and the date 27th September, which is when the PM had read it. This indicates the importance Churchill attached to the British-Polish intelligence co-operation.
81 TNA (PRO) PREM 7/6, D. Morton's note to H. Dalton of 26th September 1940.
82 More in Parts I, V, VI and VIII.
83 *British Intelligence*, op.cit., vol. 1, pp. 276-277.
84 P. Cradock, *Know*, op.cit., p. 15.
85 *British Intelligence*, op.cit., vol. 1, p. 333.
86 J. Colville, *Strange Inheritance*, Salisbury 1983, p. 167. After the war J. Colville wrote: 'Probably the best all-round players in the game were the Poles'.
87 P. Howarth, *Intelligence*, op.cit., p. 200 – Cavendish-Bentinck said that 'The Poles were the best people by far'.
88 More in PRO, HS 4/268, Intelligence Services of the Polish Resistance Movement – captured German document.
89 *British Intelligence*, op.cit., vol. 2, pp. 203, 249 and 292.
90 Ibid., p. 125.
91 Ibid., vol. 3, pp. 461-462.

14
Special Operations Executive

Eugenia Maresch

The Fourth Arm

In pre-war Great Britain, various governmental departments pursued clandestine special operations. Most prominent was Military Intelligence (Research), MI(R) branch of the War Office (WO) which at the outbreak of war, was controlled by the three Chiefs of Staff through the Director of Military Intelligence (DMI) Maj-Gen. Frederik G. Beaumont Nesbit.[1] Section D was controlled by the Foreign Office (FO) through 'C' the Chief of Secret Service (CSS) better known as the SIS (Secret Intelligence Service) or the C organisation. The Ministry of Information was also involved, acting through the unlikely name of 'Electra House', (a building in London) which was responsible for war propaganda, as was the Ministry of Economic Warfare (MEW), which inherited the Industrial Intelligence Centre. These disparate Departments were shortly re-named SO1 (propaganda), SO2 (special operations) and SO3 (plans). Soon only SO2 was retained as a viable organisation, and was re-designated as SO (E), later SOE (Special Operations Executive).[2] The structure was in place; all it needed was a co-ordinating machinery and a suitable Minister to run it.

On 1 July 1940 a paper was presented at a ministerial meeting chaired by Lord Halifax the Foreign Secretary and attended by Lord Hankey, Chancellor of the Duchy of Lancaster; Dr Hugh Dalton, Minister of Economic Warfare;[3] Sir Alexander Cadogan, Permanent Under Secretary of State in the FO;[4] Maj. Desmond Morton[5] representing the Prime Minister; Col. Stewart Menzies,[6] Chief of SIS and Gladwyn Jebb[7] of the FO. This meeting virtually decided on a separate formation of the new organisation headed by a civilian rather than regular officer. Not much attention was paid at this stage to the political consequences of such a structure. Later, this was bitterly regretted by Anthony Eden the Foreign Secretary, who laid the blame on his predecessor Lord Halifax.[8]

The War Office, responsible for giving strategic advice to the government, in its brief to the Chiefs of Staff Committee (COS) on 8 July 1940, asked to be fully informed of all activities that might affect the conduct of future operations. On 16 July 1940, Prime Minister Winston Churchill formally offered the post to Dalton, a Labour MP, hoping no doubt that he might successfully harness the movements of the Left in Europe for subversive purposes. Dalton was at liberty to recruit his own desk officers, which he did, mostly by absorbing personnel from MI(R) and Section D. True to the spirit of the Secret Service, no public announcement was made. The War Cabinet decided that '...it would be very undesirable that any Parliamentary Question in regard to the SOE should appear on the Order Paper.'[9]

In October 1940, a paper was issued for limited distribution within Whitehall, which recorded official recognition of subversion as a 'Fourth Arm' of offence against the enemy. It was in fact the foundation charter of Special Operations. It stated that 'subversion is an essential element in any large scale offensive action and as no one of the fighting services is in a better position to undertake such activities than another, it should be recognised by all three as another and independent service'.[10]

This was a far more reaching claim than other Services were prepared to allow. It also implied that the Head of SOE was entitled to a status equal to that of the Chiefs of Staff. How much independence was allowed for SOE, or how disabled 'the Fourth Arm' became – is debatable. It was certainly vulnerable and relied almost entirely on the goodwill of the COS and the FO, who reasserted control over the political aspect of all SOE's work. Frictions persisted between SIS and SOE, primarily because SOE was acquiring importance as a source of tactical operational intelligence.[11]

The internal structure of the Executive was sound and self contained in spite of unavoidable personnel changes. Dalton as ministerial head of the organisation, identified by the symbol SO, stayed in post until February 1942, when Lord Selborne[12] succeeded him. Successive Directors of the SOE were: Sir Frank Nelson[13] (August 1940–May 1942); Mr, later Sir Charles Hambro[14] (May 1942–September 1943) and Brigadier, later Maj-Gen. Colin McV. Gubbins[15] (September 1943–1946). The Director always used the codename CD.

Unlike 'C', CD had no permanent seat at the meetings of the Joint Intelligence Committee of the War Cabinet, but he had a right of direct access on matters that concerned his departments. CD also had no permanent place at the weekly meetings of the Chiefs of Staff Committee (COS), where again he would be invited only if matters were considered to affect SOE. In effect, he was on a par with that other great inter-service organisation, Combined Operations Headquarters.

Sixteen members of the Council ran the organisation: Directors and Deputies, Advisers and Administrators, representing all Services and Regions where operations were to be undertaken. There were three internal Service Directorates: Director of Finance, Group Capt. J.F. Venner RAF (D/Fin) who was responsible for all finances, including Polish arrangements. Director of Research, Development and Supply run by Col. F.T. Davies and Director of Signals, Lt-Col. F.W. Nicholls RS whose role was crucial for the success of Polish Signals. The Chief Executive Officer to Dalton was Gladwyn Jebb (V/CD), seconded from the FO. All matters destined for the Minister went through him. Jebb as an Assistant Under Secretary at the FO was responsible for decision making on major questions of policy or about operations proposed by SO2. After his departure in May 1942, Harry N. Sporborg took his place, also as V/CD.

The Assistant Chief (A/CD), was Air Commodore A.R. Boyle RAF[16] who combined the posts of Security and Personnel, while the Chief Staff Officer to CD Lt-Col. R.H.Barry[17] liased with Chiefs of Staff. Most of all he acted as a Director of Plans and was instrumental in presenting plans derived from the Polish General Staff through the Polish VI Bureau'. There were five regional directors responsible for running their separate groups, starting with the London Group headed by Hambro (AD/A), from spring 1941 until May 1942, when Brig. Eric E. Mockler-Ferryman[18] (AD/E), took control over France, Holland and Belgium. There were other groups covering the Mediterranean area; Cairo; the Middle East; and the Balkans, where the Poles were actively involved on various missions. Poland and Czechoslovakia formed a separate Group ('M'), for which Gubbins was ultimately responsible.

The Polish Section MP

In November 1940, Brig. Gubbins joined SO2 as Director of Training and Operations. His involvement with the Poles was as much political as it was military, and his personal attachments to them did not escape sardonic remarks from his fellow officers and superiors. Even after becoming CD he kept his overall control and remained in close touch with Polish affairs up to the end of the war and after.[19] Gubbins relied mainly on his General Staff Officers who had served under him in the Military Missions to Poland and France. These included the French, German or even Polish speakers, Capt. Harold Perkins,[20] who was in charge of special work carried out by the reconstituted Polish Mission after the collapse of France and Capt. Peter A. Wilkinson RF[21] whom he had appointed GSO2. Two other officers who made their distinctive mark in the Polish Section, who also had Polish connections, were the Polish speaking Capt. Richard Truszkowski[22] (MPX) and Capt. Ronald Hazell[23] (MPO). The work of the Polish Section of SOE was entirely different from that of any other Section associated with occupied countries such as Holland or France, where field operatives with ready made schemes for resistance were almost non existent and recruitment far from simple. Poland was different; there was a historical tradition of conspiracy and insurrection against oppressors.

SOE, at the beginning, was dealing with three separate executive bodies of the Polish Government and their Chief of Staff. First, the VI Bureau (military arm) of the Polish General Staff at the London HQ of the Polish Home Army in Poland. Second was the Ministry of Interior (political arm) which represented the exiled Polish Government inside Poland; and the third, so called by the British, 'Kot's organisation' (civilian arm) whose duty was to look after Polish nationals and their interests in foreign countries. The creation of a fourth one – that of the Ministry of National Defence (MON), under Gen. Kukiel in 1942 – was undertaken after much consideration.[24] Under the influence of Brig. Gubbins, Gen. Sikorski agreed to reorganise the Continental Action due to dissatisfaction with Minister Kot's interference in military matters. In spite of SOE's conciliatory gestures, acrimony between the two Ministries persisted.[25]

The Polish Minorities EU/P

In December 1940 a nine page memorandum entitled 'Allied Propaganda in France' was put before Brig. Gubbins by Prof. Stanisław Kot the Minister of the Interior and his secretary Mr Jan Librach, the main author of the scheme.[26] The object of the plan was to engage some of the half a million Poles living in the occupied and unoccupied parts of France; to link many Polish communities by establishing regular clandestine inter-communication between them. The main task was to be dissemination of propaganda, passive resistance and gathering useful information. SOE's intention however, was to employ both Polish and French nationals for sabotage activities. According to Gubbins, the scheme had additional advantages for SO2, which was to give much needed reception committees, who would welcome and conceal operatives dispatched to France by sea or air. There were other benefits, such as establishing radio communications with the Anglo–Polish authorities as well as courier services across the Franco–Spanish border.[27] By mutual agreement, a new Section EU/P was established, initially co-ordinated by Maj. R. Truszkowski (January to July 1941) and later by Maj. R. Hazell (July 1941 to September 1944). It was a parallel Section to P5 of MI6. In the last year of war, the Section desk officer was Maj. C. B. Ince. Broadly speaking the Polish organisation incorporated a network of intelligence cells in Belgrade, Bucharest, Budapest, Buenos Aires, Cairo, Istanbul, Lisbon and Stockholm. After protracted negotiations between Dalton and Sikorski, the British Treasury made a substantial credit of £600,000 available. However, it carried certain conditions of control by SOE over the intended use of the funds.[28]

Political and Military Tasks of Polish Section SOE

The task of MP (SOE's Polish Section) was to co-ordinate the demands placed upon it by the military side of the Polish General Staff and the political parties of the Government in exile, based in London. Control of couriers and communications was vested in the VI Bureau. With the growth of the Underground Movement in Poland and the support of staff officers from London, control of policy and the role of the VI Bureau was reduced to liaison. Technical control of radio and coded traffic as well as courier work was retained by agreement with the Ministry of the Interior.[29]

According to the orders of the Chief of General Staff of 9th of October 1941, the prime responsibility of the VI Bureau was to pass the directives of guiding principles to the Home Army, set out by the Polish Chiefs of Staff. Secondly, they were to prepare briefs on the military situation in

Poland, select suitable personnel for training in preparation for parachuting into Poland or despatch as couriers. They were also to keep records of Polish military establishments, material dumps and personnel.[30] the VI Bureau, worked under four chiefs, first Gol. Marian Józef Smoleński (July 1940–December 1941), Lt-Col. Tadeusz Rudnicki (December 1941–March 1942), Lt-Col. Michał Protasewicz (March 1942–July 1944) and finally Lt-Col. Marian Utnik (July 1944–1946).

An essential reorganisation of the VI Bureau, undertaken in January 1941, creating an independent special section S, virtually run by one officer, Capt. Jan Jaźwiński. His duties were many, the outstanding one was to prepare technical plans for proposals of air operations into Poland and present these to SOE. This also involved the instruction of personnel in special operations and techniques such as clandestine communications, sabotage and combat. These men named by the Poles as 'Cichociemni' (Silent and Unseen) were eventually parachuted into their areas of operation, together with weapons, explosives, radios, money etc. The training of field operatives, whether for offensive action or support and courier work, was handled by Polish instructors in conjunction with facilities provided by the British authorities.[31]

Notes

1 Frederik G. Beaumont-Nesbitt (1893–1971) Maj-Gen., Military Attaché in Paris (1936-1938), Deputy Director of Military Intelligence WO (1938-1939), Director (1939-1940), Military Attaché in Washington 1941, ADC to King George VI 1944.
2 W.J.M. Mackenzie, *The Secret History of SOE, The Special Operations Executive 1940–1945*, London 2000.
3 Hugh Dalton (1887–1962), Dr., studied Law, served in 1914–18 war, lecturer at LSE, Parliamentary Under Secretary FO (1929–1931), Labour MP 1924–31 and 1935–59, Minister of Economic Warfare 1940–42 and Head of SOE, President of the Board of Trade 1942–1945, Life Peer 1960. See his *Second World War Diary*, ed. B. Pimlott (1986).
4 Alexander Cadogan (1884–1968) Sir, Permanent Under Secretary FO (1938–1946), knighted 1941. See *The Diaries of Sir Alexander Cadogan, O.M., 1938–1945*, ed. D. Dilks, London 1971.
5 Desmond J.F. Morton (1891–1971) Sir, ran Industrial Intelligence Centre in 1930s, Churchill's personal secretary and adviser on secret matters 1940–45, knighted 1945. See R.W. Thompson: *Churchill and Morton*, London 1970.
6 Stewart G. Menzies, (1890–1968), Sir, Col., later Maj-Gen., Life Guards, knighted in 1943, Chief of Secret Intelligence Service 'C' (1939–1952). See A. Cave Brown, *The Secret Servant, the life of Sir Stewart Menzies Churchill's spymaster*, London 1988.
7 Gladwyn H. M. Jebb (1900–1996) Sir, FO Official, Private Secretary to Sir Alexander Cadogan, Chief Executive Officer of SOE 1940–42 acting as Permanent Under Secretary, knighted 1949, Ambassador to Paris 1954–1960, Lord Gladwyn 1960.
8 W.J.M. Mackenzie, chapter IV, p.56
9 Ibid., p. 69–70
10 TNA (PRO) HS 7/211, *The War Diary*, introduction.
11 F.H. Hinsley, E.E. Thomas, C.F.G. Ransom, R.C. Knight, *British Intelligence in the Second World War*, (later as Hinsley), Vol. 3, London 1984, p. 462.
12 Lord Selborne (Viscount Wolmer), (1887–1971), Conservative politician, worked in the Ministry of Works and Buildings (1940–42), Minister of Economic Warfare responsible for SOE (1942–1945).

13 Frank Nelson (1883–1966) Sir, India merchant, knighted. 1924, Conservative MP (1924–1931), Consul at Basle 1939, CD of SOE (1940–1942).

14 Charles Hambro (1897–1963) Sir, distinguished line of Norwegian bankers, Director of Bank of England, on FO's Russia Committee, head of SOE Scandinavian Section 1940, CD of SOE (1942–1943), left SOE in 1944 for Washington.

15 Colin McVean Gubbins RA (1896–1976) Lt-Col., later Maj-Gen., Sir, member of numerous intelligence missions. Chief of Staff (GSO1) to Maj-Gen. Adrian Carton de Wiart's MI(R) abortive Military Mission to Poland in 1939. Commanded the force of Independent Companies in Norway in 1940 awarded DSO, appointed director of operations and training for SOE with special responsibility for Poland, Director (CD) of SOE September 1942 to December 1946. See *Gubbins & SOE* by P.A. Wikinson, J.Bright Astley, *Gubbins and SOE*, London 1993.

16 A. R. Boyle (1887–1949) Air Commodore, Director of Intelligence at Air Ministry, with SOE as Director of Planning and Personnel

17 Richard H. Barry LI, (1908–1999) Col., with the intelligence branch of the War Office since 1939, joined SOE in 1941, Gubbins' Chief of Staff (1944–1946), head of German Section, Director of Plans (A/Col).

18 Eric E. Mockler-Ferryman (1896–1978) Brigadier, with SOE 1943-45, Chief of Intelligence, 'Director' for Western Europe within SOE under control of SHAEF (Anglo-American Command) responsible for TORCH.

19 P.A. Wilkinson, J. Bright Astley, *Gubbins and SOE*, London 1993, pp.130–2.

20 Harold Perkins (1905–1965), Capt. RE, later Lt-Col., master mariner, engineer, before 1939 run a business in Poland, commissioned by MI(R) for the Military Mission to Poland in 1939, in 1940 stayed with Gubbins, joined the newly formed SOE in the rank of Captain, appointed Head of Polish Section (MP) of SOE (1941–1945). In February 1945 sent by WO on a mission to Gen. Anders in Italy, purpose unrecorded.

21 Peter A. Wilkinson (1914–2000) RF, Lt-Col, Sir, Staff Officer Military Mission to Poland 1939, GSO2 under Gubbins and Liaison Officer between MI(R) and Section D, head of the Central and East European Section SOE until 1943, sent on special missions to the Middle East and the Balkans, Deputy Director in the Planning Section, in charge of operations in Yugoslavia, Italy and Austria; knighted 1970.

22 Richard Truszkowski (1897–1988) Capt., later Lt-Col. London born of Polish émigrés, educated at (Chemistry University College), sent with British Expeditionary Force to Archangel in 1919, studied in Poland, PhD in 1926, joined the British Military Mission in Poland in 1939, then SOE in 1940 as Major, sent to Russia on Military Mission in 1941, worked as (MPX) for the Polish Section of SOE, on missions to Cairo, Italy and Germany, left SOE in the rank of Lt-Col.

23 Ronald Hazell (1902–NN) Capt., later Lt-Col., employed by United Baltic Corporation Ltd as a shipping agent in Gdynia, in Poland from 1929 till 1939, joined the Military Mission to Poland in 1939 in the rank of Capt. Sent on mission to Romania, joined SOE, in charge of the Polish Minorities Section (1941–44)

24 IPMS A.XII.52/18, L.dz.554/tjn/42, 12 November 1942 official note by Gen. Sikorski to Minister Mikołajczyk informing him of an agreement with SOE, whereby the two Polish Ministries (Defence and Internal affairs) would share the responsibilities on clearly defined lines; a note by Brig. Gubbins to Gen. Kukiel dated 17 November 1942 informing him of the reorganisation of the Continental Action to simplify liaison with SOE, a joint office would be formed so that the military organisation of the Defence Ministry would collaborate with Ministry of Internal affairs and work amicably side by side in France.

25 TNA(PRO) HS 7/184, *Index to History of the Polish Minorities Section* written by Lt-Col. R. Hazell with comments by Lt-Col. Truszkowski dated 1946. It refers to Operations Adjudicate and Bardsea, as well as Poland. Other interests in the Balkans and the Americas. The history contains an appendix C that is an official

formulation agreed by Gen. Kukiel and Brig. Gubbins dated 30 Dec. 1942 of the tasks of the Continental Action both in the political and military spheres. The Ministry of National Defence (MON), together with SOE were to engage in the preparation of certain schemes for the Continental Action, backing the Allied forces during the invasion of the Continent.

26 Ibid., HS, 4/319, ref. PB.19 Memorandum entitled *Allied Propaganda in France* dated 17 December 1940, [written by J. Librach with the help of the then Maj. Truszkowski], it became a blueprint for the 'Continental Action'.

27 Ibid., HS 4/319, ref. M/PD/81, official note dated 11 January 1941 written by 'M' [Gubbins] to 'CD' [Nelson] about the new organisation in France, its object, plan of action as well as additional advantage for S.O.2 work, in using the Polish reception committees, their safe houses and established courier services across the Franco-Spanish border. The plan of action, together with finance was agreed upon with Mr Librach chief of Central Bureau of the Continental Action of the Ministry of Internal Affairs.

28 TNA(PRO) HS 4/326, ref.M/PD/142, note by Gubbins to Dalton dated 6 Feb. 1941 expressing dissatisfaction with the financial transactions of the Ministry of Interior, his reluctance to support Kot's organisation due to its general insecurity and its amateurish nature.

29 Ibid., HS 7/183, *War Diary Poland*, contains the history of Polish Section SOE probably written between 1946-1948, based on reports, official notes and correspondence which passed through the Central Office of SOE.

30 IPMS, A. XII 30/2, L.dz. 1782/sztab/tj/41 official note dated 9 October 1941 showing the guidelines of responsibilities to be undertaken by various sections of the Polish Intelligence organisation, especially the contacts with Poland.

31 Studium Polski Podziemnej (SPP, Polish Underground Study Trust), ref. SK 16/9, *Dziennik Czynności*, (War Diary), written by Capt. J. Jaźwiński, Head of 'S' Department of VI Bureau PGS.

PART III
POLISH-BRITISH INTELLIGENCE CO-OPERATION

15
Polish-British Intelligence Co-operation

Gill Bennett

When German forces invaded Poland on 1 September 1939, leading to the British declaration of war two days later, there was already an active Polish Intelligence organisation operating in Poland and in close contact with the British Secret Intelligence Service (SIS). For a short while, indeed, SIS provided the only Wireless Telegraph (W/T) channel operating out of Poland and enabling contact between Polish General Staff (PGS) and London, but when after the invasion intelligence gathering in Poland became impossible the greater part of the Polish organisation left for France. Polish PGS, with a British Mission attached under Gen. Carton de Wiart, was evacuated to Paris where large numbers of Polish Service personnel also escaped.

Once in Paris, the Poles lost no time not only in re-establishing their Intelligence organisation but also in developing a network of posts in other countries. SIS were keen to tap into information gathered by the Poles, although warned by a report from an 'unimpeachable source' that since the Polish SIS had left their complete archives in a cellar in Warsaw, where they had been found by the Germans, 'any offers that are received by us of ex-Polish Intelligence officers or sources they may have used' must be considered as suspect. Nonetheless, they endeavoured to set up a closer liaison with the Poles, but the French authorities, on whom the Poles were of course dependent, insisted that all liaison with SIS must be conducted through French channels.

An SIS minute of 10 December 1939 noted, however, that since any information that the Poles obtained and handed to the French was then passed on to the British, 'we do not wish to interfere with this arrangement, and so should not take any steps to contact any of the Polish Intelligence in Paris without the permission of the French'. The Polish General Staff, however, maintained that their II Bureau must have complete independence from French control, and had more or less achieved this by the spring of 1940.

An SIS minute of 14 March 1940 set out the current position on Anglo-Polish liaison. Col. Colin Gubbins, in Paris as liaison between the Polish forces and the British War Office, was in close contact both with Polish Intelligence and with Cmdr. Wilfred 'Biffy' Dunderdale, head of an SIS station in Paris responsible for liaison with the French *Deuxième Bureau*. Gubbins passed to Dunderdale any information received from the Poles, including the fact that Polish Intelligence now had intelligence cells at Budapest, Belgrade, Bucharest, Riga and Stockholm, and were establishing one at Oslo. It was arranged that Gubbins should vet any proposals received by SIS for the employment of Poles in those places, 'so as to ensure our not crossing any of the Polish lines or vice versa'.

Meanwhile, Gubbins put Dunderdale in touch with Colonel Stanisław Gano, the officer responsible within the Polish II Bureau for intelligence activities. This was the beginning of a close and friendly liaison between the two men, and between SIS and the Polish Intelligence Services, which was to last throughout the war. For the whole period Dunderdale was to remain in charge of the section responsible for contacts both with the Polish II Bureau in London and with Polish networks in France, as well as for SIS operations carried out in France by non-Gaullists. As described in Chapter 12, this section was called successively A4 (July 1940–April 1942), P5 (May 1942–December 1943) and SLC (December 1943 onwards).

After the fall of France in June 1940, the Poles had to escape yet again, this time to England, though a number of their Intelligence operatives remained in France and were to set up effective networks and channels of communication. Gen. Sikorski and what became the Polish Government in Exile were established with full British support in the United Kingdom, and were unique among the governments in exile in being permitted to maintain and run their Intelligence service independently, including maintaining their own wireless communications, and their own communications base and training establishment. They were permitted to send and receive messages uncensored in their own codes, and their signals remained uncontrolled until special security precautions came into force before the Normandy invasion in June 1944. The Poles were also unique in arriving in London with a number of clandestine networks, so-called intelligence stations or *réseaux* already operating in enemy-occupied Europe and in touch by wireless telegraph (W/T), and because of their separate communications and resources in the field remained more independent of SIS than any other exiled clandestine service operating from Great Britain.

Despite this independence, however, once the Polish Government in Exile was established in London, with the General Staff's Intelligence Bureau installed in the Hotel Rubens in Buckingham Palace Road, liaison with SIS became more regularised and wide-ranging. Through Dunderdale and his A4 section, SIS provided funds, supplies and logistical support, and in return the Poles agreed that all information obtained through their clandestine sources would, where it did not directly affect internal Polish affairs, be passed to the British authorities. At the same time, relations with French Intelligence (though not with clandestine French networks) were to be broken off, and instructions were sent through SIS channels to Polish agents in the field that they should in future hand over all information to British contacts.

A minute of 6 August 1940 from Dunderdale to the head of SIS, Brig. S.G. Menzies (known as 'C' or, internally, as 'CSS'), enclosing a memorandum on the Polish Intelligence Service, reported that 'Liaison with all sections of the Polish IS is now working smoothly and satisfactorily'. The enclosed memorandum, however, described a complex situation.[1] It explained the earlier division of the Polish Central Intelligence Bureau into Naval Intelligence ('A') and Military Intelligence ('B'), the former funded by the French Admiralty, and the latter, under the direction of the II Bureau of the Polish General Staff, gathering all except naval information. Both sections were now to work as a Central Organisation in close co-operation with SIS.

This Organisation would be responsible for 'the direction of work executed by the representatives abroad, organisation of research and recruiting, classification and distribution of information and documents obtained from all sources'. 'A' and 'B' sections, though in theory autonomous, would be co-ordinated, and while each would confine itself primarily to naval or military information, 'representatives will be asked to extend their activities to all spheres so that the results obtained may be to a great extent reciprocal'. 'A' would rely largely on financial assistance from its British counterpart (though SIS would pay for specific information), while 'B' would be funded from the Polish Army budget. In addition, a special military Underground organisation within Poland was carrying out Intelligence work within the occupied territories, liaising with the central authorities through the VI Bureau of the Polish General Staff. Reports from this organisation, which worked according to instructions received from the VI Bureau, were passed to the II Bureau for study, and also reached SIS through this channel.

While Dunderdale may have felt this clarified the situation, not everyone in SIS agreed. A minute of 12 August listed five different Intelligence services that appeared to be maintained by the Polish Government in London:

- Foreign Office service under the Polish Foreign Minister;
- a political bureau under Professor Kot, working directly to Gen. Sikorski;
- a military Intelligence service, in touch with the War Office;
- a naval security service, in direct touch with the Admiralty; and
- a further organisation run by the Polish General Staff.

A young Polish officer was reported as 'apprehensive about the activities of these different organisations in England...He, for his part, would be heartily glad if the British War Office were to order them all to co-ordinate their operations in one Bureau and say that the only alternative would be to close them all up.'

Dunderdale explained to CSS on 21 August that not all of those listed constituted Intelligence services 'proper', and that Col. Gano had 'expressed regret that any confusion should have arisen over the purpose of or the extent to which any given organisation is over-lapping', but some confusion clearly remained. A manuscript annotation on the 12 August minute teased Dunderdale that while his 'friends' seemed to fall into category (iii), 'With 46 Generals on active list in UK there are bound to be some funny Polack activities!'

The situation was made more complex with the establishment in the summer of 1940 of the Special Operations Executive (SOE), with whom Polish Intelligence also established close relations and from whom they sought facilities and equipment. On 26 September 1940, on the Prime Minister's instructions, his Intelligence adviser Maj. Desmond Morton arranged a meeting between Brigadier Menzies and Col. Mitkiewicz, Assistant Chief of the Polish General Staff and Director of Military Intelligence. Although no formal record of this meeting has been found, Major Morton's minute to Mr. Churchill later the same day reported that Brigadier Menzies and Col. Mitkiewicz had reached agreement regarding future channels of communication between British and Polish Intelligence Services:

> The difficulty was that the Poles appeared to control several Intelligence Services. Persons representing themselves as agents of one or other of these services would ask Brig. Menzies to help them and he had no means of finding out whether they were genuine. It has now been arranged that when any person asks for facilities saying he is working for the Poles, Brigadier Menzies will communicate at once with Colonel Mitkievich [sic] and the latter will assume responsibility for saying whether the man is to be helped and to what extent.[2]

Despite agreement at a senior level, the records show that a degree of confusion and 'crossed wires' persisted during the autumn of 1940. In these circumstances, it is understandable that liaison with the British authorities did not always run smoothly. However, the willingness of the Polish authorities to co-operate fully with SIS made any clashes far less serious than they might otherwise have been, and the underlying relationship was a strong one. The situation also improved when, as Dunderdale noted on 18 January 1941, the naval and military sections of Polish Intelligence were united under the direction of Col. Gano by order of Gen. Sikorski. In future, Gano should be the sole channel through which intelligence should pass to SIS, where the point of liaison would remain Dunderdale's section A4.

From the summer of 1940 Polish Intelligence-gathering networks were being established in both occupied and unoccupied territories: information from the British Intelligence archives regarding these networks is in Part VI. The results of their activities reached SIS both through Polish II Bureau channels, and through local contacts with SIS operatives. In either case the information was handled and distributed by Dunderdale and A4. In France, the distinction between Polish and French networks often became blurred, the same network containing both French and Poles, but A4 handled them both.

In December 1942 Dunderdale reported to SIS that there were to be a number of organisational changes to the Polish security services, which were now to come under the control of the Polish Ministry of Defence. The Poles estimated that during the coming financial year their expenditure on account of security would be £32,400, and had asked MI5 to notify HM Treasury that this sum was approved. Dunderdale noted 'that the money in question is really the Poles' own money and that it is advanced to them by our Treasury on a certificate that the amount is reasonable. These certificates are signed by various people; for instance the certificate in the case of Polish agents is signed by CSS, while the certificate on account of expenditure for the Polish Navy is signed [by] the Admiralty...unless we have any special reason for doing so, there is no object in querying the amount. All that is necessary is either for us or MI5 to tell the Treasury that in our opinion the amount is reasonable.'

Throughout 1943 the Polish Intelligence services continued, together with the French *Deuxième Bureau,* to provide a wide range of valuable information to SIS. A report on P5 organisation as at 30 June 1943 stated that Polish sources supplied military, naval, air, economic, political and counter espionage information (the last not handled by P5 itself). P5 organised travelling and transport facilities to and from foreign countries, while a Polish SOE factory at Stanmore, manufacturing radio equipment and supervised by a committee under the Radio Security Service (RSS), produced and supplied special material for agents, such as W/T sets.

Polish Intelligence operated from approximately 30 stations in occupied and neutral countries in Europe, while approximately 300 accredited agents were engaged in intelligence activities, in addition to numerous informants. Material received from Polish Intelligence was passed by a member of P5, according to the subject of the reports, to one of the SIS sections such as military, naval, air and economic, or Russian, for onward distribution to departments like the War Office, Foreign Office, Ministry of Economic Warfare or the Service ministries.

Requirements and questionnaires
It was SIS's job to pass on the requirements of its customer departments to its agents and other sources of information. It is clear that such requirements, sometimes in the form of questionnaires, were passed to the Polish Intelligence authorities. Unfortunately, however, very little documentation concerning Intelligence requirements has been found in SIS archives. It is likely, of course, that such requests would have been destroyed after the information had been received and circulated, since their utility was at an end.

A few documents have been found indicating the sort of question-naires or specific requests for information that were made. In June 1940, for example, a questionnaire was drawn up listing information sought on Albania, Bulgaria, Romania and Yugoslavia. It was not addressed only to

Polish Intelligence, but it was hoped that Polish sources might be able to supply some of the answers. For Romania, the questions were:
- What formations or units have their headquarters at the following towns, and what are the names of their commanders: IAŞI, RĂDĂUŢI, VASLUI, MĂRĂŞEŞTI, T. OCNA, TULCEA?
- What is the location and who is the Commander of 22nd, 23rd and 24th Infantry Divisions?
- Details wanted of locations, composition and Commanders of any Divisions that have been formed since 1st Jan 1940?
- What Mechanized Brigades exist, and where are they located?

For Yugoslavia, SIS wanted to know:
- What is the location of the Divisions forming the 7th Army?
- Who is the Officer commanding Sibenik Command?
- What formation Headquarters are located in: Novi Sad, Velika Kikinda, Subotica, Sombor, Osijek, Brod, Banjaluka, Sisak, Zagreb, Varaždin, Maribor, Ljubljana?

A report on the allocation of responsibilities in A4 section, drawn up in August 1940, indicates further areas on which SIS sought information. These included USSR military reports, Orders of Battle, reports on the Russian aircraft industry, railway and factory reports, military and geographical survey of countries adjoining the USSR, military aerodromes in the Baltic States and Occupied Poland, and details of the air forces of Bulgaria, Czechoslovakia, Austria and other countries.

In 1942 documents indicate areas of ongoing penetration by Polish Intelligence, such as Italy and Portugal. Economic information had already been received but it was hoped that a 'constant flow of military information' might be achieved. In Greece, Bulgaria, Romania, Hungary and Yugoslavia very little information was being received, partly due to communications difficulties. Reporting from Scandinavia was predominantly on naval issues. It was noted, however, that in the previous year Polish Intelligence had been concentrating on the penetration of Germany by agents operating from the occupied territories: some of these had been dropped as part of SOE operations, while resident agents had been instructed to penetrate German ports and industrial centres.

A rare example of a direct request to the Poles is contained in an unsigned letter to Maj. J. Żychoń ('Janio') of 19 December 1942, asking for information on the following points:
- Maj. Paul LEVER KUEHN, German Assistant Military Attaché, Istanbul, said to be an expert in Arab affairs, has for many months been collaborating with Germans in Sofia in receiving agents and sabotage material in Turkey and passing them on to Syria and elsewhere. For this purpose his chief agent in Istanbul is Egon von BADENFELD. Their activities now appear to be directed against the Caucasus and Northern Persia. Major SCHULZE-BERNETT, German Assistant MA and head of an intelligence organisation at

Ankara, co-operates with LEVER KUEHN in this work. Any details of LEVER KUEHN's agents, activities and contacts would be welcome;
- any information about the Italian espionage system in Turkey;
- espionage by the German Consulates in Trebizond, Adana and Alexandretta. Any details of activities or personalities;
- activities of the Spanish Intelligence Service in Turkey.

There were some SIS complaints about the amount or the quality of information. In September 1940 it was noted that information supposedly coming from Polish sources in Lithuania was identical to information already passed to SIS by their own sources in Finland some weeks before, and a plea was made for the Polish Intelligence authorities to be asked to avoid 'crossing wires' in this way. In September 1942 it was noted that almost no information had been received from Polish counter espionage sources in the Middle East, implying that organisation and personnel difficulties were to blame.

A further report, dated December 1942, noted the achievements of Polish naval intelligence, particularly in North Africa where useful details had been passed on about coastal batteries, French war and merchant vessels and the fact that the French North African ports were not protected. Equally, Polish sources on the south coast of France were very efficient in keeping SIS informed on the state of the French fleet in Toulon and the movement of merchant ships and their cargo. Other reports noted were from Poland, on gas and on naval matters in Danzig and Gdynia. The SIS report concluded with a request for further technical naval information from Germany and on the movement of Axis war vessels off the French Mediterranean coast.

P5 issued a total of 11,477 reports in 1943, an increase of 54% over 1942. 539 of these were graded A and 6210 B, with the War Office and Air Ministry as the most appreciative recipients. Of the total, 5,667 emanated from Polish sources but there is no indication of how these were divided according to value. In regard to air reports from Polish sources, 1148 were received, 120 graded A and 720 B. These bare statistics, though interesting as showing the importance of the contribution made by Polish Intelligence in terms of volume, cannot, unfortunately, be expected to put flesh on the bones of the story of Anglo-Polish Intelligence liaison. It is clear from SIS documents from the immediate postwar period that the decision was taken to destroy all but the summary details of wartime reporting. This applied, of course, to reports from all sources, not just Polish. None of the original reports, which were translated if necessary, sanitised and distributed to customer departments on receipt, appears to have survived, although it is possible some may have found their way into the National Archives.

There are a few fuller summaries of the work of the Polish II Bureau. One such covers the period 1 January to 30 June 1944, and reports that during that period 3,973 reports were issued, an increase of 12% over the second half of 1943. The greatest increase was in military reports, while those on air matters maintained the high quality they had attained in 1943. On military subjects, particular praise was given to reports on the regrouping of divisions on the Eastern Front, which were described as 'excellent both as regards accuracy and importance of information sent'. On communications, the time-lag of approximately two months in receipt of information from Poland reduced its value, but reports from France had improved both in speed and accuracy.

Following the Allied landings in Northern France in June 1944, the emphasis within SLC (which P5 had now become) began to change, with the Polish organisation in France beginning a process of liquidation, and SLC's involvement with the French decreasing generally. Increasingly, SLC was concerned with collating, analysing and distributing intelligence on the USSR, received from a variety of sources including the Polish General Staff. At the same time, Polish Intelligence continued to supply information on military and other matters concerning Germany and Poland. A report on SLC activities for September 1944 noted a total of 528 reports submitted to SIS HQ, singling out as of special interest reports on the Orders of Battle for *Flak Abteilungen* (Poland and Germany), the identification and location of German divisions in Poland and the defences and movement of air force divisions.

Polish Intelligence continued to provide useful information to SIS although, as the war in Europe drew to a close and Poland's postwar position appeared increasingly vulnerable, the focus of their information-gathering, like that of SLC as a whole, was increasingly on the Soviet Union and Soviet Intelligence. The quantity and quality of this contribution, however, was undeniable and it is clear from the small amount of surviving documentation that a high value was placed on it. The Polish Intelligence effort – which had continued no matter where or in how difficult a position the members of their organisations found themselves—was praised not just by British Intelligence authorities, but by a range of government departments and military authorities alike.

The Prime Minister, Winston Churchill, had a keen appreciation of the Polish contribution and the sacrifices it had entailed. At the end of the war in Europe, in response to a request from the Prime Minister, Dunderdale prepared a summary report on SLC's wartime record.[3] This showed that of 45,770 reports produced by SLC between 3 September 1939 and 8 May 1945, 22,047 were received from Polish sources. This information was said to have been supplied by 1500 French and 600 Polish agents, but the latter figure represented only those Poles who had worked in France, and was not comprehensive. In an appendix to this document Dunderdale listed some of the more interesting and important subjects covered by the Polish reports, including submarine construction, V-weapons, synthetic petrol manufacture and air raid damage. He concluded:

> It will thus be seen that Polish agents worked unceasingly and well in Europe during the last five years, and that they provided, often at great danger to themselves and to their relatives, a vast amount of

material of all kinds on a wide variety of subjects. The Polish IS made an invaluable contribution to the planning and the successful execution of the invasion of Europe, and to the ultimate victory of the Allied forces in Europe.

Technical liaison between British and Polish Intelligence

British and Polish Intelligence authorities worked closely together in more technical areas, most notably in that of cryptography. As described in Part VIII below, the Polish government's willingness before the war to share the notable achievements of their cryptographers in breaking the ENIGMA code made a major contribution to the Allied cause. During the war Polish cryptographers, whom SIS was able to help to escape from Poland to Romania and thence to France, continued to play an important part through their work in the cryptography department of the French *Deuxième Bureau* under Col. Bertrand until 1942–3 when, again with SIS help, some were able to escape over the Pyrenees to the UK.

Rejewski and Zygalski, who arrived in England on 30 July 1943, were assigned to a small Polish intercept and cryptographic station at Felden (near Hemel Hemstead), (operated from 21 June 1943 after being moved from Stanmore). Stanmore station had been set up in 1940 following an approach to the British authorities by Colonel Banach of the Polish General Staff. He provided details of Russian military radio networks and cyphers and, although the information was already available at GC&CS, it was decided that co-operation on interception and decryption of the Russian target would be advantageous and representatives from Bletchley Park visited the Poles at Stanmore on 3 December 1940.

The provision of premises, finance and equipment for a new station was agreed and technical co-operation began immediately. The British provided Russian code books and regular feedback and guidance (the Poles had lost all their code books and other records during successive evacuations from Poland and France, and had been forced to recreate records entirely from memory). All correspondence and exchange of material was conducted through Dunderdale's section of SIS, with technical matters such as the supply of receivers and aerials handled by RSS. GC&CS ceased to work in Felden on Russian communications soon after the German invasion of Russia (feedback was last noted on 2 September 1941). The Poles continued to work on Russian communications throughout the war, but there is no evidence for further co-operation with Bletchley Park, where GC&CS were running an 'ENIGMA factory' and maintaining the tightest security.

The Poles also operated under RSS supervision a radio factory at Stanmore producing, *inter alia*, equipment for clandestine purposes. This factory also developed equipment for high speed radio transmission capable of sending 100 groups in two seconds.

Poles at Stanmore, using their own cyphers and W/T operators, also ran their own clandestine radio network with stations in England, Europe and the Middle East. This was under the general control of Dunderdale, with RSS responsible for detailed supervision of radio networks and provision of equipment. This aspect of Anglo-Polish relations did not always run smoothly. There were predictable tensions over equipment and facilities, and anxiety at times on the British side concerning security and the content of some of the messages sent overseas in Polish cyphers. For example, in March 1944 British authorities in the Middle East took remedial action after finding that Polish Consular traffic between Istanbul, Jerusalem and Cairo was in a very low grade cypher; decodes of Polish messages between London and Grenoble were observed in Abwehr (ISK) messages in August 1944; in the same period German decodes of Polish governmental and military messages appeared in German high level communications and in Japanese military attaché communications; and British captures at the end of the war confirmed that some high-level Polish cyphers had been read by the Abwehr.

Anxiety increased towards the end of the war, when it appeared to SIS that Polish intelligence-gathering was increasingly directed against the Soviet Union, while the British Government was keen to improve the relationship with her Soviet ally. Overall, however, the collaboration was a fruitful and important one, and the release into the public domain of the files of the Radio Security Service, a process begun after the establishment of the Anglo-Polish Historical Committee in 2000, means that further research in this area is now possible.

Notes
1   The full text of this memorandum is reproduced in Volume II of this Report.
2   TNA (PRO), PREM 7/6.
3   A full summary of this report and its attachments is reproduced in Volume II of this Report.

1. "Enigma" – a German cipher machine.

2. Marian Rejewski (1905–1980) Polish cryptologist, co-author of the discovery, in 1933, of the theoretical basis for the operation of "Enigma".

3. Henryk Zygalski (1907–1978) Polish cryptologist, co-author of the discovery, in 1933, of the theoretical basis for the operation of "Enigma".

4. Jerzy Różycki (1909–1942) Polish cryptologist, co-author of the discovery, in 1933, of the theoretical basis for the operation of "Enigma".

5. London, 10 Downing St. Left to right: Lord Halifax Secretary of State for Foreign Affairs, Polish Prime Minister W. Sikorski, Prime Minister W. Churchill, A Zaleski Polish Foreign Minister

6. Gen. Stewart Menzies (1890–1968), the Chief of British Secret Intelligence Service (1939–1952).

7. Gen. Colin McVean Gubbins (1896–1976), Director of SOE (1943–1946).

8. Col. Harold Perkins (1905–1965), the Chief of polish Section SOE (1941–1945).

9. Cmdr. wilfred Dunderdale (1899–1990), "Wilski", SLC of SIS in liaison with the II Bureau Polish General Staff.

10. Col. Peter Wilkinson (1914–2000), Head of South-East European SOE Sections.

11. Col. Stanislaw Gano (1895–1968), Chief of the II (Intelligence) Bureau of the Polish General Staff (1941–1946).

12. Col. Leon Mitkiewicz (1896–1972), Chief of the II Bureau of the Polish General Staff (1940–1941), Head of the Polish mission at the Combined Chiefs of Staff in Washington.

13. Lt-Col. Leon Bortnowski (1899–1976), Chief of the Records and Studies Department II Bureau of the Polish General Staff (1942–1945).

14. Lt-Col. Władysław Gawel (1897–1978), Head of Radio-Intelligence Polish General Staff.

15. Col. Tadeusz Skinder (1897–1952), Deputy Chief of the II Bureau of the Polish General Staff (1943–1945).

16. Lt-Col. Jan Leśniak (1898–1976), in the years 1944–1945 – Asistant to the Chief of the II Bureau of the Polish General Staff.

17. Lt-Col. Stefan Mayer (1895–1981), Commandant of the Polish Intelligence Officers School in Scotland 1941–1945.

18. Maj. Jan Henryk Żychoń (1902–1944), the Chief of the Intelligence Department of the II Bureau of the General Staff (1940–1944).

19. Maj. Maksymilian Ciężki (1898–1951) participated in the deciphering of "Enigma"; Chief of the German Codes Department at P.C. Bruno (1939–1940), Deputy Chief of Station "300" (1940–1943).

20. Lt-Col. Marian Romeyko
(1897–1970), Chief of the Polish
Intelligence Station "F" in France fom
january 1942 to January 1943.

21. Lt-Col. Wincenty Zarembski
(1897–1966), Chief of Station "F"
(1940–1942) and the Russian Section
of Records and Studies Department
of the II Bureau (1942–1945).

22. Maj. Roman Czerniawski
(1910–1985), "Walenty", "Armand",
Chief of the Interallie Station in France
"Brutus" in XX system.

23. Maj. Jan Józef Graliński, an
expert in Soviet codes, worked in
the "Z" team and Station "300"
in France.

Mieczysław Słowikowski

Stwierdzam, że wyż.wym.,wła-
ściciel paszportu służbowego
Seria...B:........ Nr ....
.............., jest oficerem
Armii Polskiej w stopniu......
....
I certify hereby that the
above-mentioned, bearer of the
service passport Series...B...
No.............is an Officer
of the Polish Army in the rank
of............................
Je certifie que le porteur du
passport de service, Serie.B..
No.............est Officier
de l'Armee Polonaise, dans le
grade de....................

Podpis właściciela legitymacji.
Signature of the owner of the
Service Card.
Signature du porteur de la
Carte de Service.

24. Maj./Lt-Col. Mieczysław Słowikowski (1896–1989), "Rygor", Chief of Polish
Intelligence Station "Afr." in Algiers (1941–1944).

25. Capt. Wacław Gilewicz
(1902–1992), Chief of the "Płn"
("North") Station in Stockholm
(1940–1941).

26. Capt. Tadeusz Szefer, intelligence
officer of the Station "A" in Athens
(1940–1941) and of the "T" Station in
Jerusalem (1941–1945).

16
Intelligence Co-operation during the Second Half of the 1930s

Andrzej Pepłoński, Andrzej Suchcitz and Jacek Tebinka

Initial contacts with British Intelligence were established by the II Bureau of the Polish General Staff during the Polish-Bolshevik war. Representatives of the British mission who observed the war took steps aimed at obtaining sources of information among the Polish population and Russian emigrés. The tasks concerned predominantly the public mood and morale of Polish officers during important military operations at the eastern front. On 25 June 1921 Kazimierz Olszewski, an official at the Ministry of Foreign Affairs (the VII Department) co-operating closely with the II Bureau, established a contact with Capt. Derbyshire from the British Embassy in Warsaw. During a conversation Derbyshire admitted that he was interested in receiving information about persons suspected of engaging in subversive activities.[1] At that time both sides were not interested in making intelligence co-operation any closer; it was stated, though, that all British Intelligence elements functioning in the Embassy were involved in studying the domestic situation in Poland[2] and followed closely the Polish petroleum, lumbering, textile and food industries, as well as the biographies of Polish politicians, their financial status and morale. The Passport Section had a vast file of persons suspected of being engaged in subversion and espionage or of having committed crimes. However, monitoring of the Soviet and German intelligence services was a priority.

Poland was assigned a rather distant place in British policy with the exception of the period 1918–1921 when she was delineating her frontiers. Since Poland did not represent any greater strategic or economic importance, until the early 1930s she remained rather a function of the attitude of London towards the Soviet Union and especially towards Germany.[3] The II Bureau officers who held the posts of military attachés in London signalled little interest in co-operation on the part of British Intelligence. Moreover, local regulations hindered the information work since personal contacts and correspondence with particular bureaux of the War Office were forbidden unless permitted by the Intelligence Department. Nevertheless, it was possible to obtain in London political and military information of essential significance to the Polish authorities, as proven by Maj. Władysław Michałowski who for that purpose exploited his contacts with the French Military Attaché.[4] At the same time he gradually tightened the co-operation with British Intelligence and officers from the Air Ministry and the Admiralty as well as persons employed in the Committee for Imperial Defence.[5]

The exchange of information usually pertained to reconnaissance of the situation in the Soviet Union.[6] In the course of increasingly closer co-operation Maj. Michałowski gained access to the more detailed information that British Intelligence had. He used this opportunity to examine the British attitude towards a possible German-Soviet confrontation from the point of view of current war potential of both sides.

Polish-British Intelligence contacts related also to joint undertakings outside Europe. The conference held in the Grosvenor Hotel (London) on 3 November 1934 was attended by Capt. Jerzy Niezbrzycki, head of the East ('Wschód') Section, Col. Stewart Menzies, deputy chief of the Secret Intelligence Service (SIS), Maj. J. P. Shelley, Chief of an SIS cell in Jerusalem, and Maj. R. H. Plowden. One of the topics discussed at the meeting were preparations for installing a Polish-British Intelligence cell in Persia, soon given the cryptonym 'Radames'. Its Chief, Capt. Stanisław Orłowski, a II Bureau officer using a forged passport issued to 'Oskar Sanders', was to become acquainted with the local conditions and then create an intelligence network in Iraq and Afghanistan. That would enable him to prepare a study on possible recruitment in the Soviet front-line with due attention paid to the technical possibilities of working across the border and communications with resident agents as well as to organise a communications network and a courier service. The II Bureau expected only that through the SIS the British would help to set up communications with Warsaw and provide counter-intelligence co-operation in Persia[7]. It turned out, however, that the SIS obviously treated that mission as a symptom of 'the expansion of a foreign intelligence in the area of British influences';[8] Maj. Shelley proved incapable of ensuring any communications and despite further promises he never even left for Persia. Consequently, during a meeting with Capt. Orłowski in Baghdad on 6 June 1935, Capt. Niezbrzycki decided to 'have a final talk with the English about the communications and obtaining information concerning the work and the territory of Persia, and in case of a negative response from the English consider the possible closing down of the cell',[9] which in fact happened in November 1935.

Capt. Niezbrzycki's visit to London also provided an opportunity to discuss current possibilities of organising intelligence 'along the European-Soviet border (recruitment, communications, transfer of persons)'. The proposal of using Russian emigrant groups for intelligence work was rejected. Attention was drawn to the specific conditions prevailing in the Soviet Union which created enormous obstacles for setting up a network of resident agents and obtaining military documents.[10]

In the second half of the 1930s Polish-British intelligence co-operation, previously limited to an exchange of information about communist
movements and other subversive organisations, became more active. As
a result of an agreement between the II Bureau and the SIS, Capt. H.
Hamilton-Stokes,[11] the head of the Warsaw cell established direct contact
with the West ('Zachód') Section of the Intelligence Department,
expecting assistance in conducting active intelligence as well as access to
the information materials. The whole undertaking was organised by Capt.
Niezbrzycki who informed Section 'Zachód' about the co-operation with
Capt. Stokes also in other areas.[12] Despite the fact that the co-operation
showed certain gaps the intelligence obtained in this way and
supplemented, if necessary, by the II Bureau, constituted a valuable
additional source of information, although the British side regretfully did
not respond to the II Bureau's proposals of May 1938 to exchange
information about the Luftwaffe.

Within the framework of co-operation the Polish side permitted
British Intelligence to conduct operations in other countries from the
Polish territory. There can be no doubt that a retired Gen. Adrian Carton
de Wiart and Lt. Harold Perkins, the owner of a factory in Bielsko, used
their positions to supply British Intelligence with various information, also
about Poland.[13] Naturally, such a covert co-operation or rather assistance
which Polish intelligence provided to the British obviously did not stem
from sentiments but from the simple calculation that in this way London
would perceive Warsaw as a potential partner in Central Europe. This is
precisely why at the beginning of October 1938 Lt-Col. Edward R. Sword,
the British Military Attaché in Warsaw, was the only representative who
could freely tour the regained lands around the Olza River.[14]

The same reasons were behind the co-operation between the two
intelligence services in various parts of Europe. For example, in December
1935 Maj. Chidson, the British Military Attaché in Bucharest, asked his
Polish counterpart, Lt-Col. Jan Kowalewski, to examine the possibilities of
getting his agents across the Polish border into the Soviet Union. Crossing
the Romanian border was much too difficult and Maj. Chidson did not like
the presence in the area of representatives of French intelligence, who
pursued similar activity.

The exchange of files and technical co-operation were accompanied
by joint surveillance activities related to persons suspected of conducting
espionage for the Soviet Union. Such operations even led to the exposure
of dangerous Soviet agents operating in Great Britain.[15]

In the years preceding the outbreak of the war co-operation between
the II Bureau and British Intelligence became more intensive, although a
true breakthrough did not take place until 18 March 1939, when the British
Cabinet debated the security of Romania. The discussion about building
an alliance against the German aggressor led to the preparation of a
Foreign Office draft of a declaration that was to be proposed to France,
the Soviet Union and Poland, which in January 1939 was still suspected of
inclinations towards establishing a Berlin-Warsaw axis.[16] The planned

declaration foresaw joint consultations in the event of another aggression on the part of a European state. Although Józef Beck, the Polish Minister of Foreign Affairs, feared that Poland would be dragged into an agreement with Moscow, which would further deteriorate the already tense relations with Berlin, the initiative itself facilitated efforts to make relations with London closer. This is the reason why on 22 March he suggested to the British a secret bilateral agreement maintained in the spirit of the declaration.[17]

The Polish proposal was well received in London – Neville Chamberlain recognised Poland as a state which in the event of war could establish the second front and in this way to hold Hitler in check. The standing of Poland rose in the light of reports sent by Col. Firebrace, the British Military Attaché in Moscow, who showed that the Red Army was incapable of offensive actions. Although the British Chiefs of Staff took into consideration the fact that Poland would be conquered by the Germans in two or three months, they also predicted large Wehrmacht losses in the course of this campaign. The British military assumed from the outset that they would be unable to provide assistance to the Polish Army, nor did they take into account the possible threat posed to Poland by the Soviet Union.[18]

The British decision about guarantees for Poland was preceded by information from intelligence of 28 March 1939 about an imminent German attack against Poland; the information turned out to be false. The information was confirmed the following evening by Ian Colvin, a correspondent of the *News Chronicle* in Berlin, who informed Chamberlain about German preparations for an invasion of Poland.[19] As a result, on 31 March 1939 the British Prime Minister, speaking in the House of Commons, promised to grant, immediate support to the Polish government;[20] an agreement signed on 6 April 1939 during a visit paid by Minister Beck in London replaced unilateral British guarantees with obligations to render mutual assistance in the event of a German attack. In the secret part of the joint communiqué both sides pledged to hold a full and quick exchange of information about threats facing both countries.[21] It did not mean a formal establishment of co-operation by the special services of Great Britain and Poland, but in practice paved the way towards it.

Obviously, the British guarantees did not immediately lead to closer relations between the Polish and British intelligence services. Apart from distrust this distance was caused by the fact that the SIS did not really have valuable information about the German military potential. Without having fully capable agents of its own in Germany the SIS had nothing substantial to offer.

Moreover, the first Polish-British Staff talks and, as it turned out, the last ones before the outbreak of the war, did not take place until the last week of May 1939 in Warsaw. Upon the arrival in the Polish capital the British delegation received instructions from London to destroy documents describing British-French Staff talks of 3 May 1939, during which the British military learned that in the event of a German attack against Poland the French Army did not intend to launch operations along the western front but would prepare for an offensive against Italy. The British found this fact highly disturbing because it meant that the concept of threatening Hitler with war on two fronts was beginning to break down.[22] Obviously, the Western Allies did not intend to make these plans known to the Polish side.

Instead, at the beginning of June 1939 they showed only lengthy documentation concerning the Soviet Union and Czechoslovakia and containing, among others, information about the Soviet railway industry as well as the export of aeroplanes in 1936 – mainly 'SB' bombers and 'I-15' and 'I-16' fighters – to Spain (200), China (300) and Czechoslovakia (70). The detailed information related to the aircraft industry works, their output, the number of employees and the types of the planes produced.

Paradoxically, establishing closer co-operation was possible only because during the 1930s British strategic planning took it for granted that the main British contribution to the war against Germany would be air and sea battles, and that land operations would be limited to subversion and sabotage. The first of the structures created for this purpose, soon after the annexation of Austria, was General Staff Research – cryptonym GS (R) – in the General Staff at the War Office, later known as Military Intelligence Research (MI/R/), which studied the techniques of irregular warfare,[23] co-operating with an independent section 'D' of the SIS, headed by Maj. Laurence Grant, a 37-year old sapper and a Cambridge University graduate.[24] The head of GS (R) was Maj. John C. F. Holland, one of whose chief co-workers was Maj. Colin McVean Gubbins, later the Chief of Special Operations Executive (SOE). In the spring of 1939 efforts were undertaken to study the possibilities of conducting sabotage and subversive activities in those states which according to British assessments could become occupied by the Nazis.[25] One of the elements of that undertaking was a mission by Maj. Gubbins, who travelled around Romania in May, the Baltic states and Poland; while in Warsaw he talked with Maj. Shelley, among others.[26]

Another intensifying factor in the establishment of contacts was the anxiety about certain trends in Polish policy, which made the British Cabinet send Gen. Edmund Ironside, Inspector General of Overseas Forces to Warsaw (17–20 July 1939) in order to become acquainted with Polish intentions. Without intending to conduct any Staff talks or even more so to create plans of military co-operation, the instruction mentioned that 'if Gen. Ironside is asked what military action he will take in a situation causing a sudden military reaction of Poland he is to say that the Government of His Majesty will provide immediate assistance on the ground, in the air and at sea. In the light of the outcome of the talks held with the French military those assurances obviously lacked credibility. Nonetheless, they brought the British Cabinet and the military comforting news since it became obvious that the Poles did not intend to provoke the Third Reich, although Marshal Edward Śmigły-Rydz did express the opinion that in view of Hitler's aggressive plans war was inevitable.[27]

The growing German threat to Poland and a simultaneous tendency to ignore the signals about a possible German-Soviet rapprochement,[28] which as a result came as a total surprise,[29] were the reasons why Maj. Gubbins paid another visit to Warsaw, this time with a very concrete proposal concerning the establishment of co-operation in propaganda warfare in Germany. Its purpose was the prevention of war by bringing about a change of government and even the ousting of Adolf Hitler, and in case of an outbreak of war – to reduce its duration to a minimum. After contacting Lt-Col. Stanisław Gano, Chief of the Technical Section of the II Bureau of the Polish General Staff (19 July 1939), Maj. Gubbins proposed to Col. Marian Józef Smoleński, Chief of the II Bureau, and Lt-Col. Józef Skrzydlewski, Chief of the III Department, responsible for the planning of subversion and war propaganda, that if such co-operation was to be approved he would guarantee permanent and secret communications between London and Warsaw and between Poland and Germany. In this situation, having obtained consent from his superiors, Lt-Col. Skrzydlewski put forward only one condition, namely, that such a campaign would not trigger a 'flood' of German counter-propaganda. After all, that country had a much larger technical potential in this respect. The II Bureau was, ready to consider each attempt on a case by case basis and to provide assistance in the penetration of certain regions of Germany and neighbouring countries, so as to avoid a false impression of 'ill will'. For its part, the Bureau expressed a wish for portable short-wave W/T stations with a range of about 300 km, which were to be used along the frontier with Germany so that the Germans would suspect that the signal came from within their territory.[30] Although possible co-operation in the domain of sabotage and subversion was not discussed – as reported by Maj. Gubbins and Lt-Col. Skrzydlewski – some issues were most certainly agreed on; at the end of August 1939 two sappers – Lt-Col. Stefan Rueger and Maj. Michał Protasewicz – arrived in London to purchase special equipment and explosives 'which were to be used in Poland, among other things, for the possible destruction of railway and road connections between Poland and Romania in the event of a deep German penetration in the south' so as to hamper quick exploitation and transport of Romanian crude oil.[31] In order to make co-operation more harmonious Maj. Stefan M. Dobrowolski, who was to be appointed deputy Military Attaché at the Polish Embassy in London, was entrusted with the task of liaising between the two intelligence services.

During the final days of peace II Bureau officers forwarded almost every day to the Military Attaché at the British Embassy in Warsaw reports about the concentration of German troops near the Polish borders, receiving in return British information on the same subject. That co-operation received a new framework after 24 August 1939 when a British Military Mission in Poland was established. It was headed by Gen. Sir Adrian Carton de Wiart who resided in the Polesie region. The Mission was composed of officers from the Military Attaché's office and the SIS –

i.e. the Embassy's Passport Control Office. They were joined by Col. Gubbins together with twelve officers, sabotage specialists, on the third day of the war.[32] They set off from London for Warsaw *via* Alexandria, Athens and Bucharest on 26 August.[33]

In London Col. Gubbins received a number of secret instructions which requested him to determine the premises for Polish-British co-operation and to present the results of intelligence reconnaissance, to obtain maps and information communiqués about ongoing operations, and to indicate transportation routes for the arms supplies for the Polish Army. Having established contact with the General Staff, members of the British Military Mission monitored the course of war activities. The most important observations, such as information about the exceptional effectiveness of the German Air Force, were forwarded to London. Already on 4 September the Mission determined that German penetration conducted from the territories of Silesia and eastern Prussia had made such progress that the Polish Army was threatened with being cut off.

Gen. Carton de Wiart talked with Marshal Śmigły-Rydz on a number of occasions, and Lt-Col. Gubbins maintained contact with Gen. Wacław Stachiewicz. They discussed the current situation, the predicted development of war activities and planned operations. The British also accompanied the Headquarters after its transfer to Brześć and then to Włodzimierz wołyński. Throughout the whole period Lt-Col. Sword maintained contact with Col. Smoleński, Chief of the II Bureau, in order to conduct current identification of German formations.

On 12 September attention was drawn, among other things, to the growing threat to the Southern Front posed by a German mountain division marching from Slovakia and two armoured divisions approaching Jaworów. On the following day Lt-Col. Gubbins, accompanied by Group Capt. Davidson, left for Lwów, to the Headquarters of Gen. Kazimierz Sosnkowski GOC Southern Front. On 14 September Gubbins met with Col. Józef Jaklicz, Deputy Chief of the General Staff, and Col. Smoleński, who, having analysed the current situation, announced that in view of the general breakdown of the Northern Front, the irreparable situation in the centre and the threat facing the left flank, the Marshal decided to immediately withdraw from along the entire front.[34] A day later Lt-Col. Gubbins spoke with Gen. Stachiewicz once again communicating to him recommendations made by Gen. de Wiart, who had suggested widening the bridge head on the right flank and strengthening the protection of the Stanisławów–Czerniowce train line. On that evening Lt-Col. Sword contacted Gen. Stachiewicz and Col. Smoleński and then communicated to the head of the Mission their conclusions regarding the bombing of cities by German Air Force (a report was instantly sent to London). On 16 September Gen. de Wiart talked again with Gen. Stachiewicz, Chief of the General Staff, who, unaware of the Abbeville agreement,[35] requested once more that the British Air Force attack targets in Germany so as to reduce 'the pressure on Poland'.

It also seems that at the beginning of September the British still did not know the contents of the secret protocol to the German-Soviet pact. Although its existence and content were widely gossiped in European capitals, as evidenced by the telegrams decrypted by the Government Code and Cypher School, London continued to regard the Soviet Union as a state which could ensure supplies for fighting Poland.[36]

That conviction began to change rapidly, and on 5 September 1939 a note written by R.A. Butler, Parliamentary Under-Secretary at the Foreign Office, stated that thanks to intelligence an outline of the conditions of the Soviet-German pact had been known earlier and had reached the Foreign Office. A conviction was increasingly stronger that Berlin and Moscow had come to an agreement concerning the division of Poland and that the USSR would capture eastern Poland the moment the Wehrmacht reached the positions determined in advance. The British also realised that they lacked possibilities for preventing Soviet aggression against Poland.[37]

The Soviet invasion launched on 17 September 1939 did not, therefore, come as a great surprise to the Foreign Office, which assessed that the offensive would accelerate the anticipated fall of Poland by several days at the most.[38] In the evening of that day the Military Mission, having contacted the Chief of the General Staff and the Marshal himself, expressed the opinion that the efforts of the previous two weeks had come to an end, and at about noon on 18 September it crossed the Romanian border, thus terminating the first stage of the co-operation with the Polish Armed Forces.

During the co-operation numerous crucial observations about the course of the defensive activities in Poland were made, drawing attention first of all to the disproportion's between the military potentials of the warring sides. It was stressed that the rapid advance of the armoured troops and the crushing air superiority enabled the Germans to achieve victory in less than three weeks. Gen. de Wiart expressed his regret that in the resulting situation he was unable to fulfil the task of 'making sure that the programme of co-operation with the Polish Army as part of a general plan was implemented – as has been agreed during the Staff talks'.[39] In an assessment of German strategy and tactics it was underlined that the enemy had carefully concealed general mobilisation, masked identification information and the numbers of vehicles, and openly exchanged units near the Polish border. The Luftwaffe began its attacks by destroying Polish airports and hangars. As a result, within several days the airports became useless. Furthermore, the co-operation with armoured units rendered Polish counter-attacks futile, while the intensely bombed Polish arms industry had already practically ceased to exist by 4 September.

The head of the Mission also expressed many detailed observations and criticism with regard to the Polish High Command, claiming, among other things, that: 'The Polish General Staff was much too slow and probably too obstinate to take into consideration implications of the deep and strong penetration of the Polish positions in the early phase of the struggle [...]' due to which the orders to withdraw issued by the

Headquarters were 24 to 48 hours late'.[40]

The course of war in Poland made it impossible for Lt-Col. Gubbins to carry out some of the tasks received from London. The most important one, concerning the co-operation with the Polish Army, had already ceased to be valid at the beginning of the war since the British General Staff, upon government instructions, did not intend to launch any military operation on the Continent. Nevertheless, observation of the course of the defensive war provided members of the Mission with many valuable conclusions about the German army. Furthermore, the presence of the British contributed to the establishment of contacts with Polish officers, who became partners in organising help for the Polish Resistance movement almost a year later. On the British side a special role in this co-operation was played by future SOE representatives: Lt-Col. (Gen.) Gubbins and Capt. (Lt-Col.) Perkins. The officers, despite having limited authority, frequently demonstrated their understanding and support for Polish political and military initiatives, a fact which had a particularly positive influence on co-operation with Home Army intelligence.

In fact, the established co-operation was by no means one-sided. During a visit of Lt-Col. Rueger and Maj. Protasewicz which lasted until 9 September, the first joint expedition was undertaken. Its purpose was to check the equipment and sabotage procedure in combat conditions. At the invitation of his British colleagues, including Capt. Diggins *vel* Diggens, Maj. Protasewicz was parachuted into Germany on the nights of 5 and 6 September 1939. The aim of the expedition was to blow up a 30-40-metre long steel railway bridge by using explosives with a 24-hour delay mechanism, thanks to which the whole group managed to walk safely to Denmark, from where they were taken by plane to England while the bridge was destroyed.[41]

Although the possibilities for intelligence co-operation were rather limited, there were various examples showing that it encompassed not only the British Military Mission, to which Capt. Jan Chmarzyński was assigned as a liaison officer. A letter from Rear Adm. John Godfrey, Director of Naval Intelligence Division (NID) of the British Admiralty addressed to Col. Smoleński, thanking him for valuable co-operation with H.M. Embassy in Warsaw illustrates concrete assistance rendered to the western Ally. The effects of this particular co-operation were to be of important for British Naval Intelligence.[42] On the following day Col. Smoleński sent a telegram to London to immediately inform the British Admiralty that the Germans had laid mines in the southern part of the Belt and the Sound, so that the passage was possible only near the Sterborg buoy.[43] Valuable information was also passed over after the arrival in Great Britain of three destroyers (1 September) and two submarines: the ORP 'Wilk' (20 September) and ORP 'Orzeł' (14 October); while in Rosyth the latter was boarded by the deputy head of the NID. All the collected information provided a detailed picture of the situation on the Baltic Sea and the passage to the North Sea. Moreover, while in Constanta, the head of the newly established Independent Foreign Navies Section of the Polish

Navy Command – handed over to the British Consul a W/T station brought over from Warsaw.[44]

Notes

1 CA MSW, Section 'W', call no. 262/122/1, Report of the Information Department at the Ministry of Foreign Affairs, 25 June 1921, l. dz. D VII 2525/21.
2 Ibid.
3 M. Nowak-Kiełbikowa, *Polska-Wielka Brytania w dobie zabiegów o zbiorowe bezpieczeństwo w Europie 1923–1937* (*Poland-Great Britain at the Time of Efforts for Collective Security in Europe 1923–1937*), Warszawa 1989, pp. 567–575; M. Nurek, *Polska w polityce Wielkiej Brytanii w latach 1936–1941* (*Poland in British Politics in 1936–1941*), Warszawa 1983, pp. 316–317.
4 CA MSW, Section 'W', call no. 262/122/1, Report by the Information Department at the Ministry of Foreign Affairs, 25 June 1921, l. dz. D VII 2525/21.
5 AAN, A-II/101/1, Letter from Maj. Michałowski, the Military Attaché in London, to the Chief of the II Bureau, 25 August 1927.
6 P.A. Wilkinson, J. Bright Astley, *Gubbins and SOE*, London 1993, p. 31.
7 CA MSW, Section 'W', call no. 262/97, Report from the conference held on 3 September 1934.
8 A. Misiuk, *Służby specjalne II Rzeczypospolitej* (*Special Services of the Republic of Poland*), Warszawa 1998, p. 119.
9 IPMS, A.II.27/56, Report from Maj. S. Orłowski to Lt-Col. S. Mayer, 14 December 1935, leaf 3.
10 CA MSW, Section 'W', call no. 262/97, Report from the conference held on 3 September 1934.
11 Capt. H. Hamilton-Stokes was the head of the Warsaw Passport Control Office until June 1936, and then was transferred to Madrid (N. West, *MI-6. Operacje brytyjskiej Tajnej Służby Wywiadu 1909–1945* (*MI-6. The operations of the British Secret Service*), Warszawa 2000, p. 61)). In September 1936 he was replaced by Maj. J. P. Shelley, who held this post until September 1939 (see: IPMS, vol. 251/5, letter of recommendation for Maj. J. P. Shelley of 24 September 1936, issued by Col. V. G. (?) from the War Office).
12 CA MSW, Section 'W', call no. 262/145, Note from Lt. J. Niezbrzycki to the Chief of Section West ('Zachód'), 18 March 1933.
13 See, i. a.: A. Carton de Wiart, *Wspomnienia* (*Memoirs*), 'Zeszyty Historyczne', 1988, fasc. 86, pp. 30–63.
14 E. Turnbull, A. Suchcitz (ed.), *Edward Roland Sword: The Diaries and Dispatches of a Military Attaché in Warsaw 1938–1939* , London 2001, pp. 95–99.
15 CA MSW, call no. 615/232/6, Telegram from the Chief of Section 'W' to the Military Attaché in London, 17 December 1937.
16 TNA(PRO) FO 371/23015, C 1169/54/18, Note by Strang of 17 January 1939.
17 TNA(PRO) CAB 23/98, Conclusions (39) 12, 18 March 1939; Conclusions (39) 13, 20 March 1939; *Documents on British Foreign Policy 1919-1939*, ed. by E. L. Woodward and R. Butler, third series (further as: DBFP), vol. IV, London 1951, pp. 453–454, 463–464.
18 *The Diaries of Sir Alexander Cadogan, O.M. 1938–1945*, ed. D. Dilks, London 1971 (further as: Cadogan Diaries), p. 162; TNA:PRO FO 371/23688, N 1542/485/38, memorandum by Firebrace, 7 March 1939 ; CAB 23/98, Conclusions (39) 16, 30 March 1939.
19 *The Diplomatic Diaries of Oliver Harvey 1937–1940*, ed. by J. Harvey, London 1970, p. 271; Christopher Andrew, *Secret Service. The Making of the British Intelligence Community*, London 1992, pp. 587–588.
20 *Poland in the British Parliament 1939–1945*, ed. by W. Jędrzejewicz, vol. I, New

York 1946, pp. 5–6; on guarantees see: M. Zacharias, *Geneza układu o wzajemnej pomocy między Polską a Wielką Brytanią* (*The Origin of the Mutual Assistance Pact between Poland and Great Britain*) [in:] *Władze RP na obczyźnie podczas II wojny światowej* (*Polish Authorities in Exile during the Second World War*), London 1994 and H. Jackiewicz, *Brytyjskie gwarancje dla Polski w 1939 roku* (*British Guarantees for Poland in 1939*), Olsztyn 1980.

21 D. C. Watt, *How War Came. The Immediate Origins of the Second World War, 1938–1939*, London 1989, p. 190; M. Nurek, *Polska w polityce*, op. cit., pp. 195–196.

22 TNA(PRO) CAB 23/99, Conclusions (39) 30, 24 May 1939; A. Prażmowska, *Britain, Poland and the Eastern Front, 1939*, Cambridge 1987, pp. 80–84.

23 D. Stafford, *Britain and European Resistance 1940–1945*, Polish edition, Warszawa 1984, p. 34

24 N. West, *MI-6*, op. cit., p. 79.

25 T. Panecki, *Polonia zachodnioeuropejska w planach Rządu na emigracji (1940–1944) – Akcja kontynentalna* (*The Polish Community in Western Europe in Plans of the Government-in-exile (1940-1944) – Continental Action*), Warszawa 1986, pp. 54–55.

26 E. Turnbull, A. Suchcitz, Edward Roland Sword, op. cit., p. 42; TNA:PRO HS 8/260, Report by C. Gubbins, 1 June 1939.

27 TNA(PRO) CAB 27/625, FP (36) 55th Meeting; PREM 1/331A, Memorandum of 12 July 1939 'Visit of Gen. Sir W. E. Ironside to Warsaw'; CAB 23/100, Conclusions: (39) 35, 5 July 1939, (39) 37, 12 July 1939, (39) 39, 20 July 1939 r.; WO 106/1677, report by Ironside of 20 July 1939.

28 The testimony of Walter Krivitsky was ignored as well as the articles by Leon Trotsky, intelligence signals and the opinions of Robert Vansittart, the main diplomatic advisor who already in the spring of 1939 warned against a rapprochement between the two dictators (see: *Foreign Relations of United States: Diplomatic Papers, 1939*, vol. I, Washington 1956, p. 287; TNA:PRO FO 371/23697, N 2624/1459/38, Collier to Washington 31 May 1939; FO 371/23686, N 4146/243/38, memorandum by L. Collier of 26 August 1939; N 3335/243/38, memorandum of 10 July 1939).

29 First information about the progress made by the negotiations reached Foreign Office through American diplomats as late as 22 August 1939 (see: TNA:PRO FO 371/23686, N 4146/243/38, note by Butler of 25 August 1939; Christopher Andrew, *Secret Service*, op. cit., pp. 598–599; S. Żerko, *Stosunki polsko-niemieckie 1938–1939* (*Polish-German Relations 1938–1939*), Poznań 1998, pp. 433–435).

30 TNA(PRO) HS 4/165, Report by Lt-Col. C. Gubbins of 31 July 1939; IPMS, B. I. 6i/2, report by Lt-Col. J. Skrzydlewski, 24 November 1939, leaf 15.

31 IPMS, Kol. 77/3, Diary of Col. Michał Protasewicz, leaf 234.

32 Information reports of the Second Bureau were relayed to the British Military Mission, see: TNA:PRO WO 208/118; see also: *Kampania wrześniowa 1939 roku. Sprawozdania informacyjne Oddziału II Sztabu Naczelnego Wodza* (*The September Campaign of 1939. The Intelligence Reports of the II Bureau of the Polish General Staff*), ed. A. Suchcitz, London 1986; P.A. Wilkinson, *Foreign Fields. The Story of an SOE Operative*, London 1997, pp. 71–83.

33 The Mission was composed of, inter alia Royal Navy Capt. N. L. Wharton, Group Capt. A. P. Davidson of the Royal Air Force, Lt. P. A. Wilkinson and Lt. Harold B. Perkins. Five British officers joined the Mission as translators together with fifteen employees of the Passport Control Office at the British Embassy in Warsaw, headed by Lt.Col. Shelley.

34 AWIH, call no. II/1/39, Translation of a report by the British Military Mission, 26 October 1939.

35 See: *Polska w polityce międzynarodowej (1939–1945). Zbiór dokumentów. 1939*

(*Poland in International Politics* 1939–1945. *Collected Documents 1939)*, selected by W. T. Kowalski, Warszawa 1998, pp. 552–556; *Cadogan Diaries*, p. 216.

36 TNA(PRO) FO 371/23147, C 12715/1110/55, H. Kennard to FO 1 September 1939; HW 12/242, no. 075538; HW 12/243, no. 075734.

37 J. Tebinka, *Polityka brytyjska wobec problemu granicy polsko-radzieckiej 1939–1945* (*British Policy and the Polish-Soviet Border 1939–1945*), Warszawa 1998, pp. 60–62.

38 TNA(PRO) FO 371/23699, N 4491/4030/38, Note of 15 September 1939; *Harvey Diaries*, p. 319; Bodleian Library, Simon Papers, Oxford, box 11, diary of 17 September 1939.

39 AWIH, call no. II/1/39.

40 Ibid.

41 While saying good-bye the Englishman said to Maj. Protasewicz: 'Thank you for your co-operation. This is the first time that I have worked with a Pole. I am glad that everything went so smoothly', and two days later he added: 'You know, it was blown up' (report by Maj. Protasewicz about the subversive action in Germany in September 1939, 'Przegląd Kawalerii i Broni Pancernej', 1988, no. 128, pp. 262–268. This report, written for the Chief of the General Staff in September 1940, was sealed in an envelope: 'The deed of Lt-Col. Protasewicz Michał, awarded with the Order of Virtuti Militari' with an instruction that it should not be opened until after the war. The envelope remained unopened for more than forty years. In his memoirs, written in the 1960s and 1970s, Col. Protasewicz made no mention of the whole issue).

42 SPP, TP-3, Portfolio of Brig-Gen. Marian J. M. Smoleński, letter from Rear Adm. J. Godfrey to Col. M.J. Smoleński, 6 September 1939.

43 IPMS, A.12.53/26, leaf 70, Coded telegram no. 4 of 7 September 1939 to the Polish Embassy in London.

44 IPMS, Kol. 90/6, Report by Cmdr. Lt-Col. Brunon Jabłoński for Rear Adm.l J. Świrski, Chief of the Royal Navy Command, London 26 August 1940.

17
Co-operation Between the II Bureau and SIS

Andrzej Pepłoński

Contact between Polish and British Military Intelligence was established during the first years after Poland regained her independence. Initially, the prime aim of this co-operation was to gather information on the military, economic and political situation in Soviet Russia. The Polish authorities, who were worried principally about their eastern neighbour, attached great importance to all information about the threat of war, which is why they established a network of intelligence outposts in the countries adjoining the Soviet Union. Apart from intelligence networks operating in Russia itself, II Bureau also had intelligence cells in Finland, Latvia, Estonia, Lithuania, Romania, Turkey, Central Asia and the Far East. As the threat of war increased, intelligence exchanges began to include information concerning the Third Reich and other European states. At the beginning of the 1930's, the chiefs of II Bureau were aware of the differences in the range of the interests pursued by the two intelligence organisations. The British, involved in a global policy, sought information of strategic significance and were interested in details concerning the position, equipment and training of Soviet forces in the Far East. Polish Intelligence concentrated its attention on the aggressive plans of Poland's closest neighbours, although it, too, tried to monitor the situation in Siberia and even in Manchuria. The exchange of information between the two Intelligence organisations took place mainly through the military attachés in Warsaw and London. Joint intelligence activities were also occasionally carried out. In 1938, British Intelligence provided II Bureau with information about the organisation and positioning of Czechoslovak armies. On the eve of war, II Bureau provided the French and British Intelligence with the methods used for decrypting German dispatches sent by Enigma.

In the months following the outbreak of the Second World War, II Bureau officers were evacuated to Romania and began to operate on territories occupied by the USSR and the Balkans. Station 'R', set up in Bucharest, worked with among others Capt. Stephen Ernest Carlton, a

British Intelligence officer stationed there (see more: chapter 4: T. Dubicki, *Romania*). The establishment of the Polish military and civilian authorities in France revived contacts between II Bureau and British Intelligence, though for understandable reasons, contacts with French Intelligence were more vigorous. The basic exchange of information took place during conferences held by representatives of both sides. Wider co-operation with British Intelligence was intensified after French Intelligence deployed a group of Polish cryptologists to work on the German Enigma coding system. Direct contact with the head of the Polish team, Lt-Col. Gwidon Langer, was maintained by Captain (later Major) Kenneth MacFarlane, a British liaison officer who had a direct teleprinter line to the British cryptological centre in Bletchley. The Bletchley centre provided the majority of keys used for deciphering dispatches. Thanks to the co-operation between the Poles, the French and the British, systematic decoding of correspondence between German units was possible. In the first half of 1940, over 8,000 dispatches were deciphered with the aid of Polish cryptologists. These dispatches contained data on the location of German armies, the composition of operational-tactical units and on orders on their battle readiness. The dispatches also showed the concentration of German armies on the eve of the invasions of Norway, Denmark, the Netherlands, Belgium and Luxembourg. Information confirmed by French Intelligence showed the deployment of more than one hundred German divisions, including over ten armoured ones.

Following the fall of France, most II Bureau officers were evacuated to Great Britain. The new position in which the Polish civilian and military authorities found themselves influenced the activity of the Bureau. In accordance with the political targets set by the Polish government, intelligence co-operation was, first and foremost, to increase the contribution made by the Polish Armed Forces and its allies to victory over Germany. Since it was anticipated that in future battles Polish units would be fighting under Allied command, it was expected that the Allies would supply information about the enemy in those theatres of operation where Polish units were to be engaged. Furthermore, the Poles expected to receive information from battle reconnaissance, an area in which the Allies had superior means.[1] In accordance with the assumptions made by PGS, co-operation with the Allies was to consist of providing them with intelligence in the form of documents and reports. In return, II Bureau was to receive analytical reports. In effect, co-operation was to be based on the principle 'insight into the whole in return for details'.[2]

Similar assumptions applied to intelligence conducted by II Bureau of the Home Army GHQ, which supplied London with information not only from the General-gouvernement and the Reich, but also from the occupied and neutral parts of Europe. After the outbreak of the German-Soviet war, Home Army Intelligence was also active in the vicinity of the Eastern Front. Only some of this information was useful for the purposes of Polish armed resistance and for the preparation of an uprising in Poland, but most of it usually had great value for the Allies.

The chiefs of the II Bureau intended to conduct their co-operation with Allied Intelligence, especially the British, so that in return for the information supplied the Polish side would receive not only political and military benefits, but also financial assistance and technical equipment for intelligence work, both abroad and in Poland. It was expected that British special services would help in the training of the Polish Armed Forces and would prepare them for intelligence duties. These objectives could not be met immediately, since the intelligence services of their current and future Allies were not on a war footing yet. Moreover, the Allies did not always wish to meet all the earlier obligations and arrangements. Despite their considerable expertise and experience in establishing co-operation with other intelligence services, it took British Intelligence some time to make up for the delays in their preparations for war. In this situation the chiefs of SIS were very interested in the personnel of the II Bureau, PGS. The first contacts between the two, before the new Polish Intelligence structures were put into place, show how cautious British Military Counter-intelligence (MI5) was initially. Apart from the usual procedures applied in relation to new arrivals to the British Isles, the British were also aware of various tensions between II Bureau officers.

The British wished primarily to use those officers who effectively organised pre-war anti-German Intelligence. But in fact most of the appointments to the top posts in the II Bureau were of officers who specialised in intelligence in the East (Col. Leon Mitkiewicz and Lt-Col. Stanisław Gano). At the end of June 1940, SIS verified those persons whom they intended to use for intelligence purposes. Poles arriving in Great Britain were subjected to detailed observation and selection in transit camps and in the so-called Patriotic School.[3] In July 1940, British Intelligence organised a training course to prepare a group of liaison officers who were to facilitate co-operation with the Polish military and civilian institutions. Two Polish officers attended a study course in Cambridge, Capt. K. Załuski and Capt. A Szarski, both spoke four languages. The Chief of the Intelligence Department of the II Bureau was Maj. Jan Żychoń, the pre-war Head of Station no. 3 in Bydgoszcz. His deputy was Major Witold Langenfeld, who worked with Żychoń for many years. Żychoń was a controversial figure, who owed his appointment both to his professional skills and to the support of Gen. Władysław Sikorski. British Intelligence was right in its high regard for Żychoń's pre-war intelligence achievements and his work for the French Admiralty. At that time several other II Bureau officers established close contacts with British Intelligence. The British side asked for Major Tadeusz Szumowski to be appointed to the Polish Embassy in London.[4] His contacts with Capt. Graham, an SIS officer, contributed to the selection of a group of officers employed by the II Bureau.

Official co-operation between the Chief of the II Bureau, Col. Mitkiewicz, and Brig. Frederik Beaumont Nesbitt, Director of Military Intelligence between 1939–1940, was established on 29th July 1940. General principles of co-operation and the exchange of information and reports were established, as was the financing of Polish Intelligence abroad and in Poland. The Chief of the II Bureau was assured that British Intelligence would supply daily communiqués ('Intelligence') and reports of radio monitoring conducted by the BBC. From the very beginning, the co-operation between both intelligence services was contained within an organisational framework. A liaison office with Polish Intelligence was established at HQ level. The liaison office, headed by Cmdr. Wilfred Dunderdale 'Wilski',[5] co-ordinated all intelligence co-operation between the various British special services and those Polish military and civilian institutions which participated in the gathering of information of military significance. The establishment of the liaison office was necessary not only because of the complicated structure of British Intelligence, but also to keep secret both organisations and the principles of their activity. The requirement for secrecy was shown even by the fact that all correspondence between SIS and the II Bureau guaranteed the sender absolute anonymity.

British Intelligence wished to use the potential of Polish Intelligence, both civilian and military, to the full extent possible. In addition to the Stations and Cells controlled by the II Bureau, intelligence was supplied also by the VI Bureau of PGS, the Evacuation Department and the Special Affairs Department of the Ministry of National Defence, the Ministry of Internal Affairs and the Ministry of Foreign Affairs. A leading role was played by II Bureau, with the other services providing supplementary information. The process of spreading the networks onto the Continent was initiated by the British authorities. Originally, they suggested rather unrealistic ideas, which would have entailed an excessive use of those Polish soldiers who had not been evacuated to Great Britain. A positive impact on shaping Polish-British intelligence co-operation was played by the introduction into the Polish Section of SOE of officers who were familiar with pre-war Poland. A key role in contacts with PGS was played by, among others Capt. Harold Perkins, who until 1939 managed a textile factory in Bielsko, and by Ronald Hazell, a pre-war shipping agent in Gdynia (see: T. Dubicki, *Romania*).

For security reasons, a group of MI5 officers acted as intermediaries in contacts with particular Polish special services. Among them were Lt-Col. Norman, Capt. F. A. Scott and Lt-Col. McCook.[6] Independently of the activity of the British, Counter-intelligence remained in the hands of Security Department at the Polish Ministry of National Defence, which kept suspicious persons under surveillance. Counter-intelligence dealt also with the protection of military secrets and censored correspondence. The Correspondence Control Section worked closely with the British Postal and Telegraph Censorship. Their joint aim was to prevent Intelligence information leaks and to collect information from correspondence. According to the agreements signed with Military Intelligence 12, all the private correspondence of soldiers was subject to censorship. A total of 554,556 incoming letters and 329,905 letters sent out of the United Kingdom were censored during the war.[7] In the course of 1944 alone, the

Security Section of the Counter-Intelligence Department at the Polish Ministry of Defence provided British Counter-intelligence with 2,318 items of information.[8] The II Bureau also worked with MI9, which facilitated the escape of British officers from German camps.

From the very beginning, the resistance networks in Poland were an essential source of information about the wartime potential of the Third Reich, even more so since they had almost a year's worth of experience behind them. In time, the role of the Home Army Intelligence grew. The first contacts between the representatives of Polish resistance and British Intelligence were established by the 'Muszkieterowie' (Musketeers) organization, which in February 1940 had intelligence and counter-intelligence cells in 32 towns within the pre-war borders of Poland.[9] Their contact with British Intelligence was established through Krystyna Skarbek-Giżycka 'Granville'. A year later 'Muszkieterowie' had their networks in the Reich, the Soviet Union, Hungary and the Balkans, although their activity was concentrated in occupied Poland.

In early July 1940, the II Bureau outlined the intelligence tasks in Poland, Romania, Hungary, Yugoslavia and Turkey. Polish Intelligence was to provide information on the attitude of the occupiers towards the Polish population, food supplies, the transit of fuel and military equipment across Poland and on industrial production. But the bulk of those tasks related to purely military issues, namely the composition and distribution of large military units, changes in the distribution of forces along the demarcation line, the production of war material and battlefield gasses, and the morale of the army.[10]

Brig. Beaumont Nesbitt assessed positively the first phase of Polish-British intelligence co-operation. His farewell letter of 26th December 1941, addressed to Col. Mitkiewicz (who was to be replaced as Chief of the II Bureau by Lt-Col. Gano) expressed his appreciation for Polish Intelligence. The contents of this letter, which was communicated to the officers of the II Bureau, confirmed that the British were already receiving information from Polish outposts operating all over Europe, including the USSR and the Third Reich.[11] The Chief of the II Bureau warned, however, against too close a relationship with the British in the belief that British Intelligence intended to assume a dominating role among the Allied special services. This, in his opinion, could reduce the chances of attaining the political goals as formulated by the Polish Government. Despite such reservations, co-operation between the two intelligence services developed harmoniously, as shown by the first inter-Staff conference held at the War Office on 25th January 1941. Attended by officers specialising in German and Soviet problems, the British side was represented by Maj. Eric Birley (Head MI14(d) of German Section), Capt. Derek Tangye and Lt. Pryce-Jones (from the same Section) and Major Guy Tamplin (Head of Russian Section). The Polish participants, all from II Bureau, were Lt-Col. Ignacy Banach (Head of Research Department), Maj. Stefan Jędrzejewski (Head of Russian Section) and Maj. Jan Leśniak (Head of German Section). The conference was to deal with such issues as Order of Battle, the organisation and deployment of German units, the current state of parachute units, the economic situation, and fuel and lubricant supplies – and the same matters in relation to the USSR. This exchange of views showed how much the two intelligence services did not know, for example about the organization of Panzer divisions[12] or the parachute units.[13] During the conference it was decided not to discuss the economic situation or the supplies of fuel and lubricants. In his interesting statements Maj. Tamplin predicted that the USSR would not attack Germany in view of the weakness of the Soviet State and the decomposition of its army. On the other hand, he was of the opinion that Germany could launch a winter offensive in the east, although he did not exclude further agreements between Germany and Russia. The course of the debate showed that the British officers were interested in an exchange of information with II Bureau representatives. A report from the conference noted that 'The British spoke openly, the attitude of the participants of the conference was friendly, and the lunch which ended the conference was rather lavish'.[14] It was decided that similar meetings should be held once a month. The next one was to take place in the Rubens Hotel – Polish GHQ which included the offices of the II Bureau, PGS.

Both Intelligence services carefully monitored the German preparations for war in the east. Information from Poland indicated that initial operations had been started during the winter of 1939/1940. The Germans embarked upon the expansion and repair of communication lines – roads, rail tracks and bridges. They also began building barracks for an enlarged army, an intensive training of soldiers, and military units were brought up to full strength. In the early spring of 1940, the enemy commenced a systematic expansion of roads leading from west to east, mainly across southern Poland. In the wake of the French defeat, the Germans accelerated the construction of roads and the expansion of railway stations in the area between the Vistula and the Bug rivers. In the autumn of 1940 they concentrated on airfields and airstrips between the two rivers, and to the west of the Vistula. During the winter of 1940/1941, Polish Intelligence informed London about increased transports of war material and ammunition as well as the setting up of depots to the east of the Vistula. From the spring of 1941 mention was made of increased supplies of aerial bombs and fuel, as well as of an influx of technical personnel needed for servicing airfields. The existence of several Air Force staffs was disclosed in May 1941. Military activity grew markedly from the end of May. Transports came in from the Balkans and the west. In mid-June 1941, Polish Intelligence confirmed the presence in Poland of about 90 large military units, including between 7 and 11 armoured divisions. The size of the Air Force also grew, and Army staffs were being positioned.[15]

Information acquired by Polish Intelligence was being confirmed by other sources. At the end of February 1941, William Cavendish-Bentinck, the then chairman of the Joint Intelligence Committee (JIC), drew attention to news from Poland, namely, that the Germans were extending landing strips and strengthening their surfaces. On the basis of this information the JIC chairman commissioned a SIS advisory sub-committee to prepare a report on the possibility of a German attack against the Soviet Union.[16]

By mid-1941, co-operation between the Chief of the II Bureau and Lt. Commander Dunderdale was satisfactory. The way in which tasks and conclusions were presented indicates, that at that time the heads of British Intelligence tried to ensure a degree of autonomy for the II Bureau. A meeting held on 25th July 1941 between Gano and Dunderdale discussed the functioning of radio communications of the Ministry of Internal Affairs, the control exercised by the II Bureau over the totality of the Polish wireless network, and the use of ciphers by the VI Bureau. Both the latter and the Ministry of Internal Affairs maintained contact with Poland using II Bureau equipment and procedures. When the British Intelligence representative suggested that the II Bureau should assume total control over the 'political' communications (that is, that of the Ministry of Internal Affairs), Gano replied that 'Polish wireless communications do not pose a threat to British interests'.[17] He considered the British proposal to be unrealistic, since communications with the Home Army GHQ was overloaded with intelligence reports from Poland. The British accepted the detailed technical suggestions made by the II Bureau without any reservations.

The suggestions addressed to the II Bureau were undoubtedly linked to the outbreak of the German-Soviet war. In mid-August 1941 British Intelligence experienced serious omissions in information from its own sources. In a conversation with Maj-Gen. Bronisław Regulski, the Polish Military Attaché in London, Brig. Whitefoord declared that the War Office had no detailed information from the Eastern Front, because Gen. Frank Noel Mason-Macfarlane, Head of the British Military Mission, 'not only does not have any possibilities for visiting the front, but does not receive detailed information from the Soviet HQ in Moscow'.[18] In this situation, the War Office had at its disposal only fragmentary, individual items of information provided mainly by its military attachés in Turkey and Sweden. Brigadier Whitefoord thought that the Soviet operational situation along particular fronts could rapidly deteriorate at any moment. He did not trust the efficiency of the Red Army HQ in Moscow. He also believed that the Soviet war communiqués which appeared in the British press were suspect, since they were 'fabricated' in London by Ambassador Ivan Maysky. The War Office at the time was unfamiliar with the actual losses suffered by the belligerents. Communiqués about the fivefold superiority of the German Air Force raised serious doubts. Whiteford's conversation with Gen. Regulski has shown deep insight into the general situation at the Eastern Front and stressed the importance of defending the Leningrad region. His most favourable assessment pertained to the central section of the front, but he was anxious about the fate of the oil fields in the Caucasus. Furthermore, he admitted that he had no information about the reserves at the disposal of the Soviet Command.

The II Bureau, PGS, also did not have full knowledge of the situation in the East. On 19th June 1941, the II Bureau received from Berne (agent no. 594) information about a planned German attack against the USSR, which was expected to take place around 22nd June.[19] On 22nd June 1941 Gano reported to Gen. Sikorski that the only available source of information was radio monitoring, and presented a summary of a speech given by Viacheslav Molotov about the commencement of the war by Germany. The flow of information about the situation on the Eastern Front, from the II Bureau cells in various European states, began to increase only several days after the German attack. After a few days, British Intelligence, too, began to receive better intelligence on the situation in the east, as shown by a report which presented in detail the distribution of forces of the two warring sides and the dynamics of operations between 22nd June and 27th August 1941.[20]

The heads of the II Bureau, PGS, mobilised their intelligence sources, indicating the prime areas on which information was required, which included the war in the east. At the beginning of July 1941 Maj. Żychoń, Chief of the Intelligence Department, instructed Station 'W' in Budapest that, in addition to normal work, it should concentrate on obtaining information about the organisation of the warring armies and the course of battles conducted by armoured-motorised, Air Force and parachute units. The Station was also to seek material on the supplies, new battle measures, losses, and the morale of German, Romanian, Slovak and Hungarian units. He also wanted data on the impact of British and Soviet air raids and the attitudes in occupied countries.[21]

The war in the east increased British interest in the work of the Home Army Intelligence, as shown by numerous questionnaires, instructions, inquiries and detailed tasks sent to Warsaw *via* the VI Bureau, PGS. As for naval issues, as a rule, these were simply the translations of British questionnaires used by Naval Intelligence. British Intelligence not only tried to assign tasks, but also to explain the significance of the information it was after. In order to facilitate the work performed by Home Army agents, detailed instructions were prepared on the observation of particular ports.

During the first months following the outbreak of the German-Soviet war, the British frequently pressed for intelligence from areas adjacent to the Eastern Front. Information was requested on the whole hinterland of the German armies, from the Baltic to the Black Sea, with special emphasis on the main communication routes and staging centres. The prime task was to rapidly set up intelligence cells at those communication junctions, where land and sea transport could be observed. The greatest significance was attached to such towns as Riga, Memel, Minsk, Homel, Kiev and Dniepropietrovsk. Successive cells were to be set up in other prominent localities. The third step was to increase the density of the network of cells. The plan was to organise intelligence in the east by Polish officers trained in British centres and transported to Poland by air. This difficult and important task was efficiently fulfilled by Home Army Intelligence. The tasks for the emerging intelligence network were frequently modified. During the decisive operations along the Eastern Front the tasks allocated to Polish Intelligence were influenced by the requirements and questions forwarded by the Soviet HQ.

Home Army GHQ devoted much effort to carrying out the assignments received from London. In accordance with the wishes of the Allies, the systematic expansion of military resistance structures was accompanied by the creation of intelligence cells throughout the whole country. It must be stressed, however, that until March 1940, the organisation of Home Army Intelligence and its tasking was in Polish hands. Following the establishment of communications with the Polish authorities in Paris, intelligence work was adapted to new requirements. Because of Polish patriotism, the resistance authorities were virtually flooded with detailed information, which required supplementation and verification. Though the number of pre-war intelligence officers working for the resistance was relatively modest, methods of collecting and checking the information adapted to wartime conditions were quickly devised. Home Army intelligence network gradually began to spread beyond Polish territory. Intelligence work was carried out by Poles deported as forced labourers to the Reich and to other occupied countries. Underground organisations in POW camps also contributed to the information collected by the II Bureau of the Home Army. Information obtained from such sources was mainly on industrial production, the economic situation, the morale of the German population and, rarely, on Wehrmacht units and military installations. At the end of 1940, Home Army GHQ embarked upon creating a centrally controlled intelligence network, in accordance with the recommendations of the London-based authorities. At the same time it was decided to unify all intelligence undertakings in Poland into a cohesive whole. The offensive intelligence network called 'Lombard', created in August 1942, had the greatest range. Its principal task was to obtain information on the enemy's forces, their equipment and dislocation, as well as on the armaments industry in the Reich. Apart from systematic information about the location of German armies in the General-gouvernement and next to the Eastern Front, the greatest successes of 'Lombard' were the discovery of the secret experimental testing site in Peenemünde, the acquisition of information and material about the tests of the new V-1 and V-2 weapons, the penetration of the Focke-Wulf aircraft manufacturer, the information about the new type of Panther tank (Pz. Kpfw. V Panther), and the capture of plans of new types of submarines (Taschenuboot) from the Hamburg shipyard.[22] Alongside the Lombard network, the Offensive Intelligence Bureau of the Home Army GHQ also had a central Intelligence network known as 'Stragan' ('Marcjanna'), created at the beginning of 1941. The complicated Home Army Intelligence organisation was systematically expanded. In time, it became the best service of its kind in Europe.

From the autumn of 1941, British Intelligence frequently requested information about the situation in various ports, from the North Sea to the Baltic. After the US joined the war, the importance of naval intelligence grew considerably. Instructions asked for information on the construction of surface ships and submarines, the training of their crews and on movements in transshipment ports. Just as essential was the location of factories producing the most important parts for shipyards, in view of Allied plans to bomb such enterprises.

Intelligence on the German ports was frequently mentioned in correspondence between the Home Army GHQ and its intelligence. Tasks formulated by British Intelligence were passed on to II Bureau, where they were modified if the need arose. The next step was to transmit these tasks to the VI Bureau, which in turn relayed them to Poland by radio. In mid-September 1942, London requested the creation of a network of intelligence outposts, which were to duplicate the work performed by the apparatus supervised by the II Bureau, PGS. Home Army Intelligence was to establish two separate intelligence cells in Gdynia and Gdańsk, equipped with small radios, making it possible to send reports directly to the VI Bureau.[23] The prime purpose was to accelerate the flow of information to London. At the same time a request from British Intelligence was relayed to the Home Army: whether it would be possible for intelligence to cover the Baltic coast from Riga to Hamburg, or at least to Szczecin (Stettin). The plan was to equip the resident agents, who were to organise naval intelligence, with radios, so that they could maintain direct communications with the VI Bureau in London. This new requirement meant that it was necessary to select from among Home Army Intelligence personnel candidates for heads of intelligence cells to be set up in Vienna, Prague, Berlin, Wrocław (Breslau) and Bucharest, as well as in select towns in Italy, Denmark and Norway. The II Bureau intelligence cells were already operating in some of these towns, but it was planned to duplicate them. This requirement was justified by the fact that 'it is much more difficult to send people out from England than from Poland'.[24] Apart from appointing heads of intelligence cells, who were to be placed under the direct control of the II Bureau, the Home Army GHQ was to supply them with instructions, money and radios, to facilitate their legalisation by preparing suitable 'covers', and to provide them with identity documents.

Complying with the suggestions made by British Intelligence, and the requirements of PGS, the II Bureau organised intelligence stations in numerous parts of the world. The location of intelligence Stations and Cells was influenced by earlier contacts, the development of wartime events, and local conditions. Station 'F', established in Toulouse after the fall of France, was followed by Station 'Interallié' in Paris, both set up on the initiative of II Bureau officers who found themselves in the unoccupied zone. Meeting the requirements of British Intelligence, the II Bureau successfully built a network of intelligence cells in North Africa, supervised by Station 'Afr.', whose Chief was Maj. Mieczysław Zygfryd Słowikowski.

Co-operation between the II Bureau and US Intelligence started in the middle of 1941, clearly with the approval of the British side. This led to the establishment of a network of intelligence cells, controlled by Station 'Estezet' in New York, which stretched across North and South America. Information obtained by those cells reached American and British Intelligence via II Bureau. The exchanges of counter-intelligence information with representatives of British special services took place in South America. In view of the information requirements of both Allied intelligence services, the II Bureau, PGS, organised intelligence networks in Scandinavia, the Baltic states, Czechoslovakia, Germany, Switzerland, Italy, Belgium, the Netherlands, France, Spain, North Africa, the Balkans, Turkey and the Near and Far East. At the beginning of 1944, there were eight Stations, two Independent Intelligence Stations and thirty-three Intelligence Cells. Two Stations and eight Cells operated on the territories seized by the enemy, four Stations and seventeen Cells in neutral countries, and two Independent Cells and eight Intelligence Cells in Allied states. In addition, the II Bureau included the Radio Intelligence Service, the Intelligence School, liaison sections and Army, Air Force and Naval attachés. All together, the staff of the II Bureau consisted of 162 officers and 755 other ranks.[25] On 25th October 1943, the field operatives included 70 officers, 776 agents and 85 informants. Nine officers were arrested by foreign counter-intelligence services and two were killed. Three Intelligence officers and 34 agents were interned in POW camps. The monthly budget of the II Bureau was some £19,000, and together with subsidies from the Ministries of Foreign Affairs and National Defence, intended for military attachés and liaison missions, it exceeded £24,000.[26] These sums do not include the costs of the intelligence of the II Bureau, the Home Army GHQ.

An important breakthrough in the co-operation of the two intelligence services was achieved in France where, in addition to intelligence operations, the Poles were engaged in diversion and sabotage. Initially, significant results were delivered by Station 'Interallié', headed by Capt. Roman Czerniawski. In the autumn of 1941, the Germans uncovered the network and liquidated it. They discovered various connections with the non-ocupied zone, and this led to arrests among members of Naval Intelligence in Toulouse. Capt. Czerniawski, who was arrested, pretended to agree to collaboration with the Abwehr, and after an escape staged by the Germans, he arrived in Britain, where he revealed all the circumstances of his arrest. Subsequently, regarded as a double agent for the British, codename 'Brutus', he played an important part in the disinformation campaign, misleading German Intelligence on the eve of the invasion of the Continent. As early as June 1941, British Intelligence intended to set into motion a resistance organization, whose members were to include Polish officers present in Vichy France. This proposal led to a dispute with the II Bureau, which was anxious not to link conspiracy activities with intelligence.

Following this dispute, the task of organising resistance in France was taken over by the Special Affairs Department of the Ministry of National Defence and the Ministry of Internal Affairs. The so-called Continental Action, organised following a British request by the Ministry of Internal Affairs among the Polish community in France, was an operation on a significant scale. The Polish Organisation of Struggle for Independence (POWN – for simplicity it will be referred to in future as the Polish Secret

Army in France) 'Monika', established in France and headed by Aleksander Kawałkowski 'Hubert', not only engaged in propaganda and political diversion, but also acquired valuable information. Between mid-June 1940 and 11 November 1942, the Information Department of the Polish Secret Army in France supplied London with some 2,000 reports and dispatches containing intelligence information. The Special Affairs Department of the Ministry of National Defence, headed by Maj. Tadeusz Szumowski, carried out diversion activities and provided intelligence. The organisers of military resistance, trained in special centres in England, were parachuted into France, where they received technical and financial support. 15 such operations involving 24 parachutists were carried out in the brief period between July 1943 and August 1944.[27] The task of creating an intelligence network, which would help with preparations for the invasion, was entrusted to Capt. Władysław Ważny 'Tygrys', who in early March 1944 took over as the Intelligence Officer to the Chief of Staff of Polish Secret Army in France 'Monika'. The network continued to work until 28th August 1944, though Ważny died before this (see more: Chapter 21 on Polish Intelligence in France). Over 100 dispatches containing some 170 various reports, including 48 notes and sketches (see: Chapter 11 on the Functioning of the Intelligence Services of the Ministry of Internal Affairs and the Ministry of National Defence), were sent to London. These dispatches contained information on the distribution and movements of German forces, on coastal fortifications and on the location of unit HQs. The Department of Special Affairs of the Ministry of National Defence received 67 items of information about the location of flying bomb launch sites, 17 on the transport of such bombs and 15 describing the results of air raids against specific launch pads and depots.[28]

A picture of the trends and intensity of the information reaching British Intelligence is provided by the correspondence between the II Bureau, PGS, and Cmdr. Dunderdale. From 1st May 1941 to 1 May 1942, it was dominated by information from France and included reports from Station '300' about radio intelligence, reports from Station 'Interallié' (Capt. Czerniawski), described as Intelligence Cell 'Walenty' – Paris, a report about Maj. Żychoń's return from the United States, data on the organisation of intelligence in the Middle East, reports from Intelligence Stations 'Afr.' in Algiers and 'Estezet' in New York, news from Poland, some dozen reports from II Bureau agents, reports about the transfer of Station 'Interallié' agents to Barcelona, and news about the arrest of Capt. Czerniawski 'Walenty'. On 9 August 1941 alone, Comdr. Dunderdale received 13 documents containing II Bureau intelligence material.[29] This list shows that the II Bureau acted as an intermediary not only with respect to records, but also on organisational issues.

The Radio Intelligence Section of the Radio Centre, PGS, played a significant role in the acquisition of information on the Red Army. It employed 18 radiotelegraphists and conducted wireless monitoring. Whenever possible, it deciphered the contents of radio traffic. In November 1942, for example, it was listening in to the Soviet field and Air

Force transmissions, as well as those of the central radio station in Moscow. An average of about 44 telegrams were intercepted daily, and every tenth one was deciphered. The telegrams contained information on the organisation of Soviet Army units, battle reports of the Army and the Air Force, and data on the supplies. 8 codes and 52 cipher keys were broken in this period. In mid-November, the British authorities presented the Radio Intelligence Section with three new, American-made, National H. R. O. monitoring sets. (See Chapter VI E. Maresch).

Intelligence Station 'T' in Jerusalem, directed by the II Bureau, PGS, whose establishment was large (118 persons), conducted radio intelligence focused on the eastern Ally. Apart from its Radio Intelligence Section, it included an Intelligence Section (19 persons) and a Counter-intelligence Unit (12 persons). The Station had cells in Tel Aviv, Cairo, Tehran, Baghdad and Beirut. Its work indicated that it was being prepared for post-war activity.[30]

The II Bureau reports show that co-operation with British Intelligence included also an exchange of counter-intelligence information and reports containing intelligence material used for disinforming the enemy. In the second half of 1943 alone, 538 counter-intelligence reports and 194 reports relating to Operation 'D' reached the British.[31]

The Allies regularly assessed the work carried out by Polish Intelligence. This procedure was indispensable, since it was necessary to verify sources and make decisions on further activity. British Intelligence assessed both individual, important items of information, and also presented more complex assessments, based on the analysis of information obtained in the course of several months. Some of these assessments were relayed by the II Bureau to other interested services, in order to motivate Intelligence staff and eliminate shortcomings. One such evaluation, pertaining to the second half of 1943, reflects both the successes and the numerous faults of Polish Intelligence. All together, British Intelligence prepared 3,546 various reports on the basis of 1,407 reports presented to it by the Polish side. In comparison to the first half of the same year, this was an increase of as much as 67%. The number of reports containing strictly military and naval data grew by 29%. An even greater increase took place in the case of reports on the German Air Force (94%) and industry (163%). The number of assessments received by SIS from its various clients also grew considerably. The basic problem mentioned in numerous assessments was the great delay in the receipt of material from Poland, and especially from areas next to the Eastern Front. There were cases where reports on the organisation of particular units reached London several months after the information had been obtained. This complaint undoubtedly referred to periodic reports supplied via couriers. In the case of information on military transports, Home Army Intelligence reports were considered to be of more value than those from the II Bureau, PGS. The reports from Poland were regarded as precise and 'extremely useful'.[32] British Intelligence was critical concerning some of II Bureau agents, indicating that their information on German fortifications in Western Europe was exaggerated. Most sought-after material from Germany and Austria included the information on shipbuilding, the production of tanks and planes and the accuracy of air raids. The work of Naval Intelligence, conducted in the region of Toulon and along the Atlantic coastline, especially by French agents 'VIR' and 'Nina', both from the 'Cecile' network earned high praise. Similar opinions were expressed about intelligence in Germany, run from Poland and Sweden. The highest praise went to Polish Intelligence in Gdynia and Gdańsk. By comparison, reports from other ports appeared to be much too general and only rarely contained construction data. This is the reason why British Intelligence suggested, that Polish agents should establish contacts with sailors in such ports as Hamburg, Bremen and Kiel. British Intelligence stressed that 'wherever possible, we would like precise information about submarines under construction, the number of ships being outfitted whilst already in water, tonnage, progress made, and the scale of production'.[33] The vast demand for information about war production influenced the general assessment of II Bureau efforts in particular regions of Europe. Intelligence in France – which supplied numerous reports about motor vehicles, train engines, railway rolling stock, and the production of chemicals, aluminium, armaments, munitions and explosives – was criticised for an insufficient number of reports on aircraft production, the effectiveness of air raids, and especially the time required to repair the damaged factories or to shift production to new sites.

A survey of British assessments shows that the best work was carried out by Home Army Intelligence, which provided the most important information, meticulously prepared and supplemented by German documents or photographs. The British assessment stated that 'Industrial reports have improved considerably. We have received useful reports concerning iron, engine building, tanks and train engines as well as armaments and chemicals'.[34]

The II Bureau received good marks for information sent from Switzerland. This included data on monthly output of factories working for the Germans, for example the Oerlikon works, as well as information on new inventions in the production of incendiary bombs, flame-throwers and oxygen tanks. British Intelligence was worried, however, about the considerable fall in the number of reports on fuel production. On the other hand it highly appreciated reports on the methods used for making synthetic fuel and gas generators, which proved especially useful for the Ministry of Economic Warfare (MEW). Economic information from Scandinavia, France, Italy, Russia, Belgium, the occupied states and the German satellites was considered insufficient.

During 1944, the organisation of Intelligence Stations and Cells of the II Bureau, PGS, changed significantly due to the development of the situation in Europe, in the wake of successive German defeats at the Eastern Front and the Allied landing in Normandy. In mid-1944, the field force of the II Bureau consisted of 100 officers, 1,666 agents, 51 civilian employees, 26 privates and 10 female volunteers. In December of that year,

Stations 'Afr.' and 'F II', as well as nine Cells controlled by them, were closed. During the same period, the II Bureau suffered considerable losses: enemy counter-intelligence arrested 11 officers and 78 agents; 13 agents were executed. As the preparations for the invasion of France were undertaken, Maj. Langenfeld, Chief of the Intelligence Department, attended numerous conferences of representatives of British, French and American intelligence services. The II Bureau also carried out operations, which involved delivering money, equipment, weapons, radios, photographic equipment and food to the Continent. The direction of the work of some Intelligence Cells was modified. The 'Wschód' (East) Section of the II Bureau attempted to develop activity aimed against the Soviet Union. Station 'T' was moved to Cairo and changed its name to 'Eswu'. It now had eight Intelligence Cells located in the Middle East, Turkey and Greece, which were to carry out discreet intelligence operations against the eastern Ally. Its daily activity consisted of close co-operation with British and American Counter-intelligence in the Middle East.[35]

The II Bureau, PGS, co-operated not only with the Western Allies. For a time it also worked with Soviet Intelligence and maintained contacts with Finnish and Japanese intelligence services. Nonetheless, its co-operation with British Intelligence was of a different character, as is confirmed by statistical data illustrating the number of reports reaching other intelligence services during consecutive phases of the war, with Home Army Intelligence dominating in every respect. The total number of reports passed on to British Intelligence grew steadily: in the second half of 1940 there were 3,091 and in 1941 – 3,098. By 1942, it had already reached 9,881, and a year later there were 10,400 items of information and intelligence material. In 1944, British Intelligence received 7,351 reports. In addition, British Intelligence was in receipt of counter-intelligence reports (1,121 in 1944), as well as of information sent by Radio Intelligence unit of the II Bureau (25,510 in 1944).[36]

But the volume of information supplied was only one measurement of mutual co-operation. The tasks and detailed questions addressed to Polish Intelligence demonstrated the significance of some of the information. It is quite possible that sometimes information, which at first glance appeared to be rather unimportant, ultimately proved to be of exceptional value – especially where British Intelligence did not have any other sources of knowledge at its disposal. This appraisal is confirmed by some of the assessments made by the British partner. The contents of the monthly and individual reports by Home Army Intelligence show that it was able to penetrate many areas of the military activity of the Third Reich and its allies. The depth of this penetration was accompanied by the wide geographical scope of intelligence activity. The delays sometimes suffered in delivering the information were caused by the serious difficulties with operating in, and moving through, the Reich and the occupied countries. Not all the recipients of the information were aware of this fact. They rarely considered the obstacles encountered in the course of intelligence work, or the losses suffered by Polish Intelligence, especially in Poland itself.

Notes

1 CA MSW, VI Bureau 295/580, Note entitled 'Praca Oddziału Wywiadowczego na emigracji' (*Work of the II Bureau in Exile*) (no date), leaf 184.
2 Ibid., leaf 185.
3 More in: J. Curry, *The Secret Service 1908–1945, (MI-5)*, 1999, pp. 254–262.
4 Between 1936 and 1939, Maj. Tadeusz Szumowski was the Chief of 'Sajgon' Intelligence Cell at the Polish Legation in Stockholm, and from 19 March 1939 to 15 August 1939, chief of 'Zachód' (West) Section, the II Bureau, Polish General Staff.
5 Between 1922 and 1926, Cmdr. W. Dunderdale, RNVR, headed SIS cell in Istanbul, and between 1926 and 1940, the Station in Paris. As a result, he had excellent contacts with Polish Intelligence. F.B. Richards, *Secret Flotillas. The Clandestine Sea Lines to France and French North Africa*, London 1996, pp. 61, 107.
6 Institute of History at the Polish Academy of Sciences, call no. 93/60, A. Korejwo, *'Działalność polskiego rządu emigracyjnego' (Activity of the Polish Government-in Exile)*, account leaf 44.
7 IPMS, A.XII. 24/6c, Report of the Protection Section of the Security Department of the Chief Staff, 5 November 1945.
8 IPMS, A.XII. 24/6c, Report on the activity of the Protection Section of Defensive Intelligence at the Ministry of National Defence, 4 January 1945.
9 Archive of the Institute of the History of the Peasant Movement (further: AZHRL), Prof. Kot's Papers, vol. 80, Report no. 9 from the Captain of 'Muszkieterowie' to Supreme Commander, 13 February 1940, leaf 9.
10 SPP, file 2.3.6.1, Intelligence tasks in Poland, 9 July 1940.
11 L. Mitkiewicz, *Z gen. Sikorskim na obczyźnie (With General Sikorski in Exile)*, Paris 1968, p. 100.
12 The composition of 13 armoured divisions has not been determined precisely. It has been only ascertained that two heavy armoured divisions consisted of about 400 tanks, and the light divisions – of about 200 tanks; in accordance with their establishment, as of July 1940 and 10 February 1941, armoured divisions had on the average up to 209 combat vehicles, while the light divisions no longer existed. In 1940, they had been transformed into armoured divisions. Operation 'Barbarossa' involved 19 armoured divisions, see: T. Sawicki, *Niemieckie wojska lądowe na froncie wschodnim czerwiec 1944-maj 1945 (German Armies at the Eastern Front, June 1944-May 1945)*, Warsaw 1987, p. 84; H. Guderian, *Wspomnienia żołnierza (A Soldier's Reminiscences)*, 2nd ed., Warsaw 1991; on mistaken British calculations concerning German forces see also: *British Intelligence in the Second World War*, F. H. Hinsley, R.C. Knight, C.F.G. Ransom, C.A.G. Simkins, E.E. Thomas, vol. 3, part 1, London 1981, p. 468.
13 Reconnaissance showed that at the time the Germans deployed about 50,000 specially trained soldiers. British Intelligence did not have at its disposal information about the creation of special *Luftlandetruppen*, and assumed that only some commanders and staff officers were trained for this purpose.
14 IPMS, A.XII.24/48, Report from an inter-Staff conference with representatives of the British War Office, 25 January 1941.
15 IPMS, A.XII. 24/1, Note for Chief of the II Bureau, PGS, 12 July 1941.
16 D. Mc Lachlan, *Admiralicja. Pokój 39. Brytyjski wywiad morski w akcji 1939–1945*, Warsaw 1971, p. 279.
17 CA MSW, VI Bureau 295/580, Note from Lt-Col. S. Gano of 25 July 1941 on his talks with Lt. Commander W. Dunderdale, leaf 6–7.
18 IPMS, A.XII. 24/48, Note from Military Attaché, London, to Chief of Staff, PGS, 15 August 1941.
19 IPMS, A.XII. 24/1, Note from Lt-Col. S. Gano, Deputy Chief, the II Bureau, to Supreme C-in-C, 22 June 1941.

20 IPMS, A.XII. 42/72, Review of the Russo-German campaign between 22 June and 27 August.

21 SPP, 2. 3. 6. 2. 2, Note from Maj. J. Żychoń to the Chief of the VI Bureau, PGS, 9 July 1941.

22 This general name concealed small submarines which the Germans classified as 'Küsten-Uboote', experimental types Wa 201 (269/294 t) and Wk 202 (236/259 t), as well as vessels from the XVII (312/345 t), XXII (155/ ? t) and XXIII (234/258 t) groups. J. Lipiński, *Druga wojna światowa na morzu* (*The Second World War at Sea*), 4th ed., Gdańsk 1976, p. 723.

23 SPP, file 3.7.4.1, Ciphered dispatch to Kalina no. 3195/ tjn 41, 10th October 1941.

24 SPP, 2.3.6.2.2, Note from Lt-Col. S. Gano, the Chief, II Bureau, PGS, to Chief of the VI Bureau, 15 September 1942.

25 IPMS, A. XII. 24/56, Draft of a speech given by Chief, II Bureau, on 30 April 1944.

26 IPMS, A. XII. 24/3, Survey.

27   Members of the organisation were supplied with about 40 radio sets, 104 stens, 111 pistols, over 25,000 pieces of ammunition, about 950 pounds of explosives and approximately 100 hand grenades. Furthermore, the military organisation received 18,850,000 francs, 47,650 dollars and 48 diamonds.

28 AWIH, V/20/11, Report of Information Section, Special Department, Ministry of National Defence, leaf 20–21.

29 IJPL, Col. S. Mayer collection, kol. 100. 11/1, Mail register, II Bureau (to Dunderdale).

30 CA MSW, VI Bureau 295/577, Official note from Maj. Gaweł, to the Chief, II Bureau, PGS, on the organisation of a Radio Section in Station 'T' in Jerusalem, leaf 199.

31 IPMS, A. XII.24/37, Report on the work of the II Bureau, PGS, from 1 July 1943 to 31 December 1943.

32 IPMS, A, XII.24/37, SIS Note, l. dz. W/4017, of 4 March 1944 – Polish II Bureau. Half yearly assessment of work from July to December 1943.

33 Ibid.

34 Ibid.

35 IPMS, A. XII24/37, Report on the work of the II Intelligence Bureau, PGS, for 1944.

36 IPMS, A. XII24/37, Survey of material supplied to British War Office by the II (Intelligence) Bureau, PGS.

18

SOE and Polish Aspirations

Eugenia Maresch

There is scant information in Polish literature on the relationship of the British organisation SOE – Special Operations Executive, with the Polish Government in Exile and their Chief of Staff. Likewise, in comparison with the French or other resistance movements in Europe not much is written in English about the extent of the British involvement in sustaining the Polish Resistance. Recent releases of SOE documents (1995 & 2002) contain a great deal of new material, which revealed complex relationships, trials and tribulations on some scale. Notes, letters, memoranda and war diaries should attract historians to tackle the subject afresh and view it from different perspectives.[1]

'Honesty of purpose'
The Polish General Staff was fully aware that the underground movement was not equipped to carry out full scale operations against a modern army such as the German. The only option available was to undertake subversion warfare against the enemy. Even then, only limited acts of sabotage were possible, due to severe reprisals by the Germans. Paris, a temporary refuge for the Polish Government in exile, became a venue for clandestine talks with the British on the ways and means of helping occupied Poland.

Lt-Col. Colin McVean Gubbins RA, a member of the British Military Mission to Poland arrived four days after the war had started and hardly had time to make any joint strategic plans or form stay-behind parties that would eventually co-operate with the Polish underground movement. Back in London, Gubbins accepted the proposition made by his friend and mentor Lt-Col. J. C. F. Holland,[2] head of Military Intelligence (Research) MI(R), branch of the War Office (WO), to continue the work of the Military Mission in Paris.[3] This time, Gubbins' task was not a conventional liaison mission. He was more involved with covert activities, making tentative arrangements to assist with supplies for guerrilla warfare.[4]

Gubbins had frequent clandestine meetings in Paris with a high-ranking Polish officer Lt-Col. Stanisław Gano. At that time, he was a deputy chief of the Intelligence Service of the Polish General Staff, Oddzial II (O II), (commonly referred to by the British as 'II Bureau').[5] Between them, they shared the same sense of purpose and a friendship developed. Gubbins, in one of his letters described Gano as: 'a personal friend of mine, whom I know to be completely honest and unself-seeking; he is a soldier first and foremost, but is very intelligent – in fact the soundest man in the Polish Headquarters.'[6]

These early informal contacts dealt with immediate problems – to secure material aid to Poland, especially radio transmitters and automatic pistols. It was assumed that the British would assist to procure and deliver these limited supplies directly to Polish agents in Budapest and Bucharest via the diplomatic bag. In the first half of 1940, the shortage of arms and ammunition as well as knowledge of sabotage methods had rendered the operations sporadic and almost negligible.[7]

Gubbins soon realised that the sheer volume of supplies needed by the Poles was problematical, unless MI(R) set up its own organisation. Having established the criteria, Gubbins returned to London for negotiations, hardly expecting a series of catastrophic events, which followed. The invasion of Norway by the Germans, his subsequent service in the campaign as well as his engagement in the building up of the stay-behind Auxiliary Units in expectation of the imminent invasion of Britain by the Germans and finally, the fall of France. The next meeting with the Polish officials would be in London, the permanent home of their second exile.

'Desirable and useful'

After regrouping in London, the Polish Government had to face a new challenge – how to bring about concrete plans for co-operation with the British Services, among them Intelligence. Important matters were at hand and these needed to be presented to the British Intelligence Services which were in the process of being restructured. The machinery was convoluted with its operational divisions and sub-divisions in the Service Ministries; the Joint Planners, Chiefs of Staff and Special Services were at odds.[8]

Unaware of these changing structures and how Whitehall operated, Gen. Sikorski[9] wrote letters to CIGS (Chief of Imperial General Staff)[10] and FO (Foreign Office). General disorientation persisted, as to which channel these various requests should go. A series of meetings were eventually arranged, starting with the Prime Minister, followed by other ministerial bodies from the Foreign Office, the War Office and the newly formed MEW (Ministry of Economic Warfare).[11] All had an authoritative and instrumental role to play in setting up the infrastructure to assist the beleaguered country of Poland.[12]

The documentary evidence found in the SOE files stipulated the spheres of responsibility and the degree of subordination to the British Secret Intelligence Service.[13] There was also the question of interdependence of the Polish Intelligence Services, which also needed restructuring. These matters were discussed at the Conference, held on 29 June 1940 between Gano, representing the II Bureau, together with Col Smoleński[14] in charge of the VI Bureau Polish General Staff (Polish Intelligence Services), took on the two MI(R) officers – Lt-Col. Holland and Maj. Wilkinson. Gano began with a statement that it was Gen. Sikorski's wish that both these organisations should be closely linked with the corresponding British departments and asked Holland to facilitate this.

It was agreed that the II Bureau, would be put directly in touch with SIS to whom all intelligence would be transmitted direct. Information with reference to diverse activities was to be controlled by the special branch of the VI Bureau.[15] There were proposals to establish a station in Cairo, equipped with a radio transmitter to be in direct contact with the Polish underground movement as well as London HQ.

Captain A. Douglas Dodds-Parker[16] was posted to Cairo as a GSOII, to co-ordinate Polish activities in the Balkans. It would be through him, that MI(R) the War Office and the British General Staff was briefed. Thus, the hierarchical structure of power and influence was devised. Nevertheless, these initial appointments were fluid and liable to change.

MI(R) prepared their own report, laying down long and short-term policies of co-operation with the Poles. Dated 17 July 1940, it recognised the possibility of a major rising in Poland and to this end, they would endorse a close contact with their counterpart, the Polish II Bureau. The British Intelligence in the East European countries functioned within the passport control office of diplomatic missions, which were closed down due to war. To substantiate these inherent difficulties, the Polish proposition of co-operation was keenly accepted. The report also acknowledged the pressing need to improve and set up communication lines for supplies of arms and equipment as well as the training of agents. The short-term policy recommended immediate action to stop Germany's transfer of crude oil and other goods from the Balkans. Above all, the report advocated British assistance to the Poles in supplying them with all necessary sabotage material, to facilitate transit of Polish agents from Poland to their fields of operation.[17]

Maj. Desmond Morton, Churchill's private adviser and confidante was responsible for bringing the two respective sides together. On 23 September 1940, Sikorski raised six current problems with Churchill. Each was substantiated by Aides Memoire; the first points at issue were the supply of arms for the Polish Forces, the financial terms and provision of monies and the fate of the Polish gold. The recruitment via Canada of the Poles living in USA and the question of equipment for the Polish Division. Last of all, the 'agreement', which would formulate the policy on which, the Intelligence Services of the two states would work together.[18]

Three days later, at a separate meeting on 26 September 1940, of the heads of both Secret Intelligence Services, the British (SIS) run by Col. Stewart Menzies known as 'C' and Col. Leon Mitkiewicz[19] as Chief of the II Bureau met. Mitkiewicz in the absence of Smoleński, represented all Polish

Intelligence Services, military and civil, or better termed, political intelligence service, emanating from several political parties finding themselves under the umbrella of the Ministry of Interior run by Prof. Stanisław Kot.[20]

For the British authorities, this structure sounded complex and not very secure. They would have to deal with several individual Polish agencies such as: the military Intelligence information gathering, the civil and political Intelligence not only from Poland but other countries as well as the courier traffic.

Matters did not improve by creating yet another body – the Special Operations Executive (SOE), an organisation responsible for covert activities. However, this created another impulse for further discussions. Hugh Dalton, head of MEW, consulted Gen. Sikorski about Gubbins' new post with SOE, which was to be responsible for special operations and training, as well as matters related to Poland. The appointment was well received by the Polish General Staff. Maj. Perkins, who was also known to the Poles from the pre-war period, was going to be the head of the Polish Section (MP).

Menzies was adamant that individual Polish agencies were not to approach SIS direct, as it had no means of finding out which they represented. All requests for facilities were to be channelled via the II Bureau. Moreover, Menzies feared that the open acts of sabotage would endanger the long-term Intelligence plans.

At one stage, there was an attempt by the Director of Military Intelligence, Maj-Gen. Frederik G. Beaumont-Nesbitt at the War Office, to subordinate Kot's political Intelligence Service to the II Bureau, but apparently Sikorski was against it as he stipulated that the II Bureau was involved with information alone, while Kot's department carried out policies of the Polish Government in exile to the Poles in Poland.[21]

An additional meeting was held at Rubens Hotel, which was requisitioned for the Polish Government as its HQ. It was to formulate the policy of Anglo-Polish co-operation. Present, were the three invited British officers, Gubbins, Wilkinson and Perkins. Gen. Sikorski, the Polish Prime Minister and Commander-in-Chief, attended with Kot the Minister of Interior and Gen. Sosnkowski,[22] Commander-in-Chief of the newly formed Home Army. Gen. Sikorski outlined the structure of the organisation in Poland, whose political delegate he was to appoint separately.

His immediate and pressing problem, was the state of the partially dismembered army in Poland, which had to be re-grouped and re-armed. Its fate and its actions were entrusted to the then named Union of Armed Struggle – the Home Army (Związek Walki Zbrojnej – Armia Krajowa), at GHQ in London headed by Gen. Sosnkowski. The effectiveness of the Home Army depended on military considerations. It had its own structure of four territorial commands in German occupied Poland and two in the Russian occupied Polish territory. The inner cadre consisted of reliable men numbering approximately 3,500 officers and 48,000 other ranks. Not counting the first reserve, which would probably double the other ranks of loyal men to be trusted with clandestine tasks, only 35,000 of the total had small arms or ammunition. Apart from the Home Army, there were sabotage groups working under their direction in collaboration with the Trade Unions in most industrial towns.[23]

Prof. Kot tried to emphasise his prerogative of dissemination of propaganda material via the radio, press and leaflets. He raised matters relating to subversion the setting of safe routes and reception centres for the couriers and other agents.

Another suggestion was made, although not innovative – to utilise the vast number of Polish immigrants settled at the turn of the century, mainly in France and Belgium. There was also a substantial number of Poles trapped in Romania and Hungary. Kot was enthusiastic and quite determined to form some sort of clandestine civilian organisation for active anti German operations in those countries. Likewise, over a million Poles working for the German economy as a forced labour could be used for that purpose.[24]

Gubbins was keen to grasp the necessities of this irregular political organisation; it interested him, whether it extended over Russia as well as German occupied Poland. As an experienced MI(R) officer, he was aware of the for need co-ordination the political and military demands placed on them by the Poles. Dalton, in a letter to Churchill of 12 November 1940, put the problem in a nutshell:

> It was at once clear to me that, what was really needed was a first rate liaison officer who would know not only Kot's secrets and plans but also those of the Polish Military. The point, which I need not elaborate unduly, is that Kot is Sikorski's protégé, but is not on good terms with a number of other Poles, including Sosnkowski. For a reason the whole matter requires the most delicate and skilful handling, unless all the wires are to be hopelessly crossed and general effort impeded. Fortunately my own personal relations with the Poles have been good, much better than their relations with one another'.[25]

Inauspiciously, matters in France took a turn for the worse and Churchill, in his dark moods, expressed dissatisfaction with the volume or quality of information coming from SIS. He demanded to know to what extent foreign agents were being used. Morton, as his personal Intelligence adviser, took the brunt of Churchill's wrath and arranged a series of meetings.

The SIS and the II Bureau became an unlikely partnership where the Poles would participate and collude with the British, to further the cause of the war as far as that may be 'desirable and useful'.[26]

'The Fourth Arm'
Attached to a memorandum submitted by Dalton to Chiefs of Staff (COS) on 20 August 1940, was an Annex entitled *Probable state of readiness and ability of certain countries to rise against the Nazi Regime.*[27] In it, he stated that there was no likelihood of any serious rising against the Nazis in

Germany itself. On Poland, he was more optimistic, predicting that by March 1941, there may not be enough arms and materials to merit a general rising, but none of the countries, except possibly Poland and Czechoslovakia were likely, from its own resources to be in a position to initiate a rising on an effective scale. Even then, such uprisings were likely to be brought about as a result of carefully laid plans and assisted by Great Britain.

It must be stressed that Sosnkowski kept Dalton fully informed on the passive resistance in Poland, he talked about intelligently directed propaganda and about the conditions of everyday life. In fact at the time of writing the memorandum, Dalton was receiving information of successful sabotage carried out against stores and depots of munitions and food supplies for the Germans.[28]

Dalton's and the Chiefs of Staff's main concern however was that these spontaneous acts might develop into a premature national rising, which would be disastrous if not co-ordinated and backed up by the Allies' major operations. Sikorski and his Chiefs of Staff initially expressed these sentiments on several occasions.[29] Dalton was aware that the Polish Home Army was not an offshoot of SOE as it took its orders from the Polish Government in exile. By their orders, only subversive activities on Polish territory were allowed to take place, which would not bring mass reprisals by the Germans on the Polish population.

The British Government had no control over the Polish policy or radio communications for that matter. True, the Poles were part of SOE through the Polish Section (MP), which acted as intermediary between COS and Polish Chief of Staff. The Poles were dependent on SOE's administrative services, the provision of arms, explosives, training facilities and most of all air support for Poland.

The Polish government literally took the meaning of the original SOE charter as a beacon of hope. Like Dalton's faith in the power of the 'Fourth Arm', they kept reminding the British of that view. They believed, that since the SOE was responsible for Polish affairs, sufficient power should have been vested in SOE by the British, vis-à-vis other Ministries, to ensure that all Polish requests for help were met.

'Polish pride' and the Treasury
The method of financing the Polish Intelligence Service and its diverse operations was very important to the British. No matter what course of action was desirable, the British were in no position to issue orders to the Polish Government. They had to resort to persuasion and what ever pressure they could exert through financial control. Wilkinson, in one of his comprehensive reports referred to the attitude taken by Gen. Sikorski, that, to ensure credit was given to the Polish nation, the Polish Government had to be financially independent. Wilkinson refers to it as the 'Polish pride', of which, he personally was not overtly concerned, but about the relationship with the Poles, which was already delicate and depended largely on personal contacts if certain objectives were to be achieved.[30]

According to the 1940 Anglo-Polish Finance Agreement, known as the Polish Military Credit, an initial lump sum of £5 million was available to the Polish Government, primarily for the upkeep of all Polish Armed Forces abroad. However, it was arranged between the War Office and the Treasury that expenditure on Intelligence could best be dealt with outside the lump sum. A Protocol dated 25 February 1941 contained a separate arrangement, which was to be revised annually.[31]

A Most Secret note to the Treasury revealed more information on this particular subject. Rear Adm. John H. Godfrey RN, Director of Naval Intelligence in the Admiralty, expressed a desire to use the services of the Polish Navy Intelligence unit and suggested that the running costs be paid by the British whilst the overheads like salaries would be the liability of the Polish Naval Staff. In August, Sikorski confirmed the arrangement by requesting the Treasury to advance to Adm. Jerzy Świrski a sum not exceeding £75,000 per year commencing 1 June 1940. It was to be regarded, as a 'book debts' owed to the British Treasury, to be recovered after the war.[32]

The Polish II Bureau was functioning on a separate budget. It had to be 'invited' to obtain the consent of 'C'. Once approved, funds went straight from the Treasury into the Lloyds Bank branch at Pall Mall.[33]

Similarly, the budget for the military and political activities in Poland, executed through the VI Bureau, was sanctioned sometimes by 'C', other times by SOE (Col. J. F. Venner, Finance Director) who administered it and passed onto Wacław Mohl, Financial Director at the Polish Embassy. The first payment to the VI Bureau, advanced by WO through SO2, for urgent assignments in 1940, was 100,000 dollars. This sum was later credited to SOE as soon as formalities were completed.

One of 'C''s notes of approval, stated: 'I have examined the request and in view of the valuable information which has been produced (by far the best of any of our Allies), I consider that, if feasible, the demand should be met'.

Partial documentation reveals that the total budget for 1942 amounted to 7.5 million US dollars. This encompassed expenses of four million for the organisation, the underground movement arms, ammunition, couriers, ransom etc. while 3 million for propaganda, diversion, sabotage, and 500,000 for Intelligence work. Transactions were made in foreign currency, usually in US dollars or gold, which the Treasury had difficulty in getting hold of. It had to resort to clandestine purchases in Stockholm, Lisbon, Zurich or Jerusalem, by discreet approaches to Jewish organisations in Great Britain.

After the death of Sikorski in 1943, the Military Credit was duly revised, likewise, the Protocol, which dealt with the 'Secret Votes' of individual Intelligence Stations. As the war developed, new factors played their part. Changes had to be made regarding the 'Big Scheme' project, involving transport sabotage on the railway lines leading towards the Eastern Front. Initially, SOE supported financially up to $2/3$ of the cost of operations and $1/3$ was covered out of Polish Credit. This scheme ceased to function fairly soon, without much spending, due to advancing Russian

Army to the West. The other new expenditure which had to be integrated into the 'Secret Vote', was that of the Polish Ministry of Defence, which had to take care of the evacuation of the Poles.[34]

On receiving the combined preliminary budget for 1945, the Treasury and the Foreign Office were perturbed, not necessarily because it was outside the scope of the existing credit limit, but the worsening situation of the Polish–Russian relations which was a big issue for the British. Revision of policies and agreements were called for. The Cabinet decided to postpone the signature for the Military Supplies and only just approved the Air Force Agreement on the intervention of Churchill.[35] The tide for Poland has already ebbed, and the 'Polish pride' had to be swallowed yet again.

Collateral Source of Military Intelligence

Unlike the II Bureau which had direct contacts with the British SIS through Cmdr. Wilfred Dunderdale (P4 then P5, in 1944 SLC),[36] the Polish Section (MP) of SOE had a different role to play. It acted for two distinct Polish authorities: the Polish General Staff for military matters, building up supplies in support of the Home Army, as well as with subversion and sabotage. The other was the Polish Government, acting through the Ministry of Internal Affairs linking London with political organisations in Poland. The Ministry had another responsibility towards the Poles who happened to be in all parts of Europe outside Poland. They were involved with another section of SOE, called European Polish Minorities – EU/P. Later, operational responsibilities notably in France and the Balkans, were transferred from the Interior Ministry to the Ministry of Defence of the Polish Government.

Polish Intelligence information coming from the military or political sources in Poland was incorporated into vast number of messages which were sent from far and wide to the Polish Radio Centre in Stanmore, North London. These messages were transmitted in two different codes, one for the II Bureau and the VI Bureau. Once registered, they were sent by telegraph-printer to the Polish Cipher Office in London. They were segregated according to their codes, de-ciphered, translated and dispatched to the recipients. Information of interest to SIS and SOE would be passed onto them by the II Bureau and the VI Bureau, respectively.

In general, intelligence destined for the Polish Ministry of Interior was incidental and if it was of interest to SOE, it was conveyed to them. The Ministry had a Central Bureau run by an individual seconded from the Polish Foreign Ministry, named Jan Librach.[37] He was instrumental under Minister Kot's directives, in creating an operation called 'Continental Action', in which the EU/P Polish Minorities was functioning. Librach was very liberal in dispensing important bits of information in exchange for small favours, from the Americans. SOE was aware of the situation but did not take him to task, in fact, they did not object.

Another means of gathering Intelligence was through carefully organised operations. The precursor of Anglo-Polish operations in France was 'Adjudicate'. It lasted from September 1941 to February 1942 and was led by Lt. Teodor Dzierzgowski (Nurmi). His sizeable network of 180 agents unfortunately was compromised. Nevertheless, 'Adjudicate' became a template for future SOE operations, such as 'Monika' which brought important intelligence on the locations of V1 and V2 rockets.[38]

There were also successes in Anglo-Polish co-operation, such as establishing overland communications for couriers and Polish escapees, who were forcibly drafted into the German Army and served in the Balkans. New escape routes were set up in Romania, Serbia and Albania, all leading towards the Italian port of Bari. Operations 'Harbourne', 'Polaxe' and 'Workroom' were managed by Lt. Col Patrick Howarth of SOE and Lt-Col. Mercik of the VI Bureau, both based in Cairo. Operation 'Harbourne' claimed the life of Lt. Józef Maciag (alias John Nash) in December 1943. Operation 'Polaxe' with Capt. Alfred Link, had bad experiences with local partisans. While Lt Michał Gradowski (alias Michael Lis), who was parachuted into Albania as part of operation 'Workroom', had to contend with Albanian guerrillas. Polish evaders became a rich source of intelligence information for the British.[39]

Relations with the Soviets and FO

While co-operation with the Americans was understandable for the Poles, similar aspects of 'sharing' Polish intelligence with the Soviets, which was undertaken by the British, was totally abhorrent to them. Perkins was sure that a very considerable quantity of Polish information was passed to the Russians, as almost they alone would benefit from it.[40] There was however, an understanding between the Russians and SOE that Poland was a British commitment and liasing with the Home Army was their sole responsibility.

With the growth of Soviet supremacy, allegations were made that both Polish Intelligence Services of the General Staff and Ministry of Internal Affairs lacked co-ordination, that their policies conflicted and quite probably, the material sent to Poland intended to be used against the Germans was used against the Soviets. Clearly, the British closely watched the Polish Ministry for every slight deviation to act as a pretext to tighten the reigns on the new Polish government and subordinate the rest of its Intelligence Services.

To convince the FO of the importance of keeping supplies to Poland at all cost, Gubbins wrote a note to Frank Roberts (FO). He reminded him of earlier directives of Gen. Sikorski and his Chiefs of Staff soon after the commencement of the German Campaign against the Soviet Union. Enclosing a long list of sabotage, faithfully carried out by the Poles, he referred to it as the outward sign of assistance, which the people of Poland were affording the Allies including the USSR. He assured Roberts that other independent reports received in London confirmed his perception that these acts of bravery played deeply on the morale of the Germans. Gubbins exposed the fact of obtaining vast amount of operational intelligence from Poland – has always been at the disposal of the Russians and Allied Staffs.[41]

It was an impressive list of mass damage or destruction of the railway system covering the period from June 1942 to January 1943: 1,268 locomotives, 3,318 railway trucks and coaches, 76 railway transports set on fire, 25 derailments, 90 interruptions caused in railway traffic, 7 bridges destroyed, 148 points cut, 22 assorted damages and 2 railway workshops set on fire. A list of industrial sabotage was just as impressive.[42]

Oddly enough, Gubbins picked up this subject again after the war. While preparing a report for Lord Selborne, he sought Perkins' opinion on the accuracy of the information regarding railway sabotage. Perkins' reply was a fitting accolade to Anglo-Polish collaboration:

> We have never been able to check the actual figures of derailments etc. The figures mentioned in the statement conform to the totals, which we compiled from individual reports received from Poland. At one time, the figures were so high that I accused the Poles of destroying more locos than ever existed in Poland. They stuck to their figures however. Personally I believe them to be correct, and though it may be dangerous to mention concrete facts and figures, without them the magnitude of the action cannot be assessed, and we can also rest assured that there is no evidence in existence to refute them.[43]

On 25 March 1942 a proposal was submitted by SOE to the Defence Committee that a directive should be given to the Polish Secret Army requesting them to sabotage German lines of communications through Poland to the Eastern Front. This was known by SOE as the 'Big Scheme'. It was proposed in spite of the fact that during the winter 1941/2, not more than a few tons of explosives for sabotage purposes had been delivered to Poland. There were doubts, at least in London about the success of this daring operation.

In spite of these circumstances, during the summer of 1942, the Home Army attacked bridges and German lines of communications as far as Minsk.[44] A message dated 20 October arrived in London informing the Polish Chiefs of Staff that as an experiment, an agent (Cichociemny)[45] trained by SOE in England for a specific sabotage, was despatched to Poland on a mission to disconnect simultaneously seven railway lines passing through Warsaw (Operation Wieniec).[46] This was accomplished on six lines on 8 October, causing considerable traffic confusion, which had a direct bearing on the operations on the Eastern Front. Other acts were to follow. A document listing substantial list of sabotage over the period of two months was sent by Hambro ('CD') to Lord Selborne with an additional comment: 'At last we reap the benefit of one's labours and our training, even though they are at present limited.'[47]

Support of a kind for the Polish war effort, was shown by the Foreign Office in May 1943. It concerned the Soviet Government's complaints about Poland's attitude towards the incitement to active resistance in Poland.[48] Alexander Cadogan brought this confidential news to Gubbins' attention, after a FO meeting. According to the British Ambassador in Moscow, Sir

Archibald Clark Kerr, it may have been Stalin's wish to settle now the problem of the eastern front, or it could have been his urge to provoke changes in the Polish Cabinet.

To overcome any apparent divergence of views between London and Moscow, a meeting at the FO was chaired by Sir Orme Sargent, Permanent Under Secretary of State FO. A note was prepared for the Ambassador not intended for passing on to the Russians, but merely to put him in the picture when he saw Stalin personally. It followed that the British in collaboration with the Poles, were working together towards a directive layed down by the Chiefs of Staff that disruption of Germany's communications was the best assistance the Poles could give.[49]

The Ambassador was also instructed to hand over samples of Polish reports, (confirmed previously by the British as authentic), which would prove that the Polish Government-in-Exile has built up in Poland an extremely efficient organisation. There followed a statement: 'The Polish resistance movement, is certainly the most effective and best controlled of all such allied movements it is in our view important that it should not be sacrificed to Soviet short-term designs or become a pawn in Polish-Soviet political dispute.'[50]

In spite of this, the relations between the Poles and the Soviets in the second half of 1943 detoriated and consequently became problematical for the British. Very limited support was shown for subsequent Polish requests for help. While acknowledging the need to sabotage the German communications as of prime importance, the COS held a different view of the supply of equipment to the Secret Army for organised military action.[51]

Relations with COS
The Polish contribution to the wide field of operations undertaken by SOE depended largely on circumstances of the war, which were beyond their control. The Polish Government may not have been aware of the contents of a document discussed at COS's meeting on 25 November 1940. The Chiefs of Staff's paper was prepared with a view to guide SOE, in how it could apply the offensive strategy in Europe and elsewhere. A laborious piece of writing, entitled *Subversive Activities in Relation to the Strategy*. In very simplistic terms, it gave instructions how to create economic disorganisation and dislocation of communications, whilst at the same time maintaining the national spirit and passive resistance. It defined those areas where subversive activities would help British strategy or interfere with that of the enemy. Against this background, priority was attached to interference with communications in Northern France, Belgium and Holland. The second priority was the preparation for eventual operations in Tunisia, Sicily and Southern Italy. A third priority included Southern Norway, Brittany and South-West France. Poland was not even mentioned.[52]

Ever since the Polish Section was established in December 1940, the outstanding problem, which blighted this section throughout the war, was air communications. It was slightly alleviated by a promise of three Halifax aircraft attached to 138 Squadron (RAF), but Sikorski complained that it was an unsatisfactory arrangement and asked in a letter to the CAS of 2 October 1941 for at least twelve aircraft, complete with Polish crews and ground staff as a basic requirement. Gubbins supported the idea of the formation of a separate Polish flight, he thought the Poles would make a great success of it. However, the Air Ministry on account of limited resources rejected it.[53]

COS imposed limitations. They did not feel that at this stage of the war, the Polish Secret Army was worth a squadron of 12 aircraft. On 1 June 1942, the Polish Government put forward to SOE their detailed proposals for operations during 1942/3 to commence as soon as the nights were long enough to permit flights to Poland. Adverse weather conditions or technical difficulties or reluctance on the part of the Air Ministry who had other priorities in mind continually dogged these operations.

Gubbins, whilst disclaiming any wish to criticise the COS, felt, like the Poles, that in view of the strategic importance of the work in Poland and the sacrifice which the Poles were making to the common cause, they were perhaps entitled to more support than the British were giving them at the time. It was impossible for SOE to argue the point, and interfere with the Air Ministry's supreme task (as expressed by Air Chief Marshal Harris) – 'to sustain the battle waged by Bomber Command, which might prove decisive, if the support aircraft is drawn away from the resources by less essential calls.'[54]

It was a bitter disappointment for the Polish Government to accept the Air Ministry's ruling, that the support of their indomitable resistance should be accorded a lower priority than the bombing offensive, especially as the successes of the Polish airmen in the Battle of Britain was so vividly fresh in their memory. The truth unfortunately was that these requests lay entirely outside SOE jurisdiction. SOE was in no position to dictate to the Air Ministry or any other Service for that matter.

A statistical review of air operations to Poland from the UK and Italy, from its inception on 15 February 1941, until the last operation on 28 December 1944, indicate that there were 731 sorties with the loss of 58 aircraft, out of which 366 were successful. The total number of personnel sent to Poland amounted to 344, with the loss of eight. Supplies were vital and SOE was often the only source. Official statistics on this subject reveal that 666 tons of weapons was dropped into Poland throughout the war. It greatly contrasts with 10,000 tons sent to France and an astonishing 18,000 tons into Yugoslavia.[55]

The Poles observed a visible change in strategy after the death of Sikorski, in the second half of 1943. Relations with COS became more tense after discovering that the Polish Chief of General Staff went over their heads with a request for help to the Combined Chiefs of Staff in Washington, (through Col. Mitkiewicz). SOE was visibly upset when they learnt about a request from Gen. Sosnkowski, then Polish Commander-in-Chief, to Gen. A. Brooke CIGS, on three vital matters. First, employing the Polish Corps in one formation for future engagements, second the necessity for preparing the Polish Home Army for offensive operations.

The third request was in fact a change in principle, that operational problems concerning the Polish Home Army, should be the subject of direct talks between British and Polish Chiefs of Staff, and that they should not be the responsibility of SOE.[56] The reaction to all these requests was negative.

On 24 September 1943 the Combined Chiefs of Staff reaffirmed their previous decision – not to engage the Home Army in any plans in connection with 'Overlord' and recommended no military equipment for the planned general insurrection. CCOS's arguments were given as lack of assurance by the Allies that they would arrive in time to relieve the Home Army and that the airlift of 73 thousand men was beyond their present resources.[57] Finally, SOE was directed to present a revised plan for Poland, solely for the increase of supplies of sabotage material and adequate allocation of the aircraft.[58]

Furthermore, SOE was apprehensive of Stanisław Mikołajczyk the new Prime Minister and his ability to control such communications with Poland, whether through military or civil channels. How changeable was this opinion, is reflected in the report entitled: 'Internal Polish Control of the Home Army'. At the FO meeting, chaired by Assistant Under Secretary FO Sir William Strang, and attended by Perkins and Sir Owen O'Malley, (British Ambassador to Poland), further drastic measures were taken against the Poles.[59] It fell onto SOE to stand firm and repudiate an accusation expressed at a COS meeting, that the air containers with ammunition destined for Poland were dropped to a compromised Home Army (AK) reception committee. Perkins reiterated that under the existing control and existing personnel of the VI Bureau, SOE had a reliable and smooth organisation upon which they could rely. As an example, he indicated that a Reception Committee would meet every aircraft despatched to Poland, furthermore, the whole business of reception, collection and dispersal of material and money would be arranged in a most efficient manner. Whereas the civilian authorities responsible for underground action had proved themselves not nearly so efficient.[60]

The unpleasant duty of stricter control of the contents of the containers to Poland fell upon the SOE. Packed by the British with arms and ammunition material, they were unlikely to hold messages, although as stated in the COS report, packages with the official diplomatic seal found in the containers remained untouched and their contents unknown.[61] Strang, however, had no reservation about giving a red light to Mikołajczyk, suggesting certain pretexts for the approach. SOE depended for political guidance on the Foreign Office, accordingly, representations were made to the Central Department but in reality it was a signal for the FO to start the process of dismantling the power of the Government in exile, and with it the influence of SOE upon it.

Ever since the Tehran Conference, the British were hoping for better relations between the Poles and the Soviets. Their only hope was to promote collaboration between the Home Army, the Red Army and partisans on Polish territory. As an inducement, the British government wanted something tangible to assure the Soviets that the Poles did not foster anti-Soviet or pro-German activities in Poland. However, they could not prove it, as they had no control over communications between the Poles. The Polish government, was alone among the Allied Governments in Britain who managed their own wireless stations and their own ciphers. Although SOE provided the transmission facilities, they did not hold the Polish codes and could not read their messages, which the British only suspected to be anti-Russian in nature.[62]

The War Cabinet Office (WCO), together with FO, COS and SIS, with the visible exception of SOE, favoured one option but did not know how to induce the Polish authorities to deposit copies of their ciphers while allowing them to keep their own wireless stations which could not give a firm guarantee to the Russians that the Poles were sending no instructions to Poland of which the British were not aware. Nor could they check that the despatches of messages in diplomatic ciphers and bags to neutral capitals were retransmitted to Poland.

Another matter that weighed down the Polish Government at the beginning of 1944 was the accusation by the Defence Committee that the Polish clandestine political movement, which was under the control of the Minister of Interial Affairs was to some degree penetrated by the Germans. This was caused by the apparent loss of radio transmitters, seized by the Germans. The Minister of Internal Affairs Władysław Banaczyk asked Lord Selborne for replacements. Further investigations proved the networks were intact and useable. Nevertheless, the FO, WCO and COS were invited to give an opinion prior to Churchill's consent. The request for the radio transmitters, according to Roberts, was to be conditional. The Polish reaction was not recorded, but feelings must have been high as the radios were of Polish design and manufacture (with American and British parts).

Documents reveal that members of the SOE Polish Section were also involved in censoring the outgoing messages from London. As expected, this abhorrent decision had devastating consequences during the Warsaw Uprising and after, when the Polish Government could not freely communicate with their own people. Sir Alexander Cadogan had doubts about the Russians and knew that the possession of Polish ciphers by the British would not stop Stalin's suspicions nor would he be likely to accept assurances about the goodwill of the Home Army. In his opinion it was 'an insulting demand to address to a loyal ally'.[63]

With the Red Army advancing into Poland, it was imperative to the British to keep the stranglehold on all clandestine and official activities of the Polish Government-in-Exile.[64] Dark clouds were gathering over Poland.

Notes

1   D. Dilks, *Epic and Tragedy. Britain and Poland 1941–1945*, Hull, 1996. Published also as an essay in *Dzieje Najnowsze* in Poland, 1996; E.D.R. Harrison, *The British Special Operations Executive and Poland. The Historical Journal*, 43, 4 (2000), Cambridge University Press.

2   J.F.C. (Jo) Holland RE, DFC, Col. later Maj-Gen., assigned to the War Office GS(R)

General Staff (Research) wrote a secret report for DCIGS on the possibility of providing British support for insurgency in any country of Eastern Europe overrun by the German Army, joined MI(R), produced various reports on irregular warfare with Gubbins as deputy.

3 Holland and Gubbins on the instigation of the Director of MI(R), Maj. F. G. Beaumont-Nesbitt, worked together just before the war on most secret instructions by the Chief of Imperial General Staff (CIGS), under the auspices of D section of the Secret Intelligence Service (SIS), on the sabotage and subversive actions aiming at the Axis powers.

4 W.J.M. Mackenzie: *The Secret History of SOE Special Operations Executive 1940–1945*, London 2000, chapter III p. 44.

5 Stanisław Gano (1895–1968) Lt-Col., studied in Moscow, took part in 1918–20 Russo-Polish war, since 1924 Intelligence Officer (1928), Military Attaché in Helsinki (1933–1935), chief of Technical Section of the II Bureau in Warsaw (1939), Chief of Polish II Bureau (1941–1946).

6 TNA(PRO) HS 4/325, M/PD/80, note from Gubbins to Sir Frank Nelson, CD, Operational Head of SOE dated 10 Jan. 1941, gives characteristics of Gano and Kot.

7 P.A. Wilkinson and J. Bright Astley: *Gubbins and SOE* (1993), The MI(R) Mission in Paris chapter 7 p. 46.

8 F.H.Hinsley: *British Intelligence in the Second World War: From the outbreak of war to Spring 1940*, Vol. 1 chapter 3 p. 89 (1979).

9 Władysław Sikorski (1881–1943) Gen., Polish Prime Minister in exile from 1939, Commander in Chief, Minister of Military Affairs.

10 TNA(PRO) FO 371/24472, C6832 note from Maj. Gen. Beaumont-Nesbi-t DMI of the War Office to G. Jebb of FO dated 1 May 1940.

11 Ibid., PREM 7/6 note from Desmond Morton Churchill's Security Adviser dated 26 Sept. 1940 to Minister Dalton, advising him to make arrangements with Kot's organisation (MSW).

12 The inter-departmental bodies, which dealt with economic intelligence, created in September 1939 a single department the Ministry of Economic Warfare (MEW), which had its own Intelligence Branch, with Morton as its head. The Branch had in turn two departments: Blockade Intelligence servicing everyday activities and Economic Warfare Intelligence whose aim was to provide Intelligence for the Services and other agencies of the British Government.

13 TNA(PRO) HS 4/194, note on meeting of Colonels: Lt-Col. Kwieciński, Col. Smoleński, Lt-Col. Gano, Lt-Col. Holland and Maj. Wilkinson on 29 June 1940 at the MI(R) War Office subject: initial arrangements for the Polish Intelligence activities. Document revealed that the first SIS-II Bureau meeting took place on 22 June 1940.

14 Marian Józef Smoleński (1894–1978) Col. Commander 2nd Lancers Regiment. Chief of the II Bureau of the General Staff (February–September 1939), Chief of the VI Bureau General Staff (1940–41).

15 Hinsley, vol.1 ch.9, p.276–7, the Polish Gov. agreed to hand over to the SIS all the intelligence that it gathered, except that dealing with Poland's internal affairs. As from January 1941, the II Bureau became the sole link for passing this information and for receiving British requests for information.

16 A. Douglas Dodds-Parker, GG (1909) Col. employed on special duties in 1940, mission commander for SOE, served in North Africa, France and Italy, Col. in 1944.

17 TNA(PRO) HS 4/194, report dated 17 July 1940 on MI(R) activities in connection with the Poles, stating short and long term policy, on the lines of communication with Poland.

18 TNA(PRO) PREM 7/3 and 7/6, notes by Desmond Morton to Prime Minister Churchill dated 26 Sept. 1940, informing him of an agreement between two heads of Intelligence Services – Menzies (SIS) and Mitkiewicz (II Bureau). (no written

agreement was found).

19 Leon Mitkiewicz (1896–1972) Col., Chief of II Bureau in 1940–1941, Deputy Chief of Polish General Staff, Chief of Polish Military Mission to the Combined Chief of Staff in Washington (1943–1945).

20 Stanisław Kot (1885–1975) Prof., historian, in 1940–1941 Minister of Internal Affairs, Polish Ambassador to Moscow (1941–1942), Minister of Information and Documentation (1943–1944).

21 TNA(PRO) HS 4/325 note from Sir Frank Nelson (CD) to Gladwyn Jebb (Executive Director SOE) dated 14 Oct. 1940; HS 4/326, extract from a note on meeting with Prof. Kot and Prof. Namier, 11 Nov. 1940.

22 Kazimierz Sosnkowski (1885–1969), Gen. An army inspector in 1939, GOC Southern Front in September 1939. In France Commandant-in-Chief of the Polish Home Army, from 8 July 1943– 30 September 1944: Supreme C-in-C Polish Armed Forces.

23 TNA(PRO) HS 4/325, M/PD/11/MX, note on meeting between Sikorski, Sosnkowski, Kot, Gubbins and Wilkinson at the Polish General Staff on 6 Dec.1940; HS/4/136 18785, part II note on 'SOEs work with the Poles' written by Wilkinson dated 24 Dec. 1941.

24 Ibid., HS 4/270, report from Polish Ministry of Internal Affairs dated 4 Oct.1944 gives a list of Polish workers and prisoners of war employed in German industry as 52,446 persons and 1,187,000 persons in all regions of Germany, list from P.W.I. Intelligence ref.1.111/243 compiled on 15 August and 28 November 1944.

25 Ibid., HS 4/147, note from Dalton to Churchill dated 12 Nov.1940.

26 TNA(PRO) CAB 120/746, note from Churchill to Gen. Ismay for Col. Menzies dated 5 Aug. 1940.

27 Ibid., CAB 80/16, COS (40) 683 Appendix 1 dated 20 Aug.1940.

28 Ibid., HS 4/197, L1570/41, 6 page letter addressed to Gen. S.G. Menzies from Gen. Sosnkowski dated 9 May 1941, a first comprehensive report on sabotage undertaken so far in Poland.

29 Ibid., FO 371/26783, statement concerning sabotage and diversion in Poland prepared by VI Bureau dated 16 Dec. 1941.

30 TNA(PRO) HS 4/136, 18785, note on SOE's work with the Poles, dated 24 Dec. 1941.

31 Ibid., T 160/1412, 0173/326 note from J. Cash War Office to William L. Fraser (Treasury) dated 13 Dec. 1943 contains extract of the original Protocol.

32 Ibid., T 160/1332, F16208, note from Rear Adm.l John H. Godfrey (DNI) to A.L. Waterfield (Treasury) dated 19 July 1940, setting out conditions for employing the Poles by Admiralty for Intelligence purposes.

33 Ibid., T 160/1412, 84177, note from Gano to Menzies dated 5 Dec. 1941; C/8297 note from Menzies to H.Brittain (Treasury) dated 10 Dec. 1941, gives consent to the payment, expresses satisfaction with Intelligence information received from the Poles.

34 TNA(PRO) HS 4/297, note on contribution by the Treasury dated 3 Feb. 1944, as approved by the War Cabinet Defence Committee, stipulating sums for 'Big Scheme' operation in the Eastern front, as well as separate budgets for operations inside Poland and inside the Reich (ref. 1354 of 12 April 1942)

35 Ibid., T 160/1412, W3527/3527/64, note from D.L.Stewart (FO) to T.J. Cash (WO), dated 22 Mar. 1944, informing that the Cabinet decided to postpone the signature on Military Supplies because of the Polish-Russian political differences; the Military Credit to be revised by the Cabinet.

36 Wilfred Dunderdale (1899–1990) RNVR, Cmdr. (known as 'Wilski' or 'Dun'), son of British sea merchant in Odessa, educated in St. Petersburg, made himself useful to the British Naval Intelligence Service. Joined SIS in 1921, served in Istanbul. In 1926 sent to Paris where he remained until the fall of France in 1940. Responsible for

French and Polish Intelligence Services, worked in London throughout the war in close collaboration with Polish II Bureau.

37 Jan Librach, Chief of the Central Bureau of the Continental Action of the Polish Ministry of Interior,

38 TNA(PRO) HS 4/236, ref. M /PD /573, note by M [Gubbins] to CD [Nelson] dated 28 March 1942, contains Nurmi's report on his French organisation and plans for action on German communication lines into Spain.

39 Ibid., HS 5/889, brief for 'Harbourne' dated 26 May 1943; HS 4/205 brief on Michael Lis by Lt-Col. Threlfall, (Force 139) to Maj-Gen. W. Stawell dated 15 Aug. 1944; HS 4/312, folio 19431, Force 133 telegram dated 3 January 1944, with information of death of John Nash [Józef Maciag] and requesting assistance to organise a safe house for another courier. Included in the folder is Col. Bailey's order to evacuate the Poles, who were part of the British Mission, from Mihailović's territory.

40 Ibid., HS 4/138, MP /INT /6111, note from MP [Perkins] to A/CD [Cmdr. A.R.Boyle] dated 26 June 1944; HS 4/138, ref. 3587 FO cipher telegram to Moscow dated 27 June 1944, announcing dispatch of reports on sabotage undertaken by the Home Army, for onward transmission to NKVD.

41 TNA(PRO) HS 4/142, 75400, Plans 410/419/ P10/18, note by Gubbins on Polish activities, dated 11 May 1943.

42 Ibid., HS 4/142, cipher telegrams no.690 and 691 from FO to Moscow dated 13 June 1943 for transmission to NKVD, listed acts of sabotage undertaken by the Polish Home Army, between June 1942 and January 1943.

43 Ibid., HS 4/293, hand written letter dated 3 May 1946 from Gubbins to Perkins asking for his opinion regarding Polish claim on railway sabotage and Perkins' reply.

44 TNA(PRO), HS 4/203, ref. 1463,13 wireless intelligence reports on German transport movements to the North and South fronts of USSR territory, compiled by Chief of the VI Bureau Lt-Col. Protasewicz for Brig. Gubbins, dated 25 April 1942. Reports contain information on railway bridges and transport of troops and weapons towards Minsk at the rate of 35 in 24 hrs. and Kiev 10 transports. These were to be used as targets for sabotage purposes, as part of the 'Big Scheme' operation.; See J.Garliński: *Poland SOE and the Allies* (1969) p. 108

45 'Cichociemny' – a nickname/cryptonym given to 362 (inc. 2 women) Polish trained parachutists who were dispatched to Poland at night time. Literally means 'silent, dark and invisible'.

46 'Wieniec' – code name for a successful sabotage operation on railway line connections around Warsaw on 8 October 1942, lead by Capt. Z. Lewandowski (codename Szyna).

47 TNA(PRO) HS 4/310, CD /3612 note from CD [Hambro] to SO [Lord Selborne] dated 31 Oct. 1942.

48 Ibid., HS 4/142, MCD /1111, note from M /CD [Gubbins] to MP [Perkins] dated 5 May 1943

49 Ibid., HS 4/323 ref. CD /5283, minutes of a meeting held at FO, attended by Gubbins, Wilkinson, dated 25 May 1943, subject: operation of radio Swit, co-ordination of British-Soviet policy regarding resistance in Poland and Europe generally.

50 Ibid

51 TNA(PRO) CAB 79/67, COS(43)271st mtg. held in November 1943.Subject: Polish Resistance Movement and assistance by SOE. Discussed: limited allotment of aircraft for flights to Poland; Polish resentment towards non-committal use of the Secret Army in connection with Overlord; rejection by the CCOS to support Home Army's general insurrection in Poland. In conclusion, Poland was to accept the means already allocated to her and her needs were not allowed to take precedence over other operational requirements.

52 Ibid., CAB 80/56, COS (40) 27 meeting 25 Nov. 1940.
53 Ibid., HS 4/321, ref. M /PD /1393, note from M [Gubbins] to CD [Dalton] dated 12 Dec.1941; FO 371/39423, ref. C4046, report dated 23 March 1944, compiled for S of S [A. Eden] on ' Air Support for the Polish Resistance Movement'. Lists operations carried out, problems involved and the control of supplies to be carried.
54 TNA (PRO), FO 371/39422, COS (44) 84 dated 28 Jan.1944, ref. C1885 extracts from two COS meetings, includes opinions expressed by the Prime Minister Churchill, Lord Selborne, Secretary of State [Anthony Eden] and Air Chief Marshal Harris. Matters discussed: control of special operations with a possibility of tripling the load dropped in Poland, without reducing support for Yugoslavia, Greece and France. Decided, to wait for more opportune moment to change the conditions for the Polish Military Credit.
55 TNA (PRO) HS 7/183, History of Poland, appendix H, a list of British Air operations undertaken on behalf of occupied countries. Compares air sorties and tonnage of materials dropped.
56 Studium Polski Podziemnej (SPP), Polish Underground Movement Study Trust, ref. 232111, letters by Gen. Sosnkowski and Gen. Brooke dated 20 November 1943.
57 TNA (PRO) FO 371/34557, C11634, ref. CCOS 119 mtg. dated 23 September 1943, where 'The Armed Forces and Secret Military Organisation of Poland as a Factor in General Allied European Planning' was discussed. Also a telegram (JSM 1198) dated 21 September 1943 from the British representative in Washington to WO in London, in support of CCOS' negative decisions regarding Polish requests.
58 TNA (PRO) CAB 79/67, minutes of COS meeting 4 November 1943 with recommendations to submit a cut down plans (by SOE & the VI Bureau) for helping Poland; FO 371/34558 ref. C15104/129/55.
59 TNA (PRO) HS 4/144, C9117/34/G, minutes of the meeting at FO, dated 6 Aug. 1943, to discuss Polish internal control over the Secret Army. Present: Strang, Harrison, O'Malley and Perkins, all expressed fear towards the new Prime Minister Mikołajczyk, who had an ambition to control civilian and military communications with Poland.
60 Ibid., HS 4/144, note 1083, from AD/H [Lt-Col. D. Keswick] to K/AIR/P, dated 3 Feb.1944.
61 Ibid., FO 371/39423, COS (44) 179 Mtg. 20 Feb. 1944, report by the Chief of the Air Staff, on arrangements for closer supervision of the contents of packages conveyed to Poland by SOE.
62 Ibid., HS 4/144, a memorandum prepared by Roberts (FO) in consultation with 'C' [Menzies] for Gen. Hollis (WCO) dated 8 Jan. 1944, introducing closer control of the Polish Government's communications with organisations in Poland. It was done to placate Stalin, according to S of S' assurances given at the Tehran Conference.
63 TNA(PRO) HS 4/144, K.POL/14, note from K /POL [W.Houston-Boswall] political advisor to SOE to CD [C. Gubbins] dated 7 Jan.1944.
64 Ibid., FO 371/39422, F.1550/125, note arising out of Defence Committee meeting from [Lord Selborne] to Deputy Prime Minister [Clement Attlee], dated 18 Jan. 1944, reporting a conversation with Minister Władysław Banaczyk, relating to worsening internal conditions in Poland. A Russian document, captured by the Home Army, had instructions for the Polish Communist Party to destroy the underground movement. Intelligence information also revealed orders being given to Gen. Zhukov's parachute troops to exterminate the Home Army.

PART IV
OPERATIONS OF FIELD STATIONS OF POLISH INTELLIGENCE

19

The Functioning of Polish Intelligence Stations in the Field: Information from British Intelligence Archives

Gill Bennett

Introduction

As stated in Chapter 3, documents in British Intelligence archives record that by early 1940 the Polish Intelligence Service had intelligence cells at Budapest, Belgrade, Bucharest, Riga, Stockholm and Oslo, in addition to their activities in occupied Poland and, after June 1940, in both occupied and unoccupied France. The networks quickly expanded to include most of Occupied Europe, North Africa, the Middle East, Far East, Scandinavia, the Americas and neutral countries such as Switzerland. Reports from all these areas were passed to the British Intelligence authorities, through local contacts, through direct contact with the UK and through Polish-British liaison in London.

Many of the reports based on Polish information were destroyed after their content had been distributed to military and government customers. What survives in the closed archives is sparse, and both general narrative and detail must be reconstructed from scattered references and reports, sometimes written considerably after the event. Nevertheless, a picture emerges of active and resourceful Polish agents and networks, interacting both with British and other countries' Intelligence services in countries across the world. Despite the difficulties and restrictions of wartime travel, Polish agents, informants and contacts were always on the move, setting up courier lines and escape routes across Europe and beyond, enabling their fellow Poles and other Allies to reach safety in the UK and elsewhere.

The scale and diversity of Polish Intelligence activities was impressive, but could also make them vulnerable to penetration by the enemy. This was one reason for the practice of setting up parallel Polish Intelligence organisations in the same country, supposedly ignorant of each other – a security device that could also cause confusion. Some of the stories unearthed from the archives are stories of betrayal and failure; others portray bravery, ingenuity and creative determination. All are interesting and illuminating.

The information on Polish Intelligence activities that follows has been divided up for ease of reference into geographical areas and individual countries. Often, however, these distinctions are blurred and artificial, as networks operated across borders, and agents, and informants travelled across Europe and beyond. The confused and confusing nature of the picture presented was deliberate, and should be seen as a mark of the success of Polish Intelligence in its constant struggle against the enemy.

20
France and North Africa

Gill Bennett

France

F2, Interallié and Marine

The Polish Intelligence network in France was set up in July 1940, immediately after the fall of France, by a group of Polish officers in Toulouse. Intelligence Station FII (later as FII) was originally set up with one home-made radio post and three Polish officers, organising an escape route for Allied forces to the UK from Toulouse. These officers were joined by many French recruits, whom they trained, and by other compatriots escaping from Occupied France throughout 1940.

The officers concerned were Wincenty Zarembski, code named 'Tudor', Mieczysław Słowikowski ('Ptak', later known as 'Rygor'), and Roman Czerniawski ('Armand', 'Valentin'), all of whom had served as Intelligence officers with the Polish army. Without contact with London, without money, codes or radio, they set about creating an Intelligence network from the escape route they had already organised. By means of messages sent to the UK with Poles whose escape they organised, the group had received codes and a wireless telegraph set from London by August 1940. The Polish HQ in London, with the agreement of SIS, sent out Tadeusz Jekiel ('Doctor') to help 'Tudor' organise the station. Słowikowski remained responsible for running the escape lines until sent to North Africa in the spring of 1941 to build up a clandestine organisation there for obtaining military information.

By the end of 1940 four Polish intelligence cells of F in France had been set up: 'Tudor' at Marseilles, 'Panhard' at Lyon, 'Rab' at Toulouse and an intelligence cell in Paris set up by 'Armand'. Armand's cell, known as Interallié, covered most of Occupied France and received messages that were sent (via the *Wagons-Lits* attendants on the Paris/Marseilles Express) to 'Tudor' for transmission to London. 'Doctor' was based in Bordeaux, where his second in command was Leon Śliwiński ('Jean-Bol'). Doctor's cell specialised in information concerning enemy submarines and shipping, and became known as cell 'Marine'. It prided itself that no submarine left Bordeaux, Brest or Le Havre without London's being notified. This information was regarded as extremely valuable by the British Government, although Naval Intelligence wished that the service also extended to U-boat destinations and patrol areas.[1]

Doctor also organised a cell, 'Italie', through which information was passed on German troop movements on Italian railways, Italian industry and port movements. This route provided the first reports to London that the Germans might invade North Africa, and in June 1943 Polish sources signalled the exact situation of the 'PC du Grand Quartier Allemand' at Taormina which was obliterated by Allied bombardment immediately before the Sicily Landings.

At the end of 1940 W. Potocki a Polish officer with contacts in the highest Vichy circles, joined 'Doctor's cell with the code name 'Calixte'. By mid-1941 Calixte had an intelligence station of his own, entirely concerned with politics. Certain 'hautes personalités militaires et politiques' found it convenient to use their aristocratic Polish friend as a means of contact with London. Intelligence Station 'Calixte' also ran a clandestine newsletter, and this was the reason that the Vichy police arrested 'Calixte' in November 1941. His other activities were not known to the police so he was imprisoned for only a short time, but as his position was now compromised. 'Calixte' had to hand over his political reportage to Cell 202 in Lyon, which thenceforward gave news of and from neutral officials in Vichy as well as the French government. From August 1942 a 'secteur spécial' of cell Marine, headed by W. Rozwadowski ('Pascal') also filled the gap left by 'Calixte' in high-level political and economic intelligence.

By early 1941, the French recruits trained by the Poles were ready for action as secret agents and W/T operators, and they began to outnumber Polish agents by an increasing margin. By the end of the period 1940-41 intelligence station F, though still Polish-led, was staffed by 210 French to only 40 Poles. However, 'Marine' and other cells operating in Marseilles and Nice remained almost exclusively Polish, and Polish agents provided nearly all information on Mediterranean ports and Axis troop movements to North Africa. In addition, an FII cell at Lyon and headed by a Pole, W. Obrembski ('OB'), provided information on industrial production in the Lyonnais area. A parallel cell, P.O.2 Lyon, reporting on Axis troop transports in the Midi, was also headed from August 1941 by a Pole, Z. Wilkoński ('Orient'), parachuted in from London.

In July 1941 'Armand' in Paris established direct W/T contact with London, and was able to operate independently of 'Tudor'. His intelligence cell, Interallié, covered more or less the whole of Occupied France and even had a cell in Belgium. It had as its objective the discovery of the 'ordre de bataille allemand complet (terre, marine, aviation, fortifications, industries de guerre en France, transport de troupes', and its work was described as 'outstanding, particularly on German Order of

Battle'. Both 'Armand' and 'Tudor', from the cells in Paris and Marseilles centres, provided industrial information from reports they each received from the two zones of France. The output of munition and aircraft factories working for the Germans, and movements of *matériel* by land and rail, were reported quickly to London.

Tudor was also responsible for liaison with the various indigenous French Resistance movements that began to appear, for training their members as W/T operators, and for making sure that targets were not duplicated. 'Calixte' also helped with this, and in organising escapes to the UK, via Spain or by boat. Tudor and his Marseilles intelligence cell were also the chief means at this period of making Resistance requirements known to London.

In November 1941, disaster struck both 'Armand' and 'Tudor'. Interallié was penetrated by the Gestapo and 'Armand', together with his chief of staff Mathilde Carré ('Victoire', 'La Chatte', 'Bagheera'), was arrested, and his five transmitting posts in Paris were captured, together with 100 agents. Both 'Armand' and 'La Chatte' were accused of collaboration, and the latter, together with a French W/T operator also 'turned' by the Germans, provided them with an almost complete picture of Interallié. 'Armand', however, later went on to become a double agent, codenamed 'Brutus', who played a central part in the plan that fooled the Germans into diverting their troops away from the proposed Allied landing places in Normandy.

A stream of arrests followed those of 'Armand' and 'La Chatte', and the collapse destabilised FII. 'Tudor' was 'burnt', and was withdrawn to London (his network was later rebuilt with the help of the 'Panhard' group, and renamed 'Tumars', communicating with London via Marseilles). There is no doubt, however, that both Czerniawski and Zarembski had made outstanding contributions to the Allied cause through their work in France. These two men, starting from nothing, had set up the first Intelligence network for the Allies in France, and maintained a valuable supply of information at a time when other sources were unavailable. Their departure led to a considerable reorganisation of FII and changes in personnel.

Cell Marine under 'Doctor' and 'Jean-Bol' continued into 1942 despite the collapse of the networks in Marseilles and Paris, but 'Doctor's position had been compromised and he left to start a new cell in North Africa, leaving Jean-Bol in charge. By now he had sources in Toulon, Marseilles and Port-Vendres, and later re-activated agents in Brittany who had been lying low after the Paris arrests. Naval reports were typed out in FII's cell in Nice and sent to London by two different routes, with a third copy being given to the US Naval Attaché in Vichy. (In March 1942 an arrangement had been made with the US Ambassador to Vichy and his colleague in Bern, to allow use of the American diplomatic bag to and from Vichy/Geneva where they were passed to SIS for transmission to London.)

None of the reports from Marine survives in British Intelligence archives, but Station FII claimed that in 1942 Marine had:

- given quick news of [Order of Battle] of enemy shipping;
- reported on troop transports leaving the Mediterranean ports for North Africa (including the tiny Port Vendres, used extensively for small transports);
- run a little boat, under Lt. Buchowski, every month from St Raphael to Gibraltar carrying couriers, mail and escapers;
- survived the decimation of cell BÓR *réseau* in Marseilles in August 1942 and continued sending Intelligence by the safe hand of a *Wagon-Lit* guard who took documents to Station FII/Paris.

The greatest contribution of Polish Intelligence in France in 1942 was their reportage on Axis troops going over to North Africa, either from the Mediterranean ports of France or from Italy and Sicily. None of the emerging French cells seems to have paid much attention to their southern coastline.

With the collapse of Interallié Intelligence Station FII was badly bruised, but had largely recovered by the summer of 1942. It continued to report on a wide range of subjects including German troop movements to North Africa, fortifications and enemy shipping in the French Atlantic ports, and political activities in the Vichy Government. According to information from German sources, in the summer of 1942 one network of Polish and French agents, based in Paris, Lille and Douai, was being organised by a Polish Colonel, Wiktor Hennoch ('MAR'). Another Polish member of the group, Starorypiński ('Star', 'Rota') was apparently responsible for collecting agents' reports, administering funds and forwarding the material to Nice for transmission to the UK by W/T or air. Both these officers managed to escape capture when the network was infiltrated by German agents and rolled up in September 1942.

A further group of Polish and French agents appears to have been the target in December 1942 of a German operation codenamed Zarathustra. This group was led by a Polish ex-cavalry officer, Capt. Gołogórski (also known as Lipski), who was thought to be running a number of agents in unoccupied France. Also under suspicion were Capt. Macherski, Commandant of the Polish Legion for the Nice area, M. Fuksiewicz, formerly Polish Consul at Toulouse, and Madame Wanda Łada, Polish delegate to the French Red Cross, who was thought to have an *entrée* to the Vichy Foreign Minister. When this group was infiltrated, the Germans apparently uncovered details of plans by Polish Intelligence to evacuate to Aix-les-Bains or Spain in the event of an Italian attack on Nice; and for the formation of a group of agents for the liberation of captured British agents, parachutists and airmen.

By the end of 1942 FII was also involved in running lines across the Franco-Swiss border, and setting up a sea link with Gibraltar. In addition, FII became involved with some of the French Resistance organisations. After the Allied landings in North Africa, when the Germans occupied the whole of France, Intelligence Station FII was hit again, with widespread arrests following the influx of German and Italian security units into southern France. Nevertheless Station FII still managed to provide valuable information, as witnessed by two brief reports on the Polish organisation in France by Dunderdale, dated 30 September 1943 and 17 January 1944.

According to the first report, there were 159 registered agents, helpers, couriers etc controlled by the HQ in the south of France, and 5 W/T stations operating in turn. During August and September 1943 481 reports had been received, of which 356 were circulated, comprising 138 military, 130 naval, 44 air and 44 economic. Between June and September 20 reports had been graded A, 352 B, 66 C, 5 D and 9 ungraded. The second report, of January 1944, covered the whole of 1943, and stated that a total of 1,161 reports had been issued on the basis of material submitted by the Polish organisation in France. These comprised 303 military, 393 naval, 254 air, 190 economic and 21 political reports, with gradings 48 (A), 879 (B), 150 (C), 12 (D) and 28 (ungraded). No further details of these reports appear to have survived, but the figures show a continued high level of activity despite the problems suffered by the Polish networks.

Arrests continued throughout the spring of 1944, but despite this Station FII contributed to the intelligence on German order of battle and fortifications, both in North West and southern France, prior to the Allied landings in these regions. In July a further 16 agents were arrested, among them the chief of the Normandy sector. An SLC minute dated 25 September 1944 noted that Station FII was now in the process of being liquidated, and that the Polish authorities were in touch with the French *Deuxième Bureau* to whom they were handing over lists of Frenchmen who had worked for the Polish organisation in France during the previous four years. A Polish mission, comprising Jan Leśniak, Bogusław Feuer, Bolesław Łaszewski and Tadeusz Opiel, was being sent to France to deal with winding up the cell. Meanwhile another Polish agent, de beauregard ('Łoś', also known as 'Toun' and 'Gregoire'), was representing Polish interests in France. By the end of 1944, FII's operations appear to have been subsumed into French Intelligence.

'Bertie' and Intelligence Station Z

In 1940, while Zarembski, Słowikowski and Czerniawski were putting together the networks that were to become Intelligence Station FII, another valuable Polish source was already supplying information to London. Following the German invasion of Poland, the Polish cryptographers responsible for breaking the Enigma code and building a replica of the Enigma machine (see Chapter 6) had escaped to France via Romania with SIS help, and in October 1939 were integrated into the *Deuxième Bureau*'s cryptography department *Le Section d'Examen* (SE), run by Colonel Gustave Bertrand ('Bertie', known to the Poles as Col. Bolek). Bertrand's close relations with the Polish cryptographers predated the outbreak of war, when he had facilitated their liaison with SIS over Enigma. He was to work indefatigably on their behalf throughout the war.

This group of 18 Polish cryptographers formed a centre of radio interception known as 'Equipe 300' or 'Cell Z'. Following their escape to France, they worked from November 1939 until June 1940 at Cell 'PC Bruno', a chateau near Paris. On 10 June 1940 Bertrand and his aides 'requisitioned' several buses (actually stolen from the Parc de Vincennes) and drove the Poles and their machines south, to near Brive. From there they were flown to safety in Algiers in July, when the SE was dissolved under the terms of the French Armistice. Bertrand, however, was determined both to continue his own work – contriving, with the help of his patron Col. Rivet, to remain employed by the Vichy police – and to ensure that the work of the Polish cryptographers should also continue.

By October 1940 the Poles had been brought back from Algiers, and were settled in the Chateau des Fouzes, near Nimes (PC CADIX), which had been secured for Bertrand by Gen. Weygand himself. There, together with a group of Spanish Republican cryptographers and 5 Frenchmen, they continued until November 1942 to work on Enigma and to send out immensely valuable messages dealing with all aspects of Axis activity, Abwehr agents in France and intelligence acquired from Rivet's *réseau* KLEBER. Bertrand also managed to set up Enigma cells in Algiers and Rabat during this period.

Bertrand had established independent contact between the *Equipe* 300 and London between July and August 1940, through a colleague in Geneva, Commandant Perruche. Communication continued to be channelled through Geneva until March 1941, when Bertrand travelled to Madrid to meet Dunderdale, who handed him a W/T set for future use. From November 1940 Station 300 was also in liaison with 'Tudor' in Marseilles, and remained in close contact with Intelligence Station FII until November 1942. It appears that both Bertrand and Station FII used the 'Vichy Valise' – i.e. diplomatic bag – to communicate with Spain, Switzerland and London, and also used the *Deuxième Bureau* radio transmitter at Clermont-Ferrand. (Later Bertrand was to claim that members of his Station 300 also communicated with London without his knowledge.)

Following the Allied landings in North Africa, Bertrand again managed to smuggle the members of Station 300 out of France. Some went to North Africa, to join the intelligence cell there, but the principal Polish cryptographers were smuggled over the Pyrenees to Spain, whence their evacuation to the UK was facilitated by SIS. Bertrand himself remained in France, working with the *réseau* KLEBER directed from Algiers by Gen.Rivet, until he was arrested in Paris in January 1944. He managed to escape and evade recapture until picked up by SIS in June 1944 and taken to London.

The work of Intelligence Station 300 was both specialised and important. Its staff were expert cryptographers and had the most modern equipment. Most importantly, its interests and communications were protected constantly by the ingenious Col. Bertrand, who arranged for them to be funded first by the *Deuxième Bureau* and later by the Vichy authorities. Through his efforts the work on ENIGMA was able to continue undiscovered, passing on to London German and Italian Army intercepts.

North Africa

As mentioned earlier, in the spring of 1941 Słowikowski ('Rygor'), who had remained in charge of the Polish escape lines out of France, was sent to North Africa to build up a clandestine organisation for obtaining military information. This he achieved successfully, with the help of French contacts, for by the time of the Allied North African landings in November 1942 his intelligence station (also known as 'Rygor') had cells reporting from most of the ports and main centres along the North African coastline

According to a minute by a member of A4 section dated 15 May 1941, the Polish deputy Director of Military Intelligence had reported that an Intelligence sataion had been established in Algiers under Słowikowski, and that subsidiary cells were to be established at Tunis, Oran, Casablanca and Dakar. Communication between the stations, subsidiary cells and Polish General Staff would be maintained by W/T. The network was expected to come into operation by the end of May 1941, but a number of reports had already been received from Casablanca, particularly dealing with counter-intelligence matters. Other SIS sections had already submitted to A4 a number of questionnaires that had been summarised and transmitted by mail to North Africa, though subsequent requests would be sent by W/T.

It was, indeed, from Algiers that the last message was received by SIS on 8 November 1942 before the Allied landings, warning that the Vichy French were prepared to fight: a telegram received from Rygor at 00.27 a.m. that morning stated that from 6 November all shipping movements in the Port of Algiers had been suspended, and ships at sea had received orders to return to the nearest port. Submarines 'Caiman and 'Marsouin' were held in readiness at Algiers.

Unfortunately, very little information concerning Rygor has survived in British Intelligence archives. Although Rygor was noted as having good political sources and port watchers, and commended for valuable information during the planning and execution of the North African landings (for which Słowikowski subsequently received an OBE), no reports have been found, nor details of particular cells, nor evaluations. As far as individual Polish agents or contacts are concerned, few substantive references have surfaced. Mieczysław Komar ('Pingo') was reported to have been arrested in Tangier by the French in late 1942, and instructions were sent to the SIS representative to try and help him. Stanisław Szewalski of the Polish Army, who had worked in North Africa and was evidently an expert on Oran, was in Scotland in December 1942, but the Americans were very anxious that he should return to Oran 'to help them in trying to cope with the pro-Axis and pro-Vichy elements which still abound'. Their request appears to have been made to the Polish authorities through SIS, but it was refused by the Polish Chief of Staff on the grounds that the request should have been made through the proper channels in

Washington; and that in any case, Capt. Szewalski was 'not suitable'.

Other brief references relate to operations to transport Polish officers to and from North Africa. Orkan, a member of the Polish organisation in North Africa, was embarked off the coast of North Africa on 12 July 1942, arriving in the UK on the 17th; in the Casual/Zebra operation on 11/12 September 1942 three Polish officers were landed off the Algerian coast, and six embarked; five Polish Intelligence agents were embarked successfully off the coast of North Africa on the night of 5 October 1942 in the Giraffe operation. Such references are tantalising, but unfortunately they appear only as notes in brief SLC summaries noting the number of reports received in a week or month.

There are also a few references to the means of communication employed. 'Rygor' and his intelligence station worked closely with the American authorities (OSS and diplomatic) in North Africa, and used the US diplomatic bag as a means of sending material to London. Their reports were handed open to the Americans, who took copies and passed them on, making use of the information themselves. In return, equipment, money and correspondence could be passed from London to Rygor by the same route: a group of telegrams dated June 1942 refer to instances of packages going astray, instead of reaching Rygor through the 'usual channel' of the American Embassy in Algiers.

Despite some contradictory reports (Polish Intelligence authorities in London also told SIS in November 1942 that 'Rygor and friends have had no dealings with US Consulate [in Algiers] and do not wish any'), it seems clear that 'Rygor' did have close US contacts; one account commented that Słowikowski 'unfortunately preferred the OSS to SIS'. A report of December 1942 from Algiers suggested that following the Allied landings 'Rygor' had even 'hinted' that the Americans should take over the Polish intelligence station altogether, and from December 1942 onwards US links appear to have been very close.

No further information has been found in British Intelligence archives concerning 'Rygor', although some communication through British channels evidently continued: in May 1944 the SIS representative in Algiers was asked to contact Słowikowski and 'arrange to collect from him until further notice such II Bureau mails as he may have for despatch to London'. It is a pity that so little documentation has survived on this evidently successful intelligence station.

Note
1   See *Hinsley*, vol. 1, p. 333.

21
Polish Intelligence in France 1940–1945

Rafał Wnuk

At the time of the German offensive against France the latter was the seat of the exiled Polish government and the Polish General Staff, thus the II (Intelligence) Bureau of the General Staff, which directed Polish networks. The defeat of France came as a total surprise to the Polish Command. Because of the pace of the German offensive the heads of II Bureau were unable to take steps to prepare future intelligence networks in France. As a result the initiative to resume intelligence activity originated in the lower ranks – among those intelligence officers who had not been evacuated to Great Britain.[1]

The Franco-German armistice signed on 22 June 1940 totally subjugated France to German influences and divided the country into two zones: northern – occupied, and southern – unoccupied, a division of a great significance from the point of view of intelligence activities. The absence of Germans in southern France was the reason why there were more favourable conditions for organising intelligence than in the occupied part of the country. It was there that the first networks were set up by Maj. Mieczysław Zygfryd Słowikowski 'Rygor' and Maj. Wincenty Zarembski 'Tudor', intelligence officers who at the same time supervised the evacuation posts. In a short span of time they gathered a group of Poles who spoke excellent French and whose personalities and skills predestined them for intelligence. As a result Polish intelligence cells were already created in August 1940. They were steered by Maj. Słowikowski. On 15 September 1940 Słowikowski's network established direct radio communication with the II Bureau of the Polish General Staff in London and began sending reports. That was the first Allied intelligence network in France.[2]

On 17 September 1940 Słowikowski was ordered by Col. Leon Mitkiewicz, Chief of the II Bureau, to separate the evacuation posts from the intelligence network. In accordance with those instructions Maj. Słowikowski retained his control over the evacuation and handed over the intelligence network, functioning as Station 'France' (cryptonym 'F'), to Maj. Zarembski 'Tudor'. In accordance with the directives of the Chief of the II Bureau the new chief carried out organisational changes which consisted in the intelligence being based on the work performed by officer cells (PO), which in turn built field cells on their own. 'Tudor' controlled the following cells:

- PO-1 in Toulouse, under: Maj. Stefan Korwin-Szymanowski 'Rab';
- PO-2 in Lyon, the head: Lt. Jan Kamieński 'Franty';
- PO-3 in Marseilles, under: Lt. W. Krzyżanowski 'Panhard';
- PO-4 (cryptonym 'Marine') in Nice, under: Lt. Tadeusz Jekiel 'Doctor', as well as Intelligence Cell. No. 1, cryptonym 'Interallié' – ('INT') in Paris, under: Capt. Roman Czerniawski PAF 'Armand'.[3]

From the very beginning Intelligence Station 'F' remained in the centre of attention of the British, whose Secret Intelligence Service networks in France as well as other occupied European countries had been totally surprised by the course of events and proved unprepared for activity in conditions caused by the German occupation. In this situation the Allies could count only on Polish intelligence and that of the Free French.[4] Polish intelligence was in a special position since SIS officers would trust the Free French only to a limited extent, fearing that some of the French networks might be infiltrated or subjected to infiltration by the Abwehr. Doubts with regards to the loyalty of Free French intelligence agents, especially those coming from the special services of the pre-war Republic, were intensified by the existence of Vichy France with which numerous Frenchmen identified themselves. Such a reserved attitude proved to be fully justified since a large group of members of pre-war French intelligence worked for Vichy and actively fought against all forms of organised resistance.[5]

Distrust was additionally deepened by the clear conflict between British and American politicians, on the one hand, and Gen. Charles de Gaulle, on the other. The leader of the Free French tried to conduct an independent policy which was aimed at limiting the role played by America and Great Britain, and ensuring future French domination in post-war Europe. Those circumstances adversely affected the reliability of the information forwarded by the Free French and enhanced the importance of Station 'F' networks.

In 1941 Polish intelligence systematically supplied the Allies with reports concerning French industry with particular attention being paid to armament factories and all kinds of undertakings involving railway lines and roads, where at the same time constant monitoring of the rail transports was conducted. Station 'F' agents gathered intelligence regarding the distribution of German units in France. In the period of September-November 1941 they managed to obtain an extremely important report of Swiss Intelligence, describing the German Order of Battle on the French territory,[6] and verifying findings made by Polish and Free French intelligence services. At that time more significant reports were communicated by W/T, whereas their full versions and the particular telegrams were forwarded to London by couriers.

In the spring of 1941 French ports on the Mediterranean became particularly important because they supplied German armies fighting in Africa. Intelligence in the ports of southern France was successfully conducted by the naval network headed by Capt. Jekiel (Intelligence Cell PO-4), who discovered the destination ports of ships and provided detailed characteristics of imported and exported cargo.

The British were also unable to rely on their own intelligence network in French North Africa which gained prominent strategic significance from February 1941 and after the landing in Libya of the troops of General Erwin Rommel's Africa Corps. The attempt made by the SIS at the beginning of 1941 to build a network based on French officers who presented unfavourable attitude towards the Germans and the Vichy authorities ended in May 1941 in a complete failure. As a result of betrayal most of the conspirators were arrested by Vichy Counter-intelligence.[7]

In view of the difficulties with creating its own intelligence cells the SIS turned to the II Bureau with a request to establish a network based on Polish intelligence members from unoccupied France. This mission was entrusted to Maj. Słowikowski, who arrived in Algiers in July 1941 together with experienced officers of Station 'F': Capt. Jekiel and Lt. Stanisław Rombejko.[8] They began to build an intelligence structure under the codename Station 'Afryka' ('Afr.').[9] In October of that year 'Afr.' cells were operating along the whole African littoral, from Casablanca to Tripoli. That intelligence network comprising nearly a hundred agents managed to provide a lot of valuable information, although it was relatively small considering the size of the penetrated region. According to an assessment made by Stephen Dorril, Station 'Afr.' was 'the most wide-spread and the best Allied intelligence network on the territory of the French North Africa which remained under the Vichy regime; in 1941–1942 it played a leading role in planning of the operation 'Torch', that is the Anglo-American invasion of Algeria and Morocco in November 1942'.[10]

For the sake of precision it should be added that the effective planning and conduct of the invasion of French North Africa was only possible owing to the information from the reports transmitted from unoccupied France, especially the naval cell in Nice (PO-4), combined with information from Station 'Afr.'.

Station '300', directed by Lt-Col. Gwido Langer 'Luc', functioned in unoccupied France from October 1940. The station's team was engaged in deciphering German reports sent by the Enigma coding machine. Polish cryptographers closely co-operated with a French underground cryptographic centre (code named 'Cadix'). Station '300' had its own W/T station and thus was capable of immediately relaying the deciphered German telegrams to London. Furthermore, it received reports from Station 'Afr.' which it then passed on to London (see Chapter 46: J. S. Ciechanowski, J. Tebinka Cryptological Co-operation: Enigma).

The activity of Station 'Interallié' – ('INT') – deserves to be discussed in greater detail. In October 1940 Capt. Czerniawski[11] left Toulouse for

Paris in order to conduct intelligence work in the occupied part of France, where he started to build a network of agents together with Bernard Krótki 'Christian'. Both men recruited agents in the Northern basin, Brittany and Normandy and even created intelligence cells in Belgium. In the first half of November 1940 Capt. Czerniawski sent Maj. Zarembski the first of periodical, weekly reports. Correspondence was transported in dead letter boxes installed in lavatories of the express train en route from Paris to Toulouse.

Although 'INT' was a cell of the II Bureau of the Polish General Staff its structures included many Frenchmen and Belgians as well as several Spaniards, Czechs and Germans. The rapid expansion of the network was the reason why it became necessary to decentralise it. Scattered over a large area the cells gained considerable independence; the positive aspect of this situation was that the Chief of the Station was relieved of some duties, but the negative effect was less effective control over the compliance with the rules of operational security.

'INT' informed London by December 1940 about the plans for transferring Afrika Korps to Tripoli. However, the British Command, which had not received confirmation of this news from other sources, deemed it unreliable. Soon afterwards the Germans launched the invasion of North Africa. MI5 analysts also ignored an 'Int.' report about miniature submarines built by the Germans. The sub-assemblies were shipped from Germany to ports along the French Atlantic coast, where they were assembled and launched. The British Navy was soon to pay a high price for that mistake. Agents of Intelligence Cell no. 1 also established the locations of about a hundred German airfields in northern France and Belgium, informed about the reconstruction of sea ports as well as the installation of new fortifications and coastal batteries. Capt. Czarniawski's cell reported about the location and size of Wehrmacht units, the quantity of industrial production, and German rail and sea transport.

Much of the information obtained by the station had to be immediately/sent to London. In order to make the network more efficient and to expedite the reports quickly, the Chief of the Station provided Capt. Czerniawski with a W/T station and funds. However, the insufficient power of the transmitter made it impossible to establish wireless contact with London; communications with London-based II Bureau of the Polish General Staff became possible only after the installation of the W/T station on top of a high building next to Trocadero (10 May 1941). From that moment 'Armand' could send more important information instantly, thus increasing the importance of his network.[12]

In the autumn of 1941 'Armand' was summoned to London; on the night of 2 October 1941 an aeroplane from England picked him up at a sports airfield in Compiègne. In London the Chief of 'INT' met with Colonel Stanisław Gano, Chief of the II Bureau, Maj. Jan Żychoń, Head of the Intelligence Department of the II Bureau, and Gen. Władysław Sikorski, Prime Minister of the Republic of Poland. 'Armand' presented a progress report on the results of activity, and received instructions to reorganise the cell and provide a deeper cover. He also tried to establish official contacts with representatives of the Free French because he wanted the Frenchmen working in 'INT' to be assured that they would be treated by Gen. de Gaulle's movement according to the same principles as members of the French 'Résistance'. However, the British, who did not fully trust the General, prevented the normalisation of relations between Polish and French intelligence networks.[13]

On 11 October 1941 Capt. Czerniawski was parachuted into the region of Tours and upon arrival in Paris he immediately started reorganising the cell, which at that time totalled 160 agents. He created an independent cell which conducted intelligence exclusively within the area of Paris, and divided local networks into 14 independent sectors. He also changed the method of sending reports from sectors to the HQ so that the couriers would not have direct contact with the addressees. On 16 October 1941 Intelligence Cell no. 1 was finally separated from Station 'F', and began functioning as an independent Station 'Interallié' – ('INT'), controlled directly by the II Bureau in London.[14]

The Germans, who conducted wireless monitoring, were well aware of the fact that a W/T station working for the Allies was situated in Paris, and suspected that it was sending reports obtained by some sort of intelligence network. Hence, they took efforts to track it down at all costs. In the second half of October 1941 the Abwehr finally traced Station 'Interallié'.[15] The Germans arrested 'Paweł', Chief of the 'Interallié' sector in the department of Calvados, who, in turn, led them to Lieutenant Krótki, deputy Chief of the Station. The Abwehr found the apartment where Czerniawski lived together with Mathilde Lily Carré 'La Chatte', the Station's secretary responsible for contacts with the field structures. Both were arrested on 16 November (according to other sources – on 18 November). After initial interrogations Mathilde Carré agreed to collaborate with the Germans and showed them the secret spot containing documents and money. Her active co-operation enabled the Germans to arrest about half of all the members of the 'INT' network. Although the Station ceased to exist the intelligence work was continued in occupied France and the Germans failed to stop it. Envoys from Station 'F' established contact with those agents of the uncovered 'Interallié' network who had escaped the arrest. That allowed for a new intelligence structure to be established to function within Station 'F'. From September 1941 to November 1941 the Chief of Cell, and subsequently Station 'Interallié' sent 95 weekly reports which averaged from 20 to 50 pages, while the most comprehensive one, describing transportation traffic, was 400 pages long.[16]

The arrest of Capt. Czerniawski, which put an end to the first Allied intelligence network, in occupied part of France, closed an important chapter in the history of Second World War intelligence. Nonetheless, it did not terminate the intelligence activity of its author. In the course of interrogations concerning Station 'Interallié', Oskar Reile, a Colonel of the Abwehr, recognised that Capt. Czerniawski was an excellent candidate for a German agent, and that 'Armand's' accomplishments rendered him reliable in the eyes of the Allies. His experiences and personality indicated that he could easily convince the heads of Polish and British Intelligence services that he was a trustworthy officer. In May Col. Reile proposed co-operation, promising at the same time to guarantee safety to the 65 imprisoned members of 'Interallié'. In return, 'Armand' was to make his way to London and begin working for the Germans. The Polish officer agreed and his former colleagues became hostages ensuring the loyalty of the new German agent.

On 14 August 1942 the transfer of the prisoner to Paris was interrupted by an 'escape' arranged by Col. Reile. The 'escapee' arrived in Madrid and then went to Gibraltar, from where he was transferred to London on 10 October (according to other sources on 2 October). For two weeks British and Polish counter-intelligence specialists tested the 'cover' devised by Col. Reile and finally acknowledged that it was credible. Subsequently, Czerniawski reported directly to Col. Gano, Chief of Polish Intelligence, and described the true state of affairs. Col. Gano summarised the course of this meeting to Prime Minister Sikorski, who ordered an immediate contact with the War Board. With the knowledge and consent of Prime Minister Sikorski and Col. Gano British Intelligence decided to use Czerniawski to disinform the Germans and put clandestine influence on them with the assistance of double agents. The operation was known as the 'Double Cross system' after the 'XX' symbol standing for the cell responsible for the details of the operation.[17] For security reasons no other Pole apart from Gen. Sikorski, Col. Gano, Gen. Klimecki, Maj. Lagenfeld and Col. Orłowski knew the truth about Czerniawski's 'escape' and the role which he was given by the 'XX' cell supervising the operation.

From January 1943 Capt. Czerniawski, who then used the codename 'Brutus', began sending information to the Germans. For a year he dispatched thoroughly prepared true information so as to become fully trusted by the Abwehr.[18] Once he succeeded the second, much more difficult phase of the intelligence game began, namely, convincing German Intelligence that the invasion of the Western Allies would take place at another time and place than actually planned. That operation, code named 'Fortitude', was undertaken as part of a wider effort aimed at deceiving the Germans. That included the erection of a dense network of W/T stations in south-east England, conducting intensive correspondence, the construction of mock-up military camps, and concentrating air raids of the north-eastern coast of France. All that was to produce the impression that the invasion would be carried out in the Pas de Calais and Dunkirk region. The key role in 'Fortitude' was performed by four agents: a Spanish journalist Juan Pujol 'Garbo', a Dane Wulf Schmidt 'Tate', a French woman of Russian descent Lili Siergieyev 'Treasure' and Capt. Czerniawski 'Brutus'.[19] The latter played a special part since he was the only German agent in the Allied Staff and, in the eyes of the Germans, a liaison officer to Gen. Dwight D. Eisenhower.

In the third week of May 1944 Capt. Czerniawski sent a telegram giving notification that the invasion of France would take place at the beginning of July. The Allies would first land in Normandy, but this would be only a tactical manoeuvre aimed at distracting the German forces from the actual site of the landing, whose true target would be Calais. The Germans fully trusted the report. The British and American troops landing in Normandy found the Germans unprepared. When a report about the attack reached Berlin neither Gen. Alfred Jodl, Commander-in-Chief of the Wehrmacht, nor Adolf Hitler made any decisions for a long time to regroup the armies, being firmly convinced that this was not the actual invasion. One of the SIS reports assessing the role played by Capt. Czerniawski during the preparation and conduct of the operation 'Overlord' (the invasion of Normandy), stated that at the critical moment the value of 'Brutus' was almost impossible to be overestimated.[20]

The last important misinformation operation conducted by 'Brutus' was connected with the bombing of London by V-1 and V-2 rockets. The Germans, wishing to know the effects of the air raids, asked 'their' agent about their effectiveness. Capt. Czerniawski replied that most of the rockets fell several kilometres short of London. Consequently, the Germans corrected the trajectory and many of the rockets flew over London and dropped outside city limits.[21]

The above mentioned German destruction of Station 'Interallié' seriously weakened Station 'F'. Arrests conducted by Vichy special services adversely affected the cells in Lyon (from December 1941 under Lt. Zygmunt Wilkoński), Marseilles and Toulouse. The naval station in Nice, headed by Lt. Leon Śliwiński after Capt. Jekiel left for Africa in July 1941, remained unimpaired.[22]

After the arrest of Capt. Czerniawski, Maj. Zarembski, Chief of Station 'F', left for Paris where he got in touch with 'Interallié' agents, albeit violating principles of operational security. On several occasions he travelled to Spain carrying reports but without any documents which would ensure a minimum of safety. Maj. Zarembski managed to save some elements of the network, but the Chief of the II Bureau in London decided that his further presence in France involved too many risks and ordered Zarembski to leave the country.[23] In February 1942 Zarembski was transported by plane to London.

In January 1942 Station 'F' was entrusted to Lt-Col. Marian Romeyko 'Mak', who in six months thoroughly rearranged its structures. What remained of the Toulouse cell served for the creation of Sub-Station 'Rab', headed by Maj. Korwin-Szymanowski 'Rab'. It was composed of a field cell 'Felicja' in Toulouse headed by Capt. Gustaw Firla Benz, an industrial cell in Lyon headed by Lt. Zygmunt Wilkoński 'Toul', an evacuation cell (to Spain) headed by Lt. Feldhausen, a railway cell in Pau (on the border with Spain) organised by 'Biały' (PALOME Julian Eysmond), and the naval cell in Marseilles – Lt. Marian Serafiński 'Bór'. Sub-Station 'Bolesław', headed by Leon Śliwiński 'Bolesław' ('Jean-Bol'), was based on the staff of the Nice cell. Its structures engaged three Naval intelligence cells in Toulon (one of them was headed by Gaston Havard 'Foch', and another by Capt. Trolley de Prevoux 'Vox'), a cell controlled by Lt. Wiktor Hennoch 'Mar' in Marseilles, a central Air Force cell directed by a French- man Filip ('Lundi'), with subordinated cells in Belgium and Paris, an Italian cell run by cavalry Capt. Leon Gołogórski 'Filip', a cell in Lille headed by Bernard Manceu 'Germaine', a cell in Bretagne organised by Gilbert Foury 'Edwin', a cell in Toulouse headed by Andrzej Kuśniewicz 'Bondy' ('Karol'), an economic-political cell of Wincenty Jordan – Rozwadowski 'Pascal', an independent cell in Lyon run by Lt. Stanisław Łucki 'Arab' and 'Rota' Henryk Starorypiński and an industrial cell directed by Witold Obrębski 'OB'.

Cells and persons engaged in particularly sensitive and important tasks were supervised directly by the Chief of Station 'F'; they included the bureau of the Station, created in June 1941, the counter-intelligence cell of Maj. Kazimierz Kwieciński, and female couriers who provided communications between Vichy and the occupied zone (Maria Sapieżyna 'Mania', 'Matka Mani' – name unknown, and Maria Krakowska 'Mura'), 'Mania' and Władysława Śliwińska 'Marysia', both of whom conducted intelligence work among the Italian aristocracy, as well as 'Dąb '(Jerzy Zdziechowski), who maintained contact with Vichy political circles.[24]

Each of the sub-stations was built of field networks and independent specialised cells, closely supervised by the chiefs of sub-stations. Field intelligence networks were interested in all events taking place in their regions, while specialised cells focused on a single problem.

The equipment of Station 'F' improved considerably when it was headed by Col. Romeyko (January–December 1942). With the purchase of specialist photographic equipment it was possible to microfilm reports and in this way it was no longer necessary to carry intelligence materials in suitcases. The II Bureau of the General Staff provided two modern W/T stations for immediate contact with London. In the opinion of Col. Romeyko communications were 'extremely efficient, to such an extent that we receive replies from Headquarters without moving away from the set. On important issues (a report about the departure of a ship) we get communications outside scheduled hours'.[25]

The above changes, like the reorganisation of the existing structures, which entailed separate the specialised branches (W/T stations, a cipher section, an expert office and a section responsible for finding accommodation for the staff all functioned independently of each other) brought about a considerable improvement in operational security.

Written reports of Station 'F' were forwarded regularly every two weeks, and sometimes amounted to 700 pages. They were made in two copies, one of which was delivered by the American Naval Attaché in Vichy while the other was carried by couriers across Spain to Lisbon. As a result courier reports reached London in about ten days.[26]

In the second half of 1942 the conditions of work of Polish Intelligence deteriorated considerably once the Polish Organisation of Struggle for Independence (POWN – for simplicity it will be referred to in future as The Polish Secret Army in France), controlled by the Ministry of

Internal Affairs, became active in the south of France. The Polish Secret Army in France assumed the form of a large-scale network involved in current combat and subversive activities. The presence in one region of two organisations pursuing different goals but seeking support among the same social group (Poles living in France) led to a conflict of interests. In the opinion of Col. Romeyko the establishment of The Polish Secret Army in France had a very negative impact on the possibility of conducting intelligence work. The Poles became a particularly suspected group and found themselves at the centre of attention of the Italian police. According to the Chief of the Station: 'All this produced a particularly unhealthy atmosphere for the Poles. The French authorities changed their attitude and were against us. A number of arduous restrictions for foreigners were introduced. All trips, even to the neighbouring commune, were controlled. Moreover, German counter-intelligence had grown roots in large cities [...] It even had villas of its own for research [...] A special counter-intelligence police was set up in Vichy under German supervision'.[27]

For that reason the bureau of Station 'F' decided to gradually replace the Polish personnel of the networks with the French who were less suspicious. The changes pertained first and foremost to the courier services and led to the employment of French radio-telegraphic operators; they also involved a transition from Polish codes to the French ones. The creation of a counter-intelligence sub-cell in all cells of Station 'F' was initiated.

The changes did not protect the network from setbacks. On 15 August 1942 a special group of the French police arrested members of the Marseilles naval cell, including its Chief, Lt. Serafiński 'Bór'. In this situation the remaining cells of the Sub-station run by Maj. Korwin-Szymanowski 'Rab' suspended or considerably limited their activity for security reasons. In mid-October 'Rab', threatened with arrest, was ordered to leave his position which was taken over by Maj. Kwieciński 'Wiktor'.

At the end of October the Vichy political police traced two W/T stations, one in Lyon and the other in Nice. This was most likely caused by new radiolocation equipment used by the Frenchs considering that the arrests occurred during the transmission of messages. More arrests followed, at the turn of October and November when Members of Sub-station's cells headed by Śliwiński 'Bolesław' were arrested in Lyon, Nice and Paris. Station '300' mentioned above was also affected.

German and Italian troops entered the Vichy state on 11 November 1942, accompanied by Abwehr functionaries who were already familiar with the local conditions. Sapieżyna 'Mania', a courier of the Chief of Station 'F', was arrested on 17 November while carrying many intelligence reports. Her arrest was the work of Rev. Kwiatkowski, the parish priest of the Korybut-Daszkiewicz parish in San Remo, who probably worked for the Italian security service. The arrest of Sapieżyna and a series of earlier arrests posed a direct threat to the bureau of Station 'F'. German internment of personnel of the U. S. Attaché's office and the simultaneous elimination of the evacuation cell to Spain disrupted courier communications. This was the reason why at the end of December 1942 Col. Romeyko decided that given the circumstances the network was forced to suspend further activity and destroy all of its archives and notes, etc. Its main personnel was ordered to leave France.

W/T communications almost stopped; it was limited to the contact of the Station 'F' bureau with London. The 'defrosting' (reactivating) of the network was planned for the second half of January 1943, following the implementation of far reaching changes. After handing over of duties to Śliwiński, Col. Romeyko crossed the border into Switzerland on 27 December 1942, ending the period of directing the Polish intelligence network in France.

The resumption of intelligence work, as planned by Romeyko, never took place. Śliwiński was arrested at the beginning of January 1943 and he had not designated his successor in advance. At the same time about thirty of his closest colleagues, including 17 Poles, were detained. The Chief of the II Bureau of the Polish General Staff determined that maintaining the network further would be too risky and ordered the disbandment of Station 'F'.[28]

While active, Station 'F' sent to London a great number of intelligence materials: 5,302 reports and information notes forwarded by couriers and in the form of W/T telegrams, of which 2,482 were sent when the Station was headed by Maj. Słowikowski 'Rygor' and Maj. Zarembski 'Tudor'; 2,770 reached London during the tenure of Col. Romeyko 'Mak'.[29]

Many of the reports were responses to questions put by the OSS and the SIS. For example, when in the early spring of 1942 the Allied Command, anxious about the security of Gibraltar, feared that neutral Spain would be attacked by Germany, Station 'F' was entrusted with the task of checking the disposition of German troops in France from the point of view of possible preparations for such an operation. At the turn of March and April 1942 British and American intelligence services received a report from Polish intelligence and a map showing the German Order of Battle in France, Belgium and the Netherlands. The American Military Attaché in Lisbon evaluated the report as 'excellent' and immediately forwarded it to the Director of Military Intelligence in Washington, while Lt-Col. Robert A. Solborg, working in the Attaché's office, concluded that 'the current deployment of German troops in no way points at the concentration of troops or preparations for the invasion of the Iberian Peninsula'.[30]

In 1942 the Allies, concerned with the safety of their planes engaged in operations over the Continent and fearing possible German preparations for an invasion of Great Britain, tried to obtain comprehensive knowledge about the potential of the Luftwaffe. Polish intelligence supplied London with detailed information concerning the disposition of the Luftwaffe, new technical solutions applied in aviation and other details. For those reasons the networks conducted a meticulous reconnaissance of German anti-aircraft batteries deployed along the coast and around the more important industrial centres. The battle for the Atlantic meant that foremost importance was attached to reports about the

Kriegsmarine, especially about the production in those shipyards which assembled miniature submarines and their mooring sites. The naval cells of Station 'F', specialised in monitoring movement at sea, forwarded many reports concerning that issue, and regularly wired detailed telegrams giving the hours of the departure of particular vessels together with a description of their cargo.[31]

Particular significance was ascribed to Polish assessments of the public feelings of the French population as well as the influence and popularity of clandestine movements in France. The English and the Americans feared that the Free French would try to present themselves in a favourable light and overestimate public support for their movement. If military and industrial information was interesting predominantly for staff officers responsible for preparing plans for military operations, reports discussing social moods and the influence of various political trends were of interest primarily to political circles. The most essential reports of this type reached the American President and Secretary of State through the OSS. An October report of Station 'F' informs that Pierre Laval, the Prime Minister of Vichy France, believed that the war would probably be over by the end of 1942 and that peace would create conditions conducive for the future of France since she had not participated in the war nor suffered war losses, therefore she would enjoy new opportunities for development. That document contains an in-depth analysis of the realities and stresses the growing impact of the communist party as well as shrinking support for Vichy and the remaining 'actors' on the French political arena. It says, 'the split in the Action Française [ultra-right, monarchist-conservative political movement – R.W.] caused by the church's adoption, with regard to the Jewish question, of an attitude [condemnation by the French Roman-Catholic Church of the persecution of Jews – R.W.] of anti-collaborating convictions of the right wing expressed in *Le Figaro* has brought about evolution of the French right wing and its definite departure from any collaborating ideas. [...] French left wing, now represented first of all by Léon Blum and Édouard Herriot and it is they whom the left will consolidate around again. Full support that de Gaullist Movement received from the socialists as well as acceptance for temporary dictatorship of General de Gaulle, as a historic necessity, is bound to influence the entire left wing [...] political support of a great group provides political and social base for de Gaulle Movement [...] de Gaullist Movement in France has reached a turning point and is a step away from the transformation into a serious political direction that decides about the future of France. If this movement is well organised and adequately active [...], it will become the most important movement deciding on the new reality.'[32]

The contents of this report, highly valued by the Americans, indicates that Polish intelligence well knew the social mood in France and possessed profound knowledge about French official and underground political life. The report's author had correctly predicted the development of events in France two and a half years before the end of the war, which at that time was a highly unpredictable country.

To summarise the one year of intelligence work conducted by Station 'F', headed by Col. Romeyko, a particularly important event should not be ignored, namely, an understanding with the French 'Resistance', achieved in the middle of 1942. The Poles reached an agreement with such prominent figures associated with the Resistance as Gen. Laurant, Gen. Jean de lattre de Tassigny, Deputy Ferdinand Laurent, Gen. Henri Giraud, Lt-Col. Ronin and others. Within the framework of co-operation with the French Air Force intelligence network, headed by Lt-Col. Ronin, the Poles were supplied with much information; in return, the Polish side provided Ronin with possibilities to contact the British.[33] Presumably it was thanks to those contacts that Station 'F' learned about the relations between various trends of the Resistance movement and the attitudes dominant among its members.

The departure of Col. Romeyko and the evacuation via Switzerland and Spain of several score members of his group did not mean that all activity had ceased, since some 200 agents of Station 'F' network, which was disbanded upon the orders of the Chief of the II Bureau, remained in France. Many of them continued to pursue intelligence work. In January and at the beginning of February 1943 the W/T stations left behind by the Station sent fifty reports. Already in January 1943 Maj. Zdzisław Piątkiewicz 'Lubicz', Lt. Wincenty Jordan-Rozwadowski 'Pascal', Capt. H. Starorypiński 'Rota' and Lt. Zbigniew Morawski 'Lao' started to rebuild a communication network encompassing particular cells. In view of the fact that from the end of 1942 the crisis appeared not to be spreading the II Bureau in London decided to establish a new intelligence network – Station 'F II', composed of personnel still remaining in the field. Formally, this structure was created on 13 February 1943 by the order sent by the telegram no. 951-955; the new head was Maj. Piątkiewicz. The former chief of intelligence, Col. Romeyko, who at that time was staying in Geneva, was instructed to create a cell in Switzerland which would constitute a mail transfer point and technical base for Station 'F II'.[34] The new network took over from its predecessor all wireless communications under the control of Lt. Jerzy Krauze 'Błysk' (two broken W/T stations and one ready to work), a spare manned W/T station headed by Jeremi Stroveiss 'Karbo', a small amount of photographic equipment and money, as well as seven cells of the former Sub-station 'Bolesław' and two of Sub-station 'Rab' – all in various condition.[35]

Meanwhile, on 1 March 1943 Station 'F II' sent its first general report for February. On 6 February Lt. Jordan-Rozwadowski crossed the Swiss border carrying a lengthy report. Having reached Geneva he established contact with representatives of Swiss Intelligence and managed to conclude an agreement between the respective intelligence services, according to which the Swiss were not to hinder the anti-German activity of Polish Intelligence. This made it possible to organise a safe courier route in Switzerland, to create favourable conditions for despatching reports from Geneva to London and to receive funds from London needed to cover the expenses of 'F II'. The establishment of a secure base in

Switzerland was an extremely important step towards rebuilding allied intelligence in France.[36]

After the Germans overran the unoccupied part of France conditions for intelligence work deteriorated considerably. The German reprisals against the French for providing any sort of assistance to, not to mention collaboration with, secret anti-German organisations, generated far-reaching restraint among the people. An interesting characterisation of France was outlined by Lt. Jordan-Rozwadowski, one of the main organisers of the 'F' network and an excellent intelligence officer: 'A country integrally occupied by the Germans but whose élite, noticing the division and inertia of their own Resistance organisations (the consequence of an absolute lack of clandestine experiences in a country that enjoyed long-lasting freedom) is favourably inclined towards the cause of the Allies and willingly remains at the disposal of non-French organisations.

The Polish element – officers or civilians – left behind in a region drained by evacuation is composed either of blunderers or persons of meagre moral qualities. The majority of both groups either speak French poorly or not at all. Meanwhile, one of the results of the German integral occupation of the country is the special attention paid to the Poles. In other words, only a person capable of being taken for a German or a Frenchman can work underline{effectively} [emphasis in the original]. [...] The Germans followed a similar line of thinking, being aware of the fact that their agents would not be able to operationally penetrate the work carried out by the local Underground. Hence the German recruitment of about 40,000 agents of the French Gestapo, a hundred times more dangerous to us than any purely German organisation because it operates predominantly by means of provocation. The prime task of a French agent working for the Germans was to make his way into the ranks of the 'Resistance".[37]

In a situation when there was a lack of suitable Polish personnel and the Germans were particularly sensitive to the Poles, Station 'F II' network became gradually dominated by people born in France. Practically, only the bureau remained purely Polish. More importantly, only a few Poles with professional intelligence training, received in the pre-war II Bureau, stayed in the organisation. The others were self-taught and had gained their experience during the occupation. Frenchmen drawn into intelligence worked without financial reward, exclusively for patriotic reasons, and were treated as colleagues in a common cause and not as paid agents. Lt. Jordan-Rozwadowski maintained that only three groups in French society were successful in intelligence work: clergymen, Jews and Gypsies,. Thanks to the fact that the organisation based its work on ideological elements only a few of the agents broke down when arrested. None of the more important members of the network betrayed their colleagues despite the universal application of the death penalty and torture.[38]

Compared to its predecessor the structure of Station 'F II' changed considerably. The division of duties in its bureau assumed final shape in the mid-1943. Maj. Piątkiewicz 'Lubicz' was responsible for general administration, finances, personnel and contacts between the 'F II' command, the base of Lt-Col. Romeyko 'Mak' in Switzerland, and the II Bureau in London. Together with his secretariat, 'Lubicz' stayed in hide-outs on farms in the region of Grenoble-Chambéry. The organisation of the courier communications network, the transfer to Switzerland and Spain, distribution of funds in the field, looking after those detained and their families, and contacts with other Polish organisations remained in the domain of Morawski 'Lao', who was simultaneously the head of Cell 'Magda'. The most prominent branch of Station 'F' was supervised by Jordan-Rozwadowski 'Pascal', responsible for the organisation of intelligence, the development of the network, tactics and the preparation of reports. The leadership of the Station had their own assessment office, a cipher office and other auxiliary cells as well as a mobile control cell[39] whose task was to check information which appeared to be false or exaggerated. Its members included the most experienced agents.

Station 'F II' included field cells which, in turn, were divided into smaller territorial sectors. Cell 'Magda' – 'Madeleine', headed by Lt. Morawski, mentioned above, covered the Rhône and the Alpine region, including Lyon, Grenoble and Chambéry, while Cell 'Anna', controlled by Capt. Trolley de Prevoux 'Vox', encompassed Provence, Cell 'Metro' – 'Cecylia', headed by Gilbert Foury 'Edwin' – the region of Paris, Normandy, Brittany and the Northern Basin; 'Felicja', under Capt. Gustaw Firla 'Benz' encompassed Toulouse; 'Maria', headed by Lt-Col. Stanisław Lasocki 'Łoś' and then by Jean Coudert 'Rett' – the region of Lyon, while 'Azur', supervised by Marius Comolli 'Ariel' and Ambroise Massei 'Puck' was probably a supra-regional network.[40]

Station 'F II' network grew rapidly and in 1944 had more than 1,500 members.[41] Information was sent by a network of W/T stations at the disposal of the Station or particular cells. Written intelligence reports (the longest ones totalled 800 pages) were made in four copies. One remained in the studies and assessments office of the Station, two were sent by courier via Spain and Switzerland, and one was picked up by an aeroplane from Great Britain.

The architects of the network dwelt on the experiences gained from the activities of Station 'F', and while adapting intelligence to a new and more difficult situation they placed great emphasis on maximum protection against exposure. Prior to commencing work on a given territory the leadership of 'F II' created a support base that included dead letter boxes, accommodation for agents and spare operational premises, safe contact points, networks of couriers, a back-up network and a system of isolation for persons and networks traced by the enemy. According to 'Pascal', responsible for intelligence in 'F II': 'Each of the independent cells required at least 15 dead letter boxes (10 operational and 5 spare ones), four liaison agents [...] two-three offices used interchangeably for editing and photographing reports, and two premises for ciphers – all in the place of work of the head of a given cell – with the provision that none of the agents could live in the place where he worked'.[42] The principles of operational security were strictly obeyed: a ban on carrying compromising materials, reports were to be carried exclusively by trained couriers, it was obligatory to have a 'cover story' for those performing any sort of intelligence tasks, and a categorical ban on entering premises without previously checking if they are 'clean' (signalled by using items placed on window sills or on staircases). Adherence to the principles of security and complete isolation (temporary severance of contacts with persons detained by the Germans) enabled the remaining members of 'F II' network to avoid arrest despite the detention of individuals or whole cells. The existence of duplicated independent networks whose members were not aware about each other was the reason why a direct hit against one of the networks did not hamper the continuity of intelligence over the whole territory.[43] Thanks to such an organisation of work despite the constantly growing terror of the German authorities and the collaborating French police the 'F II' network survived in good condition until the complete liberation of France, supplying the Allies a lot of information of prime importance. As early as March 1943 Polish intelligence provided the Allies with a map of German defence lines in the Netherlands, Belgium and France.[44] Later on, networks operating along the Atlantic coast and the English Channel conducted a regular and detailed reconnaissance of German fortifications in Normandy, Brittany and Flanders.[45] At the same time intelligence assessment was conducted with regard to the German defence lines on the Mediterranean coast and along the French-Italian border, as well as fortifications further inland.[46] Polish intelligence provided complete and detailed reconnaissance of the German Order of Battle (both Wehrmacht units and Luftwaffe), constantly updating it.[47] Such information was priceless during preparations for the invasion of Normandy and after the creation of the second front.

Submarine bases as well as the movement of naval and freight ships and trains were continuously monitored. Reports transmitted by Station 'F II' analysed the domestic situation in France and evaluated public mood. Information about the destruction of industrial centres due to Allied bombing and the impact of air raids upon the morale of the German troops became increasingly important.

British and American evaluations of reports obtained from 'F II' networks, now in NARA (College Park, Maryland), leave no doubt as to the quality of the materials. The following evaluating grades prevail: 'new information', 'valuable information', 'very useful data', 'clearly true, reliable and valuable data'. Only rarely the following formulations can be found: 'true data but already outdated' or 'probably a good report but useless in its current form'.[48]

Once the front moved (June 1944) the area of operation of the Polish network shrank. The last 'F II' cell worked on the fortified bridge-head in Nantes, which the Germans held until May 1945. That was the source of the last wireless reports from France received by the Allies before the end of the war.[49]

In the course of its activity Station 'F II' sent more than 10,000 pages of professional intelligence. Efficient organisation made it possible for wireless telegrams and written reports to reach London quickly. Besides the contents of the intelligence reports it was the speed that decided that the network's accomplishments were valued very highly. The price paid by the Station for this success was very high – 85 persons were executed, 151 were deported to camps, and 60 were interned.[50]

To complete the overall picture reference should be made to the Polish Secret Army in France, established in 1941 and headed by Aleksander Kawałkowski 'Hubert'. Its basic aim was to organise Poles living in France for the purpose of conducting subversive activities in the German rear areas. Less importance was attached to intelligence, nevertheless the intelligence section of this organisation provided several thousand reports. From the point of view of intelligence the Polish Secret Army in France assumed greater significance after the invasion of Normandy, when telegrams from behind the front line were useful for the Allied forces. The network performing this task was created by Capt. Władysław Ważny 'Tygrys', parachuted in March 1944; It played a special role in the summer of 1944 when it was directed to establish the location of V-1 launching sites. In response, 162 telegrams were sent with information concerning that matter.[51] Unfortunately, on 16 August 1944 'Tygrys' was arrested by the French police and executed. His death did not, however, halt the work of the network and last reports concerning V-1 rockets were transmitted at the beginning of September. The Polish Secret Army in France achievements include also the discovery of the largest French depot storing V-1 rockets in the St. Leu-d'Essernet caves where the Germans kept 70 missiles used for attacking London.[52]

After Germany seized France Polish intelligence was the first to organise itself and to send information from the occupied country. Throughout the whole war it forwarded almost uninterruptedly highly valued reports, providing the Allies with a complete picture of German activity as well as of the social, political and economic life in France. An extremely valuable network active in North Africa was created by engaging officers from Station 'F'. Intelligence based in France had its cells in Luxembourg, Belgium and the Netherlands, and occasionally penetrated North Italy. The last intelligence W/T station to send telegrams from the part of the country still under occupation was in the structures of Station 'F II'. Unquestionably, the Polish intelligence in France had a considerable contribution to Allied military successes in Africa and West Europe.

Notes

1 M. Z. Rygor Słowikowski, *In the Secret Service. The Lighting of the Torch*, London 1988, pp. 15–16.
2 IPMS, Kol. 96, Interview given by Leon Śliwiński to Maciej Morawski on Radio Free Europe, 21 XII 1984.
3 IPMS, Kol. 242/63, Station 'F' – France, pp. 3–9.

4 N. West claimed that the II Bureau Intelligence networks left behind in France '[…]
   rapidly became for British Intelligence the only source of information about the
   situation in the occupied region which is yet another testimony the weakness of
   SIS structures in Europe'. N. West, *MI-6. Operacje brytyjskiej Tajnej Służby
   Wywiadu (MI-6. The Operations of the British Secret Intelligence Service
   1909–1945)*, Warszawa 2000, p. 114.

5 NARA, RG 165, MID France, Box 805, File 2910, Navy Department. Office of the
   Chief of Naval Operations. Washington, February 19. 1942. French Espionage and
   Propaganda, pp. 11-15.

6 NARA, RG 165, MID Germany, Box 1201, File 6170, Organization of the German
   Army November 6. 1941, pp. 1-36.

7 J. E. Zamojski, *Profesjonaliści i amatorzy. Szkic o dziejach polskiej służby
   wywiadowczej we Francji w latach 1940–1945 'F-2' (Professionals and Amateurs.
   Sketch about the History of Polish Intelligence in France in 1940–1945–'F-2')*,
   'Dzieje Najnowsze', 1980, nr 4, pp. 89–91.

8 IPMS, Kol. 242/63, leaf 1, Station 'Afryka' – Algiers.

9 M. Z. Rygor Słowikowski, *In the Secret Service*, op. cit., pp. 127–163.

10 S. Dorril, *MI-6. Fifty Years of Special Operations*, London 2000, p. 250.

11 Having made his way to France Flight Capt. Roman Czerniawski graduated from a
   Staff course at the École Supérieure de Guerre (Paris) and then in March 1940 was
   sent to the Second Department of the First Grenadier Division. He was the author
   of the famous command 4444 – the signal for disbanding the division. A. Pepłoński
   *Wywiad Polskich Sił Zbrojnych na Zachodzie 1939–1945 (The Intelligence Service
   of the Polish Armed Forces in the West 1939–1945)*, Warszawa 1995, p. 107.

12 J. Piekałkiewicz, *Szpiedzy, agenci, żołnierze. Tajne oddziały w II wojnie światowej
   (Spies, Agents, Soldiers. Secret detachments during the Second World War)*, Kraków
   1993, p. 3.

13 TNA(PRO), KV 2/72, Memorandum concerning the statement by Fl/Lt. Roman
   Czerniawski, formerly of the 'Progress' Intelligence Office, on the subject of the
   liquidation of the I. O. by the Germans on 12.10.1942 in the presence of Maj.
   Witold Langenfeld, Lt. Rudolf Plocek, pp. 1-7. A. Pepłoński, *Wywiad PSZ*, op. cit.,
   pp. 110–111.

14 IPMS, Kol. 242/63, Ekspozytura F. Placówka wywiodowcza no. 1 Paris p. 18; TNA
   (PRO), KV 2/72, Memorandum concerning the statement by Fl-Lt. Roman
   Czerniawski, pp. 24–27. R. Garby-Czerniawski, *The Big Network*, London 1961, p.
   201. For the structure of 'Int.' network see: i. a. N. West, *MI-6*, op. cit.

15 According to A. Pepłoński the crisis was caused by the fact that the Germans had
   detained the newly recruited agent 'Emil' who drunkenly boasted in a tavern that
   he was working for Intelligence. On the other hand the report by R. Czerniawski
   claimed that a penetration of the network was rendered possible by Tadeusz
   Biernacki, an Abwehr agent. See: TNA (PRO), KV 2/72, Memorandum concerning
   the statement by Fl/Lt. Roman Czerniawski, pp. 7-10; A. Pepłoński, *Wywiad PSZ*,
   op. cit., p. 111.

16 A. Pepłoński, *Wywiad PSZ*, op. cit., p. 113; R. Garby-Czerniawski, *The Big Network*,
   op. cit., pp. 181–197.

17 Cell 'XX' employed specialists representing numerous disciplines, such as
   physicians, psychologists, sociologists, etc. As a rule these were civilian scientists
   and frequently outstanding academic professors. The cell was also known as a
   'Committee of twenty'. On the 'double-cross' system see: J. Masterman, *The Double
   Cross System*, Polish ed., Warszawa 1973.

18 IPMS, Kol. 96, Interview given by Roman Czerniawski and broadcast by Radio Free
   Europe on 26 December 1974, leaf 2-12.

19 E. Volkaman, *Espionage. The Greatest Spy Operations of the 20th Century*, New York
   1995, p. 45.

20 TNA (PRO), KV 4. 83, Report on the activities of the security service during August Special Agents 1944, p. 2.
21 IPMS, Kol. 96, Interview given by Roman Czerniawski and broadcast by Radio Free Europe on 16 December 1974, Lewes 12-20.
22 IPMS, Kol. 96, Chief of the II Bureau of the Polish General Staff in London, document signed by Lt.Col. Marian Romeyko, former head of Station 'F', report on the activity of Station 'F' in 1942, p. 2.
23 A. Pepłoński, *Wywiad PSZ*, op. cit., p. 102.
24 IPMS, Kol. 96, Marian Romeyko, former Chief of Station 'F', report..., pp. 89; ibid., Polish chiefs and administrative personnel; ibid. Dismissed Polish superiors and administrative personnel; ibid. Explanations of codenames; J. E. Zamojski, *Profesjonaliści i amatorzy*, op. cit., pp. 102–107; IPMS, col. 242/63, Station 'F' Marseilles, p. 1.
25 IPMS, Kol. 96, Marian Romeyko, former Chief of Station 'F', report..., p. 10.
26 Ibid., pp. 11–13.
27 Ibid., p. 16.
28 Ibid., pp. 18–49.
29 A. Pepłoński, *Wywiad PSZ*, op. cit., p. 105.
30 NARA, RG 165, MID Belgium, Box 127, File 6905, German Order of Battle in Holland, Belgium and France, April 2 1942, British and Polish, Reliability: Excellent, pp. 1–4.
31 NARA collections contain several score Polish reports from this period, with detailed information and situational plans. See, e. g.: NARA, RG 165, MID France, Box 888, File 6905; Box 897, File 7905; Box 906, File 9505; Box 911, File 9900; Box 914, File 7; Box 904, File 9815; Box 928, File Misc., Box 1280, File 6320.
32 See, e.g.: NARA, RG 165, MID France, Box 811, File 3020, Strictly confidential. November 6, 1942. For the president, the secretary and the under-secretary. A. J. Drexel Biddle, Jr. Attaching copies of a strictly confidential report from Polish secret sources in France, on internal developments in France.
33 IPMS, Kol. 96, Marian Romeyko, former chief of Station 'F', report..., pp. 21–22, 54.
34 IPMS, Kol. 96, Dr. Marian Zdzisław Piątkiewicz, former Chief of Station F II, London 1945. Secret. Chief of the Intelligence Bureau, ibid., pp. 2-4.
35 Ibid., pp. 6-7, also IPMS, col. 96, Polish chiefs and administrative personnel; ibid. Dismissed Polish chiefs and administrative personnel; ibid. Explanations of codenames. The legacy of Sub-station 'Bolesław', taken over by the 'F II' network, included the cell in Marseilles (although its chief, Lt. Wiktor Rozwadowski 'Tor', had been burned), a cell in Lyon, composed of several persons and headed by Lt. Stanisław Łucki 'Arab' and Cavalry Capt. Henryk Starorypiński 'Rota', an embryo of a cell controlled by Zbigniew Morawski 'Lao' in Grenoble, the untouched political cell of Lieutenant W. Jordan-Rozwadowski 'Pascal', a naval cell under Capt. 'Vox' (NN) in Toulon, composed of several persons, the functioning Toulon network 'Foch' headed by Gaston Havard, and remnants (a few persons) of the network of Gilbert Foury 'Edwin' in Paris. The legacy of Sub-station 'Rab' included the sub-station staff composed of several persons and headed by Capt. Gustaw Firla 'Benz', as well as several persons-strong intelligence cells located in Toulon and Bordeaux.
36 IPMS, Kol. 96, Dr Marian Piątkiewicz..., pp. 8–9.
37 IPMS, Kol. 96, Notes concerning the work of F II in 1943–1944. Lieutenant Rozwadowski Wincenty 'Pascal' February 1945 in London, pp. 2–3.
38 Ibid., pp. 4–5, 13.
39 Such cells included the studies office of Tadeusz Heinrich 'Cor', a cell specialising in receiving parachuted supplies and headed by Lieutenant Brunon Semmerling 'Fitton', a W/T cell – cryptonym 'Karcial' – under Jean Milgram 'Gemar', and a

ciphers office of the Chiefs of Station 'F II', directed by Lt. Henryk Mikołajczyk 'Mirek'.

40 J.E. Zamojski, *Profesjonaliści i amatorzy*, op. cit., pp. 110–112., IPMS, kol. 69, Explanations of codenames.

41 IPMS, Kol. 96, Dr Marian Piątkiewicz…, p. 4.

42 IPMS, Kol. 96, Notes about the work conducted by F II in 1943-1944. Lt. Wincenty Rozwadowski 'Pascal' February 1945 in London, p. 9.

43 Ibid., pp. 10–13.

44 NARA, RG 165, MID France, Box 885, File 8610, Germany coast defences system, defensive works, prepared defences in Belgium, Holland and France. 3 March 1943, Polish Official.

45 NARA, RG 165, MID France, Box 885, File 6810, France Fortifications. Attached are photos of reports in French on German fortifications in the Somme, Paris, Normandy and Brittany, ibid., Box 962, File Misc. German Fortifications in Brittany., ibid., Box 885, File 6810, France. Military. German fortifications in Brittany and Normandy, October 10 1943 r., ibid., Box 962, File Misc. France. Military. German fortifications in Brittany, and many other documents from this collection.

46 NARA, RG 165, MID France, Box 928, File Misc. France. Military Defenses in the Toulon region. March 11, 1943 r., ibid., France. Military. German fortifications in the South of France, and many other documents from this collection.

47 NARA, RG 165, MID France, Box 910, File 9815 (this box contains numerous Polish Intelligence reports about the German Air Force), Box 962, File Misc., France. Military, February 1944, Box 900, File 7800, France. Geography. German, Coast cities. German bases. 4. Nov. 1943, and many other documents from this collection.

48 NARA, RG 165, MID France, Box 851, File 4610, Evaluations of Polish Intelligence Reports.

49 IPMS, Kol. 96, Interview with L. Śliwiński, p. 2.

50 A. Pepłoński, *Wywiad PSZ*, op. cit., p. 107.

51 IPMS, Kol. 95/19, Aleksander Kawałkowski, Minister Plenipotentiary, *Underground Struggle in France*, p. 15.

52 A. Pepłoński, *Wywiad PSZ*, op. cit., pp. 162-169.

22
North Africa

Andrzej Pepłoński

The activity undertaken by the II Bureau of the Polish General Staff in North Africa was the consequence of the development of the political and geopolitical situation in the whole Mediterranean basin after the fall of France. Once the local French authorities in Algiers, Tunis and Morocco subjugated themselves to the government of Marshal Henri Philippe Pétain the Axis states enjoyed greater freedom in launching military operations, being able to better concentrate their forces in preparation for an attack against Egypt which was controlled by the British.

Those events coincided with the arrival of the Polish government in London and the initiation of a new stage in the co-operation between the II Bureau and British Intelligence. The fact that interest of Polish Intelligence was focused on North Africa stemmed from the agreements concluded by Col. Stewart Menzies, Chief of the Secret Intelligence Service, and Col. Leon Mitkiewicz. The Chief of II Bureau expressed his negative attitude towards the Vichy government and specified the intentions of his Staff. As a result, II Bureau stations in France, Portugal and Spain became more active in acquiring information about the situation in North Africa.[1] On 18 November 1940 Gen. Juliusz Kleeberg ordered a group of Polish officers to leave France for Algiers and Morocco, where they were to create a network evacuating Polish and Allied soldiers from France via Africa to Gibraltar.

Initially the effort was concentrated on rendering help to Polish soldiers interned by the Vichy government. The evacuation was directed by artillery Capt. Stanisław Szewalski. Only after contacting the Polish team in Gibraltar and the local SOE station did Szewalski's group embark upon co-ordinated evacuation and intelligence work. Since the circumstances were conducive it was possible to establish contacts with patriotic groups among the French officers and the US Consulate. Support provided by French Intelligence and members of the 'Réseau d'Astier' clandestine organisation proved essential. In mid-May 1941 Maj. Maigasson and Lt.

Cordier passed over to Capt. Szewalski the contact with two female agents who maintained close relations with officers of the German control commission in Algeria, which considerably facilitated access to secret documents. Capt. Szewalski, who was fluent in German, examined the contents of the briefcases which the Germans carried during their intimate encounters, and photographed or copied the most valuable documents. This procedure continued for almost half a year. The knowledge obtained was forwarded to representatives of British and American intelligence services.[2] Capt. Szewalski's group conducted intelligence work up to 7 April 1942;[3] later organising the evacuation of several II Bureau officers to Algiers.

In view of the growing interest in the information coming from North Africa, at the beginning of May 1941 on the orders of the II Bureau of the General Staff work was initiated to create station 'Afryka' ('Afr.'). This task was entrusted to Maj. Mieczysław Zygfryd Słowikowski 'Rygor', an anti-Soviet intelligence officer before the war, most highly valued among the Polish officers in France. These opinions were confirmed by his thorough preparation of the new and difficult missions covering the area outside Europe, with its central point located in Algiers and extending to Tripoli and Dakar. In the initial organisational work two other Intelligence officers took part: Lt. Tadeusz Jekiel 'Doctor' and Lt. Stanisław Rombejko 'Mustafa', 'Nord', who had earlier participated in establishing station 'Francja'. Considerable assistance was provided by Maj. Maksymilian Ciężki 'Maciej', who headed a communications cell, which during the evacuation was a branch of the 'Cadix' centre in Algiers.[4] Słowikowski obtained a forged French passport with the name of Stawikowski Mieczysław Józef. The entry visa was signed by Marcel Dubois, the Police Commissioner in Morocco. The border control procedure was operationally assessed.

Cautious preparations, however, did not eliminate the risk associated with travelling to Algiers, as the contents of Maj. Słowikowski's luggage, contained 500,000 francs, a codebook, and telegrams containing the tasks for the station. Having overcome those difficulties Słowikowski encountered new obstacles caused by instructions issued by the II Bureau, forbidding him to request assistance from the Polish Consulate General in Algiers, the Honorary Consulate in Casablanca, or contacting the local Polish community.[5] In this situation the Chief of station 'Afr.' began to look for collaborators among the French who were familiar with the area and local contacts especially those who were bona fide legal residents. Work progressed slowly and London-based headquarters kept putting forward new tasks, some of them impossible to realise. A coded telegram of 21 July 1941 contained detailed questions about anti-aircraft defences in North Africa and military transports to Germany. On the following day the II Bureau wanted to know about the technical condition of the battleship 'Richelieu',[6] moored in the port of Dakar, its current armament and gun calibre as well as various information relating to coastal defences. Further assignments included making plans of towns and ports, and a list of Allied ships requisitioned by the Vichy government, together with their current names. All the instructions arrived during the first five days of Maj. Słowikowski's stay in Africa.[7]

After an initial assessment of the local conditions the Chief of station 'Afr.' had orders to create intelligence cells in Algiers, Oran, Tunis, Casablanca, and Dakar. The internal structure of the station's HQ was simplified because of great distances and the lack of radio communications. For those reasons the stations were considerably independent. The technical section was directed by Lt. Rombejko, while the remaining sections: economic, naval and political were entrusted to Lt. Henryk Łubieński 'Banuls', 'Start'. Both heads of sections assigned tasks and drafted instructions for field cells. Maj. Słowikowski was personally in charge of the ciphers.

The station began its work on 31 July 1941. The first intelligence cell, established in Oran, was directed by Capt. Paul Schmidt of the merchant Navy (agent no. 1812). The cell in Tunis commenced working at the beginning of October. Agent no. 1820, had valuable contacts with the French Army Command in Tunis. In October 1941 alone as many as 65 telegrams sent to London dwelt on the information acquired by the two cells. The significance of station 'Afr.' became obvious once British intelligence signalled that it did not have its representative in the region. This information became an impulse for developing further activity. Soon a way was found to improve the financial situation, which initially was unsatisfactory. On 6 August 1941 economic activities were initiated within the 'Flock-Au' Company, which became an official cover for the whole staff of the station.[8] The station's agents became employees of 'Flock-Au' branches in numerous North African towns.[9] Słowikowski officially held the post of commercial director. A dynamic development of agents' network followed, when an average of six agents and operatives were recruited monthly. In November 1941 nine new agents were recruited, and a further fifteen in June 1942, when the station fully developed its potential.[10] In October 1942 the intelligence network was composed of as many as 70 agents and informants registered with Bureau II.

For a while Station 'Afr.' maintained radio communications with London through the cell No. 1 of station '300' in Algiers, headed by Maj. Ciężki. Furthermore, it would use a mailbox in Tangier (Jaima Bueno, 'the Continental' Hotel).[11] As the intelligence network acquired progressively more intelligence materials and documents, it became indispensable to establish courier communications. In this respect, the assistance provided by Robert Murphy, a special representative of President Roosevelt, proved to be particularly useful.[12] It was necessary to act swiftly because the Allies were preparing to seize the southern coast of the Mediterranean, and invasion had to be preceded by a thorough intelligence reconnaissance.

American intelligence, also, received reports from station 'Afr.' at that time through the II Bureau and it valued them highly. In October 1941 the contents of the 65 telegrams mentioned above included, inter alia, information about the reinforcement of the corps in Dakar by two companies 250 strong from a Foreign Legion regiment, the military garrison in Constantine, the La Senia airfield, and the transfer of a group of fighter planes from Maison Blanche airfield to Blida airport. Furthermore, the station informed that the El Aouina airfield north of Tunis was used by the Italians as well as passed over technical specifications of the 340 mm guns deployed near El Metline, east of Bizerta. In December 1941 the station informed London about the condition of coastal defences in the port of Sfax and provided detailed descriptions of the artillery positions. Additionally, it reported that the El Aouina airfield was used not only by the Italians but also by the Germans in their flights to Tripoli. 'Afr.' provided an assessment concerning the road transport movement to Tripoli with food, petroleum and munitions, and informed about inspections of the Mareth defence line on the border between Tunis and Tripoli by German and French officers. The station learned that Marshal Pétain allowed the Germans to use the ports in Bizerta, Bône, Philippeville and Mers-El-Kebir. Agent no. 1880, recruited in May 1942 together with seven other persons, provided 'Rygor' with a copy of the protocol from an international conference in Algiers, attended by the Germans, on increasing industrial and mining production in North Africa. In response to the information received the Intelligence Department requested new information about the French-German agreement on facilitating the use of sea ports and airfields by Axis states.[13]

When the United States joined the war the contacts between Maj. Słowikowski and the American consulate in Algiers grew closer. The Americans permitted their channels to be used for sending the station's correspondence pouch to London.[14] With the coming visit of an OSS representative from Washington, who was described in correspondence as Col. 'X' Col. William A. Eddy further consultations were undertaken replacing the scope of future cooperation. The Americans tried to convince the Chief of 'Station Afr.' to include the intelligence network in the sabotage campaign. Since such a step was hazardous, Maj. Słowikowski categorically refused, saying that 'an entirely separate network of agents has to be organised, unconnected with the work of intelligence agents in the field', and that he 'will not use his own network for that purpose'.[15] The talks were held in consultations with Col. Stanisław Gano, Chief of the II Bureau, who advised 'Rygor' to maintain friendly contacts with Col. Eddy, to render all possible assistance and to provide 'organisational and professional advice, if he asks for it'.[16] Col. William A. Gano reminded him that in accordance with current regulations the chief of Station 'Afr.' should not organise a network for the Americans but could supply them with counter-intelligence information.

These contacts coincided with the efforts of the British and American staffs, which on 20 July 1941 initiated the next stage of preparations for the landing operation. Several days later a decision was taken to begin the realisation of the plan for the invasion of French North Africa, from then on code named 'Torch'. In the winter and spring of 1942 Station 'Afr.' systematically sent new information, e.g. about the research conducted by Air France staff into the possibilities of adapting aeroplanes for military transport. A week earlier the arrival of four troop carriers in the port of

Tunis and a French torpedo boat with shipwrecked men on board had been signalled. The appointment of a new commander of the cruiser 'Dunquerque' was reported as well as the inauguration of a voluntary recruitment of drivers in Tunis.[17]

From mid-April 1942 the station passed the answers through its own W/T station,[18] to the questions from HQ about a possible extension by the French authorities of the Tunis-Gabes railway line in the south-east direction from Tripoli, and by the Italians from Tripoli to the west towards Tunis, as well as a possible stay of Japanese ships with merchandise in African ports. In June 1942 'Rygor' confirmed the construction of railway lines in Tunis and the purchase by Germans of about 1,200 lorries. He traced the shipment route of India rubber marked K.Z.-523 from Dakar to Casablanca and then by train to Algiers and by ship to France. In mid-June 'Rygor' compiled information on the munitions stocks for the French Navy vessels.[19] Further important economic information was forwarded to HQ in the summer. The contents of the French-German and the French-Italian agreement were revealed concerning the supply of 640,000 tons of iron ore for the Germans and 15,000 tons for Italy in return for coal and olive oil.[20] At that time the station reached full organisational effectiveness and acquired without difficulties the information sought by HQ. This was confirmed by Col. R. A. Solborg, a liaison officer of Intelligence OSS with SOE in Lisbon also an envoy of President Franklin D. Roosevelt, who in August 1942 had arrived in Africa for a while after visiting several European capitals and the Intelligence Department of the General Staff. His conversation with Maj. Słowikowski concerned primarily the assessment of the current situation in North Africa and the Mediterranean.[21] The Chief of the station stated that he had information about the growing German interest in North Africa and thus potential difficulties in Allied troop movement along the western coast of Africa and across the Mediterranean. He suggested that the 'landing operations themselves should be conducted simultaneously in all of North Africa. The resistance of the French troops will be symbolic because their Army includes many supporters of Gen. de Gaulle and there is a lack of ammunition and modern weapons. North Africa will be captured in 24 hours'.[22] Maj. Słowikowski said that he maintained constant communications with London by sending two telegrams daily, while the ciphers at his disposal made it possible to conduct correspondence in all languages. However, the information forwarded by Maj. Słowikowski was not the only source of knowledge about the situation in North Africa available to Col. Solborg. In a report submitted to his superior, Col. William J. Donovan on 11 June 1942, he used information and assessments coming from the Portuguese, Spanish and French political and military circles as well as his own observations.[23]

Maj. Słowikowski's opinion about the efficiency of the intelligence station under his command was by no means exaggerated. A comparison of the results of work in the period from 1 October 1941 to 1 May 1942 clearly indicates that 'Afr.' was the best station. With only two cells and 16 agents at its disposal it supplied HQ with as many as 936 reports, while the largest Station 'F' with five cells and 56 agents, sent 1,227 reports. Furthermore, 13 agents of 'F' had been arrested, while 'Afr.' had lost only two.[24]

On 18 October 1942 Station 'Afr.' forwarded information about the coastline defence plans and artillery positions as well as the defence plans of the town and port of Dakar. It also informed HQ about the state of the ships in the port, their ammunition reserves and equipment. Furthermore, information was obtained about two tank divisions and the state of an airfield as well as the aeroplanes using it, in the region of Dakar. Two days prior to the invasion 'Rygor' had sent to London confirmed information regarding the coastal defence in Philippeville and reported that Italian officers had inspected the fortifications. On 7 November 1942, on the eve of the Allied landing, Station 'Afr.' informed HQ about an alarm and the combat alert in the La Senia, Blida and Maison Blanche airfields.[25]

On 8 November 1942 British and American troops landed in three French ports in North Africa: Casablanca, Oran and Algiers. This operation encountered the resistance of those French forces which served the Vichy regime. Ultimately, upon the order of Adm. Jean-François Darlan, Commander-in-Chief of the Armed Forces, French detachments surrendered and the Allies recognised the Admiral as head of the civilian administration in the region. Gen. Henri Giraud assumed supreme command over those French soldiers who decided to join the war against the Axis.[26]

The course of operation 'Torch' confirmed the results of the intelligence gathered by the station. The Americans and the British awarded 'Rygor' with the highest military distinctions. During the ceremony, held on 28 March 1944 in Place du Gouvernement in Algiers, Gen. Jacob Devers, Deputy-Commander-in-Chief of the Allied forces in North Africa, decorated the Maj. with a Legion of Merit Degree of Officer. The citation was signed by President Roosevelt. The British presented Maj. Słowikowski with OBE The Most Excellent Order of the British Empire, which corresponded to the high assessment of his work expressed by Cmdr. Wilfred Dunderdale,[27] head of the SIS liaison unit. The Polish military authorities had already shown their appreciation to Maj. Słowikowski in August 1943, when they awarded him the Gold Cross of Merit with Swords. Similar decorations were awarded to several French agents and Lt. Rombejko.[28]

After the invasion the tasks of the station gradually changed passing back translated text to the British. At a II Bureau briefing 'Rygor' received detailed instructions for intelligence work in parts of occupied Africa occupied as well as southern Italy, especially Sicily and Sardinia. Additional instructions related to South France and Spanish Morocco. The chief of the station was to continue co-operation with the French (Col. Louis Rivet), American and British intelligence services.[29] The new assignments proved to be extremely demanding. One of the prime reasons for less effective work were difficulties with maintaining regular communications with the Italians.

At the beginning of May 1943 'Rygor' reported that 'our Allies, too, had not all achieved positive results'. In the same letter he indicated other causes of the set-backs: the lack of suitable candidates for agents among the Italian population in North Africa, the lack of cover documents, and the scarcity of clandestine contacts in Italy.[30]

The proverbial last nail in the coffin was the directive of Col. Rivet requiring his permission for each recruitment of agents thus limiting the possibilities for expanding the network. 'Rygor' informed HQ about the problems[31] and in view of all these circumstances he suggested closing the Station. This suggestion was approved. At the end of January 1944 a decision was made to set up Station 'ITA' in Italy. At the beginning of September 1944 the network of Station 'Afr.' was taken over by a liaison officer Maj. Adam Świtkowski, Ph.D. Maj. Słowikowski was assigned to a new post at the Infantry Training Centre in Scotland.

Notes

1 L. Mitkiewicz, *Z gen. Sikorskim na obczyźnie* (*With General Sikorski in Exile*), Paris 1968, p. 82.
2 IJPL, Kol. 100/13/1, An account by Col. S. Szewalski from April 1970 entitled 'Droga do zwycięstwa prowadzi przez Afrykę Północną' ('The path towards victory leads across North Africa').
3 IJPL, Kol. 100/13/1, Note from the Evacuation Station 'Lizbona' to Capt. Szewalski, 11 May 1942.
4 HIA, M. Z. Słowikowski, Box 1, Note from the chief of Station 'Afr.' to the chief of the II Bureau, 24 September 1945.
5 M. Z. 'Rygor' Słowikowski, *W tajnej służbie* (*In Secret Service*). *Polski wkład do zwycięstwa w drugiej wojnie światowej*, (*The Polish Contribution for Victory in the Second World War*), London 1977, p. 15.
6 About the cruiser 'Richelieu' and Allied attempts at eliminating it (operations 'Catapult' and 'Menace') see: A. Perepeczko, *Od Mers El-Kebir do Tulonu* (*From Mers El-Kebir to Toulon*), Gdańsk 1979, pp. 87–88, 97–139.
7 Ibid, pp. 128–129.
8 Capt. Tadeusz Jekiel 'Doctor', an engineer by profession, an Intelligence officer, carried a French passport with a Moroccan visa issued for Thomas Jequel, born on 7 June 1907 in Maubeuge. His cover as a representative of a firm 'Carpentras' Chemical-Optical Society specialising in buying up silver.
9 HIA, the M. Z. Słowikowski Collection, Box 1, Note by the Chief of Station 'Afr.' to the Chief of the II Bureau of the Polish General Staff, l. dz. 5/tjn. of 8 January 1942.
10 M. Z. 'Rygor' Słowikowski, *W tajnej służbie*, op. cit., p. 162.
11 IPMS, Kol. 242/63, "Communications of Station 'Afr.'." The II Bureau was given an address to which the radio transmitter was to be delivered – Alger 6 rue Arago, Hotel 'Arago', Madame Rombejko, password 'Michous', response 'Jenwerrais'.
12 HIA, the M. Z. Słowikowski Collection, Box 1, Note from 'Rygor' to the Chief of the II Bureau of the Polish General Staff, l. dz. 25/tjn., 6 May 1942. J. de Launay, *Secrets Diplomatiques 1939–1945*, Bruxelles 1963, pp. 55–56.
13 M. Z. 'Rygor' Słowikowski, *W tajnej służbie*, op. cit., pp. 179–181.
14 The Allies did not keep their promise. The pouch no 1 and 2 were kept in the U.S. Embassy in Lisbon for several months. CAW, VI Bureau, vol. 483, telegram from the Chief of the II Bureau Station 'Estezet', no. 2283 of 27 March 1942, leaf 200.
15 Ibid., leaf 201.
16 CAW, VI Bureau, vol. 483, Dispatch from 'Rygor' to the Chief of the II Bureau, no. 317 of 30 May 1942.

17 M. Z. 'Rygor' Słowikowski, *W tajnej służbie*, op. cit., pp. 215–216.

18 The W/T station functioned uninterruptedly till the closing of the station on 14 September 1944.

19 In June 1942 15 new agents and informers were recruited.

20 M. Z. 'Rygor' Słowikowski, *W tajnej służbie*, op. cit., pp. 291-292.

21 HIA, the M. Z. Słowikowski Collection, Box 1, Note from 'Rygor' to the Chief of the II Bureau, l. dz. 54 of 17 June 1942. Since Col. Solborg's mother was Polish so he spoke Polish well, he served in a regiment of dragoons stationing before the First World War in Mińsk, near Warsaw, comradeship between the two officers was quickly established enhancing the co-operation.

22 HIA, the M. Z. Słowikowski Collection, Box 1, Note from the Chief of Station 'Afr.' to the Chief of the II Bureau of the Polish General Staff, l. dz. 54/tjn. of 17 June 1942.

23 TNA(PRO) HS 3/62, Report by Col. R. A. Solborg to Col. W. J. Donovan from 1 June 1942, concerning the Iberian Peninsula and North Africa.

24 IPMS, A.XII.24/37, A list of consignments and their results from 1.10.41–1.5.42 compilede by II Bureau (Intelligence) from 1 October 1941 to 1 May 1942.

25 M. Z. 'Rygor' Słowikowski, *W tajnej służbie*, op. cit., p. 228.

26 Ibid., p. 370.

27 The decorated men included agents Paul Schmidt (no. 1812), Robert Ragach (no. 1845), and Joseph Briatte (no. 1850).

28 Ibid., pp. 442-445.

29 HIA, the M. Z. Słowikowski Collection, Box 1, Minutes of a briefing with the Chief of Station 'Afr'. on 21 February 1943.

30 HIA, the M. Z. Słowikowski Collection, Box 1, Note from 'Rygor' to the Chief of the II Bureau of the Polish General Staff, l. dz. 145/43/tjn. of 2 May 1943.

31 HIA, the M. Z. Słowikowski Collection, Box 1, Note from 'Rygor' to the Chief of the II Bureau of the Polish General Staff, l. dz. 672/tjn. of 4 September 1943.

23
The Iberian Peninsula

Gill Bennett

Spain

The picture of Polish Intelligence activities in Spain that emerges from documentation found in British Intelligence archives is a confused one. A great deal of human traffic was involved, since Spain was the regular escape route for Polish and other Allied agents, contacts and informants forced to leave France. Consequently, the Polish authorities in Spain worked closely with British Intelligence, who often arranged for the evacuation to the UK of those who made the journey to Spain successfully with Polish help.

The confusion arises from the existence, according to British records, of several parallel and in some cases competing Polish organisations in Spain. These appear to have been controlled by different Polish authorities in London – the II and VI Bureaux as well as military Intelligence, and were not supposed to be aware of each other. It appears that all of them contacted SIS through British Embassy channels, however, so that there were also competing demands for money and other assistance.

No comprehensive account of these Polish activities has been found. A group of documents dating from late 1943 gives a representative impression of the complex situation. These concern the arrival in Madrid in the summer of 1943 of Kasimierz Kraczkiewicz, apparently sent by Kowalewski (in Lisbon) with the assignment of re-organising and taking charge of the escape route for Polish refugees; his real, and very secret mission, however, was thought to be gathering political and military information.

The task of running the escape routes was already being carried out in Madrid by Leonard Leonardów, who had escaped from France in 1941 and was now engaged in passing 'parcels (including wireless-sets) and bodies' across the frontier. Neither the British nor Polish authorities were impressed by Leonardów, who demanded 9,000 pesetas a month to run a courier service into Spain on behalf of SOE (although the courier was thought to cost only 2,500 ptas). Leonardów appears to have had difficulty in writing in Polish and employed a Polish lawyer in Madrid, Czesław Konarek, to write reports for him. Konarek himself was suspected by the Polish Minister in Madrid of being a German spy, but in SIS's view this was only because Konarek's activities had attracted Abwehr attention.

Leonardów had received instructions to work under Kraczkiewicz and in future to take orders from him. However, there appears to have been friction between them from the start, with Leonardow anxious to achieve Kraczkiewicz's removal. One apparent reason for this was to avoid too close scrutiny of Leonardów's financial arrangements. Kraczkiewicz, for his part, was unimpressed by Leonardow, and when he discovered that the Spanish police appeared to have a very detailed and comprehensive knowledge of his secret mission in Spain soon after his arrival, he became convinced that Leonardów was responsible for betraying him, either through malice or indiscretion. However, although Leonardów remained unco-operative and bypassed Kraczkiewicz at every turn, the latter was unwilling to accuse him. The documents suggest, in fact, that information may have reached the Spanish police through other channels, such as through Lisbon. Kraczkiewicz himself was described as having made a number of 'unreliable' contacts in Spain, although SIS considered him 'very competent, extremely tough and ready for anything that might come along'. The development of this power struggle is not documented after the end of 1943. The only other reference that has been found mentions that an SIS agent in Spain – not the one involved in liaison with the Poles – had been asked to keep an eye on and report on Polish Intelligence activities.

At the end of 1943, however, there was a new development. A minute dated 16 December stated that the Polish Intelligence authorities in London had informed SIS that they intended to send a new representative to Spain, Henryk Łubieński (codenamed 'Start'), to establish an independent organisation. He would operate under the direct control of the II Bureau and would have no contact with any other Polish representatives in Spain or Portugal. 'Start' would operate under journalistic cover as a correspondent for the Polish and American press.

SIS were asked to afford facilities for 'Start' through the British Embassy. He was to be given a password to identify the SIS representative concerned with Polish liaison, who would then pass mail through the diplomatic bag to London for onward transmission to the Poles through liaison channels. The 16 December minute stated that SIS's chief interest in all this was that 'Start's new courier lines might be used to speed up the transmission of information to the UK. While the Poles were obtaining very valuable information from their own country, it was taking a very long time to reach the UK: it reached France within a few days, but could take 6 or 8 weeks from then on.

The minute admitted that there were risks attached to a new Polish organisation. Once 'Start' began to build up an organisation for the collection of information in Spain, the danger would increase both of the information being redundant, and of lines getting crossed with other sources. On balance, however, it was felt that provided contact with Start was kept to a minimum and that he worked independently, the risk was worth taking.

Apart from these organisational intrigues, the bulk of references to Polish activities in Spain concern requests for SIS to try and help Poles who had escaped to Spain accomplish the onward journey to the UK. Often they had been working for the Polish and French *réseaux* in France. In some cases these Poles had then been arrested and imprisoned by the Spanish authorities. A number of telegrams have been found, all couched in very similar terms: the Polish Intelligence authorities in London had received information that X was in Spain, either on the run or in prison, and asked SIS to provide help and facilities. Minimal detail is given. Documents have been found concerning requests for assistance for the following:

- Pierre Naquet ('Peter Nichols', 'M. Dumontagel')
- Alexander Olechowski ('Ratauld')
- General Kleeberg ('Andrzej')
- Gabriel Heumann ('Ducros')
- Omer Lacroix ('Omer Catron', 'Omer')
- Stefan Szymanowski ('Louis' Stefan 'Corvin', 'Rab')
- Zygmunt Wilkoński ('Orient')
- Roehr ('John Royston')
- Felicjan Korycki ('Bey', due to arrive in Gibraltar)
- Jerzy Pietraszewski ('Pit',   "   "   ")
- Roman Koperski
- Wanda Morbitzer ('Eva')

In all the above cases the surviving documentation is restricted to a few brief references or a single telegram. (For more details see Chapter 24. J.S. Ciechanowski).

Detailed information has survived concerning Corp. Józef Węgrzyn, also known as Luis Goricochea Tarín, Carlos Rossel, Joseph Dawson and by the code names of 'Carlos' and 'Luis'. Originally a soldier in the Polish armed forces, Węgrzyn escaped from a series of prisons and internment camps and from early 1943 ran several very successful escape routes for Poles from France to Spain via Andorra, managing to arrange the safe evacuation of 550 Poles (as well as a number of British and Americans) before his arrest in March 1944. Although released, his position was compromised and he himself was evacuated via Gibraltar and Algiers to the UK, where he was interrogated at the Royal Victoria Patriotic Schools in Wandsworth.[1] A report prepared on Węgrzyn on the basis of that interrogation is reproduced in Volume II of this Report. His story was described as 'one of the main threads in the annals of the Polish Evacuation Service in Spain...It is difficult to rate too high the services which Węgrzyn rendered to the Allied cause by organising, mainly by his own efforts and initiative, the Andorran Evacuation network'.

The 'Enigma' escapes

Particular efforts were made to secure the safe return of the Polish cryptographers whose escape from France had been arranged by Col. Bertrand. Known as the 'Wicher' group after the code name of Col. Gwido Langer, they included two of the three cryptographers who had cracked the enigma code: Marian Rejewski ('Oksza') and Henryk Zygalski ('Benol', 'Remor'). Also in the group were Tadeusz Suszczewski ('Longinus'), Wiktor Michałowski ('Lubicz'), Stanisław Szachno ('Radwad') and Sylwester Palluth ('Marek', Czarny).

On 29 December 1942 a telegram was sent from 'C' to SIS in Spain stating that 'a party of thirteen Polish cryptographers under Col. Langer password Wicher' were expected to cross from France with French help:

> They are of great importance. If they arrive please make every endeavour to help them. Consider they should be regarded as special case and worth special steps to keep them out of Spanish hands. Would rather they were in Miranda [prison] than that.

Further telegrams on 9 January 1943 stated that the 'most important party' was due to cross the frontier making for Barcelona in the week beginning 11 January:

> If they call on you for use of car to save this party from arrest by Spaniards, you must comply with request and do all you can to help...I attach the utmost importance to the safety of these men...They are specialists, having information which it would be disastrous for the Germans to obtain.

It did not prove easy, however, to track down the 'Wicher' group or offer them help. On 26 January Bertrand telegraphed that a party of eight had left Toulouse on 13–14 January, while a further party of five was due to leave on 20–22 January. However, a message from Lubicz on 5 February reported that some of the Poles had given themselves up to the Spanish authorities at Guardiola; by 23 February Langer ('Wicher') was still in France, but Palluth, Zygalski and Rejewski had all been interned by the Spaniards. Rejewski and Zygalski were eventually released and in July 1943 travelled to the UK via Portugal and Gibraltar. They were then assigned to a Polish cryptanalytic unit at Stanmore where they worked for the rest of the war.

Portugal

Virtually no information on Polish Intelligence activities in Portugal has survived in British Intelligence archives, though the references that have been discovered suggest that arrangements were similar to those in Spain. Portugal, like Spain, was an escape route from France, and indeed a number of Poles were sent from Spain to Lisbon and thence to the UK. It appears that there were also parallel Polish organisations utilising the same channels of communication, providing information to several Polish agencies in London.

Among the few Poles to whom reference has been found are Eugenia Miładowska, the wife of a Polish prisoner of war, who appeared to have an intimate connection with both Polish and Czech Intelligence in Lisbon; Wacław Śledziewski, whose return to London was requested urgently by the Polish II Bureau in December 1941; and Zygmunt Cedro, representative of Polish Naval Intelligence in Lisbon, who was to be granted mail and W/T facilities by SIS in order to transmit his information to London. Other papers concern arrangements in 1943 for Mrs Sylvia Wallace née Wokołowska, a secretary to the Polish General Staff in London, to be officially attached to the staff of the British Passport Control Office in Lisbon so that she could, in fact, work as a secretary to a Polish Intelligence representative.

Gibraltar

Documents discovered on Gibraltar relate exclusively to transit arrangements for Poles en route to the UK. One such was Col. Stanisław Orłowski, who left Cairo for Gibraltar in July 1942 to take up a post as Chief of the Counter-intelligence Department at the Polish Defence Ministry in London. Through the good offices of SIS he was given a priority passage from Gibraltar. The SIS representative in Jerusalem wrote to London on 7 July 1942 recommending Orłowski, with whom he had worked for more than a year in the Middle East, in glowing terms. Orlowski had been:

> ...an excellent colleague. We have worked in perfect harmony the whole time and no request to fill gaps in our organisation has ever been refused. The output of his show has always been of a consistently high order, and I have the greatest respect for his abilities and character. I am not sure who is our liaison officer with the Poles, but I feel that it would be to his advantage to know Col. Orłowski.

Other officers for whom transit facilities were provided by SIS included Cmdr. Bogusław Żórawski, whom the Polish General Staff wanted brought back from Algiers for employment in German Occupied Territory; and Stanisław Korboński, a Polish lawyer recently escaped from France, whose return was arranged in December 1942. Instructions were sent to Gibraltar in December 1943 that if Stanisław Lesiński and Jan Bartke should arrive in Gibraltar, they should be sent to the UK by the first available means of normal transport. In January 1944 two Polish agents, Jan Czarnocki and his wife, who had been working with one of the intelligence cells in France and had just managed to escape, were given facilities and help to travel to the UK. No further information has been found.

Note

1   See *Hinsley*, vol. 4, pp. 71–2 and Appendix 10.

24
Iberian Peninsula

Jan Stanisław Ciechanowski

Following the fall of France, Portugal and Spain became one of the most important communication crossroads of the belligerents. This is also where their interests crossed. For the anti-Nazi coalition, the Iberian Peninsula was a window on Europe and America. Lisbon and Madrid, and also other capitals or largest cities of neutral states (Stockholm, Berne and Istanbul) became significant espionage centres.

Polish Intelligence became extensively interested in the Iberian Peninsula during the Spanish civil war (1936–1939), when it treated this region as an excellent observation area for Soviet activity, German, and to a lesser degree Italian military units and their equipment.[1] Portugal performed the role of a principal base for the numerous ad hoc missions sent for this purpose by II Bureau of the Polish General Staff.[2] The importance attached by Polish Intelligence to the Spanish civil war was demonstrated by the appointment of Karol Dubicz-Penther to the post of the Polish Minister in Lisbon (1 February 1937). At the same time he ran a single person intelligence cell 'Anitra', set up by Section 'Wschód' ('East') of II Bureau, to observe Soviet Intelligence work in Spain.[3] Lt-Col. Aleksander Karol Kędzior was the Military Attaché there from January 1937, accredited primarily to observe the Spanish Civil War.[4] After September 1939, the continuity of Polish Intelligence on the Iberian Peninsula was almost totally interrupted, by the removal of leading staff of Section 'Wschód', which organised expeditions to Spain during the Civil War.

Since 1928, Portugal was ruled by the authoritarian government of António de Oliveira Salazar.[5] After the outbreak of the Second World War, the Portuguese authorities, officially neutral, were forced into an extremely dangerous game. On the one hand, they were bound by an alliance with Great Britain, reinforced by considerable economic dependence upon the British, whilst on the other, constantly growing German pressure gave the Third Reich increasing political and economic influence in Portugal. Up until the end of 1943 a German invasion of the Iberian Peninsula, and thus also of Portugal, was considered to be likely.[6] But the majority of Portuguese remained pro-British.[7]

The attitude of the Portuguese authorities towards Polish interests, institutions and refugees was, on the whole, rather friendly. Consequently, their observance of the principles of neutrality was much greater than was the case in Spain. Most of the time Portugal and Spain granted Polish refugees transit visas only, and even these were combined with numerous restrictions. It therefore became extremely important for the Portuguese Ministry of Foreign Affairs to grant Polish officials diplomatic status, thus ensuring their diplomatic immunity and privileges, as well as visas with no specified term. Thanks to this, the Polish Legation 'changed from day to day from a small mission into the most important representation of Poland in the western part of the European Continent'. The Germans in vain demanded its liquidation.[8]

The Poles in Portugal did not encounter any danger similar to France or constant harassment and infiltration by the Spanish. The Portuguese 'international police', PVDE,[9] was interested in the operations of the Polish II Bureau and Ministry of Internal Affairs, but to a lesser degree than was the case with British and German Intelligence. In any case, the attention of the relatively small Portuguese counter-Intelligence was for a long time concentrated on the threat of a German invasion. The Poles attracted less attention, which is not to say that there were no obstacles. In his reminiscences, 'Kim' Philby, an SIS officer and a Soviet agent, who between 1941 and 1945 headed the Iberian Department of Section V (counter-intelligence, dealing with enemy operations against Great Britain, abroad), claimed that a very high percentage of intelligence operations carried out by the Abwehr against the United Kingdom took place on the Iberian Peninsula.[10]

Lisbon was, then, one of the most important centres of Polish Intelligence in Europe. In 1943 an officer of the Lisbon station wrote: 'I am not sure whether [...] before 1939 anybody in Warsaw expected, that Lisbon would become the headquarters of intelligence work during this war'.[11] The most significant station on the Peninsula was Station 'P' of II Bureau, PGS, in Lisbon.[12] From the second half of 1940 it was headed by Lt-Col. Stanisław Kara ('Profesor'), working under the cover of an official of the Polish Legation. Between 1932 and 1934 Kara had been Polish Consul-General in Lille, and between 1935 and 1939 had held the same post in Paris, and until the outbreak of war in Berlin. Portuguese archives show that initially the local authorities were not aware of the real character of his activity.[13] Kara was recalled in January 1944, and was replaced by Maj. Feliks Albiński ('Paz'), employed in II Bureau since February 1939. When war broke out, he was the Chief of Strategic Intelligence Cell in Berlin, and later in II Bureau HQ in France; between 1940 and 1942, following the fall of France, Albiński headed Station 'M' in Madrid.[14]

Station 'P', established after the defeat of France, was gradually enlarged and its establishment consisted of eight intelligence officers.[15] The

Station was known among the Poles living in Portugal as the 'Consulate', because of its cover of as a passport issuing section. Its counter-intelligence Section specialised in Polish refugees, whose majority came from France via Spain, and also from occupied Poland.[16]

After the defeat of France, Portugal became an important transit country for those Poles, who legally and illegally set off either for the United Kingdom or across the ocean.[17] The evacuation of Polish soldiers and war industry specialists across Portugal to Great Britain, was illegal under Portuguese law. It was supervised on behalf of I Bureau, PGS, by Col. Fryderyk Mally (Legation counsellor and unofficial Military Attaché), and from September of 1943, by Capt. Roman Kazimierz Badior (stock exchange broker by profession and officially legal counsel to the Legation).[18] The same route was also used by couriers from Poland to Great Britain.

Station 'P' had at its disposal several intelligence cells. Naval Cell no. 1 in Lisbon was headed by Lt. Zygmunt Cedro ('Henzyg'), representing Naval Intelligence of Polish Naval Command. Cedro acted under the cover of a shipbroker of 'Baltic Union Ship–Brokers' in Lisbon.[19] Station 'P' also controlled intelligence cells in Spain ('Pomar') and Genoa ('Pardilla').[20] Station 'P' also had a Cell in Belgium, headed by Dumont, one of the chiefs of the Belgian underground Sûreté de l'État.[21] Co-operation with the Belgians was initially established on the initiative of Lt-Col. Kara at the end of 1941. The decision to maintain the Belgian network via the Lisbon Station was made by the Chief of Polish II Bureau. With this in mind, it was planned to create the 'Leopold Intelligence Cell no 1. of Station "P"', composed of Belgians living in Portugal. Their prime task was to gather information about the German army and its allies. There is no file relating to this co-operation, and we do not know whether this plan was implemented. Presumably, the attempt to create 'Leopold' had failed, or its work did not satisfy the Chief of the Station. Consequently, the intelligence cell headed by Dumont was the only one in Belgium, though not the only one controlled by Station 'P'. The other was Cell 'Jamart' (no. 1) in Casablanca, whose activity presumably ended when its head, betrayed by his French co-conspirators, was arrested in December 1941. In 1942 the only Belgian mission under Lt-Col. Kara was, therefore, the Dumont Cell.[22]

In addition, Station 'P' had at its disposal intelligence cells in Lisbon: no. 1, headed by 'Janek' (agent no. 1349, their radio transmitter was serviced by 'Roman' – agent no. 1354), no. 2 ('ProDeO'), no. 3, headed by 'Herculano' (agent no. 1344), which probably co-operated with Józef Count Potocki – a prominent figure in the pre-war Polish Ministry of Foreign Affairs and during the war the representative of the Polish Red Cross in Lisbon,[23] and no. 5, headed by 'Nicol' (agent no. 1353), whose radio was operated by 'Ferra' (agent no. 1357).

Table 1. Statistical survey of Station 'P' in Lisbon

Period	Cells	Officers	Civilian officials and NCOs	Agents	Informants
1 October 1941	5 and 5 in the course of organisation	46			
1 May 1942	7	47			
Between May 1942 and 1943	12				
Second half of 1943	7	8	4	41	
5 May 1944	4	7	38	31	
End of 1944	4	5	6	36	
Beginning of 1945	4	4	29	9	
1 February 1945	28	2			
July 1945	4	at least 3			

Source: prepared by the author on the basis of lists from the documentation of II Bureau, PGS, (A. XII), kept in IPMS, and documentation from CAW, VI Bureau (II. 52. 481 and 486).[24]

Notes:

1. 15 agents were recruited and 14 arrested or compromised between 1st October 1941 and 1st May 1942. The intelligence material delivered totalled 299, thus giving the Station third place in Europe, after Stations 'F' (1227) and 'S' (309).

2. In 1943 Station 'P' controlled as many as 12 intelligence cells: 'Nicol' and 'Herculano' in Lisbon, 'Pardilla' in Genoa, 'Pilao' in the Azores, 'Pomar' in Bilbao (all had their own radios), 'Parga', 'Peco', 'Peso' and 'Pomona' in Lisbon, 'Pelada' in Porto, 'Pola' on Cape Verde and 'Pingo' in Casablanca.[25]

3. In the first half of 1944, there remained: 'Pena', 'Pardilla', 'Peco', 'Pelada', 'Peso', 'Pomar', and 'Pomona'.[26]

The tasks of Station 'P' were to conduct military and political intelligence on Germany, Italy and in both unoccupied and Vichy France; study and the preparation of press reviews; seeking and interviewing persons travelling across Portugal to obtain information of interest to the Station; counter-intelligence work in Portugal and offensive Counter-intelligence in order to collect information on those states against whom the Station organised intelligence activities; the fulfilment of tasks formulated by HQ and liaison with Stations 'M' (Spain), 'F' and 'F. II' (France), 'S' (Switzerland, i.e. via Portuguese diplomatic bag) and "W" (Hungary). The vast scope of those tasks meant that funding for Station 'P' was considerably and steadily enlarged.[27]

The Station maintained communications with London via radio and couriers. Throughout the existence of the Station, courier post was sent through the British Embassy in Lisbon.[28] As for communications in the other direction, on his arrival in the Portuguese capital in March 1941, Lt-Col. Bertrand received from the British, via the Lisbon channel, a transmitter intended for Station '300' of II Bureau, PGS. Station '300' was active in the region of Nîmes (see Chapter 46: *Cryptographic Co-operation. Enigma*).[29] Station 'P' provided, for example, regular reports on goods traffic. These were needed by the British Ministry of Economic Warfare, which appreciated the information. Similar reports from Spain were less frequent, although these were also regarded as useful.[30] On the other hand the Centre was of the opinion that the quality of information on air matters was markedly inferior. The Air Intelligence Section of the Air Force Command described the Lisbon station as 'weak'.[31] On the other hand, American Intelligence praised Polish Intelligence missions in Portugal (II Bureau and Continental Action) as 'probably the best offensive intelligence system in Lisbon'. The US Military Attaché, Col. Robert A. Solborg, was of the opinion that the Chiefs of both Polish Cells – Lt-Col. Kowalewski, Head of the Ministry of Internal Affairs Station, and Lt-Col. Kara, Chief of the Military Intelligence mission, were 'extremely able men'.[32] The latter's co-operation with the Americans was particularly good, especially following the agreement between the intelligence services of the two States, which was signed in September 1941. In June 1942 it was decided that the Chief of Station 'P' was to supply the representatives of the Office of Strategic Services (OSS) primarily with information concerning offensive counter-intelligence, as well as with intelligence material requiring its immediate use. Kara was also to offer the OSS resident advice and assistance.[33]

In 1942 the British evaluation of Station 'P' was no longer so positive, especially since its costs were relatively high.[34] In Lisbon, co-operation between Polish Intelligence and SIS in terms of disinformation (called 'Action D') was known under the cryptonym 'Olek'. As was the case with similar undertakings carried out in Stockholm and Istanbul, the target was the Japanese. At the beginning of 1944 the leadership of Polish Intelligence were dissatisfied with the outcome of such operations in Portugal and planned to end them.[35]

After the closure of an independent Intelligence Cell in Madrid (May 1941), Station 'P' covered all of the Iberian Peninsula. Since Polish Intelligence considered the Peninsula to be a traditional German 'gateway to the world', the Station became more active in offensive counter-intelligence. To meet this requirement, two cells controlled by Station 'P' were created in Spain; their purpose was to gather intelligence mainly about Germans travelling through Spain. This is why, in May 1944, consideration was given to a proposal of transferring the Station to Spain, but the project was abandoned following the arrest of its Chief, Maj. Albiński on 7 June 1944 at the Spanish border.[36]

The significance of the Iberian Peninsula for Polish Intelligence diminished considerably in the wake of the Allied landings in Normandy (6 June 1944). Consequently, in October 1944 the staff of the Lisbon Station was reduced for the first time. By the end of 1944 Station 'P' was one of the three Polish Military Intelligence missions that remained on territories supervised by the Central Section.[37] At the end of June 1945, the II Bureau in London decided to completely separate

Station 'P' from the Legation. At the time when official recognition was withdrawn from the Government-in-Exile, there were two intelligence officers in Lisbon.[38]

Co-operation between the Polish and British Intelligence was, for example, instrumental in the organization, in 1941, of the escape from Spain of Carol, the former King of Romania. His arrival in Portugal was prepared and supervised by Maj. Zdzisław Żórawski, formerly a journalist with the Polish Telegraph Agency, in co-operation with Lt-Col. Jan Kowalewski in Lisbon. The Portuguese Ministry of Foreign Affairs regarded him as an SIS agent, deployed by the British Ambassador in Madrid. In reality Żórawski did not work for British Intelligence, but co-operated with it. But the Portuguese reaction testified to the close relationship between the Allied intelligence services. Upon his return to Spain, Żórawski was arrested, despite the fact that he carried a diplomatic passport. Released in the late summer of 1941, thanks to the intervention of the Polish Legation in Madrid with the Spanish Foreign Ministry and the police, he made his way to Portugal, only to be briefly arrested again. From 1944 Żórawski was Chief of the Intelligence Cell 'Mexico City' in the capital of Mexico, supervised by the Independent Intelligence Station 'Estezet' in New York.[39]

The second country on the Iberian Peninsula where Polish Intelligence was active, was Spain. But the role played by the Poles in Spain was less prominent, since the conditions there were much more difficult: the Spaniards were more submissive to German pressure. Wartime Madrid was one of the most important centres for the German secret services.[40] On the other hand, the activity of SIS there was to a certain degree constrained by Sir Samuel Hoare, the British Ambassador in Madrid from 1940 to 1944, whose clashes with SIS were common knowledge.[41]

During the war the Spanish dictator, Gen. Francisco Franco y Bahamonde, had to play a very complex role. On the one hand he was grateful to, and financially obligated towards, Germany for its help at the time of the Civil War. On the other he was the recipient of food and fuel supplies, mainly from the US, indispensable for a country devastated by the recent conflict. As a rule, the Spanish authorities and population were quite amiable towards Poland and the Poles, though Spanish society was sharply divided in terms of its wartime sympathies. The attitude towards the Poles was coloured by anti-communism, the most important determinant of Franco's policy, and by Catholicism.[42] But the prime consideration in the intricate game played by the Spanish was to protect the country against the negative effects (for itself) of Allied victory. The fact that during the Civil War Polish diplomats, especially the Minister, Marian Szumlakowski, had saved a large group of Spanish supporters of the national camp in Madrid, also played its role.[43] On the other hand, the Spaniards remembered the supplies of Polish arms for the Republican army.

The harshest conditions for Allied agents in Spain lasted from the moment Italy joined the war and the fall of France, to the German defeats in 1942, especially the Allied invasion of North Africa. Subsequently, both

Madrid and Lisbon did not believe in the eventual German victory and initiated a slow rapprochement with the Allies.

Polish Intelligence operations in Spain were directly linked with the situation of the Polish Legation in Madrid, which constituted the main cover for the officers of II Bureau, PGS, though officially Spanish authorities refused to include the newly arrived diplomats on the diplomatic roll.[44] Polish Intelligence in Madrid informed London that the Spanish police tried to collect material compromising the Poles, even more so since it knew about the radio transmitter in the Legation.[45] On 21st January 1942, under growing German pressure and due to the considerable activity of Polish agents and blundered illegal evacuation of Poles, Madrid decided to demand the closure of the Legation and Consulate under the pretext of a violation of diplomatic regulations.[46] Although the Spanish note called for the suspension of the missions and not for the severance of diplomatic relations, a subsequent note of 6 March 1942 insisted on the closure of the Polish missions and the departure of its staff within fourteen days. Thanks to the intercession of Włodzimierz Ledóchowski, the General of the Jesuit Order, who approached Pope Pius XII, and of the Allies, and because of the skilful endeavours of Minister Szumlakowski, the decision about the closure of the Polish Legation was implemented only in part.

The issue of Intelligence work and the considerable restrictions on its activities in Spain was linked to the pressing matter of the evacuation of Polish soldiers from France, across Spain and Portugal, to Great Britain. Since the evacuation was often conducted extremely ineptly, the Spaniards rapidly discovered that their transit visas and border control stamps were forged. The majority of illegal refugees from Polish military units in France, intercepted by the Spaniards, were interned in a camp in Miranda de Ebro (Castille). The Spaniards did not yield to German pressure to hand over the several hundred Polish soldiers, just as they did not turn back those Poles who were stopped along the border with France. From March 1943 – at a time when Madrid began to consider Hitler's defeat as increasingly probable – they were steadily being released, together with Poles held in other prisons. The route for evacuating Polish Intelligence personnel also ran across Spain,[47] and was used by emissaries from the Home Army GHQ on their way to Gibraltar and PGS in London.[48]

Polish Intelligence began to work in Spain immediately after the defeat of France. Prior to the establishment of a Station, there was Cell 'M', about which there is little information.[49] From the autumn of 1940, the Chief of Station 'M' in Madrid was Maj. Feliks Albiński ('Marcel'), who used a diplomatic passport and acted under the cover of an official of the Polish Legation in Madrid. Until its closure, the Madrid Station employed at least three Intelligence officers.[50]

Communications between Station 'M' and HQ and with Stations 'P' and 'F' were maintained by radio, Allied couriers and smugglers who carried mail across the border between Spain and France and vice versa, and couriers of Station 'F'. In these ways, reports, money, and radio sets circulated between Polish Stations in France and London via Madrid and Lisbon.[51] The Iberian Peninsula played a similar role for the 'Monika' Base, the Polish underground sabotage organisation in France.[52]

Table 2. Statistical survey of Station 'M' in Madrid

Period	Cells	Officers	Civilian officials and NCOs	Agents
1 October 1941	6	5	3	67
1 May 1942 (undergoing closure)	2	38		

Source: prepared by the author on the basis of documents from IPMS and CAW.
Notes:
1. From 1st October 1941 to 1st March 1942, the Station provided 156 items of Intelligence, which ranked it fourth among nine European Stations.
2. Station 'M' provided a total of 2 369 intelligence reports, of which 2 212 by the end of 1941.

Station 'M' conducted land, naval and air intelligence in Germany, Italy, occupied and Vichy France, Spain, and occupied Poland. Its prime task was to seek information about German and Italian forces and the internal situation as well as various military, political and general intelligence relating to Poland. The secondary task was to gather political, military and economic data regarding occupied and non-occupied France and all possible information about the war potential of the Axis states, with particular attention paid to the Order of Battle and the distribution of military units (predominantly armoured and Air Force), new combat measures, and fuel and raw material supplies.[53]

Funds intended for the Madrid Station were slightly lower than those for the Polish Intelligence Station in Lisbon.[54] May 1942 marked the end of the wider-scale activity of the Station. From that time on, Polish Intelligence activities in Spain were controlled by Station 'P', though from 25th December 1943 to July 1945 some work was carried out by the Independent Intelligence Cell 'Iberia', with a single officer and one civilian, but without any agents.[55] The Cell conducted intelligence directed against France. It was also expected to observe the German presence in Spain, and was probably dealing with the evacuation of Polish soldiers from France. Its head was Lt. Henryk Count Łubieński ('Banuls', 'Start'), who came to Spain as a *Polish News* journalist. The Count was a prewar Warsaw correspondent of 'Słowo', and from August 1940 to the beginning of 1941 head of the evacuation cell in Perpignan; subsequently he was sent on a special mission to Vichy to establish valuable contacts, a task which he fulfilled admirably. From July 1941 to October of the following year, he acted as liaison officer of Station 'Afr.' in Algiers.[56] In Madrid, Łubieński worked in the Legation under the cover of a Press Attaché, and was not directly controlled by the Chief of Station 'P' in Lisbon.

Capt. Edward Bratkowski ('Wołowski'), previously an officer of

Station 'P' in Lisbon and deputy to Lt-Col. Kara, who dispatched him to Spain, arrived in Madrid in the middle of December 1943; here, he created and directed intelligence cell 'Wołowski', focused primarily on France. The mission was subordinated to Station 'P'.

Many Polish Intelligence officers were arrested in wartime Spain. On 30th May 1942, Maj. Albiński was expelled by plane to Portugal, after the Head of Dirección General de Seguridad (DGS)[57] issued (on 17 March) an order to find and arrest him and to remove him from Spain.[58]

The remaining officers of the Polish Station shared a similar fate. Maj. Kazimierz Stanisław Zarębski ('Adam'), Deputy to Albiński (and from May 1941 the treasurer of the Polish Red Cross in Madrid), was arrested on 18th February, despite the fact, that he had a diplomatic passport.[59] 2nd Lt. Mikołaj Rostworowski ('Tap', 'Michał', 'Brunon'; agent no. 120), the press officer of the intelligence cell acting under the cover of the Chief of the Madrid section of the Polish Telegraph Agency, was arrested in Madrid on 21st February 1942 suspected of anti-German propaganda and espionage. Five days later he was released and forced to leave Spain.[60]

Whilst the Madrid Station still existed, it had at least three cells. Cell no. 2 was headed by 2nd Lt. Włodzimierz V. Popławski ('Paul'), an expert on Spain, whom Zygmunt Zubrzycki, a Legation official, described as the 'most credible Intelligence agent whom I had encountered during the war'.[61] During the Spanish Civil War, Popławski stayed both in Republican and Nationalist Spain.[62] He returned there in September 1940, working under the cover of an employee of the Evacuation Section of the Polish Legation in Madrid, his real task being the illegal evacuation of Polish soldiers from France to Great Britain. In November of that year, he was dismissed after a misunderstanding with the Minister, Szumlakowski, and with Col. Mally, and assigned different Intelligence tasks.[63] Finally, on 1 September 1942, Popławski joined the 7th Cadre Rifle Brigade.

Intelligence Cell no. 3 (Naval) was headed by Capt. Roman Koperski ('Torero'), a pre-war II Bureau officer, who in Madrid acted as a so-called cover official of the Legation ('Koparski'). As early as on 6 January 1942 he was arrested and charged with spying for Great Britain against Spain and Germany. Threatened with the death penalty, Koperski was ultimately sentenced to five years imprisonment[64] and spent two years in prison, initially in San Sebastián and then in Burgos. In May 1943, he was transferred to the Porlier prison in Madrid, from which he was released at the beginning of 1944.[65]

Rudolf Parr, a Polish citizen of Jewish descent who worked for Polish Intelligence, was arrested on 19 February 1942. Parr travelled together with Koperski to Malaga, a fact which became known to the Spanish authorities, who accused him of 'secret activity aimed against the current socio-political order in Europe' and deported him to Portugal. In the opinion of Spanish counter-intelligence, Parr worked under the name of Primulter or Prlmutir.[66] His real name was Rudolf Perlmutter, and until 1937 he was a contract employee of the Polish Honorary Consulate in Valencia, headed by the industrialist Vicente Noguera Bonora, killed by leftist militia in August 1936.[67]

At the head of Cell no. 7, in Barcelona, was Wanda Halina Morbitzer-Tozer ('Ewa'), who before the war was a contract employee at the Honorary Consulate in Barcelona and an assistant to Eduardo Rodón y Blasa, the Honorary Consul (since 1922). During the Second World War, this Cell played a prominent role in evacuating Polish soldiers from France via Spain.[68] The contribution made by Tozer to the Polish war effort was simply invaluable.[69] The fact that her husband was a British citizen probably facilitated cooperation with SIS representatives in Barcelona. Persons recommended by Tozer, including Polish citizens, became members of the British Intelligence network.[70] In 1943, the Gestapo uncovered her activity and demanded from the Catalonian DGS that she be arrested as the organiser of a wide-scale campaign intent on secretly conveying Polish soldiers across the Pyrénées. Under interrogation, Tozer was threatened with being handed over to the Germans. Accused of participation in the illegal evacuation of Polish citizens and with espionage, and warned by a high-ranking functionary of the Guardia Civil, she managed to flee to Portugal before being officially charged and arrested.[71]

Station 'M' had two other Intelligence Cells, no. 1 in Rome, headed by Lt. Zygmunt Count Skórzewski ('Włodzimierz'), acting under the cover of a Polish Red Cross inspector. Dispatched in January 1941 from Madrid, where he also fulfilled the same function,[72] Skórzewski was responsible for organising illegal evacuation.[73] Cell no. 2 in Casablanca was run by Capt. Alfred Józef Birkenmayer ('Burmistrz'), officially also a representative of the Polish Red Cross.[74]

From the beginning of 1944, Polish Intelligence in Madrid also employed Gustaw Findeisen, a lawyer and an Attaché of the Polish Legation, a former contract employee of Consulates-General in Vienna and Paris, and an inmate of the Miranda de Ebro camp. Findeisen was a regular II Bureau operative when in France, and from the middle of August 1943 in Spain. His counter-intelligence assignments consisted of interviewing refugees arriving in Madrid. He also worked closely with the Minister, Szumlakowski.[75]

The co-operation between Polish Intelligence and Minister Szumlakowski, who maintained direct contact with Lt-Col. Kara, Chief of Station 'P' in Lisbon, began in the summer of 1943. The Minister relied on several trusted informants,[76] supervised the questioning of Polish soldiers, and established 'post boxes'[77] in Barcelona and in northern Spain.[78] At the request of Kara, the Minister also maintained contacts with the pro-British and pro-monarchist Gen. Alfredo Kindelán Duany.[79] Kara trusted Szumlakowski and indicated, that information obtained from the Minister was extremely valuable. In one of his letters, Kara wrote: 'In Spain the Minister is really capable of achieving a lot'.[80]

A series of intrigues in London and amongst the Polish refugees in Madrid and Lisbon as well as conflicts with the Minister following his protest against the Sikorski–Mayski pact led to Szumlakowski's dismissal. Officially, he was charged with insufficiently energetic intervention in favour of the internees of the Miranda de Ebro prison, or of an outright campaign against their release, an accusation totally unsupported by the available source material. On the contrary, Szumlakowski's endeavours were not only intensive, but also ultimately effective. He was dismissed on 30 September 1943.[81] Meanwhile, at the end of 1943, the Spaniards planned to accredit their own representative to the Polish Government-in-Exile in London.[82] Their attitude towards the Polish Legation depended upon Szumlakowski retaining his post. Furthermore, diplomatic privileges of the Polish Legation were restored by the decision made by Count de Jordana, Minister of Foreign Affairs and a friend of the Polish Minister from the Civil War days, who justified his support by the special position enjoyed by the Minister in the Spanish Establishment.[83] The false charges against Szumlakowski were also refuted by Lt-Col. Kara, who was recalled from the Lisbon post in January 1944 as a result. Moreover, Kara was ordered not to co-operate with Szumlakowski any further, despite the fact that the latter provided valuable information, inaccessible to other Polish Intelligence operatives.[84]

Wide-ranging, albeit rather chaotic, activity was conducted in Spain by the Continental Action mission.[85] It was unofficially headed by Lt-Col. Jan Kowalewski in Lisbon, to whom reports were sent directly. After the fall of France the first Continental Action representative in the Spanish capital was Dr. Jan Kaczmarek, who in 1941 was forced to leave for South America.[86] The next representative of, in the words of Spanish Counter-intelligence, 'the Polish diplomat named COT, head of the extreme leftist party',[87] was Dr. Zygmunt Zawadowski ('de Ribeiras'), a diplomat with over twenty years' experience in the Ministry of Foreign Affairs, and at the outbreak of the war, Deputy Polish Commissioner-General in Gdańsk. From 1940, Zawadowski officially held the post of Counsellor at the Polish Legation in Madrid, although this was an internal nomination, that was not disclosed to the Spaniards. His other function, with the rank of 2nd Lt., involved the preparation of press reviews for Station 'M', where he was known as 'Traper'. In addition, and for a time at the end of 1941, Zawadowski was in charge of the (legal) Evacuation Section and was the head of the Section dealing with care for the internees and prisoners in Spain at the Polish Legation. In other words, Zawadowski worked for four Polish organisations – the II and I Bureaux of PGS, the Ministry of Foreign Affairs and the Ministry of the Interior. His first function was kept secret even from Minister Szumlakowski, with whom – as indeed later with Minister Dubicz-Penther in Lisbon – Zawadowski remained at odds.[88]

Much as his successors did later, Zawadowski organised a small-scale but rather efficient system of communication with France and, to a lesser degree, also with Poland. Initially, Spanish counter-intelligence regarded him as the Chief of Polish Intelligence in Spain. This would indicate that the Germans were also not very familiar with the duality of the Polish secret services, as demonstrated by the arrest of Rostworowski of II

Bureau. At the turn of March 1942 Zawadowski (known to the Spaniards as 'Sabadowsky') was at risk of being arrested – this was the result of the effectiveness of Spanish counter-intelligence[89] – and so he was transferred to Lisbon.

The next representative of the Ministry of Internal Affairs in Madrid was Leonard As. Leonardów (known as 'Ribeirrinho' for the purposes of Continental Action, and as 'Gustaw' in terms of his illegal evacuation activities), a half-Russian and half-Italian Wilno-born engineer, universally suspected of involvement in large-scale currency trade in France.[90] At the end of 1941 Zawadowski drew him into the illegal evacuation work. In time, however, Leonardów was suspected of working also, or even primarily, for the Germans. As a result, the Ministry of Internal Affairs broke off all contacts with him and forced Leonardów to leave Spain at the end of March 1944.[91]

Officially, Karol Kraczkiewicz ('Filip'), a young Foreign Ministry employee and the successor of Leonardów, was controlled only by Librach and the Minister of Foreign Affairs; in reality he was supervised also by Lt-Col. Kowalewski from Lisbon ('Ludwika'), with whose help he maintained contact with the Centre in London. Kraczkiewicz's chief task was the maintenance of communications (mail, money, and radios) between London and 'Monika' in France, although this contact broke down after the invasion of Normandy. His other assignment was the observation of political and economic life in Spain.[92] Kraczkiewicz also organised permanent courier routes, whose functioning did not fully satisfy the Polish Ministry of Internal Affairs, and obtained extremely valuable information from France. At the same time, Kraczkiewicz enjoyed excellent contacts with the Americans ('Samowicze') – his main partner was Gregory Thomas ('Tomcio Paluch') from OSS, from October 1943 the Attaché at the US Embassy in Madrid ('Maciej'), with the Hungarians and, to a lesser degree, with the Italians. In April 1944, Kraczkiewicz started, with the assistance of 'Karp' and despite enormous obstacles and an almost total lack of help from the British ('Gospodarze', or 'Hosts'), to organise an auxiliary evacuation outpost of the Ministry of the Interior for Polish refugees from France in Barcelona.[93] The Spaniards threatened that his visa would not be prolonged and even threatening arrest, while the German Ambassador intervened several times with the DGS, calling for the expulsion or detention of Kraczkiewicz, who on 10th June 1944 was finally forced to leave Spain.[94]

In Madrid, Kraczkiewicz was replaced as the representative of the Ministry of the Interior by Dr. Wiktor Jerzy Makow ('Poppy'), who worked closely with Polish Military Intelligence and with successive Ministry representatives. Moreover, Makow represented the 'Hydro-Nitro' Swiss chemical firm in France and Spain. In the spring of 1943, he organised Polish clandestine support bases (hide-outs) working alongside the British ones, intended for Polish citizens making their way from France to Portugal without any visas and frequently without documents. These channels were also used for dispatching information, money and radios along the France-Great Britain route via Spain and Portugal. For this purpose it was necessary to use French and Spanish smugglers, recruited primarily from members of the Spanish left wing.[95] While co-operating with the British, the Poles nevertheless retained their separate channels, which were also much less expensive. Makow also organised intelligence in the Vichy Embassy in Madrid.

Lt-Col. Jan Kowalewski informed from Lisbon that the delegate of the Minister of Internal Affairs in Madrid maintained excellent relations with representatives of British Intelligence. At the end of the war, however, the situation changed fundamentally: with the consent of the Polish authorities, Makow co-operated with SIS to the end of March 1944 when his contact was severed because '[...] the 'hosts' disliked his excessive expenses'. From that time on, his relations with the British were, at the very least, complex.[96] On the other hand, Makow's contacts with the Americans, the French and the influential representatives of the Spanish Government remained invariably satisfactory.

The Spanish chemist Juan Abelló Pascual, chairman of the Commercial and Navigation Chamber in Madrid, provided particularly valuable services rendered both to 'Poppy' and to 'Filip'. Officially, 'Poppy' came to Spain to supervise the installation of a chemical factory for Pascual. When the secretary of Abelló, Francisco Casas ('Pilarski'), whose home acted as a 'dead letter-box' and a 'hide-out' for a courier caught near the border, was arrested on the night of 17 June 1944,[97] he confessed to all contacts known to him giving away, among others, the codenames of Kraczkiewicz and Makow. The case implicated also II Bureau, with whose representative Casas worked, by meeting people arriving from France whom he directed to Bratkowski. The police linked Casas with 'Filip', who had been trailed and suspected for a long time. When on 21 June Bratkowski left for Lisbon, he confirmed the suspicions harboured by the Spaniards, convinced that he was the deputy of Kraczkiewicz, Chief of the Polish Intelligence network.

Kraczkiewicz meanwhile, unaware of this turn of events, left two days after the arrest of Casas. The Spaniards also detained the driver, Pablo, sent by Bratkowski to San Sebastián. From that moment on, Makow was carefully watched since he was associated with the arrest of several 'Red' smugglers detained at the frontier, although the subsequent investigation showed that the Poles had nothing to do with them.[98] 'Poppy' was arrested on 7 September in San Sebastián, suspected of espionage, although admittedly not against Spain. The Legation, headed by Józef Potocki, frequently intervened on his behalf. He was released at the end of December, and in January 1945 ultimately cleared of all charges due to the lack of evidence. Casas was released from prison in February.[99]

During the Second World War, Polish Intelligence attached particular significance to Portugal and Spain. In the former, Polish Military Intelligence managed to carry out effective operations, which the Allies assessed higher than did II Bureau of PGS. The effective measures taken by Spanish counter-intelligence against Polish Intelligence activity meant that Lisbon became one of the foremost centres of Polish Intelligence, at least until the Allied landings in Normandy – although it could not boast of such spectacular successes as the ones enjoyed in Algiers or Stockholm. The most important contribution made by the Polish secret services in the Iberian Peninsula was the mission carried out by Lt-Col. Jan Kowalewski (see Part VIII).

Notes

1   The only known mission conducted by Polish Intelligence on the Iberian Peninsula prior to 1936 was Cell 'Carlos', created in 1933, whose tasks entailed the assessment of German influence in this country and the collection of counter-intelligence information. The cell, situated in Barcelona (from 1934 to 1936 in Berlin), was headed by Józef Postel, an Austrian of Czech origin (for more see: A. Woźny, *Niemieckie przygotowania do wojny z Polską w ocenach polskich naczelnych władz wojskowych* (*German Preparations for War Against Poland in the Assessment of Polish Supreme Military Authorities*), Warsaw 2000, pp.198–199).

2   See: file on Polish Intelligence missions in Spain during the Civil War in: Rossiyskiy Gosudarstvienniy Voyenniy Arkhiv, Moskva (further: RGVA), fond 308 (II Otdiel Gienieralnogo Shtaba Polshi, g. Varshava), description 3–5, 11, 19. Supplementary documentation is available in CAW, II Bureau of the Polish General Staff, 1921-1939 (further: II Bureau), I. 303. 4. 1917–1922.

3   This rather curious marriage of the functions of a head of a diplomatic and intelligence missions has been ascertained on the basis of II Bureau documents in Moscow (RGVA, fond 308). 'Anitra' ceased all activity after the outbreak of WW II.

4   Lt-Col. Kędzior was officially accredited in Spain in February 1939. In September 1939 Gen. Stanisław Burhardt-Bukacki, Head of the Military Mission in Paris, appointed him Chief of General Staff of the recreated Polish Army detachments in France. Soon afterwards he became Chief of Staff at the Ministry of Military Affairs and subsequently Chief of General Staff, a function he performed until June 1940. In January 1942, Kędzior became Head of the Polish Military Mission in Chungking, at the same time acting as Military Attaché in China. The Mission did not begin its work until November of that year (A. Woźny, *Niemieckie*, op. cit., p. 198; A. Pepłoński, *Wywiad Polskich Sił Zbrojnych na Zachodzie 1939–1945* (*The Intelligence Service of the Polish Armed Forces in the West 1939–1945*), Warsaw 1995, p. 203; P. Stawecki, *Oficerowie dyplomowani wojska Drugiej Rzeczypospolitej* (*Staff Officers of the Armed Forces of the Second Polish Republic*), Wrocław 1997, p. 167).

5   See his political archive (so-called Arquivo Salazar) [in:] Instituto dos Arquivos Nacionais/Torre do Tombo, Lisbon (further: IAN/TT).

6   Constant apprehension connected with this fact can be discerned also amongst Polish refugees and workers of the numerous Polish institutions created in Lisbon after the fall of France. Lists of Polish citizens particularly threatened in the case of German invasion were prepared together with the British Embassy (see: S. Schmitzek, *Na krawędzi Europy. Wspomnienia portugalskie 1939–1946* (*On the Edge of Europe. Portuguese Reminiscences 1939–1946*), Warsaw 1970, passim, and numerous British plans in the event of the invasion of Portugal [in:] TNA(PRO), FO 898/246, 248, 249 and 250).

7   Ibid., FO 898/246, study concerning Portugal, 15 December 1942.

8   S. Schmitzek, *Na krawędzi*, op. cit., pp. 214, 331 and 345.

9   PVDE, Polícia de Vigilância e Defesa do Estado, the secret political police of the regime, commonly known as the 'international police', supervised by the Ministry of Internal Affairs, fulfilled also counter-intelligence tasks according to the Iberian model. Poles who lived in Portugal during the war maintained that German impact

on PVDE was extremely strong (S. Schimitzek, *Na krawędzi*, op.cit., p. 331), although it did not exclude certain Allied presence in this institution (see: IPMS, Ministry of Internal Affairs, A. 9. VI.10/1, organisational scheme of the PVDE).

10 K. Philby, *My Silent War*, New York 1968, p. 43, see: pp. 47–76.

11 IJPL, Kol. no. 100 (Col. S. Mayer), Lt. Z. Godyń to Col. S. A. Mayer, b.m., 3rd April 1943. The author wishes to thank Mr Zbigniew S. Kowalski for making this document available.

12 Most of the data concerning the personnel structure, communication tasks and subsidies of the foreign outposts of II Bureau, PGS, to 1943 is given on the basis of a notebook containing information about the structure of Polish Intelligence networks, which the author managed to find in IPMS, Kol. 242/63.

13 A list of the Diplomatic Corps, prepared by Serviço de Estrangeiros PVDE for the Portuguese dictator, mentions Lt-Col. Kara as Kara (first name), Stanisław (surname), 'female functionary' (sic!) of the Polish Legation (IAN/TT, Arquivo Salazar, AOS/CO/IN-8C, list of diplomats accredited in Portugal; see: S. Schimitzek, *Na krawędzi*, op. cit., p. 211).

14 More extensive information about the pre-war service performed by Albiński in: CAW, Personnel Files 501 and 527, Feliks Albiński. During WW I Albiński served in the German army and fought, for example, at Verdun. His family surname of Alankiewicz, which later on he rejected, was restored in 1922. In 1921 he became a reservist and returned to the Army at the beginning of the 1930s. Promoted to Capt. in January 1933.

15 The Intelligence officers of this station included Lt-Cmdr. Feliks Jasłowski ('Tomasz Jasiński'), Capt. Edward Bratkowski ('Wołowski'), Lt. Wacław Zbigniew Rago ('Raap'), Lt. Zygmunt Godyń, Dr. Zygmunt Bednarski, Capt. Mściwoj Kokorniak, Capt. Mieczysław Jaworski (who on his return to London became the Chief of the Central Section of the Intelligence Department), Capt. Adam Ehrenberg *vel* Dzierżanowski, Capt. Witold Treger, Lt. Fedorowicz, Lt. Odrowąż Władysław Łaniewski and 2nd Lt. Dr. Mieczysław Liparski. The Station employed at least four civilians: Michał Pilarski ('Jadwiga') – ciphers, Lt. Stanisław Dembiński ('Hrabia', 'Teska'), Bohdan Szmejko (during the Spanish Civil War an unofficial representative of the Polish Ministry of Foreign Affairs with the Nationalist authorities in Salamanca, at the same time working for the 'Wschód' Section of II Bureau of Polish General Staff , up to June 1940 an official of the Polish Consulate in Lyon), radiotelegraphist Szymczak, Stanisław Wadowski ('Milton'), Rabczewska, Netzel and Sylvia Wallace. The typist Antonina Mackiewiczowa ('Stanisława') was employed whenever the Station required her assistance.

16 In 1942 the Chief of Offensive and Local Counter-intelligence was Jan Rabczewski ('Lt. Jan Rudowski'). Until May 1941, the head of this cell was Capt. Konstanty Hartingh ('Narkiewicz').

17 More in: S. Schimitzek, *Na krawędzi*, op. cit.

18 From 1940, the military evacuation mission transported about 5,500 persons to Great Britain. Another 3,000 were transferred from Spain directly to British Gibraltar. The overall number of Polish refugees who crossed Portugal during WW II amounted to 6,000-7,000 (ibid., pp. 695–696).

19 In November 1941 he left for the United States, where, in time, he became Assistant to the Navy Attaché in Washington.

20 The first cell was headed by agent no. 1380, whose codename was identical with the name of the outpost. The Chief of the second cell – agent no. 1376 – used the codename 'Date'.

21 The civilian Sûreté de l'État was established in March 1940. It was supervised by the Belgian Minister of Justice and during the German occupation it acted as part of the Resistance (more in: P. André, *La libération d'Anvers* [in:] *Les grandes énigmes de la Résistance en Belgique*, ed. by B. Michel, Geneva 1972, pp. 189–246).

22 IPMS, Kol. 242/63, notebook with information about the structure of Polish
    Intelligence; CAW, VI Bureau, II. 52. 483, 'Stanisław' (Col. S. Gano) to Lt-Col. S.
    Kara, Chief of Station 'P', location unspecified, 17 November 1941; Station 'P' to II
    Bureau, PGS, Lisbon, 4 and 10 December 1941. On the co-operation of Polish
    Intelligence with the Belgian Staff and Sûreté de l'État, initiated by Station 'S' in
    Berne in October 1942, and on work conducted for Polish Intelligence by 2nd Lt.
    Duchamps ('Rivert', agent no. 539) see: correspondence [in:] ibid. For general
    information on the co-operation of Polish and Belgian Intelligence Services during
    WW II see: A. Pepłoński, *Wywiad*, op. cit., pp. 226–230.
23 This assumption is based on knowledge, obtained elsewhere, that during the war
    Potocki was involved in intelligence work in Portugal; the street where the Polish
    Red Cross had its offices since March 1942 was rua Alexandre Herculano. The
    'Herculano' radio station, which belonged to Station 'P' did not work at least until
    September 1943, since it was to come into service in case of German invasion of
    Portugal. When this danger passed, it began working in 1943. Ultimately, the radio
    was closed on 20 December 1945 (correspondence in IPMS, Kol. 242/70 and PRO
    HW 34/8).
24 The data is based on estimates, established from extant material.
25 IPMS, A. XII. 24/37, list of Stations and independent intelligence cells of the II
    Bureau, PGS, no place or date.
26 Ibid., A. XII. 24/35, list of cells of the Central Section of Intelligence Department
    during the first half of 1944.
27 In January-February 1941, the subsidies amounted to £120. Between March and
    May, this sum grew to £300 and in June and July it totalled £400. From August to
    December the subsidies totalled some £600, and between August and October an
    additional £400 was provided for intelligence cells. Between January and June 1942
    the subsidies amounted to £900, and in June 1943 it was planned to lower the
    expenditure, as of 1st August, from an undetermined sum to £500 (IPMS, Kol.
    242/63, notebook with information about the structure of Polish Intelligence
    networks).
28 S. Schimitzek, *Na krawędzi*, op. cit., p. 641. In the opinion of 'Kim' Philby, British
    Intelligence secretly read the diplomatic post of numerous countries (including
    Poland), which passed through British territory (K. Philby, *My Silent War*, op. cit.,
    pp. 63–64).
29 W. Kozaczuk, *W kręgu Enigmy* (*The Enigma Circle*), Warsaw 1979, p. 179.
30 IPMS, A. XII. 24/37, assessment of half-yearly work performed by II Bureau
    (July–December 1943), 4 March 1944.
31 Ibid., A. XII. 24/56, Lt-Col. A. Kowalczyk, Head of Air Force Intelligence, to the II
    Bureau, PGS, London, 6th May 1944. Favourable opinions were expressed about
    the VI Bureau, Stations 'F. II.', 'S', and 'SKN', and the Independent Cell 'Belgijska'.
32 NARA RG 156, MID, Records of the War Department, Box 2847, Col. R. A. Solborg,
    US Military and Attaché in Lisbon, Chief of Military Intelligence Services, 16
    November 1943.
33 CAW, the VI Bureau, II. 52. 483, 'Janio' (Maj. J. H. Żychoń), Chief of Intelligence,
    to Station 'Estezet', no place, 16 June 1942.
34 M. Z. Rygor-Słowikowski, *W tajnej służbie . Polski wkład do zwycięstwa w drugiej
    wojnie światowej* (*In Secret Service. The Polish Contribution to Victory in WW II*),
    London 1977, pp. 417–418.
35 CAW, the VI Bureau, Hand-over certificate of the Intelligence Department of the II
    (Intelligence) Bureau, PGS, 15 February 1944.
36 IPMS, A . XII. 24/37, Report on the Central Section of the Intelligence Department
    of the II Bureau, PGS, for 5 May 1944, and CAW, the VI Bureau, II. 52. 481, Hand-
    over certificate of the Intelligence Department of the VI Bureau, PGS, 15 February
    1944.

37 IPMS, A. XII. 24/37, Report on the work by the Central Section of the Intelligence Department of the II Bureau, PGS, in 1944. Spain and Portugal were the domain of the Central Intelligence Section.

38 CAW, the VI Bureau, II. 52. 486, 'Paz' to HQ of the II Bureau, PGS, Lisbon, 25th and 26 June 1945, and the Chief of the II Bureau, PGS to the Chief of Station 'P', 27 and 28 June 1945.

39 Ibid., II. 52. 480, Overseas Section of the II Bureau, PGS. Personnel, posts and salaries, O. I. in North and South America, no place, 29 May 1945.

40 W. Schellenberg, *Los secretos del Servicio Secreto alemán*, Barcelona 1958, p. 124; D. Pastor Petit, *Espionaje. La Segunda Guerra Mundial y España*, Barcelona 1990, pp. 38–43, 225, 539.

41 During WW I, Sir Samuel John Gurney Hoare, Lord Templewood, headed British Intelligence in Russia; subsequently he was Secretary of State for Air (1922–1929), Secretary of State for India (1931–1935), Foreign Secretary (1935), First Lord of Admiralty (1936–1937) and Home Secretary (1937–1939). When in Spain, he attempted to limit intelligence work there to an indispensable minimum, in order not to provoke the Spaniards (D. Pastor Petit, *Espionaje*, op. cit., pp. 513–514; N. West, *MI-6. Operacje brytyjskiej Tajnej Służby Wywiadu 1909–1945* (*MI6: British Secret Intelligence Service Operations, 1909–45*) Warsaw 2000, passim; see: Lord Templewood, *Ambassador on Special Mission*, London 1946; M. Allen, *El rey traidor. De cómo el duque de Windsor traicionó a los aliados*, Barcelona 2001, p. 216 and P. Starzeński, *Trzy lata z Beckiem* (*Three Years with Beck*), Warsaw 1991, p. 19).

42 It is worth recalling a very pro-Polish and the wide-scale campaign in Europe conducted by Spain in 1943 and concerning the Soviet murder of Polish officers in Katyń (correspondence in IPMS, A.9.VI.10/1).

43 J. S. Ciechanowski, *Azyl dyplomatyczny w poselstwie Rzeczypospolitej Polskiej w czasie hiszpańskiej wojny domowej (1936–1939)* (*Political asylum in the Polish Legation during the Spanish Civil War (1936–1939)*), 'Przegląd Historyczny', vol. 41, 2000, fasc. 4, pp. 551–584.

44 On 16 June 1941, the Spanish Ministry of Foreign Affairs issued a note stating that it would no longer recognise a further expansion of the staff of diplomatic and consular missions (see: the Marian Szumlakowski Collection, Centre for Studies on Classical Tradition in Poland and Central-Eastern Europe at Warsaw University, further: KMS /the author wishes to thank Prof. Dr. Jan Kieniewicz for making available the private papers of Minister Szumlakowski/, M. Szumlakowski to Col. F. Mally, Madrid, July 1941.

45 Archivo General del Ministerio de Asuntos Exteriores, Archivo Renovado, Madrid (further: AG MAE), Leg. R. 2221, exp. 20, Vice-Secretary of State for Public Order in the Ministry of Internal Affairs to the Minister of Foreign Affairs, Madrid, 24 January 1942. Spanish services claimed that similar transmitters functioned in Barcelona and Valencia.

46 Ibid., note by the Spanish Ministry of Foreign Affairs to the Polish Legation in Madrid, Madrid, 21 January 1942.

47 By way of example, 2nd Lt. Leon Śliwiński, an officer of Station 'F. II' ('Orzeł Biały', no. 1565/LIX, London, November 1999, p. 58) or Capt. Roman Czerniawski ('Walenty'), Chief of Independent Station 'Int' (IPMS, Kol. 242/63). See: correspondence [in:] CAW, VI Bureau, II. 52. 478.

48 They included Elżbieta Zawacka in April 1943 (letter of Prof. Dr. E. Zawacka to grateful author, Toruń, 3 June 2000). The cryptonym of the VI Bureau cell in Madrid was 'Waleriana', and in Portugal – 'Lisa', 'Salamandra' and 'Migdał'. The single-person cell 'Lisa' maintained radio communications with the VI Bureau HQ in London and with Switzerland (Station 'Wera') and Hungary (Station 'Liszt') thanks to Hungarian diplomatic bag (A. Pepłoński, *Wywiad*, op. cit., p. 279; see: J. Garliński, *Polska w drugiej wojnie światowej* (*Poland during WW II*), London 1982,

p. 123; T. Dubicki, *Bazy Wojskowej łączności zagranicznej ZWZ-AK w latach 1939–1945. Studia i materiały*, Częstochowa 2000, s. 7, 11, 167–168.

49 See: IPMS, A. XII. 24/45, Information from Col. L. Mitkiewicz, Chief, the II Bureau, PGS, London, 15 August 1940.

50 They included Maj. Kazimierz Stanisław Zarębski, 2nd Lt. Zbigniew Dohnalek ('Aleksander'), 2nd Lt. Mikołaj Rostworowski and 2nd Lt. Dr. Zygmunt Zawadowski. The cell also employed several civilians: Cadet Officer Antoni Cimoszko ('Colt'), an engineer, Master Corp. Franciszek Rudzki ('Kuba'), typist Helena Brandt, Maria Rostworowska née Dunin-Borkowska, wife of Mikołaj, assistant press official, and Corp. Franciszek Nazarko, radiotelegraphist.

51 More in: reports in IPMS, Kol. 96. It is characteristic that contact was maintained with the Spanish communists (predominantly the so-called Maquis), especially as regards smuggling across the French-Spanish border and to a lesser degree across the Spanish-Portuguese frontier.

52 IPMS, Kol. 95/19, Polska Organizacja Walki o Niepodległość (Polish Organisation of Struggle for Independence), May 1945.

53 On the basis of a summary of organisational instruction of 9 September 1940 and the tasks and Navy questionnaire of 20 February 1941 [in:] IPMS, Kol. 242/63, notebook with information on the structure of Polish Intelligence networks.

54 The subsidies in October–November 1940 totalled £300, in December – £500, in January 1941 – £250, in February – £600, in March–May £460, from June to July £500, and between August 1941 and March 1942 – £800 (ibid.).

55 Ibid., A.XII.24/35, List of Central Section networks in 1944, and CAW, the VI Bureau, II. 52.481, Hand-over certificate of the Intelligence Department of the II Bureau, PGS, 15 February 1944.

56 More in: M. Z. Rygor-Słowikowski, *W tajnej służbie*, op. cit., passim.

57 In Spain, as in Portugal, counter-intelligence was the domain of appropriate police authorities. Dirección General de Seguridad, supervised by the Ministry of Internal Affairs, was an efficient police service which controlled foreigners in Spain (cf. the not exact opinion that counter-intelligence for all practical purposes did not exist until 1944 [in:] J. Bordavío, P. Cernuda, F. Jáuregui, *Servicios secretos*, Barcelona 2000, p. 75). Together with Guardia Civil, the DGS was entrusted with the task of combating communism; hence its considerable prerogatives and funds. The Germans had significant influence in DGS, the gendarmerie (Guardia Civil) and Intelligence (SIM, Servicio de Información Militar and the Third Section of the Supreme Staff, Tercera Sección de Alto Estado Mayor), which during WW II provided them with information, particularly from Spain and neighbouring regions (Portugal, France, Gibraltar and Morocco).

58 Two further attempts were made to transport Major, subsequently Lt-Col. Albiński to Spain. In both instances he was arrested and deported to Portugal (in June 1942 and June 1944). Consequently, during the penultimate year of the war, it became impossible to transfer II Bureau's Station in the Iberian Peninsula from Lisbon to Madrid. Archivo Histórico Nacional in Madrid contains an extract from a DGS dossier on Albiński (Archivo Histórico Nacional, Madrid, further: AHN, Fondos Contemporáneos, Expedientes Policiales, further: FC, EP, H-555). In June 1943, Servicio de Información de Dirección General de Seguridad claimed that the Polish Legation maintained an operational intelligence organisation focused on Central Europe, directed against Germany, and working for Great Britain and Poland. Its head was supposed to be 'Albinski' or 'Albiniski' (see also: S. Schimitzek, *Na krawędzi*, op. cit., pp. 579–580).

59 KMS, M. Szumlakowski to the Minister of Foreign Affairs, Madrid, 19 February 1942.

60 IPMS, A.9.VI.10/1, Report by M. Rostworowski, Lisbon, 4 March 1942, M. Szumlakowski to the Ministry of Foreign Affairs, Madrid, 3 March 1943; M.

Szumlakowski to the Polish Legation in Lisbon, Madrid, 26 February 1942.

61 Z. Zubrzycki, Note for the Polish Ambassador in Madrid, Madrid, 10 May 1992, Ms, property of Prof. Jan Kieniewicz, whom the author would like to thank for making this source available.

62 More in: RGVA, fond 308, description 4, item 113, File of W. Popławski on his intelligence missions to Spain in 1937; AG MAE, Leg. R. 2221, exp. 20, report 'Un nuevo elemento de la Organización polaca', Madrid, 6 February 1942.

63 KMS, M. Szumlakowski to General W. Sikorski, 18 November 1940.

64 General Alonso, Deputy Minister of Military Affairs, supposedly said that Koperski, working for the 'Foreign Office', was interested in military transports to Morocco, (KMS, M. Szumlakowski to the Minister of Foreign Affairs, Madrid, 29 January 1943).

65 CAW, the VI Bureau, II. 52.481, Hand-over certificate of the Intelligence Department of the II Bureau, PGS, 15 February 1944; AHN, FC, EP, H-555, Secretary-General of Police HQ in Madrid (DGS) to a judge dealing with espionage, Madrid, 3 July 1943; IPMS, A.45.763/7, list of persons to be placed on the next list of evacuees.

66 AHN, FC, EP, H-537, excerpt from the personal files of R. Parra.

67 More in: J. S. Ciechanowski, *Z dziejów humanitaryzmu. Azyl dyplomatyczny w ambasadach i poselstwach madryckich w czasie hiszpańskiej wojny domowej (1936–1939)* (*From the History of Humanitarianism. Diplomatic Asylum in Legations and Embassies in Madrid during the Spanish Civil War (1936–1939)*), in print.

68 For many Polish soldiers the address of the Polish mission in the capital of Catalonia (10 Fontanella Street) became a synonym of the comprehensive care provided by the official Polish mission in unfriendly Spain. Emphasis should be placed on the role played by Casto de Zavala Eizaguirre, the honorary Polish Consul in Bilbao, and by the Polish Red Cross mission in Madrid, in particular Juliusz Babecki (S. Schimitzek, *Na krawędzi*, op. cit., p. 535).

69 See: account by Zbigniew Stanisław Kowalski (2000), to whom the author would like to express his gratitude.

70 An account by one of the agents in contact with W. Morbitzer-Tozer, Spain, 21–22 July 2001. During WW II, this person worked for SIS. Contact with SIS representatives in the capital of Catalonia was established *via* Tozer. The tasks involved predominantly observing the airport in Barcelona. The Polish agent was arrested in May 1942, for her involvement in the illegal evacuation of Polish soldiers across Spain. A month later she was released from the Barcelona prison.

71 W. Tozer, *Druga wojna światowa* (*The Second World War*), and *Do Portugalii na zielono* (*To Portugal by illegal border*), typescripts and letters of W. Tozer (author wishes to thank Mrs. Krystyna M. Tozer de Fuster for access to these materials). IPMS, A.9.VI.10/1, M. Szumlakowski to Minister of Foreign Affairs, Madrid, 23 November 1942; Ibid. Kol. 242/63, Zeszyt z informacjami o strukturze placówek polskiego wywiadu (Information about the structure of Polish Intelligence agencies) and a letter by T. Malinowski from Oviedo, 'Polonia. Boletín Informativo de la Colonia Polaca en España', December 1993, no. 8, p.12.

72 In his capacity as a Polish Red Cross representative, Skórzewski probably worked also for the II Bureau in Madrid.

73 More in: TNA(PRO), FO 371/34556, correspondence of July 1943; CAW, the VI Bureau, II. 52. 483, Memorandum of the II Bureau, PGS, and K. Strzałka, *Między przyjaźnią a wrogością. Z dziejów stosunków polsko-włoskich 1939–1945* (*Between Friendship and Hostility. From the History of Polish-Italian Relations 1939–1945*), Kraków 2001, pp. 212, 220–232.

74 A. J. Birkenmayer served in the II Bureau between 1918 and 1927. During the rule of the 'Colonels', he was one of the best organisers of the pro-government press. From 1930 to 1935, he was a parliamentary Deputy as a representative of the Non-Party Bloc for Co-operation with the Government (BBWR). Arrested by the French

authorities in Casablanca, probably in August 1942, and released after a time thanks to the intervention of Marcel Dubois, police commissioner and friend of Maj. M. Z. Słowikowski, Chief of Station 'Afryka'. From September 1942 to the end of war, Birkenmayer was Chief of Intelligence Cell (from 1943 – Independent Intelligence Cell) 'Manchester' in Ottawa (CAW, II Bureau, I. 303. 4.393, Chief of the II Bureau to the Minister of Military Affairs, Warsaw, 7 July 1927 and I. 303. 4 .7812, information card on Birkenmayer; M. Z. Rygor-Słowikowski, *W tajnej*, op. cit., pp. 149, 158, 227, 245; *Kto był kim w Drugiej Rzeczypospolitej* (*Who was Who in the Second Republic*), ed. J. M. Majchrowski, Warsaw 1994, p. 236; A. Adamczyk, *Bogusław Miedziński (1891–1972). Biografia polityczna Bogusław Miedziński (1891–1972). A Political Biography*, Toruń 2000, pp.198 and 212).

75 Correspondence in KMS; S. Schimitzek, *Na krawędzi*, op. cit., p. 625.

76 They were Lt. Zbigniew Słupecki 'Luis' ('George'), active mainly in San Sebastián, Lt. Jarosław Głowacki 'Jarosław', por. Kaiser 'Fernando' and 'Hiszpan'.

77 A trustworthy person who, given the right password or sign, received the post and passed it on.

78 They included Tadeusz Rakusa-Suszczewski, formerly of Station '300' in France, 2nd Lt. Stefan Śmigaj, Father Efrem, a Capuchin monk working in Madrid and Barcelona, Antoni Jankowski, Stanisław Błaszczyk, who interviewed Polish soldiers traveling through Madrid, and Stanisław Niedzielski, a resident of Malaga from 1943 and Kara's trusted co-worker in Paris and Berlin.

79 He was one of the six Spaniards whom the British in Spain were to protect at all costs in case of a threat (D. Pastor Petit, *Espionaje*, op. cit., p. 515).

80 KMS, Lt-Col. S. Kara to M. Szumlakowski, 16 September 1943.

81 Due to numerous misunderstandings, he continued to act as chief of the cell until February 1944.

82 IPMS, A.9.VI.10/2, 'Ribeirrinho', Information from Spain, Madrid, 23 November 1943. Such an intention was to have been expressed by Count de Jordana, head of Spanish diplomacy, to an ambassador of one the Allied states.

83 KMS, Count de Jordana to Duke de Alba, Madrid, 27 December 1943. The Minister requested Duke de Alba, the Spanish Ambassador in London, to delicately draw the attention of the Polish decision-makers to this fact. However, the Ministry of Foreign Affairs did not change its decision.

84 IPMS, A.45.599/2, Polish Legation in Madrid, Col. S. Gano, Chief of II Bureau, PGS, to W. Radziwiłł, 19th January 1944, and CAW, VI Bureau, II. 52.481, Hand-over certificate of the Intelligence Department of the II Bureau, PGS, 15 February 1944. In March 1944, Lt-Col. Kara became Military Attaché in Rio de Janeiro.

85 IPMS, A.9.VI.10/1 i 2. This archive preserved the almost complete documentation of Continental Action networks in Spain and Portugal.

86 Ibid., A.9.VI.17/2, J. Librach, Head of Continental Action, to Lt-Col. J. Kowalewski, 15 March 1941.

87 This diplomat was Stanisław Kot, see : AHN, FC, EP, H-537, Secretary General of Police Headquarters in Madrid (DGS) to the Head of DGS Political-Social Brigade, Madrid, 21 October 1942.

88 IPMS, A.9.VI.10/1 Ministry of Internal Affairs.

89 AG MAE, Leg. R. 2221, exp. 20, G. Caballero, Director General of DGS, to Head of European Section of MAE, Madrid, 6 February 1942.

90 KMS, L. As. Leonardów to Wierzejski, Madrid, 20 December 1942.

91 More in: correspondence in KMS. In order to explain this probably unprecedented incident, it is necessary to go back to the Spanish Civil War. In April 1937, the Polish Legation in Madrid organised the evacuation to Poland of a group of Spaniards who sought refuge in the Polish mission. They were transported to a port in Valencia, where they were supposed to board the Polish warship O.R.P. 'Wilja'. When their passports were checked in the port security station, taken over by a

leftist militia, Victoriano Martín Martín, a former police lt., was recognised and was to be shot immediately, despite protests by Polish diplomats, predominantly First Secretary Juliusz Sakowski. Having arrived at the scene of the incident, Minister Szumlakowski stood in front of the firing squad and thus prevented the execution of Martín Martín. In 1943 Count de Jordana, the Spanish Minister of Foreign Affairs, wrote to Duke de Alba, the Spanish Ambassador in London: 'Minister Szumlakowski faced the firing squad in order to prevent an execution of a certain officer, thus risking his own life' (KMS, Count de Jordana to Duke de Alba, Madrid, 27 December 1943; more details about this particular incident and the equally hazardous and dramatic smuggling of another Spanish officer dressed as Polish Consul onto the 'Wilja' with the assistance of Szumlakowski, see: J. S. Ciechanowski, *Z dziejów humanitaryzmu*, op. cit.). Martín Martín was the only police officer among the evacuees. During WW II, as Police Commissaire in Madrid, he rendered great service to the Poles, although his position in the local hierarchy was not very high. He was one of the Polish 'insiders' in the Dirección General de Seguridad (see: correspondence in KMS and an account by Zofia Snawadzka, to whom the author expresses his thanks).

92 IPMS, A.9.VI.10/2, Ministry of Internal Affairs, Instruction by Minister S.; ibid., Mikołajczyk for K. Kraczkiewicz, London, 31 March 1943, A. 9. VI. 17/3, M. Piotrowski to Lt-Col. J. Kowalewski, no place, 11 February 1944.

93 Ibid., 'Filip' to 'Nart', 12 June 1944.

94 See: correspondence in IPMS, A.9.VI.10/1 and 2.

95 S. Schimitzek, *Na krawędzi*, op. cit., pp. 600-601. The author, a representative of the Ministry of Labour and Social Welfare, highly praised the results of Makow's activity.

96 IPMS, A.9.VI.10/2, Ministry of Internal Affairs, 'Filip' to 'Nart', 21 March 1944 and 11th April 1944.

97 This was the 'man with a scar', an agent from Pamplona and a former driver of General Emilio Mola, one of the leaders of the 'generals' rebellion' of July 1936, a member of the Falanga, and, as it became apparent later on, for two years a Gestapo agent, who transported post and people from the frontier.

98 IPMS, A.9.VI.10/2, Ministry of Internal Affairs, 'Poppy' to 'Nart', 28 June 1944; and a note of 20 July 1944. Markow intended to employ for intelligence work Józef Łobodowski, later a famous poet ('Poppy' to 'Nart', 22 July 1944).

99 Correspondence in KMS and IPMS, A.9.VI.10/2 Ministry of Internal Affairs.

25

The Soviet Union

Andrzej Pepłoński

The range of the activities conducted by Polish Intelligence in the USSR changed substantially as the war went on. The Polish Eastern territories found themselves under Soviet occupation twice. On 17th September 1939 the inclusion of Eastern Poland into the Soviet state was accompanied by large-scale repressions against the Polish population and by the recruitment by NKVD of agents, who were to supply information on the Polish civilian and military authorities, as well as on the situation in Western Europe.[1] Consequently the situation in that part of Poland which was overrun by the Red Army became the concern not only of the Polish Government established in France, but also of the Western Allies.

Almost immediately following the invasion of 17th September, the intelligence structures of the Polish émigré authorities attempted to set up intelligence activities on the occupied territories. In parallel, spontaneous resistance organizations were emerging. One of the first intelligence networks in Lwów (Lviv), which was a part of the 'Loyal to Poland' military organization, was headed by Lt. Karol Trojanowski. Later a new organization was set up, under the name 'Association of Organisations for the Liberation of the Homeland', it had an Intelligence Department, led by Lt. Roman Kędzierski. On 22nd December 1939 Maj. Aleksander Klotz 'Niewarowski', an emissary of the Service for Poland's Victory – the Union of Armed Struggle HQ, arrived in Lwów, and this led to the unification of all the military organisations there. As a result, a number of diversionary actions were successfully undertaken, along the railway routes in the Borysław Basin and in the Przemyśl region. These actions did not develop further, having been crushed in early 1940 by mass repressions carried out by the NKVD. The effectiveness of Soviet measures was assisted by the betrayal of several members of the military clandestine organisation, especially by Maj. Emil Macieliński 'Kornel'. Lack of communications with the Union of Armed Struggle – further the Home Army GHQ in Warsaw was a serious impediment to any expanding underground and intelligence work. Couriers from Wilno and Lwów were rarely able to cross the heavily guarded German-Soviet demarcation line. Polish Intelligence had therefore to rely on the information supplied by persons who managed to make their way to France. On the basis of such information II Bureau, PGS, prepared reports about the situation in those parts of Poland, which were under Soviet occupation.[2]

After the outbreak of the German-Soviet war the knowledge of the situation in the Soviet Union acquired new meaning. Some of II Bureau officers predicted that the Red Army would be defeated within a few weeks. British Intelligence did not share this view. General F. H. N. Davidson of SIS was firmly convinced, that 'Russia would bear as much as would be necessary and would fulfil her tasks as part of the general Allied effort'. In order to gain certainty on this, an influx of new information was required, especially on the war potential of the eastern Ally. Difficulties with crossing the front line made it possible to embark only upon sporadic spot intelligence operations in the USSR. The participants of one of such actions were two representatives of Home Army Intelligence in Lwów – an officer called 'Jur' and his colleague, 'Andrzej'. From 24 September to 18 November 1941 they travelled to Moscow along a difficult route through Zhitomir, Korosten, Ovruch, Homel and Smolensk to Dorogobuz, located near the front. On the way the agents assessed war damage and the effectiveness of the Soviet Army by paying attention to the large numbers of abandoned military equipment, including artillery and tanks. Their observations were confirmed during a several days long stay in Moscow (22–25 October 1941), where the Poles noticed significant damage and a large number of anti-aircraft guns protecting the capital during raids that recurred day and night. The morale of the military units was good, food supplies for the civilians were satisfactory, but prices tended to increase quickly. The local authorities encouraged the population to leave Moscow due to increasing difficulties with food supplies.[3]

The Allies, however, expected a regular flow of precise information on the military, economic and political situation in the Soviet Union. It became possible to gather such material after the establishment of Polish-Soviet military co-operation – as a result of the Polish-Soviet Agreement. One of the elements of collaboration between the Poles and the Soviets was an exchange of information about the situation on the German side of the eastern front. Contacts between the two intelligence services were, however, weighed down by the confrontations between them dating from the inter-war period. Furthermore, Polish Intelligence in Poland feared that co-operation with the Soviets might lead to the disclosure of military clandestine organisation in Poland. In their opinion the Soviet Military Mission to PGS in London was not prepared to share the most important information from the areas near the front. Nevertheless, under pressure of the Soviet authorities, on 25 August 1941 General Władysław Sikorski approved the principles of co-operation between the two sides. Maj. Leon Bortnowski was given authority to relay to the Home Army the intelligence tasks formulated by Soviet Intelligence. He was also asked to supply the Soviets with information received from Poland. Further agreements led to the creation of a radio communication system. Nonetheless, the distance between the intelligence services of both sides was maintained. This co-operation lasted throughout the spring and summer of 1942. Home Army Intelligence, through its radio station called 'Ada' and the intermediary of Maj. Bortnowski ('Wisła'), provided the Soviets with the most important reports about the concentrations and movements of the German armies, indicating the probable directions of offensive operations. Such reports included information on the number and contents of military transports. In March 1942, for example, Home Army Intelligence identified 871 complete and 9,313 incomplete transports, adding that in comparison with transports from the front, the surplus of men sent eastward was about 240,000. Report no. 1 of 28 April informed the Soviets of the transfer of two Bavarian divisions from Wilno to Smoleńsk.[4] A report of 29 April provided the location of 14 Luftwaffe bases, i.e. in the region of Riga, Pskov, Mińsk and Kharkov. There were also reports of continuing reinforcement of the southern part of the front with armour. By the end of April, Home Army Intelligence reported a grouping of armoured and mechanised forces composed of eight divisions, reinforcing the southern area of the front. It is most likely that what Home Army agents had been observing was a concentration of forces within the so-called Directive no. 41 (Fall Blau), approved on 28 March 1942. Fall Blau was the attack along the central Don river, and further towards the Caucasus, with the participation, among other units, of 3rd Panzer Corps, commanded by General von Mackensen.[5] Home Army assessment was that between 1 and 16 June 1942, the Germans concentrated about 50 divisional units there, 28 of which were identified. It reported that 738 artillery pieces, 394 anti-aircraft guns, 480 anti-tank guns and 54 tanks were being moved south. In mid-July Home Army Intelligence informed about the movements of Hungarian, Italian and German troops towards the regions of Kiev, Równe, Homel, Orel, and Dyneburg.[6] The overwhelming majority of information gathered by Home Army coincided with data originating from Soviet sources. Despite this, the Soviet side rarely expressed its approval for the authors of the Polish reports, hence the co-operation was carried out in an atmosphere of mutual suspicion.

On the other hand the British and the Americans were interested in obtaining information about the current state of the Red Army, which would make it possible to assess the Soviet chances for stopping the aggressor and eventual victory. For the Polish Government, knowledge of the Soviet war potential and of its strategic and political plans was regarded as essential. Polish Intelligence was required to supply information from sources independent from the official Soviet agencies. This task was given to Maj. Bortnowski. While organising co-operation with Soviet Intelligence in the Soviet Union, he was at the same time to create Station 'Rosja' ('R'), which would operate without the knowledge of the host country.

The first source of information for Bortnowski were statements by Polish Army officers released from Soviet prisons. Their accounts showed that Soviet Intelligence attempted to gain the co-operation of those officers, who before the war worked in the II Bureau, or who were arrested while working for the Home Army. One such was 2nd Lt. Stanisław Żymierski 'Łazowski', whom the Polish authorities in Paris sent to Poland together with his brother, an artillery officer. Both were arrested by the NKVD and, after training, were to be parachuted into the German-occupied Poland, to establish contact with Col. Stefan Rowecki 'Rakoń'. Their mission was cancelled after the two men suffered injuries during training jumps. The NKVD tried to use Lt-Col. Stanisław Pstrokoński, who before the war worked in the 'Wschód' ('East') Section. Both Pstrokoński and Lt-Col. Antoni Szymański, a former military attaché in Berlin, undertook the analysis and operational assessment of the anticipated German attack against the Soviet Union. Attempts were also made to obtain data from other II Bureau officers[7] about the network of Polish agents in Germany. Reports on such attempts were forwarded to London and were considered as important, since they drew attention to the grave threat posed by the Soviet Intelligence both to the resistance in Poland and for Polish Intelligence in the West.

Despite the agreements on co-operation, Bortnowski encountered various obstacles on the part of the Soviet military authorities. As early as the beginning of September 1941, Bortnowski was reporting a lack of information about the situation at the front. His contacts with representatives of the Soviet General Staff were limited to the organisation of the Polish Army in the USSR.[8] In the course of his talks, the Soviet side would not mention the issues of interest to Bortnowski. Consequently the primary source of his information were Polish officers, who shared with him their impressions from their official travels across the USSR. The Chief of Station 'R' collated such data and attempted to assess the situation of the Red Army along particular sections of the front. In September 1941, for example, he reported on the considerable losses suffered by the Germans in the Leningrad region and the mass evacuation of the population of that city, the continuing defence of Kiev, which was being intensively shelled by the German artillery, and on the battles on the Dniepr river, stressing that the capture of Dniepropetrovsk and Krivoy Rog seriously weakened the Soviet arms industry.

In his assessment of the position of the Soviet troops along the central section of the front, Bortnowski referred to opinions expressed by Gen. Frank Noel Mason-Macfarlane, the British representative in Moscow, who at the time was in the front-line region of Viazma. The Maj. also sent reports about the construction of new airfields in the region of Vologda, and highly praised the efficiency of rail transport and effective anti-aircraft defences around Moscow and Leningrad. He was also impressed with the rate with which new units were formed, despite shortages of uniforms and modern equipment. Nonetheless, the Polish agent regarded the overall situation of the Red Army as very difficult,[9] an opinion, which appeared to be confirmed by the behaviour and proposals made by the intelligence services of the eastern ally. On 20th September 1941, General Georgiy

Zhukov, a representative of the NKVD, suggested to the Head of the Polish Military Mission in Moscow an immediate establishment of wireless communication with Home Army Intelligence, in order to relay data on the German troop movements behind the eastern front. He suggested that the Polish side treat this as a 'friendly favour'.[10] In order to meet the expectation of his partners, Bortnowski drew the attention of his superiors to the division of tasks between the NKVD and Military Intelligence (GRU). The latter established co-operation with the II Bureau of PGS, while the NKVD dominated contacts with the Polish Army in the USSR. Such dual approach guaranteed decisive NKVD superiority in the issues associated with the functioning of Home Army resistance.[11]

Independently of his official contacts with the Soviet authorities, Bortnowski embarked upon creating a field network. In October 1941 he reported the establishment of the 'Sandomierz' cell in Buzułuk, whose head, Maj. Wincenty Bąkiewicz, had at his disposal an operational fund of 500 dollars and 5,000 rubles. Since before the war Bąkiewicz directed the 'Russian' Section of the Records and Studies Department, there were fears for his life. It was therefore intended to send him to London. Bortnowski was also concerned about the lack of information on the fate of the officers of former Station no. 1 in Wilno and the Independent Information Sections of the District Corps HQ in Eastern Poland.[12]

The organisation of intelligence activity was seriously hampered by the transfer of the Polish Embassy from Moscow to Kuybishev, where the only hotel was at the disposal of British and American officers, including representatives of intelligence services. All that Maj. Bortnowski had at his disposal was a single officer and a radio. He had to work in very difficult circumstances, which impaired his ability to gather information. There was no access to the local press, no protection for his codes and he did not even have a room of his own. In these circumstances, the Maj. devoted most of his efforts to expanding for recruitment to the army network. Information about the internal situation in the Soviet Union was to be supplied by persons arriving at the newly created recruitment centres, and the 'Sandomierz' cell. The increasingly loose discipline of the Red Army provided him with an opportunity to acquire information on Soviet operational plans. Information on the morale in the Polish Army in the USSR and on the activities of the Polish civilian authorities was also collected. Restricted access to the radio, which remained at the disposal of the Polish Embassy in Kuybishev, was another problem.[13] On the plus side, there was increasing willingness on the part of the Russians to speak about events at the front and on the general situation in the USSR. The prevailing mood was that of defeatism and anti-Soviet sentiments. Bortnowski reported that German troops entering terrain abandoned by the Red Army were welcomed by the local population 'with bread and salt', while further inside Russia serious deficiencies with transport and food supplies began to manifest themselves.[14]

Despite the growing tension in Polish-Soviet relations, caused by the preparations for the evacuation of the Polish Army to the Middle East,

Polish Counter-intelligence loyally participated in countering German espionage. In November 1941, the NKVD was presented with information about a German Intelligence network functioning in the region where the 6th Infantry Division was stationed. An Abwehr agent, who contacted the Polish authorities, revealed a list of twenty Poles working for German Intelligence.[15]

The information obtained in the Soviet Union testified to the limited possibilities of Station 'R'. The reports were dominated by incomplete data about the situation at the front, current propaganda slogans, and a description of prevailing moods.[16] More valuable information was provided by Station 'SKN' in Stockholm, which co-operated with Scandinavian intelligence services. The reports from Stockholm contained information on shorter training time for new recruits to the infantry, the artillery and the Air Force and on the methods of enhancing the battle readiness of front-line units, for example by supplementing them with experienced soldiers discharged from hospitals. Station 'SKN' reported on the improvements in the efficiency of higher commands and offered opinions on the capability of the Red Army to plan and conduct war operations on a larger scale. In 1942, the Station presented a detailed technical characteristic of the new 'Simonov 41' rifle, a 127 mm. incendiary bomb projector, and the T-70 and K.V.S. I (Klim Voroshilov S.I.) tanks, which were used as KV-1 and KV-2. There was also more general information on the new 100-ton tank known as F. D. H.,[17] reportedly produced in Chelabinsk and Gorkiy.[18]

Attempts were made to renew the relationship with Japanese Intelligence, with which the II Bureau co-operated during the inter-war period, to bolster information about the situation in the Soviet Union. General Sikorski personally prepared the instructions for Col. Aleksander Kędzior, sent to China as the Head of Military Mission to carry out 'a detailed study of Soviet penetration and intentions in the Far East'.[19] The information obtained by Kędzior proved to be of little value.

A more important source of knowledge on the situation in the USSR was General Makoto Onodera, the Japanese Military Attaché in Stockholm, who co-operated with Lt-Col. Michał Rybikowski ('Peter Iwanow'), Chief of Intelligence Cell no. 1, under the control of Station 'SKN' in Stockholm.[20] In early 1942, General Onodera, who used information from Finnish Intelligence, provided information on the strength of the Red Army in the Far East, Siberia, the Caucasus, Iran and the Volga-Ural region. He estimated that at the European front the Soviets had at their disposal about 4,400,000 men, and another 3,300,000 elsewhere. A further 2,000,000 were being trained, and more than 1,000,000 wounded and sick servicemen were hospitalised.[21] Successive reports from Station 'SKN' described the mobilisation of men born between 1901 and 1922.[22] Other information acquired from Japanese Intelligence and relayed by Station 'Bałkany' at the end of May 1943, indicated serious difficulties experienced by the Soviet Union. The report claimed that the Red Army although well trained and equipped has shown fatigue, even exhaustion and the human resources were low. The establishment of Soviet divisions had been reduced to 8,000 soldiers, and infantry regiments were composed of only two battalions.

Soviet forces at the Eastern Front were estimated to total 400 divisions, 190 tank brigades (with about 100 tanks per brigade) and 18,000 planes, including 6,000 in the first line. Soviet-made tanks and planes were used in battles, while equipment received from the Western Allies was introduced to the front as the need arose. Monthly production was estimated at 900 planes and 1,000 tanks. A comparison of the current balance of forces in the Far East showed, that in the middle of 1943 the USSR was not capable of entering the war against Japan.[23]

Similar opinions about the Red Army were voiced at the time by the II Bureau, PGS. Attention was drawn to information about the transfer of several aircraft bases to the west of Kursk. Moreover, a concentration of considerable Soviet forces in two locations in the region of Moscow and in the area of Voronezh-Tambov was recorded.[24] In November 1943, the II Bureau prepared an initial analysis of the course of the Kiev operation, dominated by favourable opinions about the skill of the Soviet High Command. The analysis anticipated that the Red Army intended to seize communication centres around Kiev and to cut off the southern group of the German forces from the rest of the Eastern Front in order to destroy it. The state of German fortifications in the east was presented in great detail, with particular attention paid to the defensive positions in Poland and in eastern Prussia.[25]

Information about the political situation in the Soviet Union, obtained during the first half of 1944, indicated the emergence of a difference of opinion between Stalin and the NKVD leadership, caused by the decisions made at Tehran. The emergence of political groups around Beria, Voroshilov, Molotov and Vyshinski was noted. 'Stalin and the government circles attach little importance to the Union of Polish Patriots. The Russians want to establish their own government the moment they enter Warsaw'.[26] Consequently the II Bureau, closely following the development of the situation at the front, sought also information about any Soviet plans relating to post-war Poland.

In mid-June 1944 there were reports on the war industry production, which attained a level satisfying wartime needs, only the labour force was in short supply. It was expected that the exhaustion of human resources would force a decrease in the size of the army. On the other hand, successes at the front started to exert a positive impact on the mood prevailing among the Soviet people.[27]

Information obtained by intelligence was used for various assessments prepared for Polish military and civilian authorities. The situation at the Eastern Front and in the Soviet Union was examined against the background of global events. At the beginning of February 1945, the PGS expressed a view very different from the one formulated in 1941, that 'the military victory over Germany, or decisive participation in it, could well be the accomplishment of the USSR and not of the Anglo-Saxon powers. Military victories which grant the Russians a privileged position in the war effort of the anti-German coalition will also make it possible [for Moscow] to take political initiative, especially in Eastern Europe'.[28] Such conclusions were supported by detailed information about the forces participating in the war.

Notes

1 IPMS, A.XII.24/38, Intelligence and Counter-intelligence Report no. 1, l. dz. 11320/IItjn. 40, the II Bureau, PGS in Paris, 10 March 1940. At the beginning of 1940, a number of persons approached the II Bureau, who of their own accord revealed that they had co-operated with the NKVD. As a rule, they had been recruited in Lwów and included representatives of various occupations, with civil servants, railway workers, former soldiers and policemen among them.

2 IPMS, A XII/24/40, Summary no. 12, News on the situation in Poland under Soviet occupation, March 1940. More in: Polskie Podziemie na terenach Zachodniej Ukrainy i Zachodniej Białorusi w latach 1939–1945 (The Polish Resistance in Western Ukraine and Western Belorussia in 1939–1945], vol. 1, 2, Warsaw – Moscow 2001; Polska i Ukraina w latach trzydziestych-czterdziestych XX wieku. Nieznane dokumenty z archiwów służb specjalnych (Poland and Ukraine during the 1930s and 1940s. Unknown Documents from Special Services Archives),vol. 1, Warsaw-Kiev 1998.

3 Report by 'Jur' from III Bureau, Lwów, 16th December 1941 [in:] Żołnierze Komendy Głównej...(Soldiers of the HQ...) , pp. 95–99.

4 CAW, O VI, 1777/90/644, Dispatch from 'Ada' to 'Wisła' no. 145 of 27 April 1942, leaf 8.

5 P. Carell, Operacja Barbarossa (Operation Barbarossa), Warszawa 2000, pp. 407–430.

6 CAW, O VI, 1777/90/644, Dispatch from 'Ada' to 'Wisła' no. 197 of 17 July 1942, leaf 56.

7 IPMS, Kol. 138/161, Dispatch from the Chief of Station 'R' to HQ, 22 August 1941.

8 Ibid., Situation report from Station 'R' to the Chief of the II Bureau, PGS, 4 September 1941.

9 Ibid.

10 Ibid., Dispatch from the Chief of the Polish Military Mission no. 49 of 20 September 1941 to the Supreme Commander.

11 Ibid., Dispatch from the Chief of Station 'R' to 'Stanisław' no. 61 of 26 September 1941.

12 Ibid., Dispatch from the Head of Station 'R' to 'Stanisław' of 21 October 1941.

13 Maj. Bortnowski informed HQ that he did not have a car but possessed 'a fountain pen, very little paper (in Kuybishev it is impossible to buy even a school notebook), a broken typewriter (Olivetti) and 12 000 invalid Soviet rubles'. Ibid., Dispatch from the Chief of Station 'R' to 'Stanisław', 22 October 1941.

14 Ibid., Dispatch from Station 'R' to 'Stanisław', 21 October 1941.

15 Ibid., Dispatch from Station 'R' to 'Stanisław', 27 November 1941.

16 Ibid., Dispatch from the Military Attaché in Kuybishev to the II Bureau, PGS, l. dz. 192/43, 5 March 1943.

17 This was probably exaggerated information about the heaviest JS-2 and JS-3 (Josif Stalin) tanks, produced since 1943/44, weighing 46–46,5 tons and fitted with a 122 mm. gun.

18 IPMS,A.XII. 24/61, Dispatch from Station 'SKN', 10 March 1943 (agent 'Hei').

19 IPMS,A.XII. 24/76, Instruction for the H of the Military Mission in China, l. dz. 42/O. Wyw. tjn. of 11 March 1943.

20 Contacts between Lt-Col. Rybikowski and Japanese Intelligence dated back to 1939 and the establishment of co-operation with General Onouchi Hiroschi, the Military

Attaché in Riga; E. Pałasz-Rutkowska, A. T. Romer, *Historia stosunków polsko-japońskich 1940–1945* (*The History of Polish-Japanese Relations 1940–1945*), Warsaw 1996, pp. 245–247.
21 IPMS, Note from the II Bureau, PGS.
22 IPMS,A.XII. 24, Dispatch from Station 'SKN', l. dz. 194/R, of 15 May 1943.
23 IPMS,A.XII. 24/61, Dispatch from Station 'Bałkany', l. dz. 213/43, of 31 May 1943.
24 IPMS,A.XII. 24/16, Periodic communique no. 14/43 of II Bureau, PGS, 21 May 1943.
25 Ibid.
26 IPMS,A.XII. 3/28, Dispatch from Cairo from Col. A. Szymański to the Supreme Commander, 26 February 1944.
27 IPMS, A XII/24/16, Note by Lt-Col. W. Zarembski from 'Rosja' Section of the Studies Department, the II Bureau, PGS, 13 June 1944.
28 IPMSA.XII. 3/10, Study by the Operational Bureau of PGS entitled '*Ogólne położenie wojenne na tle politycznym oraz przewidywany rozwój wydarzeń*' (*General wartime situation against the political background and the anticipated development of events*), 6 February 1945.

26
Northern and Central Europe

Gill Bennett

A search for information on Polish Intelligence activities in this region has yielded very disappointing results. Despite a number of hints and oblique references to the activities of Polish secret organisation and resistance movements, no substantive documentation has been found and no information from British sources. Hints and references indicate a large amount of clandestine activity within Poland itself, carried out by a number of different organisations. But no reports survive in SIS archives, partly of course because liaison with the Home Army was carried on through other channels.

From the small amount of information available, however, it is clear that despite danger and difficulty Polish agents succeeded in maintaining courier lines from Warsaw to London through various staging posts including Paris. One tantalising item is a note by Dunderdale listing some of the concealing devices used for transporting mail out of Warsaw (valuable articles were never used, as liable to be stolen): 'Backs of pocket mirrors, backs of hairbrushes, backs of nailbrushes, hollow toothbrushes, shaving brushes, shaving sticks, cakes of soap, fountain pens, pencils (Eversharp type), suitcases with false bottoms, soles of shoes.'

No information has been found relating to Polish activity in other countries of northern Europe.

27
Southern Europe and the Balkans

Gill Bennett

For this region the only information found in closed British records relating to Polish Intelligence activities concerns the following countries: Bulgaria, Hungary, Romania, Turkey and Yugoslavia. However, it is clear that Polish agents and contacts working in the area also travelled to, and had dealings with contacts in other countries such as Italy and Greece. Most of those concerned passed at some time through Istanbul, an important focus for Intelligence because of its links with the Middle East as well as Europe. There is, therefore, considerable overlap between the countries on which information has been found. This is particularly true of Hungary and Turkey where the Polish Intelligence relationship appears to have been especially close.

Bulgaria
Only one document has been found relating specifically to Polish activities in Bulgaria, and it draws upon information received from German sources that may not be reliable. The document, dated January 1942, relates to the activities of a Polish agent called Kowalewski (also known as Bobrowski and Noris) who was said to be engaged in smuggling Poles out of Bulgaria. He was assisted by another Pole, Zembrzuski, who had previously worked in the Polish Legation. Kowalewski also worked in close liaison with the Polish Consul in Istanbul.

Other contacts mentioned were: Maria Pozigowska, formerly the cook to the Polish Minister in Serbia, and in 1942 running a restaurant in Sofia (the *Ruska Stolowka*) which was a meeting place for Poles in Bulgaria; Danka Dobrewa, a Post Office worker; and two other Polish agents, Fuchs and Jarzambek.

It appears that a Pole working as a German agent had some success in penetrating Kowalewski's network, and was given various assignments as a courier. The documentation indicates that he was regarded with some suspicion by Kowalewski and his colleagues, but no further details of the story are available.

Hungary

Documentation on Polish activities in Hungary is fuller than that on Bulgaria, though fragmented. Budapest was an important focus for gathering information on German movements and activities, and liaison between Polish and Hungarian Intelligence services was already in place before the outbreak of war. Following the invasion of Poland this co-operation was continued; some references have been found in 1940 to the liaison activities of an Austrian refugee, Fritz Gartenberg, who appears to have been close to both the Hungarian authorities and Polish Intelligence through the medium of the Polish Military Attaché in Budapest. Other names mentioned include Nini Fortini, the widow of a Pole executed by the Gestapo in Warsaw, Col. Adam Rudnicki, and Zbigniew Jazmanowski.

References have also been found to questionnaires prepared by Polish Intelligence that had fallen into German hands, asking, for example, about details of German troops occupying Slovakia (March 1940), and about British air raid damage in Germany (July 1940). Another questionnaire of August 1940 asking about war factories, troop movements and the morale of workers in Germany also fell into German hands through another Polish agent, Marjan Bajerlein known as 'Zdrevecki'. Penetration of Gartenberg's circle by German Intelligence led to his arrest and that of Fortini, Rudnicki and Jazmanowski in November 1940, but the influence of friendly Hungarian officials secured their release under house arrest.

In August 1940 SIS received reports about two parallel Polish Intelligence networks in Budapest, neither of which appeared to be aware of the activities of the other. The Polish authorities in London informed SLC that it was important to maintain this dual system in order to check the sources and authenticity of information received. The 'official' II Bureau representative in Budapest was Capt. Otto Pawłowicz, working from the Polish Legation, and it was with him that arrangements were made for liaison with SIS in Hungary and the establishment of communications with London.

Other reports from the same period indicated the existence of as many as three separate Polish Intelligence networks in Budapest in addition to that run by Pawłowicz. Firstly, Lt-Col. Emisarski, Maj. Bastgen or Bas and Col. Kornaus (Dochnal) of the Polish Military Mission were said to be smuggling Polish soldiers to England (the latter two were apparently arrested in July 1940). Another network, part of the Polish secret military organisation in Warsaw and run from the UK by Gen Sikorski, was said to be directed by Lt-Col. M. Krajewski of the Polish Embassy in Budapest (also arrested in July 1940), assisted by Lt-Col. Bezeg 'Longin', Col. Siewanowski, Bolesław Huebner, Konrad Żylechowski, and Capt. Michał Jaroszewicz (the latter three arrested in September 1940 together with many other members of their organisation). Finally, Col. Rowecki was said to represent the Polish Resistance Movement.

This somewhat chaotic situation was clearly compromising the effectiveness of Polish Intelligence in Hungary. In November 1940 SIS received a report stating that there were 'some half-dozen Polish organisations' in Budapest 'which not only do not repeat not work together but actually work against each other', mentioning in particular the names of Billewicz and Fietowicz. A further report noted that 'it appears in general that spirit of Polish activities here is 'each man against every other' and even 'some against Britain'.' Following the arrest of Emisarski no Polish representative appeared to be able to mediate between different factions, and the resulting confusion was thought to be a threat to SIS's own activities. In these circumstances it was suggested that the Polish authorities in London should be asked to designate a representative in Budapest to act as central liaison, and to control all Polish networks 'in the interest of their own country'.

An unsigned letter of 18 November 1940 from the Polish Intelligence authorities in London acknowledged this information from SIS as confirming reports received from other sources, and stated that 'the necessary measures have been taken already'. It pointed out, however, that Capt. Pawłowicz was the only official representative of the II Bureau in Budapest: Billewicz was 'one of the personnel of the local post of the VI Bureau which is directed in Budapest by Lt-Col. Bezeg 'Longin', while Fietowicz 'acts on behalf of Minister Kot as liaison agent for the political organisations in Poland'. Instructions were accordingly sent to SIS representatives in Budapest that full collaboration only with Capt. Pawłowicz was desirable 'to exclusion of all other self-styled heads of Polish II Bureau'.

In March 1941 the Polish II Bureau PGS sent a further memorandum to SOE (copied to SIS), confirming that Maj. Pawłowicz was 'the sole person authorized by the Polish authorities to get in touch with our representative in Hungary', and that Col. Gano was 'strongly opposed to his cells having anything to do with sabotage or subversive activities'. A letter of 13 March from SIS to SOE warned that in view of this, 'it would seem very undesirable to establish any channels, either for intelligence purposes, or in regard to sabotage, that have not the approval of the Polish authorities here and on the spot'. For the Polish II Bureau or SIS representatives in Budapest to be compromised would mean 'an almost complete breakdown of W/T communication between Warsaw, Budapest and London', since this was the one remaining link (other than the secret W/T stations in Polish occupied territory working with Polish stations in London and Istanbul) through which intelligence reports were being received from the network of Polish agents. SOE were urged not to take any action that might jeopardise this, and to avoid other 'self-styled Polish liaison officers' such as Count Rozwadowski (working for Professor Kot), Mr. Stypiński (Polish Ministry of Finance representative) and Mr. Szczeniowski (formerly secretary to the Polish Legation).

Very little information has been uncovered relating to Polish activities in Hungary after 1941. According to German sources a former Polish Intelligence officer was recruited by German Intelligence and infiltrated a group of Polish agents in Budapest working on intelligence, sabotage and propaganda: the names Pomerański/Hermański (also known as Koehler) were mentioned, in contact with Władysław Kawecki in Kraków (Cracow), Barbara Sobolewska and Mieczysław Stabrowski in Warsaw. Some reference has also been found to an agent known as ROMAN, formerly employed by the Polish Legation in Budapest, who by May 1943 had moved to Istanbul. Again, however, the line of investigation dries up and no further details have been found.

Romania

As in other countries, there were a number of Polish individuals and networks carrying out Intelligence activities in Romania at the same time, either working together or in competition with each other. References in closed British archives indicate a particularly close relationship between Polish and French Intelligence in Bucharest. Because of this close relationship, contacts with SIS were restricted. An SIS minute of 30 March 1940 noted that it had been agreed with Commandant Perruche of French Intelligence that in all cases of approaches by Polish organisations abroad to SIS representative, the latter would always consult with the French representative on the spot: 'we have definitely agreed with the French that we will not play with the Poles abroad except with their knowledge'.

This agreement affected the British response to a proposal by Polish Intelligence in Romania to share information on Soviet Russia gathered from a group of young Russians opposed to the Soviet regime. The group was trained by a Polish officer who spoke Russian fluently and was thought by them to be Russian, an important factor as 'all are ideologists working for the redemption of their country'. They were to be based in Russian-occupied Poland, and to send back information by radio.

This elaborate scheme was expensive to set up and run, and the Poles offered to share the information with British Intelligence in return for the latter's bearing half the costs of transport, maintenance, equipment and expenses. Although SIS thought the idea had possibilities, they were unwilling to proceed without approval from Polish HQ in Paris and French Intelligence authorities – neither of whom had been told about the scheme. It is not clear from British archives whether the plan went ahead, but if so it was not on a joint basis.

Detailed information about Polish activities in Romania is patchy. In early 1940, a Col. of the Polish General Staff, Wilhelm Heinrich or 'The Chief', was described as working in Bucharest with Zygmunt Szpotański (apparently working for Gen. Sikorski), and Józef Poznański, a Major at the Polish Military Bureau; a former Polish official, Kościałkowski, was described as working for French Intelligence. Heinrich was said to have a good knowledge of the organisation of German and Russian armies and of German domestic politics, and to have an 'undying hatred' of the Soviet Union. According to a German source, Polish Intelligence activities in Bucharest were centred on an address in Calea Roma, from where contacts were maintained with Belgrade, Zagreb and Budapest. Until May 1940 Heinrich was assisted by Poznański, whose areas of special interest were the transfer of prisoners of war, the administration of Polish transport in Romania and the collection and distribution of information; after Poznański went to Chile, Tadeusz Ignaczewski, a Polish General Staff Capt. who had served in the First World War, took his place.

SIS minutes of August 1940 refer to Maj. Stanisław Orłowski, also known as 'Ostaszewski', as the official representative of Polish Intelligence in Bucharest. However, he was arrested by the Romanian police in October. It was hoped that his release might be secured through an approach from Polish to Romanian Intelligence contacts, so that with SIS help he could escape to Turkey. No information has been found to indicate whether this was achieved.

Bucharest formed part of a courier link from Warsaw to London, used for passing both information (gathered from the General-gouvernement, Germany and the Ukraine) and escaping Poles. In addition to an office in Berlin, the organisation used an estate at Cranguri for transmitting W/T messages to London, and also had transmitters installed in the office of the Japanese Military Attaché in Bucharest where two Poles, employed by the Japanese on anti-Soviet intelligence, were – unknown to their employers – also relaying messages for Polish Intelligence. This link was apparently infiltrated by a German agent in May 1943, leading to the arrest of two of the Polish couriers, Adolf Zawalski (Rudolf) and Teodor Zarembiński (who attempted to escape by diving through a window, leading the Germans to name the operation *Fensterspringer*). These and other arrests appear to have paralysed the courier link, and no evidence has been found as to whether it was later reactivated.

Romania also served as a communications link between Poland and Turkey. However, it appears that this link was precarious, partly due to shortage of funds. It relied heavily on the crews of Romano-Turkish shipping lines, who tended to be unreliable and willing to work for whoever paid the most.

Turkey
Istanbul was an Intelligence capital, where most countries' consulates appear to have been engaged in intelligence activities. Despite this, very little information has been found about Polish activities there. References have been found to Polish Intelligence operating through contacts in the Spanish and German Consulates as well as their own, as well as through the Turkish Police. However, the Poles considered British links with Turkish Intelligence to be closer and more productive than their own. An SIS minute of December 1940 stated that 'the Turks are not very keen on giving the Poles cover', and that the Polish authorities in London wished SIS to take charge of a network set up in Turkey by a Pole named Zakrzewski.

Again, a number of different individuals and networks appear to have co-existed in Turkey. Among those to whom reference has been found are: Tadeusz Berdziński, Vice-Consul at the Polish Consulate in Istanbul; Jerzy (George) Kurcyusz, also a Polish Vice-Consul; Pawel (Paul)

Białobłocki, a chauffeur at the Polish Consulate, and an official at the Polish Legation called Wdziekoński.

In November 1943, SIS were informed that Col. Sadowski of Polish Intelligence would shortly arrive in Turkey to co-ordinate Polish activities in the Balkans and Middle East. He had previously been the Polish representative in New York and was highly thought of. Sadowski was keen to establish direct liaison with SIS in Istanbul and a telegram was sent asking for the SIS representative's views on such collaboration (24 November). Unfortunately, no response or further papers have been found.

Yugoslavia

Very little information has been found concerning Polish Intelligence activities in Yugoslavia, but the few references uncovered indicate a close relationship with French Intelligence, as in Romania. For example, in early 1940 documents from a German source refer to Oktavian Spitzmuller, also known as Fritz Muller, who held both French and Polish passports and was suspected by the Germans of being a French agent. Another French connection can be traced to Capt. Witold Szymaniak, who in March 1941 was living in Belgrade as a French citizen under the name of Victor Senner. A minute by SIS's A4 section of 31 March 1941 noted that Szymaniak might have to leave Yugoslavia, and that the Polish General Staff had asked SIS to offer him assistance in doing so if the need arose.

In late 1941–1942 Countess Potocka, President of the Polish Refugees' Welfare Committee in Cirkvenica, was said to be carrying on Intelligence as well as welfare activities in Yugoslavia. Closely connected to church circles and to the Vatican, she was assisted by the Archbishop of Belgrade, and operated an information office in the Vatican, staffed by an Army chaplain named Kwiatkowski, for passing information to London.

In December 1944, information reached SIS about a Polish organisation in Belgrade concerned with the evacuation of Poles from enemy territory. According to a man known as Vlastimir Janković, who had become involved in April 1941 when Alois Kotnik, also known as Zvonko Pavischa and Tadeusz Kobal, approached him for shelter, the organisation reported to the Polish Government in Exile in London and was well supplied with funds. Janković and Kotnik opened a guesthouse in Belgrade to use as cover for their activities, but later had to leave Yugoslavia to avoid police interest. Further details are not available, although both Kotnik and Janković appear to have come to the notice of the Gestapo and were arrested more than once.

28
Hungary

Andrzej Przewoźnik

The Home Army Liaison Base No. 1, 'Romek',[1] organised in the autumn of 1939 in Budapest, was the first military station serving as a communications link between the resistance movement being formed in occupied Poland and the Polish Government and military authorities in Paris, and later in London. In addition to its tasks relating to the maintenance of communications, at first exclusively by courier and later also by radio, 'Romek' dealt with diversion, the transfer of people to the Polish military units being formed in exile and with the underground life of the Polish community in Hungary. One of the most important elements in the organization of this Base was its Intelligence Section run by Capt. Jan Billewicz 'Bliżewski'.[2] As the Deputy Commander of the Base, he in fact directed 'intelligence activities in Hungary, aided by the local Station of the II Bureau' (at the time known as Station 'W').

Station 'W', subordinated to the II Bureau of PGS, acted almost in parallel to 'Romek',[3] creating its own network of contacts to ensure the operation of courier routes, the collection of information from the territories occupied by the Soviets and supporting the secret attempts to evacuate interned Polish officers. One of its tasks was to collect information on the development of the political situation in this part of Europe. Such information was passed on via Polish intelligence to Paris and later to London, to the British secret services.

An important spur to this activity and to the expansion of available contacts was provided by a trip of Lt-Col. Stanisław Gano, then Deputy Chief of the II Bureau, PGS, who in December 1939 visited Polish intelligence stations in Budapest, Bucharest and Belgrade.[4] One of the effects of this trip was the re-organisation of Polish intelligence in that part of Europe and the intensification of intelligence gathering which, from that point on, was not limited to mainly Polish affairs. Economic affairs, disposition and movement of troops and any German or Soviet activity in the region were of interest.

The changing political situation in 1940, and in particular the threat of closing down Polish diplomatic and military missions in Hungary and Romania, caused the II Bureau, PGS, to issue (on 24 April 1940) an instruction to all intelligence stations in these countries. The instruction ordered the preparation of plans to evacuate and to establish deep undercover intelligence cells, which were to remain in Hungary and Romania. The 'Romek' Base was, in addition, to set up a safe house for a radio station in Salonika.

The first organisational contacts and co-operation with British intelligence in Hungary can be traced back to 1940. These contacts were, however, sporadic, and limited to the necessities, such as the need to pass correspondence or to establish contacts and construct communication links into Yugoslavia. Broader co-operation was made impossible by the arrests of Station 'Romek' and Station 'W' personnel by the Hungarians in mid-1940. The blow delivered by the Hungarian intelligence was not, however, severe, and it did not delay the recruitment of informants in the Balkans. But it caused a significant weakening of Polish-British contacts. Between October 1940 and March 1941 only one pouch was transferred via British channels.

The existence of several (at that point) unco-ordinated Polish underground centres in Budapest clearly impacted on co-operation with the British in Hungary. It is clear that it was the 'Muszkieterowie' (Musketeers) organisation, set up in occupied Poland by Stefan Witkowski ('Tenczyński'), which had the most intensive contacts with the British intelligence services. Andrzej Kowerski 'Kennedy' and Krystyna Giżycka-Skarbek, both constantly visiting Hungary, represented Witkowski's organisation. Mrs Giżycka-Skarbek made regular courier journeys to Poland. Both maintained regular contacts with the SIS station in Hungary, using this route to pass on reports on the political and military situation in occupied Poland, prepared there by Witkowski's organisation. Giżycka also provided the British side with a safe route into Poland for escaping British POWs, held in camps on Polish territory.[5] Later, in view of the evacuation of diplomatic missions and threatened with arrest, she, too, was evacuated by the British.

In March 1941 the leadership of the British secret services told the Chiefs of II Bureau, PGS, that for security reasons in the future it would maintain contacts with the local representative of their Station in Budapest, and not with any other of the numerous agencies of the Polish Government and Polish political organizations active in Hungary.[6] In other words, the Station in Budapest accepted full responsibility for contacts with British Intelligence.

The first half of 1941 brought an intensity of reports concerning German preparations for the war with the Soviet Union. Reports from Hungary indicated troop movements and setting up depots for arms and ammunitions sent from Germany and its satellite countries. Fundamental news which was recieved in May 1941 was, that there is a concentration of troops transported from the Balkan region. The majority of such reports on the preparation for an attack against the USSR were transmitted via II Bureau, PGS, through direct contacts in Hungary or via Polish w/t stations supported by the British.

In 1942 Col. Stanisław Rostworowski 'Rola', the commander of the 'Romek' Base, established closer contacts with British intelligence in Hungary. This enabled him to maintain permanent radio contact with PGS, and also to strengthen his courier routes, including the ones to Lisbon and Bern. Communications with the Vatican, where Station 'Nuncjusz' (Nuncio) was set up, were also established.

In 1943, when Polish underground work in Hungary was re-organised, there were also changes in some of the Polish intelligence structures. In accordance with the decision of th VI Bureau, PGS in London, in the spring of 1943 the Communications Base, as well as Station 'W', were subordinated to the Home Army Commander-in-Chief. From then on, their orders would come from the Home Army GHQ in Poland.

On 30th September 1943 Col. T. Howie,[7] an SOE officer who escaped from a POW camp in Germany, arrived in Hungary, made contact with the 'Liszt' Base and began to co-operate closely with Polish intelligence officers, including courier communications in the Balkans. The Base provided SOE with accounts of Howie's current activities.

In 1944 Col. Howie worked closely with Prince Andrzej Sapieha, 'Tokaj', who was in Budapest as special emissary of the Home Army Commander-in-Chief, Gen. Bór-Komorowski. The Prince was empowered to conduct talks with the Hungarian military and political leadership on the possible Hungarian assistance in creating Home Army units from among Polish officers interned in Hungary. Such units were to participate in the general uprising in Poland, planned by the Home Army GHQ. Hence Sapieha's attempts to secure arms for the Home Army units being secretly organised in Hungary.

Sapieha managed to obtain Howie's[8] support in this respect, and the British Col. helped the Prince to establish contacts with the appropriate Hungarians. Sapieha had talks with the Chief of Staff of the Hungarian Army, Gen. Ferenc Sombathely,[9] and later with the Regent, Admiral Miklós Horthy himself. Close contacts with Polish representatives, in turn, allowed for better support for British intelligence during the German occupation of Hungary, as – unlike Polish civilian structures – the Polish intelligence was not broken up and continued to operate. They provided high quality information on the political and military situation in Hungary and in its neighbour states. In a report presented to his superiors after successfully reaching Italy from Hungary, Col. Howie spoke highly of his co-operation with Polish intelligence and with Prince Sapieha in Hungary. It is obvious from Col. Howie's report that without the assistance of the Poles he could never have survived and could cerainly not have engaged in any useful work.

In December 1944 Base 'Liszt' received a message from PGS for Howie concerning the air-drop of equipment for an operation called 'Natal'. PGS asked the Base whether it would be able to mount this operation with its own resources. Though the Base responded in the positive, the operation did not take place.

Almost from its beginning, Station 'W' in Budapest actively participated in the establishment of communications into Yugoslavia and further, to stations, among others, in Athens and Rome. The commanders of the Station were also in contact with British missions to Gen. Draža Michailović's partisans, and later also with those to Josip Tito.

The last Maj. operation undertaken together by Polish and British intelligence was air transport to Hungary provided for the courier of the VI Bureau, PGS, L/Corp. Zygmunt Pales 'Szum', in September 1944. SOE's Hungarian Section provided transfers from Italy to Hungary, as well as the required documents. The London headquarters informed Col. Perkins of this.

'Szuma' was to jump over Hungary, reach Budapest and establish contact with the commanders of Base 'Liszt' to help with communications with London. The expectation was that once this had been accomplished, 'Szum' was to be used to establish a courier route between Budapest and Istanbul. Having reached Turkey, he was to work for Base 'Flora' there. Col. Marian Utnik, the Chief of the VI Special Bureau, PGS, saw him off on 1 September 1944, and 'Szum' was flown to Base 'Capri' in Italy. Though he was ready to go, the operation was cancelled due to unfavourable military developments in the region, and in particular because of its heavy penetration by the Soviet intelligence.[10]

Notes

1 The Communications Base No. 1, in Budapest, operated from the autumn of 1939 until October 1946 under successive codenames 'Romek', 'Liszt' and 'Pestka'. It was run, in turn, by Lt-Col. Alfred Krajewski 'Polesiński', Acting Commander Lt-Col. Zygmunt Bezeg 'Longin', Col. Stanisław Rostworowski 'Rola', Col. Franciszek Matuszczak 'Dod', Capt. Maria Gleb-Koszańska 'Jankowska Maria'. For personnel of the Base, see T. Dubicki, *Bazy wojskowej łączności zagranicznej ZWZ-AK w latach 1939–1945* (*ZWZ-AK Bases of Military Communications Abroad in 1939–1945*), *Studia i materiały* (*Studies and Sources*), Częstochowa 2000, pp. 144–150.

2 As Lt-Col. Krajewski 'Polesiński', arrested by the Hungarians in July 1940. After numerous interventions, released after some time and evacuated to Turkey.

3 Station 'W' was also known as 'Jan'.

4 TNA (PRO), HS 4/163, Zapis rozmowy z ppłk. S. Gano po jego powrocie z rozpoznania w Budapeszcie, Belgradzie i Bukareszcie (A note on the conversation with Lt-Col. Gano upon his return from reconnaisance trip to Budapest, Bucharest and Belgrade). Document prepared on 20 December 1939.

5 TNA (PRO), HS 4/291.

6 L. A. B. Kliszewicz, *Placówki wojskowej łączności kraju z centralą w Londynie podczas II wojny światowej* (*Bases for Military Communications between Poland and HQ in London During WW II*), vol. 1, *Baza w Budapeszcie* (*The Budapest Base*), Warsaw–London 1998, p. 147.

7 SPP, 5.2.2.4, Polski podziemny ruch oporu na Węgrzech (Polish Underground Resistance in Hungary).

8 SPP, 5.2.2.4; TNA(PRO) HS 4/226 27 October 1944 MPP to CD.

9 *Armia Krajowa w dokumentach 1939–1945* (*Documents on the Home Army*), vol. 3, Wrocław 1990, p. 201. A Report by 'Tokaj' to 'Lawina' of 6 November 1943.

10 SPP, Personal papers of Zygmunt Władysław Pales.

29
Yugoslavia

Andrzej Przewoźnik

The establishment of a cell in Belgrade was being considered in March 1940, when the evacuation of the 'Romek' Base in Budapest was a distinct possibility. The plan was that, should the military situation develop unfavourably, first the radio and then all of the staff of 'Romek' would be transferred to Yugoslavia.[1]

The idea of setting up a cell in Yugoslavia was well justified, since it was the country criss-crossed by courier routes leading to Western Europe, as well as by the routes used by Polish soldiers and officers attempting to join the Polish Forces being formed in France.

In the spring of 1940 several 'Romek' officers, including Capt. Władysław Guttry 'Grot', Capt. Tadeusz Werner 'Ostoja' and W/O. Zygmunt Burghardt 'Lipczyński', were sent to Belgrade from Budapest. One of their tasks was to establish a Cell 'Sława'. Maj. Wiktor Zahorski 'Tramp', also from 'Romek', who was to command the cell, arrived from Budapest in early August.[2]

In Yugoslavia there was already a Station of the II Bureau of PGS, called 'J', which supported the organisation of 'Sława'. 'J' was run at first by Capt. Adam Piasecki, and later by Capt. Stefan Maresch 'Czarny'. The Chief of the II Bureau ordered 'J' to support the commander of 'Sława'.[3]

The German attack on Yugoslavia significantly complicated the activities of 'Sława', like breaking up of courier routes and radio links: for a time there had been no means of reaching the London HQ by radio. Further problems were created when a number of 'Sława' personnel were arrested, including its chief. The command of 'Sława' was taken over by Capt. Guttry who, together with his brother, Kazimierz, set up an additional post in Jagodina. This allowed for permanent radio contact with 'Romek'. But the break in systematic contacts between 'Sława', 'Bey' and 'Romek' caused complications and, in effect, a break in the cell's work.

The base's activities picked up only after the arrival of Capt. Jerzy

Szymański from the 'Muł' Base in Cairo, whose task was to reactivate courier routes (and especially those through Yugoslavia) with the co-operation of the British intelligence services. At a conference with the British on 28 December 1941, attended among others by Col. Guy Tamplin, who headed the SOE's Polish Section in Cairo, it was decided to place an intelligence cell run by 'Muł' with the units commanded by Gen. Mihailović.

In March 1942 'Sława' changed its name to 'Drawa'. During the night of 15/16 June Capt. Józef Maciąg was transported to Yugoslavia and joined Mihailović's troops. Within a few days he managed to establish radio contact with Cairo. The British, who wanted to use Polish networks and routes for anti-German diversion, supported him. Col. Tamplin used those Poles who deserted from the German army to join Mihailović. With SOE, which provided the necessary supplies, 'Drawa' organised the first Polish unit in Yugoslavia attached to Gen. Mihailović. This soon caused some differences of opinion between the Poles and the British. The former thought that the latter were giving in to Soviet pressure by transferring their sympathies to the partisans commanded by Gen. Tito whilst at the same time reducing their support for Mihailović.

In November 1943 Gen. Colin McVean Gubbins received a report prepared by SOE's liaison officer for Polish affairs, Capt. Patrick Howarth, containing an assessment of the feasibility of using Polish units for operations in Yugoslavia. This report caused a difference of opinion as to the role such units should play in view of the political situation there. In consequence the Poles were evacuated from this territory and 'Drawa' ceased to function. As for Capt. Maciąg, he was killed in December 1943 during a German attack on a British mission.[4] 'Drawa's' activities were fraught with difficulties from the very beginning. Capt. Maciąg, presenting himself as a British officer, managed nevertheless to organise and build up an intelligence network on Romanian, Serbian and Bulgarian territories on both sides of the Danube. The information gathered was passed on to the British. In that time the 'Muł' Liaison Base in Cairo, with the support of the II Bureau, PGS, and of the British intelligence services, managed to set up four cells in Yugoslavia, called 'Drawa', 'Pristina', 'Ohrida' and 'Larissa'. Together they employed 12 persons.[5]

Notes
1 More on the evacuation plans in: T. Dubicki, *Polska konspiracja w Rumunii w latach 1939–1945*, vol. 1, 1939–1940 (*Polish Clandestine Organisations in Romania, 1939–1945*), Warsaw 2002.
2 In August Maj. Zahorski 'Tramp' was arrested by the Yugoslav authorities. On the basis of an order of 30th November 1940 'Sława' was to be run by Lt-Col. A. Krajewski, the commander of Station 'Grzegorz' in Athens. See L.A.B. Kliszewicz, *Placówki wojskowej łączności kraju z centralą w Londynie podczas II wojny światowej (Bases for Military Communications between Poland and HQ in London During WW II)*, vol. 6, Bazy w Belgradzie i Atenach (Bases in Belgrade and Athens), Warsaw–London 2002, pp. 6–7.
3 Ibid., p. 7.

4   Capt. J. Maciąg died on 11th December 1943 in the village of Luka near Boru. See J. Tucholski, *Spadochroniarze* (*The Parachutists*), Warsaw 1991, pp. 155–156.
5   A. Pepłoński, *Wywiad Polskich Sił Zbrojnych na Zachodzie 1939–1945* (*Intelligence Services of Polish Forces in the West 1939–1945*), Warsaw 1995, p. 277.

30
Greece

Andrzej Przewoźnik

The idea of setting up a communications and intelligence cell in Greece emerged in the autumn of 1940, when there were serious problems in maintaining communications with occupied Poland, caused by the war in the Balkans and the Middle East. Its implementation was accelerated by the Italian attack on Greece and the British decision to support the Greeks. In October 1940 Gen. Kazimierz Sosnkowski asked the Polish Foreign Minister August Zaleski to support the activities of the VI Bureau, PGS, aimed at setting up a cell in Greece, to be called 'Grzegorz'. Mutual recriminations and the negative attitude to the idea of the Polish envoy in Athens, Władysław Schwarzburg-Günther, delayed the emergence of this cell, which came into being only in January 1941.

The organisation of 'Grzegorz' was undertaken by Col. Alfred Krajewski, 'Adam Korab'. While still in Istanbul, working with the commanders of Base 'Romek' in Budapest and of Base 'Bey' in Istanbul, this officer presented the concept of its organisation. In view of the difficulties in reaching agreement with the Polish Legation in Athens, 'Korab' began his work with the valuable assistance of both Station 'A', the Greek Station of the II Bureau of PGS and of British intelligence. The Greek authorities were also helpful with the necessary documentation and in particular with servicing the radio communications.[1]

One of the tasks of 'Grzegorz', set up in Athens and attached to the Greek Station of the II Bureau of PGS, was to maintain communications with the bases 'Romek' in Budapest, 'Bey' in Istanbul and 'Sława' in Belgrade. A single-person communications cell was located in Salonika.

In reality the conflict between Gen. Sosnkowski, in practice represented by II and VI Bureaux of PGS, and the Polish Foreign Ministry and its Greek Legation, paralysed the work of 'Grzegorz'. Moreover it led to the British secret services withdrawing their promised assistance. The cell was therefore supported only by Station 'A'. Its fate was sealed by the fluid and, to British interests detrimental, war situation in Greece.[2]

In April 1941 the personnel of Station 'A' were evacuated from

Greece, and 'Korab' with his radio operators followed on 11th April, going to Cairo and leaving behind only some well-hidden contacts. Thus ended the brief history of cell 'Grzegorz' in Greece, which did not meet its tasks. The opportunity to transfer couriers, mail, funds and radio equipment was lost. The Athens cell would have been well suited for this purpose, it would have opened new opportunities to build additional courier routes into Poland and would have shortened communications with Egypt, and likewise with the Polish authorities in London.

It was not until the end of 1944 when Polish intelligence set up a new cell in Greece in co-operation with the VI Bureau of PGS. Called 'Hellada', its main purpose was to establish a courier route from Greece via Bulgaria or Yugoslavia and then Hungary and Romania to Poland. But the military situation in this part of Europe made it unworkable. The territories of these states were already deeply infiltrated by Soviet intelligence. New courier routes were not established in spite of British support (Capt. Fox). As the Soviet sphere of influence reached all the way to the Greek border, this forced the staff of 'Hellada' to evacuate Poles from Greece and indeed from the Balkans. Its activities rendered, however, much valuable intelligence information. The cell, led by Lt. Leon Wujek 'Chmurny', ceased to exist in August 1945.[3]

Notes

1   A. Pepłoński, *Wywiad Polskich Sił Zbrojnych na Zachodzie 1939–1945* (*Intelligence Services of Polish Forces in the West 1939–1945*), Warsaw 1995, p. 271.
2   L. A. B. Kliszewicz, *'Grzegorz'. Placówka Wojskowej Łączności w Grecji* (*Military Communications Cell in Greece*), 'Zeszyty Historyczne', no. 65, p. 92.
3   CA MSW, 295/399/IX-48, pp. 133–138.

31
Romania

Tadeusz Dubicki

The decision to set up a Polish intelligence station in Romania was taken during the inspection trip there of the newly appointed Chief of the II Bureau, Col. Tadeusz Wasilewski who was accompanied by Lt-Col. Stanisław Gano, on 12 and 13 December 1939. The final form of discussion was creation of Station 'R' (Romania), headed by Lt-Col. Tadeusz Skinder. Unofficially, he was already in charge of the Intelligence Service which according to original plans, was to become an important link – the so-called 'Action South'.

As decided on 13 December 1939, the Romanian Station was to be 'the only intelligence network working for the II Bureau of PGS', and its main function was to '[...] ensure permanent communications with Poland through reliable Poles'. Its other tasks were 'to collect and report information on all the aspects of life in Poland and the military and administrative situation under occupation'.[3] It was to direct its attention towards 'the Soviets'. After some time it was expected to reach as far as the Odessa, Kiev and Kharkhov (Char'kov) Military Districts. This was to be done in co-operation with Romanian intelligence, which to some degree was to be informed of the work carried out by the Poles in the East.

Station 'R' consisted of HQ in Bucharest, led until June 1940 by Skinder, and later by Maj. Stanisław Orłowski 'Ostaszewski'. The Station was subordinated to the Chief of the II Bureau, via the Chief of its Intelligence Department, Lt-Col. Gano. The HQ consisted of several sections: Intelligence (led by Maj. Józef Bińkowski), Counter-Intelligence (Maj. Stanisław Kuniczak) and General (Capt. Stefan Konarski). Lt-Col. Kazimierz Florek and Capt. Jerzy Fryzendorf also played important a role.

There was another, main and most secret structure, a special unit consisting of some 10 persons, led until May 1940 by Lt-Col. Ludwik Sadowski. It is known that the unit 'worked with the knowledge of Romanian intelligence', therefore almost certainly against the Soviets and possibly on sabotage. Maj. Bińkowski, the former Chief of Station 5 in Lwów, later commanded the unit.

There were other intelligence cells in Romania, closely linked to Station 'R', called 'Roman', 'Stasia' and 'Cezar'. The latter, in Czerniowce (Černovcy), was led by Maj. Henryk Nitecki 'Zaremba', aided by Capt.s Aleksander Kolasiński and Edward Grabowski. The Bukowina (Bukovina) region, with Czerniowce being its capital, proved to be crucial for activities directed towards the East, as the courier and communication trails to and from Lwów, where the Home Army GHQ for Soviet occupation (Area 3) was located, passed through this region. Station 'R' and the 'Bolek' Base usually used the same persons as couriers. Until June 1940 alone there were some 50 instances of courier missions across the border. The Czerniowce cell was later reinforced with two more, 'Czesław' and 'Leon'. This formation remained until the end of June 1940 when, following the entry of Soviet troops to Bukovina and Bessarabia, 'Cezar' was moved to Suczawa, where it remained until November 1940.

It must be stressed that Station 'R' could only operate thanks to the approval by the hosts. Co-operation with the Romanians was good until autumn of 1940, when the Iron Guards and Gen. Ion Antonescu took power.

Station 'R' was expected to remain in contact with the intelligence services of Great Britain, France and Japan.[4]

The contacts with the British were of special importance for the Poles. The British were very interested in the various aspects of politics and economics both in Romania and in occupied Poland. Station 'R', the number of whose personnel eventually reached 50, was a significant source of information and inspiration. Polish-British contacts began in autumn of 1939. One of the main British contacts in Romania for the Poles was Capt. Stephen Ernest Carlton. According to Lt-Col. Iranek-Osmecki, Skinder's Deputy, maintained that Carlton was placed in Bucharest 'to become the nucleus of a Special Operations Executive Cell'.[5] In the opinion of Col. Stanisław Rostworowski, who headed the 'Bolek' Communications Base the Home Army in Romania, Carlton '[...] was informed on Polish matters – he already has an organization under both occupiers'.[6]

The same source provided the information that it was Capt. Carlton who passed on to Station 'R' the warning, originating from British intelligence and delivered via France, about Samson Mikiciński, whose activities on behalf of German intelligence were later proved. In addition to Carlton, with whom Skinder personally remained in touch performing the role of the liaison officer with the British,[7] Capt.s Ronald H. Hazell and and W. Harris Burland played important roles in Bucharest. In the recent past both had Polish links.

In 1929–1939 Capt. Hazell resided in Poland, among others as British Vice-Consul in Gdynia. In September 1939 he was a member of Gen. Carton de Wiart's mission, and later was delegated to work in the Balkans. On Col. Colin Gubbins's orders he maintained contacts with the Poles.[8] Burland, in turn, was a member of the Military Mission to Poland, and after September 1939 was transferred to the British Military Mission in

Bucharest, which worked for Military Intelligence (MIR). Following the changes in the organization of British intelligence they were both transferred to SOE. They remained in Bucharest as intelligence operatives; Capt. (later Maj.) Hazell designated D/H 43 and Capt. Burland – D/H 44. The other British agents were B. Young – D/H 5, J. Toyne – D/H 7 and A.G.G. de Chastelain – D/H 13. The latter worked on Romania from Istanbul.[9] There are numerous examples of attempts to develop Polish-British intelligence co-operation in Romania from both sides. Such co-operation is also confirmed by the conference held in Paris in December 1939 by Lt-Col. Gano with British Intelligence representatives, whose names are not known to us.

Their report on this conference, transmitted to London on 20th December, confirms that the Polish side had every confidence in their British partners, who were presented with the Polish plans to organise resistance under both occupying powers. The British representatives agreed with the principle of Gano's current tactics, which was to halt for a time sabotage and guerrilla activities in Poland.[10] The time was to be used to provide for arranging military supplies (pistols or revolvers, grenades and nitroglycerine-based explosives), and stocking them within 40 kilometres from the border and later to be transported from the areas adjacent to the Romanian border to underground arsenals deeper in Poland.

From the conversation it indicated that the British partners were to participate in this by supplying '[...] w/t sets working on dry batteries, so urgently needed in Poland'.[11] Gano told his British colleagues that the Polish authorities had already established radio communications with Poland. The agreement between the Poles and their British colleagues assured supplies of materiel required for special operations. On 29 January 1940 the Chief of the II Bureau informed Col. Skinder that 'the English are to provide for Poland some 40 kilograms of arms and special materials per week. An authorized person shall on each occasion report to Boguszewski [Skinder's passport name – T.D.]. Goods to be smuggled through as per orders'.[12]

Col. Gano outlined the Polish plan to conduct sabotage and diversionary action on the Romanian stretch of the Danube, to which the British side paid special attention. This was envisaged as sabotage directed against German interests, though conducted on the territory of a neutral country. A detail plan, aimed at the disruption of transport on the Danube, used to supply Germany with various materials. It envisaged the use of some 150–200 river craft, at the time stationed in Bratislava. They were to be brought to a chosen place and linked by chains. Every second craft was to be equipped with delayed explosives to cause a fire. The British were to 'organise' some 100 such bombs.[13] This Polish plan mentioned here in some detail, provided the inspiration for another, purely British and regretfully unsuccessful, attempt to block the Danube in the vicinity of Iron Gates, undertaken in April 1940. Alfred Poniński, Counsellor at the Polish Embassy, reported on the discovery of preparations to this action: in Giurgiu the Romanians detained several British ships carrying arms and explosives.[14]

Closer links with the British Intelligence at the time are also reported by Lt-Col. Franciszek Demel (Deputy Chief of Staff, the Home Army GHQ), who on 12th February 1940 noted down 'first contact with Gubbins', and under 17 February that 'first transport of explosives, arms and radio sets' had been received from the British.[15]

The co-operation with the British took a multitude of forms and included posts not specializing in intelligence – such as the mission of the Polish Consulate-General in Constanţa. It is from there that in early March 1940 came the information of a significant inflow of Germans onto the Black sea coast. According to the intelligence obtained from the British Consul in Constanţa, these Germans were members of training teams for German Heinkel bombers and conducted this activity on Mamaia beach.

The Poles had learned from Romanian sources that Romanian fishing boats had part-German crews. The German fast patrol boat, 'Ernst Guenther', which arrived via the Danube in the autumn of 1939, was in Constanţa. In the winter of 1940 it was renamed 'Marea Negra', and by the spring had returned to its original name.

Special tasks were undertaken by couriers sent into Soviet-occupied Poland to gather information. In addition to their liaison work, they also gathered information on various aspects of life there, including the military. Such missions were undertaken by Zbigniew Chaszczyński 'Polniaczek', Jan Kowalski 'Dowbor', Stanisław and Zbigniew Skotnicki, Mieczysław Lisowski, Janina Kowacka 'Wacek', Jadwiga Rusińska 'Zwoliński', Antoni Boski 'Strzała' and many others – who were sent out and came back – but only for a time. To provide an example of their work: in July 1940 one such courier sent to Bukowina, newly occupied by the Red Army, came back with the Order of Battle of Soviet troops in the region.[16]

The materials collected by Station 'R' staff were prepared by Bucharest HQ, and then sent to the Centre in Paris, and later to London, as special bulletins (in the form of 'General Information Communiqués', 'Economic Intelligence Communiqués' and 'Military Information Communiqués'). They were also passed on to other recipients (such as other Stations or the offices of military attachés). The broad spectrum of these bulletins reflected the work of the Station, which penetrated first of all the territories under Soviet occupation, but also those under the Germans. The information contained in them was divided into the following groups: 1. Administration, 2. The Attitudes of the occupiers to the general public, 3. Economic relations, 4. Social and Cultural Relations. The Order of Battle of both occupiers was a separate matter. Some carried information on Romania, especially on the oil industry, transport and food supplies.[17]

The product of Station 'R' work was also of interest to the French, and the Japanese not well disposed to the Soviets.

One can say, that after the fall of France, the British tred to activate the Poles who were somewhat passive. Close associations with the French gave way to the British. But the contacts with these intelligence services, even the French, began to be overshadowed by those with the British. It would be probably fair to state that, following the fall of France, it was the

British who were attempting to make the Poles, who became somewhat passive, more pro-active.

In early July 1940 this was the subject of a meeting between the Chief of the VI Bureau, Col. Marian Smoleński, and Capt. Harold Perkins of SOE. Perkins accepted that for a time the Poles suspended their sabotage and diversionary activities – but, this did not mean that their work was no longer of use. This was reflected in Romania in so-called the case of Lt. Jerzy Klimkowski, who was to be used for the transport of arms to the territories under Soviet occupation. According to the Polish side, Klimkowski initiated this privately, with the British station in Bucharest.[18] On 21 September 1940 Maj. Orłowski reported as follows: 'Today I had contact with an Englishman, D/H 43 [Capt. Hazell – T.D.], who is charged with, and equipped for, diversion activities in Poland, under both occupations. I informed D/H 43 of the latest orders from HQ forbidding any engagement of diversion in Poland for the time being. I informed him of the closure of subsersive activities on Romanian territory'.[19]

The matter of British involvement in this affair is explained, at least in part, in a dispatch from station 'A' in Cairo, whose commander, Lt-Col. Józef Matecki 'Ostry', had talks with the British. It appears the British had already the goods in stores in Cairo, Romania and Hungary and wanted to get rid of to Poland. Ostry's judgment was that what was needed was 'an assessment of the current situation on the three B territory [Bucharest, Budapest, Belgrade – T.D.], and their ability to store the equipment, as the local operational plans depends on this'.[20]

In spite of the differences concerning the scope of intelligence activities in Romania,[21] there was co-operation between the two sides, even when Polish posts there were being closed, as happened in November 1940. The reason was the anti-Allied policy adopted by the new Romanian authorities (Iron Guards and Gen. Antonescu). In the case of the Poles the result of this new policy was a wave of arrests in October 1940, which included Station 'R' staff, with its Chief, Maj. Orłowski. The Romanians also discovered the Station's radio set and some materiel, which was hidden in Bucharest and in the provinces.

An anti-Polish campaign was started, in Romania and in Germany. Under the title 'Polish Spy Organisation Discovered in Romania', on 26 October 1940 *Frankfurter Zeitung* informed its readers that the Romanian police 'found more proof that a [spying – T.D.] network was being constructed and that it was linked to the English legation'. The author maintained that 'it appears that the Polish spying apparatus in Romania is formally a part of the Intelligence Service, run by military attaché Nabb [...] it is obvious that the Polish organization receives its means from an English source, including technical equipment'.[22]

In early 1941 the so-called 'secret evacuation' of Polish military personnel from Romania took place. The team which undertook this mission (included Col. Dr. Franciszek Bałaszeskul, Jerzy Giedroyc, Capt. Bolesław Ziemiański) received support from the British, who were also obliged to leave Romania at the same time.

Thus in early 1941 in the broad sense a painful gap appeared in the intelligence activity in Romania. In mid-1941 a decision was finally taken that Polish intelligence there would be organized by Capt. Bolesław Ziemiański, in Romania since September 1939. Ziemiański, 'Mościbrodzki', was an expert intelligence operative. From 1929–1935 he commanded the security team for Marshal Józef Piłsudski at the Belweder Palace. In his early days in Romania he worked for Base 'Bolek', among other assignments as chief of its evacuation post in Sighet. Thanks to his experience and with very limited resources for organizational and technical skills, Ziemiański managed to organise an intelligence network, which began to operate in the second half of 1941. In August of that year, after the German-Soviet war broke out, Ziemiański received an order (initially via radio; this was later confirmed in correspondence from Istanbul) to begin intelligence work aimed mainly at gathering information on the military potential of Romania and Germany.[23] Among those willing to undertake this work, were the Polish military escapees (of whom there were some 4,000 in addition to 80,000 ethnic Poles living in Romania. Henryk Jagiełło and Mieczysław Karpiński, both former staff of the Counter Intelligence Section of Corps HQ in Łódź, were from the first group. The other 'professionals' were Marian Koziarski and Stanisław Milewski, former staff of the Counter Intelligence Department of the II Bureau in Warsaw. All together, Ziemiański's organisation included some 20 persons, three of whom were women. One of them, Anna Schuman, was considered to be Ziemiański's deputy – as well as his cryptographer. Ziemiański stated that he personally recruited and trained most of those working for him.[24]

An analysis of their domicile indicates that this was an important factor in the recruitment of agents. In addition to the inhabitants of Bucharest, the group consisted of those living in Craiova, Piteşti, Ocnele Mari, Caracal, Brasov, Turnu Magurele and Giurgiu. This geographical spread enabled the collection of information from a significant part of Romanian territory. The first important task of the network, which it received from Turkey as early as the spring of 1941 (from the military attaché there, Col. Andrzej Liebich), was to verify the outcome of the diversionary activities on the Danube, in the vicinity of the Iron Gates, by Secret Intelligence Service agents (Ziemiański described them as the Romanian-British diversionary network).[25] The purpose was to ascertain the damage, to assess the time required to resume shipping on the river could be resumed and what impression this action created.

To find answers to these questions, Capt. Ziemiański managed to reach some Romanians employed by a shipping line based in Bucharest. He also travelled to the Iron Gates region, ostensibly to visit some Polish refugees living, in Turnu Severin. This led him to conclude that the explosion at the Iron Gates caused significant damage and made shipping difficult – but not to the degree anticipated at first. He thought that the explosives used were not powerful enough. This information was passed to Istanbul through Maj. Niewiarowski, who was leaving Romania to join Polish forces in the Middle East.

Another task carried out by Ziemiański's network was to collect information on the German and Romanian preparations for war against the USSR. The most vexing task was finding the approximate date of a German attack from a 'German' contact – a soldier stationed in Bucharest. He was an ethnic Pole, distantly related to one of the Polish refugees, and employed in the printing shop of the German Corps staff. It was this Corps which was to prepare the attack from the Romanian side. After some 'preparatory work', this soldier revealed the 'approximate' timetable for the German attack on the USSR. Capt. Ziemiański passed this information by radio to Istanbul.[26]

After the German-Soviet war broke out, the next task for Ziemiański's organisation was to inform on the actual course of the Romanian Army's battles in the Odessa and Sebastopol regions. This was accomplished by constant observation of railway stations and hospitals. This allowed an estimate to be made of Romanian casualties and of Bucharest's involvement in the war. Ziemiański thought that one of the most important items of information passed on to Istanbul was the use of artillery shells with compressed air used near Odessa.[27]

The degree of organisation undertaken by Ziemiański's network is supported by the account of one of the participants, Maksymilian Osman, a Pole from Bukovina and a teacher by profession, who escaped Bukovina just ahead of the Soviet troops entering the area in June 1940. The above-mentioned Jagiełło and Karpiński, offered Osman 'participation in the sabotage and intelligence work against the Germans'.[28] One of Osman's duties was to provide a safe house for a radio set used in Bucharest by Jagiełło – but his most important solo activity was in the port of Giurgiu on the Danube, some 60 kilometres from the capital. Through the intermediary of his brother-in-law, Lucjan Androchowicz, Osman managed to obtain employment in the local, Austrian-owned Danubian shipping line, DDSG, which provided him with the opportunity of observing military, equipment and fuel supplies for the front, as well as the transport of wounded from the front. Osman passed such information to Karpiński, with whom he met at intervals in Bucharest, in a pre-arranged location. Later, having forged a key to a strong box where documents were kept during a transport from Giurgiu to Constanţa. According to Osman, once this information was passed on, the Allies frequently bombed Giurgiu and its environs.[29] There was a pipeline from the Ploieşti oilfields to the port of Giurgiu, and oil was pumped from storage tanks onto ships in the port. This was of particular interest to the Allies.

Between spring of 1941 and autumn of 1943, Capt. Ziemiański's network carried out a number of valuable tasks for the Allies. By then it was supported by a second network of Polish intelligence in Bucharest, commanded by Capt. Bronisław Eliaszewicz 'Bruno Ortwin'. Both were run by Station 'R', at first located in Jerusalem, and later in Istanbul (as Station 'Bałk.'). To facilitate matters, they were given numbers: Cell no. 1, 'Tandara', ran by Capt. Eliaszewicz, and Cell no. 2, 'Tusla', under Capt. Ziemiański.[30] Eliaszewicz was officially employed in the office of the military attaché of Japan, having forged papers as a citizen of Manchukuo. He was supported by Eugeniusz Szadurski (a long-standing employee of Polish intelligence), Jan Kowalik (Adamczyk), Stanisław Łoza and Janina Puciato.[31]

Cell no. 1 was in radio contact with a similar intelligence cell in Istanbul (no. 3) and with Station 'T'. Contact was maintained via the radio set operated by Kowalik and situated in the office of the Japanese attaché!

Until July 1943, when Base 'Bolek II', run by Capt. Bogusław Horodyński, was penetrated by the Romanian intelligence and the Gestapo, Ziemiański used the communications facilities at Base 'Bolek II'. This did not halt radio communications, which were taken over by Eliaszewicz – until autumn of 1943, when the German direction finding D/F, located the radio set at the office of the Japanese military attaché. This led to the arrest of Capt. Eliaszewicz, and later to that of Capt. Ziemiański (on 24 October 1943).[32] The flow of intelligence out of Romania did not stop – thanks to the small team run by Dr. Zdzisław Gałaczyński. It was thought at the time that this group worked directly for the British. Gałaczyński was described as 'a technical expert of the English intelligence station in Romania'.[33]

The subject and scope of interest of Polish intelligence activities in Romania clearly shows that reports were prepared mainly for the benefit of the Allies. Military, political and economic information indicates its prime destination, though they were sent first to the Chief of the II Bureau of PGS, to the Chief of similar Bureau at the Headquarters of the Polish Army in the Middle East, the Chief of Station 'T' and to the military attaché in Ankara.

The remaining fragments of intelligence reports from Romania indicate that the Chief of 'Bałk.' Station directed them to his superiors.

The information transmitted was dealt with on a multitude of issues. For example on 1 August 1942, Maj. Boxshall of SOE-Romania delivered his appreciation for reports on the displacement of Romanian units at the Eastern Front 'as well as for the other information received from you from the usual sources. This information is very interesting and very helpful'.[34]

Information from Romania was dominated by reports on the Romanian and German Order of Battle, the oil industry in Romania and the internal situation in that country.

The material held mainly at NARA indicates that the Western Allies had extensive knowledge at their disposal, including on such crucial matters as the state of the Romanian Air Force. In August 1943 Polish sources provided the Western allies with a document entitled 'The Study of the Situation at Romanian Airfields', based on the information obtained from Romania by the PGS (Air Intelligence) in London. This contained, among other things, a detailed map showing active airfields. These included 43 airfields classified as B1 and B2, serving heavy bombers and fighters, and 30 airfields of type C, for light aircraft. Polish intelligence also identified some 60 runways. The map showed that most airfields were in the vicinity of Bucharest and Ploiești.[35]

Polish Intelligence also supplied the Allies with information on the strength of the Romanian Air Force, which, following its re-organisation in mid-1943 had at its disposal some 500 combat and transport planes. Combat aircraft (250 planes) were organised into 10 squadrons, with some German equipment (as, for example, in Tiraspol).[36] There was also more detailed information, for example on the 9th Air Group stationed in Tecuci.

Polish Intelligence identified many factories engaged in war production, such as the Malaxa plant in Bucharest (Cotroceni Street) and its branch in Târgoviște, both working for the aircraft industry. In this particular matter, the British asked for further information.[37] Another report confirmed the existence, also in Bucharest, of a plant repairing aircraft engines, capable of dealing with 120 engines per month (February 1943). Its planned enlargement would have given it the capacity of repairing 1 thousand units monthly.[38]

The Poles also reconnoitred Romanian anti-aircraft defences, which was especially important in view of planned – and soon carried out – air raids on the most important industrial plants. Their reports dealt, for example, with the strategically important Cernavoda on the Danube, where many reinforced anti-aircraft batteries and balloon barrages were found. 10 guns, whose deployment were carefully planned, defended the airfield there.[39]

Similar intelligence was obtained on Giurgiu and on the Baneasa airfield outside Bucharest (where underground hangars were constructed by the Germans). Another report pointed to the construction of a Danube bridge between Giurgiu and Ruse on the Bulgarian side. It was thought that the large number of barges laden with fuel, used for the construction, would assist an attack from the air.[40] There were also very valuable reports on the location of German anti-aircraft batteries along the Danube and around Ploiești. The report presented by the Poles contained 29 items, which included information on the listening posts and defensive positions. It established that their supplies came from Piatra Neamt, where headquarters were situated. It was suggested that the Otopeni airfield (wrongly described as Motopeni), situated near to the Bucharest–Ploiești road, should be bombed.[41]

The task of destroying the Romanian oil fields was undertaken by Allied (British and American) aircraft in mid-1943. An important role in guiding the bombers onto targets and subsequently in assessing the damage caused, was played by Polish Intelligence. During the first, 'trial', raids, in June 1942, the Poles supplied the information on the successful bombing of railway yards in Bucharest. On 12 June 1942 the same squadron bombed the 'Astra' refinery in Ploiești, and then the railway station in Buzau and the ports in Braila and in Constanța. All this was confirmed by Polish Intelligence.[42]

Careful preparations of these operations brought the success to the Allies. For example, on the construction of a dummy Ploiești, located some 40 kilometres to the north of the real town. As for the genuine oilfields, it identified various attempts to minimise possible air raid damage, including concrete walls around the refinery and oil tanks. Strengthening of air defences and camouflage of installations were reported on.[43]

The Poles provided information on the transfer of key installations underground – but not of oil tanks, which could be bombed. Reports were submitted on the modern refineries equipped with automatic valves to close the pipe, in the case of fire (this had the effect of reducing any damage). It was thought, nevertheless, that the Astra Romana, Steaua Romana, Concordia and Creditul Minier refineries would explode on being hit, since many other installations remained on the surface. There was a suggestion to employ incendiary bombs, which did not require low flying or precision bombing.

The mass bombing by the Allies in August 1943 was concentrated in the Ploieşti region, and the Poles reported on its outcome. Based on information from an engineer employed there, on 12 August a report was sent to London via Istanbul that the raids were successful. The refinery, and the oil wells, were on fire. According to the informant the air raids delivered a heavy blow to the Romanian oil industry. The British side gave much attention to this report, described as 'top secret'.[44]

The next air raid, on 15 August 1943, was considered to be very successful. The expectation was that the break in production in damaged plants would last 8–10 months.[45] The same source reported that the defences around other refineries 'appear to be very robust'. There was also information that despite the heavy damage, the export of Romanian oil increased – though that was the raw material, not usable petrol.[46]

Polish Intelligence also provided accurate information concerning the export of Romanian oil. It confirmed, for example, the transit of oil via Germany to Italy. This was a regular transaction, though moderate in size (some 10–12 cisterns per day). There was other important information concerning oil, too – for example, that every day five trains were being sent to the Eastern Front, using tankers on the Black Sea.[47]

Information on food supplies and on the provision of other goods was also considered to be of strategic importance. Polish intelligence was reporting the steady increase in grain export to Germany. In July 1942 in the port of Giurgiu the contents of 30–35 rail cars daily were being transferred onto barges for transport via Danube to Germany. The same source informed on the trade with Italy, where grain was being exchanged for cotton. It was thought that the indebtness of the Axis countries to Romania increased constantly.[48]

For the British, the Poles were the main source of information on the complicated internal politics of Romania. This included the attitudes of the Romanian authorities towards the opposition there and the efforts to decouple the country from its alliance with the Germans. Such attempts were undertaken in 1941–1943 with the significant participation of the Poles (Continental Action Romania – Akru).[49] The Romanian-German political and military relationships were also of much interest.

The ability of the Poles to work in this area was the result of their political communications network (the British referred to it as Kot's network). Its Balkan and Middle Eastern centre was located in Istanbul and was led by Dr. Jerzy Kurcyusz. In 1940 this network had its own cell in Romania, 'Kask', directed by Władysław Kański.[50] From 1941 he was replaced by Władysław Wolski 'Rafał', who had good contacts with prominent Romanian politicians, thanks to his previous diplomatic and consular work.[51] 'Rafał's' reports were sent to Istanbul, to a Romanian specialist, Stefan Werner 'Ster', who evaluated them and dispatched these to London. There, via the VI Bureau, they reached the Polish Section of SOE (Capt. R. Truszkowski – MPX) and Capt. Hazell of MPO-EP/U, and Romanian Section of SOE – (Maj. Edward Boxshall – D/H109). The others who participated in the discussions on these reports were Col. Pearson (D/HV) and Col. Peter Wilkinson (MX).[52]

In March 1942 the British considered expanding this initiative. They knew that the Poles were primarily interested in maintaining communications with Poland;[53] while themselves wanting to reduce the German influence. For this reason, information on the tensions and misunderstandings in the Romanian-German relations was very useful to the British. From this perspective, they analysed what was said at a meetinhg (13.IV.43) between Hitler and Antonescu, namely a significant difference of opinion on Antonescu's attitude towards his political opponents. A Polish informant in Bucharest stated later that: 'Antonescu will never agree to hand them [the opposition] to the Germans'.[55]

There are numerous indications of Polish activities to which much importance was attached by the British. London was very interested in the fate of Iuliu Maniu, the leader of the Peasants' Party, who in British opinion could have played a role in extricating Romania from the Axis. The Poles had access to this politician, as well as to the Liberal leader, Bratianu. Based on information obtained from Polish sources, Capt. Hazell told the Romanian Section of SOE that on 19 January 1941 Maniu and Bratianu delivered a memorandum to Marshal Antonescu. Hazell reported that: '[...] our Polish friends told us also about the negotiations between Antonescu and the Germans which have been going on for 3 months, concerning the number of Romanian divisions which were to join the fighting in the spring of 1942'. According to this source, the Germans demanded 600 thousand soldiers, whilst the Conducător [Leader – T.D.] talked about 10 divisions.[56]

As already mentioned, the activities of Polish intelligence in Romania slowed down following the arrests of Base 'Bolek II' staff (June–July 1943) and of the intelligence operatives in the autumn of the same year. But important information from Romania was still getting through, as already mentioned, thanks to the actions of the group led by Zdzisław Gałaczyński (Mieczysław Wieraszko, Lt. Włodzimierz Czupryk, Maria Wilczyńska, Maria Gałaczyńska),[57] which was active until 8 January 1944. On that day the radio station served by Wieraszko was 'burnt', and the group was exposed.[58] Prior to that, however, and as late as November 1943, important intelligence was being delivered to Turkey. This referred to the Order of Battle of the army as of September 1943, with Army, Corps and Division details, the location of their headquarters and the names of the commanding officers – it covered 34 tactical units. There was also information (not verified) of a political nature, namely on the peace talks between the USSR and Romania, which were to have taken place thanks to the intermediary of 'Turkish factors'.[59]

The information passed on in January 1944, in turn, provided intelligence on the precise distribution of Black Sea defence troops. Among others, the location of the Headquarters of Vice-Admiral Lautenbacher, the Commanding Officer of the German Black Sea submarine fleet, was revealed – in hotel 'Ballino' in the town of Eforia. At the same time Polish intelligence uncovered the presence of 11 German U-boats in the ports of Constanţa, Odessa and Sulin. Nearby, in the Mangalia docks, two destroyers were under construction: their hulls were being completed in January 1944. Further reports arrived at Station 'Bałk.' in February, March and June of 1944. We can only speculate as to their sources – by then Władysław Wolski was free again, though his 'Akru' initiative was spent, as a result of British caution, which began to recognise Romania as belonging to the Soviet sphere of influence.

Such an attitude was dominant following the coup in Romania on 23 August 1944, when its armed forces switched sides and joined the Allies. The last serious British attempt in Romania was 'Operation Autonomous', led by de Chastelain at the end of 1943.[60]

Operation 'Yardarm' in 1944 constituted a symbolic end to the British wartime presence in Romania. Its purpose was to safely evacuate British agents.[61] Only some of the Poles were extracted, including the Gałaczyński group, and taken to Italy. But the fate of most active co-operators, Capt. Bolesław Ziemiański, Capt. Bronisław Eliaszewicz and Capt. Bogusław Horodyński, was very different, they were arrested by the Soviet secret services. Ziemiański finally found himself in a Warsaw prison, whilst the other two were deported to the USSR. Unfortunately this happened because the British refused to come to Ziemiański's aid when in October 1944 he approached Col. Wiesner (British Mission) asking for his group and for Horodyński's people to be evacuated.[62] Wiesner said that he had no instructions from his superiors in this matter! A later and badly misjudged attempt to help the Poles ended in disaster, when Wiesner's superior asked the Soviet General, Vladimir Winogradov, for permission to evacuate 'a Polish military group'. Gen. Winogradov (Vice Chief of Allied Control Council) requested a report on the activities of this group, which Ziemiański, already compromised, naturally refused.[63]

Notes

1 IPMS, Romanian Files, the dossier of Lt-Col. Tadeusz Skinder, point 2; Organisational Order of Chief of II Bureau, PGS, 13 December 1939.
2 IPMS, A.XII.55/1, Organisation of Communications with Poland (temporary). 'Action South', Bucharest, 13 October 1939.
3 *Armia Krajowa w dokumentach* (*Documents on the Home Army*), op. cit. vol. 6, doc. No. 1645, p. 117.
4 T. Dubicki, *Konspiracja polska w Rumunii 1939–1945* (*Polish Clandestine*

Organisation in Romania 1939–1945), vol. 1, 1939–1940, Warsaw 2002., pp. 77–84.

5 SPP, Kol. 2/28, Col. Kazimierz Iranek-Osmecki.
6 Ibid.
7 *Armia Krajowa (Home Army)*, vol. 6, l. dz. 1125/40, 23 September 1940.
8 SPP, O.VI,L.dz.1125/40, 23 September 1940.
9 D/H signified the Balkan Section of SOE. Romania was described as D/H 109.
10 TNA (PRO), HS 4/163, Record of interview with Lt-Col. Gano on his return from reconnaissance at Budapest, Belgrade and Bucharest, 20 December 1939.
11 Ibid.
12 IPMS, A.XII.55/33. HQ no. 400, 29 January 1940.
13 TNA(PRO), HS 4/163, L. 2/M/Poland/3.
14 IPMS, A. 26, Coded radio dispatch no. 179, 9 April 1940.
15 SPP, Kol. 11/3, material from Col. F. Demel.
16 T. Dubicki, *Kurier do Lwowa (Courier to Lwów). Zbigniew Roman Chaszczyński – 'Kazimierz Polniaczek', 'Kozak'*, 'Mars. Military Problems and History', no. 2/1994, p. 157; SPP, Kol. 39/7, ibid. Military Information from Agent no. 83 'Dowbor'; ibid, Military Tasks for the Czerniowce Garrison (agent no. 107 'Strzała').
17 T. Dubicki, *Konspiracja (Conspiracy)*, op.cit., vol. 1, pp. 106–107.
18 Ibid., pp. 285–287.
19 AAN, Polish Consulate in Constanţa, 18, coded dispatch from Bucharest, 21st September 1940.
20 *AK w dokumentach (Home Army Documents)*, vol. 6., doc. no. 1616, plac 'A', l.dz. 10/K tjn. 14 August 1940.
21 In spite of the contacts with the British, certain details were kept from them, especially those relating to Poland. The Head of Station 'R' ordered that, matters of intelligence passed from 'R' to Base 'Romek' in Budapest: should be passed immediately to the Centre. You may not pass this information to the British Intelligence. CAW, Armia Krajowa (Home Army), vol. XII, B I. 31, 'Biuletyn Informacyjny' (Information Bulletin), Note no. 32 to 'Romek' Base.
22 Alexandrian microfilms (WIH Archive) 289655, vol. –81, film no. -524.
23 T. Dubicki, *Bazy wojskowej łaczności zagranicznej ZWZ-AK w latach 1939–1945. Studia i materiały (ZWZ-AK Military Communications Bases Abroad in 1939–1945.Studies and materials)*, Częstochowa 2000, p. 115.
24 Archiwum Państwowe miasta stołecznego Warszawy, IV K 291/56, Protokół przesłuchania podejrzanego (Ziemiańskiego) (Transcript of Interrogation of the suspect Ziemiański), 11 June 1951.
25 Ibid.
26 Ibid.
27 Ibid.
28 An account and biography of Maksymilian Osman (held by the author).
29 Ibid.
30 IPMS, Kol. 242/63.
31 The salary of the chief of Station was £38; the other staff earned £20–30.
32 T. Dubicki, *Bazy (Bases)*, op.cit., pp. 122–123.
33 Ibid, p. 120.
34 TNA (PRO) HS 4/235, D/H 109, 1 August 1942.
35 NARA, RG 165, MID Romania, Box 2882, file 9185, Rumania Aerodromes, Polish Intelligence, Confidential, 20 August 1943.
36 Ibid., Box 2884, Rumania, Air force, Polish Intelligence, Confidential, no. 2227/43, 11 July 1943.
37 Ibid., Box 2883, f. 9505, Rumania Aircraft Industry, Polish Intelligence, Confidential, no. 2483/43, 8 July 1943.
38 Ibid., Romania. Aircraft repair workshops in Bucharest, Polish Intelligence,

Confidential, no. 422/43, 15 February 1943.

39 Ibid., The Cernavoda Aerodrome, Polish Intelligence, Confidential, no. 101/43, 12 November 1943.

40 Ibid, Box 2874, f. 1530, Polish Intelligence, Confidential, no. 2822/43, 5 August 1943.

41 Ibid., Box 2883, f. 9505, Germany, Air Polish Intelligence, Confidential, no. 1237/43.

42 Ibid., Box 2874, no. 305817/42.

43 Ibid., Box 2882, f. 9185.

44 Ibid., MID Germany, Box 2870. The source of the report is indicated by a note made by A. J. Drexel Biddle jr., who received the report from the Chief of Polish intelligence.

45 Ibid., MID Romania, Box 2870, Polish Intelligence, Rumania. Effects of bombing on oil supplies, Confidential, no. 5230/43, 15 August 1943.

46 Ibid.

47 Ibid, Box 2869, f. 4115.

48 Ibid., Box 2871, f. 4220, information concerning Rumania.

49 See also J.S. Ciechanowski's chapter, 'Lt-Col. Jan Kowalewski's Mission'.

50 T. Dubicki, *Conspiracy*, op.cit., pp. 222–239.

51 IPMS, A 9 VI 22/2. To The Minister of Internal Affairs in London, Secret. Concerning 'Akra', Istanbul, 3 October 1941.

52 TNA (PRO) HS 4/235, D/H 109/Ro/2627, do D/H V 5 III 1942; ibid., MPO/PD/848 do MX, 20 February 1942, Notes on the Polish-Romanian situation; D/H109 E.G. Boxhall (1899–1984) born in Bucharest.

53 TNA(PRO) HS 4/235. Notes on a conversation between Mr Librach – Chief of the Polish SOE in London, MX 9 (Col. Wilkinson) and D/H 109 (Maj. Boxshall) at Stratton House, 23 March 1942.

54 NARA, RG 165, MID Romania, Polish Intelligence, Marshal Antonescu relations with Hitler, 22 May 1943.

55 Ibid., Rumania, Political. Polish Intelligence. Confidential, no. 1401/43, May 1943.

56 TNA(PRO) HS 4/335, MPX (Capt. R. Truszkowski) to D/H 109 (Maj. E. Boxshall), 6 March 1942. It was ascertained that on this issue the Romanian Chief of Staff rejected German demands mainly because it was not possible to provide the Romanian Army with complete and modern equipment. It was therefore concluded that 'The reports indicate therefore that in practice the preparations for the spring campaign have been completed and that the main body of the German Army would attack in early April at the southern end of the Russian front'. Ibid., MPO/PD/107 do D/H 109, 17 March 1942.

57 T. Dubicki, *Bazy* (*Bases*), op.cit, pp. 56–66.

58 SPP, 5.2.1, PGS VI Bureau. Copy of Appendix no. 2 to l. dz. 124/tj.45, 24 November 1944.

59 IPMS, Kol. 138/192, Station 'Bałk.', 8 December 1943.

60 TNA(PRO), HS 5/834.

61 TNA(PRO), HS 5/835.

62 SPP, 5.2.6.6., Neptun 12, 31 January 1945.

63 Ibid.

32
Turkey

Jan Stanisław Ciechanowski and Tadeusz Dubicki

Polish Intelligence was active in Turkey since before the war. Its prime task was to observe the growing Soviet penetration both in the Balkans and in the Middle East.[1] This continued after the outbreak of the Second World War. Until 1940 the Polish Intelligence mission attached to the Polish Embassy in Ankara conducted intelligence there.[2] In the summer of 1940 Station 'T' was established in Jerusalem, to which the Intelligence Cell No. 3 in Istanbul (and others) was subjected. It conducted land, sea and air intelligence directed against Germany and the Soviet Union, as well as carefully monitored Turkey's neutrality and her ambivalent attitude to the world conflict.[3] Istanbul, where interests and influences of the opposite parties criss-crossed, became one of the most important centres of the intelligence game in the Second World War. In view of the police state characteristics, Turkey was not an easy territory on which to conduct intelligence activities.[4]

In November 1940 Capt. Jerzy Fryzendorf 'Feliks Jurewicz', ('Kresowiak') was the temporary head of Cell No. 3 of the II Bureau. In the same month he was replaced by Maj. Józef Bińkowski,[5] in turn later replaced by Capt. Wacław Zalewski (Wiktor Zaleski), working under the cover of an official in the Polish Consulate General in the former Ottoman capital. Not later than in 1942 Zaleski was replaced by Capt. Witold Szymaniak ('Alfred'), former head of Cell No. 1 in Belgrade working to Station 'J' in Zagreb.[6] One of the successes of the Istanbul Cell was to gain access to the encrypted telephone messages (easy to decipher), being sent from the German Consulate.[7]

In 1941 and again in 1944 there was a plan to move Station 'T' from Jerusalem to Turkey, but the authorities in Ankara would not agree to this. Since such a response was anticipated, in 1941 it was planned to create in Istanbul a clandestine Station 'T', run by Maj. Edmund Władysław Piechowiak ('Edward Panasiewicz'), a former officer of Station No. 3 (in Bydgoszcz) of the II Bureau of Polish General Staff in Poland. During the war he served as Deputy Chief and Intelligence Officer of Station 'T' in Jerusalem, working under the cover of Polish Red Cross Delegate for the Far East. Towards the end of 1943 Maj. Piechowiak was given the command of the independent Station 'Bałk.' in Istanbul. 'Bałk.' worked closely with Station 'T', which passed information about recruitments in the M.E. for work in Germany.[8]

The co-operation between these two Stations brought measurable results, especially valuable in terms of counteracting the various German intelligence ploys involving persons of Polish origin or presenting themselves as such.

As far as Turkey and the Middle East were concerned, such German ploys often took the form of sending German agents with the mission to reach Polish Army units in the East, or to gain the trust of Polish authorities by pretending to be the emissaries of the various resistance organisations in Poland. A number of such agents were even given sabotage missions by their German masters.

Available materials describe several such incidences. With time it became clear beyond any doubt that the following agents participated in these ploys: Ryszard Mączyński, Tadeusz Dębnicki, Bronisław Biernacki, Mieczysław Bratkowski, Stanisław Swedkowicz, Jan van der Linde.[9] They were sent out by the Gestapo in Warsaw in 1942–1943 (with the exception of Swedkowicz, who was trained in the Berlin office of Sicherheitsdienst). All these affairs show a pattern employed by the Germans: the agents would be delivered to the Turkish border, having crossed it, the 'agents' would present themselves at a Polish office as 'escapees'.

One task of Polish counter-intelligence was to verify the authenticity of the stories told by such people. In the case of the agents named above, their stories did not add up. A special procedure was then invoked: the suspects were taken to territories under British control. In most cases they were first taken to the Information Centre in Beirut, where they were subjected to questioning at the Interrogation Centre. Many were questioned (in German) by Capt. P. N. O'Leary-Fox of 1st Defence Security Corps, Syria. Capt. Rowton was another of the interrogators.[10]

The transcripts of these interrogations were then made available to the Poles. In the case of Swedkowicz, suspected also of sabotage, one of the interrogators was Lt. H. Mascewicz (?) of II Bureau, Polish Army in the East. The questioning lasted many hours and its results were carefully analysed. The resulting conclusions were sent to London, via Stations 'T' or 'Bałk'. To find out the real identity of such agents required consultation with Poland underground organisation, since only they could verify the facts.

To demonstrate the complexity and difficulties which faced the interrogators and without going into too many details, suffice to say that Swedkowicz, for example, was using also the names of Waldemar Seidemann, Stanisław Czudakow, Joseph Krusch; Dębnicki (born as Kawa) was also called Orsza and Piotr Kmita.

It would appear that those agents who initially managed to create a 'good impression', after some time and following the verification of their cover stories, tended to gradually change their stories, until finally they would admit to working for the Germans – though providing different reasons for this. One such reason, of special interest to the British, was co-operation with 'White Russians'. This was the case, for example, with Tadeusz Dębnicki, who introduced himself as an emissary of Maj. von Regenau (real name Borys Smysłowski-Holmston).[11] The latter was a former officer in the Tsarist army who during the Second World War II was Sonderführer with the Nachrichten Abteilung Osten OKW. The British investigation, later joined by the Poles (by a team from Intelligence Cell No. 1, led by Capt. Franciszek Wierzbicki with the participation of Lt. Kazimierz Krenz and Dr. Jan Krupiński), established that: 'Dębnicki, beyond doubt a German agent, was used with good results for recruitment of others among secret resistance organizations in Poland'.[12] He also had close links with earlier German intelligence operations, for example with the mission of Maj. Abramowicz and of 'Zaremba' Szadkowski (together with 3 people from the 'Musketeers' organisation) on Russian territory, directed by Maj. Regenau.[13] Dębnicki was a former Legionnaire (that is, a soldier of Polish Legions of Marshal Piłsudski in World War I who enjoyed high status in Poland). He was a Maj. in the Polish Army and a Director of the 'Pocisk' (The Bullet) factory in Rembertów between the wars. London was interested in him because the offer presented on Smysłowski-Holmston's behalf was considered a threat to relations with the USSR. The Dębnicki case was being investigated from January to November 1943, when it was abandoned – '[...] since there are legal obstacles in trying Dębnicki, it is necessary to ask the English authorities to intern him until the war ends'.[14]

The same conclusion was reached in the cases of other detainees. Their further fates are not known. It is reasonable to assume that they were later released, as was the case with another agent held in England, Stefan Starykoń-Kasprzycki.[15] Jan van der Linde, who arrived in Turkey in October 1943 calling himself Hans Merz, was in a different category. He was probably a Dutchman in German service, though this is not certain, since according to the British his Dutch was poor. He presented himself as a representative of 'Miecz i Pług' (Sword and Plough), which in the context of the recent execution in Poland of the leaders of this organisation, charged with collaborating with the Germans, sounded peculiar. Today, his activities are beyond doubt. It has been proven, for example, that in Warsaw Merz arrested Col. Janusz Albrecht (Home Army Chief of Staff), and others![16] The many items of information on Poland obtained from Merz at his interrogation were passed on to Lt-Col. Stanisław Sulma (who was Chief of the Communications Base of the Home Army in Istanbul).[17] The assessment of the material brought by Merz (which included letters to Gen. Anders and Minister Kot, among others) was that it was '[...] damaging, and the circumstances of [Merz's] trip and the way the material was smuggled...highly suspicious'.[18] Maj. Richard Truszkowski of SOE was equally clear. In his letter to Capt. Krzyżanowski of the VI Bureau, PGS, he stated that van der Linde confirmed his collaboration with the Gestapo in Warsaw.[19]

The uncovering of many agents and informants of German intelligence in Turkey and the Middle East were among the most important results of the work of Polish intelligence there. Among them were: Dr. Graeve, Chief of Amt VIc RSHA (Foreign Intelligence) for the Middle East, who directed this work from Berlin, his Deputy B. Beissner and officers Mehring and Eylitz. The personnel of German outposts in Athens and Sofia was also known.[20] Information was also obtained from agents being interrogated. At the same time, as testified to in the reports from 'Bałk.', intensive offensive counter-intelligence operations were undertaken. Reports no. 7 of 1943 and no. 3 of 1944, for example, contained exhaustive dossiers on the current personnel of the Reich's Embassy in Istanbul, a list of German agents in Turkey, information on the activities of German Intelligence directed against the USSR and the methods employed by the Soviet Intelligence.[21] Report no. 3 contained several dozen names of persons identified as working for German Intelligence and of 'suspicious foreigners', and photographs of 22 were enclosed.[22]

In May 1944 the Station 'Bałk.' had at its disposal four cells 'Tandara' and 'Tusla' in Bucharest, 'Tatar' in Cairo and 'Turnu' in Ankara.[23] In practice the Romanian cells were at that time inactive, since their heads, Capt. Bolesław Ziemiański 'Mościbrodzki' and Capt. Bronisław Eliaszewicz 'Ortwin', released from prison where they were held since the autumn of 1943, were under close Romanian and German supervision (more on this in the 'Romania' chapter). 'Bałk.' also had two recruitment cells, 'Tirana' and 'Turlaki', again inactive at the time. Altogether, the Station had 15 agents, 3 recruitment agents and 22 informants.[24]

In May of 1944 the immediate evacuation of both Romanian cells was being planned; their place was to be taken by two new ones. If the Red Army were to enter Romania, the heads of both were to be recalled, since they were known to Soviet Intelligence. Prior to that they were to designate and prepare their successors, lack of communications meant that they could not be informed of this task. In the spring of 1944 the fate of the Romanian cells was discussed in Cairo by the Chief of the II Bureau of PGS, Col. Gano, and Maj. Piechowiak. The decision was that newly arrived officers could not be compromised by maintaining contacts with those agents whose identities were known to the enemy.[25] The role of the go-between was entrusted to the former Commander of the Home Army Communications Base in Bucharest, Capt. Bogusław Horodyński, who was ordered to break all his previous contacts and to work on his own. Horodyński's mission ended in his arrest by Soviet Intelligence on 11th March 1945.[26]

At the same time the 'Tatar' cell, led by Capt. Gilewicz, was disbanded by the Chief of II Bureau. Its personnel was subsumed by the Stations 'T' and 'Bałk.'s. It is established that in May 1944 Station 'W' in Budapest had one-way communications with Station 'Bałk.', which in turn was in contact with the Centre. 'Bałk.' was hoping to place a Polish officer in the American station in Turkey, to serve as Chief of the Polish Section. This job was to be entrusted to Lt. Jerzy Piotrowski from the Office of Deputy

Chief of Staff in Washington. Such an arrangement would have been very advantageous, in view of the significant American ability to operate courier routes in the Balkans and in Hungary. While in Cairo, Col. Gano was also to talk to the Chief of 'Bałk.' about this Station becoming more active.[27]

At the end of 1944 the 'T' Station was located in Cairo and after some time it merged with 'Bałk.', assumed the responsibilities of both and changed its designation to 'Eswu'. In view of the new political and military situation in the Balkans and as 'Bałk.'s' task was exclusively aimed at the Germans, it was closed on 1st January 1945. On 31st January 1945 a new cell, No. 7 'Turcja' was created, led by Capt. Tadeusz Zdzisław Szefer ('Tadeusz Rayski'), formerly an intelligence officer with Station 'A' in Athens and of Station 'T' in Jerusalem. The task of this new cell, with five officers and subordinated to Station 'Eswu' in Cairo, was – in agreement with SIS – to work on preparing the post-war intelligence directed against the USSR. In addition to its observation (without setting up intelligence networks) of the countries within the Soviet sphere of influence, it conducted very careful monitoring of Soviet and Communist penetration. As the USSR expanded its influence in Turkey and Asia, this task was of some importance. Cell No. 7, 'Turcja', observed events in Soviet-occupied Yugoslavia, Bulgaria, Romania and Albania and monitored developments in Turkey. 'T's' work was directed primarily against the Germans and those Balkan countries occupied by them. When possible, it also conducted intelligence and offensive counter-intelligence against the Axis powers in Turkey and the Balkans.In the assessment of the 'East' section, the cell obtained much interesting and, in the main, well-regarded intelligence information, though it had only a small number of staff (nine officers and one civilian).[28]

The activities of an Allied agent Jerzy Iwanow-Szajnowicz were also indirectly linked to the Polish intelligence effort in Turkey. Iwanow-Szajnowicz was recruited to work for Polish Intelligence by Station 'A' in Athens, subordinated to the II Bureau, PGS, in 1940. In the spring and early summer of 1941 the heads of Station 'T', planning to use an agent in Greece, were in dispute with the Base of the VI Bureau in Cairo ('Alek', 'Muł'), led by Lt-Col. Walerian Mercik ('Jakób Alek'), who wanted Iwanow-Szajnowicz to be handed over to the Carpathian Brigade (of the Polish Armed Forces) to be used for establishing communications with Poland in Greece. A compromise was finally reached: Iwanow-Szajnowicz was to take over the 'Muł' contacts in Greece and to serve as liaison between the VI Bureau's bases in Istanbul and in Cairo. Formally not working to the former, at the same time he was to carry out tasks given to him as 'Athos' (agent no. 2882)[29] by Station 'T'.

The 'Wojskowa Organizacja Propagandy Dywersyjnej' (Military Organisation for Diversionary Propaganda – the Military Organisation for Diversionary Propaganda) was also active in Turkey, having been moved there from Bucharest in August 1940. It was led by the former military attaché in Romania, Lt-Col. Tadeusz Zakrzewski. Whilst in Turkey, in addition to its previous directives aimed at obstructing the Soviet and German interests in the Balkans, the Military Organisation for Diversionary Propaganda successfully carried out another mission: to obstruct and counteract the political activities of the Third Reich's ambassador there, Franz von Papen.[30]

Capt. Tadeusz Werner 'Ostoja', an excellent conspirator and an expert on technology, sabotage and communications, played a prominent role in the Military Organisation for Diversionary Propaganda. His achievements already included the running of laboratories in Budapest and Belgrade, whose weekly production of new documents amounted to 400–500 items, including stamps, forms etc.[31] As part of the Military Organisation for Diversionary Propaganda in Yugoslavia, he managed a diversionary unit which, among others, managed to provoke anti-German demonstrations in Zagreb and Parchev, set fire to a camp full of German resettlers he participated in mining three tankers transporting fuel on the Danube, from Romania to Germany. The magnetic mines were supplied by British Intelligence in Oblicewy Vence.[32]

The effects of the Military Organisation for Diversionary Propaganda's work were quickly noticed, as demonstrated by the arrival from London of a British Major, who wanted to find out about the methods employed. Soon afterwards an unexpected order followed the Major: 'In view of the political situation in the Balkans, by 1 December Lt-Col. Zakrzewski is to hand over his work to the British or to close his organization and operations'.[33]

The intelligence agency of the Polish Ministry of Internal Affairs was also active in Turkey. The Continental Action in the Balkans, as part of a unit dealt with general and political communications between the government and Poland in Turkey, was run by Jerzy Kurcyusz ('Thieme', 'Azis', 'Ali', 'Adam Nowina-Kurcjusz'). A Doctor of Law, pre-war a member of various right-wing organizations and during the Second World War head of communications bases with Poland in Rome and Athens.[34] The tasks of the Continental Action cell in Istanbul were described as 'JU-RU-TU-BU'. JU signified occupied Yugoslavia, where Roman Kowalik ('Kowal', 'Hanka') was responsible (from Istanbul) for communications with the Rome cell, at first on his own, and later as part of the 'JU-RU-TU-BU' in Istanbul.[35] 'RU' (or 'AKRU') stood for Romania, where work (again, from Istanbul) was directed by Stefan Werner ('Ster'), an expert on Romania and a former press attaché at the Polish Embassy in Bucharest. His job was to keep open communications with Romania, and through it, with Hungary, to maintain contacts with prominent Romanians and to create an anti-German centre there.[36] 'TU' was for Turkey, the main centre of all this activity, and 'BU' for Bulgaria. From April 1943 the observer of Bulgarian affairs in Istanbul was Apolinary Kiełczyński ('Niko'), officially vice-consul in Istanbul, and in Bulgaria itself the 'correspondent' of Continental Action: until 1941 Karol Iwanicki, and later Zbigniew Kowalski ('Kowalewski', 'Witold', 'Zbyszek'). In the spring of 1943 communications with the latter were lost – he was arrested by the Gestapo.[37] In other words, there were three Sections of Continental Action (Romanian, Bulgarian and Yugoslav) and the separate Turkish section.[38]

The Ministry of Internal Affairs' cell had a relatively wide network of informants, providing valuable information on the political, economic and military situation in the Balkans and in the USSR. The cell also participated in the maintenance of communications with the Polish Embassy in the USSR.[39] One of the main tasks of the Continental Action Post in Istanbul was to promote the idea of a Central European federation. The most important talks on this, with the Romanians in Portugal, were conducted by Lt-Col. Jan Kowalewski. But, via a series of careful steps, there was a lively and steady exchange of ideas and correspondence, also in Turkey, with former allies. Kurcyusz and Stefan Werner 'Ster' were the main participants in these contacts. It is in part thanks to such contacts that the Romanians were prepared to aid the Poles in maintaining their diplomatic courier traffic. Romania was of importance for the representatives of the Polish Ministry of Internal Affairs, mainly because of such opportunities to communicate with Poland. It was Werner's mission in Istanbul, which worked on communications with Poland via Romania. The British were putting pressure on the Polish Government in Exile in London to disallow Werner to talk about the Free Romania Movement, or about the Central European Federation, planned for the post-war period. Werner – in SOE's opinion – was, in any case, not the only Pole who, in the British opinion, conducted such irritating (to London) talks. It was thought that the representatives of other secret Polish organizations were also involved.[40]

Information gathering, however limited, was undertaken by the Home Army Foreign Communications Base in Istanbul, 'Bey', also conducted intelligence work.[41] 'Bey' was established on the basis of the Base 'Bolek', evacuated from Romania in the summer of 1940. The documents preserved at the Polish Underground Movement Study Trust in London show that in the autumn and winter of 1940 'Bey' had an intelligence section, in November 1940 run by the Acting Chief of the local II Bureau (of PGS) cell, Capt. (of the pre-war Frontier Defence Corps) KOP Jerzy Fryzendorf. Counter-intelligence and records were in the hands of the Istanbul II Bureau cell. From the beginning of 1941, when the personnel situation of the Polish military cells in Turkey was stabilised, the tasks and the organisational and staffing structure of the Base of the the VI Bureau were clearly separated from those of the cell of II Bureau. The organizing principle was that 'Bey' collected intelligence only occasionally, at the margins of its main activity. This changed only in 1944, with the increased Soviet expansion in the Balkans. The co-operation of the Base with the Station of the II Bureau was good.[42]

The notorious case of Samson *vel* Stanisław Mikiciński, the secretary of the Chilean Legation at the Polish Government-in-Exile in France and at the Turkish Government,[43] accused of spying for the Germans, as well as the spy affairs of Paluchowicz and Wiktor Kutten, who were charged with having been double agents for the Germans,[44] can be traced to inadvertent policies of the Polish Ministry of Internal Affairs and the II Bureau.

Notes

1 More in: Dokumentacja Referatu 'Wschód' Wydziału Wywiadowczego Oddziału II SG (Documentation Section 'East' of the II Bureau of Polish General Staff) [in:] Rossijskij Gosudarstviennyj Vojennyj Archiv, Moscow, Russia (further: RGVA), fond 308 (II Otdieł Gienieralnogo shtaba Polshi, g. Warszawa) and [in:] CAW, II Bureau of General Staff from 1921–1939 (further: II Bureau); A. Pepłoński, *Wywiad polski na ZSRR 1921–1939 (Polish Intelligence in the Soviet Union)*, Warsaw 1996, passim.

2 CAW, Oddział VI Sztabu Głównego Naczelnego Wodza z lat 1940–1949 (the VI Bureau of PGS, 1940–19949 (further: the VI Bureau), II.52.481, Protokół zdawczo-odbiorczy Wydziału Wywiadowczego Oddz. Inf.-Wyw. Sztabu NW (Hand-over Certificate of the Intelligence Department of the II Bureau, PGS), 15 February 1944.

3 More in: M. Sokolnicki, *Dziennik ankarski 1939–1943 (The Ankara Diary 1939–1943)*, London 1965, passim. In addition to the evidently 'wait and see' attitude of the Turkish government towards events, a German invasion of Turkey could also not be excluded (L.A.B. Kliszewicz, *Placówki wojskowej łączności kraju z centralą w Londynie podczas II wojny światowej (Military Communications Bases Between Poland and the Centre in London During WW II)*, vol. 3 Baza w Stambule (The Istanbul Base), Warsaw-London 1999, p. 139).

4 Ibid., pp. 207–208.

5 Ibid., pp. 9–10, 13, 16–17.

6 A Naval Intelligence Cell was also active in Istanbul. Once Naval Intelligence was submitted to the II Bureau, PGS, it was working for Station 'T'. At the time the following served as intelligence officers of Cell No. 3: Capt. Bolesław Piłecki, Lt. (Navy) Tadeusz Berdysiński (officially an employee of the Polish Consulate General in Istanbul), 2nd Lt. Zdzisław Martyszus (formally Vice-Consul in Istanbul), and civilian employees were Lt. Włodzimierz Ledóchowski (see 23 below), Staff Sergeant Adam Praga, L/Corp. Julian Horowitz, Able Rating Tadeusz Bykowski (office employee in an aircraft factory in Ankara) and 2nd Lt. Wacław Fedorowicz (under the cover of an official in the 'Polish Iron Export in Istanbul'). Lt-Col. Tadeusz Zakrzewski ('Zyndram'), in 1937-1940 military attaché in Bucharest, was active for the II Bureau until December 1940. There were also Maj. Tadeusz Tokarz (as was the case with Zakrzewski, the Turks did not allow him to remain there), Lt-Col. Marian Zimnal, who later became the military attaché in Ankara, and in 1944–1945 Capt. Zygmunt Łupiński ('Lester'). Cell No. 3 maintained radio communications with Station 'T' in Jerusalem and with Cell No. 1 in Bucharest using a radio set placed in the summer residence of the Polish Embassy in Ankara. IPMS, Kol. 242/63, Folder with information on the structure of Polish Intelligence cells; A.XII.24/71, Gen. W. Sikorski, Commander-in-Chief to Lt-Col. T. Zakrzewski, b.m. 22 November 1940; A.XII.24/46, Lt-Col. T. Zakrzewski to Chief of the II Bureau, PGS, Istanbul, 8 November 1940; L.A.B. Kliszewicz, *Placówki (Cells)*, op.cit., p. 21; W. Ledóchowski, *Pamiętnik pozostawiony w Ankarze (A Diary Left in Ankara)*, Warsaw 1990, p. 260.

7 Ibid., p. 262—264.

8 IPMS, Kol. 242/63, Folder with information on the structure of Polish Intelligence posts and II Bureau, A.XII.24/56, A Report on the Activity of the Intelligence Department for the period 5 May to 14 May 1944, b.m. 13th May 1944; W. Ledóchowski, *Pamiętnik (A Diary)*, op. cit., p. 264, and M. Sokolnicki, *Dziennik (Diary)*, op.cit., p. 487 (the Polish Ambassador to Turkey, Michał Sokolnicki, maintained that the secret military cells, including Intelligence, had 'no regulated relationship' with himself, ibid., p. 134).

9 IPMS, Kol. 24/1, 24/5, 24/6, 24/40.

10 Ibid., Kol. 24/50, A Report on the Interrogation of Maj. Tadeusz Dębnicki in Beirut between 25 April and 3 May 1943, in German; ibid., Kol. 24/5, A Summary of the Interrogation of R. Mączyński at the Information Centre in Beirut. Counter-

intelligence. Appendix no. 1 to l. dz. 6979, tjn. 43.

11 Ibid., Kol. 24/4a, A Report..., between 25 April and 3 May 1943.

12 Ibid., Kol. 24/46, Head of Cell no.1 Capt. F. Wierzbicki to HQ Polish Army in the East Chief of Station of II Bureau. Secret, l.dz. 3630 kw (tjn. /43, 6 November 1943).

13 T. Dubicki, A. Sepkowski, *Dzia łalność wywiadowcza organizacji 'Muszkieterowie'. Nieudana misja na Wschodzie (Intelligence Activities of the 'Muszkieterowie' Organisation. A Failed Mission in the East)*, [in:] *Historyk i Historia (Historian and History)*. In *honorem Henrici Dominiczak* [ed. J. Walczak], Częstochowa 1999, pp. 93–114.

14 IPMS, Kol. 24/46, Chief of Cell no. 1 Capt. F. Wierzbicki..., 6 November 1943.

15 T. Dubicki, A. Sepkowski, *Afera Starykonia czyli historia agenta gestapo (The Starykoń Affair or History of the Gestapo)*, Warsaw 1998.

16 M. Foedorowitz, *W poszukiwaniu modus vivendi (In the Search of Modus Vivendi)*, 'Mars. Problematyka i historia wojskowości' (Mars. Military History), 1994, no. 2, p. 168.

17 In respect of the van der Linde affair, Maj. Truszkowski informed the VI Bureau, PGS, that 'Andrzej', the former head of 'Miecz i Pług' and a collaborator of Herr Spilker (SIPO head in Warsaw) told van der Linde that a British officer, who found himself in Poland with three Polish officers, was to contact with the Home Army and co-operated with 'Miecz i Pług' near Kraków – at a time when van der Linde left Poland. IPMS, Kol. 24/13, Maj. R. Truszkowski to the VI Bureau, PGS, 24 December 1943.

18 IPMS, Kol. 24/13, Maj. Truszkowski, RT/INT/666, 24 December 1943.

19 Ibid.

20 Ibid., Kol. 24/45, persons employed by German Intelligence.

21 IPMS, Kol. 138/192, Report of Offensive Counter-intelligence no. 7 'Bałk.', l.dz. 25/43, 17 December 1943.

22 Ibid., Report of Offensive Counter-intelligence 'Bałk.', l.dz. 540/44, 17 March 1944.

23 The Station's personnel consisted of 2nd Lt (Rtd) (later Lt.) Włodzimierz Ledóchowski ('Alan', 'Halecki', 'Jupiter'), the nephew of the General of the Jesuit Order and one of the first couriers between Warsaw and Bucharest, who arrived in Istanbul in July 1942. He worked there under the cover of 2nd Secretary – much to his dissatisfaction. In December 1942 II Bureau despatched him to Ankara where he continued to work in intelligence at the Polish Embassy under diplomatic cover. In March 1944 he was transferred to the 'Sara' military communications base in Cairo (W. Ledóchowski, *Pamiętnik (Diary)*, op.cit., pp. 252–275; M. Sokolnicki, *Dziennik (Diary)*, op.cit., pp. 450, 538–539; IPMS, A.XII.24/56, list of issues to be discussed with cells by Col. Gano during his inspection tour to Italy, North Africa and the East in spring of 1944; L.A.B. Kliszewicz, *Placówki (Cells)*, op. cit., p. 170). In January 1944 the cells in Yugoslavia and Bulgaria were being organised – but in the event these were probably not established (IPMS, A.XII.24/35, Note, 12 January 1944).

24 As of April 1944. (IPMS, A.XII.24/37, Capt. J. Piękosz, Chief of 'East' Section of Intelligence Department, Note for Chief of Intelligence Department, 5 May 1944). In January the Station had establishments for 15 officers and 6 civilian officials and had at its disposal 20 agents and 21 informants (ibid., A.XII.24/35, Note, 12 January 1944; A.XII.24/37, Note, 8 May 1944). In April 1943 'Turda 2', a cell working to Station 'T', was active in Istanbul (L.A.B. Kliszewicz, *Placówki (Military Missions)*, p. 139).

25 IPMS, A.XII.24/56, list of issues to be discussed with chiefs of the II Bureaux cells by Col. Gano during his inspection tour to Italy, North Africa and the East in spring of 1944.

26 T. Dubicki, *Bazy (Bases)* op. cit., Częstochowa 2000, pp. 73–74.

27 IPMS, A.XII.24/56, list of issues to be discussed with chiefs of the II Bureau cells

by Col. Gano during his inspection tour to Italy, North Africa and the East in spring of 1944, and Report on the work of the Intelligence Department for the period 5 to 14 May 1944, b.m. 13 May 1944; A.XII.24/37, Maj. Billewicz, Chief of 'East' Section, Report on intelligence work of Stations 'T', 'Bałk.' and 'W', 12 May 1944.

28 For more see: CAW, Oddział VI (VI Bureau), II 52.481, General guidelines for the 'Syria', 'Iran', 'Palestyna', 'Turcja', 'Grecja' Cells concerning the Soviet penetration; II 52.486, Maj. F. Wierzbicki ('Wierzynek'), Chief of Station 'Eswu' to Chief of Cell no. 7, 24 April 1945., to Cell no. 5, b.m., 26 April 1945, to Chief of Cell no. 3, b.m., 12 October 1944., to Chief of Cell no. 1, 30 November 1944.; Lt-Col. L.L. Sadowski ('Sadwik'), Chief of Station 'Eswu' to Chief of Cell no. 8, b.m., 11 March 1945., and II.52.481; IPMS, Oddział II, A.XII.24/37, Capt. Piękosz, Chief of 'East' Section, Intelligence Derpartment, Annual Report on intelligence activity in the East for 1944,L.A.B. Kliszewicz, *Placówki (Military Missions)*, op.cit., pp. 199–200.

29 More in: A. Pepłoński, *Wywiad Polskich Sił Zbrojnych na Zachodzie 1939–1945 (Intelligence of Polish Armed Forces in the West)*, Warsaw 1995, pp. 145–148, and a more popular work: S. Strumph Wojtkiewicz, *Agent nr 1 (Agent no. 1)*, Warsaw 1988.

30 T. Dubicki, *Konspiracja polska w Rumunii w 1939–1945, Polish Clandestine Org. in Romania 1939–1945*, vol. 1, 1939–1945, Warszawa 2002, pp. 43–44.

31 T. Dubicki, *Działalność kpt. Tadeusza Wernera na rzecz polskiej konspiracji bazowej na terenie Węgier i Bałkanów w l. 1939–1945 (Capt. Tadeusz Werner's Activities for Polish Bases in Hungary and Romania in 1939–1945)*, [in:] T. Dubicki, *Bazy (Bases)*, op.cit., pp. 135–137.

32 Dossier of Capt. T. Werner, no ew. 1661/III/1898, (held by T. Dubicki).

33 T. Dubicki, *Konspiracja (Clandestine organisations)*, op.cit., p. 45.

34 More in: J. Kurcyusz, *Na przedpolu Jałty. Wspomnienia z tajnej służby w dyplomacji (At the Forefront Before Yalta. Memoirs of Secret Service in Diplomacy)*, Katowice 1995; L.A.B. Kliszewicz, *Placówki (Military Missions)*, op. cit., and the documentation of the Istanbul Cell held at IPMS, MSW. Some of those who worked in the unit responsible for communications with Poland were: Tadeusz Cieplak ('Tadeusz Nowak', 'Tad', 'Tadeusz'), Kurcyusz's deputy, who in the autumn of 1943 was transferred to Lisbon, and Paweł Zaleski, Adam Macieliński, Józef Olszewski, Władysław Zachariasiewicz ('Zawisza', in 1943 r.). Kurcyusz led the Istanbul cell from September 1940 under the cover of vice-consul, and from October 1942 as 1st Secretary of the Embassy in Ankara. He was recalled in February 1944 following an attempt at his life, probably undertaken by German Intelligence, which was tantamount to the cell being burnt. Kurcyusz was replaced by 'Jan Rudowski' (real name Jan Rabczewski), a pre-war public prosecutor from Wilno and in 1942 Chief of Counter-intelligence in Station 'P' in Lisbon (J. Kurcyusz, *Na przedpolu (At the Forefront)*, op.cit., pp. 18 and 398; IPMS, Kol. 242/63, notebook on the structure of Polish Intelligence cells; L.A.B. Kliszewicz, *Placówki (Missions)*, op. cit., p. 170). Kurcyusz, as he writes himself, was considered in Istanbul to be the emissary of the Sikorski Government, whom he knew well from before the war, with the mission to control Polish missions held by pre-war diplomats (J. Kurcyusz, *Na przedpolu (At the Forefront)*, op. cit., p. 38).

35 In 1944 Kowalik was sent to Yugoslavia by the Ministry of Internal Affairs and the Evacuation Department of the Ministry of National Defence. One of his co-workers was a Yugoslav, Kniaziewicz, and in Yugoslavia itself – Józef Mirowski ('Jasna'). Another person active there in 1941 was Tadeusz Trawiński ('Tadeusz Kowal', 'Bajerowicz'), who worked as the chief of a communications base with Poland. A lawyer from Śląsk, following the fall of Yugoslavia he was arrested by the Gestapo. One version of the subsequent events has it that it he was later released, having faked his willingness to co-operate with the Germans (more in: J. Kurcyusz, *Na przedpolu (At the forefront)*, op. cit., pp. 222–307, 369–371, and IPMS, MSW, A.9, a

list of cryptonyms used by the Ministry of Internal Affairs).

36 The following co-operated with Werner in Romania: Dr Tadeusz Wróbel ('Tadek', who provided intelligence information and was a go-between with the Deputy Prime Minister Mihai ('Ica') Antonescu, and Władysław Wolski ('Rafał'), who was arrested and interned in June 1943 (IPMS, MSW, A.9, a list of cryptonyms used by the Ministry of Internal Affairs); L.A.B. Kliszewicz, *Placówki* (Military *Missions*), op.cit., p. 144, and J. Kurcyusz, *Na przedpolu* (*At the forefront*), pp. 336–352). In March 1945 Werner was sent to France.

37 The testimony of Ryszard Mączyński, who informed on the Bulgarian cell, IPMS, Kol. 24/1, the case of Ryszard Mączyński.

38 J. Kurcyusz, *Na przedpolu* (*At the forefront*), op.cit., p. 335. The Home Army cell in Istanbul also had a special section for contacts with the Czechs, Slovaks and Serbs ('AS', 'Slav Action'); ibid., pp. 55 and 335). Contacts with the Home Army correspondent in Istanbul was maintained by, among others, the emissary of Continental Action in the Middle East and the liaison with the Tartars and other Muslim nations, Izmael-Bek Pietrucin-Pietruszewski ('Izmael', 'Bek', 'Aga', 'Kiszkurno'), and Witold Rajkowski ('Omar'), sent to the Middle East in August 1941 to work in Egypt, Palestine and Syria, operating out of Beirut (IPMS, A.9, a list of cryptonyms used by the Ministry of Internal Affairs, see T. Dubicki, *Rumuńskie aspekty w Akcji Kontynentalnej (1940-1944)* (*Romanian Aspects in the Continental Action [1940-1944]*), 'Biuletyn Instytutu Filozoficzno-Historycznego w Częstochowie' (The Bulletin of the Philosophy and History Institute in Częstochowa, no. 29/8 2001, pp. 22–48.

39 J. Kurcyusz, *Na przedpolu* (*At the forefront*), op. cit., p. 70.

40 Ibid., p. 348, and TNA(PRO), HS 4/235, Polish negotiations with Romania, MX.1, 10 June 1942, and D/HV (J. Pearson) from MX (P.A. Wilkinson), 28 February 1942.

41 Also 'Farys', 'Selim', 'Kot', 'Team', 'Hasan', 'Neptun', 'Flora'. The Base was run by Lt-Col. Stanisław Sulma ('Stanisław Suliman', 'Sulman', 'Selim', VII-XI 1940, XII 1940-VI 1941, IX 1941-I 1945; he obtained diplomatic cover only in October 1943), Col. Stanisław Rostworowski ('Rączy', XI-XII 1940), Col. Alfred Krajewski ('Adam Polesiński', 'Adam Korab', VI-IX 1941) and Lt. (Reserve) Stanisław Patkowski ('Stanisław Prus', 'Żarnowicz', from January 1945). In the summer of 1940 Capt. Bolesław Piłecki was a member of the Base, then being formed, as a representative of the II Bureau. See T. Dubicki, *Bazy* (*Bases*), op. cit., pp. 163–165.

42 L. A. B. Kliszewicz, *Placówki* (*Military Missions*), op. cit., passim, and J. Kurcyusz, *Na przedpolu* (*At the forefront*), op. cit., p. 70.

43 Por. T. Dubicki, *Konspiracja* (*Clandestine organisation*), op.cit., pp. 230–236; R. Buczek, *Człowiek do złotych interesów* (*A Man with the Golden Touch*), Warsaw 1991; J. Kurcyusz, *Na przedpolu* (*At the forefront*), op.cit., pp. 43–50.

44 More in J. Kurcyusz, *Na przedpolu* (*At the forefront*), op. cit., pp. 29–30, 40, 43–50; W.T. Drymmer, *W służbie Polsce* (*In the Service of Poland*), Warsaw 1998, pp. 243-245, 256; TNA(PRO), HS 4/213, Note on the Kot Organisation in the Middle East, draft; W. Ledóchowski, *Pamiętnik* (*Diary*), op. cit., p. 264.

33
Scandinavia and the Baltic States

Gill Bennett

Documents found in the British closed archives indicate that Polish Intelligence was extremely active in Scandinavia, particularly in Sweden where an extensive Polish organisation was built up and a close relationship developed between the Polish and Swedish Intelligence services, based in part at least on their shared distrust of the Soviet Union. Indeed, the evidence suggests that this close liaison affected the flow of information to British and American Intelligence authorities, with whom the Poles were reluctant to share information acquired from Scandinavian sources. The situation was further complicated by the existence of a large number of German agents in Sweden, and of the pro-German sympathies of certain Swedish and Polish officials there.

In these circumstances it is not surprising that the surviving documentary evidence is patchy and at times inconsistent. The general picture conveyed is that the Polish organisation in Sweden controlled their regional Intelligence activities, including those in Norway, Denmark and the Baltic States. This is complicated, however, by the fact that in common with Polish practice parallel networks were set up, intended to operate in ignorance of one another, so that it is often difficult to tell which activities were 'official' and which due to local initiative. The information that follows, concerning principally Polish activities in Sweden, indicates both the scale of the activity and the confusion that could result from its means of operation.

Sweden
The majority of documents that have been found referring to Polish Intelligence activities in Sweden date from 1943 onwards. These indicated that early wartime attempts to set up an effective Polish Intelligence operation in Sweden in co-operation with the Swedish authorities were hampered by distrust and treachery. For example, references have been found to a Pole, Bernard Smolarczyk (also known

as Szmularczyk), who was evacuated from Poland at the beginning of 1940 and sent to Sweden with the intention that he should travel from there to France. He remained in Sweden, however, where his conduct aroused suspicions that he was in fact working for the Germans. He left for Poland in 1943.

Meanwhile, further difficulties were caused by the activities of a Swedish officer, Capt. Carl Florman. An unnamed Polish officer had uncovered evidence of an illegal German organisation operating in Sweden, and reported this to Florman in July 1940. The information, however, was apparently used to obtain the expulsion from Sweden of a Polish Intelligence officer, Capt. Gilewicz, leading to friction and a temporary breakdown in communication between the two services.

Polish Intelligence in Stockholm appears to have been penetrated by a German agent in 1942. A Pole with a *Volksdeutsch* pass, working as a steward on a Swedish ship plying between Danzig and Swedish ports, contacted the Polish Legation in May 1942 and was enlisted by Maj. Edmund Różycki, also known as Mazepa and Dziennikarz, to supply political information under the cover name Orzeł. According to German sources, after being 'tested' by being offered help to escape to England (an offer he accepted but did not take up), he was given a salary, and a questionnaire on shipping and harbour intelligence (in reply to which the Germans supplied 'chicken feed' information). He was also asked to procure a coat of new German transparent material for testing. When he did this, he was given further questionnaires and was asked to procure a German seaman's book, samples of German articles made from *ersatz* materials and other items. He was given the names of Polish agents to contact in Gothenburg and Malmö if his ship called there. No information has been found as to when this arrangement came to an end or what happened to Orzeł.

Such episodes, if discovered, put a strain on relations between Polish and Swedish Intelligence, and of course compromised the integrity of information supplied to Polish and British sources in London. Overall, however, Polish-Swedish relations were close and cordial, and even when official squabbles, arrests and deportations of Poles and dissensions within the ranks of the Swedish Intelligence services marred official relations, there was still very close unofficial co-operation. This enabled the development of at least one extensive Polish network based in Stockholm, SKN), headed until June 1944 by Maj. Edmund Różycki, and thereafter by Lt-Col. Władysław Łoś (also known as Bilecki).

In addition to SKN, other networks were known or suspected to exist, but SIS had little information about them. These included a cell headed until July 1944 by Cmdr. Edmund Piotrowski (also known as Pilewski), operating under cover of the Polish Red Cross; working to the 'Polish Ministry of the Interior', carrying out underground work in German-occupied countries; and an organisation known as 'Base RENIFER', which may have been connected with the VI Bureau.

Station SKN, comprised a military headquarters in Stockholm, with

Intelligence, counterintelligence, economic and political sections.[1] It covered all types of Intelligence, including counterintelligence, and its agents attempted to operate in Poland, Germany, Russia and all occupied territories from its Swedish base. On occasion, it also carried out intelligence operations against Sweden itself, leading to considerable friction with the Swedish authorities and the arrest and deportation of Polish Intelligence officers (including SKN's head, Różycki). After the latter had been removed, his successor Łos proposed to set up two networks, one unknown to the Swedes.

SKN had working cells subordinated to it, numbered 1–4, and a cell known as Cell GUSTAV that was acting as liaison between the Polish and Swedish Intelligence services. GUSTAV, which was headed by the assistant chief of SKN, Maj. Szymaniak (Lim) also had cells at Stockholm (known as 'Ilgrim', and headed by Lt. Olszowski) and Malmö (known as 'Erik', and headed by Lt. Piotrowski (Colt)). The cells were composite units, handling all types of intelligence, and sometimes were involved in resistance movements. Although supposed to deal with different areas, there was a good deal of overlapping which led to jealousy between them.

Cell 2, headed by Lt. Borys Żukowski (Wilk), dealt chiefly with intelligence from Danish and Baltic ports, principally concerning ship-building. Most of its agents were sailors. Cell 3 was headed by Rosenmayer, whose real name not known by SIS but who was described as 'an extremely valuable officer... in personal touch with all his valuable agents'. Cell 3 was particularly interested in naval intelligence, including Swedish waters. It had close links with networks in Norway, and had also achieved limited penetration of German ports. It also worked closely with Cell 4, headed by Lt. Masłocha (Pasek), which operated in Denmark. After a crisis in February 1944 when several Poles from Cell 4 were arrested, it was decided that it was too dangerous to use Polish agents in Denmark. Attempts to recruit Danish agents, however, were opposed by the Danish 'Frihedsraad' organisation, thought by the Poles to be under British influence.

Information received by SIS indicated that resistance groups in occupied countries were contacted by SKN ostensibly with a view to assisting them, but actually in order to establish a Polish Intelligence network in the country concerned. These plans appeared almost entirely anti-Soviet in character, and directed towards serving Poland's post-war needs. SKN met with a certain amount of success in their liaison with the Intelligence services (underground or legitimate) of the Baltic and Balkan states, Others, notably the Norwegian and Danish patriot organisations, were suspicious and unwilling to co-operate. This unwillingness was based partly on a suspicion that the Poles might be pro-German and partly – so the Poles believed – on pressure from British sources, although no evidence of this has been found.

Up until the summer of 1944, Polish-Swedish Intelligence co-operation was close. An example of this is the relationship between Maj. Carl Petersen and Maj. Felix Brzeskwiński of the Swedish and Polish

General Staffs respectively. Petersen, who had served in the Polish Legation in Stockholm between 1919 and 1922, offered to supply Brzeskwinski with information about Russia in exchange for information about Germany. Another example was the relationship between the Polish Maj. Szymaniak and a Swedish Intelligence officer, Lt. Bent Erik Hultgren, who was particularly interested in counter espionage against Soviet and Swedish communists.

Despite the breach caused by the expulsion of Różycki and the arrest of Polish agents, both the Polish and Swedish Intelligence authorities were keen to maintain good relations. Although the Swedes were bound to condemn Polish breaches of Swedish law and diplomatic privilege, alarm at recent Soviet military successes and fear of their intentions in Scandinavia was a strong impetus towards co-operation. The Swedes appear to have attempted to exert greater control over the Poles, for example by insisting that Polish agents, equipment and communications must be sent through Swedish channels. In addition, they insisted that no Intelligence operations should be conducted against Sweden and that the Poles must carry out their activities 'discreetly': as an SIS document noted, the Poles 'are prepared to agree to, but not necessarily fulfil' the Swedish conditions.

Norway and Denmark

Liaison with Norwegian Intelligence was handled by Cell 3 of SKN, but attempts to establish a similar liaison with Norwegian Intelligence to that established with the Swedes were largely unsuccessful. Although the Norwegian authorities were willing to co-operate on counter-espionage matters, their co-operation was strictly limited and they tended to be suspicious of Polish approaches. Equally, the Poles found it difficult to set up any kind of organisation without official Norwegian assistance.

Cell 2 tried to set up joint Polish-Danish networks in Denmark, and succeeded in setting up two known as 'Lupus' and 'Wolf', but they were short-lived and of limited efficacy. Again, the Poles alleged that Danish unwillingness to co-operate was due to British pressure. The same reason was given for the failure of a network set up in Denmark by Cell 4, under Lt. Masłocha. Accusations of lack of co-operation were, however, also made by the British and American authorities. For example, a request made to the Poles for help in penetrating Japanese Intelligence in Scandinavia was refused on the grounds that it might harm Polish-Japanese relations. Maj. Szymaniak, head of the Gustav liaison section, was also put in contact with Danish Intelligence in the early months of 1944. He was given an introduction to Lt-Col. Nordentoft, said to be chief of Danish Intelligence in Sweden, but did not pursue the connection for fear of compromising the Polish networks in Denmark.

By the end of 1944 SIS was receiving information that Polish Intelligence activities in Scandinavia were experiencing serious problems. Several cells had closed or come almost to a standstill. It was thought that there were four main factors responsible for this: recent shipping restrictions in the Baltic, which meant that the Poles had to rely on

German ships to maintain contact with agents; the hostility of Danish patriot organisations, which impeded the passage of Polish agents or material through Denmark to Germany; the personality of Lt-Col. Łos, who was thought to lack the drive and experience of his predecessor; and, most importantly, the attitude of the Swedish authorities. The close co-operation on which the Poles had relied had never really been re-established after the expulsion of Różycki, and Polish information was said to have lost its 'market value' in Sweden; in addition, it was said that the Swedish authorities 'do not mind by what means they defend their neutrality'.

Conditions were clearly difficult, but the scant surviving documentation indicates that a residual level of Polish activity persisted until the end of hostilities. A report of January 1945 reported that Cell 2 was now concentrating on servicing a permanent intelligence cell in Hamburg, while Cell 3 was achieving better results through working with a large number of probationary agents on German ships. Cell 4 had been overtaken by disaster, however, with the death of Masłocha in a gunfight with German police on 2 January, leading to the suspicion that his networks had been penetrated. Finally, on a lighter note, the report mentioned cell 'Erik', planning to use a fishing vessel as cover for intelligence activities. A boat, the 'Lilly', had been purchased. Unfortunately, according to the report:

> The agent neglected to buy a fishing net, and promptly fell under Swedish suspicion. He was accused of smuggling ball-bearings to Denmark, and much explanation, plus the purchase of a fishing net, were [sic] necessary before he was cleared of the charges.

Note
1 An organisational chart of SKN found in SIS archives, dated September 1944, is reproduced in Volume II.

34

Scandinavia and the Baltic States

Andrzej Pepłoński

During the inter-war period in the several cells of II Bureau were active Baltic region. They gathered intelligence directed mainly against the Soviet Union. Such cells were established in Finland, Estonia, Latvia and Lithuania. In Sweden, intelligence tasks were in the hands of the military attaché. Before the war, there was also a cell of II Bureau in Stockholm, led by Capt. Gustaw Firla, who succeeded Tadeusz Szumowski 'Steyer' in March 1939.[1] His work was supported by the military attaché Maj. Feliks Brzeskwiński and by the naval attaché, Capt. Podjazd-Morgenstern. Since the results of the work carried out by the Swedish cell were disappointing, following the establishment of II Bureau in Paris, Lt-Col. Gano ordered Capt. Wacław Gilewicz, the Chief of Station 'Reggio II' in Copenhagen, to set up a station in the Swedish capital. Its objective was to concentrate on 'Germany itself and everything connected with Germany in Northern Europe'.[2] This decision was taken at a time when there were difficulties with the 'Witold' Base, which was to be set up in Kaunas (Lithuania), under the command of Lt-Col. Tadeusz Rudnicki 'Wierzba'.[3] The lack of success of this Base and the occupation of Lithuania by Soviet troops in June 1940 forced Rudnicki to move it to Stockholm and to change its name to 'Anna'. The new Station 'Północ' ('North') became a part of the 'Anna' Base, which led to complications and demarcation disputes between staff working for II Bureau and those responsible to the VI Bureau.[4] Co-operation between them was, however, established.

The selection of Capt. (cav.) Gilewicz was a wise move, since he was one of the few II Bureau officers familiar with both the Third Reich and Scandinavia. He also was experienced in naval intelligence and had many valuable contacts, especially in Denmark. Moreover, in the period preceding the outbreak of the war, he established contacts with officers of British and French intelligence.

Station 'Północ' was set up in Stockholm in January 1940. At the beginning Gilewicz, working under the cover of 2nd Secretary of the Polish

Legation, used his informants recruited before the war. One of these was 'Majer', who lived in Malmö and had numerous contacts among the employees of its port and on the island of Bornholm. Col. Nishimura, the Japanese military attaché in Stockholm, was supplying the Station's Chief with information from the ports of Haparanda and Boden. But the ability to watch the movements of ships, naval and merchant, through the straits was better developed than the observation of ports. The Station discovered, for example, German transports of cows from Bornholm, but more importantly, the departure of the Kriegsmarine fleet for the invasion of Norway. Among the identified warships was the heavy cruiser 'Blücher', sailing in the direction of Oslo as part of the V Invasion Group, commanded by Rear Adm. Otto Kummetz. Gilewicz was sharing such information with the Chief of SIS Station in Copenhagen, Maj. Bernard J. O'Leary, and the Chief of the French intelligence cell, Capt. Miller.[5] Intelligence material on naval matters was also made available to Cmdr. Henry Denham, British naval attaché in Stockholm. Capt. Sidney Smith, the Chief of SIS Station in Stockholm, was interested in German industry, in the construction of new factories, in war production, in the construction of new types of airplanes and in human resources. Gilewicz found it difficult to understand how a country like Great Britain, with such industrial potential, could have had so few sources of information and had to rely on the Polish Intelligence. This did not prevent him, however, from gathering information of interest to British Intelligence, especially since in return Capt. Smith delivered one thousand pounds sterling per month, which was several times more than the operational budget provided to Capt. Gilewicz by the II Bureau. As Capt. (cav.) Gilewicz saw it, 'Smith was an old intelligence hand and had good knowledge on my position and potential. Consequently he neither demanded nor expected that which was beyond our reach'.[6] The two usually met every 10 days, and the exchange of information and the division of labour was harmonious. In one of the most interesting reports of 1940, Gilewicz stated that in response to the British submarines' torpedo attack on several German ferries in the straits between Denmark and Sweden, the Germans had constructed an anti-submarine net made of steel cables.[7]

Gradually, the Chief of Station 'Północ' recruited new agents. He also intended to set up a unit to analyse the press. His first new recruit was Tadeusz Nowacki, a journalist and economist with a good knowledge of German and Russian and completely fluent in Swedish. More than that, Nowacki had contacts among the employees of the Swedish Ministry for Industry and among journalists, that enabled him to obtain good information. To assist Nowacki, Capt. Gilewicz employed a Mr Mikołajewski 'Orwid', who was an accountant with excellent German.[8] Gilewicz's sister, Irena Przyjałkowska, who had good command of German, French and Russian, also joined the analytical unit. With Mikołajewski, she would select the relevant articles, while the analysis and report writing was the province of Nowacki. Klara Osińska, a former employee of the Polish Consulate in Szczecin (Stettin), was the secretary of the Station. The analytical unit concentrated on some 50 technical periodicals and of the local German newspapers, in which much interesting information was to be found. Copies of the reports sent to the II Bureau were then made available to Capt. Miller of French Intelligence and to the two British officers.

Following the transfer of the Polish authorities to Great Britain and the changes in the management of the II Bureau, Capt. (cav.) Gilewicz was confirmed as Chief of Station 'Północ'. He was also given an operational budget of £300 per month, but was required not to forward intelligence material directly to the British. This particular requirement was not implemented in practice, since British Intelligence was paying for the information-gathering network, and lack of direct radio communications would have prevented immediate transfer of important information to the Centre. In any case Capt. (cav.) Gilewicz, despite possible official consequences, was of the opinion that 'war is not normal peacetime clerking' and did not stop the flow of information to the British Intelligence.

Among instructions received by Capt (cav.) Gilewicz from the Centre was the requirement to act as liaison (passing instructions and tasks) for those officers of the II Bureau who resided within Japanese diplomatic mission. As agreed between Lt-Col. Gano and the Japanese military attaché in Paris, intelligence materials and reports obtained or prepared by such officers were to be relayed to Stockholm via the Japanese diplomatic bag. Gilewicz was empowered to make selected intelligence information available to the Japanese. Such contacts with the Japanese were the result of very good co-operation between the two services during the inter-war years.

Station 'Północ' was active in the Third Reich, in the Baltic states and in Poland. Once Maj. Michał Rybikowski was placed with the Japanese post in Riga, new opportunities emerged. Rybikowski's task was to establish contacts with Capt. Alfons Jakubianiec 'Kuncewicz', who was in Kaunas at the time, and to organise an anti-German network in Lithuania, Latvia and Estonia. Since the Latvian authorities did not agree to extend Rybikowski's visa, following the fall of France he took up a Japanese offer of help and went to Stockholm. There, he found employment on a contract as an official in the press unit of the Japanese attaché's office. At the same time Rybikowski set up Intelligence Cell 'L', to continue gathering anti-German intelligence. Being formally subordinated to Capt. Gilewicz as Chief of Station 'Północ', through whom he would receive his tasks from the II Bureau. Rybikowski was trying to avoid the intermediary of a junior officer and was passing intelligence to London via the military attaché of the Polish Legation in Stockholm, Lt-Col. Feliks Brzeskwiński.[9] The information related mainly to the situation in the Third Reich. In mid-October the Centre was being informed of further developments indicating that Wehrmacht was concentrating its forces in Poland, for example of the appearance in Warsaw of a group of five German generals, led by Gientah and Baron von Schenkendorf. The presence of new generals was also observed in Lublin, Jarosław, Radom and Tarnów.[10]

Other officers of the II Bureau were also able to avail themselves of Japanese assistance. In the second half of 1940 in Kaunas, for example, and thanks to the Japanese Consul there, Sugihara, a very successful operation was mounted: 2,139 Japanese transit visas were obtained for Polish citizens of Jewish origin. A substantial proportion of these visas were fabricated by the Document Unit of the Home Army Wilno Region[11] – and thanks to this, a significant group of Jews managed to reach Vladivostock without difficulties, and from there travelled to the US or to the Middle East.[12]

In October 1940 the then Japanese military attaché in Stockholm, Col. Toshio Nishimura, was made Chief of the II Bureau of the Quantun Army in Manchukuo. In November his place in Sweden was taken by Col. (Gen.) Makato Onodera. This change was advantageous to Maj. Rybikowski's further work, since he managed to become friendly with Onodera. As a consequence, the activities of Polish Intelligence in Sweden were gradually concentrated around Rybikowski's network, which reached directly to Germany.

Maj. Edmund Różycki recruited a valuable agent, 'Eden', who operated in Helsinki, and who managed to assemble a network in Latvia and Estonia. Meantime 'Majer' an official of the Polish Foreign Ministry, and Jarosław Pieniężny 'Schwarz', were working in Malmö. They were instructed to establish contact with an informant called 'Peters', who collected information of interest to naval intelligence. 'Peters' provided information on, for example, the extensions to airfields in Denmark and the construction of 15 U-boats in Bremerhaven. He obtained it from another informant, 'Anders', who had business dealings in Norway. Capt. Gilewicz contacted 'Peters' with Capt. Smith, who in return for more detailed information offered 'Peters' 2,500 Swedish crowns.[13] To improve the flow of information from the Reich and from Poland, the Chief of Station 'Płn.' was trying to maintain an alternative network, as he did not fully trust the Japanese, and thought that Maj. Rybikowski was providing exaggerated information ('was too inventive').[14] These plans coincided with the initiatives of the Base 'Anna', whose main purpose was establishing communications with Home Army HQ in Poland. An important role in securing communications between Warsaw and Stockholm was played by Capt. Jakubianiec 'Kuba' ('Kuncewicz'), employed at the Manchukuo Embassy in Berlin. In addition to running the intelligence Cell no.1 of Station 'Płn.', he acted as an intermediary in communications with Stockholm, using Japanese diplomatic bag.[15] Sabina Łapińska 'Sabina', also employed by the Manchukuo Embassy, dealt with courier communications. 'Sabina' assisted in, for example, the transfer of mail between Station 'Płn.' and the intelligence cell 'Zygmunt', set up in Warsaw by Maj. Zygmunt Trzaska-Reliszko on the instructions of Capt. Jakubianiec.

Drastic changes took place in Station 'Płn.' in mid-July 1941. Capt. Jakubianiec was arrested in Berlin with a group of his colleagues, and on 29 July Capt. Gilewicz was forced to leave Sweden, following the discovery of his true role by counter-intelligence and the police. The Station, renamed 'SKN', was now run by its former records officer, Maj. Edmund Różycki 'Dziennikarz'. The staff now consisted of intelligence officer Capt. Stanisław Skrobecki 'Rudolf', two Polish Foreign Ministry officials, Pieniężny 'Schwarz' and Frankowski 'Florian', typist Zabłocka and of seven persons employed in the press office run by Czechowicz.[16]

Since the Base 'Anna' continued to experience difficulties in maintaining radio communications with London, the radio equipment of the three Polish submarines interned in Sweden was used for this purpose. The Commander of 'Żbik', Lt-Com. Michał Żebrowski, was ordered to intercept coded German dispatches. The radio communication staff from the other two submarines participated in this work. In the period immediately preceding the closure of Station 'Płn.', its field operations were run by Intelligence Cell no. 1 in Stockholm (Maj. M. Rybikowski 'Adam Mickiewicz' ['Michał']), who controlled the following Intelligence Cells: no. 1 in Berlin (Alfons Jakubianiec 'Kuba'); no. 2 in Prague[17] (Stanisław Daszkiewicz 'Perz' ['Herman']); no. 3 in Riga (Mirosław Giedroyc 'Kit'); no. 4 in Dyneburg (Zofia Wojewódzka 'Krysia'), no. 5 in Kaunas (Klimek Lutkiewicz 'Józef').[18] At the beginning of October 1941, following the change, Station 'SKN' had 33 agents and informants, and another 12 were recruited within the next six months.[19]

People returning to Sweden from Poland, Germany and the areas adjacent to the Eastern Front also supplied valuable information.[20] Most of the material gathered by Station 'SKN' was, however, from Germany. In April 1943, for example, one of its agents supplied important information from the Lübeck and Travemünde regions, where new anti-aircraft units were located. He also discovered a shipyard on the Western bank of the river between the two towns where small submarines were being constructed, and further down a large factory whose purpose he was unable to determine. On the Eastern bank he found large armaments plant and some 500 metres away another shipyard, this one building trawlers.[21] Other information referred to the Blohm und Voss shipyard in Hamburg. One of the agents reported on the current volume of U-boat construction. He discovered that work was continuing on 12 submarines of some 800 tonnes each. His estimate indicated that this particular shipyard completed some 400 U-boats since the war began.[22]

Observation of military transports crossing South-Western Sweden was vital for an assessment of German forces. In that part of Sweden the Germans used several railway lines, with most traffic between the ports of Helsingør in Denmark and Helsingborg in Sweden. Rail transports were directed to the South of Sweden, to the port of Trelleborg, and also through railway junctions in Vanersborg, Olskroken and Krylbo. Some were reaching as far as Stockholm and Göteborg. Transit via Sweden unabled transports intended for the Eastern front. Station 'SKN' agents observed such traffic, reporting details including departure times, the number of carriages, and their passengers. In the case of military equipment, reports included the type of train carriages with ammunition, tanks, armoured cars and other vehicles. The conditions in Sweden at the time allowed for the registration of the train's direction of travel, especially in the case of those transiting through Helsingborg. Not all the transports could be precisely identified. In the case of goods trains, for example, the only information available was often its starting point or station in Germany. Frequently such information could include dozens of cars making up a train. The contents of such cars were frequently reported. To provide some examples: Station 'SKN' reported that on 20 June 1942 at 16.00 the ship 'Deutschland' with some 300 soldiers from a unit stationed in Sassnitz in Germany entered the port of Trelleborg. Three days later the same ship brought to Trelleborg a similar group of soldiers.[23] Other reports contained information on the ages of officers and even the makes of cars being transported. As for reports on the passenger trains, these usually contained information as to the destination, the number of carriages and departure times of each train. At the end of September and in October 1942 the Station reported an increase in the movement of German transports arriving in Göteborg from Norway, through Krylbo. On average, German transports were reaching this town every four hours. Five such transports were capable of carrying over 30 tanks, 45 pieces of anti-tank artillery, several 150 mm guns, several dozen various vehicles, 53 carriages with soldiers and 20 tankers with petrol.[24] In the next few months the frequency and character of such transports did not change significantly.

Good results were also obtained from the monitoring of German transports through the Olskroken station. On 7 January 1943 alone, 11 trains went through this station, in the direction of Vanersborg or Trelleborg. Each report was analysed. The usefulness of the reports on German transit via Sweden was varied, but in the main they were assessed by the allies as useful.[25]

In early 1943 Station 'SKN' provided increasing amount of information on the growing Soviet Intelligence activities in Sweden. It discovered, for example, that Soviet Military Intelligence (GRU) agents were interested in the poor food supplies to the village of Tranenberg, where Polish refugees were living. The USSR Embassy wanted to use this information for propaganda purposes.[26] There was also increased activity of Communist organisations. On one of the information meetings attended by USSR Embassy representatives, was a military attaché Col. Nikitushev and Col. Riazin, who was an intelligence agent.[27]

In mid-1943 Station 'SKN' began co-operating with Swedish Intelligence. The Chief of the II Bureau instructed the Station discreetly to inform the Swedish authorities of Soviet intelligence activities there. This led to the first contacts with Swedish counter-intelligence, that developed over the next few months. The scope and principles of information exchange were agreed, and a representative of the II Bureau, Maj. Szymaniak, arrived in Stockholm as the liaison officer between the two intelligence organisations.[28]

Maj. Rybikowski maintained contact with Capt. Heikki Aulio of the Finnish General Staff, established in March 1942. The Finnish officer suggested an exchange of information on the USSR. All the material he provided was passed on to British Intelligence, who thought it valuable. The British reciprocated only once. The II Bureau, PGS, wanted to cultivate such contacts with a view to the post-war period, but the British advised that these links be broken off, as they might have led to complications in the diplomatic relations between Finland and the USA.[29]

In the next few months, the efficiency of Station 'SKN' weakened. The reason was the continuing lack of radio communications with the Centre, and with individual cells and agents. Information from the field was received late and was becoming worthless. It was important to supply a new radio transmitter for Cell no. 4 in Denmark. New codes and radio protocols were established. The II Bureau considered, that one of the most important tasks was 'to preserve absolute secrecy concerning the very fact of monitoring of Russian stations'. In addition, the Station was given guidelines on monitoring.[30]

By the second half of 1944 Station 'SKN' had an increasing volume of information of significance to the Polish Government in London. Activities of the left-wing Polish groups in Sweden were observed. The staff of the Soviet Embassy often acted as intermediaries in the contacts between PKWN (Polish Committee for National Liberation – the Polish proto-government established by the Soviets) and ZPP (Union of Polish Patriots, an organization set up under Soviet tutelage) in Stockholm. In August 1944 at a meeting in the flat of Halina Moor the decision was taken to change the name of ZPP to the branch of Związek Wyzwolenia Narodowego (National Liberation Union). ZPP acted under Col. Riazin's supervision. Riazin, quoting agreements with the Lublin Committee, stressed the need to spy on the staff of the Polish Legation in Stockholm.[31] In April 1945 the Centre in London was informed that a course has been set up in Stockholm for those Poles who were to be sent to Poland to take responsible positions in the emerging administration at the voivodship (provincial) and district levels.[32]

Notes

1 A. Woźny, *Niemieckie przygotowania do wojny z Polska* (*German Preparations for the War with Poland*), Warsaw 2000, p. 321.
2 L. Gondek, *Na tropach tajemnic III Rzeszy* (*On the Trail of the Secrets of the Third Reich*), Warsaw 1987, p. 44.
3 Order of Gen. K. Sosnkowski to the Commander of Stockholm Base, l.dz. 3564/Tjn./40 of 1 June 1940 r. [in:] *Armia Krajowa w dokumentach* (*Documents on the Home Army*), Warsaw-Kraków 1991, vol. 6, pp. 59–61.
4 R. Mackiewicz, S. Steckiewicz, *Z dziejów polskiego wywiadu na Litwie w czasie II wojny światowej* (*Polish Intelligence in Lithuania During WW II*), 'Mars', vol. 8, London-Warsaw 1998, pp. 170–175.
5 L. Gondek, *Na tropach* (*On the Trail*), op.cit., p. 60.
6 IPMS, Kol. 206, copy of letter of Capt. Gilewicz of 20 June 1981.
7 SPP, 2.3.6.3.1, Intelligence Report no. 1 of Cell 'Sajgon', l.dz.123/40, 27 June 1940.
8 IPMS, Kol. 206, copy of Capt. Gilewicz's letter of 20 June 1981.
9 L. Gondek, *Na tropach* (*On the Trail*), op.cit, p. 60.
10 SPP, sygn. 2.3.6.3.1, Despatch of Lt-Col. Rudnicki 'Wierzba' to the Chief of the II

Bureau, PGS, no. 2635 of 15 October 1940.

11 H. Levine, *Sugihara's List*, *The New York Times*.

12 E. Pałasz-Rutkowska, A.T. Romer, *Współpraca polsko-japońska w czasie II wojny światowej* (*Polish-Japanese Co-operation During WW II*), 'Zeszyty Historyczne', 1994, no. 110, pp. 5–11.

13 IPMS, Kol. 206, copy of Capt. Gilewicz's letter of 20 June 1981.

14 Ibid.

15 J. Łopuszański, H. Matuszewicz, *Baza 'Anna' w Sztokholmie w latach 1940–1945* (*The 'Anna' Base in Stockholm in 1940–1945*), [in:] *Z dziejów wydziału łączności zagranicznej Komendy Głównej ZWZ-AK 'Zagroda'* (*Some Aspects of the History of Foreign Communications Office of the Home Army GHQ*), ed by K. Minczykowska and J. Sziling, Toruń 1999, pp. 57–67.

16 IPMS, Kol. 242, Note on Station 'SKN' – Stockholm.

17 The cell operated from the autumn of 1940. Thanks to Japanese support, its Commander was moved to Prague, where he worked officially in the Japanese Consulate. In reality he concentrated on setting up an intelligence network. AMWP, Collection of M. Rybikowski, statement of Lt. S. Daszkiewicz 'Perz' of September 1948; J. Łopuszański, H. Matuszewicz, *Baza 'Anna'* (*Base 'Anna'*), op. cit., p. 78.

18 IPMS, Kol. 242/63, Personnel of Station 'SKN' in Stockholm.

19 IPMS, A XII.24/37, Report on the Work of the Intelligence Department for the Period from 1 October 1941 to 1 May 1942.

20 SPP, 2.3.6.3.1, Copy of report from the Stockholm cell of 9 January 1942.

21 NARA, RG 156, MID, Germany, Box 1054, Folder 1190, Report of Station 'SKN' of 2 April 1943.

22 NARA, RG 165, MID, Germany, Box 1172, Folder 420, Report of Station 'SKN' no. 1870/44.

23 Ibid, MID Sweden, Box 2992, Information concerning Germany.

24 Ibid, MID Sweden, Box 2992, Sweden. Transport of goods, war materials and German troops through Sweden.

25 Ibid, MID General, Box 3329, Evaluation of Polish Intelligence Reports 1943–1944.

26 IPMS, A.XII.3/41, Letter of Chief of the II Bureau Col. Gano to Foreign Ministry Counsellor Wierusz-Kowalski of 21 August 1943.

27 IPMS, A.XII.3/41, Letter of Chief of II Bureau to Foreign Ministry of 13 April 1943.

28 IPMS, A.XII/56, Official note of Chief of the II Bureau Col. Gano for the Chief of Staff, PGS, of 28 February 1944.

29 IPMS, A.XII.24/56, Note of Deputy Chief of the II Bureau Lt-Col. Skinder for Commander-in-Chief of 12 January 1944.

30 IPMS, A.XII.24/56, Guildelines for 'SKN', l.dz. 311/SKN/44 of 26 July 1944.

31 IPMS, A.XII.3/41, Note of Chief of the II Bureau Col. Gano to Ministry of Foreign Affairs, l.dz. 5523/Wyw.KW/44 of 14 September 1944.

32 The course was run by Tierentiew and the lecturers Małgin and Czernov. The participants were paid 300 crowns per month.

35
Switzerland

Gill Bennett

A reference has been found to Roman Malinowski, a Polish Consular officer formerly in Leipzig, living in Basle in December 1939-April 1940. He was assisted by Ratajczyk, Józef Motłoch and Anton Wiliński, Following German penetration of this organisation, Ratajczyk and Wilinski were arrested.

In September 1944, an SLC minute noted that the Polish authorities in London were seeking assistance for two Polish Intelligence officers to travel from Switzerland to France: Maj. Zdzisław Piątkiewicz (Biz) and Lt-Col. Marian Romeyko (Mak).

36
Switzerland

Andrzej Przewoźnik

The Polish communication cells in Switzerland were established in 1940, on the initiative of the then Home Army Commander-in-Chief, Gen. Kazimierz Sosnkowski. The first such cell, called 'S'[1] based on the Military Attaché's office at the Polish Legation in Berne, began its work In August 1940. From its inception it was run by Lt-Col. Bronisław Noel ('Antoni Kobelin'), the Polish Military Attaché in Switzerland. The cell established courier links with Hungary (Base 'Romek'), Yugoslavia (Cell 'Sława') and with Portugal, as well as setting up contacts with the Vatican. To a large degree, its activities were framed on the British diplomatic and intelligence services, operating in Switzerland. Important support was received from PGS's II Bureau Station there, run by Maj. Szczęsny Chajnacki ('Darek' 'Lubiewa').[2]

The neutrality of Swiss territory was conducive for comparative intelligence gathering. This explains why the personnel of the cell established there by the VI Bureau, PGS, consisted of highly qualified, long-standing intelligence officers. The geographical position of Switzerland meant that the cell became an important intermediary in many secret intelligence and political operations and provided much high-quality information.

On 7 May 1942 the command over all the agencies subordinated to Cell 'S' was taken over by Maj. Choynacki, who combined his work as the Polish Deputy Consul at the Legation in Berne with directing the Intelligence Station. Maj. Choynacki took over from Lt-Col. Noel 'Kobelin', who was recalled to London. His closest co-worker and Deputy was Maj. Franciszek Brzeziński 'Brzoza' ('Buk'), an officer of the II Bureau, who until war broke out was a Polish Intelligence agent in Germany.

Organisational changes required by the VI Bureau, PGS, were introduced in 1943. Cell 'S' was transformed into the communications Base called 'Wera'. With increased responsibilities it required more personnel, which enabled 'Wera' to work on several issues at the same time. Information delivered by couriers from Poland was passed via radio to HQ in London. Permanent communications with Lisbon Station was achieved due to diplomatic courier network of the British, Hungarian and Polish services, and through the intelligence network built up by the II Bureau, PGS. In the second half of 1943, 'Wera' succeeded in establishing a courier route through France to Spain. With the assistance of Hungarian diplomats, it also constructed a permanent link to Base 'Liszt' in Budapest. As a result, in 1943 'Wera' had at its disposal Cell 'Szafa' and 13 personnel: 7 officers and 6 civilian officials.[3]

The work load of the II Bureau's Station in Berne was passed on directly to PGS in London. It consisted of numerous reports on the armaments industry and the economy in Germany. These reports were then passed on to the British Intelligence. On the basis of available archival documents, it is possible to state that the reports contained additional information on the French and Italian arms industry serving the military needs of the Third Reich: data on the production volumes of specific branches of industry, or particular plants, new designs and on technological improvements being introduced to German weapons.

The Station also provided reports on the Swiss-German co-operation in arms production and on the political situation in this part of Europe. Through the intermediary of 'Wera' and of the II Bureau Station, the Poles had access to secret talks between the Hungarians on one side and the British and Americans on the other. Such talks were held in Lisbon and Switzerland, ostensibly on participation in the war by Hungary – but in reality on the possibility of them joining the Allies. Using the advantage of good Polish-Hungarian relations, the Poles acted as intermediaries, supporting the aspirations of the Hungarians.

The setback, which took place in the spring of 1944 in the Home Army GHQ's Foreign Communications Department, had its impact on 'Wera', too. As a result of 'Jarach's' provocation, the Germans had arrested the entire network leading to 'Janka' in Paris, through the 'Regina' cell in Alsace. The communications throughout the Swiss-French border region also suffered. As a result, the communication with France were conducted through the route build up by the II Bureau, which led via Belfort and Montbeliard in France, to Porrentruy in Switzerland.[4]

For a time, the courier routes to France were paralysed. In this situation, the Chief of the II Bureau's Station, Lt. Stanisław Appenzeller 'Krucz', managed to obtain permission from the Swiss authorities to set up a radio station near Les Sairains, in the Jura plateau in north-west Switzerland. Having their own, fully independent radio station enabled the m to maintain direct communications with London, as well as with Lisbon and Budapest, in this difficult periods.[5]

In the second half of 1944, there were more organisational staff changes in 'Wera–Panorama'. On 18 September 1944 Maj. Bronisław de Ville 'Ludwik'[6] became the Chief of 'Panorama', replacing 'Lubiewa'. There were also changes in the II Bureau Station in Berne itself. Lt. Appenzeller 'Krucz', the Chief of the 'Porrentruy' Cell in Lausanne, was replaced by Maj. Stanisław Młodzianowski 'Dąbrowa' ('Serge'), who previously managed the 'Atlas' Post in Geneva.

One of the last operations undertaken by 'Panorama' was the transfer of a courier from Poland, Jan Nowak (Zdzisław Jeziorański) 'Zych' with his wife, Zofia Wolska 'Greta'.[7]

The Communications Base in Berne ended its operations in the spring of 1945.

Notes

1 The cell, later Communications Base, was known, in turn, as 'S', 'Wera' and 'Panorama'. For its personnel, see: T. Dubicki, *Bazy wojskowej łączności zagranicznej ZWZ-AK w latach 1939–1945* (*Military Foreign Communication Bases, 1939–1945*), Częstochowa 2000, pp. 165–167.
2 CA MSW, the VI Bureau, PGS, sign 295/167-VI/65, k. 109.
3 CA MSW, the VI Bureau, PGS, sign 295-1/11, Establishment of Military Communications with Homeland Bases and Cells and Personnel Changes for 1943, as of 15 February 1944.
4 An account by A. Smulikowski 'Kotwicz' (in the collection of A. Przewoźnik). Smulikowski was an employee of the Home Army GHQ's Foreign Communications Bureau, and later, from 1942, of the 'Wera' Base in Switzerland.
5 An account by A. Smulikowski (in the collection of A. Przewoźnik).
6 SPP, Personnel files of Bronisław de Ville.
7 Jan Nowak, *Kurier z Warszawy* (*Courier from Warsaw*), Warsaw 2000, pp. 387–411.

37
Latin America

Gill Bennett

Only a few documents have been found relating to Polish Intelligence activities in Latin America. These refer to Polish agents in Uruguay, Argentina, Brazil and Mexico. As elsewhere, there was some confusion on both sides between competing Intelligence activities undertaken by the Poles. In February 1941 Col. Tokarz was referred to both as chief of Polish Counter-Intelligence (by A4 section of SIS), and as chief of the Polish II Bureau (by Col. Gano, in conversation with a member of A4). In both cases the question at issue was a possible contact between Lt-Col. Fabiszewski, Polish representative (of either the II Bureau or Counter Espionage) in Buenos Aires, and British representatives there.

In April 1942, an SIS representative in Montevideo reported that a local Polish Intelligence representative had 'received instructions from his chief to work closely with us and give us all important information which he obtains from his agents in Argentine, Uruguay, Brazil and Chile when his organisation in last named country is functioning'. The message also referred to another Polish agent in Uruguay, Dr. R. Ciechanow, and to a Polish agent in Rio de Janeiro, J. Szulc or Shultz, also known as Jankowski.

One document only survives concerning Polish activities in Mexico. It refers to the Polish Military Attaché, Maj. Stefan Dobrowolski, who was 'also in charge of Intelligence'. Maj. Dobrowolski's relationship with his British colleagues was cordial, and they were 'inclined to trust him on all matters except those pertaining to USSR activities'.

38
North and South America

Jan Stanisław Ciechanowski

Polish Intelligence was not very active in the Americas until 1941. In the summer of that year it was decided to establish Station 'Estezet' in New York, with the cover provided by the Polish Consulate General. Between 1941 and 1945, the Consul General was Sylwin Strakacz, formerly personal secretary to Ignacy Jan Paderewski, and the Station's Chief was Lt-Col. Ludwik Lucjan Sadowski ('Sadwik'), officially the Counsellor.[1] The Station covered the US, Canada, Brazil, Argentina and, indirectly, Peru, Bolivia, Chile, Paraguay and Uruguay.[2] Its tasks included reporting on the military and political situation, the Polish community agitations and penetration of Communists, with particular attention to attitudes towards the US, Canada and Polish issues; also the stage of development and attitude of Ukrainian associations and the press published by the national minorities (Polish, German, Ukrainian, Czech, Slovak, Lithuanian and Jewish).[3] By comparison with other Polish Intelligence networks, Station 'Estezet' had more of a counter-intelligence brief.

The co-operation of Polish and American Intelligence services began in the summer of 1941, when Maj. Jan Henryk Żychoń, then Chief of the II Bureau of PGS,[4] visited the US and held talks with Col. (later General) William J. Donovan, who from 11 July was the Coordinator of Information. Donovan was trusted by President Franklin Delano Roosevelt, with whom he was in regular contact, and was charged with building an effective American intelligence system. The establishment of Station 'Estezet' was agreed in August, and on 10 August 1941 the two officers signed a secret initial agreement on intelligence co-operation between the Polish and American special services. The agreement also provided for a regular exchange of documents and information relating to the conduct of the war. They also agreed to appoint liaison officers; on the Polish side this role was played by Lt-Col. Sadowski.

In October 1941 the Poles began to supply the Americans with various materials, which were considered to be valuable from the very beginning.[5]

American Intelligence cells, or their representatives, co-operated with their Polish colleagues, especially in North America, the Soviet Union and in Portugal.[6] Polish Intelligence contemplated the creation of separate Polish-American cells, which would be completely independent from both countries' national missions,[7] but this idea was not put into practice.

The material delivered to the Americans concerned mainly the identification and positioning of Axis armies, military transports, the navy, war industry, the air force, the results of air raids and enemy losses and morale. Although the planned co-operation was to consist of an exchange of information, in practice it was the Poles who supplied intelligence to the Americans. In return, the Polish Government in Exile hoped to benefit primarily in political terms. In the field, it was expected that the two partners would provide each other with technical support, in line with their respective abilities. In practice, assistance meant American communications support in those areas, where the Poles conducted the intelligence work.[8]

A breakthrough in the development of American Intelligence, and in their co-operation with the Poles, came after the Americans joined the war, following the Japanese attack on Pearl Harbor on 7 December 1941. Only five days later Sadowski suggested to Donovan that the Intelligence co-operation, which for all practical purposes had been initiated in October, be broadened and made closer. On American proposals, the Poles started to supply them with information on the Soviet Union and various issues connected with the impact the Soviets were making.[9] From March 1942, the materials reaching Donovan, passed through a special liaison office in New York chiefed by Allen Dulles, who later was to acquire some notoriety. The Poles maintained a working relationship with him and his successors, tackling more important issues with the Co-ordinator of American Special Services. In the spring of that year, once Donovan's organisation became more robust, co-operation between the two partners became broader. The Office of Strategic Services (OSS), chiefed by Donovan, was established in 13 June 1942.[10]

At the time the Americans were receiving large amounts of comprehensive material requested by them. The Poles shared with their American partners their experiences on methods of technical exploitation of information, as used at PGS. In Washington this knowledge was made available to the chiefs of individual units of the initially weak – in 'Sadwik's' opinion – research department of OSS,[11] with whom periodic conferences were also held. Official contact between the Polish Station and the Military Intelligence Division (G-2) was finally inaugurated in September 1942. Previously, Donovan wished to limit the contacts between the Poles and the US Military Intelligence, although he tolerated secret liaison with the MID, which begun after the American visit of Col. Leon Żółtek-Mitkiewicz, Deputy Chief of PGS.[12] OSS and MID were provided with specific intelligence material. In January 1942 Col. Gustav B. Guenther informed Mitkiewicz that all the documents relayed to G-2 were very useful and contained important information.[13]

Until 1943, the Chief of Station 'Estezet' carried the sole responsibility for co-operation with OSS, Military Intelligence Division (G-2), Naval Intelligence and the Federal Bureau of Investigation – that is, for the transmission to the Americans of intelligence obtained by his agents or passed on from HQ. The Chief of Station was the only representative of the Chief of the II Bureau in the Americas and the liaison officer with the organisation chiefed by Col. Donovan. One of his tasks was to make sure that the Americans presented their assessments of the material received and of intelligence assignments carried out.[14]

The Station head maintained contact with the FBI through the intermediary of OSS or directly. Co-operation with this security institution, begun towards the end of 1941, was not extensive. The Polish side provided the Americans with counter-intelligence material on Americans of Ukrainian and German descent, as well as pro-Nazi White Russians living in the eastern states. On this last matter, the Station Chief co-operated with Percy E. Foxworth, the FBI chief in New York.[15]

As far as South America was concerned, here, too, the co-operation between the II Bureau and the FBI was not extensive, though the Federal Bureau of Investigation was responsible for Intelligence activity there. In the opinion of Station 'Estezet', the reason was the negative attitude of the State Department, whose relations with OSS were strained.[16] A major part of the intelligence provided to the FBI from South America related to the Germans in Argentina.

Polish material was also provided to the New York office of the Foreign Economic Administration (FEA). This was the only American institution, which was supplied with material directly by Maj. Marian Stanisław Chodacki, from 1943 Chief of the Independent Intelligence Cell 'Estezet', and not by Col. Mitkiewicz's Mission in Washington. The FEA was particularly interested in information on the German economy.[17]

The number of reports passed on to the Americans was very large, as illustrated in the table below.[18] Particularly noteworthy is the quantity of information supplied in the second half of 1943 and the increasing volume of material intended for the G-2 at the expense of OSS.

In Washington, Polish Intelligence was regarded as the best among all Allied Services. The Americans also preferred the more cautious Polish analyses to, in their opinion, overly optimistic studies by the British, especially as regards the Soviet Union.[19] In a letter of 8 October 1942 Col. Ivan D. Yeaton, Chief of the Eastern Europe Section of American G-2, declared that by 'providing reliable and topical information, the Polish II Bureau reinforces the position of the American Chiefs of Staff to a considerable degree'. On 20 December 1942 General Hayes A. Kroner, Deputy Chief of Military Intelligence Division, told Gen. Władysław Sikorski: 'The Polish Army has the best intelligence in the world. Its value for us is beyond estimation. Regretfully there is little we can offer in return'. And in a letter of 21 October of that year, Gen. Donovan wrote: 'II Bureau reports are of immense value to the (US) Chiefs of Staff. They make one of the most important contributions that we receive'.[20] In early January 1943, during his visit to the United States, the Polish Commander-in-Chief, General Sikorski, was told by Generals Strong and Kroner that they were greatly interested in profiting further from the accomplishments of Polish Intelligence. In return, the Americans were to support the Poles in obtaining communications equipment. Another indication of the American appreciation for the importance of Polish intelligence activity was the letter by Earl Brennan (Italian Section OSS), who wrote to Maj. Jędrzejewski: 'I can say frankly that the Polish reports are at present among the very best intelligence from Italy which comes over my desk. I have been particularly impressed with the concrete, highly specific nature of the information, and the reports are obviously made by an agent or agents of keen ability'.[21] In 1944 R. H. Scannell, an FEA Intelligence officer, wrote to the Chief of 'Estezet': '[...] the Polish Intelligence reports are considered among the most useful of the many varieties of intelligence received by the Economic Intelligence Division'.[22] Polish Intelligence was considered to be the best source of information for the Chiefs of Staff.[23]

Table 3: Intelligence supplied by II Bureau of PGS to US intelligence organs during WW II

Period	Number of reports supplied	Notes
1 October 1941–30 June 1942	610	Until 16 September 1942, 74% of the information, studies and reports was supplied to OSS, 19% to G-2, 4% to FBI, 2% to Psychological Warfare Branch and 1% to Naval Intelligence Service. 176 were on Germany, 80 – France 54 – North Africa, 38 – Russia, 29 – Italy, and 74 – other states.
1 July 1942–30 June 1943	6,041	of which 3,195 were delivered *via* 'Estezet'
1 July–30 December 1943	9,761	
1 January–30 June 1944	6,006	of which 3 002 reports for OSS, 2,302 for G-2 and 702 for NIS.
1 July–31 December 1944	6,062	of which 1,832 reports for OSS, 124 for G-2 and 1,106 for NIS.
1 January–15 February 1945	869	of which 88 items for OSS, 720 for G-2 and 61 for NIS.
16 February–May 1945	?	

Source: prepared by the author on the basis of IPMS, A. XII. 24/37 and 56, reports on the activity of Intelligence Department of the II Bureau, PGS.
Notes:
1. This is an incomplete list. Various reports contain different figures.
2. In addition to the material supplied by Station 'Estezet', a considerable number of reports were provided to American attachés in London, who, in turn, passed these over to the OSS.
3. The US Chiefs of Staff provided the Poles, *via* Col. Mitkiewicz's office, with monthly and half-yearly assessments of information.

Polish-American Intelligence co-operation was reflected in uneasy relationship with SIS. During a typical conversation held in October 1942 between Lt. Eugeniusz Piotrowski ('Robert'), an officer of Station 'Estezet', and Col. Yeaton, the latter complained that the British wished to preserve their monopoly in intelligence work and that the War Office provided them with subjective and outdated information. On this score, relations between London and Washington were tense. Moreover, Col. Yeaton suspected the British of passing on information originating from PGS, but presented as their own. The British actually did supply the Americans with Polish reports, which the Americans then made available to the Poles as coming from a reliable London source (sic!). 'Robert' concluded that by providing the Americans with valuable information, the II Bureau contributed to the reinforcement of their position *vis à vis* the British.[24]

A thorough reorganisation of Polish Intelligence networks in the Americas took place in 1943, in the aftermath of a visit by the Polish Commander-in-Chief, Gen. Sikorski, to the US. On 4 January 1943 by mutual consent a high-ranking liaison officer to the Combined Chiefs of Staff (CCS), with the rank of Deputy Chief of PGS was appointed.[25] On 11 February 1943 Col. Mitkiewicz, the former Chief of the II Bureau (between 1940 and 1941, and the Deputy Commander of the 1st Armoured Division) was appointed to this post. His tasks included co-operation with the US Army Staff and the CCS, exchanging information about the enemy, presenting Polish reports on operational issues (particularly related to Poland), planning proposals for enemy surrender and the organisation of post-war security. Informing the relevant American planning bodies about the Polish position with regard to the war aims (together with the Polish Ambassador), dealing with the material needs of Poland and the Polish Army in the East (APW), and carrying out tasks assigned to him by the Commander-in-Chief or the Chief of Staff. Col. Mitkiewicz also co-ordinated the work of the Military, Air and Naval Attachés and the Chief of the Station, and later that of the Independent Intelligence Station 'Estezet', which he supervised only in administrative matters. This led to the considerable independence of 'Estezet' in relation to the Deputy Chief of PGS.[26]

From the time when Col. Mitkiewicz took over the new post, it was his office that supplied the Americans with intelligence.[27] His obligations towards the II Bureau, PGS, included passing on information about the enemy, obtained from the Americans, derived from press surveys or from other sources; assessments of the American internal situation in the form of monthly reports, which were supplemented by the reports prepared by the attachés. For his part, Chief of the II Bureau informed Mitkiewicz in detail about the most important issues associated with Polish Intelligence.[28]

The Chief of 'Estezet' prepared a plan for the reorganisation of Polish Intelligence field cells in both Americas. In accordance with the suggestions made by HQ, Lt-Col. Sadowski initiated the closure of cells in the US, but did not change those in Canada and in South America. The 'Estezet' Station was finally closed on 31 August 1943. Having completed the changes, Sadowski was recalled to HQ, which thought his work to be very good. In 1944, after brief service in the Records and Studies Department of the II Bureau, PGS,[29] he was appointed Chief of Station 'T'. The Independent Intelligence Cell 'Estezet', newly organised on 1 September in New York, acted, as did its predecessor, under cover, within the Polish Consulate General, and was a lower-rank intelligence unit. From the end of 1943 it was chiefed by Maj. Marian Stanisław Chodacki ('Maracz'), who between 1936 and 1939 was the Polish Commissioner General in Danzig.[30] As did its previous incarnation, the unit maintained contact with HQ in London and with its subordinate cells in Rio de Janeiro and Buenos Aires by radio, coded dispatches sent by post, and by couriers – its own, British and American.[31]

As part of the reform, the cells previously controlled by Station 'Estezet' within the United States were closed. Cell 'Mandan' in Detroit, chiefed by Wacław Żarski ('Peowiak'), a Consulate employee,[32] was closed on 31st March 1943. The 'Magellan' in Pittsburgh, managed by Dr. Jan Kasprzak ('Magellan', 'Jan Rembowski'), whose contacts with Slavic communities were regarded as extremely useful and were highly praised,[33] was also closed. Cell 'Mackenzie', ran in Buffalo by Marian Wójcik ('Ojciec'), was closed on 31 March 1943, following its chief's departure for New York and new duties. On 31 March 1943 Janusz Stamirowski ('Nowakowski'), Chief of the 'Mackay' in Chicago, was discharged and re-appointed chief of the local Polish Information Centre, which led to the closure of the intelligence cell. Lt. Jerzy Piotrowski ('Peters'), Chief of Cell 'Magog' in Washington, who was particularly close to the Americans, was transferred to Col. Mitkiewicz's office after the latter's arrival in the American capital.[34] The 'Magdalen' Cell in New York, chiefed by Zygmunt Krosnowski ('Tabasz'), was closed in the first half of 1943, as was 'Madame' in Washington, run by Edward Weintal ('Karpiński', agent no. 5015), a 'Foreign Correspondence' journalist.[35]

Until its re-organisation, Station 'Estezet' supervised the following Intelligence Cells: 'Manchester' in Ottawa, 'Sabanilla' in Rio de Janeiro and 'Salvador' in Buenos Aires. The reform raised the rank of the 'Manchester' mission to that of an Independent Intelligence Cell, which became equivalent to 'Estezet'. 'Manchester', established on 15 August 1942, functioned at the office of Polish Military Attaché in Ottawa, and until the following year was controlled by 'Estezet'. The area of its activity was Canada and a small part of the US. Its chief, Capt. (Retired) Alfred Birkenmayer ('Burmistrz'), acted under the cover of a contract official of the Polish Attaché's office.[36] The basic tasks of the cell included the observation of organisations, groups and persons acting to the detriment of the Polish State, in particular of Ukrainians, and to a lesser degree Germans, the investigation of Soviet and communist influence, observing Polish communities, and acting as intermediary in passing over of mail from 'Estezet' to the London HQ. Its work was assessed as highly favourably. As a principle they decided not to establish a network of agents, but to rely on personal contacts.[37] When at the beginning of 1944

Maj. Jan Henryk Żychoń handed over the duties of Chief of the Intelligence Department of II Bureau to Maj. Witold Langenfeld, he declared that the Canadian station was important due to Soviet penetration, the role played by Canadian Ukrainians, and the expansion of relations with Canadian military authorities.[38]

Brazil as well as Argentina were places where British and German influences intersected. The Abwehr was particularly active in neutral Brazil, where there were many German émigrés and developed commercial co-operation with Germany. The country played an important role in controlling the South Atlantic and the seas between Africa, Europe and South America. German agents even planned coups d'état in Brazil, Argentina and Chile by exploiting the considerable popularity of fascist ideas in the largest Latin American states – and Germany made large-scale purchases of South American food and raw material for its war industry.

The reorganisation carried out in 1943 retained the 'Sabanilla' and 'Salvador' intelligence cells, which continued to be supervised by 'Estezet', although no longer by the Station, but by the Independent Intelligence Cell. Cell 'Sabanilla' in Rio de Janeiro was originally headed by Jan Schulz (vel Szulc, 'Jankowski', agent no. 5153),[39] who at the beginning of 1943 was replaced by Lt. Bohdan Pawłowicz ('Pedro'),[40] officially the deputy Military Attaché in Rio de Janeiro.[41] A network of informants was organised in Sao Paulo and the port of Santos, where communist and German influences were strong. Intelligence work was conducted also in the states of Santa Catalina and Rio Grande do Sul and in the western part of Parana, to a large measure upon the basis of the local Polish community. Co-operation with the British and the Americans, who were supplied with Polish Counter-intelligence reports (which was also the case throughout the Americas), was good. As a rule, it took place upon the Allies' request and consisted primarily of local Counter-intelligence assessment regarding indicated persons or groups.[42] 'Sabanilla's' activities embraced also Brazil, Peru and Bolivia. It reported to the 'Salta' cell, which was also located in the Brazilian capital and was chiefed with excellent results by the celebrated Polish journalist and publicist Konrad Wrzos ('Spryciarz', agent no. 1315), acting under the cover of the chief of the press bureau.[43] From the summer of 1944, on the basis of an agreement between Maj. Chodacki and Lt-Col. Stanisław Kara, the Polish Military Attaché in Rio de Janeiro and previously Chief of Station 'P' in Lisbon, the latter supervised Cell 'Sabanilla'.[44]

Cell 'P. A.', later known as 'Salvador', was formally established in Buenos Aires on 1 January 1942. At first it reported to Station 'Estezet', and later to the Independent Intelligence Cell. Its Chief, Lt-Col. Stefan Fabiszewski ('Steffall'), worked at the Polish Legation in Buenos Aires, and was later replaced by Lt. Ludwik Karol Lubicz-Orłowski ('Piotr').[45] The Cell covered all of South America, with the exception of Ecuador, Colombia and Venezuela. Most of its attention was concentrated on Argentina, Brazil, Chile and Uruguay, and to a lesser degree on Paraguay. In the most important issues 'P. A.' maintained contact with HQ via the radio station in the Legation, though 'Estezet' would have been copied on the traffic. In more routine matters, radio contact was maintained with 'Estezet', and the cell also used British and American couriers, and airmail for press and general material.

One of the basic tasks of the cell, as was the case with other Polish Intelligence networks in both Americas, was local co-operation with representatives of the US and British Intelligence and Counter-intelligence, who received all-important political, military, economic and Counter-intelligence information. The main task of the cell was the observation of the economic and war potential of Latin American countries in view of German influences in these countries. The greatest importance was attached to relations between Argentina and the Third Reich.[46] The work conducted by the cell was evaluated by 'Estezet' as good.

Intelligence Cell 'Salvador', in turn, supervised the smaller cells: 'Sinalca' in Santiago de Chile, 'Sambrerette' in Montevideo (Uruguay), 'San Antonio' in Buenos Aires and 'San Feli' in Asunción (Paraguay). The first of these, chiefed by Wiktor Stanisławski ('Rolski', agent no. 5154) was seen as weak, and at the end of 1943 it was decided to close it. 'Sambrerette', shut down at the end of 1943, was run by Józef Makowski ('Legun', agent no. 5157), the Polish Honorary Consul in Montevideo. 'San Antonio', chiefed by Dr. Roman Czesław Ciechanow ('Korsak', agent no. 5152), was closed at the end of 1942. Ludwik Krotoszyński ('Łodzianin', agent no. 5160), Chief of the fourth cell (shut down at the end of 1943), had excellent contacts with the local politicians; communications difficulties resulted from the fact that the British did not have an Intelligence representative in Asuncion.[47] In 1944 Maj. Żychoń advised Maj. Langenfeld, (his successor) to retain the South American cells at the very least to the end of the war, since they rendered considerable service to the local American and British Intelligence at a time when the role played by Latin American states, especially Brazil, grew markedly.[48]

In Mexico, Polish Intelligence was represented by Navy Lt. Jacek Rewkiewicz. A single-person Intelligence Cell 'Mexico' worked in its capital from the second half of 1944; it was supervised by the Independent Intelligence Cell 'Estezet' and chiefed by Maj. Zdzisław Żórawski, who previously worked for Polish Intelligence on the Iberian Peninsula (see *The Iberian Peninsula*), under the cover of a press agency bureau chief. His assignment involved reporting on the Soviet penetration and anti-Polish activity in Mexico.[49]

Table 4: Structure of Polish Intelligence Cells in the Americas from mid-1941 to mid-1943

Posts	Officers	Civilians	Agents	Informants
Station 'Estezet'	2	At least 5	13 (to May 1942); 19 (to September 1943); total: 23 persons.	–
Intelligence Cell 'Manchester'	1	2	–	21
Intelligence Cell 'Sabanilla'	–	–	1 (Chief of Cell, Intelligence Agent of Cell 'Salvador') + 8	–
Cell 'Salta'	–	–	1 (Chief of Cell) + 8	–
Intelligence Cell 'Salvador'	1	–	17	–
Cell 'Sambrerette'	–	–	1 (Chief of Cell)	–
Cell 'San Antonio'	–	–	1 (Chief of Cell)	–
Cell 'San Feli'	–	–	1 (Chief of Cell)	–
Cell 'Sinalca'	–	–	1 (Chief of Cell)	–
Intelligence Cell 'Magdalen'	–	1	–	–
Intelligence Cell 'Mackenzie'	–	1	–	–
Intelligence Cell 'Mackay'	–	1	11 (to Sept. 1943); 8 (Oct. 1943 to mid 44, agents taken over after the closure of the Cell); total: 11 persons.	–
Intelligence Cell 'Magog'	1	–	–	–
Intelligence Cell 'Magellan'	–	1	9 (to end of 1942); 7 (Jan.-Sept. 1943); total: 9 persons.	–
Intelligence Cell 'Madame'	–	–	1 (Chief of Cell)	–
Intelligence Cell 'Mandan'	–	2	–	–

Source: prepared by the author on the basis of IPMS documentation (II Bureau), CAW (VI Bureau) documentation and R. Świętek, *W służbie (In the Service)*, op. cit.

Table 5: Structure of Polish Intelligence Cells in the Americas from the second half 1943 (re-organisation) to the summer of 1945

Posts	Officers	Civilians	Agents	Informants
Bureau of Special Services to the Commander-in-Chief	7; 8 (from March 1944)	11	–	–
Independent Intelligence Station 'Estezet'	2	2; 3 (from 44)	4; 2 (from the first half of 44); 0 (second half of 44)	2 occasional unpaid informants (former agents, from mid-44)
Independent Intelligence Station 'Manchester'	1	2	–	21; 22 (from the first half of 44)
Independent Intelligence Station 'Sabanilla'	1	0; 2 (from second half of 44)	11	–
Cell 'Salta'	–	–	1 (Chief of Cell) + 8	–
Intelligence Cell 'Salvador'	1	0; 1 (from 44)	5	2 (former agents)
Intelligence Cell 'Meksyk'	–	1	–	–
Independent Intelligence Cell 'Siła'	–	4 (?)	–	–
Independent Intelligence Cell 'Savoy'	1	–	–	–

Source: prepared by the author on the basis of IPMS documentation (II Bureau), CAW (VI Bureau) documentation and R. Świętek, *W służbie (In the Service)*, op. cit.

Notes:
1. The Bureau of Special Services to the Commander-in-Chief dealt with Intelligence as only a part of its duties.
2. The 'Siła' and 'Savoy' Independent Intelligence Cells were being set up from February to July 1945.
3. Unwitting informants were not taken into consideration.
4. All data are estimates.

The Polish II Bureau was also by tradition responsible for the military attachés accredited to Polish diplomatic missions in the Americas. From 25 April 1941, the Military Attaché in Washington was Col. Włodzimierz Onacewicz, particularly highly regarded by Naval Intelligence for his reports on the US Navy and merchant shipping and on the operations in the Pacific. His reports were considered the best amongst the material supplied by military attachés.[50] Onacewicz was also highly praised by HQ and Col. Mitkiewicz.[51] Col. Onacewicz was in contact exclusively with the MID, which he supplied with 'assessments of the general situation', sent periodically *via* HQ; he also took part in discussions and conferences, using for this purpose material obtained from the Chief of the Cell 'Estezet'.

Following the reform of Polish Intelligence in the Americas, the main burden of representing PGS fell on Col. Mitkiewicz, who at the turn of November 1943 warned about the threat of complications involving the representation of PGS in CCS in view of the possible creation of a British-American-Soviet Staff. This body, placed in London, was to be an extension of CCS. On the other hand should the Council of Four be established, a similar joint staff would have been set up in Washington. Mitkiewicz drew attention to the fact that in such a situation it would be better to make him the chief of the Polish Military Mission to the US. Otherwise, due to complex Polish-Soviet relations, there was a risk that he might be ignored as the official liaison officer to CSS: 'The Americans are very interested in news from Russia, principally in an objective assessment of the current Soviet war potential. They would like to know not only what is supplied to them by their own Military Mission in Moscow and by Soviet propaganda, but the objective truth. In one of the conversations held with a G.2 representative, I heard that several Polish Intelligence officers would accomplish much more than 200 members of the British-American Military Mission in Moscow. Emphasis was placed on our objectivism in relaying news from Russia.' At the time G-2 intended to end the intermediary role played by the American Military Attaché accredited to the Polish Government in London. From that point, all intelligence was to pass through the office of Col. Mitkiewicz in Washington. In the opinion of the Deputy Chief of Staff, this would have been a considerable improvement.[52]

The year 1945 brought decisions, which were to ensure a Polish Intelligence presence in South America after the war. The Independent Intelligence Cell 'Siła' in Rio de Janeiro, headed by Jerzy Chmielewski, was opened on 15 February 1945 under the cover of a commercial enterprise – a trade firm for Latin America, based on foreign representatives. Its task was to cover the whole region with a network of agents in order to gather long-term economic and political information. The Cell was to pay attention to the possibility of trade between Poland and Latin American countries, the fluctuation of prices and the demand for raw materials of interest to Polish buyers, as well as to outside economic penetration in the region.

During the first, organisational phase, that was to last for six months 'Siła' was to have cells in Buenos Aires, Montevideo and Sao Paulo, and was to be supervised directly by the Information and II Bureau of PGS. Four Polish Intelligence agents, who were to begin normal trade activities based on a returnable loan, were sent from Great Britain.[53] In 1945, the costs of setting up the Cell and its subsidiary units, together with the salaries of its Chief and his assistant, amounted to £300, £960 and £600, respectively. The establishment of 'Siła' was closely connected with a plan for creating an information network (S.I.A.Ł) independent of all official

27. Capt. Bronisław Eliaszewicz (1897–1958?), Chief of the "Tandara" Intelligence Cell No. 1 in Bucharest.

28. Maj. Edmund Piechowiak (born in 1896), Chief of the "Balk." Intelligence Station in Istanbul from 1943.

29. Lt. Mikołaj Rostworowski (born in 1914), officer of the "M", Intelligence station in Madrid.

30. Maj. Mieczysław Jaworski (1897–1949) in the years 1942–1944 Head of the Central Section of the Department of the II Bureau of the General Staff in London.

32. Maj. Bolesław Ziemiański
(1900–1976), Chief of the "Tulsa"
Intelligence Cell No. 2 in Bucharest of
the "T" Station (1941–1943).

31. Lt-Col. Stanisław Kara (1893–1955),
Chief of the "P" Station in Lisbon and a
liaison officer with the Home Army
(1940–1944).

33. Maj. Michał Rybikowski (1900–1991), Chief of Intelligence Station "L" and "SKN" in Stockholm.

34. Lt. Stefan Ignaszak (1911–2005), "Cichociemny" officer of the Home Army Intelligence responsible for reconnaissance of Peenemünde.

35. V-1 and V-2 weapon production facilities at Nordhausen.

36. Col. Kamizierz Iranek-Osmecki (1987–1984), Chief of Intelligence GHQ Polish Home Army (second from right) at a meeting with Maj. Alfons Kotowski and Lt. Stanisław Jankowski on 1 August 1944, on the day the Warsaw Uprising was launched.

37. Maj. Henryk Schmidt, Chief of the counter-espionage cell of the "Estezet" Station in New York (1941–1943), intelligence officer of the "Estezet" Independent Intelligence Cell (1943–1945).

38. Maj. Marian Stanisław Chodacki (1898–1975), Chief of the "Estezet" Independent Intelligence Cell in New York, Polish liaison officer with OSS (1943–1945).

39. Col. Stanisław Rostworoski (1888–1944), Commandant ZWZ-AK (union of Armed Struggle – Home Army) Liaison Bases in Bucharest (1939–1940) and Budapest (1941–1942) responsible for communications with occupied Poland.

representatives of the Polish Government or the Army. The information network was to serve the purpose of long-term intelligence penetration of the area. The annual cost of S.I.A.Ł. was to exceed 8 000 US dollars. The funds for the network were to be transferred by the Chief of Information and the II Bureau, PGS, so as not to leave any traces in the accounts.

In addition to 'Siła', the Poles established another 'future-oriented' cell, known as the Independent Intelligence Cell 'Savoy',[54] in New York. Initially, 'Savoy' was also expected to act under the cover of a commercial enterprise, and to begin with, with a single operative. Initially its network of agents was to cover North America, and in the future also Europe, where it was planned to locate 'trade branches' in enemy countries or those which were of interest to the Polish state for other reasons. Until the anticipated expansion of the cell, its main task was to gather information about moods prevailing in the Polish community. The budget for 1945 was temporarily put at 2,000 US dollars. The Chief of Cell was to be Lt. Col. Karol Piasecki.[55]

At this time, the importance of Polish affairs in the US had diminished. Between 1944 and 1945, Col. Mitkiewicz informed HQ about the growing popularity of the Soviet Union among the American establishment at the expense of Polish interests. He warned about support for the idea of the Curzon Line, the increased activity of the Communists, who portrayed the Polish Government in Exile as reactionary and fascist, and of the tendency to compare the attitude of the Soviet Union towards small Central European countries to the relations between the US and Latin American states.[56] Since the ultimate Allied decision was to hand over Poland to the Soviet sphere of influence, on 4 July 1945 it was decided to reduce the number of officers in Cell 'Estezet', thus limiting its liaison functions to a minimum. As was the case with other intelligence stations, 'Estezet', too, was to remain at the disposal of HQ or, after its possible closure, to act as the embryo of a Polish information service 'independent of Warsaw'.[57] Two days later Washington withdrew its official recognition of the Polish Government in London, and recognised the communist-dominated Government in Warsaw as the sole representative of the Polish state. In July and August 1945, PGS decided to close 'Estezet'.[58] Col. Mitkiewicz represented PGS in the United States until August 1945, when he completed the closure of his Bureau.

The Polish Ministry of Internal Affairs had an intelligence service of its own in the Americas. In July 1941 the Ministry and the II Bureau, PGS, signed a written agreement providing that all anti-sabotage, anti-diversion as well as any diversion and terror, conceived as reprisals against the Germans for their bestial occupation of Poland, were to be conducted by the Ministry as part of Continental Action. The agreement was a reaction to the organisation of the New York-based 'Estezet'. Consequently, PGS halted the organisation of terrorist actions in South America, previously initiated by the Chief of the II Bureau, as well as all anti-sabotage and anti-diversion activities in North America. Nonetheless, PGS claimed that the Ministry's campaign did not produce results until the spring of 1942.

Meanwhile, the Polish authorities in London received categorical demands from the Commander-in-Chief of the Home Army and the Government Delegate for Poland to 'apply physical reprisals in retaliation for the bestial acts committed in Poland' in areas inhabited by the Germans. During his visit to the United States at the end of March 1942, the Commander-in-Chief, upon American request, issued an order that the II Bureau was to take over 'special duties', that is Continental Action, in the USA and Canada. This job was to be entrusted to Cell 'Estezet' and the Military Attaché in Ottawa – Lt-Col. Janusz Iliński. Jan Drohojowski ('Eryk') and Tomasz Kuźniarz, members of the Polish Embassy staff in Washington, who until then conducted Continental Action (under the cryptonym 'Maya'), were expected to hand over all the relevant issues to Iliński, to continue observing, for the Interior Ministry, the relations within the local Polish community, and to conduct political Intelligence 'within the range of Polish matters'.[59] Ultimately, the influence of the Ministry proved dominant. In May 1942, General Władysław Sikorski, the Commander-in-Chief and Minister of Military Affairs, ordered the Chief of Staff to immediately halt 'Continental Action' in the Americas conducted by the military. The Cells specially created for this purpose and supervised by PGS were to be closed or used by the Intelligence. Lt-Col. Iliński was forbidden to take any further part in Continental Action[60] and was told to inform Col. Donovan that the Action had been taken over by the Ministry of Internal Affairs.[61] Once again, the initiative belonged with Jan Drohojowski, who chiefed Continental Action in the US until his departure for China.

In South America, the Continental Action was carried out under the cryptonym 'Soledad' (in SOE terminology 'Saintly'). A Cell of the same name, established in February 1942, was operating through South America, especially in the south. Its Chief, working in Buenos Aires, was Edward Paciorkowski ('Gomez', 'Roca'). In October 1941, a network of 'correspondents' was organised in Buenos Aires, Misiones, Montevideo, Paraguay, Bolivia, Chile and Brazil.[62] 'Soledad' was engaged in intelligence activity and attempted to politically counter-balance German activity in Argentina, Uruguay and Brazil.[63] As an example, the cell managed to place one of its agents in a German air transport enterprise in Buenos Aires. 'Gomez' maintained direct contact with SOE representative in the Argentine capital, and through him, conveyed reports to London. In addition, reports were sent by a post office telegraph and the radio station in the Polish Legation.[64] Relations between Continental Action representatives in Buenos Aires and those of Military Intelligence were not the best possible.[65]

A Continental Action cell, part of the 'Soledad' campaign, existed also in Santiago de Chile, where it dealt mainly with German political and economic penetration and conducted pro-Allied propaganda by resorting to lectures given by Dr. Jan Kaczmarek ('Diaz', 'Juan Diaz'), the Chief of Cell, a former chairman of the Union of Poles in Germany and a representative of the Interior Ministry in Madrid. Dr. Kaczmarek began his mission in early 1942 and remained in Santiago de Chile until the spring of 1943. In December of that year he left for the US, where he became a Continental Action 'correspondent' in Washington. In the same month Władysław Banaczyk ('Orkan'), the Minister of Internal Affairs, asked Zbigniew Golędzinowski (under a new codename 'Ombu'), who was previously Paciorkowski's deputy, to travel to Chile. There, from February 1944, Golędzinowski worked with Polish Military Intelligence, from which he obtained valuable information: in addition to various German issues, on the communist movement, which at the time spread across Chile and included the activity of the pro-Stalinist 'Committee of Polish Patriots'. The Ministry Cell in Santiago de Chile was closed in December 1944.[66] Continental Action was also conducted in Brazil, under the cryptonym 'Juca'.

As early as in the autumn of 1941, Col. Donovan had meetings about attempts at Polish-American sabotage co-operation with Col. Adam Koc, who from 1940 represented the Finance Ministry in the United States. Donovan tried to persuade Koc to join sabotage planned abroad. The participants of a briefing held on 15 April 1942 by Col. Mitkiewicz, Deputy Chief of Staff, with Col. Gano, Chief of II Bureau, and Maj. Żychoń, Chief of Intelligence Department, agreed that Lt-Col. Sadowski, Chief of 'Estezet', was to organise a terrorist organisation in South America, which would act on the orders of PGS. Its tasks were to include sabotage and terror against persons of German nationality in those cases when, in the opinion of PGS, revenge was necessary. The campaign was to be conducted by Col. Koc, acting in concert with the Chief of 'Estezet'. The organisation, which was to be financed by an American loan of half a million dollars, was not to be conducted 'under a communist label', and was to be undertaken with the knowledge of the Commander-in-Chief but not that of the Ministry of Internal Affairs.[67] Col. Koc was getting ready for an inspection of Polish military cells (attaché offices, evacuation and recruitment centres) in South America, to be carried out in the name of the Chief of General Staff, Maj-Gen. Tadeusz Klimecki. In reality, the purpose of the inspection tour was to organise the above-mentioned action. The planned three month long tour of Latin America by 'Witold Warmiński' (a codename chosen by Col. Koc) never took place, probably because General Sikorski decided to entrust Continental Action once again to the Ministry of Internal Affairs.[68]

Polish Intelligence in the Americas concentrated on tasks closely co-ordinated with the Western Allies. Use was made of familiarity with some of the minority communities. The most important aspect, however, was the activity of the Polish II Bureau and Continental Action in the United States, where Polish Intelligence cells acted as intermediaries in Polish-American Intelligence co-operation. It delivered much greater results than has been assumed until now. A skilful management of relations with OSS and MID, which competed against each other, testified to the professionalism of the Polish officers. The intelligence sent to the Americans since 1942 was assessed very highly.

Notes

1 Lt-Col. L. L. Sadowski was a Legionnaire (member of Piłsudski's Legion in WW I), an employee of the Intelligence Service since 1920, and in the mid-1920s the Chief of II Bureau Cell no. 4 in Katowice. He was regarded as an outstanding officer (for more on this see: A. Pepłoński, *Wywiad Polskich Sił Zbrojnych na Zachodzie 1939–1945 (The Intelligence Service of the Polish Armed Forces in the West 1939–1945)*, Warsaw 1995, p. 127. At the time when he chiefed 'Estezet', its intelligence officers included Lt. Eugeniusz Piotrowski and Lt. Janusz Kazimirski. The Chief of Counter-intelligence was Capt. Henryk Schmidt. Among the civilians and agents employed by the Cell were: Michał Glazer ('Czarny'), Józef Śliwowski ('Mazur', agent no. 1321), Helena Sworakowska ('Helena Monwid'), Dr. Aleksander Gawlik ('Hopkins', agent no. 5023, director of the New York branch of PKO/Polish Universal Savings Bank, who carried out counter-intelligence tasks and had wide contacts in the US, and had been associated with Polish Intelligence before the war), Alfred Ronald 'Norton', an American citizen, Franciszek Pawliszak, Michał Pilarski and Stanisław Sławik.
2 For more, see: R. Świętek, *W służbie polskiego wywiadu w Ameryce Północnej i Południowej 1941–1945 (In the Service of Polish Intelligence in North and South America 1941–1945)*, 'Przegląd Historyczny', vol. 79, fasc. 3,1988, pp. 539–572.
3 IPMS, A. XII. 24/37, Overseas Section of the Intelligence Department in the II Bureau of PGS, London 20 January 1945. See preserved Intelligence studies and correspondence with the British and American Intelligence Services: IJPA, New York, Collection 'Independent Intelligence Cell 'Estezet', call no. 16-17, 30-33.
4 The establishment of contacts between the Intelligence Services was initiated during the first visit paid by General Sikorski to the United States at end of March 1941.
5 For correspondence and the text of the agreement see: CAW, VI Bureau, PGS, II. 52 .483 and IPMS, A. XII. 24/37, report on the results of the work performed by the Intelligence Department from 1 October 1941 to 1 May 1942.
6 CAW, VI Bureau, II .52. 483, Chief of the II Bureau of PGS to Cell 'Estezet', location unspecified, 27 March 1942; 'Stanisław' (Col. S. Gano) to Col. L. Żółłtek-Mitkiewicz, Lisbon, 2 June 1942.
7 Ibid., Maj. J. H.Żychoń, note for the Chief of II Bureau of PGS on co-operation with American Intelligence, 22 April 1942.
8 Ibid. 'Sadwik' to the Chief of II Bureau, PGS, New York, 16 January 1942.
9 Ibid. 'Sadwik' to the Chief of II Bureau, PGS, New York, 18 January 1942 and 22 September 1942. Col. Żółłtek-Mitkiewicz, Deputy Chief of PGS, gave his consent in the middle of February 1942.
10 P. Grose, *Szpieg dżentelmen (A Gentleman Spy)*, Warsaw 1998, p. 129. Under the pressure exerted by bureaucracy, the Col. was deprived of the radio-propaganda section. The OSS was supervised by the Joint Chiefs of Staff. This move weakened the position held by Donovan, but guaranteed better relations and co-operation with Army and Naval Intelligence. On American Intelligence organisations, see: IJPA, New York, Collection 'Independent Intelligence Cell 'Estezet', call no. 4, Maj. S. M. Dobrowolski, Deputy Polish Military Attaché in Washington, Organisation of Intelligence and counter-intelligence in the United States, Washington, 4 October 1941; J. Srodes, *Allen Dulles. Master of Spies*, Washington 2001; R. Dunlop, *Donovan. America's Master Spy*, Chicago-New York-San Francisco 1982, pp. 293–475; A. C. Brown, *The Last Hero. Wild Bill Donovan*, New York 1982; R. H. Smith, *OSS. The Secret History of America's First Central Intelligence Agency*, Berkeley-Los Angeles-London 1972.
11 CAW, VI Bureau, II. 52. 483, 'Sadwik' to the Chief of II Bureau, PGS, New York, 12 August 1942. The G-2 Research Department was also reputed not to be the best. Lt Col. Sadowski stressed that in both cases the fault lay with assessment of material

obtained. Hence the greater interest in copious detailed material than in individual information (ibid., 'Sadwik' to the Chief of the II Bureau of PGS, New York, 16 January 1942). Sadowski indicated that Donovan's office had considerable problems with recruiting personnel which could be immediately employed in effective Intelligence work, as well as the frigid relations between the OSS and the State Department, the FBI, and Army and Naval Intelligence. Sadowski preferred to co-operate closer with the MID; this, however, was impossible without Donovan's consent (ibid., 'Sadwik' to the Chief of the Information and the II Bureau of PGS, New York, 7 December 1941).

12 Further as: Mitkiewicz.

13 CAW, (VI Bureau, II). 52. 483, Col. G. B. Guenther from G-2 to Col. L. Mitkiewicz, Washington, 14 January 1942.

14 IPMS, A. Xll.24/35, Proposal on the scope of work and competencies of the Chief of Cell 'Estezet' in New York concerning co-operation with the American Information Service in the United States. Co-operation with American Intelligence was to take place strictly via the Post. The Attaché was not to deal with Intelligence, although he was expected to assist 'Estezet' when needed. His traditional tasks included, apart from representation, inquiry into the armed forces and military questions (CAW, VI Bureau, II. 52. 483, Maj.-Gen. T. Klimecki, Chief of the General Staff, to the Military Attaché at the Polish Embassy in Washington, 12 October 1942).

15 Ibid., questionnaires.

16 Ibid. 'Sadwik' to the Chief of the II Bureau, PGS, New York, 18 January 1942 and 22 September 1942.

17 IJPA, New York, Collection 'Independent Intelligence Cell "Estezet"', call no. 4, R. H. Scannell of the FEA to M. Chodacki, New York, 15 November 1944, and reports relayed to FEA in 1944–1945, call no. 33–36.

18 Material supplied by the Poles to G-2 is kept in NARA, College Park, Maryland, USA, Records of War Dept. General and and Special Staffs, Entry 77, MID, 'Regional File' 1922–1944.

19 CAW, VI Bureau, II. 52. 483, 'Sadwik' to the Chief of II Bureau, PGS, New York, 12 August 1942.

20 Cited after: IPMS, A.XII.24/37, Report on work of the Intelligence Department, PGS, from 1 July 1942 to 30 June 1943, London, 28 August 1943.

21 CAW, VI Bureau, II. 52. 483, E. Brennan of the OSS to Maj. S. Jędrzejewski, Washington, 16 September 1942.

22 IJPA, New York, Collection 'Independent Intelligence Cell "Estezet"', call no. 4, R. H. Scannell of the FEA to M. Chodacki, New York, 15 November 1944.

23 IPMS, A. XII. 24/56, Report on work of the Intelligence Department II Bureau of PGS from 1 January to 30 April 1944. It is worth recalling that British assessments were similar. By way of example, among 9 761 reports dispatched by Polish Intelligence between 1 July 1943 and 31 December 1943, the British considered 8% as being extremely valuable, 70% as of great value, 18% as valuable, 3% as of little value and 1% as of no value (ibid., II Bureau, A. XII .24/37, Report on the work of the II Bureau, PGS, from 1 July to 31 December 1943, and CAW, the VI Bureau, II. 52. 483, Col. A. Marecki to PGS, Washington, 18 December 1942.

24 Ibid., 'Robert' to the Chief of II Bureau, PGS, New York, 14 October 1942. On co-operation between 'Estezet' and SIS in the United States see: AIJP, New York Collection 'Independent Intelligence Cell "Estezet"', call no. 31–32.

25 CAW, VI Bureau, 11.52.483, Col. A. Marecki to PGS, Washington, 18 December 1943, and Col. A. Marecki to the Chief of Staff, PGS, Washington, 4 January 1943. The Americans did not agree to a Polish Liaison Officer being assigned to the Staff of General Eisenhower 'due to Allied pressure'.

26 IPMS, A.XII.24/70, Gen. K. Sosnkowski to the Deputy Chief of Staff, 29 July 1943.

The duties of the liaison officers co-operating with the British and American elements of CCS were still performed by the Military Attaché, Col. Onacewicz, to the American Joint Chiefs of Staff, and his Assistant, Capt. Dr. Stefan Zamoyski to the British Joint Staff Mission. For more on the activity of Col. Mitkiewicz, see: L. Mitkiewicz, *W Najwyższym Sztabie Zachodnich Aliantów 1943–1945 (In the Supreme Staff of the Western Allies 1943–1945)*, London 1971, passim; L. Mitkiewicz *Z generałem Sikorskim na obczyźnie (fragmenty wspomnień) (With General Sikorski in Exile (Fragments of Reminiscences)*, Paris 1968; W. Onacewicz, *Komentarze do książki Leona Mitkiewicza Z generałem Sikorskim na obczyźnie' (Commentaries on Leon Mitkiewicz's book With General Sikorski in Exile*, 'Zeszyty Historyczne', fasc. 18, Paris 1970.

27 In 1944, while passing over the duties of Chief of Intelligence to his successor in this post, Maj. Langenfeld, Maj. Żychoń recommended that the former should return to the practice of relaying material to the Americans via the Chief of 'Estezet' and not the Bureau of Col. Mitkiewicz (CAW, VI Bureau, II. 52. 481, Hand-over Certificate of the Intelligence Department of the Information and Intelligence Bureau, PGS, 15 February 1944). The Bureau of the Deputy Chief of General Staff in Washington included: Maj. Stefan Jędrzejewski, Chief of Polish Military Mission Staff, Lt. (later Capt.) Jerzy Piotrowski, Intelligence Officers Lt. Włodzimierz Czaykowski and Lt. Arnold Ronke, Cipher Officer Lt. Janusz Kazimirski, and in New York the Supply Officer, 2nd Lt. Tadeusz Jaroński. The Bureau also employed civilians: Michał Pilarski, Lesław Bodeński, Zofia Talmontowa and Kazimirska (IPMS, A.XII.24/70, correspondence; CAW, VI Bureau, II. 52. 480, Overseas Section of the Information and Intelligence Bureau, PGS, The organisation and budget of Intelligence Cells in North and South America as of 1st June 1944.

28 IPMS, A.XII.24/1 6.

29 CAW, the VI Bureau, II. 52. 481, Hand-over Certificate of the Intelligence Department of the II Bureau, PGS, 15 February 1944.

30 When he was in charge of 'Estezet', the Intelligence Officer was Capt. Henryk Schmidt ('Hudson'), and civilian employees included Stanisław Sławik, Wanda Musiałówna and Hanna Abłamowicz.

31 IPMS, A.XII.24/37, List of Stations, Cells and Independent Intelligence Cells of the II Bureau of PGS. In 1944, radio communications between HO in London, the Independent Intelligence Stations 'Estezet' and 'Manchester' and the Deputy Chief of PGS were interrupted as a result of restrictions imposed by the British, and was not re-instated until the end of the war (ibid., Kol. 242/62, Note for the Commander-in-Chief on radio communications of the II Bureau, PGS, London, 1 May 1944, and the diagram of communications of the clandestine network of agency radio stations of the Information and II Bureau, PGS, as of 1 May 1945; ibid., II Bureau, A. XII. 24/56, Report on the activities of the Intelligence Department from 5 to 14 May 1943, 13 May 1944).

32 More on this in: R. Świętek, *W służbie*, op. cit., p. 545. 'Sadwik' was of the opinion that the presence of an agent in Detroit was necessary in view of the radicalisation of the workers in that town. On agents and informers of Polish Intelligence Cells in the Americas, see: correspondence in CAW, IPMS and R. Świątek, *W służbie*, op. cit. 539–572 (on the basis of Col. Leon Mitkiewicz's notebook held in the Józef Piłsudski Institute in New York).

33 'Magellan' was to have been transferred to the Station's HO, but continued to maintain contacts with its agents and informants.

34 This was probably Jerzy Piotrowski, who between 1933 and 1939 worked in the Polish diplomatic and consular service (ibid., p. 546).

35 More in: ibid., p. 550.

36 The civilians employed in the Independent Intelligence Cell) 'Manchester' in Ottawa were Adam Bobrowski and Kamila Choma-Iberszerowa.

37 CAW, VI Bureau, II. 52. 486, Temporary organisational instruction for the 'Manchester' Cell, 'Sadwik', Chief of Cell 'Estezet', New York, 19 August 1942; Station 'Estezet', organisational report for the first quarter of 1943, 'Sadwik', Chief of Cell 'Estezet', New York, 14 May 1943.
38 CAW, VI Bureau, II. 52. 481, Hand-over Certificate of the Intelligence Department of the II Bureau, PGS, 15 February 1944. See also: AIJP, New York, Collection 'Independent Intelligence Cell 'Estezet', call no. 4 and material related to Intelligence work in Canada, call no. 28-29.
39 Schulz was an agent of Cell 'Salvador', which could mean that up to the time when Cell 'Sabanilla' was handed over to Lt. Pawłowicz, it was a subordinated to the former network. Before the war, Schulz worked in the Security Department of the Ministry of Internal Affairs in Warsaw (R. Swiętek, W służbie, op. cit., pp. 555–556).
40 CAW, the VI Bureau, II. 52. 486, Lt-Col. S. Kara to Col. S. Gano, Rio de Janeiro, 12 September 1945. More in: Polski Instytut Naukowy w Ameryce (Polish Institute of Arts & Sciences of America, PIASA), New York, Bohdan Pawłowicz Papers, col. 29; IJPA, New York, Bohdan Pawłowicz; R. Swiętek, W służbie, op. cit., p. 546 and W. Baliński, Brazil [in:] Akcja niepodległościowa na terenie międzynarodowym 1945–1990 (Independence Campaign on an International Arena 1945–1990), ed. by T. Piesakowski, London 1999, p. 580.
41 Until the second half of 1944, he did not have an Intelligence Officer or a civilian official, though the authorised strength provided for such posts. At the time, the new civilian employees were Jan Schulz and Piotr Górecki ('Pegar'). 'Salvador's' agents included Andrzej Count Tarnowski ('Ochotnik', agent no. 5302), a graduate of Oxford and a former member of the Vickers board, who was extremely well connected in Brazil, especially among the Americans and the British, as well as in diplomatic circles. Another 'Salvador' agent was Lt. Mikołaj Count Rostworowski, previously a Polish Intelligence officer in Madrid, whose work was highly regarded. In early 1945 he was transferred to Chile (more in: IJPA, New York, Collection 'Independent Intelligence Cell 'Estezet', call no. 18; cf. A. Rostworowski, Ziemia, której ż nie zobaczysz. Wspomnienia kresowe (A Land You Shall Never See Again. Reminiscences from Eastern Borderlands), ed. by S.J. Rostworowski, Warsaw 2001, pp. 418–419.
42 IJPA, New York, Collection 'Independent Intelligence Cell "Estezet"', material concerning intelligence work in Canada, call no. 18–24 and 26–27.
43 CAW, VI Bureau, II. 52. 486, Cell 'Estezet', Organisational report on the first quarter of 1943, 'Sadwik', Chief of Post 'Estezet', New York, 14th May 1943 r. Between 1929 and 1943 Konrad Wrzos (real name: Henryk Rosenberg) was the editor-in-chief and political reporter 'Ilustowany Kurier Codzienny' daily. In February 1945 he resigned from the II Bureau and died in Brazil in 1974 (more in: IJPA, New York, Collection 'Independent Intelligence Cell 'Estezet', call no. 4, K. Wrzos to M. Chodacki, Rio de Janeiro, 9 February 1945, and M. Chodacki to the Chief of the II Bureau, PGS, New York, 23 March 1945; correspondence, call no. 18 and R. Swiętek, W Służbie, op. cit., p. 547).
44 IJPA, New York, Collection 'Independent Intelligence Cell 'Estezet', M. Chodacki to the Chief of the II Bureau, PGS, New York, 30 September 1944.
45 He carried a diplomatic passport. Orłowski was the son of Count Ksawery Franciszek Orłowski of Jarmolińce, the Polish Envoy in Brazil (1920–1921) and Spain (1921–1923) (more in: X. W. Meysztowicz, Gawędy o czasach i ludziach (Tales About Past Times and People), London 1993, p. 139, and the Marian Szumlakowski Collection, Centre for Studies on Classical Tradition in Poland and East-Central Europe at Warsaw University, further as: KMS – the author offers his thanks to Prof. Jan Kieniewicz for making available the private papers of Minister Szumlakowski – note by M. Szumlakowski, the Polish Envoy in Madrid. K.F. Orłowski died in 1926. During the Spanish Civil War, Karol, whose mother was

Argentinian, served with the Nationalists (J. L. de Mesa, *Los otros Internacionales. Voluntarios extranjeros desconocidos en el Bando Nacional durante la Guerra Civil /1936–1939/*, Madrid 1998, pp. 197–198). At the beginning of 1941, Orłowski headed the Cell in Madrid which on behalf of the I Bureau of PGS conducted an illegal evacuation of Polish soldiers from France to Great Britain. He was imprisoned in March and April 1941, and subsequently left Spain (see: correspondence in KMS).

46 IJPA, New York, Collection 'Independent Intelligence Cell 'Estezet', material concerning intelligence work in Canada, call no. 18–24.

47 In 1943, the Chief of Cell 'Estezet' estimated that the good work performed by the local cell produced useful albeit not sensational results. He regarded Asunción as a 'counterpart of our Kutno or Rzeszów' (correspondence in IJPA, New York, Collection 'Independent Intelligence Cell 'Estezet', call no. 4; CAW, VI Bureau, II. 52. 486, Instruction for Post 'P. A.', together with annexes, 'Sadwik', Chief of Cell 'Estezet', New York, 1 February 1942; Post 'Estezet', Organisational report for the first quarter of 1943 'Sadwik', Chief of Cell 'Estezet', New York, 14 May 1943). The civilian officials of 'Salvador' were Józef Soboliński and Jeremi Stempowski 'Junosza'.

48 Ibid., II. 52. 481, Hand-over Certificate of the Intelligence Department of the II Bureau, PGS, 15 February 1944.

49 Ibid., the II. 52. 480, Overseas Section of the II Bureau, PGS, Personnel, posts and salaries in Intelligence Posts of the II Bureau, PGS, in North and South America, 29 May 1945; IJPA, New York, Collection 'Independent Intelligence Cell 'Estezet', material concerning intelligence work in Canada, call no. 25.

50 IPMS, A.XII.24/56, Lt-Col. C. Janicki, Deputy Chief of the Intelligence Department of The Polish Naval Command to the Chief of the II Bureau, PGS, London, 5 May 1944.

51 The Deputy Chief of Staff stated that for two and a half years, Col. Onacewicz fulfilled his duties very well, enjoyed a deservedly good opinion, and maintained extremely good relations with the American Staff (ibid., A. XII. 24170, report by Col. L. Mitkiewicz, Deputy Chief of Staff, 4 December 1943).

52 IPMS, A.XII.24/70, Report by Col. L. Mitkiewicz, Deputy Chief of Staff, 4 December 1943.

53 The training of 2nd Lt. Edward Kolasa and 2nd FLt. Antoni Kalinowski, who were to join Cell 'Siła', began in March 1945 (A. Pepłoński, *Wywiad*, op. cit., p. 137).

54 They signed agreements concerning official status as members of the II Bureau, PGS. Furthermore, on 15 February 1945 Col. S. Gano, Chief of the Polish II Bureau, signed with J. Chmielewski, 'a resident of Rio de Janeiro' an agreement concerning the establishment of a two-person commercial company 'Siła' for the purpose of trading in Great Britain, South America and Poland. The profits were to be divided into two, and quarterly accounts were to be presented. Col. Gano was entitled to cede the whole of his share, or its part, to a third party without obtaining Chmielewski's consent (IPMS, A.XII.24/65, Agreement between Col. S. Gano and J. Chmielewski of 15 February 1945 and an instruction for the 'Siła' Cell. See: CAW, the VI Bureau, II. 52. 480, Overseas Section of the II Bureau, PGS, Personnel, posts and salaries in Intelligence Cells of the Information and II Bureau, PGS, in North and South America, 29 May 1945).

55 The agreement on the establishment of a two-person company was also signed with him on 19 February 1945. The division of profits was to be defined later. Precise instructions were to depend on the development of the 'enterprise' (IPMS, A.XII.24/65, Agreements between Col. S. Gano and Lt-Col. K. Piasecki, of 19 February 1945, instructions for the 'Savoy' Cell, Note on the organisation of an Information Network in Latin American countries, and CAW, the VI Bureau, II. 52. 480, Overseas Section of the II Bureau, PGS, Personnel, posts and salaries in

Intelligence Cells of the II Bureau, PGS in North and South America, 29 May 1945).
56 AIPMS, A. XII. 24/70, Cal. L. Mitkiewicz, Deputy Chief of Staff, Situation Report for February 1944, Washington, 15 March 1944.
57 CAW, VI Bureau, II. 52. 486, Chief of the II Bureau, GHQ, to Independent Stations 'Estezet' in New York and 'Manchester' in Ottawa, no place, 4 July 1945. The subsidy for 'Estezet' was to total £800, and for 'Manchester' £250.
58 See: correspondence in: ibid., II. 52. 480.
59 Ibid., Gen. W. Sikorski, Chairman of the Council of Ministers, to the Ministry of Internal Affairs, Chief of the General Staff and Lt-Col. J. Iliński, location unspecified, 2 April 1942. Soon afterwards it became apparent that Iliński co-operated earlier with representatives of the Ministry of Internal Affairs as regards Continental Action, without the knowledge and consent of PGS (ibid., Note for the Commander-in-Chief concerning 'Continental Action', 30 April 1942).
60 In fact, between 1941 and 1943 he represented Continental Action in Canada, chiefing a propaganda and information cell. For the purposes of Continental Action, Lt-Col. Iliński used the codenames 'Lees' and 'Ott'.
61 Ibid., Gen. W. Sikorski to the Chief of Staff, Field Headquarters, 31 May 1942; A. Kułakowski, Secretariat of the Chairman of the Council of Ministers, to Maj-Gen. T. Klimecki, London, 6 May 1942; Chief of the Staff to Lt-Col. J. Illiński, 30 April 1942; J. Iliński to the Deputy Chief of Staff, Ottawa, 20 April 1942.
62 IPMS, A. 9 List of cryptonyms used by the Ministry.
63 On German infiltration in Latin America see: D. Pastor *Petit, Espionaje. La Segunda Guerra Mundial y España*, Barcelona 1990, pp. 141–142, 659–660.
64 TNA(PRO), HS 4/221, The Kot Organisations, 14 January 1941.
65 Paciorkowski and Golędzinowski, whom the II Bureau accused of an unnecessarily ostentatious display of contacts with American Intelligence. Both men were apparently closely observed by German Counter-intelligence (CAW, VI Bureau, II. 52. 483, 'Sadwik' to the Chief of II Bureau, New York, 6 February 1942).
66 For more on Continental Action in Latin America, see: IPMS, A. 9. VI. 4/1-2 (Argentina, 1941-1945), A. 9. VI. 4/5 (Brazil 'Inca', 1943–1945), A. 9. VI. 4/6 (Chile 1941–1945). Continental Action in Argentina was conducted under the cryptonym 'Perełka', and in Chile 'Almagro'.
67 CAW, VI Bureau, II. 52. 483, Maj. J. H. Żychoń, Chief of Intelligence, Note on briefing of 15 April 1942.
68 See: ibid., 'Sadwik', Chief of Cell 'Estezet', to Col. Mitkiewicz, Deputy Chief of Staff, 20 May 1942; Chief of Staff to Station 'Estezet', location unspecified, 30 May 1942.

39
The Middle East

Gill Bennett

Documents found in the closed British archives suggest that the relationship between British and Polish Intelligence operatives in the Middle East was a close one. An SIS letter dated 10 October 1944, reviewing Anglo-Polish Intelligence co-operation in the Middle East, noted that SIS had 'always maintained a general liaison' with Polish Intelligence at all places where the latter had a presence, 'with the idea of guiding them as far as possible, and seeking their assistance in the task of gaining intelligence about the enemy – principally in Europe'. By late 1944 British Intelligence authorities were worried that Polish activities in the Middle East (as elsewhere) were now dominated by their anti-Soviet motivation, but in the earlier part of the war close co-operation with the Poles was directed exclusively towards defeating the Axis powers.

The first specific reference found to Polish activities in the Middle East is in December 1940, when it was reported that Maj. Józef Bińkowski ('Binky'), formerly Polish Intelligence Service representative in Bucharest and in Istanbul, had been refused a residence permit by the Turkish authorities on the grounds that he was working against the Soviet Union and this might prejudice Russo-Turkish relations. Bińkowski was therefore moving to Jerusalem to set up a station there, with SIS's approval.

By July 1941, however, Bińkowski was being recommended by the Polish authorities as 'suitable and willing' to move to Tehran and work closely there with British Intelligence. An SIS minute of 12 September 1941 noted: 'the Poles consider him a good man, therefore the sooner he gets to Tehran and starts work for us the better'. Further minutes betray some frustration at the time it was taking to achieve this: 'It is well over a month since Poles decided to try to send him out as Polish Red Cross Representative. In view of Polish-Russian Alliance and of Allied occupation of Iran there should now be no difficulty in getting him sent out in any capacity they please' (18 September). The matter was discussed with Col. Gano, who promised a decision would be taken 'soon'.

Bińkowski finally left Jerusalem for Tehran via Baghdad on 9 October, together with Capt. Mazur and Private Lorenz of the Polish Army. However, they arrived in Iran without the requisite visas, holding only military documents that were not sufficient to obtain residence permits. A minute by A4 section of 15 November stated that this would give Bińkowski 'little scope for moving about in Persia and [he] will therefore be unable to execute the urgent mission on which he is engaged [liaison with Allied Russian, British and British Indian forces]'. It was suggested by Maj. Orłowski, of the Polish Intelligence station in Jerusalem, that the three Poles might be attached to the British Command in Iran as liaison officers. Orłowski stressed that Bińkowski should not assume the cover of Polish Military Attaché in Tehran, as Polish Intelligence needed that post for the chief of a larger military mission that they were planning to send.

On 20 November two telegrams were sent to the SIS representative in Tehran, explaining the proposal, which 'would have the advantage of not repeat not placing them under control of Polish Minister in Tehran', and requesting that 'in order to regularise Bińkowski and party's position in Iran as soon repeat as soon as possible, could you help to arrange matters locally'. A telegram from Tehran of 26 November reported that Bińkowski's appointment as liaison officer with British forces had already been notified to the Iranian government, and asked that arrangements should be made in London between British and Polish military authorities so that the necessary documents could be issued.

In December 1941 Bińkowski proposed that Capt. Mazur should be attached to the British Consulate General in Meshed, 'partly in connection with Polish Army in Russia, but also for intelligence work'. This proposal did not, however, find favour in SIS, on the grounds that 'such an attachment would...inevitably attract unfavourable notice on the part of the Russian authorities'. It would be more 'natural' for Mazur to be accredited to the Russian military authorities in Meshed, 'where he would be nearer the Polish armed forces in Russia, *provided that* the princi[ple] of Polish military liaison with the Russians in Iran has been, or is, accepted by the Russian authorities...Such liaison, and any information gained by Mazur while in any such capacity in Meshed, could only be to our advantage.' At this point, unfortunately, the documentation ceases, and no more information has been traced about Bińkowski, Mazur or their activities in Iran. By mid-1943, however, Bińkowski appears to have been back in Jerusalem.

References in 1942 are brief and incomplete. A telegram from Tehran dated 21 May informed SIS that an engineer called Tarvit had left with one of the first parties of Polish evacuees for Palestine. Tarvit had acted as assistant to another engineer, Col. Piotr Kończyc, chief of the Polish commission responsible for moving Poles round the Soviet Union. It was suggested that 'much of railway information you want' could be obtained by arranging with Orłowski for special interrogation of Tarvit, or by arranging with Polish General Staff for Kończyc, who had been ill, to go to Tehran or Cairo on leave and speak to him then. No further information on this has been found.

The only other reference in 1942 is in a telegram from Cairo dated 10 September, complaining about Polish counter-intelligence in the Middle East, which was 'separate from their operational intelligence and of much lower quality with tendencies towards worse aspects of continental secret police methods'. Similar complaints had been received from Turkey, where there were 'strong indications' of leaks of information from Polish Intelligence in Ankara to 'Spaniards and Germans'. However, it was noted that Orłowski, who had just been appointed Chief of Polish counter-intelligence, was 'far better type. If you can encourage him to take our view of counter-intelligence as opposed to security and secret police methods it will be most useful.' Polish Intelligence should be able to produce 'most useful' information from the Caucasus.

As stated above, by 1943 Bińkowski is referred to as being in Jerusalem. There he was joined by Lt. Piękosz of Polish General Staff, who was reported in January 1943 as travelling via Lagos and Cairo; and by Lt. Fedorowicz who had been recalled from Istanbul to take up post in Jerusalem. These movements appear to have been part of a general reshuffle aimed at transferring the headquarters of Polish Intelligence in the Middle East from Jerusalem to Istanbul. It was hoped that this would lead to an improved flow of information, and to an improvement in the quality of written reports. Under the new system Polish reports from the region would be sent through Istanbul to London, from where they would be passed on to Cairo for distribution as necessary. This procedure followed that set up earlier in Jerusalem by Orłowski, in order to avoid reports arriving in Cairo 'by devious channels and thus causing confusion'.

The new Polish Intelligence representative in Istanbul, according to a telegram of 4 June 1943, was to be Capt. Galewicz. He, and the new chief of Polish security in the Middle East, Lt-Col. Bąkiewicz, were reported to be travelling to Istanbul via Cairo in June and July where they would call on SIS representatives 'to discuss points of mutual interest'. Meanwhile, SIS were asked by the Polish authorities to facilitate the passage to the UK of Capt. Maresch, working with Polish Intelligence in Tehran. Notices of all these movements are brief and incomplete.

In July 1943 the SIS representative in Baghdad, visiting Jerusalem, contacted headquarters about a Polish Intelligence officer he had known since 1940, Col. Rudziński. They had met in June 1940 in Estonia, when Rudzinski was charged with the evacuation of Polish military internees in the Baltic States, but had been put into great danger with the Soviet invasion of Estonia. British and French Intelligence had helped him to escape to Stockholm, from where he had travelled to Moscow in the summer of 1942 and had worked closely with British Intelligence there. In May 1942 Rudziński had accompanied Gen. Sikorski on his visit to the Polish armed forces in Iraq and elsewhere. In July 1943 he met up with his former SIS contact in Jerusalem, and gave the latter 'a considerable amount of information'. Rudziński told him that he had now been appointed to Tehran, but was travelling there via Baghdad and would call on his SIS friend there.

The SIS representative considered that Rudzinski's visit would be of considerable value, partly 'to get me into friendly touch with authoritative [Polish] sources in Iraq', and to provide information. He accordingly asked London to supply a short questionnaire for him to give to Rudzinski on the subjects on which his information could 'be expected to be complete and authoritative', including Polish, Soviet and French subjects, and German subjects viewed from a Soviet and French perspective.

As noted above, by late 1944 British Intelligence authorities were concerned about the direction of Polish Intelligence activities. In October a representative of British Intelligence in Cairo recorded a conversation with Lt-Col. Tysowski, Chief of Polish Intelligence in Jerusalem. Gustaw Tysowski had told him that he had been summoned home to discuss the future of Polish Intelligence in the Middle East, and plans to put officers in place to get information on Soviet penetration in the Middle East. The British representative explained that the British Government were treating the Soviet Union as allies, and that their attitude towards them was 'strictly correct'. Tysowski agreed that 'his future workings would have to be the subject of agreement between his headquarters and ours in London', and had given no hint of immediate action, though Polish agents were, apparently, already being deployed.

Nor did Tyskowski mention the visit to Baghdad, apparently on Tysowski's orders, of a Capt. Remkawicz to penetrate Soviet activities and find out everything possible about future Soviet policy. Remkawicz had spoken about this to a member of British GHQ, who was 'very perturbed' and asked London for clarification. The Cairo report of the conversation with Tysowski concluded: 'I quite realise that the Poles may well exploit our connection with them, which, as I have explained, has solely been done for our work against the Axis, to hint that they likewise have our support for anti-Soviet activities. This, as you will see, is quite contrary to the true state, and we are meticulously careful to show them that we are not concerned to facilitate them in this task.'

The only other document concerning Polish activities in the Middle East dates from the end of the war, when Col. Gano and CSS discussed the future of Polish representatives in the Middle East, (now under the control of Polish HQ in Italy). Though the connection with SIS was now at an end, it was agreed that 'should any of these people appear to be in danger, it might be advisable to permit our Representatives in those countries to take over from the Poles any documents, codes etc. which should not fall into other hands'. Among the names discussed in this context were Maj. Franciszek Wierzbicki (Wierzynek) and Capt. Roman Królikowski (Król), both based in Cairo, Capt. Tadeusz Szefer (Kościelny) and Capt. Władysław Marczyński in Istanbul, Capt. Michał Zawistowski in Tehran and Lt. Piotr Kurnicki in Beirut.

40

The Middle East

Jan Stanisław Ciechanowski

During the first half of the 1930s, the II Bureau of the Polish General Staff began to set up intelligence networks in Asia and the Middle East. Their task was to take over anti-Soviet intelligence work in case of war with the Soviet Union.[1] After the German and Soviet invasion of Poland, intelligence in this area was carried out until 1940 by the Polish intelligence mission located at the Polish Embassy in Turkey.[2] Due to changes made to the prewar Section East and its abandonment of intelligence activities in Poland, the II Bureau was forced to start afresh in the Near East terrain.

In the autumn of 1940 Station 'T' located in Jerusalem[3] was established. From the summer of 1941 it was chiefed by Lt-Col. Stanisław Zygmunt Orłowski ('Stanisław Orzechowski'), who came from Romania. Lt-Col. Orłowski was a pre-war II Bureau officer and in 1933–1935 the chief of cell 'Radames' in Tehran. The station conducted air, naval and land intelligence concentrated on the Soviet Union and Germany. Its chief task was anti-Soviet intelligence – which required lengthy preparations – and defensive counter-intelligence, whose significance grew as the Polish military presence in the Middle East increased. Other tasks, commissioned by the British, involved radio intelligence, assessments of the situation in enemy countries (focusing mainly on military, industrial, economic and political issues), as well as intelligence analyses of the press and publications issued by the enemy and neutral states.[4]

On account of numerous tasks received by Station 'T', supervised by 'Wschód' Section of the Intelligence Department, and the enormous area of operation, they received considerable financial assistance.[5] Communications with the HQ was maintained through the radio transmitters in London and the Polish Consulate General in Jerusalem as well as British couriers.[6] Intelligence cells[7] no. 1 and 2 operated in Bucharest (after the disbandment of Station 'R' which functioned in 1939–1940) and no. 3 – in Istanbul. The Intelligence Cell no. 4, with offices in Tehran, the capital of Persia, was chiefed by Maj. Jerzy Bińkowski ('Buderski').[8]

It was characteristic for the activities of the Polish intelligence in the Middle East that the operations in this area were closely connected with the activity in the Balkans. This also affected the personnel issues. From 1943 Station 'T' co-operated with Station 'Bałk' which was established at that time in Istanbul. The scope of the co-operation included mainly the selection of candidates for recruitment and the transfer of newly recruited agents from the Middle East to work against Germany and its allies in the Balkans. The station in question also functioned as an intermediary between Station 'Bałk' and the military attachés to the Yugoslav and Greek governments in exile with the seat in Cairo.

The scope of activity of Station 'T' developed due to the growing threat to Allied interests in the area of operation of the Polish station. In mid-July 1942 the concentration of Polish forces was shifted from Palestine to northern Iraq, which was also the destination for the Polish Army in the East, commanded by Gen. Władysław Anders. The II Bureau of the Polish Army in the East focused its attention on the Soviet Union,[9] especially effectively since Lt-Col. Wincenty Bąkiewicz became its chief. He had been Chief of the Independent Branch 'Rosja' in the pre-war Studies Department of the II Bureau of the PGS.

With the activities of Station 'T' the work of one of the most famous World War II Allied agents – Jerzy Iwanow-Szajnowicz[10] was associated. He had lived in Greece since 1925 being brought up by his Polish mother. During the 1930s Iwanow-Szajnowicz was one of the best swimmers in Europe. He studied in Belgium and France. When the war broke out and the first tide of Polish refugees arrived in Greece Iwanow-Szajnowicz was engaged in organising the evacuation of soldiers from the region of Saloniki. In 1940 Iwanow-Szajnowicz was recruited to work for the Polish Intelligence by Capt. Tadeusz Zdzisław Szefer ('Kościelny'), an officer of Station 'A' of the II Bureau of the PGS in Athens.[11] The new agent initially carried out counter-intelligence tasks; after the fall of Greece he moved, together with Capt. Szefer, to Palestine. At the end of May 1941 the commanders of Station 'T' planned to use Iwanow-Szajnowicz in Greece. He completed special training for that purpose. On 21 October 1941 Iwanow-Szajnowicz was transported to Saloniki on a British submarine. He was recruited by the SIS at the beginning of his mission, without informing the Poles. That was evidenced by the severance of all ties with Station 'T' immediately after his arrival in Greece. At the beginning of 1942 Iwanow-Szajnowicz conducted, upon British orders, reconnaissance of German fortifications in the area of Marathon. He also inspired the sabotage in the 'Malziniotti' factory in New Faleron, which produced aeroplane engines, thus causing numerous German planes to crash during air battles over Africa. Iwanow-Szajnowicz also carried out a number of daring diversionary actions, such as destroying the German submarine 'U-133' and the destroyer 'Hermes' by using mines. The Germans issued a warrant for his arrest with an award for his capture. 'Athos' (agent no. 2882), the codename Iwanow-Szajnowicz used while working for Station 'T', asked Lt-Col. Walerian Mercik ('Jakub Alek') – chief of the base of VI

Bureau in Cairo ('Alek', 'Muł'), which contacts in Greece were taken over by Iwanow-Szajnowicz to be evacuated from Greece, to which British intelligence obligated itself following interventions by the Polish authorities. The SIS did not manage to keep the promise, though. Iwanow-Szajnowicz made several attempts to escape to Turkey on his own but he failed. He was betrayed by one of his collaborators, a Greek called Pandelis Lambrinopoulos in Athens. That led to the arrest of the Allied agent who was put in the Averoff prison. On 16 December 1942 he was shot and killed during an attempted escape from the execution site. The whole case of Iwanow-Szajnowicz still calls for many more explanations.

After the 2nd Polish Corps moved to Italy in March 1944, Station 'T' was reorganised in ord er to increase its effectiveness, especially that the advancement of the eastern front towards the Polish border made it necessary to intensify activities of the station directed against the Soviet Union. Lt-Col. Ludwik Lucjan Sadowski 'Sadwik', former chief of Cell 'Estezet', became the new chief of the reorganised structure. He took over from the chief of the Intelligence Bureau of the 2nd Corps the cells in Tehran, Baghdad, Jerusalem and Cairo. The bureau of the station did not engage in strictly intelligence activity, although it gathered and analysed material forwarded by field cells. According to the instruction issued in connection with the appointment of the new commander, the station was to operate in the Middle East, that is in Iran, Iraq, Syria, Transjordan, Palestine and Egypt, by conducting offensive intelligence and counter-intelligence as well as defensive counter-intelligence with regard to the Polish citizens, censorship of Polish mail and personnel training.

In March 1944 Station 'T' had official cells in Tel Aviv (no. 1) and Cairo (no. 2 'Tatar'),[12] officially functioning with the consent of the British authorities as Polish military offices, as well as undercover cells existing at Polish diplomatic missions in Tehran (no. 5), where Soviet penetration was increasingly strong, in Baghdad (no. 6) and Beirut (no. 3). Intelligence cells controlled by cell no. 1 were created in Jerusalem, Haifa and Alexandria.

Owing to specific conditions, the station ceased recruiting agents for offensive intelligence. The only form of offensive intelligence was radio intelligence. In Jerusalem station 'T' performed the function of a radio intelligence subordinate HQ. At the end of 1944 the Independent Communications and Radio-Intelligence Section was composed of a cryptology section and a radio-intelligence registry. The Section employed six officers, 64 NCOs and several dozen civilians, volunteers, trainees, radiotelegraphic operators, mechanics and craftsmen. It had at its disposal radio stations in Cairo, Jerusalem, Tehran, Istanbul and Baghdad, and dealt primarily with communications of the station for intelligence purposes and radio monitoring focused on Russia. Station 'T' was to become a kind of a Russian 'branch' of the II Bureau of the General Staff. For that reason attempts were made to guarantee its radio organisation a considerable degree of self-sufficiency.[13]

The structures of Station 'T'[14] were considerably expanded. In March

1944 there were 122 employees, including 36 officers, 13 NCOs, 15 civilians, 21 female volunteers from the Women's Army Auxiliary Service (PWSK), six junior contract clerks, 20 radio-telegraphic operators, five radio technicians, two laboratory assistants and four drivers.

Table 6: Statistical survey of stations 'T' and 'Eswu' (without field cells, prepared by the author on the basis of listing from the documentation of the II Bureau of the Polish General Staff (A XII), kept in IPMS, and documentation from CAW, VI Bureau)

Period	Officers	Civilian functionaries, NCOs and remaining staff	Agents	Informants
12 January 1944	2*	10*	3	6
March 1944	18*	40*	–	–
8 May 1944	18*	39*	3	5
end of 1944, as 'Eswu'	11+2 reserve*	13+4 reserve*	–	–
March 1945, as 'Eswu'	28	45	3	–
1945, as 'Eswu'	33	22	–	–

*Note: the data pertaining to the radio-intelligence cell not included

The main task of the station following a reorganisation that took several months in the spring of 1944 was to prepare a maximum number of intelligence officers, lower-level intelligence staff, agents and informants who could work after the war in the Middle East, Germany and other regions. HQ recommended to seek recruits in Polish administration offices, among senior members of a youth paramilitary organisation and within the Polish communities. Various studies and assessments were made on issues relating to that area, foreign influences (especially those of the enemies of Poland, including the symptoms of the impact of the Soviet influence expansion on the Middle East countries) and the Jewish and 'pan-Arabic' questions; extensive counter-intelligence activity was continued especially among the Polish Army stationing there. Emphasis was to be placed on using the available material, including those of the Bureau of Documents and the Jewish Agency in Jerusalem. HQ advised to work in such a manner so as to become deeply rooted in the local conditions 'with tomorrow in mind'.[15]

Plans were made to transfer the station to Turkey, but there was no consent from the Turkish side. Thus, at the end of 1944 the station was installed in Cairo where some time later it changed its name to 'Eswu'. The new station was created through a merger of Stations 'T' with 'Balk'. It was located in Istanbul, and was entrusted with the task of taking over the areas of operation of the former stations. The disbandment of the two stations was scheduled for 1 February 1945. 'Eswu' supervised the cell no. 1 in Palestine, no. 3 in Syria and Lebanon, no. 5 in Iran, no. 7 in Turkey and no. 8 in Greece. All of them were to prepare regular intelligence work after the war. Apart from the intelligence assessments of a given country they very carefully monitored the Soviet penetration and performed other tasks targeting the Soviet Union, though exclusively through observation and without establishing an intelligence network.[16] Between March 1945 'Sadwik' was recalled by HQ and replaced by Maj. Franciszek Wierzbicki ('Wierzynek'). The latter had served in the Tel Aviv cell and was the deputy of Lt-Col. Sadowski, who until September forwarded lengthy monthly reports about the Soviet penetration in the Middle East and the military-political situation in the countries of the region.[17]

In May 1944 it was planned to install a Polish officer as the chief of the Polish section in the U. S. intelligence station in Tehran, as Persia offered the greatest possibilities for penetrating Soviet Russia. A Polish Military Attaché, subordinated to the II Bureau of the Polish General Staff, also worked in Iran. From 1 October 1942 this function was performed by Col. Antoni Szymański, who was in turn replaced in July next year by Lt-Col. Tadeusz Rudnicki, previously Military Attaché in the Soviet Union.[18]

The Middle East was also the area of operation of the Intelligence of the Ministry of Internal Affairs represented by Włodzimierz Bączkowski ('Epstein'), who from November 1943 worked as a representative in Jerusalem.[19] His tasks included monitoring the situation in the Middle East, Soviet questions (especially southern Russia, Ukraine, the Caucasus and Turkestan) and Jewish problems. The special task of Izmael-Bek Pietrucin-Pietruszewski ('Izmael', 'Beg', 'Aga', 'Kiszkurno'), assigned to the Middle East in November 1941, was to establish, through Maj. Guy Tamplin, contacts with British SOE organisations in Cairo in order to supply information, opinions and advice concerning the Caucasus. Another representative of the Ministry of Internal Affairs was Witold Rajkowski ('Omar'), a pre-war representative of the Polish Consulate General in Jerusalem, who in August 1941 was sent to the Middle East. Rajkowski operated from Beirut and his activity encompassed Lebanon, Egypt, Palestine and Syria. He was tasked with establishing contacts with Cairo and Istanbul. In July 1942 Rajkowski became subordinated to 'Kiszkurno', as a press attaché at the Polish Embassy in Baghdad. Pietrucin-Pietruszewski left for London in April 1944 and his post was taken over by Tadeusz Szumański ('Szum.'). From September 1942 to August 1944 Wacław Loga ('Sarna') was the Tehran 'correspondent' of Continental Action.[20]

The activities of Polish Intelligence in the Middle East was closely linked with those in the Balkans. Both cases were characterised by a considerable organisational flexibility of Polish intelligence structures. A significant role was played by Polish military presence in the Middle East and the changing intelligence requirements with regard to the Soviet Union. It was in that region that 'future-oriented' intelligence cells were installed during the last years of the war on an unprecedented scale. A special part was performed by extensively developed Polish radio intelligence in the Middle East, which actually functioned as a subordinate HQ of the London base.

Notes

1 The first Polish cell in this region was probably 'Szeherezada', which functioned (at the least in 1932–1934) in Persia, a country suitable for monitoring the Soviet

Union. CAW, the II Bureau of the Polish General Staff in 1921–1939, I. 303. 4. 1910 and I. 303. 4. 2073. A successive cell was created by Col. Jerzy Grobicki in Tehran under the cryptonym 'Nabuchodonozor'. In May 1932 it was transferred to Baghdad, where it existed until April 1937. Cell 'Dragoman', chiefed by Lt. Jan Helcman, functioned in Tehran from March 1934 to May 1935. Despite some success, both stations encountered considerable obstacles; consequently, chiefs of Section 'Wschód' in the Intelligence Department of the II Bureau decided to establish another mission – 'Radames'.

2 CAW, VI Bureau of the PGS in 1940–1949, II. 52. 481, Hand-over certificate of the Intelligence Department of the II Bureau of the PGS, 15 February 1944.

3 During the initial stage of functioning the station's maximum authorised strength was six officers. IPMS, Kol. 242/63.

4 A. Pepłoński, *Wywiad Polskich Sił Zbrojnych na Zachodzie 1939–1945* (*The Intelligence Service of the Polish Armed Forces in the West 1939–1945*), Warszawa 1995, p.149.

5 In November 1940 it totalled £400, from December 1940 to January 1941 – á £250, in February 1941 – £750, in March-May 1941 – á £800, in July-August 1941 – á £700, in August-October 1941 – á £1900, in November -December 1941 – á £2000, and in January-June 1942 – á £1500 .

6 IPMS, Kol. 242/63, Notebook with information about the structure of Polish Intelligence cells. In the later period use was made of their own and American couriers. Ibid., AXII24/56, Report on the work of the Intelligence Department on 5 May–14 May 1944, 13 May 1944; col. 242/62, note addressed to the Supreme Commander concerning the radio communications of II Bureau of the PGS, London 1 May 1944, and a scheme of connections in the clandestine network of W/T stations of the agents of II Bureau of the PGS on 1 May 1945; TNA (PRO), HW 34/8, Data about Agents' Radio Sets in France, 3 September 1943.

7 In contrast to Officer cells Intelligence cells (PW) were created outside the country in which a given station was located.

8 IPMS, A.XII.24/21, List of the names of the personnel of the Polish General Staff as of 1 June 1944.

9 In 1942 accounts by the Polish soldiers about the situation in the Soviet Union were still collected. The intention was to gather material relating to the inhuman aspects of the Soviet system rather than typical Intelligence information. The campaign was initiated by Prof. Stanisław Kot at the time when he was the Polish Ambassador to the Soviet Union. S. Kot, *Listy z Rosji do Gen. Sikorskiego* (*Letters from Russia to General Sikorski*), London 1955, passim.

10 For more details see: A. Pepłoński, *Wywiad Polskich*, op. cit., pp. 145–148 and the popular publication: S. Strumph Wojtkiewicz, *Agent nr 1*, Warszawa 1974.

11 IPMS, Kol. 242/63, Notebook with information about the structure of Polish Intelligence cells.

12 Headed by Capt. Wacław Gilewicz. It was planned to disband this cell and to reassign its commander to the Tehran intelligence cell in the first half of 1944.

13 In July 1946 out of a total of 19 officers and members of the staff of the cipher section of the disbanded Polish Army as many as 11 Soviet cipher specialists serviced four W/T receivers in Jerusalem and one in Cairo. The only officer in this group was Lt. Czesław Kuraś, Chief of the Palestinian cell (CAW, VI Department, II. 52.480, II Bureau of the PGS to W. Dunderdale, 22 July 1946).

14 CAW, VI Bureau, II. 52. 486, Maj. W. Gaweł, Official note for the Chief of the II Bureau of the PGS concerning instructions for Station 'T', 4 November 1944; ibid., Instruction concerning the organisation and work of Station 'T' of the II Bureau of the PGS, London 28 March 1944, annex no. 1 (structure of the station).

15 Ibid., Instruction concerning the organisation and work of Station 'T' of the II Bureau of the PGS, London 28 March 1944 and IPMS, A.XII.24/56, report on the

work of the II Bureau on 5 May–14 May 1944, 13 May 1944.

16 For a more details see: CAW, VI Bureau. 52. 486, Lt-Col. L. Sadowski 'Sadwik', chief of Station Eswu to the Chief of Cell no. 8, 11 March 1945, 'Wierzynek', chief of Station 'Eswu' to the Chief of the Cell no. 7, 24 April 1945, to the Chief of Cell no. 5, 26 April 1945, to the Chief of cell no. 3, no place, 12 October 1944, to the Chief of Cell no. 1, 30 November 1944 and II. 52. 481, general list of tasks for the following Intelligence Cells: 'Syria', 'Iran', 'Palestyna', 'Turcja', 'Grecja' in reference to Soviet penetration.

17 Ibid., II. 52. 485. In May 1945 'Wierzynek' planned to create new clandestine cells in Greece, China, Iran, Turkey, Egypt and Afghanistan as part of preparatory work focused on the Soviet Union (ibid., II. 52. 481).

18 IPMS, A. XII. 23/3, Military Missions and Bureaux as well as Military, Air Force and Naval attachés, Lt-Col. J. Leśniak, filling in for the chief of the II Bureau of the PGS, London, 8 October 1943. This is the way Leśniak characterised him in October 1943: 'Has not sent any reports since July. Active and smart for his own purposes. In Russia responsible for a number of shortcomings'. See: ibid., the II Bureau, A. XII. 24/37, report on the work of the Central Section of the the the II Bureau of the General Staff for 1944, and A. XII. 24/56, personnel of the Central as of 8 May 1944.

19 See J. Kłoczkowski, P. Kowal, *O Włodzimierzu Bączkowskim (About Włodzimierz Bączkowski)*, in: W. Bączkowski, *O wschodnich problemach Polski. Wybór pism (About Polish problems on the East. Selection of writings)*, Kraków 2000, pp 7–28.

20 IPMS, A. 9, List of cryptonyms used by the Ministry. The cryptonym for Continental Action in Iran was 'Diana', and in Palestine 'Kali'.

41
Polish-British Co-operation in Afghanistan 1939–1945

Jacek Tebinka

During the Second World War, Afghanistan was one of the most distant and exotic countries, where Polish-British intelligence co-operation took place. From British perspective, this country, bordering India on the north-west, with a common border with the USSR, Afghanistan was important for the internal and external security of this part of the British Empire. Before the war Poland had an interest in Afghanistan since both countries had a common, though distant, neighbour – the USSR – but political and trade contacts between the two were insignificant. On 30 November 1927 Poland and Afghanistan signed a friendship treaty, but the Polish Legation in Kabul was only established on 1 December 1938, though located in Tehran. The Polish presence in the capital of Afghanistan was limited to a one-person Consulate.[1]

The Soviet invasion of Poland on 17 September 1939 gave concern for the British, that Moscow may lead a more aggressive policy towards Central Asia, possibly threatening the British rule in India. London decided to engage in more active intelligence gathering in northern Afghanistan and Soviet Central Asia – and in particular on the attitudes of the region's population towards the USSR. Such activities were the province of the Indian Intelligence Bureau, in effect the local agency of SIS. The British were hoping to obtain information from the refugees crossing the Afghani border. In October of 1939 the government of British India planned to send an intelligence officer to Kabul, to create a network of informants there. The officer would collect information on the social and political situation in the Soviet republics on the other side of the border and pass it on to the Director of the Intelligence Bureau in Peshawar, in India. The Afghani Prime Minister, Muhammad Hashim Khan, raised some objections to this idea: he feared that the Soviets would soon find out about the British emissary. What he suggested instead was that he would supply the British with information from his own intelligence network, which operated in the Afghani-Soviet border regions.[2]

Before the British took a decision on this matter, they received a proposal on intelligence co-operation in Afghanistan, Iran and Iraq. This came at the end of October 1939, through the intermediary of the Polish Minister in Tehran, Jan Karszo-Siedlewski. This proposition was due to the fact that the Polish diplomat had lost faith in the abilities of French Intelligence there and blamed the French for Polish inability to collect information in Iran. While SIS had its own sources of information in Iraq, in the autumn of 1939 the situation in Iran was much worse, following the arrest of the resident chief of British Intelligence there, Townsend-Smith. Consequently the British lost their intelligence assets in Persia. From London's perspective, the presence of some 20 Polish engineers in Afghanistan, working on government contracts, mainly involving road building in various parts of the country, created a potential source of information on internal developments and on the activities of Axis citizens.[3]

The Polish offer concerning Afghanistan was well received in London, and on 14 November 1939 the Government of India presented it to the British Legation in Kabul, suggesting that relations should be established between the British military attaché and the Polish Consul on gathering intelligence. While the British Legation in Afghanistan was also interested in working with the Poles, it saw an impediment in the person of Michał Domaszewicz, the Polish Consul, who, the British suggested, was ill-suited for this type of work.[4] There were other reasons for the delay in co-operation. The British were attempting to play a leading role vis-à-vis Polish Intelligence at the expense of the French.[5] The French responded by trying to exercise control over Polish intelligence activities in Afghanistan and Persia, though the geographical position of both these countries clearly indicated that it was British Intelligence which was better placed to be the first recipient of any intelligence gathered there. The debate between Britain and France on this subject lasted until spring of 1940. In the end it was the fall of France in June 1940 that decided the matter – Britain would be the only source of finance for Polish Intelligence in Afghanistan.[6]

The idea that the Polish Consul in Afghanistan was to run intelligence there, using mainly Polish engineers, was also of some concern to the British, who in early 1940 were worried that it might lead to a conflict with the local government there. The authorities in Kabul were prepared to assist London, but without provoking the USSR.[7]

In addition the British special services, including the Indian Intelligence Bureau, were not quite convinced of the potential value of information the Poles might have collected in Afghanistan. Such doubts were not shared by the British Minister in Kabul, William Kerr Fraser-Tytler, who saw the prospects of co-operation in intelligence in a positive light. In January 1940 the Intelligence Bureau were mainly interested in information on German and Soviet activities in Kabul, Herat and in the Afghani Turkmenistan and on the deployment and movements of the Red Army on the other side of the Afghani border.[8]

The Polish-British intelligence co-operation was delayed by the Afghan Government, which in early January 1940 refused to grant a visa to the Polish Minister in Tehran, Karszo-Siedlewski. The Minister intended to travel to Kabul in person in order to recall the Consul, Domaszewicz, and to replace him with an officer of the II Bureau, Mikołaj Bronisław Telatycki, then Polish commercial attaché in Persia. Until the end of January the authorities in Kabul were also slow in granting a visa to Telatycki, which delayed the changeover of the consul. When Telatycki finally arrived in Kabul on 4 February 1940, Domaszewicz was unwilling to hand over his post.[9]

In any case the British were not proposing to employ Telatycki on intelligence duties immediately. They were awaiting the conclusion of the talks with French Intelligence on who was to control any Polish activity in Afghanistan. Minister Kerr Fraser-Tytler thought that a Polish intelligence station would be a potentially good source of information on Soviet intelligence work there – though he doubted whether Telatycki would be in a position to collect information from north of the Afghan border. The dispatch of the British Minister to London, dated 3 February 1940, indicates that his Legation found it difficult to gather information on the German and Soviet intelligence activities in Afghanistan, except in Kabul, Kandahar and Jalalabad, where British representatives were present.[10]

As already stated, Telatycki's intelligence work was delayed by the unwillingness of Consul Domaszewicz to vacate his position – this only took place in July 1940. Lack of funds was another obstacle. The continuing French-British talks meant that from February to the end of July 1940 Telatycki was not given any money by the British. In view of the French pressure, the Polish Foreign Ministry even thought about closing the Kabul Consulate to reduce its expenditure. This possibility caused some disquiet in British Intelligence, which wanted information from the Polish engineers employed in Afghanistan.[11]

In the autumn of 1939 the British were concentrating on the Soviet threat to Afghanistan, but by the summer of 1940, after the fall of France, their attention shifted to counteracting the Axis penetration of the country. Finally, at the end of July 1940, the Foreign Office and the Government of India took the decision to finance Telatycki. The Polish Foreign Ministry approval did not arrive until 25 September 1940. The Poles asked for Telatycki to conduct his intelligence activities under the cover of Deputy Consul.[12]

Once these bureaucratic obstacles were out of the way, it seemed that nothing would further delay the Polish-British intelligence co-operation in Afghanistan. But on 18 January 1941 the Afghani Government unexpectedly refused to recognise Telatycki as the Polish Consul, and informed the British Minister accordingly. Kabul argued that it did not recognise the Polish Government-in-Exile. After some persuasion from Fraser-Tytler, the Afghani Foreign Ministry finally agreed to accept Telatycki as an unofficial representative of the Polish authorities, with a mission of looking after the small Polish community in Afghanistan. The

British Minister was pleased, since this meant that Telatycki would be able to stay in Afghanistan, collecting intelligence and quietly working against the Axis countries. The Pole was not only a channel for information – he himself was involved in intelligence. Telatycki provided counter-intelligence cover for the Polish engineers in Afghanistan, collected information on internal developments, on the activities of citizens and diplomats of the Axis powers (over 200 persons), and on those of the USSR.[13]

For a time, the outbreak of the German-Soviet war on 22 June 1941 meant that the Soviet threat against Afghanistan was reduced to a minimum. At the same time the intelligence operations conducted by the German and Italian Legations in Kabul and by specialists from these countries engaged by the Afghani Government, became the primary target for British Intelligence. The Axis powers attempted to use Kabul as a centre for collecting intelligence on India and on Soviet Central Asia. The British were also worried by attempts to cause rebellion in the regions bordering Afghanistan and India. Such attempts were made by German and Italian diplomats who were in contact with Faqir of Ipi, who was against British domination in the North-Western Province of India.[14]

The Polish ability to assist was significantly reduced due to the regulations introduced by the Afghani authorities at the end of June 1941. These prohibited foreigners to travel outside Kabul without a pass, which clearly limited Telatycki's ability to gather information. Intelligence reports submitted by the British military attaché in Kabul indicate, however, that until the end of the war the Polish representative supplied him with regular information on the internal situation in Afghanistan and on German activities there. Such information was collected by the Polish engineers working in different parts of the country, who could travel and make numerous contacts. Every few months, Telatycki would visit the Intelligence Bureau offices in Peshawar.[15]

The Axis powers suffered a significant blow in October 1941, when the Afghani authorities agreed to a demand by Great Britain and the USSR for the citizens of the Third Reich and Italy to leave Afghanistan. This limited their ability to conduct spying operations. The only operatives left in place were the Axis diplomats and secret agents.[16]

The British had one important intelligence advantage in Afghanistan: their ability to read the codes used by the German and Japanese legations and by the local Abwehr station. When combined with the information supplied by British Intelligence in Afghanistan, which in part was provided by Telatycki, this was sufficient to effectively counter the operations mounted by the Axis powers. Such operations, aimed at creating unrest in India and the Soviet Central Asia, were at their most intensive in 1942 and at the beginning of 1943.[17]

Telatycki was able to provide the British with increasing amounts of information on Soviet Central Asia, since from the autumn of 1941 a growing number of Poles, drafted to the Red Army and stationed near the border, were escaping to Afghanistan. There were also some refugees among Polish citizens freed from the Gulag following the Sikorski-Majski agreement. At first this was not a mass phenomenon – the numbers were limited to some dozen persons per month in the first quarter of 1942. As a rule, though not without difficulties, the Afghan authorities allowed Telatycki access to such refugees. Most were later evacuated to India.[18]

The breakthrough in the intelligence confrontation with the Axis powers came in the summer and autumn of 1943, when two German diplomats involved in spying were expelled from Afghanistan, and when Italy joined the Allies. This significantly reduced the potential of the Axis countries to run operations, especially since the Japanese Legation was the least effective in this activity. The Polish representative co-operated with the British until the end of the war. In November 1944, following the return to Poland, via the USSR, of two Polish engineers, Telatycki was attacked by communist propaganda, in the newspaper *Wolna Polska* (*Free Poland*), published by the pro-Moscow Union of Polish Patriots. Combined with his work as an intelligence officer, these attacks prevented him from returning to the post-Yalta Poland. The esteem in which he was held by the British was perhaps indicated by the award to him of the Order of the British Empire, 'for important services for this country [Great Britain – J.T.] of a highly confidential nature, which significantly helped to neutralize Afghanistan as a centre of hostile activity during the war'. He was also given British citizenship and assisted in his settling in Southern Rhodesia.[19]

The Polish-British intelligence co-operation in Afghanistan did not bring spectacular successes. Telatycki's activities in 1940-1945 did, however, play a part in the contribution of Polish Intelligence to the Allied war effort in many parts of the globe. This is a small-scale illustration of the intelligence co-operation between the two countries that lasted throughout the war and ended less than happily for the Polish side.

Notes

1   P. Łossowski, *Polska w Europie i świecie 1918–1939* (*Poland in Europe and in the World, 1918–1939*), Warsaw 1990, pp. 136–137. The presence of intelligence operatives of the II Bureau, Polish General Staff, in Central Asia dates back to 1932, when the 'Wschód' ('East') Section established Station 'Nabuchodonozor' in Tehran, run by Lt-Col. Jerzy Grobicki. About the beginnings of the co-operation with British Intelligence there, see Chapter 16, A. Pepłoński, A. Suchcitz, J. Tebinka, Intelligence Co-operation during the Second Half of the 1930s.

2   TNA (PRO) FO 371/23699, N 4764/4030/38, Lord Halifax to Government of India on 22 September 1939; N 4953/4030/38, Government of India to Lord Halifax on 1 October 1939; FO 371/23700, N 5513/4030/38, Kabul Legation to Government of India on 20 October 1939. See also J. Modrzejewska-Leśniewska, *Afganistan w polityce Wielkiej Brytanii i Rosji Radzieckiej 1919–1924* (*Afghanistan and the Policies of Great Britain and Soviet Russia 1919–1924*), Warsaw 2001, on the role of Afghanistan in the policies of its northern neighbour.

3   TNA (PRO) FO 371/23700, N 5107/4030/38, note of L. Baggaley of 6 October 1939; N 5608/4030/38, L. Collier to H. Kennard, 3 November 1939; FO 371/24769, N 1366/57/97, note of F. Maclean of 6 February 1940.

4   TNA (PRO) FO 371/23632, N 7291/7291/97, Government of India to Kabul, 14

February 1939, Kabul to the Government of India, 19 November 1939.

5 TNA (PRO) HS 8/263, memorandum of 5 April 1940 on the activities of MIR. This document states that the British have taken over control over the activities of Polish Intelligence in Europe and the Middle East.

6 TNA (PRO) FO 371/24768, N 923/57/91, draft dispatch of Lord Halifax to W.K. Fraser-Tytler, end of January 1940; N 1216/57/97, War Office to Foreign Office, 23 January 1940.

7 TNA (PRO) FO 371/23632, N 7717/7291/97, MI 2 to India Office, December 1939.

8 Ibid., a conference at the War Office, 19 December 1939; N 7900/7291/97, W.K. Fraser-Tytler to Lord Halifax, 28 December 1939; FO 371/24768, N 1218/57/97, Government of India to Lord Halifax, 30 January 1940.

9 TNA (PRO) FO 371/24768, N 318/57/97, R. Bullard (Tehran) to FO, 6 January 1940.

10 TNA (PRO) FO 371/24769, N 1366/57/97, W.K. Fraser-Tytler to FO, 3 February 1940. In his book on Afghanistan, Fraser-Tytler omitted the intelligence aspects: see his *Afghanistan. A Study of Political Development in Central and Southern Asia*, London 1967.

11 TNA (PRO) FO 371/24769, N 4060/57/97, note by R.T. Peel of 11 April 1940; W.K. Fraser-Tytler to FO, 6 April 1940; FO to H. Kennard, 14 May 1940.

12 TNA (PRO) FO 371/24769, N 5075/57/97, Lord Halifax to the Government of India, 22nd July 1940; N 6057/57/97, note of R. Peel of 31 July 1940; N 6720/57/97, F. Savery to India Office, 25 September 1940. Maj. E.W. Fletcher arrived in Kabul in August 1940. Working under the cover of Publicity Officer at the British legation, his job was to counteract the Axis powers intelligence activities. See M. Hauner, *India in Axis Strategy. Germany, Japan and Indian Nationalists in the Second World War*, Stuttgart 1981, p. 226.

13 TNA (PRO) FO 371/26745, C 4104/1730/55, W.K. Fraser-Tytler to A. Eden, 24 January 1941.

14 TNA (PRO) WO 106/3768A, note of MI 2 of 10 May 1943; M. Hauner, *One Man against the Empire. The Faqir of Ipi and the British in Central Asia on the Eve of and during the Second World War*, 'Journal of Contemporary History', 1981, no. 1, pp. 183–212; A. Swinson, *North-West Frontier. People and Events*, London 1967, pp. 321–332.

15 TNA (PRO) FO 371/26745, C 7195/1730/55, W.K. Fraser-Tytler to A. Eden, 28 June 1941; intelligence reports in the FO 371 set, files 31323, 34919, 39950.

16 M. Hauner, *India in Axis Strategy*, op. cit., pp. 306–339.

17 TNA (PRO) HW 1/181, S. Menzies to W. Churchill, 31 October 1941; HW 36/1, Kabul (Witzel) to Berlin, 7 and 24 July 1942; HW 38/1, Japanese Legation in Kabul to Foreign Ministry in Tokyo, 5 July 1943.

18 TNA (PRO) FO 371/31322, E 1700/79/97, Intelligence Summary no. 5 of 31 January 1942; E 2101/79/97, Intelligence Summary no. 3 and 7 of 17 January and 14February 1942; E 3393/79/97, Intelligence Summary no. 13 of 28 March 1942.

19 TNA (PRO) FO 371/47742, N 2795/1532/55, G.F. Squire to A. Eden, 3 March 1945; FO 371/56577, N 4224/205/55, Squire to India Office, 26 March 1946; FO 371/52274, E 9314/13/97, Weekly Intelligence Summary no. 35 of 31 July 1946.

Gill Bennett

Very little information has been found about Polish activities in the Far East. It is clear, however, from scattered references that a considerable number of Polish Intelligence agents managed to gain employment in Japanese Embassies and Legations in a variety of countries, and often used these positions to carry on activities of which their employers were unaware. There were, of course, instances of Poles passing information to the enemy rather than to the Allies, and sometimes to both at once, but there is no doubt that the Polish presence in Japanese diplomatic circles provided a valuable seam of information. However, no documentation has been found relating to Polish-Japanese collaboration in the region itself. The only documents that have been found relate to Anglo-Polish collaboration in China, with some reference to the Philippines.

The first references found relate to a trip to China made from October-December 1940 by Krosnowski, a Pole apparently working with SIS in Manila, who gave him money towards his trip and a questionnaire, asking him to bring back information in particular on economic matters and trans-Siberian traffic. On 26 December Manila sent London a copy of Krosnowski's report of his journey, but only a fragment has been found, in the form of part of an unsigned letter to Col. Gano dated 15 December 1940. The extract that has survived relates to a meeting in Shanghai with Col. Pawłowicz, recently assigned to the staff of the Polish Legation in Shanghai. Pawłowicz, formerly Chief of the Russia section of the Records and Studies Department in the II Bureau in Warsaw, had for some years been in close contact with his Japanese opposite numbers and had indeed helped the Japanese Foreign Ministry to reorganise their Russian research department. He had been sent to Harbin before the war as Press Attaché to the Consulate General, and although relations with the Japanese were cooler after the outbreak of hostilities, he maintained liaison with his former contacts, and managed to place several of his former officers in the Japanese 'II Bureau' in Tokyo, from where they were supplying information about Russia. Pawłowicz had lost contact with Warsaw on the invasion of Poland, but had re-established communications through Col. Levitoux, the Polish Military Attaché in Tokyo, and expressed himself to Krosnowski as eager to help.

Although the report is incomplete, further references from Manila indicate that Krosnowski also contacted the Polish Consul in Harbin, Jerzy Litewski, who had formerly been employed in counter-espionage for the Polish General Staff, and also was now keen to help the Allied war effort. Litewski apparently agreed to recruit two Polish employees of the Customs Department of the Chinese Eastern Railway, to supply regular information on contraband and general subjects. On 5 January 1941, however, an SIS telegram to Manila warned against any attempt to contact or 'interfere with' Pawłowicz, who was working for the SIS representative in Shanghai; a further telegram noted that the same 'hands-off' message applied to Levitoux, and no action should be taken in regard to Litewski until enquiries had been made with the Polish authorities in London.

On 29 January SIS were informed that neither the II Bureau nor the Polish Foreign Ministry had any objection to British contacts with Litewski, and were given the following report on him (noted as 'rather flattering' by a member of A4 on 5 February):

> Capt., Polish Army Reserve; Polish Consul in Kharbin [sic]; formerly officer of the I Ulan Regiment of KRECHOWCE; aged about 45–47; born in White Russia (now under Soviets). A man of great integrity, devoid of pose and blague. Was an excellent officer, superior and colleague.
>
> Worked in the Second Bureau since 1930; at first in C[ounter] E[spionage] – from 1931–32 was head of department there; then from 1933 onwards in the Intelligence Department; from 1934–37 was I[ntelligence] S[ervice] agent of the Eastern Department at Istanbul; was later transferred to the staff of the Polish ministry for Foreign Affairs and sent as Polish Consul to Kharbin.
>
> As Intelligence Service officer he is very calm, sober and a realist; he is courageous but careful and endowed with a great feeling of responsibility. He is very well acquainted with the methods of internal and external activity of the Soviet Intelligence Service and Counter-Espionage work. Knows all about possibilities of organising I.S. on the territory of the USSR. Has first hand knowledge of Russian emigration problems, minorities and their practical value. Less versed in theoretical research on Russian matters, he excels in organisation. Has a gift of social intercourse and tactfully exploits persons with whom he is acquainted socially.
>
> Apart from his work he was used as an expert in establishing the technical side of inspiration and Soviet disinformation. He displayed remarkable tact and firmness in his relations with the Japanese in Kharbin.

In the exercise of his duties he always showed the greatest firmness, sometimes bordering on lack of consideration for others, but he is always a gentleman.

Meanwhile, problems persisted regarding contacts with Pawłowicz. A telegram from Shanghai dated 4 June 1941 reported that the Polish Chargé d'Affaires had received a telegram asking for a report on Pawłowicz, and was likely to make an unfavourable reply, insisting that "P's cover at Legation is given up and that 'P' operates as a private individual'. Pawłowicz, however, had received a telegram from the Polish General Staff informing him that the British no longer needed him and that he should provide them with information on Russia. A period of wrangling followed as to who would employ and pay Pawłowicz. The matter was not cleared up until July, when Col. Gano asked A4 section of SIS to send a telegram to Col. Pawlowicz informing him that he had been appointed 'Chief of the Far East Intelligence Station, II Bureau, Polish General Staff, with HQ in Shanghai or elsewhere as may be indicated by your British colleague'. His office would be known as 'Wudal', and he would receive instructions and facilities from his British colleague. Col. Gano asked SIS to pay £70 monthly to Col. Pawłowicz from 1 August 1941, which sum would be reimbursed by the Polish authorities.

The A4 minute recording these arrangements concluded optimistically that the matter appeared to be settled, but difficulties persisted. Wudal (Pawłowicz) telegraphed on 9 August 1941 that the Polish Chargé d'Affaires, de Rosset, was still sabotaging his activities and showing 'signs of abnormality and irresponsibility'. He asked that the Embassy in Tokyo should be instructed to control de Rosset: 'For purpose of cover and to establish and regularise my position vis-à-vis the Polish community it is essential that I am given local rank of Consul and that de Rosset is instructed to accept this appointment and afford me all facilities in execution of my duty.' No further documents have been found relating to this dispute, nor to indicate what further contacts were pursued with Litewski.

PART V
INTELLIGENCE ACTIVITIES OF
THE UNION OF ARMED STRUGGLE – HOME ARMY

43
Intelligence Activities of the
Home Army General Headquarters

Andrzej Chmielarz

The Home Army – an underground military clandestine organisation – was created in accordance with a scheme adopted in the armed forces; therefore, its structure contained all the services, some of which were overgrown. They included the intelligence service, whose activity was supervised by the II Bureau of the Home Army General Headquartes (GHQ), and before that by the Union of Armed Struggle (ZWZ) and the Service for Poland's Victory (SZP). The vast expansion of intelligence was influenced by the fact that the Home Army emerged and acted in the areas occupied by the enemy, and by recognising that intelligence activity could prove advantageous for the Allied war effort. Polish territory was an excellent base for conducting intelligence in the Third Reich. Later, as a result of war activities that territory was crossed by the majority of communication routes leading to the eastern front.

On the eve of the capitulation of Warsaw in 27 September 1939 a new clandestine organisation was created, under the mame of 'the Service for Poland's Victory (SZP). In its scheme, an intellegence network was to be set up under Maj. Wacław Berka 'Brodowicz'.

On 13 November 1939 Gen. Władysław Sikorski created the Union of Armed Struggle, thus changing current assumptions of the clandestine organisation in Poland. At the turn of 1939–1940 In Paris, the Service for Poland's Victory was transformed into the Union of Armed Struggle General Headquarters (for simplicity it will be referred to in future as the Home Army) headed by Gen. Kazimierz Sosnkowski, who directly supervised the commands of the six regions into which the Polish territory had been divided. On account of difficulties with ensuring direct control over the regions another reorganisation was carried out in January 1940, establishing the following occupation commands: German in Warsaw and Soviet in Lwów. Following the defeat of France Gen. Sikorski appointed Gen. Stefan Rowecki, the commander of the German occupation area, to the post of Commander-in-Chief and established the Home Army General

Headquartes (GHQ) in Poland.[2] On 29 June 1940 Gen. Sikorski created an Independent Home Army.[3] Its tasks, apart from developing directives for clandestine work, involved 'general supervision of intelligence in Poland'.[4]

In accordance with the instruction of January 1941 the General Staff II Bureau set intelligence tasks for the organisation in Poland and provided technical and personnel assistance. The tasks were to be realised through the VI Bureau of the Polish General Staff responsible for getting the technical and personnel assistance to Poland and for the transfer of intelligence reports from Poland. The Home Army Commander-in-Chief was obligated to convey intelligence information 'in the most detailed and frequent manner as possible: by radio cables at least once a week and written reports once a month, additionally any seized documents' of importance.[5]

The VI Bureau provided radio and courier communications with Poland, provided funds for the underground activity, and conducted the parachute drops of arms and specially trained experts, including those involved in intelligence. In order to implement the entrusted tasks it organised a network of transfer-liaison bases located in unoccupied European countries and the Middle East. The Bureau did not have any commanding authority in relation to the organisation in Poland; on the contrary, it represented the intersests of the Home Army within the General Staff in London.

Maj. Berka began the organisation of the main cell and the construction of a field network from scratch; owing to a lack of personnel (as the majority of the staff of the General Staff II Bureau of the Polish Army was evacuated to Romania) – had to rely on people with no experience with this type of work. An attempt to recruit candidates from the intelligence of the former Frontier Defence Corps (KOP), gathered around Capt. Stanisław Orłowski, failed because they expected to take over the leading posts in the newly organised Bureau and intelligence networks.[6] Equally unsuccessful proved to be the talks held with Capt. Stefan Witkowski, an engineer and commander of the 'Muszkieterzy' military intelligence organisation, who refused to get his organisation involved in intelligence work.

Chaos and difficulties were additionally deepened by emissaries of the cells of the pre-war General Staff II Bureau of the Polish Army in Bucharest and Budapest who recruited candidates for intelligence work in networks other than those of the Home Army. Certain order was finally restored by an instruction issued in 4 December 1939 by Gen. Sosnkowski, the Home Army Commander-in-Chief, who directed: 'all those who on their own or upon orders of their previous authorities initiated, while in Romania, military undertakings at home (including intelligence and subversive activities), to hand over [. . .] all the organisational cells created in Poland' to Col. Rowecki, designated as the commander of the Home Army region in Warsaw.[7]

At a conference held in Belgrade (25 May–2 June 1940) and attended by delegates of the General Staff, the Home Army GHQ in France, and the command in the part of Poland under German occupation. It was determined that intelligence on the Polish territory would be conducted exclusively by the Home Army.[8] In January 1941, upon General Rowecki's recommendation,[9] Gen. Sosnkowski decided that intelligence in both occupied parts of the country and within the Polish borders as a whole would be carried out exclusively by the Home Army Commander-in-Chief through his intelligence organisation. In this way, all units of the II Bureau of PGS in occupied Poland, with the exception of those engaged in intelligence in the Reich and the Soviet Union, became subordinated to the Home Army Commander-in-Chief.[10]

The II Bureau of PGS, could conduct intelligence in the Reich and the Soviet Union from the territory of Poland, and had the right to create independent penetrating intelligence cells in both occupied regions. Those cells could not, however, undertake in any intelligence in Poland. Despite the decisions concerning the control over 'Muszkieterzy' (Musketeers), who maintained an independent contact with the General Staff II Bureau, the Intelligence Service (SIS) and Station '741', controlled by a II Bureau cell in Budapest, the situation lasted until June 1941, against the orders of Gen. Rowecki.[11] Eventually the 'Muszkieterzy', station 741 and the II Bureau cell active in Warsaw became subordinated to the Home Army GHQ and incorporated into its intelligence network.[12]

After its subordination to the II Bureau of the Home Army GHQ, Station '741' took on the cryptonym 'Lombard' and kept considerable autonomy. It had its own cells providing communications and a analytical work. While the incorporation of Station 741 had a successful end and the station itself marked significant successes in the history of the II Bureau, the attempt to control 'Muszkieterzy' was a total failure.

The intelligence organisation of the Service for Poland's Victory, subsequently the Union of Armed Struggle, was based on a scheme adopted by many armies. The project assumed the creation of three basic branches: supervisory-organisational; intelligence gathering and records and studies (information processing).

Security requirements of the organisation and the necessity of having a reconnaissance of enemy forces were the reasons why the Home Army intelligence service was organised in the field in parallel to other organisational branches.[13] Intelligence structures were established within every command (i.e. in cells, districts and regions). They were supervised directly by field commanders and initially worked primarily for their needs. Nonetheless, they were assigned wider tasks formulated by the chief of the Home Army intelligence, and stemming from the needs of operational planning. Since intelligence cells covered practically the whole area under the German occupation it was possible to obtain extremely detailed information – both military and economic – which, after being processed and studied at the level of the Home Army GHQ, was passed to the Headquarters in Paris and then to London.

The emerging intelligence network was, however, composed of people professionally unprepared for their tasks. In this situation, and in order to direct the work of the agents, training became an urgent necessity. It was based on direct instructions of superiors and on the directives prepared by the II Bureau of the Home Army GHQ.[14]

The directives recommended the following:

> The general rule underlying good field reports is the proverbial five W: – who is doing what, when, where, and in what way (I), furthermore, more precise descriptions of details referring to the way of obtaining information (sometimes by resorting to force), i.e. it must be said whether the given information is documentary – then it must be recorded in files (at least as a photocopy) – whether it comes from visual observation or hearsay, and in what circumstances was it obtained (while marching, stopping, transport or lodgings). The report must be brief but precise. All rumours or one's own deduction must be strictly avoided; however, if, they are included then it must be noted what represents one's own deduction or what is 'hearsay'; the same applies to drawn conclusions.[15]

Similar recommendations concerning the requirements to be met by intelligence officers trained in Great Britain were sent to London by Gen. Rowecki:

> Dwelling on the experience gained during three years of clandestine work I would like to present the remarks and recommendations formulated below, relating to the training of the future intelligence cadets:

> The purpose of intelligence work. To make the cadet aware of the purposes of intelligence through concrete answers to the questions: 1) what to look for, 2) how to report – so that he would not have to resolve those issues himself. The cadets must obtain precise instructions as to the structure of enemy organisations and its characteristic features, which are difficult to conceal in the examining objects (e.g. the organisation of the army, the system of marking, emblems, characteristic details distinguishing an air base from an airfield, the marking and silhouettes of particular types of navy ships, etc.). The cadets must emphasise the technique of editing concise intelligence reports, in accordance with certain standardised forms adapted to essential needs. For further examination I put forward a thesis concerning the specialisation of the cadets based upon a selection of priorities. In our activity three different groups of interest emerge: a) the East – military matters and all issues associated with war action, such as movement, depots, hospitals, exploitation of terrain; b) the littoral – ports, shipyards, marine traffic; c) the Reich and occupied countries – war industry.

> Techniques of intelligence work.
> 1) Accept our principle: our agents can exclusively be Polish.[16]

In general this principle was binding. Home Army intelligence did not employ paid agents and avoided recruiting agents from among native Germans. Initially, intelligence tasks were formulated by the intelligence Division of the Home Army GHQ. The material received, after being edited into reports, was sent by a courier to the General Staff in Paris.[17] By the first half of 1940 it had become clear that the intelligence from Poland constituted an extremely valuable source of information. The main problem lay in its efficient transmission to the Polish General Staff in Paris, and after the defeat of France – to London. The process of intelligence being supplied by couriers to the stations and cells in Hungary, Romania, Turkey, Switzerland or Sweden prolonged the duration of the transferring of information. This problem was resolved to a considerable extent in the autumn of 1940 only after the establishment of permanent W/T communications.

In mid-January 1940 the Home Army GHQ in Paris sent to Poland 'Guidelines for the organisation of Intelligence Service in our country'.[18] Intelligence tasks were formulated in an enclosed questionnaire. The Home Army GHQ was interested primarily in the enemy Order of Battle (the location and strength of garrisons), all changes in the Order, the organisation and description of units, the Air force, armoured and motorised weapons, army supplies and transport efficiency, fuel transport, the functioning of industry and its productivity.

Home Army intelligence provided information indispensable not only for planning its own activities, but predominantly passed the intelligence over to Allied staffs, successfully realising the entrusted tasks, despite the fact that it required organising networks outside the territory of the Polish Second Republic and building a specialised mechanism which would analyse the information obtained. In this situation the II Bureau became a highly specialised service which not only obtained information but also analysed it thoroughly and passed it on in the form of synthetic assessments for the use by the Allies.

Initially, intelligence activities co-ordinated by the II Bureau of the Home Army GHQ concentrated on intelligence reconnaissance of the Polish territory, an undertaking linked directly with a planned armed uprising which was to take place simultaneously with a victorious offensive from the west. The defeat of France and the transition to long-term activities made it necessary for the intelligence networks to reach beyond the territory of the Second Republic.

On 28 July 1940, after the establishment of permanent radio communications with London, the General Staff requested that weekly intelligence reports be sent from Poland in accordance to an established form.[19] In view of the fact that the territorial range of the assignments formulated by the Polish General Staff and the British was becoming increasingly wider, at the end of 1940 the Home Army GHQ began to organise a centrally directed intelligence network, whose prime task was to conduct intelligence in the Third Reich and on the territories it occupied. When in 1941 the information about German preparations for attacking the

Soviet Union became available, intelligence teams were organised ready to work at the rear area of the German front line in Russia.

The future tasks of Home Army intelligence finally assumed concrete shape in 1940–1941. On the Polish territory and the rear area of the eastern front intelligence was to focus on reconnaissance of all military and economic issues, while in the Reich area it was to concentrate on economic-industrial matters, including the results of air raids. Apart from these tasks the Home Army was to conduct reconnaissance of the Baltic Sea and the North Sea ports and to study the morale of the German army and society.[20]

Home Army intelligence was extremely efficient and provided a lot of information. It won its first significant success in 1940, which was to pass over the plans for the invasion of France[21] and to obtain the intelligence on the German preparations for war against Russia. The British assessed the effectiveness of the intelligence work in highest terms: 'Friends appreciate the extraordinary value of the rendered services, which have a great influence on the activities. Upon their recommendation I convey the words of highest appreciation for the good intelligence work'.[22]

On 16 July 1941 the Chief of the VI Bureau of the Polish General Staff wired Gen. Rowecki:

> Intelligence information is of utmost importance to us and our friends. This is why it is highly desirable to have daily W/T telegrams, if possible. At the same time, please reduce political reports to a maximum of 50% of the transmitted groups. The watch tower [General Sikorski] has given his consent.
> I repeat the most important currently intelligence tasks:
> * further identification of German units in the east;
> * the identification of German units transported through Poland and Prussia; basically, we are interested in monitoring of what gets across the 24th meridian in both directions;
> * German losses and the transportation of the wounded and prisoners of war;
> * possible information about operations and the use of new weapons;
> * information from the Polish and Prussian ports and those of the Third Reich;
> * information concerning the morale of the German army and the society;
> * the effects of bombing of the Reich;
> * the state and the public mood in Poland (Poles and minorities).[23]

Home Army intelligence also carried out special tasks, often very untypical, requested by the British. On 7 July 1941: 'Friends are asking for 1) samples of straw-rope used in the Reich to tie sheaves'.[24] On 3 August 1942 the intelligence Service requested: '1) information about substitute methods used for producing shoes in the Reich, their faults and merits; 2) to what extent is the alleged critical state of the Reich for the lack of: a) copper sulphate and chemical pesticides, b) phosphates and artificial fertilisers, c) fodder for live-stock, d) farming tools, e) untreated and tanned hide, f) cord used for tying, g) vaseline, iodine, castor oil and quinine'.[25]

More specialised tasks were also put forward caused by the suspicion that the Germans were using infra-red rays: 'IS requests information: 1) Do artillery, tank, searchlight and communications units use field-glasses or telescopes of abnormal shape, possibly outfitted with electrical wires, or resembling reflective cameras with wire connections 2) What sort of light is used at night for vehicles moving individually or in a column? 3) Is a device resembling a searchlight used whose light cannot be seen with the naked eye? 4) Does the equipment of units include some sort of black or dark green plates made of glass, gelatine, etc? 5) Do units use special coloured glass? 6) What is the system of making dim lights? 7) Any information about the army taking night time photographs is welcome'.[26]

The rapidly growing range of British areas of interest, which resulted in the increased number of tasks, affected also the organisational structure of underground intelligence. The expanding intelligence network as well as the need to keep the records and to segregate and prepare the reports required an expansion of essential and support cells. The organisation of the II Bureau of the Home Army GHQ gradually assumed shape in 1941–1942. The first to be created was the Intelligence Department, headed by Capt. Wójtowicz 'Bolek', deputy chief of the II Bureau, and the executive office of the Chief of the II Bureau. At the end of 1940 a unit was organised which specialised in segregating and preparing intelligence reports; later it gave birth to a Department of Studies and Analyses headed by Lt. Jerzy Jurkowski 'Wedel'.

A Counter-intelligence Department was also established in the spring of 1941, and the combined communications and financial units were split, thus creating separate departments. At the end of 1941 the II Bureau formed a department headed by Julia Krasicka 'Julia', whose task was to study the morale among the German society, and an economic studies department, organised and headed by Jerzy Chmielewski 'Rafał'. A department specialising in techniques of preparing false documents was also expanded, to be reorganised into a Cover Documents Department in 1942. Consequently, three basic branches emerged: offensive intelligence (intelligence networks), analyses and studies, and counter-intelligence. Their work was supported by specialised and service sections. The final structure of the II (Intelligence) Bureau of the Home Army GHQ encompassed nine departments:[27]

- the Executive Office of the Chief of the II Bureau – provided security of the chief of the Bureau (offices, points of contact, arrangements of meetings and briefings, dispatch of intelligence reports);
- the Studies and Propaganda Department – dealt with the morale in the German army and the society, and analyses of the German propaganda; in mid-1944 the Department totalled 30 persons;

- the Military Studies Department – was responsible for work out of the collected information, professional assessment and elaboration of conclusions; a staff of about forty in mid-1944;
- the Economic Studies Department – covered the analyses of materials concerning various domains of the economy conducted from the point of view of the defence production; 34 staff in mid-1944;
- Internal Communications Department – provided communications within the II Bureau, 39 staff in mid-1944;
- Finances and Welfare Department – responsible for the finances of the II Bureau and the welfare of the families of arrested members; 21 staff in mid-1944;
- Offensive Intelligence Department – supervision over intelligence networks controlled directly by the II Bureau of the Home Army GHQ, control over sections which direct particular networks in various areas; more than a hundred members in 1944;
- Cover Documents and Technical Support Department – forging documents and preparation of movable and permanent dead letter boxes; more than 100 staff in 1944;
- Security and Counter-intelligence Department – more than 520 members in mid-1944.

A similar structure was adopted by the field II Bureau structure of particular organisational levels. The field network of districts and regions conducted intelligence independently of the offensive intelligence networks, steered directly by the High Command (so-called central or long-range intelligence networks).[28] In those areas where the intelligence service was supervised by the commands of the Home Army regions, central intelligence networks concentrated their attention on particularly important military or industrial targets.

Considering the essential range of activity the Offensive Intelligence Department (cryptonyms 'Stragan', 'Wd 67', 'Marcjanna') was the most important. Its chief was simultaneously the first deputy chief of the II Bureau. The Department was composed of three sections : 'Zachód' (West), 'Wschód' (East) and 'Generalne Gubernatorstwo' (General-gouvernement). The Offensive Intelligence Department conducted, through the centrally steered intelligence networks, the reconnaissance of the Third Reich and the Protectorate of Bohemia and Moravia as well as the eastern front and its rear area.

Offensive intelligence organised its work by using several methods: in those areas where it was possible to engage pre-war intelligence residents (e.g. the Karol Englisch network in Austria)[29] which relied on the support from local Polish communities (the network 'August' in Cieszyn Silesia, Jan Mrózek's network in Vienna, Linz and Zaolzie),[30] while in the Polish territories incorporated into the Third Reich territorial networks were set up (stations 'Morze' (Sea), 'Wybrzeże' (Coast) and 'Śląsk' (Silesia)). Cells or individual resident agents were installed in the centre of the Reich, in north Germany, and in the Baltic and North Sea ports (e.g. the cell in Wrocław, headed by Mr. Zdzisław Maszewski, an engineer).[31] So-called mobile teams conducted on the spot reconnaissance of industrial or military targets either in the Third Reich or on the territories annexed by the Germans.

From February 1941 the offensive intelligence network of the II Bureau of the the Home Army GHQ, known under the cryptonym 'Stragan', was headed by Maj. Stanisław Rogiński 'Górski'. He supervised staffs of sections (centres) located in Warsaw which in turn controlled intelligence groups or stations. Section 'Zachód' (cryptonym: 201, 1AW, 51 KK), run by Capt. Jerzy Lewestam and after his arrest by Capt. Karol Trojanowski 'Radwan', conducted reconnaissance in the Reich and had three groups of intelligence networks: 'Wybrzeże' (Coast),[32] which penetrated the Baltic coast and northern Germany, 'Środek' (Centre), which operated in the eastern, central and western parts of the Reich and Warthegau,[33] and 'Południe' (South) in Upper Silesia, Austria, and Czechoslovakia. The headquarters of particular intelligence groups were situated in the field. The chiefs of the 'Południe'[34] group were located in Kraków, and its sub-group 'Południe-Zachód' (South-West) in Vienna.[35] In mid-1942 'Zachód' Section ran the following intelligence networks: in the Reich – the ZN, ZR, ZP, and Bavaria networks; 'Wybrzeże' Group ‾ the ZH, ZA, ZB, ZD, ZSM networks; in Warthegau – the ZSG, SZT, ZSŁ, ZSGS networks and a special group. Following arrests a reorganisation was carried out. The section was divided into WO1 (former 'Południe') – headed by J. Mrózek, WO2 – probably controlled by Jakub Wecker, and WO3 (former 'Środek') – headed by J. Fuziński. WOI was composed of the following networks: P1- Ostmark, P3 – Bavaria, P5 – the Protectorate, P7 – Slovakia, S1, S3, S5, S9 – Upper Silesia and Zaolzie. In December 1942 the following networks existed under the code names: P1, P, S1, S5, S9, S7, U1, Y20 (mobile) and A, D, C, F and G, all described as marine.[36]

In some instances intelligence in the west used networks created by other clandestine organisations. One of the earliest intelligence networks established in Pomerania, cryptonym 'A', was formed by agents of Związek Jaszczurczy (Lizard Association) intelligence and organised by Stanisław Kamiński from Tczew. Initially, the group worked for ZJ and after the ZJ intelligence network was destroyed it was taken over by the II Bureau of the the Home Army GHQ.[37] Much seems to indicate that the cell in Berlin, created by the National Military Organisation intelligence, headed by Stanisław Jeute, worked for the western section of the Offensive Intelligence of the the Home Army GHQ, as Bogusław Wojciechowski, chief of the Berlin network, co-operated with 2nd Lt. Emanuel Prower; whereas Wanda Węgierska, organised cells in the Berlin area, Westphalia and the Ruhr Basin, and maintained contacts with the Home Army.[38]

The 'centralny i kolejowy' [Central and Railway] Section (cryptonym: 202, 2BW, 52KK, Arkadiusz) penetrated the General gouvernement (GG) [German-occupied Poland]. In mid-1942 it engaged five intelligence groups (CWB, CWJ, CWI, CM, CWZ) and two subsections – central and eastern, each with four intelligence stations – as well as a railway division, which controlled railway traffic in the so-called Warsaw, southern and northern junctions. At the end of 1942 the section was composed of two subsections which maintained thirteen field stations in Warsaw, Siedlce, Lublin, Zamość, Lwów, Tarnopol, Stanisławów, Rzeszów, Kraków, Łuków, Skarżysko, Gołąb and in Białystok, outside the General gouvernement. The section supplemented the activity of the intelligence networks of particular Home Army regions in the General gouvernement and relied on stations located in particularly important regions and on observation cells.

Section 'Wschód' (cryptonym: 772, WW72, Pralnia) penetrated the rear area of the eastern front and had three centres (subsections): Centre I – the Vilnius region and the Baltic States, Centre II – Polesie and Byelorussia, Centre III – Ukraine and Volhynia. The centres included stations, which, in turn, organised permanent or mobile cells.

The Chief of the II Bureau maintained an independent station 'Lombard', focused mainly on the Third Reich, outside the 'Stragan' structure. Such an arrangement was dictated by practical reasons – the wish to obtain information from two independent sources, which defined the degree of their reliability. Moreover, in case of one of the networks being exposed the other would remain active, thus retaining the continuation of work.

The Chief of 'Lombard' was Capt. Maj. Edward Jetter 'Edward', 'Prezes'; the Studies Section was headed by Tadeusz Mystkowski 'Andrzej' and the General Section – by Maj. Tadeusz Karpiński 'Korab'. The intelligence networks were organised into four inspectorates: the Protectorate and Austria, Upper Silesia and the Poznań region, the Old Reich, Pomerania and Eastern Prussia. In 1942 'Lombard' ran 22 intelligence networks, including three headed by women.[39]

Enormous efforts made by the 'Lombard' cells headed by Maj. Jetter made it possible to obtain significant information about the situation in German ports on the Baltic Sea and the North Sea, in Kriegsmarine bases, and the Third Reich war industry. By making use of the co-operation with Polish forced labourers and POWs, as well as those Poles who had already settled down in Germany 'Lombard' penetrated all Maj. industrial centres, docks and weapons factories. In many cases the information obtained enabled the Allied air forces to bomb targets of strategic importance, e.g. in Police, Malbork, Blachownia Śląska or Halle. They conveyed detailed reports about the effects of the air raids which made it possible to assess their effectiveness and to establish a proper order of destruction. The greatest success was obtaining information about the tests of the V-1 and V-2 rockets in Peenemünde, the plans of new types of submarines, the drawings of the prototype of the Panzerfaust anti-tank weapon, and information about the production of the new 'Panther' tank.

The German police and security service as well as military counter-intelligence made numerous efforts to eliminate Polish intelligence cells.

Their achievements were sporadic and rather accidental until 1942.[40] The situation changed after the arrest in April 1942 in Warsaw of Ludwik Kalkstein, chief of one of the networks who began to collaborate with the Gestapo. The task of penetrating and destroying the intelligence structures of the Home Army GHQ was entrusted to SS-Obersturmführer Karl Heller, who headed an investigative commission (composed of 30 people) of the Main Security Office of the Reich (Sonderkommando IV E 5 des RSHA), established at the security police command in Warsaw.

On 27 August 1942 Maj. Stanisław Rogiński 'Górski', the Chief of 'Stragan', was arrested as a result of Kalkstein's betrayal and the information obtained in the course of taking down of the cells in the Reich and on the coast. Rogiński was detained together with Janina Despot-Zenowicz, his secretary, and Wanda Ossowska, Chief of Offensive Intelligence communications. The Germans also seized a list of the codenames of 280 persons co-operating with 'Stragan', which resulted in the elimination of intelligence networks not only in Warsaw but also in Gdańsk, Łódź, Silesia and Wrocław. Arrests were also made in Germany, Austria and Czechoslovakia. Most of the cells of the 'Stragan' western section were crushed. The number of detainees exceeded 300. During the same year more than a hundred members of eastern intelligence were arrested. In that situation it became necessary in many areas to establish intelligence networks from scratch.

Despite the reorganisation and a change of cryptonyms, attempts to rebuild the 'Stragan' networks failed. On 15 May 1943 the Gestapo in Warsaw arrested Capt. Karol Trojanowski 'Radwan', the new chief of the western section of Offensive Intelligence, who in effect agreed to collaborate with the Germans.

His detention coincided with the elimination of the S7 intelligence network in Warthegau, headed by Sergeant Wacław Ławrientiew from a former infantry regiment. That network, which included many officers from Poznań regiments, registered military transports in the Ostrów and Poznań railway junctions and conducted intelligence preparation on the German war industry targets in Poznań and Krzesiny near Poznań.

The majority of arrests in the Headquarters of the II Bureau of the Home Army GHQ (1942–1943) came as a result of the collaboration with the Gestapo of Ludwik Kalkstein, his wife Blanka Kaczorowska and Eugeniusz Świerczewski. This list should certainly include Trojanowski, who in his capacity as a professional intelligence officer knew most of the persons mentioned below. Those arrested were Col. Wacław Berka ('Brodowicz'), the organiser and the first Chief of the II Bureau, his successor – Lt-Col. Marian Drobik 'Dzięcioł', Lt.Col. Wacław Szczekowski 'Leszczyc', Chief of Offensive Intelligence, Trojanowski's successor – Maj. Otton Pawłowicz 'Siostra', former Chief of Station '741' and a member of WW-72.

The arrests did not interrupt intelligence work, although they did hamper it considerably. In view of the partial disintegration of the 'Stragan' offensive intelligence network, in the summer of 1942 Lt-Col. Drobik, the then the Chief of the II Bureau, reorganised the central offensive intelligence network and formed three territorial branches: General gouvernment (from 1944 the cryptonym 'Arkadiusz'); Germany, Austria and territories annexed to the Third Reich, which constituted western intelligence, taken over by 'Lombard'; Soviet territories under German occupation (eastern intelligence 'Pralnia'). This configuration of offensive intelligence functioned until the outbreak of the Warsaw Uprising. After the arrest of Lt-Col. Drobik in January 1944, the new Chief of the II Bureau was Col. Kazimierz Iranek-Osmecki 'Makary'. The activity of central intelligence was interrupted by the Warsaw Uprising. In accordance with the directives some of the networks established contact with their counterparts in the nearest regions, while the others suspended their activity. Attempts that were made to rebuild intelligence, after the capitulation of the Uprising, failed.

Intelligence in the Kraków, Silesia, Łódź and Radom regions remained active until January 1945. The regions, within their capabilities, conveyed the obtained information through the W/T directly to London. The information was fragmentary, though, and related mainly to the German forces at the front and their regrouping. Interesting material was provided by the Radom Region which in a report of December 1944 presented a detailed description of 26 large Wehrmacht tactical units, the Eighth Air Corps and several score auxiliary units.[41] The Silesia Region penetrated airfields at Udetfeld and Zendek, where at the end of 1944 the Germans tested airplanes with jet propulsion.

Generally, however, the Allies and the General Staff were deprived of complete information about the situation at the eastern front, industry in the Third Reich and other valuable information.

Special and weekly reports were transferred by radio, while monthly reports, together with annexes, more copious assessments, and microfilmed copies of seized documents were sent by courier. In London they reached British Intelligence Headquarters through the General Staff II Bureau. It was the British who then decided about forwarding them to the remaining Allies, i.e. the United States and the Soviet Union.

The information reaching the II Bureau of the Home Army GHQ from the central intelligence network and the intelligence bureaus of the regional and district commands was analysed and studied by the Military Studies Bureau and the Economic Studies Department, which co-operated with a group of researchers specialising in various fields. The information was supplied directly to the chief of the II Bureau who passed it on to the Chief of the Studies Department. After reading them he then forwarded the information, with his own comments, to particular subsections. If the reports contained unquestionably reliable information, thus of the sort which did not need to be confronted with the available evidence, then the Chief of the Studies Department personally edited a W/T telegram to London and sent it to the Chief of the II Bureau; this occurred rather rarely, though.

The activities of the Studies Department also included formulating intelligence tasks which stemmed from the need to supplement the Order of Battle with missing information or to verify that particular information. Sections submitted to the Chief of the Studies Department their doubts and possible wishes, which he passed on to the Chief of the II Bureau with a request to forward them to intelligence. Furthermore, the Bureau directed intelligence efforts on gathering information which would clarify the unclear military situation.

As the number of reports sent by intelligence grew they were no longer directed straight to the Chief of the Studies Department, but to the Distribution Desk which got them segregated and initially assessed.

Having received reports particular sections verified them and consulted with files, and if the information was valuable they immediately drafted a brief radio cable which was submitted to the Chief of the Studies Department. Once the drafts were approved, they were sent in the form of a report to the Chief of the II Bureau. Unless there were any particular obstacles such a report was transmitted to Headquarters in London on the same day.

On every 28th day of a given month the Studies Department had to present a monthly report to the Chief of the II Bureau, and he, in turn, to the Commander-in-Chief of the Home Army. Consequently, three to four days prior to that day all sections of the Studies Department provided their Chief with the summaries of monthly work, together with conclusions. This was an occasion to compile all the reports transmitted by radio by that time.

On the basis of such summaries the Chief of the Department prepared a final summary, co-ordinated discrepancies between the subsections and removed non-essential information. All the material received from the sections was used to prepare a monthly report which, together with the annexes, was often several hundred pages long.

After being rewritten, checked and signed the monthly and radio reports were handed over to the Ciphers Section of the V Bureau of the Home Army GHQ for coding. The mail of the Home Army II Bureau, addressed to the General Staff, was sent through the V Bureau of the Home Army GHQ.

A monthly report was composed of three parts. The first contained military information preceded by a summary of the situation, written personally by the Chief of the Department. Once prepared, the summary was immediately sent to London by W/T. The second part of the report included economic information, and the third – a characteristic of the morale on the German army and the society. The report was accompanied by copies of seized documents, plans of weapons factories and weapons construction drawings.

From October 1941 the monthly reports prepared by the II Bureau of the Home Army GHQ and sent by courier, provided an extremely wide scope of information – all the information obtained in the course of a month. As a rule, the written report was about 150–200 pages long, and contained up to a hundred pages of annexes. Intelligence cables sent by

W/T were usually 1–3 pages long. The analysis of intelligence telegrams presented below encompasses the correspondence from 1940–1943; all telegrams have been preserved from that period.

The preserved intelligence and identification telegrams make it possible to determine the 'geography' of the obtained information and to study the basic areas of interest of Home Army intelligence. Telegrams containing so-called intelligence tasks and assessments of the obtained information are particularly significant.[42]

The first known intelligence cable sent by radio on 9 July 1940 described a concentration of German troops in the General gouvernement. Weekly radio telegrams with situation reports started on 22 August 1940, and 17 were forwarded until the end of 1940. Most of them related to the movement of German troops as well as more important military targets or those of military significance (works). The last telegram, number '17', was dated 22 December 1940.

The first preserved report in 1941 was sent on 2 January as no. '20'. Apart from weekly telegrams, there were additional cables containing intelligence information; those were sent sporadically, such as the telegram no. 35 of 8 February 1941 about the production output of Baltic shipyards, Schwarzwald works, and the production of tanks (amphibious vehicles near Berlin), or special reports, such as the one of 15 June 1941 concerning German regrouping on the eve of the offensive against the Soviet Union.

The first identification telegram was sent on 10 June 1941. Weekly information telegrams stopped in mid-July 1941. The last weekly telegram, no. '45', was sent on 14 July 1941; afterwards there were only 'intelligence telegrams' – the first sent on 22 July 1941 as no. '46' (the numbering was retained), and the next one on 24 July 1941. The increased frequency of intelligence information was presumably caused by their importance to British intelligence: 130 intelligence telegrams were still dispatched till the end of 1941; the last one, no. '179', was sent on 27 December 1941.

32 identification cables were sent; the last one, no. '32', was transmitted on 25 September 1941. From 14 September 1941 those intelligence and identification telegrams that would become less outdated, were sent by courier, under the code name 'Rzym', to the VI Bureau of the General Staff. This fact was probably connected with the small traffic capacity of clandestine W/T stations. Four such sets were sent until the end of 1941.

In 1941 471 W/T telegrams were sent including about 200 intelligence and identification reports as well as special intelligence cables. This means that almost 43% of radio traffic was connected with the transfer of intelligence information.

In 1942 the first intelligence telegram known was sent on 8 January (as no. '184'); the first identification cable in 1942 was forwarded on 2 January (as no. '33'). The first set of reports – 'Rzym 5' – was sent on 15 January 1942, and the last one known – 'Rzym 8' – on 15 May 1942. The last preserved intelligence telegram in 1942 numbered '579' and was sent on 30 and 31 December. The last identification cable was sent on 29 December as no. '119'.

In total, 396 intelligence telegrams and 87 identification cables were transmitted in 1942. In 1943, 1156 W/T telegrams were sent; intelligence reports made up almost 42% of radio traffic.

In 1943 the first intelligence telegram was sent on 5 January as no. '581' and the first identification dispatch, no. '120' on 9 January. The last intelligence telegram, no. '1524', was transmitted on 8 December 1943. The last identification cable known, no. '207', comes from 17 September 1943. In 1943, 89 identification telegrams and 945 intelligence reports were sent, they constituted almost 49% of all cables in 1943 (2 132 sent).

In the period from 22 August 1940 to 31 December 1943 1731 intelligence reports were sent:

- 1940 – 17 weekly reports;
- 1941 – 162 intelligence reports (weekly until July) and 32 identification cables;
- 1942 – 399 intelligence reports and 87 identification cables;
- 1943 – 945 intelligence reports and 89 identification cables.[43]

The scope of the forwarded information was very wide. For example, intelligence report no. 40 of 20 June 1941 informs about the deployment of German troops before the offensive against the Soviet Union. Telegram no. 425 of 25 August 1942 informed about Hitler's Headquarters in Vinnitsa (Ukraine),[44] no. 1261 of 2 August 1943 – about the production of a secret weapon in Karlshagen on the Uznam Island,[45] no. 1464 of 7 November of that year contained the technical description of rocket planes whose serial production was being prepared by the Arado works (Arado Ar 234).[46] The report no. 1489 of 19 November described the Junkers reaction engine.[47]

Reports were passed relative to all issues concerning the German war machine: the deployment and movement of military units and their weapons, the enemy air force, naval bases and movements of ships in ports, German losses at the front and the effects of Allied air raids. Detailed information was provided about the wartime industrial production, targets to be destroyed by air attacks, the distribution and strength of anti-aircraft defence Information about the newest inventions was thoroughly gathered; police repressions were reported as well as the morale of the German army and the public mood among the German civilian population.

The effects of Home Army intelligence were most fully used by British Intelligence; however, having signed a military agreement with the Soviet Union (14 August 1941) the Poles gained an opportunity to provide intelligence information directly to the Soviet side. Moreover, they regarded it as one of bargaining chips in dealing with the Soviet side, hoping that in return they would be allowed to organise a supply base on the Soviet territory for the Polish Underground.

Moscow was to be provided directly with information concerning the disposition of German units at the eastern front, supplies transport, preparations for the offensive, etc., in other words, information obtained by eastern intelligence, whose teams followed the tracks of the German troops.

The first telegram, sent from Warsaw to Moscow on 28 April 1942, contained information about the unloading sites for military units transferred from the west at the southern and central sectors of the front. On 29 April the Russians were informed about German regrouping in the region of Kharkov. This information was invaluable for the Soviet command which had just finished preparations for pre-emptive operation (the Kharkov operation was launched on 12 May 1942). The information, forwarded on 8 May 1942 by Cell 'Wisła', was assessed as 'extremely valuable'. Direct intelligence co-operation, in which extremely valuable information was conveyed, including responses to the direct requests by the Soviet side, lasted three months. On 29 July Gen. Georgiy Zhukov informed the Polish side that there was no purpose for the further activity of Cell 'Wisła'.

An evaluation of the effects of the work conducted by eastern intelligence encountered considerable obstacles. Although it was precisely the Russians who attached greatest importance to the intelligence, they were reluctant to express appreciation. Nonetheless, judging by the tasks which the Soviet side formulated for Home Army eastern intelligence, the information obtained was valuable and trustworthy.

The British often emphasised the great value of the materials obtained by Polish intelligence. For example, in a telegram sent on 12 May 1942 from London Col. Michał Protasewicz, Chief of the VI Bureau of the Polish General Staff, informed the Home Army Commander-in-Chief that: 'Intelligence Service evaluates the information as extremely valuable and interesting. Further details about the damage incurred by the 'Gneisenau' and the progress of repairs are very welcome'. On 15 May he wrote: 'Friends are asking for information whether any factories of synthetic petrol have been recently built or are being constructed in Germany or the occupied countries'.[48]

A British intelligence assessment of the work performed by Home Army intelligence during the first six months of 1942 said, inter alia: 'Polish intelligence is our best source of information as far the Order of Battle at the eastern front is concerned [...] Polish intelligence has provided us with extremely valuable information about the railway traffic through Poland'. Home Army intelligence was praised highly for its naval information: 'We regard Polish intelligence as extremely valuable both for the information it supplies and for answering additional inquiries'. Similar opinions were expressed about the achievements of Home Army intelligence agents specialising in industry, 'one of the best sources of information'.[49]

Preserved English forms evaluating intelligence information make it possible to determine that the majority of the assessments was done by the War Office and the Air Ministry as well as HQ Air (until the end of 1943). In 1944 assessments were issued by the Ministry of Economic Warfare, the

Air Ministry and in certain cases the Admiralty and the War Office. A certain pattern can be noticed: economic questions were forwarded to the Ministry of Economic Warfare, information about air industry works and aviation equipment to the Air Ministry, naval intelligence to the Admiralty or the War Office, and military to the War Office.

The first preserved assessment form comes from 16 December 1942 and bears the number 16.[50] The opinion dated 24 December 1943 was Crit. No. 2665. The last preserved form, no. 4669, is dated 22 January 1945 and relates to the situation along the Warsaw-Radom front.

The number of assessments prepared from 3 February 1943 (Crit. No. 327) to 10 March 1943 (Crit. No. 392) totalled 75. In May 1944 201 assessments were made: (Crit. No. 3821) of 2 May 1944 and (Crit. No. 4039) of 31 May 1944. The opinions were usually prepared in two weeks. Most of the evaluations graded the information as 'of value' and frequently as 'of considerable value'.

Among the 168 assessments issued between 2 March 1943 (Crit. No 363) and 31 March 1943 (Crit. No. 531), 56 are preserved – 44 were described as 'of value', 7 as 'of considerable value', two as 'of little value', one as 'of some value', one as 'of no value' and one was not classified, although further information was requested.

April 1943: 1 April (Crit. No. 532) – 30 April (Crit. No. 845); out of 313 assessments 75 have been preserved, of which five belong to category A, 63 – to B, four – to C, and three – to D.

May 1943: 1 May (Crit. No. 854) – 29 May (Crit. No. 1003); out of a total 57 preserved assessments 11 belong to category A, 39 – to B, four – to C, and two – to D, with a single assessment unclassified.

Out of 353 assessments made from 24 April 1944 (Crit. No. 3708) to 3 June 1944 (Crit. No. 4061) 46 are preserved: 8 were classified as category A, 32 – as B, three as C, two as D and one unclassified.

British appreciation was expressed not only in praise but also in financial grants which were of great importance for the Home Army budget. Quarterly, they amounted to 1–2 million US dollars. The significance of this sum becomes visible when compared with the sum for the Home Army (10 million dollars) granted in 1943 by the VI Bureau of the Polish General Staff.

Some of the accomplishments of Home Army intelligence were of special importance for the Allied war effort. In 1940 Home Army intelligence provided a detailed analysis of German military undertakings in the General gouvernement, known under the cryptonym 'Plan Otto', with the conclusion that they are preparations for a war against the Soviet Union. In 1941 precise information related to the German concentration to attack Russia. More than 100 Maj. military units were identified, and the date of the beginning of the military action was correctly determined as the second half of June 1941. In the spring of 1942 Home Army eastern intelligence established that the target of the German offensive would not be Moscow but the Caucasus.

In 1943 information concerning German experiments with rocket weapons was forwarded; the experimental testing ground in Pustków-Blizna was identified in 1944 and Polish intelligence intercepted a V-2 rocket which dropped near Sarnaki at the end of May. On 26 July 1944 the results of studies conducted by Polish researchers, together with photographs and plans of mechanisms, were sent by a British plane to London.[51] In the same year detailed information was provided describing German tests of jet aeroplanes.

The findings made by 'Lombard' made it possible for the Allied Air Force to bomb the Focke-Wulf works in Poznań and the synthetic petroleum producers in Halle, Blachownia Śląska and Police near Szczecin, as part of the 'Synteza' assignment received in 1943.

Intelligence of the Home Army Warsaw Region provided copies of the drawings of tank equipment produced at Ursus. Copies of stabilisers were made in the works at Pabianice which produced, among others, tank parts and eavesdropping equipment. Plans of the naval base in Gdynia, stolen by Officer Cadet Józef Wawrzyńczyk, a member of the Clandestine Scout Corps, were sent to London made it possible to carry out precise bombings of the industrial target in December 1943. In 1944 intelligence of the Home Army Radom Region seized in Stalowa Wola works, where the Germans had transferred production, the documentation of an 88 mm. anti-aircraft gun, whose bullet could reach the speed of more than 1,000 metres per second, thanks to the special design of the barrel.

The examples listed above were spectacular achievements of Home Army intelligence. The greatest triumph, although not so effective, was the systematic provision of information on the economy. In accordance with the war plans the Germans concentrated their efforts on that domain of wartime production which at the given moment they regarded as crucial for operational activity. As a result, they shifted their focus from the production of aircraft equipment to submarines, then to armour weapons and, in the final phase of the war, to rockets. That information, combined with the information concerning the state and the potential of the German industry, allowed the Allies to recreate the trends in German wartime economy, to draw conclusions about prepared operations and to take pre-emptive actions.

The same can be said about the identification of German troops. The information conveyed constituted one of the fundamental elements for establishing the Order of Battle. That information was of key importance for operations on the Continent planned by the Allies. The work performed by Home Army intelligence undoubtedly supported the Allied armed effort much more effectively than subversive and guerrilla activities. The results of Home Army intelligence were directly translated into the strategic decisions of the Allies, thus contributing to the defeat of Germany.

Notes

1 At the turn of 1939 the Service for Poland's Victory was transformed, in accordance with the directives of the Commander-in-Chief, into the Union of Armed Struggle, which on 14 February 1942 was renamed and became the Home Army (AK).

2 30 June 1940, confirmed in 'Instruction No. 5'.
3 The chief and organiser of the Department was Col. Marian Józef Smoleński, the last Chief of the General Staff II Bureau before the war. From August 1941 the VI Bureau of the Polish General Staff was also known as the Special or Liaison Bureau .
4 *Armia Krajowa w dokumentach 1939–1945 (The Home Army in Documents 1939–1945*, further as: *AK w dokumentach*), vol. 1, IX 1939-VI 1941, London.
5 *AK w dokumentach*, vol. 1, p. 445.
6 Capt. Stanisław Olechnowicz, who at the beginning of 1940 gathered members of the Frontier Defence Corps (KOP) intelligence, organised an independent intelligence group under the cryptonym 'Station '741', which established direct contact with the General Staff.
7 *AK w dokumentach*, vol. 1, p. 19.
8 *AK w dokumentach*, vol. 1, p. 243.
9 *AK w dokumentach*, vol. 1, p. 445, Telegram of 4 January 1941.
10 The real ZWZ Commander-in-Chief was Gen. Rowecki (from 30 June 1940) but to 25 August 1941 an similar post existed in London (General Sosnkowski), see: M. Ney-Krwawicz, *Komenda Główna Armii Krajowej 1939–1945 (The Home Army Chief Command, 1939–1945)*, Warszawa 1990, p. 55.
11 *AK w dokumentach*, vol. 1, p. 478.
12 *AK w dokumentach*, vol. 1, pp. 548–549, Telegram of 16 June 1941.
13 Already the first instruction intended for the organisation (4 December 1939) stressed the need to conduct intelligence: 'You must urgently collect information about the deployment and strength of the occupying force. Send this information [i.e. to Paris] directly' (*AK w dokumentach*, vol. 1, p. 17). A successive instruction (no. 2) of 16 January 1940 contained a plan for organisational work; with intelligence on the first place, followed by sabotage. Ibid. p. 75.
14 AAN, 203/III/1, leaf 6. The basic document which determined the principles of intelligence work was the Secret Intelligence Instruction.
15 SPP, A.3.7.2.11, leaf 22.
16 Report no. 163 from Kalina of 9 November 1942. In 1942–1944 37 'cichociemni' trained in intelligence were parachuted into Poland.
17 The first intelligence report was forwarded on 22 February 1940 and the following one – for March 1940 – on 13 April. Ibid., pp. 99-105, 207-210.
18 SPP, 2.2.1; the date of the document was established on the basis of the number of the journal, I. dz. 1134/tjn. 40, see also: *Polskie Siły Zbrojne w II wojnie światowej (Polish Armed Forces during the Second World War*, further as : PSZ), vol. 3, *Armia Krajowa (Home Army)*, London 1950, p. 298.
19 *AK w dokumentach*, vol. 1, p. 273.
20 PSZ, vol. 3, pp. 298–299.
21 SPP, 2.3.6.3. 1, vol. 151, leaf 2, Letter from General Sosnkowski to General Sikorski informing about the receipt of materials from Poland, delivered by a special courier on 14 March 1940 and containing materials relating to a planned offensive against France.
22 Telegram of 19 May 1941, I dz. 1485.
23 SPP, A.2.3.6.2.2, vol. 50, leaf 61.
24 SPP, A.2.3.6.2.2, vol. 150, leaf. 64.
25 SPP, A.2.3.6.4, leaf 10, Telegram from the Chief of the VI Bureau of the Polish General Staff.
26 SPP, A.2.3.6.2.2, leaf 206, Telegram from the Chief of the VI Bureau of the Polish General Staff, 13 October 1942.
27 Details concerning the posts in particular sections according to M. Ney-Krwawicz, *Komenda Główna*, op. cit., pp. 87–108.
28 AWIH, III/31/20, leaf 2, 47-58, Organisational guidelines for Districts and Inspectorates.

29 B. Chwaściński, *Ostrego Pamięci zdobywcy Szczytu* (*In memory of the conqueror of the Ostry Peak*), 'Wierchy', 1974, vol. 80, pp. 105–107; T. Dubicki, *Polski wywiad w Wiedniu w latach II wojny światowej* (*Polish intelligence in Vienna during the Second World War*) [in:] *Gerda Leber-Magenau a stosunki polsko-austriackie w XX w.* (*Gerda Leber-Magenau and Polish-Austrian Relations during the Twentieth Century*), ed. by A. K. Kuczyński and D. Kucharska, Toruń-Płock 1998, pp. 249–254.

30 M. Heller, *Ruch oporu na Śląsku Cieszyńskim w latach 1939–1945* (*The Resistance Movement in Cieszyn Silesia in the years 1939–1945*), Opole 1982, pp. 110–112.

31 A. Konieczny, *Rozbicie wrocławskiej grupy wywiadu ofensywnego Komendy Głównej ZWZ-AK ('Stragan')* (*The Elimination of the Wrocław group of the offensive intelligence of the Home Army GHQ ['Stragan']*), 'Sobótka', 1973, no. 1, pp. 83–94.

32 In certain studies it appears as 'Morze'. See: B. Chrzanowski, *Konspiracja Rządu RP na Pomorzu w latach 1939–1945* (*Polish Government Clandestine Activities in Pomerania 1939–1945*), Gdańsk 1992, p. 28.

33 Group 'Środek' was probably controlled by Lt. Emanuel Prower, arrested on 21 February 1942 in Hamburg and guillotined on 24 January 1944 in Brandenburg.

34 Group 'Południe' was directed by Capt. Karol Trojanowski, succeeded by Jan Mrózek.

35 The Viennese cell which specialised in industrial intelligence was organised by Karol Englisch, who based it upon the pre-war network of the Polish General Staff II Bureau; B. Chwaściński, *Pamięci zdobywcy*, op. cit., pp. 105–107.

36 AAN, call no. III/25, leaf...; AWIH, III/22/93, vol. 9, leaf 71.

37 B. Chrzanowski, *Konspiracja Rządu RP*, op. cit., p. 28.

38 This network was disbanded in March and April 1942. See: L. Teresiński, *O działalności Sądu Wojennego w Rzeszy w okresie II wojny światowej* (*On the activity of the War Court in the Reich during the Second World War*), 'Biuletyn GKNZH w P', vol. 24, 1972, pp. 191–192; J. Pollack, *Wywiad, sabotaż, dywersja. Polski ruch oporu w Berlinie 1939–1945* (*Intelligence, Sabotage, Diversion. The Polish Resistance in Berlin 1939–1945*), Warszawa 1991, pp. 93–94.

39 AWIH, III/22/49, leaf 3.

40 In 1939-1940 the German courts sentenced 1 351 persons accused of co-operating with Polish intelligence, i.e. 34.6% of all convicts. The majority, however, were persons who had worked for Polish intelligence before the war.

41 Information based on materials belonging to Maj. Mieczysław Belenin (1983), code-name 'Ramzes', chief of offensive intelligence in the Home Army Radom Region.

42 AWIH, III/22/19, vol. 6–11 compiled and analysed by the author; including photocopy of cyphered reports in 1940–1944.

43 AWIH, III/22/19, vol. 6, K. 173.

44 Ibid., vol. 8, K. 34.

45 Ibid., vol. 10, K. 131.

46 Ibid., K. 138–140.

47 Ibid., K. 148–149.

48 Ibid., vol. 13, K. 68.

49 Ibid., K. 69.

50 SPP, A.3.7.5. 1, leaf 1, British assessments of reports from Poland; TNA(PRO) HS4/197 reports sent by Gen. Sosnkowski to Brigadier Gubbins 9 May 1941 ref. 669/TJ (866) and 775/TJ (884).

51 K. Iranek-Osmecki, *Meldunek specjalny nr 242. Pociski rakietowe* (*Special report no. 242. Rocket missiles*), 'Zeszyty Historyczne' (Paris), 1972, no. 22, pp. 67–81.

44
Intelligence Behind the Eastern Front

Andrzej Pepłoński

The German preparations for war in the East, due to its wide reach were quickly recognised and systematically tracked by the emerging structures of the Home Army and other clandestine organisations. The conducive factor in recognising German plans, was the wide Polish terrain, through which the troops of the Third Reich had to pass. The other factor, was the complexity of the Polish organisation, which enabled the Poles to observe the changes in troop dislocation by road or rail as well as air and sea movements.

The systematic expansion of intelligence field structures, communications and personnel training resulted in the increased volume of obtained information.[2] Growing number of repairs of bridges and roads going eastward were noted already in the autumn of 1939. In the winter of 1939/1940 the Germans intensified training and increased the strength of their units. They also embarked upon expanding airfields taken over by the Luftwaffe and Kriegsmarine bases in Gdynia. Simultaneously, depots, shooting ranges and hospitals were reconstructed.

In the spring of 1940 the General Staff II Bureau began to receive information on a par with character of the undertakings. The Germans commenced a planned development of roads going from the west to the east, mainly across southern Poland. At the same time they began building fortifications along the Narew, Bug and San rivers and building strongholds around the bridges of Warsaw, Dęblin and Annopol. The fall of France was followed by an accelerated development of airfields and landings strips, mainly between the Vistula and the Bug rivers and to the west of the Vistula.[3] Monitoring of the movement of German forces confirmed continuing rotations of troops stationed in Poland, Gdańsk and Eastern Prussia. By 9 June 1940 there were about 25 Maj. units. It was revealed between the end of April and the beginning of May that there were movements of units both westwards and towards the border with the Soviet Union; nine divisions formed during the mobilisation of 1939 were directed to the western front. At the same time new detachments in the strength of five divisions were spotted in the southern part of the Lublin region and Małopolska (Little Poland). Reinforced Luftwaffe units were detected in Silesia. The information came from various sources and was not fully confirmed.[4] The situation in the region of Łódź was similar. After several weeks of training the newly formed German detachments were moved in various directions and replaced by new recruits, convalescents from army hospitals and old reservists. Units were constantly shifted. Soldiers who had earlier fought in Norway and Belgium showed up in Rawa Mazowiecka. Several airfields were being built, while in those that were open, intensive training of pilots was conducted.[5]

The II Bureau more and more frequently informed about tasks assigned by British Intelligence to the Home Army. In mid-November 1940 Maj. Żychoń said in a letter addressed to the Chief of the VI Bureau that 'the English are requesting to check whether [General] Kluge is the commanding officer of the Fourth Army or whether he holds some other command post'.[6]

In the autumn of 1940 Home Army intelligence reports signalled changes related to the preparations for war in the East. Although the rail and road transport in the region of Kraków was moving with changing intensity and in various directions it was possible to identify most of the Maj. units. It was also confirmed that all fuel containers in Kraków airport, even the Polish ones, had been filled with petroleum. The construction of reserve airfields in Krościenko, Wyżne and Mądrówka was started, while the development of the airfield in Krosno continued. Nitrogen works in Chorzów launched a special department producing war gases. Registration of quarters in Kraków was continued in connection with the expected movement of tens of thousands of German troops.[7]

In late autumn of 1940 work progressed in the development of airfields and landing strips between the Vistula and the Bug rivers as well as to the west of the Vistula. Work continued in the construction of fortifications and new rail and road transport routes; Home Army intelligence found out that the deadline was set for April 1941. In the winter of 1940/1941 supplies of military equipment as well as materials and machines for constructing communication routes were observed. First groups of Luftwaffe commands showed up. Intelligence work became better adapted to the needs of London after Lt-Col. Kazimierz Iranek-Osmecki, an emissary of the General Staff, presented orders for Lt-Col. Wacław Berka,[8] Chief of the Home Army II Bureau. At the end of April 1941, upon the recommendation of Gen. Stefan Rowecki, intelligence in the Polish territory was entirely subordinated to Home Army. That decision proved to be fully justified in view of the fact that the fulfilment of new tasks required the establishing of an effective and uniform intelligence network.

From the spring of 1941 the Germans continued the construction work along communication routes[9] and began supplying airfields with bombs and fuel. Aerial communications detachments and technical personnel showed up during March and April. Sanitation staff arrived in newly opened hospitals. If in May 1941 there were barely several Luftwaffe staff HQs, then at the end of May the concentration of German troops had grown enormously.[10] Units from the Balkan Peninsula and from the west kept arriving and the number of great units reached about eighty. More staff Headquarters of high level Army and Air Force commands as well as first airborne combat units showed up. Polish intelligence found the location of the HQ of Marshal Walher von Reichenau in Tarnobrzeg, and the fact that the HQ for the Supreme Commander had been prepared in Warsaw. In a special report of 15 June 1941 Gen. Rowecki informed about a large-scale influx of armoured units in the region of Zamość and the San river as well as in Łomża, Małkinia and Siedlce. A large influx of incoming Air Force transport planes at all airfields was spotted on 12 and 13 June, and on 15 June Marshal Walther von Brauchitsch, who had been staying in the Generalgouvernement for two weeks, arranged for quarters in Warsaw. The incoming intelligence information indicated that war activities in the east would begin in a few days. The new information was that symptoms of a growing economic crisis in the Third Reich began to appear, where almost all stocks, especially raw materials, had been used up; there were shortages in food supplies, particularly fat and meat; the railways were experiencing difficulties as they were overburdened by military transports; the movement of people was limited as were the sales of petroleum. In conversations with German soldiers the forthcoming war with Russia was more frequently mentioned. Some of the speakers expressed unwillingness to participate in the war in the East; cases of suicide amongst soldiers were noted.[11] Further directives sent to Poland by the General Staff reflected growing interest in German armoured and motorised troops. Information was sought about the differences between light and heavy armoured divisions, the number of divisions of each type, their organisation and artillery, the calibre and the quantity of anti-tank and anti-aircraft guns as well as artillery pieces. Answers were expected to the questions about the presence of tank brigades, independent tank battalions and 'Panzer Jäger' divisions; such inquiries also referred to motorised divisions.[12] Moreover, information was requested about the current Order of Battle for the land and air forces in Poland and a confirmation of difficulties experienced by the German war industry. Detailed questions concerned the size of works producing aeroplanes and amphibious tanks. Home Army Intelligence was to look for classified and unclassified instructions and the field manuals for the Army, the Air Force and the Navy.[13]

Home Army Intelligence report of 8 June 1941 stated, inter alia, 'the movements and deployment of troops, the arrangement of the rear area, civilian preparations, the character of offensive activities against Russia, and a far-reaching but not completed concentration. Units are still not fully manned, services are not fully organised and in designated positions, staff (above division level) are not in place, movements and transposition of troops in the field continue'.[14]

In mid-June 1941 the II Bureau estimated that there were about 90 units in Poland, of which 7–11 were Panzer divisions. The Air Force was arriving on a large scale, Army staffs were installed, an increasingly large number of armoured units was coming in, and final concentration transfers were carried out.[15] On 21 June regional Home Army commands informed that: 'Incoming rail and road transport is composed mostly of armoured and Air Force units. Higher staffs are arriving, transposition of divisional units continue. The greatest movement of the Army and the Air Force chiefs towards the region of Lublin [...] The construction of the last section of the Jarosław-Berlin underground cable in the region of Szczakowa is to be completed by 22 June'.[16]

The long anticipated outbreak of the German-Soviet war created a new situation in Europe. The Allied staffs now requested more information about the course of battles and the chances of the belligerents. The II Bureau of the Polish General Staff PGS started to inquire about the increasing influx of wounded airmen, men from armoured units and others from the eastern front as well as information concerning the general situation of the German troops.[17] From the first days of the war the II Bureau's Studies Department analysed the events taking place on the front. From the second half of June 1941 there were problems with wireless communication and telegrams reached London with a week-long delay, one of the sources of current information was the content of the first German communiqué covering the period from 22 to 27 June 1941.

German information generally concurred with official Soviet communiqués. In that situation, the Studies Department paid attention to the fact that the Red Army engaged in combat far from its own permanent fortifications (Dniestr–Vinnitsa, Zhitomir, Berezina, Polotsk), though it did not make the information about Soviet forces and the course of the battles more precise. At the same time it emphasised the superiority of the German Air Force, fierce battles in the border area, the deployment of heavy artillery in capturing Brześć and tanks for conducting frontal attacks, as well as desperate attempts to launch counterattacks during the battle for the Dvina. The Department also expressed the opinion that the Soviet Air Force had not been defeated because new forces continued to arrive in the front area, and that Russian resistance must have been strong – as confirmed by the small number of POWs taken by the Germans (about 40,000). A similarly detailed analysis was conducted with regard to the course of battles in Lithuania, Byelorussia, and the area south of Polesie and in Bessarabia and Bukovina, with considerable attention paid to suppositions concerning the course of particular front operations.[18]

Naturally, the continuation of similar analyses required systematic influx of precise information from the front and its deep rear area. At that time Home Army intelligence registered significant changes at airfields located deeper in Poland's centre, from where pilots and technical support staff had departed eastward, leaving behind only anti-aircraft artillery detachments. It was impossible to assess the losses since the planes returned to other airfields having completed their assignments; and many small airfields were discovered with aeroplanes concealed nearby.[19]

The II Bureau of the PGS tried to mobilise field offices to collect all information relating to the German-Soviet war. At the beginning of July 1941 Maj. Żychoń, chief of the Intelligence Department, recommended that they pay special attention, apart from routine activities, to the information concerning the Order of Battle, concentrations of forces and higher commands, the course of battles of armoured-motorised units, Air Force as well as airborne detachments. Furthermore, he expected to receive information concerning communications, supplies, evacuation and losses, as well as new means of combat, the morale of the troops, and activities at sea. The information about the impact of the war in the east on the domestic situation in Russia and Germany as well as the occupied states, especially Poland, were regarded as essential.[20]

As a result of those needs new intelligence cells were activated by the offensive intelligence under the cryptonym 'Stragan'. The creation of intelligence structures most frequently involved people from the Eastern Borderlands who had already been tested in clandestine work. They had many contacts and were familiar with local conditions. As a result, the emerging intelligence cells were quite frequently manned by family members, friends and acquaintances. Station 'East-Volhynia', controlled by 'Stragan', focused its activity on taking records of German rail and road transport. The Chief of the Station, Józef Roman 'Styrski', established cells which monitored rail movement in areas of the main junctions in Volhynia and conducted reconnaissance of the strength and organisation of German garrisons and the network of regular airports and airfields. The tasks of the Station also included infiltration of German and Ukrainian authorities and offices in order to obtain information and documents necessary for the intelligence staff to function. Such documents were also used by the Chief of Station, Roman who travelled to Warsaw at least once a month for organisational purposes.[21]

In accordance with earlier directives of Gen. Kazimierz Sosnowski, on the co-operation between the Poles, the II Bureau in London sent back to Poland information obtained within its own resources intecepted by radio of German correspondence from the Eastern Front. In mid-August information referred to, inter alia, a division of the front rear area into four police sections and other organisational issues. Among others, details of the inspections conducted by the Reichsführer SS as well as the distribution of police field staffs were learnt, which was to considerably facilitate the work of Home Army Intelligence.[22]

Reports about the situation at the front rear area, which reached London in the autumn of 1941, were carefully studied by British Intelligence. That organisation was particularly interested in the information about the morale of German soldiers. Attention was paid to frequent cases of arms sales, robberies (in Siedlce, Dęblin and Brześć-on-the Bug), and considerable amounts of missing fuel, which was the reason why on 10 November 1941 400 automobiles in Biała Podlaska could not be used. Other selected information referred to the fact that maps of Turkey, Iraq and Iran were printed at the Military Geographic Institute in

Warsaw; as well as the details about railway transport movement towards the eastern front, specifying the number of transport trains and their cargo, and even the shipments of small amounts of ammunition, petroleum and food. Much attention was devoted to information about the deployment, strength and the signs of German units.[23]

With the growing significance of information concerning the war in the East and the positive evaluation of this information by British Intelligence, organisational changes were implemented in the Studies Department of the Home Army GHQ. The newly created sections were responsible for rail and road transport, the eastern front, and the Order of Battle in Poland and in the Reich, the Air Force and the Navy.[24] Other cells of the Department, staffed with officers with suitable theoretical and practical training, analysed the intelligence received from the Reich and provided numerous comments relevant for the assessments of the situation at the eastern front.

At the beginning of September 1941 Gen. Rowecki received instructions from London about the organisation of intelligence in the East by Home Army. From among the directives of a general type there were recommendations that the emerging intelligence network should encompass the whole rear areas of the German forces from the Baltic to the Black Sea, and in particular the important communication routes and transfer centres. Organisational work was also to be conducted for a future uprising and the creation of foundations for post-war intelligence structures in the East. Hence the ban on contacts with Soviet Special Services. Operational security was advised so as to prevent penetration by the NKVD. According to the detailed directives the intention was to quickly establish intelligence cells in such communication junctions that allowed the monitoring of land and sea transport. Such cells should be located first of all in Riga, Dvinsk, Minsk, Homel, Kiev and Dniepropietrovsk. During the next stage further transport routes were to be included; and then their distribution was to depend on local needs.[25]

The network operating in the rear area of the eastern front was separated from the structures of 'Stragan' offensive intelligence. Preparations for the establishment of a new network were made in March 1941. The chief of the network (cryptonym '772', 'WW-72' and 'Pralnia') was Capt. Aleksander Stpiczyński 'Wilski', an experienced officer of the 'East' Section in the pre-war II Bureau. That network embarked upon the organisation of intelligence in former eastern voivodeships and in the front's rear area. It was composed of three intelligence centres: O I – the base in Brześć on the Bug, active in the region of Polesie and Byelorussia (cryptonym '54 KK'), with five stations and subordinated intelligence cells; O II – the base in Wilno, encompassing the region of Wilno and the Baltic states (cryptonym '53 KK') with six stations; O III – base in Lwów, active in Ukraine and Volhynia (cryptonym '55 KK') with a network directed by seven stations. The first chief of Centre O I was Samuel Ostik-Kostrowicki 'Jakub'. Centre O II was led by Capt. Tomasz Zan 'Oleś'; at the turn of 1941–42 his function was taken over to Capt. Gicewicz 'Monter'. Centre O

III was headed by Maj. Aleksander Klotz 'Wizjer' ('Piotr'), a former officer of Intelligence's 'East' Section. The organisation of field structures of the centres and their personnel changed as the situation at the front developed and because of the arrests made. In 1943, following a tide of repressions which swept across Wilno a separate centre O II-b was established in Minsk and it maintained independent communications with Warsaw. Initially the chiefs of particular stations were predominantly officers of the Polish Army or the pre-war Frontier Defence Corps; later they were assisted by officers trained in Great Britain (the so-called *cichociemni*). The realisation of intelligence was usually entrusted to Home Army members, who had worked under the Soviet occupation.

The development of intelligence networks in the region of Wilno was possible owing to pre-war II Bureau agents (Station no. 1 in Wilno and Station no. 2 in Warsaw) and spontaneously emerging clandestine organisations. In July 1941 one of those organisations, known as 'The Liberation of Poland', attempted to infiltrate the German administration, simultaneously establishing contact with Home Army clandestine organisation ZWZ. Selected people were tasked with setting up contacts with the police and finding employment with the railways and in hospitals and airports. The leading men were Leon Pawłowicz, Konstanty Pawłowicz, Piotr Spogis, Henryk Ihnatowicz and Franciszek Czechowicz.[26] Apart from 'The Liberation of Poland', a Home Army network headed by Lt. Stefan Czapliński 'Wiktor operated in the region of Dyneburg (Dzwińsk). It maintained communications with the district HQ in Wilno. The eastern intelligence centre (O II) had intelligence networks in Maj. towns, those with railway junctions. The most valuable information was obtained in the Wilno, Lida, Dyneburg, Riga and Königsberg. Hotel 'George' in Wilno, frequently visited by German civilian and military dignitaries, became a particularly important source. Valuable information from German officers was also obtained by Halina Obiezierska, the hotel cleaning woman. An Italian medical doctor connected with Polish intelligence assisted in making acquaintances among the Germans. The cell in Riga provided vital information, especially about the German sea transport. Detailed information was registered concerning the movement of merchant and Navy ships, railway transport, the Air Force and the movements of German units in the rear area of the eastern front. In March 1942 about 150 representatives of the Polish community in Latvia were involved in intelligence in the region of Tallinn alone (Station 'E-VII').

After almost a year of Centre O II activity, it fell a victim of German security. Their inquiries led to the elimination of almost the whole network in the Wilno region. The head of Centre O II was now Lt-Col. Henryk Żuk 'Onufry'. Since the majority of staff engaged in intelligence were amateurs, the new chief of the cell repeatedly requested from the 'WW-72' HQ in Warsaw to send several real operatives ('cichociemni') from London. They were: Maj. Franciszek Koprowski 'Dąb', Lt. Stefan Jasieński 'Alfa' and Lt-Col. Longin Jurkowski 'Mysz',[27] but they did not reach Wilno until July 1943.

Several months before their arrival Centre O II networks revived their activity. The cells in Riga and Dyneburg functioned effectively, monitoring the movement of German transport activities; a new cell was established in Kaunas, and the one in Minsk increased its efficiency. Maj. Koprowski, who was senior in rank among the officers, was appointed as the chief of the Centre. It proved to be a serious mistake since he lacked suitable professional training (in Great Britain he was a firearms and hand-to-hand combat instructor). His violation of the fundamental principles of operational security resulted in arrests among the leadership of the Centre. This was a serious blow given the fact that a month earlier the Germans had conducted mass-scale arrests among members of the Polish intelligence in Latvia. That was caused by a mistake committed by Henryk Szostak, head of the Dyneburg cell, who had recruited, without prior checking, a pre-war boy Scout. As it turned out, he had collaborated with Latvian police for two years. Most of those arrested were executed by the Germans, and a dozen or more were sent to Stutthof concentration camp.[28]

By comparison, intelligence activity of Centre O III centre was the best developed. Its Chief was Maj. Klotz and he co-operated closely with Lt. Stanisław Łaniewski 'Dach' ('Roman'), a former II Bureau officer.[29]

As the eastern front moved, the location of Centre O III and the distribution of intelligence cells changed. On 1 September 1941 Centre O III acted as 'Południe' (South) group, only to use the cryptonym 'Cukrownia' during the last phase it its activity. The first assignments consisted in the political-economic intelligence in the south-eastern foreground of Poland and the establishment of contact with representatives of anti-Soviet circles. Subsequent tasks were of permanent character and entailed intelligence behind enemy lines with particular attention paid to monitoring communication routes. The first two-person teams were sent from Lwów, the site of Centre O III base. Maj. Klotz arrived in Berdyczów and his cover was a medical doctor. The contact was organised through a 'cover' of a local tailor's workshop.[30] All organisational issues associated with the residence were entrusted to the cell personnel. Since at the time the new German administration in Ukraine was in a state of disarray, the most frequently used cover story for the stay in Ukraine was an escape from the Soviet transport during the deportation to the East, and then a search for families lost during the war. The majority of the personnel also used the documents of fictitious or real firms active in other regions of Ukraine. Residence in various places was justified by a need to examine the terrain in connection with construction projects, a search for building materials, equipment, scrap iron, etc. Each cell used the assistance of the local population, most frequently Poles, and their personnel sought employment on the railways and jobs in economic administration.[31]

The distribution of the stations and cells was linked with the situation at the front. During the eastward movement of the German armies (from 15 September 1941 to 15 May 1942) Maj. Klotz organised three stations and 12 cells; and when there was stabilisation at the front and the beginning of the retreat of the German forces (15 May 1942 – 1 July 1943) Centre O III supervised additional six stations (Berdyczów, Kiev, Homel, Poltava, Kirovograd and Stalino) and an independent cell in Voronezh. Each station supervised several intelligence cells; 21 of them functioned in total. The reconnaissance conducted by Centre O III reached the Black Sea (Odessa) and the mouth of the Don river, near Rostov. Here, cells operated in Millerovo, Shakhty and Mariampol. The cell established in Jassy enabled Maj. Klotz to monitor railway routes and roads in northern Romania. The centre also included a border transfer station in Podwołoczyska, a report centre and a supply depot in Lwów. During the retreat of the German armies (1 August 1943–1 October 1944) the western boundary of the area of operation of the Centre O III coincided with the line along the Bug-San rivers, with 14 cells functioning in the front's rear area. The work of the 'WW-72' network was frequently interrupted by repressive activities of the German security organs due to the penetration of the network by counter-intelligence agents and the violation of the principles of operational security.[32]

The German offensive remained nearly constant in the Centre O III area of operation until the defeat at Stalingrad. That direction held double strategic significance for the Germans – the possibility of encircling the Soviet centre from the south and reaching the oil fields of the Caucasus, and then capturing Iranian oil fields. This was the reason why that region attracted the main attention of Home Army intelligence. The information relating to the German military formations around Stalingrad was also passed on to the British.[33] Apart from permanent monitoring of the German military transports going east great attention was paid to the shipment of petroleum products from the Jasło and Borysław basins. The intelligence penetration was facilitated by the fact that the dynamics of military operations in Ukraine forced the Germans to engage in various undertakings in the front's rear area, such as the construction of fortifications, airfields, military depots and roads. Since the projects were entrusted to branches of the 'Todt' organisation and various German firms which employed Polish workers recruited from the General-gouvernment, Home Army intelligence could legally transfer individual groups of agents to the rear area of the eastern front.[34]

The activity of networks supervised by Centre O III was supported by the intelligence services of regional Home Army commands: Lwów, Stanisławów, Tarnopol and Volhynia, where the chief of the local II Bureau was Maj. Henryk Pohoski 'Adolf, 'Stawisz' and his deputy was Lt. Czesław Dzierżek. Transport monitoring was carried out by a separate special network: Lt. Stanisław Lachowicz 'Wiktor' specialised in the road, motorised convoy and Air Force intelligence. Railway intelligence was carried out by Henryk Zaleski 'Włodzimierz', an engineer and a retired railway worker; he organised a network which recorded almost every transport. Hospital intelligence was entrusted to Eugeniusz Kudła 'Witold', who collected information about military formations on the basis of the files of wounded soldiers. He was helped by his wife Nina 'Figa', who worked in the local hospital, as well as nurses and nuns. In another domain, Professor Ferdynand Tarnawski 'Profesor', former Polish consul in Leipzig, conducted correspondence intelligence. For that purpose whole bags of mail (Feldpost) going from the front to Germany and the other way around were stolen; draft copies of letters and the documents of German offices were taken from wastepaper baskets by Polish women cleaners. As a result, intelligence reports were made every ten days, totalling tens of typed pages, were sent by a transport cell headed by Janusz Pratkowski. His courier was Józef Brungl, who travelled to Warsaw as a clerk of one of the German officers.[35]

Intelligence reports sent by particular centres of the 'WW-72' network contained much valuable information about the situation in areas near the front, the movement of military railroad transports and medical evacuation, and about the mood prevailing among soldiers and officers. In the middle of December 1941 the Centre O III informed that the main communication route went across Zdołbunów-Fastów-Kiev, that it had branch-lines and secondary routes, and that all the tracks had been adapted to the European gauge. Trains travelled on wide tracks only from Kriemenchug to Poltava, Kharkov, where the Soviet rolling stock was used. Further information referred to the accelerated construction of a bridge in Kiev which would take only three months to build. Detailed information mentioned two pontoon footbridges across the Dniepr river near Kiev, one pontoon bridge and a pulley for barrels with petroleum, and the fact that each ferry carried three train carriages arranged in parallel. The information about the condition of nine railway bridges in the Ukraine proved that intensive construction work was conducted and that it was scheduled to be completed at the beginning of or in the spring of 1942.

Information was forwarded that one hospital train with about 700 beds passed through Koziatyń during the day going west. From 3 December 1941 four eastbound transport trains with aircraft equipment and automobiles went through that city. Details were supplied about the organisation of the administration and attitude of the German authorities towards the local population. The report said: 'The campaign of collecting levies has begun, and the rates are higher than the Soviet ones. The attitude of the authorities in occupation towards the local population is increasingly brutal, with a simultaneous retention of external propaganda campaigns inciting Ukrainian nationalistic feelings'.[36] On 1 November 400 men of various nationalities were executed in Kiev in retaliation for cutting telephone and telegraph lines and damaging a cable factory. Home Army intelligence reports also mentioned that the Germans kept the co-operatives functioning (sovhoz and kolhoz network), so that it was difficult to estimate the volumes of basic stocks, and that there was a universal shortage of sugar, flour and fat. It was estimated that the German efforts aiming at settling economic problems behind the front lines encountered various obstacles due to the 'conditions and the population in the East'.[37]

Much information was obtained in the course of conversations held with German soldiers. One of the agents, while travelling with an SS battalion from Równo to Zhitomir, found out that they had been in Norway until August 1941 and after their leave they were sent to the front. The Germans inquired about the Soviet Air Force, cold weather and the partisans. Information provided by other intelligence networks was similar. Centre O II in Wilno informed that in January 1942 it had recorded a total of 508 railway transports going east, including 267 to Dyneburg and 241 to Mołodeczno, while 325 trains arrived in Wilno returning from those directions. The report also contained information about the transported freight, although it was not always possible to gather such information every time. Monitoring of road transport revealed traffic in both directions. The number of trucks and automobiles was established, the number and the length of artillery columns, the number of buses carrying soldiers, vehicles transporting food, etc.[38] Information in February 1942 showed that the intensity of rail transport varied. From 16 January 1942 70% of all trains went in the direction of Polotsk, and 30% to Pskov, opposite to previous months. The transports were closely guarded and masked, making it difficult to read their signs (emblems). At the beginning of March a growing number of railway transports with wounded soldiers and those suffering from frost-bite were signalled. Dissatisfaction with the war grew, even among the SS soldiers. According to the information obtained from German sources four infantry divisions, each from 18,000 to 21,000 men strong, passed through Wilno from 31 January to 11 February. The port of Riga was frozen, and on 1 and 2 February seven ships, each with a displacement of 3–5 000 tons, sailed into the port of Libava.[39]

Reports on transports contained information referring to emblems, with a precise description of each image. They were supplemented by the reports from Home Army regional commands which also monitored transport going in both directions. These reports were precise due to favourable conditions deep inside the country, so more informants could be engaged. Just as valuable was the information concerning the morale of soldiers returning from the front or sent to the east.[40]

The new cell in Odessa provided reports about the situation in southern Russia from December 1941 to 10 January 1942. It informed inter alia about the growing influx of the 150–200 mm. calibre coast artillery and the fact that trains with Italian and Romanian soldiers, all in high spirits, were on their way to Kiev. The report was supplemented with news relating to the administrative and economic issues in Odessa.

Detailed information was supplied in that period by the Centre O III. Cell 'Jastrzębiec' in Kiev reported to Maj. Klotz about the situation on the Dniepr River. On 22 February 1942 the Germans concentrated the construction effort on a railway and road bridge.[41] The rail bridge, supported by stone pillars, had a single track one kilometre long. In a letter addressed to the construction workers Hitler wrote: 'I regard the construction and completion of the bridge as extremely urgent and important'. The deadline was to be 1 March 1942, a date later postponed for two weeks. The railway transport going on tracks placed on ice was regarded a temporary solution, in which a small locomotive pulled several carriages. On 19 February 'Jastrzębiec' reported the arrival in Kiev of forty carriages of air force transport. It also provided information about the military situation in the city and surrounding areas.

At the beginning of March Centre O III reported that German detachments were being moved from the Zhitomir-Vinnitsa region to the Kiev-Biala and Tserkev-Human areas. The reserve field hospital (Armee-Reservelazaret) in Vinnitsa was evacuated, the wounded and the sick were evacuated to Lwów, and the hospital itself was transferred to the region of Human. At the same time, two motorised divisions and numerous newly formed Schupo detachments arrived to the east of Kiev. Similar tendencies were noted by a station of Centre O II in Minsk; every night 10–12 trains and 6–7 during the day moved in the Baranowicze-Smolensk direction, carrying soldiers and equipment. Precise information depicted the situation along the roads leading to the front and at the airfields as well as the growing influx of the wounded.[42]

Exact information made it possible to establish new intelligence cells. The development of the situation at the front was also favourable for getting new operatives. Station 'Minsk', which was established from scratch, built a new network composed of a dozen persons in several weeks. They began watching railway transports in the Mołodeczno region, Radoszkowice and along the main routes leading to Smolensk. Preparations were made for the establishment of cells near the railway junctions in Bobruysk, Polotsk and Vitebsk.[43]

Considerable changes in the disposition of the German troops were also noted by Centre O III. A list of railway transports chiefing towards Dniepropietrovsk-Charkov-Znamienko included information about 62 trains in the period from 15 April to 9 May 1942. The Germans sent various types of equipment and material, as replenishment intended primarily for the infantry. The next report signalled the arrival of railway transports of a motorised Waffen-SS division, which was redeployed to Belgrade following withdrawal from the eastern front. It also said that the soldiers were in excellent physical and mental condition.

In the summer of 1942 Cell 'B-8' in Piervomaysk signalled changes in deployment of troops that had already begun in the spring. In March-April a part of the 'K' army forces, concentrated in the Kiev-Biala Tserkiev-Poltava region during the winter, was moved towards Crimea and took part in the campaign in Kerch and Sevastopol. In the second half of July the same forces were quickly moved towards Lugansk-Voroshilograd. From 15 July the rear detachments of the Sixth Army led by Kleist moved along the Nikolayev-Krivoy Rog-Dniepropietrovsk line and crossed the Dnieper River, chiefing towards Stalino.[44] Cell 'B-8' indicated problems with making detailed reports about the transport movements which was caused by limited possibilities of accessing the sites of railway stations and tracks. Furthermore, in small towns German security organs made it impossible for civilians to remain near railway stations. Therefore, every attempt to obtain information posed serious risk to the agents.[45]

Information concerning German transports forwarded to the II Bureau of the Home Army GHQ were meticulously analysed by the Military Studies Department. It should be stressed that nine main lines crossed the Polish territory, 75–80% of front supplies were delivered by train, and the number of military transports totalled as many as 500 day and night. Despite the fact that not all the transports were precisely recognised the obtained information made it possible to draw conclusions regarding even the predicted operations of the Wehrmacht Supreme Command. Thanks to that the direction of the German summer offensive of 1942 was correctly predicted – that it would aim at the southern part of the eastern front and not Moscow. The prognoses about a resignation from further attempts to capture Leningrad proved similarly accurate. In the autumn of 1943 the Polish General Staff in London was informed that the defeat of von Paulus and his army at Stalingrad was only a matter of time. That was indicated, among others, by the hasty transfer to the eastern front of German armoured formations, which had initially been deployed in southern France.[46]

The new information from the rear area of the eastern front and other sources was additionally analysed by the II Bureau of the PGS before it was forwarded to the Polish authorities and the Allies.[47] Such verification limited the possibility of errors and incorrect conclusions. At the beginning of 1943, according to the information of the II Bureau the Soviet forces had 330 infantry divisions, 170 infantry brigades and 330 training divisions. During the early months of 1943 the II Bureau received information about initially 40 Maj. infantry units, then 70 and finally 110. Since the information did not seem probable the Second Department directed checking the organisation of the units mentioned in the information. It turned out that the Russians had reduced the composition of a platoon from four to three squads, and also the authorised strength of regiments in the divisions trained in the Moscow-Gorkiy-Kazan region from 3,380 to 2,517 men. Thus, it was possible to get 'an additional' 1,215,720 soldiers who formed the above mentioned 110 military units.[48]

Home Army Intelligence provided detailed information about the situation of the army of Gen. Andriey Vlasov. In September 1943, when its Main Headquarters were located in Pskov, attention was drawn to the symptoms of loyalty to Germany shown by the way in which a 300 person-strong detachment guarded 7,000 Soviet POWs in Zaslav near Minsk. German propaganda tried to show that Vlasov could soon form as many as ten divisions by recruiting volunteers from among 400,000 Soviet POWs. Meanwhile, according to Home Army intelligence he could form only 33 battalions.[49]

The II Bureau of the PGS had at its disposal information from other fronts, and thus conducted periodical analyses of the overall military situation. In December 1943 it assessed that 'the Germans continue to remain in defence in all domains and on all fronts; change is unlikely at least until spring. The Germans do not have strategic reserves and severely lack human reserves. The advantage is on the Anglo-Saxon or Soviet side at all fronts. Despite numerous domestic difficulties caused mainly by air raids there are no signs of an internal crisis in Germany'.[50]

At the beginning of 1944 the II Bureau, on the basis of information from the eastern front and the monitoring of the situation in particular sectors of the front, drew attention to the excessively slow progress westward of the Soviet troops. No significant operations were foreseen in the northern, central and southern sector. Forces were being regrouped on both sides of the front; the II Bureau assessed that 'in this situation the key to the basic changes in the east would be the deployment of Allied forces (invasion). Only the deployment of new forces can undermine the balance of forces in the east that is being rebuilt by the Germans'.[51] In the following assessment of the situation, formulated in May 1944, it was stressed that the Germans were taking into consideration a decisive Red Army offensive along the northern and central sections of the front, and therefore retained a defensive position along the whole eastern front; hence, the initiative would remain in the hands of the Soviets.[52]

The shift of the front to the west meant that the major part of the 'WW-72' network found itself on the Soviet side. This was the situation of Centre O III cells in the towns of Berdyczów, Zdołbunów, Ploskirow, Winnica, Kamienec Podolski, Złoczów, Podwłoczyska, Stanisławów and Lwów. Despite the fact that the personnel of the cells justified their presence in those areas to the Soviet authorities by mentioning compulsory labour in Germany, in a few weeks the NKVD arrested most of the members of the 'WW-72' network, several of whom were executed.[53]

Despite an explicit development of the situation at the eastern front reports from this region continued to be of interest to the Allied staffs. The reason for that lay in the approaching invasion of Western Europe. Meanwhile, some of the reports sent by Home Army intelligence reached London with a considerable delay. In some cases the encoded part of the reports arrived at the II Bureau several months later (!). Nonetheless, the received data had to be analysed by HQ, although the majority of the reports – especially those concerning the deployment of German forces – would lose their usefulness. Consequently, at the beginning of May 1944 the II Bureau of the PGS firmly called for limiting the process of encoding of fragments of intelligence reports sent from Poland. As explained by Col. Stanisław Gano, Chief of the II Bureau, that process had been introduced at the request of the British.[54]

After the Warsaw Uprising Home Army intelligence had limited possibilities for collecting information about German forces. The loss of documentation, maps and other material hampered systematic work. Lt-Col. Stanisław Kijak, who was sent to Poland, had an extensive knowledge about the earlier organisation and activity of Home Army intelligence and received instructions from the Chief of the II Bureau of the PGS and other indispensable materials. It was presumed that Intelligence cells on the German side of the front were to be located deep inside the rear area of the front in order to achieve the possibility to work longer. On the other hand, individual Home Army districts were entitled to maintain direct communications with London. The intelligence network was to restrain and even sever contacts with the combat detachments of the Home Army. The Chief of the II Bureau emphasised that since the information about the movement of German railway transports were still regarded as important he recommended that Lt-Col. Kijak take steps to create a permanent observation barrier to the west of the Vistula river, the sole purpose being the organisation of intelligence aimed against the Third Reich.[55]

During the final phase of the war the II Bureau highly valued the work performed by Home Army intelligence. The vast majority of the information from Poland referred to the situation at the eastern front or its deep rear area. Just as essential was information relating to the identification of German forces, transports of troops and materials, traffic at airports and the morale of the German troops. It was emphasised that 'the II Bureau regularly sent intelligence from Poland to the British and American intelligence headquarters co-operating with us. Intelligence materials from Poland were extremely highly valued by the Allied intelligence services, which in return for this co-operation provided a number of valuable services, including the financing of intelligence in Poland'.[56]

At the end of 1944 intelligence activities in Poland were becoming increasingly less effective. The networks which had previously functioned on the German side of the front, now became controlled by Soviet security organs. The new situation led the Home Army GHQ to use the remnants of the clandestine networks in the east in the creation of a new intelligence aimed against the Soviet Union.

Notes

1   TNA: (PRO) HS 4/322, 16876, German preparations for action against Russia, 14 February 1941
2   T. Strzembosz, *Początki oporu w Polsce. Kilka uwag* (*The beginnings of the Resistance in Poland. Several remarks*) [in:] *Armia Krajowa. Rozwój organizacyjny* (*The Home Army. Organisation and Development*), ed. by K. Komorowski, Warszawa 1996, pp. 11–17.
3   IPMS, A XII, 24 /1, Note for the Chief of the Polish General Staff II Bureau, 12 July 1941.
4   IPMS, A XII, 24/46, Polish General Staff II Bureau, Survey of the German Army Great Units on Polish territory to 25 July 1940.
5   AAN, KGAK, 203/III-55, Military report by 'Włoczka' of 27 June 1940.
6   SPP, 2.3.6.2.2, Note from Intelligence Chief Maj. Żychoń to the Chief of the VI Bureau of the PGS, I. dz. 1909/II. Wyw./40 of 16 November 1940.
7   AAN, KGAK 203/III-53, Additional report by the commander of 'Sól' of 14 October 1940.
8   See: M. Ney-Krwawicz, *Komenda Główna Armii Krajowej* (*the Home Army GHQ*), [in:] *Armia Krajowa*, op. cit., p. 24 .
9   Information was obtained on 10 May 1941 that highway construction entrepreneurs were summoned by telegraph to a briefing held in Poznań on 29 April. At the same time the Germans announced the suspension of all less important road

construction undertakings and the inauguration of work teams for repairing road behind the German Army in the east, AAN, KGAK, 203/III-55, Report by 'Kreton' of 10 May 1941.

10 TNA: (PRO) HS4/322, German preparations for action against Russia (General appreciation based on Intelligence Reports received from Poland from July, 1940 to March 1941).

11 AAN,KGAK, 203/III-53, Supplementary report by 'Rondel' of May 1941.

12 SPP, 2.3.6.2.2, Note from the Chief of Intelligence Department Maj. Żychoń to the Chief of the VI Bureau of the PGS, 26 May 1941.

13 SPP, 2.3.6.2.2, Telegram from 'Godziemba' to 'Kalina', l. dz. 1755/tjn. 41 of 28 May 1941.

14 AAN, KGAK, 203/III-53, 'Rondel' – additional report by a special source, 8 June 1941.

15 Ibid.

16 AAN KGAK, 203/III-53, 'Rondel' – additional report of 21 June 1941.

17 17 SPP, 2.3.6.2.2, Telegram from 'Łukasz' to 'Kalina', l. dz. 2206/tjn. 41 of 30 June 1941.

18 IPMS, A XII 24/78, Analysis of the situation in the German-Soviet war upon the basis of communiqués to 28 June 1941.

19 On 20 June 1941 40 new Heinkel 111 bombers were discovered at an airfield near Klikawa. The nearby forest concealed 68 planes of this type, and 23 fighters were hidden around the airfield in Zajezierze. The airfield in Sandomierz contained 30 planes of different types, including 12 fighters. AAN, KGAK, 203/III-54, Report from the Regional Command 'Malina', 28 June 1941.

20 SPP, 2.3.6.2.2, Telegram from Maj. Żychoń to the Chief of the VI Bureau, I. dz. 4934/II. Wyw./41 of 9 July 1941.

21 J. Roman, *Ekspozytura 'Wschód-Wołyń' (Station 'Wschód-Wołyń')*, [in:] *Życie na krawędzi. Wspomnienia żołnierzy antyhitlerowskiego Wywiadu (Life on the Edge. Reminiscences by Members of Anti-Nazi Intelligence)*, Warszawa 1980, pp. 220–227.

22 SPP, 2.3.6.2.2, Coded telegram from 'Łukasz' to 'Kalina', no. 3019/bn. 41 of 8 September 1941.

23 TNA(PRO) HS. 4/280, Report no. 90 of 20 November 1941.

24 B. Zieliński, *W konspiracyjnym Biurze Studiów (In the Clandestine Studies Bureau)* [in:] *Życie na krawędzi*, op. cit., pp. 305–308.

25 SPP, 3.7.4.1, Coded telegram to 'Kalina', I. dz. 3195/tjn. 41 of 10 October 1941.

26 C. Chlebowski, *Cztery z tysiąca (Four Out of a Thousand)*, Warszawa 1981, pp. 215–221.

27 H. Żuk, 'Onufry', 'Barański', *W wywiadzie Armii Krajowej 'Wschód' (In the 'Wschód' Intelligence Service of the Home Army)*, [in:] *Żołnierze Komendy Głównej Armii Krajowej wspominają (Men from the Home Army Chief Command Reminisce)*, collective work ed. by K. Wyczańska, Warszawa 1994, pp. 62–63.

28 Ibid., pp. 81–82.

29 S. Pempel, *ZWZ-AK we Lwowie 1939–1945 (the Home Army in Lvov 1939–1945)*, Warszawa 1990, pp. 52–54.

30 The clandestine premises of Maj. Klotz were situated in 8 Mala Yuridika Street.

31 HIA, The M. Z. Słowikowski Collection, Box 1, Organisation report from 'Cukrownia', 7 April 1946.

32 The Germans began arresting members of the 'WW-72' network in the spring of 1942; about 80 persons were imprisoned. A new wave of arrests took place on the night of 13 January 1943. By the summer of 1943 approximately 200 persons were detained in Lwów, Kiev, Cracow and Warsaw.

33 F. H. Hinsley, *British Intelligence in the Second World War*, vol. 3, part 2, London 1981, p. 29.

34 H. Zakrzewska, *Niepodległość będzie...*, pp. 159–162.

35 Ibid., pp. 61–63.
36 AAN, KGAK, 203/III-52, Situational report no. 6 (copy) of Centre O III, 16 December 1941.
37 Monthly report 12 /1941, [in:] *Meldunki miesięczne wywiadu przemysłowego KG ZWZ/AK 1941–1944* (*Monthly Reports from Industrial Intelligence of the Home Army GHQ 1941–1944*), facsimile prep. by A. Glass, Warszawa 2000, p. 36.
38 AAN, KGAK, 203/III-52, Intelligence report by Centre O II for January 1942. The soldiers complained about the food. They were mobilised at the end of the summer of 1942 and were to be trained until May 1942. In the course of two weeks 4,650 wounded men were admitted into the hospital on Antokol in Wilno; the majority suffered from the third-degree frost bite.
39 AAN, KGAK, 203/III – 52, Intelligence report 3/42 by Centre O II for January and February 1942.
40 AAN, KGAK, 203/III-54, Monthly report on the period from 27 January to 26 February 1942 by the Regional Command 'Malina', 3 March 1942.
41 AAN, KGAK, 203/III-52, Report from 'Jastrzębiec' to 'Piotr' [A. Klotz] – Situation on the Dnieper river on 22 February 1942.
42 AAN, KGAK, 203/II-52, Report from Station Mińsk, 21 March 1942.
43 Ibid.
44 AAN, KGAK, 203/III-52, Situation report from Cell B-8, 21 July 1942.
45 AAN, KGAK, 203/III-52, Report by Cell B-8 from 16 April to 15 May 1942.
46 B. Zieliński, *W konspiracyjnym Biurze Studiów*, op. cit., p. 309.
47 NARA, RG165, MID, Entry 77, Germany, Box 1282, Polish Intelligence, The German retreat from Russia.
48 IPMS, A XII 24/56, Note by the General Staff of II Bureau 4 May 1944.
49 NARA, RG165, MID, Germany, Box 1193, File 6000, Polish Intelligence-Germany, General Vlasov's army.
50 IPMS, A XII 24/16, Note by the Records and Studies Department of the II Bureau to the Polish General Staff, 22 December 1943.
51 IPMS, A XII 24/16, Note by the General Staff II Bureau: An assessment of the situation in the east, 1 February 1944.
52 IPMS, A XII 24/56, Note by the Register and Studies Department of the II Bureau to the Polish General Staff, 9 May 1944. A brief assessment of the general situation at all fronts.
53 HIA, The M. Z. Słowikowski collection, Box 1, Organisational report by 'Cukrownia' of 4 April 1946.
54 SPP, 2.3.6.1, Note from the Chief of the General Staff II Bureau to the Chief of the VI Bureau, 10 July 1944.
55 SPP, 2.3.6.1, Copy of a personal Instruction for Lt-Col. Kijak of 25 November 1944 prepared by the Chief of the General Staff II Bureau, l. dz. 7505/N/44.
56 SPP, 2.3.6.1, Note from the General Staff II Bureau to the Chief of the VI Bureau of the Polish General Staff, 18 October 1944.

PART VI
THE PRINCIPAL ACHIEVEMENTS OF POLISH INTELLIGENCE

45
The Achievements of the Polish Intelligence Service

Gill Bennett

British Intelligence archives contain no comprehensive detailed or summary reports on Polish Intelligence achievements during the Second World War. The greater part of the surviving evidence of the significant contribution made by Polish agents, networks, contacts and communications lies in the records of individual departments and agencies transferred to The National Archives. Many of the most notable and well-known achievements – such as those related to ENIGMA, and to Polish information on V-weapons – have already been described in published works including the British official history. In the closed records exist only fragments, brief summaries and occasional snapshots of the wider picture. This chapter will attempt to paint that picture from the scant and scattered documentation that has been found, and to add detail where available.

The only documents that have been found referring to Polish Intelligence achievements over the whole wartime period are those put together in May 1945 by Commander Dunderdale for the information of the Prime Minister. These documents, which list some of the more interesting and important subjects covered by 45,770 Polish reports that were both of high quality and quantity, are reproduced in summary form in Volume II of this Report.

All other documents refer in greater or lesser detail to short periods during the war. The main source of information on the achievements of Polish Intelligence is in the periodic summary or progress reports prepared by Dunderdale's section. No such reports have been found for 1940. The only references to Intelligence supplied from Polish sources in 1940 that have been traced are in the weekly summaries of information, which were passed to Maj. Desmond Morton for the use of the Prime Minister. These summaries do not give the source of information, but their subject indicates their possible origin. Thus the weekly summary for 7-13 October 1940 states that the total of 25 reports on the Soviet military situation included one on Red Army dispositions in Soviet south Poland, one on the calling up of the 1917, 1918 and 1919 classes in Soviet Poland for service in the Red Army, and one on railway construction in Soviet Poland. No further details are given, and the reports themselves were not kept.

More detail is available about the circulation of reports from Polish sources in 1941. An undated note by a member of Dunderdale's section states that between 1 January and 28 February 1941, numbered papers from Polish sources exceeded 900, over 400 of which had been circulated to other SIS sections, while the remainder were used to answer specific enquiries. These figures did not include telegrams from Polish the VI Bureau sources that were circulated directly to other sections. It was noted that the output of circulated reports in January and February 1941 had increased by 100% over an equivalent period in 1940.

The note continued that in addition to the production of reports, it had also been necessary to deal with correspondence with the Polish authorities, the transmission of comments, questionnaires and individual enquiries, Polish requirements for the purchase of material, assistance in the selection of appropriate W/T sites in collaboration with MI8 and GC&CS's Russian Section, and to carry out personal supervision of station personnel and workshops.

A note dated 19 May 1941 giving figures of reports received from A4 since January showed that during that period a total of 20 reports had been received from Polish sources, of which two were graded A, 13 B, 3 C and 2 unclassified. The two graded A concerned the identifications of XII Corps and 23rd Infantry Division of the Russian armed forces, and the Franco-Siamese treaty (the latter was subsequently queried and not confirmed).

Another report listed reports produced by A4 between 1 January 1941 and 1 January 1942: 3,829 from Polish sources, comprising 136 of considerable value, 1,643 of value, 256 of little value, 34 of no value, 171 with no comments marked and 1,589 with no comments received.

A list of reports issued and criticisms received by P5 during the year 1942 showed that 7,474 reports were issued, but with no indication whether they were from Polish or French sources. Some weekly report sheets have been found, however, which do break down the source of the information. Between 10 and 16 August, for example, P5 submitted 149 reports to HQ, of which 116 were from Polish sources. Between 28 September and 4 October the respective figures were 156 and 133.

Sometimes individual sections of SIS produced a report on the value of Polish Intelligence to them, though few of these survive. One such report, dated 17 December 1942, gave the comments of the Naval section covering Northern Europe, Germany, France and French Africa. It stated that the Polish Intelligence service was 'highly appreciated...both for information given and the way in which supplementary enquiries are followed up'. Particular praise was given to the 'highly efficient' North African RYGOR organisation, 'giving in great detail coastal batteries, the fact that the French North African ports were not protected by minefields, and information concerning French war and merchant vessels'; the Polish organisation on the south coast of France was also highly appreciated, particularly for its report on the condition of the French fleet after scuttling.

Sketchy figures only are available for 1943: P5 issued 11,477 reports of which 5667 were from Polish sources. Of the overall total, 539 were graded A and 6210 B, with no indication of origin. Specific items noted as of interest included a report of 8 January 1943 on Gdynia, showing the position of shipyards, anti-aircraft guns, ships and offices; three further reports in March 1943 on Gdynia, showing the position of German naval officers and information on naval units and stores; reports in August 1943 on submarine production at Danzig; a report in September containing a chart of Gdynia with the positions of guns, naval units, naval and military billets and oil tanks marked on it; and in November-December 1943, reports on air raid damage, aircraft markings and movements. None of these reports has survived.

In 1944, rather fuller progress reports have been found. On 29 August a six-monthly report was produced on the work carried out by the Polish II Bureau from 1 January to 30 June. This is a comprehensive document, commenting on Polish reports on the following areas:

Military Section
- **Order of Battle**: 'excellent both as regards accuracy and importance of information sent';
- **communications:** time-lag of two months in receipt of information from Poland still a problem, and further information sought on German railway administrative organisation in Russia, with particular reference to the effect on it of the retreat from Minsk;
- **paramilitary formations**: useful reports, but more wanted on Waffen SS depots and training units, German police and Allgemeine SS in Germany, organisation of Waffen SS divisions, preparations for continued underground and open resistance to Allied occupation forces after German's defeat;
- **organisation and equipment**: useful reports, but would like more information on organisation of mountain and light divisions, and chemical warfare indications, particularly on the Russian front;
- **defences:** useful reports received on defences of 'East Wall' on which little is available from other sources; also useful reports on defences in Western Europe, where 'in spite of occasional exaggeration' information has often been corroborated by air photographs and proved generally reliable;
- **manpower**: very little received; need indication of numbers or percentages of Poles embodied in German formations and units, what use is made of them and their promotion prospects;
- **flak:** reports scanty and out of date, though generally accurate with some interesting reports on flak strengths from Hungary.

Naval Section
- **Northern Europe:** Polish II Bureau 'continues to be most valuable and highly appreciated by us'; organisation in France provides useful information on shipping, dockyards and coast defences, but has failed to provide telegraphic reports on shipping in the Northern French ports during the invasion; Stockholm organisation provides good information on shipping in the Baltic, but 'does not appear to have recovered from its setbacks' (see Part VI); information from German naval bases Kiel, Wilhelmshaven and Hamburg is rather weak but now improving; useful information on gas in Poland;
- **suggestions for development and improvement:** to establish an organisation in the Baltic that can report by W/T matters of naval interest from Gdynia, Pillau and Königsberg; to try and penetrate German naval ports such as Kiel, Wilhelmshaven, Stettin and Swinemünde;
- **Southern Europe:** very little information received from II Bureau, but some useful coastal defence reports from Spain, greater detail required; anxious to acquire coastal defence information from Balkan Black Sea coast.

Air Section
- Polish efforts to make their reports about the German Air Force Order of Battle 'more legible and understandable' much appreciated as they are 'of a high standard of accuracy' and 'much appreciated;
- useful reports on German aircraft production, particularly where they have technical drawings attached;
- request for more reports with copies of manufacturers' nameplates attached to aircraft and components, giving useful indications of the scale of manufacture
- some criticism of time-lag, but this is improving;
- II Bureau to be congratulated on the range and accuracy of their reports over the past six months;

Economic Section
- **Shipbuilding:** valuable reports from Germany, mostly referring to Hamburg, Bremen, Lubeck and Danzig and dealing with the building of submarines and other warships; details of approximate tonnage and length would be appreciated; two reports from JOHAN-DORA seemed good at first but proved inexact; new information on trial reporting through SKN (Stockholm) whose reports on shipbuilding have been good; a report on shipyards in Stettin valued by MEW as 'the first most detailed information they received'; number of reports on Germany has increased since the beginning of 1944;
- **France:** most reports on Mediterranean ports, of which the best

have been on Toulon from BIZ; fewer reports but good quality, though details of tonnage and length still lacking;

- **Other countries:** a few reports on Denmark, two of which referred to a new type of submarine exercising in Horuphav which interested MEW.

General Industrial

- **France:** reports have increased since March but are still not producing as much information as in 1943; majority concerned railway and transport information and were nearly all of value; large proportion concerned sabotage of locomotives and rolling stock and communications, in which MEW are interested; MEW would like more information on air raid damage; information on electricity of good value, but that on armaments, munitions and explosives has been too general; reports on industries and engineering are useful, but 'detailed information concerning one particular factory is of more value than a general report attempting to cover a wider field'; no reports on iron and steel, but useful information on aluminium and light metal industry; reports concerning railways and transport are the best in quality and quantity;
- **Belgium:** reports generally valuable, but would have been more so if up to date; too many concern transport operations in 1943; more precision needed: 'one detailed report on one canal lock, or on one factory...has double the value of a long, general report dealing widely with several factories and giving no concise details'; one or two useful reports received on armaments factories, especially the DWM works at Herstal; no reports received on air raid damage;
- **Switzerland:** 19 reports received, mostly dealing with armaments, machine tools and other industrial subjects; the most recent, 'Switzerland/Germany/Machine Tools' is of value and confirms earlier information contained in 'Switzerland/ Engineering' as absolutely reliable; reports on 'Switzerland/ Armaments/ Artillery/Munitions' and 'Switzerland/Germany/ Engineering/ Machine Tools' graded A;
- **Spain and Portugal:** nine useful reports on Spain, five on the transport of commodities by rail, the others on engineering and steel; one particularly valuable as giving daily output of iron and steel; only two reports on Portugal, one on metals and minerals, and the other on transport of commodities by rail giving the traffic passing Vilar/Formosa;
- **Italy and the Balkans:** eight reports received, one of special value as confirming the existence of the factory at Verralota; other reports included two on Bulgaria, two on Greece, two on Italy (one valuable as giving the evacuation of various works to Germany and Czechoslovakia), two on Romania, one giving a valuable list of industries and useful employment figures;

- **Turkey:** useful report on storage in Turkey of chrome purchased by the Germans;
- **Poland and the Protectorate:** good reports, in particular two graded A confirming previous information on various branches of the Huta Bankowa works; another report graded 'excellent' stating that automatic ammunition machines were being erected in place of textile machinery in the Warta factory, though it would have been of greater value with approximate production date, planned output and number of workers employed; other useful reports but lacking precision;
- **Germany:** roughly 130 reports, the majority graded B, would have been higher with greater detail;
- **General remarks:** very few reports on military transport or air raid damage; monthly lists of statistical information on German train services are appreciated; reports on evacuation and new location of factories as a result of air raid damage 'of outstanding interest';
- **Baltic and Scandinavian countries:** very little received (roughly 6 reports), but always welcome; report on Norway/Aluminium graded C as it conflicted with previous information;
- **Summary on aircraft matters:** most information concerns Germany, Poland, USSR and France, regular and valued B; information on German occupied countries very infrequent and vague;
- **Poland:** very interesting reports on factories in the Lodz region and on the MWN and Bruhn works at Warsaw: 'They are well set out giving all the information required. MEW are particularly interested in the transfer of factories, the exact location, the number of workers and the output'.

Oil
- Most reports on France, always useful although a high proportion deal only with dumps; would be more valuable with production figures of oil wells, shale production, refineries and synthetic plants; best reports on Poland itself, 'very favourably commented on by MEW'; interesting reports from Hungary could usefully be expanded; 'crying need' for reports on Germany, on which information is scanty – some improvement in German information but 'not nearly so great as we wished. At present the ratio is altogether disproportionate between the importance of receiving accurate information on Germany and the number of reports that actually come in. This should be impressed on all sources.'

Political Section
- Only small number of reports, and not of great value as insufficient details are known about the background of the informants.

Rockets

- Information during last six months 'of great and increasing value'; information on whereabouts of launching ramps for V1 weapons and details of storage depots has been very useful to Air Photographic Section; reports emanating from Poland of 'very great value'.

The annexes to the above report, comprising statements of the number of reports issued during the first half of 1944 and their gradings, a note on aircraft production in Poland and a note on the work of BIZ, SEVILLE and SAB, will be reproduced in Volume II of this report.

The only other documents that have been found giving details of Polish reporting are notes of SLC activities for August, September and October 1944. Although these give the total number of reports received with no indication of origin, the subject matter of some of them, such as 'Poland-order of battle', reports on German divisions in Poland, aircraft markings in Poland and on the oil industry in Poland, are likely to have come from Polish sources. In November a report was received on the Polish electrical industry.

The following more general appreciation, although pertaining particularly to early 1944, is a good indication of the value attached to information received through Polish channels at this time:

The reports which have been reaching us during recent months from Polish sources are among the most valuable which we received and have contained information of obvious reliability, which has provided a more complete picture of the German Aircraft Industry in the east than has been obtained about any other area. In view of the importance which now is attached to German Aircraft Production, and in particular to the eastern factories to which much of the industry has been dispersed, it is requested that every effort be made to augment and accelerate the flow of this intelligence.

The information from official documents is of first class value in giving details of production planning, and now that many of the factories have been successfully attacked, it is essential that no time be lost in getting reliable ground information about the effects on production and the plans for recovery. It will be appreciated that the damage and repairs to buildings can be evaluated from photographs, but without adequate ground intelligence we are unable to say to what extent a factory has been put out of action, nor can we conclude when a particular target has recovered sufficient value to justify further attack. Ground intelligence of this sort, therefore, not only enables us to estimate production, which has a bearing on future planning, but it has a direct influence on selection of future targets.

Finally, it is necessary to mention two of the most significant and best known areas where Polish Intelligence made a Maj. contribution to Allied victory: the work of Polish cryptographers on ENIGMA, and the information supplied by Polish agents on V-weapons. Although no new or supplementary information has been uncovered in British Intelligence archives during the course of the Committee's work, other than that material which has now been transferred to the Public Record Office, certain observations can be made.

ENIGMA and Anglo-Polish cryptological co-operation
The full story of the outstanding Polish contribution in the field of cryptology represented by their work on ENIGMA was not told for many years after the war. The account given in the first volume of *Hinsley*, published in 1979, was later acknowledged to have been inadequate and misleading, and a revised version based on British Intelligence records was published in Volume 3, Part 2 of *Hinsley*, published in 1988. This Appendix sets out in detail the valuable work done by the Polish cryptographers and acknowledges that without this work British efforts to break the codes would have been delayed, and the war might have lasted longer.

Since Hinsley's Appendix was published, however, even more information on the Polish contribution to ENIGMA has come into the public domain, through the transfer of records belonging to GCHQ, as well as other Allied records. A book published in 2000 by Stephen Budiansky, *Battle of Wits: the complete story of codebreaking in World War II*, draws together a wide range of evidence, including technical information, that presents a comprehensive picture of the scale of the Polish contribution on ENIGMA that leaves no doubt as to its impact. Nothing has been found in British closed archives that adds to this detailed account.

Only one extra document relating to ENIGMA has been found in British closed archives. This is a very short memorandum presented to the Chief of SIS by Commander Dunderdale in January 1957. A transcription of this document will be included in Volume II of this Report.

Some account of Anglo-Polish cryptological cooperation later on in the war has already been given in Chapter 15. In addition, the records of the Radio Security Service (RSS), transferred to the PRO as a result of the work of the Anglo-Polish Historical Committee, give a good deal of detail about the work done by the Poles at Stanmore, and about their own communications networks and cyphers. These papers, available in class HW 47, include comprehensive notes on Polish cyphers and code books, the location of Polish overseas stations and communications, and arrangements made by RSS and SIS to provide Polish cryptographers with accommodation, facilities and equipment. RSS was under SIS control from 1941, and these papers constitute the only documentation from secret archives now extant about Polish activities in these fields. (See Chapter VI for more details – E. Maresch). No extra documentation has been found.

V weapons
Details of the Intelligence reaching the British Government on Hitler's 'secret' weapons is given in *Hinsley*, Volume 3, Part 1. Very few original

reports from Polish sources relating to V weapons have survived in SIS archives. Copies of the only substantive reports that have survived, received by SIS in 1944, together with some diagrams and photographs, are reproduced in Volume II of this Report.

Although *Hinsley* states that SIS 'had been receiving Polish reports from the Blizna area' about such weapons since October 1943, references in SIS archives indicate that Dunderdale's section A4 may have been producing reports on V weapons as early as February 1941. None of these has survived, however, and no further record of such reports has been found until the middle of 1943, when there is a reference to a 'V' report from the Polish Station in Paris.

Another reference is to a report from inside the German testing site at Peenemünde by a slave labourer from Luxembourg, who made a very rough sketch of construction work at Peenemünde and managed to escape to Luxembourg, from where he sent it by a messenger to Switzerland for passing to the British. When SIS received it they immediately recognised it as most valuable information and ordered that anything further on the subject should be telegraphed 'Most immediate'. A few weeks later the first Allied bombing raid on Peenemünde took place, and it is possible that this report played its part in exposing the nature of the work going on there. Further reports on Peenemünde from Luxembourg sources continued to reach SIS until the RAF raid on 17 August 1943. However, no trace of these reports or any map has been found.

After this date the V reports flowed in spasmodically. A batch arrived on 9 December 1943: 'Details of the Secret Weapon', 'Details of both types of rocket', 'Location of rocket emplacements', etc. These reports, which do not survive, were passed on to CSS by Dunderdale's section, but there is no indication as to whether they originated with Polish or French sources. Other reports, however, concerning the V2 testing grounds that had been moved to Blizna, in Poland, after RAF bombing of Friedrichshafen, certainly originated with Polish Intelligence. Although the adjacent forest villages were evacuated, the Polish Home Army was able to obtain information from the new German-built railway from Blizna to Lwów. By the end of November 1943 continuous reports were getting through to SIS via Warsaw. In December a Polish expert sent in a report with a photograph of a rocket in flight over trees.

In the spring of 1944 a V2 rocket fell into the sandy bank of the River Bug, near the testing ground at Sarnacki. The machine was quickly hidden by the Resistance and later smuggled into Warsaw, where it was examined by Polish scientist who extracted its fuel and sent it, via Brindisi, to London in May 1944. SIS asked to see the whole rocket, and it took until July 1944 for them to arrange, together with SOE and Polish Intelligence, for an air pick-up.

The Poles stipulated that one of their technical experts must accompany the chassis of the rocket, which only weighed 50kg: a note by SLC stated that 'The Polish agent who brought this information and material [i.e. photos, plans and sketches] has made a study of the subject and is well versed in the latest V2 developments in Poland'. With only one stop at Bari (where SIS/SOE had a base) the precious cargo arrived safely at Hendon on 28 July 1944. The passengers included Dr Rettinger, a Polish politician, who sent a telegram to Anthony Eden, British Foreign Secretary, thanking him for the ride and paying tribute to the 'efficiency of all British services concerned in this enterprise', which was codenamed Operation WILDHORN III.

Other reports from Polish sources mentioned in 1944 included a Special Report on Rocket Projectiles, received in April together with diagrams of jet propulsion engines, photographs and lists of markings on rocket parts; and a report of 30 June 1944 stating that Hitler intended to use 'flying bombs' to destroy first London and then other areas, but had been forced to change his plans by a decrease in calibre.

From mid-1944 V-reporting was frequent, though mostly confined to spotting the next position of launching sites for the benefit of the RAF. Some reports in early 1945 gave the location of V-weapon manufacture inside Germany; a reference has been found to a report in February giving details on V2 factories at Ebensbach, Leitmeritz and Frankfurt-am-Main. Dunderdale later said that he regarded work on the V-weapons as one of the most important carried out by his section, both Polish and French.

46

Cryptographic Cooperation – Enigma

Jan Stanisław Ciechanowski – Jacek Tebinka

In 1918, Dr Arthur Scherbius, a German engineer and inventor from Düsseldorf, patented an electromechanical enciphering machine known as Enigma.[1] Its continuously improved version was for a long time recognised as unfailing in passing on secret messages since it guaranteed sending an astronomical number of enciphered combinations of letters.[2] The superiority of this pioneering machine lay in the almost ideal dispersion of letters which meant that it was impossible to apply the traditional methods of breaking codes – finding references to natural language. All statistical calculations, such as the frequency of the occurrence of letters, also failed.[3]

Enigma undoubtedly constituted one of the greatest achievements in the history of cryptology. Initially, it was used mainly by large firms for protecting their secret correspondence. In 1926, however, it became part of the equipment used by the Reichsmarine,[4] in 1928 by the Wehrmacht, in 1935 by the Luftwaffe, and two years later by the police and the SD.[5] From that time on particular types of Enigma were frequently improved.[6] In 1934 Enigma became the basic instrument used by the German authorities for coding information.

Initial work on breaking Enigma, conducted by the Polish cryptologic services,[7] primarily by Lt. Maksymilian Ciężki, Lt. Wiktor Michałowski and Antoni Palluth, an engineer, failed to produce results. The breakthrough came with a cryptology course for outstanding students, organised in the Institute of Mathematics at the University of Poznań in January 1929 at the request of the General Staff.[8] The following year eight of the most talented students of Prof. Zdzisław Krygowski, director of the Institute, began to work on German ciphers intercepted by Polish monitoring stations. Although the station, located in the Poznań Municipal Command, was closed down in the summer of 1932, in September of that year three of the most promising young cryptanalysts – Marian Rejewski, Jerzy Różycki and Henryk Zygalski – became employed in the BS 4 Section (intelligence focused on Germany) of the Ciphers Office of the Intelligence Department of the II Bureau of the

General Staff in Warsaw. Originally, the three men decrypted simple hand-method ciphers but remained helpless while dealing with the growing number of telegrams which appeared to have been machine coded.[9]

Despite the purchase in 1932 of a commercial version of Enigma, the break came when Rejewski, who had been given access to German telegrams from previous years, used the mechanical combination theory (the theory of permutation), never used in cryptology before.[10] This led to the discovery of theoretical principles of the Enigma, that is the mechanisms of functioning of its particular parts, and then to devising methods of recreating the deciphering keys to the coded messages.[11] Rejewski also received help in the form of documents conveyed between December 1931 and September 1932 by Capt. Gustave Bertrand, an officer of the French ciphers bureau. From 1930 he was the Chief of section 'D' of the Service de Renseignements, supervised by Deuxième Bureau,[12] who established co-operation with the Polish Ciphers Office. From that time on, the working contacts between Bertrand ('Bolek') and Langer ('Luc') were very close. The materials were obtained from a French spy Hans Thilo Schmidt ('Asche')[13] – a member of the German Chiffrierstelle until 1934. 'Asche', however, did not have access for reaching the most protected secret, that is the diagram of the inner mechanism and the wiring of the three so-called rotors of the military version of Enigma – the E Eins – the potential of which appeared to be unbreakable. On the other hand, the Polish Ciphers Office received photographs of the military version of Enigma, a basic instruction manual, and two out-of-date monthly deciphering tables.[14] While handing over the German documentation Bertrand stressed that neither the French nor the British experts had been able to use it for breaking the code.[15] The documentation as such proved rather useless, which is confirmed by the fact that after several years of having these materials as well as others the French and the British were unable to come even close to unravelling the secret of Enigma. The significance of those documents, however, consisted only of the fact that they contributed to building a replica of Enigma, as the way towards discovering the method for establishing the deciphering keys remained very long.[16] The success was determined not so much by financial means or the number of cryptanalysts involved in the attempt to solve the issue of Enigma but by the application, first of all by Rejewski, of higher mathematics.[17] Only in combination with the science did the materials prove useful.

Enigma's code was broken for the first time during the second week of January 1933, when the Poles began reading the first telegrams, a fact about which they apparently did not inform Capt. Bertrand.[18] As a result, by the end of 1933 a method was devised for permanent reading of German coded messages.[19] In February 1933 the Ciphers Office requested the 'AVA' firm[20] to build replicas of Enigma on the basis of a prototype prepared by the three Polish cryptanalysts. Consequently, in mid-1934 there were already more than ten machines available, and the Poles were the only ones in the world to read machine enciphered German telegrams, including those of the Kriegsmarine. This was a success of international importance considering the fact that the French and the British intelligence services did not have any achievements in this field.

If Enigma was regularly read in the years 1933–1935, it was with increasing difficulty, since in 1934 the Germans changed the arrangement of the inter-connecting plugs once every quarter, from 1 February 1936 they did so every month, from 1 October every day, and finally every eight hours. Moreover, in 1936 they introduced six different sets of deciphering keys. The number of crucial elements, rotors and connecting plugs grew, too. In 1937 the Germans altered the structure of the reversal ring. Polish cryptanalysts responded by constructing a 'cyclometer' (Rejewski) and the 'clock' method devised by Różycki, which allowed them to continue reading of German coded messages and commands.[21] Consequently, the tests conducted in January 1938 by the Ciphers Office confirmed the possibility of intercepting German wireless correspondence, enciphered with the help of Enigma, of which about 75% was then effectively read.[22]

Nevertheless, on 15 September 1938 the Germans introduced obligatory changes to the initial setting of Enigma not every 24 hours but prior to the transmission of each telegram. This meant that only certain SD telegrams could be read, since the 'cyclometer' was no longer effective. Despite those obstacles the Poles also resolved this problem very quickly, because in October of that year Rejewski completed work on a mathematical model of another device – the so-called bombe – which made it possible to catch up with the Nazis.[23] In several weeks, and in secrecy, 'AVA' built a suitable aggregate composed of six Polish replicas of Enigma. In November, six such mechanical devices were produced, making it possible to obtain the most important elements of the code in two hours, and in minutes – to decipher the key. In response to the Germans introducing an individual deciphering key to every telegram the Poles used traditional keys changed every day, plus the so-called Zygalski sheets – specially perforated device invented by Henryk Zygalski.[24]

It was possible once again to read Enigma, although with unprecedented difficulties and not in a 'serial production' manner. On 15 December 1938, when the Poles had already decrypted several thousand German telegrams, the Staff in Berlin introduced a new, much improved version of Enigma, with two additional rotors despite the fact that every time only three of them were used. This innovation was implemented in connection with the introduction of wartime instructions. The Polish Staff was well aware of the fact since an agent working in the radio-intelligence service of the German Air Force from mid-1938 had informed them that codes would be changed after the declaration of war.[25]

The new modifications did not mean that the Poles had ceased reading Enigma. In January 1939 they managed to recreate the setting of the fourth and fifth rotors of the machine thanks to intercepting a slight delay of a SD code in relation to the one used by the Wehrmacht. At that time, however, the Germans changed the number of the plugboard connections, making it impossible to decrypt their information except some SD coded messages. The Polish side knew very well, though, what it would need to read Enigma once again, possibly on a regular basis.

Owing to the great increase of possible combinations it was necessary to construct ten times more 'bombes' (a growth from six to sixty). Working in parallel, they established the original setting of the rotors.[26] It was also necessary, but at the same time extremely time-consuming, to manufacture at least several hundred sets (26 sheets each) of 'Zygalski sheets', to determine the sequence of the rotors.[27] All that, however, exceeded the financial and technical possibilities of the Ciphers Bureau in a short period of time.

When the Polish General Staff realised that there was probably not enough time to make the necessary number of 'bombes' and 'sheets' prior to a possible German attack against Poland, it decided to share the invaluable knowledge about Enigma with Western Allies.

The first meeting of representatives of Polish, French and British cryptologic services devoted to Enigma took place at the invitation of Bertrand on 9–10 January 1939 in Paris.[28] The British, however, were quite reserved about the co-operation with the French and the Poles. It took Bertrand much time to persuade Alistair G. Denniston, Chief of the Government Code and Cypher School, to attend. In turn, Polish representatives – Lt-Col. Langer and Maj. Ciężki – were supposed to disclose the solution to Enigma only if it turned out that the French and the British had made some progress in this field.[29] Since the talks showed nothing of that sort, the secret was not disclosed and the number of persons aware of the Polish success was further kept limited to a minimum. However, the Poles continued to pass on decrypted German messages obtained from mechanical Enigma to the French and the British without disclosing their know-how.

When the outbreak of war became inevitable and when the British Prime Minister Neville Chamberlain declared in the House of Commons guarantees for Poland on 31 March 1939, (later confirmed on 4–6 April 1939 during talks with Józef Beck), the Polish General Staff invited representatives of the British and French radio-intelligence services to Warsaw.[30] Once again, Bertrand had to persuade Cmdr. Denniston to accept the invitation. On 25 July 1939 the Allies were shown in Pyry[31] the replicas of Enigma made by 'AVA', the 'bombes' and the 'Zygalski sheets'. Explanations and hints concerning the method of reading German ciphers were provided, and the Poles demonstrated, among others, that the rotors (each with 26 letters of the alphabet) linked with incoming and outgoing electrical wires according to the simple principle A, B, C, D..., unlike the Q, W, E, R, T, Z, U... principle applied in the commercial Enigma.[32] Two replicas intended for the Allies were sent to France by sea.[33] The replica prepared for the British was taken to London by Lt-Col. Bertrand in the company of Lt. Cmdr.Wilfred Dunderdale.[34] On 16 August it was presented to Col. Stewart Menzies, then Deputy and future chief of SIS.

Officially, the reaction of the Allies was positive. The Poles were thanked for making their accomplishments available and the French had no hard feelings. Everything seems to indicate that Rejewski was correct in his post-war assumptions that Lt-Col. Bertrand, the initiator of co-operation between the radio-intelligence services of the three countries, who was officially informed about the Polish success on 24 July, had at least guessed about those accomplishments.[35] The British behaved in a different way feeling offended by not having been informed earlier.

It was significant that on the eve of the Second World War Polish Intelligence possessed 80–90% of the knowledge of the distribution of Wehrmacht units along the Polish-German border[36] was, to a large extent, the achievement of the Ciphers Office. Despite considerable obstacles that were caused by the improvements of Enigma in December 1938 the reports were still being read, although on a very small scale since the Polish side had to wait for a suitable number of 'bombes' and 'sheets', for the production of which there was simply not enough time. Despite further changes introduced by the Germans on 1 July, the Poles still managed to solve the secret of the wartime version of Enigma by 26 August, and to read German coded messages of 6 July. Retrospectively, they deciphered commands and reports sent previously.[37]

The cryptanalysts were forced to interrupt their work a few days after the attack against Poland launched by Nazi Germany. They were evacuated on 6 September 1939 eastwards *via* Brześć on the Bug, Kowel, Łuck and Włodzimierz wołyński. After the Soviet invasion they crossed the Romanian border. Prior to that, they had to destroy most of their equipment and documentation. Rejewski, Różycki and Zygalski took advantage of the chaos in Romania and managed to avoid internment. Eventually they left for Bucharest. Embittered by France's non-existent help to Poland, they turned to the British Embassy. The Ambassador put them off by promising to consult London. The French Embassy treated them better. The Poles asked that 'Bolek' be informed about their arrival. Thanks to French assistance of Capt. de Winter the cryptologists were evacuated to France through Yugoslavia and Italy, including Langer and Ciężki, who were in a Romanian internment camp. They had two Enigma replicas with them.[38]

When Lt-Col. Langer reached Paris on 1 October 1939[39] he was permitted by the Polish military authorities to accept the French invitation and continue the cryptologic work. They were well aware of the fact that the creation of a totally independent Polish section was impossible because of lack of equipment for a separate high standard radio surveillance. Henceforth, on 29 October Lt-Col. Langer and his group, composed of 14 persons,[40] were incorporated into a cell under the cryptonym 'P. C. (Poste de Commandement) Bruno', located in 'Château de Vignolles' in Gretz-Armainvilliers, some 40 km from Paris. The cell was supervised by the 5-ème Bureau of the French General Staff, i.e. a new joint intelligence service, created after the outbreak of the war. Apart from the Poles, 'Bruno' also employed French and Spanish cryptanalysts.[41] Lt-Col. Bertrand in his capacity as chief of Section d'Examen, was responsible for radio interception and deciphering enemy reports. Langer was a representative of the Polish Army, assigned to this Allied cell together with his men. Rejewski, Różycki and Zygalski traditionally concentrated on analytical breaking of codes. The intensive work of

British cryptologists was evaluated by Lt-Col. Langer during his visit to Great Britain in December 1939. He was convinced that the Government Code and Cypher School had launched the production of the 'Zygalski sheets' and ordered cryptologic bombes based on Polish models.[42]

It was one of the reason why the British tried from the very beginning to bring over to the British Isles one of the three most important Polish cryptanalysts.[43] Although Lt-Col. Bertrand did not oppose talks and consultations, he did not intend to let the cryptologists go, being well aware of just how much he owed them. Therefore on 29 December 1939 he clearly pointed out to the British that since it was the French government which was paying for maintaining the Polish Army, the Poles would stay in France. A similar view was shared by Lt-Col. Langer, when the British turned to him in December 1939. Nonetheless, the British kept trying to invite the Poles, and indicated prophetically that the latter would lose if they refused.[44] In his letter of 9 January 1940 addressed to Col. Menzies, Chief of SIS, Denniston underlined the advantages of the enormous experiences of the three Polish cryptanalysts, requesting in this way that SIS influence the French Deuxième Bureau. On 10 January 1940 Col. Louis Rivet, Chief of the Bureau, received from his British counterpart a letter stating that: 'In order to help my experts we believe that if it could be arranged for some of the junior Polish personnel who have been engaged for many years in this specialised work, it would increase the chances of achieving early results, which are so important for both sides'.[45]

Although the original French reply has not been preserved in the archives, some circumstances indicate that it must have been negative. Quite possibly the chiefs of the Government Code and Cypher School were also to blame for that, because on 7 January 1940 Knox threatened Denniston with his resignation in order to finally obtain consent for conveying Enigma statistics to centre 'Bruno' (which was arranged in Pyry).[46] Since there was no chance that the Polish cryptologists could come to Bletchley Park for consultations, the British, including Alan Turing, went to France in January 1940 with Zygalski's perforated sheets made by the British.[47] Mutual relations improved after the first successes of 17 January 1940 when the Poles broke the Enigma coding key used by the Wehrmacht on 28 October 1939. Despite the significant delay it turned out that since the beginning of the war the Germans had not made any essential changes in Enigma and continued to use interchangeably five rotors.[48] At the time Bertrand described the co-operation with the British as 'excellent'.[49] Maj. Kenneth MacFarlane ('Pinky') was the British liaison officer, and the communications with the British radio-intelligence centre was maintained throughout the whole period. The British passed on enciphered German telegrams which were read in 'Bruno'. They supplemented those which were intercepted by the French monitoring services. Similarly the content of the German telegrams decrypted by either side was made available after the British began to decipher Enigma quite regularly (8 April 1940).

Further Enigma coded messages sent by the German army during the

September campaign which were decrypted soon afterwards, demonstrated clearly that breaking the cypher in the early stage of the next campaign could provide essential information about the intentions of the enemy. However, in February and March 1940 the Wehrmacht and Luftwaffe Enigmas were broken too late for the obtained information to be useful at the operational level. Moreover, Cell 'Bruno' sometimes received Enigma coding keys from Bletchley Park but not the telegrams which could be deciphered because the French service had not managed to intercept them.[50] Again, in the course of the Norwegian campaign, when the Government Code and Cypher School broke the army and air force Enigma (15 April 1940), for the whole month, until the change of the 'Yellow' key German correspondence was read only several hours after the coded message was sent.[51] This accomplishment, however, was not transformed into a military success, because of lack of co-ordination between intelligence and the army. In this respect, the situation did not improve much during the French campaign.

Until May 1940 the French could not manufacture necessary replicas of Enigma, modelled on the three Polish machines, two of which were constantly in use. The third one was disassembled but the attempts to build it over were unsuccessful.[52] Until 23 June 1940, when the station ceased its activity after the defeat of France, the Poles managed to decipher 8,440 telegrams, using only two machines. They were Luftwaffe wireless traffic: 1,151 referred to the Norwegian campaign[53] and 5,084 to the French one.[54] 227 telegrams came from the surveillance conducted by clandestine W/T radios used by German agents who in this way sent hand enciphered coded messages and enabled the French to take down many spies.

The coded messages decrypted by the Poles encompassed 110 days of the period from 6 July 1939 to 16 June 1940.[55] Much of the success of Cell 'Bruno' station was a part of the British who, as agreed earlier, concentrated on purely technical aspects. In the opinion of Lt-Col. Langer, out of a total of 126 solved keys necessary for reading Enigma coded messages as many as 83% were determined with the co-operation of the British from sub-section Hut 6.[56] All that made it possible to obtain information concerning the German Order of Battle in Norway and France as well as about air attacks on Paris. However, this information was of little or no use to the French authorities as in the case of air raids on the French capital.[57] Thanks to the Poles the French authorities knew about the German plans of occupying Norway and Denmark four days before the planned attack against those countries.[58] Apart from reading traditionally coded commands and reports the Poles also broke the three-letter code used by the Nazi Staffs in communicating with bomber and fighter squadrons. That was possible thanks to the hints provided by the British who were increasingly proficient in reading Enigma.[59]

Despite considerable efforts British cryptanalysts were unable to break the Enigma code before the outbreak of the Second World War and did not even come close. For a long time they regarded the monitoring of the Japanese fleet as a priority. That could have had incalculable consequences if in September 1939 they had not had a replica of the German enciphering machine, provided to them by the Poles together with adequate explanations concerning its functioning.[60] British radio-intelligence was unprepared for the challenges it faced during the war, both conceptually and practically.[61] The greater, therefore, our admiration for the quick making up for those losses. At the beginning of the war the core of the cryptologic centre was transferred to the Bletchley Park complex ('Station X') in Buckinghamshire, the new wartime location of the radio-intelligence. With time, it employed several thousand cryptologists, analysts and technical personnel.[62]

Just as the Poles before the war so now the British, who were shouldering the burden of cryptologic warfare, had to wage a constant battle in order to keep up with the changes in the Enigma system introduced by the Germans. The British contribution to the continued attempts to break Enigma was enormous and impressive. The most valuable and secret material was obtained through that decipherment known as 'Ultra'.[63] Once again, it became apparent that the decisive factor was human. Bletchley Park created a very efficient and generally reliable system of assessing and distributing information obtained through decipherment. This was the task of Hut 3 (army, air force) and Hut 4 (Navy; the famous Harry Hinsley worked here). The British were aware of the importance of this issue, and provided appropriate funding, and gathered an *ad hoc* group of outstanding specialists, including mathematicians. The achievements of the Poles were not wasted but swiftly and creatively continued and expanded.[64] Sixty sets of 'Zygalski sheets' were supplied to the Poles in Cell 'Bruno'. By taking advantage of Polish experiences, first of all of the solutions applied in the Polish 'bombe' and 'sheets', a British version of the 'bombe' was constructed based on the model devised by Alan Turing.[65] Turing himself was more of a brilliant mathematician than a cryptanalyst. He used to visit Cell 'Bruno' where the Poles shared experiences with their younger colleague even before the British began to read the Enigma.[66]

A separate problem became the struggle to decipher the naval Enigma ('M'), more complicated than the one used by the land forces and the Luftwaffe. This was an issue of essential importance for the British, as was reading the Luftwaffe reports and orders. The naval Enigma, which posed the greatest difficulties, was studied in Hut 8 (breaking the cipher of the land forces and the air force was entrusted to Hut 6). Part of the material was read in Hut 8 already in May and June 1941 thanks to captures at sea. Starting with the Norwegian campaign Enigma was intercepted together with documentation from German submarines (U-boats) and weather-ships.[67] Before the fall of France neither the French nor the Poles were informed about those successes. British soldiers and later on, to a lesser degree, the Americans often obtained this sort of material risking their lives.[68] Throughout 1942 the Germans, who had broken the British naval code, had an advantage. The British remained helpless following another change in Enigma, which resulted in many sunk Allied vessels and many casualties. The situation reversed at the end of 1942 so that by May 1945 Allied ships and aeroplanes had sunk 692 U-boats including 25 that were blown up by mines.[69] That was first of all thanks to decrypting Enigma.[70] In the opinion of Hinsley and other authors of the official history of British Intelligence the victorious battle against German submarines at the beginning of 1942 made it possible to launch the invasion of Normandy two years later. The Americans, on the other hand, broke a Japanese version of Enigma in September 1940 as part of operation 'Magic'.[71] Since 1942 this cipher partially was also no longer a secret to the Soviet Union.

The decoding of information sent by Enigma had a decisive impact on winning the Battle of Britain and the Atlantic as well as operation 'Overlord'. It also played a great role during battles against the expeditionary corps of Gen. Erwin Rommel at El-Alamain, the invasion of North Africa in 1942, and also during the landing in Sicily and the Italian campaign. In most cases decisions made by political and military authorities on the basis of information obtained from Enigma were right, although some mistakes were made. Considering the scale of the operation it was difficult to avoid them.[72]

The conditions which emerged after the fall of France made it impossible for Polish cryptanalysts to systematically pursue work on the ciphers of the German machine. In May 1940, during the first days of the German attack, a group of Polish specialists was transferred to the French Intelligence HQ in Paris. On the eve of the offensive serious changes were introduced into the system of using Enigma once again which hampered the work conducted by the Poles. The pause in reading German coded messages lasted for several days, from 16 to 21 May.[73] On 10 June the remaining cryptanalysts and the whole Gretz-Armainvilliers centre were evacuated. News about the capitulation of France reached the Polish cryptologists in Toulouse, where they found themselves after a brief stay in La Ferté-Saint Aubin and Vensat. They read some of the news from Enigma. On 24 June the Polish and Spanish staff of 'Bruno' was flown to Oran and then to Algiers. The last radio contact with London was made on 28 June. The French prevented the Langer group from being evacuated to Great Britain, which brought about considerable anxiety amongst British Intelligence, especially after receiving Bertrand's response to a letter from Col. Menzies addressed to him on 23 June 1940: 'as far as our Polish friends are concerned they were evacuated by plane before your telegram came, so it is not possible to send them'.[74] In Algeria, the Langer group was kept under deep cover.

As a result of the pressure exerted by Lt-Col. Bertrand and the approval by the Polish Staff to this plan the Poles finally returned to France in groups of two or three. They were installed in 'Château des Fouzes' in Uzès near Nîmes (department of Gard in the unoccupied zone), where out of a total of 29 staff members fifteen were Poles and seven were Spanish.[75] The French cryptonym for the station was 'Cadix'. Langer received the permission of the Polish authorities to work with the French as Station '300' of the II Bureau of the PGS. All the Poles received new identities.[76] Nonetheless, SIS was still suspicious, especially that Col. Bertrand had requested Bletchley Park to supply daily Enigma ciphering keys. For security reasons the British did not want to do it in the autumn of 1940, before determining who the centre was to work for. It was March 1941 when Bertrand met with Commander Dunderdale in Lisbon. That is when he received a W/T radio and one-time ciphers to communicate with London, though not with the Government Code and Cypher School but with SIS.[77]

On 1 October 1940 the team in France resumed its activity. Material to be deciphered was supplied by the 'Cadix' monitoring station as well as stations of the Vichy authorities. That was arranged by Bertrand, who used the name of Barsac. He was granted permission by Gen. Maxime Weygand (contrary to the provisions of the armistice). The Poles read many German commands and reports, mainly issued by the Wehrmacht, the police and the SS in northern France and the Reich, and sometimes in Poland, occupied by the Germans and the Russians.[78] The station, however, had serious problems with intercepting German coded messages. The Poles did use four receivers but a considerable part of the material to be decrypted came from Groupement des Contrôles Radioélectriques de l'Intérieur (GCR), an organisation created with German permission to fight the Resistance. It secretly supplied Bertrand with German wireless messages, although this took a lot of time.[79]

Some of the signals were intercepted from North Africa, where a branch of 'Cadix', subordinated to the Station, was created as Cell no. 1 (P.O.1, French cryptonym: 'Post Z', located in the 'Kouba' villa in the suburbs of Algiers). It functioned from April 1941 till January 1942 and used local intercept material, without the necessity of transporting it. Small groups of Polish cryptanalysts travelled there to work for 2–3 months. One such trip ended tragically: on 9 January 1942, Jerzy Różycki, one of the three Polish cryptologists and his companions: Maj. Jan Józef Graliński and Piotr Smoleński, drowned at sea near the Balearic Islands in a catastrophe of the 'G.G. Lamoricière' while returning from Algiers to the south of France.[80]

Much of the enciphered information about expeditions against the Résistance made it possible to warn French guerrillas and often individuals. The hand-method cipher of Abwehr agents was effectively broken, thus making it possible for the French underground counter-intelligence 'Travaux Ruraux' to operate. Antoni Palluth broke the cipher used by German military intelligence spies in Mediterranean ports to communicate with the headquarters in Stuttgart. Even the Swiss cipher was broken in 1941, information about this fact was sent to Poland. Altogether, Station '300' read 9,358 German coded messages, chiefly coming from Enigma.[81] That meant decrypting 4,679 reports, commands and directives. Most of them were police and SS information (3,091 reports and commands), the Wehrmacht information (679) as well as information from the Abwehr agents (518).

From 7 March 1941 the station had direct wireless communications with Polish Intelligence Headquarters in London. That also allowed for the communication between Lt-Col. Bertrand and Cmdr. Dunderdale as well as the transfer of information between the headquarters of the Polish II Bureau and Station 'Rygor' in Algiers, which passed on information of great value for the preparation of operation 'Torch'.[82] That was done behind the back of Bertrand, whose attitude towards the British was at the very least complex.[83] As a result, intercepted radiograms were no longer sent to France in 1942. Meanwhile, only Great Britain could guarantee proper conditions for breaking Enigma systematically and without greater risks. From the summer of 1942 there was a growing threat to the secret Polish-Spanish-Greek station. In addition, Lt-Col. Bertrand received confidential information about German's planned advance into the so-called unoccupied French zone. Nazi services already had information about a powerful radio station in the vicinity of Uzès or in the town itself.

In mid-October of the same year, with the threat of a direct take-over of Southern France by the Germans and Italians, and at a time of British preparations to land in North Africa, something which the Polish cryptanalysts and Bertrand could merely guess, it was decided to evacuate the Station *via* Spain. It was planned to transport twenty members of the 'Cadix' staff, including all the Poles to Great Britain. Bertrand and his wife were to join them later. Meanwhile, on 6 November, a German RDF group appeared in front of the building, but fortunately did not discover anything and was basically interested in the adjoining house. The French Col. ordered an immediate evacuation of the whole team to Côte d'Azure.[84]

With the German seizure of the unoccupied zone (11 November 1942) the hiding Poles were on the move and were forced to split up. Unfortunately, the departure of the first groups of the Station '300' staff was very poorly organised by the French. Consequently, on 13 March 1943, the Germans arrested Lt-Col. Langer, Maj. Ciężki, Lt. Palluth and civilians Edward Fokczyński and Kazimierz Gaca near Perpignan. The first two were imprisoned in Stalag 122 in Compiègne, and from 9 September in Eisenberg Castle in the Sudeten Mountains, an SS Sonderkommando camp. They were liberated on 10 May 1945 by the Americans. Palluth and Fokczyński, who were sent to the Sachsenhausen concentration camp, did not survive the war. The first died on 18 April 1944 during an Allied air raid on a Heinkel factory, where he was employed. The other died of exhaustion soon afterwards. None of them revealed to the Germans their secret, which would have told the enemy that the Allies were capable of deciphering German coded messages.

Zygalski and Rejewski were more fortunate and reached the French-Spanish border *via* Cannes, Antibes, Nice, Marseilles, Toulouse, Narbonne, Perpignan, and Aix-les-Thermes. They crossed the border on 29 January 1943 and became the victims of their guide, a Spanish smuggler who robbed them of the remainder of their funds. They were arrested in Puigcerdá and imprisoned in Belver and Seo de Urgel (until 25 March), and then in Lérida. They were released on 5 May 1943. Thanks to that and first of all with the support of MI6 they made their way to Gibraltar *via* Madrid and Portugal. From there they were transported by aeroplane to

Great Britain on 30 July.[85] Probably thanks to that the Polish cryptanalysts, upon their arrival in the British Isles, avoided a routine and extremely thorough interrogation by the British counter-intelligence.

Rejewski and Zygalski were sent to the Polish radio-intelligence and decryptment centre at Felden, in a house named 'The Arches', 16 miles from Stanmore, Middlesex. In October 1943 they were promoted from privates to second lt.s. From the autumn of 1943 they broke SS codes and ciphers, which was important as they read the coded messages of both the front armies and the detachments of this organisation stationing in occupied countries. Rejewski and Zygalski frequently obtained information invaluable for resistance movements in Europe and broke SD ciphers. They were engaged in decrypting information sent by the two formations until the end of the war. At that time, despite the pressure by the Polish Staff, Rejewski and Zygalski became totally separated from Enigma by the British who no longer needed them. For example, on 20 October 1944 the Polish authorities once again turned to the British, through Cmdr. Dunderdale, with a request to permit the Polish cryptologic unit to function normally. The unit 'whose pre-war record achievements in solving the German machine cipher was of invaluable service to the British and French staffs in this war'. Polish radio-intelligence functioned in conditions which practically excluded possibilities for a more serious work and even threatened with total elimination. As a result, Dunderdale was asked to regularly supply 2nd Lt. Rejewski in Felden with copies of the whole unsolved German material obtained by the British from monitoring. The Poles also requested the return of the Enigma replica presented in July 1939 and that Rejewski and Zygalski be provided with current experiences of British cryptanalysts from the German section. There was no reply to that request, though.[86] Until the end of the war Polish cryptologists had at their disposal extremely limited intercept material, and did not receive from the British the expected assistance which Lt. Rejewski described as 'none'.[87]

After his arrival in Great Britain Lt-Col. Langer was mistreated by Col. Stanisław Gano, head of Polish Intelligence, who had believed the imprecise French reports claiming that Langer was responsible for the unsuccessful evacuation of Polish cryptanalysts from France. Together with Maj. Ciężki Langer was sent to the Polish signal base in Kinross. He died on 30 March 1948, 'bitterly disappointed, convinced that he was betrayed by the French when they had no more use of him', Col. Stefan Mayer recalls. J. E. S. Cooper, during the war chief of the cryptologic air force section, wrote in his study (1974) about Langer: 'One would want to know what became of this man, to whom we all owe a great debt'.[88] (See Chapter VI, E. Maresch).

Maj. Ciężki died on 9 November 1951, and for the last three years of his life he survived on social welfare.[89] The end of the war and leaving Poland in the Soviet sphere of influence split the members of the former Ciphers Office. In 1946 Rejewski returned to Poland where he had left his closest family at the beginning of war. In 1978 he was awarded the Officer

Cross of the Order of the Rebirth of Poland. He died in Warsaw on 13 February 1980. Zygalski lectured at the Battersea Technical College and died in Great Britain in 1978.

The breaking of Enigma by three outstanding Polish cryptanalysts was the greatest contribution made by Poland to the victory of the Allies in the Second World War. It enabled them to attain the superiority that was of decisive influence on the course of the war and brought an early end to it. Moreover, this undoubtedly most important cryptologic success in history facilitated the British to create in Bletchley Park the 'Ultra' system which provided information about the state and activity of the German army.

The British were aware of the fact that the betrayal of war secrets, even to some extent, by those Poles or the French who had found themselves in German hands and knew the secret of Enigma could end tragically for the Allied war effort. None of the documents of the Polish Ciphers Office fell into German hands in September 1939. Nor did the Polish engineers and technicians who stayed behind in occupied Poland and who knew at least part of the truth of Enigma, betray its secrets. Some of them, like Czesław Betlewski, found themselves under direct threat. Two Polish meritorious cryptanalysts lost their lives, others, such as Langer, Ciężki and the Frenchman Bertrand, heroically kept the secret. Among all the Poles who knew about Enigma not a single one turned out to be a Soviet or a German agent. We mention this in reference to yet another fictitious Enigma story, presented recently in the motion picture *Enigma*, whose screenplay is based on a novel by Robert Harris. The screen character of a Polish traitor, revealing the secret to the Germans, has nothing in common with wartime reality.

Notes

1   See more extensively in: S. Singh, *The Code Book The Science of Secrecy from Ancient Egypt to Quantum Cryptography*, New York 2000, pp. 127–138. In 1919 Hugo Alexander Koch, a Dutch inventor, constructor and engineer patented a 'secret' enciphering machine (Geheimschriffmachine) based on a similar mechanism. In 1927 he sold his patent rights. Elements of this device were later used to improve Enigma mechanism.

2   On the mechanism of the functioning of Enigma and its maintenance see: N. Polmar, T. B. Allen, *Księga szpiegów. Encyklopedia* (*The Encyclopedia of Espionage*), Polish edition, Warszawa 2000, pp. 174 and 176. In 1939, the military version – 'Enigma W' – following improvements, had an astronomical number of cipher combinations: 4 032 925 581 343 838 699 520 000 000 3 x 7 905 875 085 625 x 100 391 791 500 (W. Kozaczuk, *W kręgu Enigmy* (*Within the Sphere of Enigma*), Warszawa 1986, p. 69, zob. *Enigma: How the German Cipher Machine Was Broken, and How It Was Read by the Allies in World War II*, London, 1984. The first model had 17 576 such combinations (S. Singh, *The Code Book*, op. cit., p.134).

3   W. Kozaczuk, *W kręgu*, op. cit., p. 18.

4   H. Bonatz, *Die deutsche Marine-Funkaufklärung 1914–1945*, Darmstadt 1970, p. 87. The mass-scale production of the military version of the Enigma for the needs of the German Army began in 1925 (S. Singh, *The Code Book*, op. cit., p. 142). At the end of the 1920s the Enigma was purchased by Swedish, American and British authorities, although the latter two countries never used it.

5   In 1935–1945 the German firm was to sell more than a hundred thousand Enigmas

INTELLIGENCE CO-OPERATION BETWEEN POLAND AND GREAT BRITAIN

to the Wehrmacht, the SS, the police, the Ministry of Foreign Affairs, the Abwehr and the SD (R. Lewin, *Ultra Goes to War. The Secret Story*, London 1978, p. 22). Various types of Enigma, predominantly its commercial versions, were also imported by countries which maintained good relations with the Reich.

6 In 1930 the basic model of Enigma was equipped with a so-called plugboard which multiplied the number of possible cipher combinations.

7 When work on breaking Enigma was initiated, the chief of the Radio-Intelligence Section of the Polish General Staff was Maj. Gwido Langer (from 1929), who in 1932 was appointed Chief of the Ciphers Office. The chief of the German sub-section was Lt. Maksymilian Ciężki.

8 It was conducted by: Maj. Pokorny, Capt. Ciężki and Palluth, an engineer.

9 W. Kozaczuk, *W kręgu*, op. cit., s. 45–46.

10 Rejewski presented the results of his observations of ciphered reports in the form of permutations. Despite the fact that the number of the unknowns practically excluded the possibility of solving the equations, the application of this method was a breakthrough in world cryptology. See more in: M. Rejewski, *Matematyczne podstawy rozwiązania niemieckiego szyfru maszynowego 'Enigma'* (*Mathematical foundations for solving the German machine cipher 'Enigma'*) [in:] W. Kozaczuk, *W kręgu*, op. cit., s. 369. A considerable although auxiliary role in breaking Enigma was played by his excellent fluent German and familiarity with German mentality (W. Kozaczuk, *W kręgu*, op. cit., s.70).

11 More on breaking Enigma: M. Rejewski, *Matematyczne*, op. cit., pp. 369–393; W. Kozaczuk, *W kręgu*, op. cit., pp. 52–59, 66–81.

12 The Intelligence Bureau of the French Staff also supervised counterintelligence. France had greater cryptologic traditions than Poland: during the first world war the French Staff boasted of numerous successes and in the first half of the 1920s it was capable of deciphering the coded messages of at least more than ten states.

13 In March 1943 he was betrayed by Rodolphe Lemoine ('Rex'), a French intelligence agent arrested by the Germans. In September Schmidt committed suicide in prison. When he was working for the French the chief of the German Ciphers Bureau was Hans Thilo's brother, Rudolf, a war criminal, then a Maj. and later a general. He was discharged from the Nazi Army after the disclosure of his brother's espionage (see: H. Sebag-Montefiore, *Enigma. The Battle for the Code*, London 2001, p. 267, 287–292, 304, 347). More on the exaggerated significance of Schmidt's work for the French intelligence, discussed below, in: ibid., pp. 9–10, 15–21, 26–32. See also: P. Paillole, *Notre espion chez Hitler*, Paris 1985, passim.

14 The key is the setting of the machine in an initial position prior to the commencement of transmitting. Part of the documentation supplied by Bertrand, primarily the keys, was made available to Polish cryptanalysts with a considerable delay, probably caused by Langer's decision to try to learn Enigma mechanism with the least possible application of keys. Col. Stefan A. Mayer believed that the documents supplied by the French were totally insignificant TNA(PRO), HW 25/16, note from MI-6 for G. F. Goodall of GCHQ concerning comments by Cmdr. Dunderdale, 1 July 1974). Up to 1940 the three Polish cryptanalysts were unaware of the origin of the documents (W. Kozaczuk, *W kręgu*, op. cit., s. 66). This was one of the numerous security measures used to protect the invaluable accomplishments of the Polish Staff.

15 See: P. Paillole, *Notre espion*, op. cit., pp. 56–57 and H. Sebag-Montefiore, *Enigma*, op. cit., p. 354. Bertrand provided the Poles and, similarly, the British, with only a part of the material about Enigma obtained from Schmidt. Thus, the Poles had smaller quantity of input material than the French (T. Heinrich, *Jeszcze o Enigmie* (*Once more about Enigma*)), 'Zeszyty Historyczne', fasc. 54, Paris 1980, p. 196.) See: G. Bertrand, *Enigma ou la plus grande énigme de la guerre 1939–1945*, Paris 1973, p. 56).

16 S. Singh, *The Code Book*, op. cit., p. 146.

17 See: ibid., pp. 149–155 and G. Bertrand, *Enigma*, op. cit., pp. 125-126. In a study from 1949 H. R. Foss, the British cryptanalyst who unsuccessfully tried to decipher Enigma reports, declared, referring to the French and British assumptions about Enigma, that: 'Later on, in Warsaw, the Poles, who must have considered us all very stupid, gave us the complete answer'; TNA(PRO), HW25/16, H. R. Foss, 'Reminiscences on Enigma', 30 September 1949).

18 G. Bertrand, *Enigma*, op. cit., pp. 23–38; TNA (PRO), HW 25/1, C. H. Alexander, 'Cryptographic History of Work on the German Naval Enigma'.

19 W. Kozaczuk, *W kręgu*, op. cit., p. 84.

20 More in: M. Danilewicz-Zielińska, *Zanim doszło do rozszyfrowania Enigmy (Before Enigma was Decrypted)*, 'Orzeł Biały', December 1974, pp. 10-11 and W. Kozaczuk, *W kręgu*, op. cit., p. 72. 'AVA', established in 1929, was located in 34 Nowy Świat Street in Warsaw. It co-operated with the General Staff supplying, among others, short-wave radio sets, and with time became its main supplier and construction works. The shareholders of this extremely modern firm included : Edward Fokczyński, Lt. Antoni Palluth, an engineer, and the brothers Ludomir and Leonard Danilewicz.

21 W. Kozaczuk, *W kręgu*, op. cit., p. 78.

22 TNA(PRO) HW 25/16, A study on Enigma, by Col. S.A. Mayer, London, 31 May 1974 (further as: S.A. Mayer's study on Enigma); a copy is also available in IJPL (Józef Piłsudski Institute, London). Lt-Col. Stefan Mayer was the Chief of the II Intelligence Department of the II Bureau of the Polish General Staff before the war. After the death of Col. G. Langer he took over and used his study papers. The British services regarded this document secret.

23 The author of the name was Jerzy Różycki.

24 W. Kozaczuk, *W kręgu*, op. cit., p. 100.

25 In the summer of 1938 Polish intelligence was warned by agent of Station no. 3 (in Bydgoszcz) of the II Bureau of the Polish General Staff who claimed that two additional rotors would be introduced into Enigma as part of preparations for war (TNA(PRO) HW 25/16, Study on Enigma by S. A. Mayer, London 31 May 1974).

26 M. Rejewski, *Matematyczna*, op. cit., pp. 384–388. The cost of constructing 54 new bombes was estimated at 1,5 million Polish złoty (about 350 000 US dollars); the Ciphers Office had at its disposal about 100,000 PZ annually for making radio-intelligence more effective (W. Kozaczuk, *W kręgu*, op. cit., p. 104).

27 M. Rejewski, *Matematyczne*, op. cit., pp. 388–391.

28 British cryptanalysts worked in the Government Code and Cypher School (GC&CS), established on 1 November 1919 to continue the undertakings of the special crypto-logic section of the British Admiralty – so called Room 40 (chiefed by A. G. Denniston), which had numerous successes in breaking military and diplomatic ciphers during the first world war. In 1919–1926 it was capable of decrypting all secret messages sent by radio or telegram by every diplomatic service in the world (including Polish) (see: TNA (PRO), HW 12, containing diplomatic coded messages intercepted and deciphered by the British in 1919–1939). See also: A. G. Denniston, *The Government Code and Cypher School between the Wars*, 'Intelligence and National Security', 1986, pp. 48–70; N. West, *MI5 Operacje brytyjskiej Służby Bezpieczeństwa 1909–1945 (MI5. British Security Services Operations)*, Polish edition, Warszawa 1999, p. 33, 42–43; N. West, *GCHQ*, London 1987).

29 TNA(PRO) HW 25/16, study about Enigma by S. A. Mayer, London 31 May 1974.

30 In his memoirs Bertrand, later a French general, wrote that Denniston had temporised probably wishing to resolve Enigma himself in order to subsequently 'bask in glory' (G. Bertrand, *Enigma*, op. cit., p. 59). This is an unjust opinion considering the fact that the British never even came close to solving Enigma and remained totally helpless. Bertrand's statement is another proof of not very good

458   INTELLIGENCE CO-OPERATION BETWEEN POLAND AND GREAT BRITAIN

relations between the French and British cryptanalysts. Many British opinions are
unfavourable towards the Frenchman (more in: H. Sebag-Montefiore, *Enigma*, op.
cit., passim).

31 The Ciphers Office was transferred there from the Saski Palace in the autumn of
1937.

32 TNA: (PRO) HW 25/12, Denniston to Birch, 11 May 1948, note by Knox of 4 August
1939 ('Notes on Warsaw').

33 The meeting was attended by Lt-Col. Bertrand and Capt. Henri Braquenié, a
cryptanalyst from the Air Force Staff (the French side), Denniston, Alfred Dillwyn
('Dilly') Knox and Cmdr. Humphrey Sandwith of Naval Intelligence – see HW25/12
Denniston's report How news was brought from Warsaw at the end of July 1939'; the
Polish side was represented by Maj. Langer, Capt. Ciężki and the three men who
broke Enigma: Rejewski, Różycki and Zygalski. It is characteristic that the talks and
social meetings were conducted mainly in German, the only language in common
for all the participants.

34 In 1922–1926 Cmdr. Wilfred 'Biffy' Dunderdale from the Volunteer Reserve of the
Royal Navy was Chief of the SIS Station in Istanbul, and in 1926-1940 of the station
in Paris, which was the reason for his excellent contacts with Polish intelligence.
See also: F. B. Richards, *Secret Flotillas. Clandestine sea Lines to France and French
North Africa 1940–44*. London: Frank Cass, 1996, p. 61, 107.

35 W. Kozaczuk, *W kręgu*, op. cit., p. 109 and 157. After the war Bertrand wrote that
Great Britain took advantage, free of charge, of the outcome of eight years of
friendly Polish-French co-operation (G. Bertrand, *Enigma*, op. cit., p. 60). In turn,
the British suspected that he only pretended to be surprised by the Polish success,
and in reality he had been informed about it much earlier; (TNA(PRO) HW 25/12,
note 'How news was brought from Warsaw at the end of July 1939'). It is difficult
to ignore the fact that the Poles passed on the secret of Enigma in their own well-
understood interest.

36 W. Kozaczuk, *W kręgu*, op. cit., p. 119; L. Gondek, *Wywiad polski w III Rzeszy
1933–1939 (Polish Intelligence in the Third Reich 1933–1939)*, Warszawa 1978, pp.
323–327; A. Woźny, *Niemieckie przygotowania do wojny z Polską (German
Preparations for War against Poland)*, Warszawa 2000, pp. 303–311.

37 W. Kozaczuk, *W kręgu*, op. cit., p. 139. See: idem, *Bitwa o tajemnice. Służby
wywiadowcze Polski i Rzeszy Niemieckiej 1922–1939 (Battle for Secrets. Intelligence
Services in Poland and the Third Reich 1922–1939)*, Warszawa 1969, pp. 191–192.

38 W. Kozaczuk, *W kręgu*, op. cit., pp. 123–130; IJPL Kol., 133, report by Col. Langer
12 May 1940, p.28.

39 Cmdr. Dunderdale, Chief of the SIS Paris Station, informed Cmdr. Alistair
Denniston, Chief of GC&CS, TNA(PRO, HW 14/1, a note 18 October 1939).

40 They were: Maj. Ciężki, Maj. Wiktor Michałowski, Lt.Henryk Paszkowski and Lt. A.
Palluth; civilians: Rejewski, Różycki, Zygalski, Sylwester Palluth, the engineer's
nephew, Kazimierz Gaca, Bronisław Krajewski and Edward Fokczyński (the
German section), Capt. Jan Józef Graliński, Lt. Stanisław Szachno, Ph.D. (one of
the best Polish cryptanalysts specialising in the east, see: A. Pepłoński, *Wywiad
polski na ZSRR 1921–1939 (Polish Intelligence Dealing with the Soviet Union
1921–1939)*, Warszawa 1996, p. 53) and the civilian Piotr Smoleński (Russian
section).

41 They were seven Spanish Republican emigrants who broke Italian and French
ciphers (G. Bertrand, Enigma, op. cit., p. 71). The Poles, all of whom gathered at
the end of October, made up Team 'Z', and the Spaniards – Team 'D'.

42 TNA(PRO), HW 25/16, *Study on Enigma* by S. A. Mayer, London 31 May 1974.

43 G. Bertrand, *Enigma*, op. cit., p. 76.

44 TNA(PRO), HW 25/16, S. A. Mayer from 1974; HW 14/2, memorandum 'Enigma-
Position' of 1 November 1939.

45 This was not the first instance since such suggestions had already been made before the outbreak of the war, immediately after the conference held in Warsaw and Pyry on 25–26 July 1939 (TNA (PRO) HW 25/12, Knox to Denniston, July 1939; note by Knox of 4 August 1939 ('Notes on Warsaw').

46 TNA(PRO), HW 14/2, note of 18 December 1939; HW 14/3, note of 25 January 1940; W. Kozaczuk, *W kręgu*, op. cit., p. 155.

47 TNA(PRO), HW 14/3, Denniston to Menzies, 9 January 1940, Menzies to Rivet, 10 January 1940. Rejewski's surname was misspelled as 'Rejewoli'.

48 TNA(PRO), HW 14/3, Knox to Denniston, 7 January 1940.

49 W. Kozaczuk, *W kręgu*, op. cit., pp. 153–154, 357–358; A. Hodges, *Alan Turing. Enigma*, Polish edition, Warszawa 2002, pp. 445–446.

50 Initially, the official history of British Intelligence mistakenly put this moment as the date of the end of December 1939, see: F. H. Hinsley, E. E. Thomas, C. F. G. Ransom, R. C. Knight, *British Intelligence in the Second World War* (further as: *British Intelligence*), vol. I, London 1979, pp. 492–493; for a confirmation that Enigma was broken on 17 January 1940 see: ibid., vol. III, part II, London 1988, p. 952.

51 TNA(PRO), HW 25/16, *Study on Enigma* by S. A. Mayer from 1974; for a list of the found keys see: IJPL (Jozef Piłsudski Institute, London), Report on the work conducted by the team of Lt-Col. Langer during the French campaign, that is 1 October 1939–24 June 1940 (further as: The Langer report), as well as a commentary by G. Welchman, *The Hut Six Story. Breaking Enigma Codes*, London 1998, pp. 227–231. *Nota bene*, teleprinter communication between Bletchley Park and Cell 'Bruno' was not established until April 1940 (see: TNA (PRO) HW 14/4, note of 6 April 1940).

52 Thus, for the first time providing current knowledge about German activity!

53 W. Kozaczuk, *W kręgu*, op. cit., p. 140. After the fall of France the French produced four Enigmas.

54 *British Intelligence*, vol. I, p. 137; TNA(PRO), HW 25/16, S. A. Mayer's *Study on Enigma*, 31 May 1974.

55 It is interesting to note that most of the 5 084 coded messages studied at Cell 'Bruno' centre originated from monitoring conducted on the British Isles – for example, on 30 May 1940 the British intercepted 650 telegrams, and the French barely 280; the reason lay in the fact that the British possessed a well-developed monitoring network which intercepted German wireless communication much more efficiently than in France (see: *British Intelligence*, vol. I, pp. 143–144; TNA(PRO), HW 25/16, S. A. Mayer's *Study on Enigma*, of 31 May 1974; TNA (PRO) HW 14/6, note of 4 June 1940).

56 Apart from German ciphers Cell 'Bruno' also worked on various Soviet ciphers and decrypted a total of 1 085 telegrams; 833 telegrams from other countries were also deciphered (TNA (PRO), HW 25/16, Study on Enigma by S. A. Mayer of 31 May 1974). See also: IJPL (Józef Piłsudski Institute, London), The Langer report.

57 It broke ciphers of the German land forces and the Luftwaffe TNA (PRO), HW 25/16, *Study on Enigma* by S. A. Mayer, London 31 May 1974).

58 W. Kozaczuk, *W kręgu*, op. cit., pp. 165–166.

59 Ibid., p. 145 and 149.

60 Ibid., p. 144.

61 After the war Cmdr. Wilfred 'Biffy' Dunderdale confessed that the representatives of the Government Code and Cipher School 'were very slow to admit that the Poles might have anything to teach them'.

62 Several persons were unsuccessfully trying to break Enigma at the beginning of the war, including Alan Turing who showed up in Bletchley Park on 4 September 1939 (A. Hodges, *Enigma*, op. cit., p. 143) and Gordon Welchman. In January 1940 their number grew from six to sixty cryptanalysts to reach the number of 6 000 cryptanalysts, analysts and auxiliary personnel at the beginning of 1943. At the end

of the second world war from 10,000 to 12,000 employees worked in the buildings and barracks of Bletchley Park. For example, in 1933–1935 the Polish Ciphers Office was composed of more than ten persons.

63 More on the mathematical aspect of this question in: S. Singh, *The Code Book*, op. cit., pp. 164–181.

64 For a more detailed discussion see: H. Sebag-Montefiore, *Enigma*, op. cit., pp. 375–388.

65 Considerable significance was ascribed to the contribution made by Gordon Welchman, a professor of mathematics at Cambridge (see: G. Welchman, *From Polish Bomba to British Bombe. The Birth of Ultra*, 'Intelligence and National Security' no. 1, January 1986, pp. 71–110). In 1944 the British used electronic enciphering machines of their own device, which were actually prototypes of computers.

66 The problem was that the Kriegsmarine used Enigma much more cautiously than the other armed forces; moreover, on the eve of the war its Enigma was thoroughly modernised. Only three rotors were used simultaneously after being selected out of a total of eight and not five, as in the case of the Luftwaffe Enigma. Hope for some progress appeared when two-three Enigma rotors were captured on 12 February 1940 on board of the U-33 before it sank in the result of an action carried out by HMS 'Gleaner', a minesweeper. A considerable number of secret documents were also seized, including codebooks: on 26 April 1940 on the patrol boat P 2623; on 23 February 1941 on the armed minesweeper 'Krebs'; on 7 May 1941 on the weather-ship 'München'; on 9 May 1941 on the U-110 (captured by HMS 'Aubrietia', a corvette, and the destroyers HMS 'Bulldog' and HMS 'Broadwater', although sunk soon); on 29 May 1941 on the weather ship 'August Wriedl' and in June 1941 on supply ships 'Gedania' and 'Lothringen'. It's worth remembering that in the category of submarines alone the Allies also captured two, practically undamaged, vessels: the U-570 (captured on 27 August 1942 by aeroplanes, the destroyer HMS 'Burwell' and the auxiliary escort vessel HMS 'Northern Chief'). It was even incorporated into the Royal Navy as the HMS 'Graph'/P-715 (on 20 March 1944 it crashed against cliffs in the region of Islay and then sunk while being hauled) and the U-505 (captured on 4 June 1944 by the escort destroyer USS 'Pillsbury'). Apart from the above mentioned U-33, U-110 and U-559 (see below) the Allies also captured the U-744 (captured on 6 March 1944 by the destroyer HMS 'Ikarus' the U-boat was sunk because it could not be hauled). It's difficult to assume that on their decks (particularly the U-570 and the U-505) something of interest could not be found! (A. Hodges, *Enigma*, op. cit., pp. 165–174; H. Sebag-Montefiore, *Enigma*, op. cit., pp. 67–77; W. Kozaczuk, *W kręgu*, op. cit., p. 298; J. Lipiński, *Druga wojna światowa na morzu* (*The Second World War at Sea*), fourth ed., Gdańsk 1976, p. 705, 706, 711, 716.)

67 W. Kozaczuk, *W kręgu*, op. cit., p. 154; S. Singh, *The Code Book*, op. cit., pp. 181–185 and F. W. Winterbotham, *The Ultra Secret*, London 1974, p. 28. For example, on 30 October 1942 Lt. Anthony Fasson and sailor Colin Grazier from the HMS 'Petard' perished in the sunk U-559, after having extracted Enigma code books (H. Sebag-Montefiore, *Enigma*, op. cit., pp. 12–13).

68 J. Lipiński, *Druga wojna*, op. cit., p. 461. According to other sources the number of U-boats was 648 (C. Blair, *Hitler's U-Boat War*, vol. 2, *Hunted 1942–1945*, Polish edition, Warszawa 1999, p.728; see *Hitler's U-Boat War*, vol. 2, *Hunted 1942–1945*, by C. Blair, 1998).

69 H. Sebag-Montefiore, *Enigma*, op. cit., pp. 5–6. On breaking the 'Naval Enigma' see: D. Kahn, *Seizing Enigma. The Race to Break the German U-Boat Codes 1939–1943*, London 1991. Peter Calvocoressi claimed that if the Western Allies had not broken Enigma in time and had not landed in France, Soviet troops would have marched all the way to the Rhine (P. Calvocoressi, *Top Secret Ultra*, London 1980, p. 198).

70 In other words, the so-called purple code, one of the four used by the Foreign Ministry (the remaining ones were : L, LA and PA); this was the most important code because it was used for the transmission of particularly significant information – it was decrypted for the first time on 25 September 1940. Moreover, American cryptanalysts from the Intelligence Communications Service, chiefed by Col. William Friedmann, broke the naval code – the so-called 5-Num, the merchant navy code, and the code used by vessels while entering and leaving bases (R. S. Stinner, *Day of Deceit: The truth about FDR and Pearl Harbor*, Polish edition, Warszawa 2002, pp. 79–103; R. Clark, *The Man Who Broke Purple*, 1977; W. F. Friedmann, E. S. Friedmann, *The Shakespearean Ciphers Examined*, Cambridge, 1958; M. Greg (ed.), *Rhapsody in Purple: A New History of Pearl Harbor*, 'Cryptologia', July 1982.)

71 F. W. Winterbotham, *The Ultra Secret*, op. cit., passim.

72 W. Kozaczuk, *W kręgu*, op. cit., p. 163, 167–168.

73 TNA(PRO), HW 14/6, Menzies to Bertrand 23 June 1940, Bertrand to Menzies 26 June 1940.

74 There were also Bertrand, his wife Mary and his deputy, Capt. Honoré Louis.

75 Rejewski was given the name Pierre Ranaud (he was supposed to be a high school professor from Nantes), Zygalski appeared as Sergeant, Langer as Lange, Ciężki as Mille, Paszkowski as Materon, Gaca as Jacquin, Graliński – Ralewski, Różycki as Julien Rouget, and engineer Palluth as Jean Lenoir.
This was a regular Polish Intelligence station, whose task was German and Soviet radio surveillance. It had its own machine cipher and communication with Station 'F', the main mission of the Polish II Bureau in France. Officially, Station '300' was located in Avignon near Marseilles. Its chief was Lt-Col. Langer ('Wicher') with a salary of 15,000 francs; his deputy was Maj. Michałowski 'Lubicz', with a salary of 13,000 francs, whose tasks included 'general maintenance and German transposition ciphers'. The station staff also included the wife of Henryk Paszkowski, as a civilian staff member, and Tadeusz Rakusa-Suszczewski, an engineer. The chief of Cell no. 1 in Algiers was Maj. Ciężki ('Maciej') with a salary of 13,000 francs, and the officers were: Capt. Graliński ('Janosik') and Lt. Paszkowski ('Casanova') with a salary of 10,000 franks, Zygalski ('Bemol') 'dealing with special German ciphers together with a seconded French officer', Gaca ('Szumieć') with a salary of 8,000 francs, and Różycki ('Rola'). The auxiliary personnel was composed of A. Palluth 'Czarny', who supervised French monitoring and occasionally 'monitoring' intended to accelerate and supplement special radio communications, Rejewski ('Oksza'), Paprocki ('Rola'), Smoleński ('Piast'), S. Palluth ('Marek'), Krajewski ('Orkan'), who had to be put in mental asylum in Algiers, and Fokczyński ('Kemlicz'), all with salaries of 8,000 francs (IPMS, Kol. 242/63, notebook on the field cells of the II Bureau of the Polish General Staff for the year 1942, with amendments).

76 According to recently disclosed documents, however, Bletchley Park sometimes shared its information in response to Bertrand's requests, TNA(PRO), HW 14/8, see note 'French Liaison' of 15 November 1940; HW 14/13, note of 5 March 1941; HW 14/16, Denniston to Director 15 June 1941; TNA(PRO), HW 14/24, telegram from Bertrand of 6 December 1941.

77 W. Kozaczuk, *W kręgu*, op. cit., pp. 201–203. At approximately the same time Rejewski improved the Polish enciphering machine 'Lacida'.

78 G. Bertrand, *Enigma*, op. cit., pp. 107–138.

79 W. Kozaczuk, *W kręgu*, op. cit., p.194. It remains unclear up to this day whether the ship sank after it struck a cliff during a storm or a German or Allied mine. At any rate, 279 persons perished out of a total of 372 passengers and crew members.

80 Ibid., p. 189, 221. In 1941 alone this Polish Intelligence cell decrypted 4,158 German and 2,435 Russian radiograms, whose texts were conveyed to Allied staffs.

81 M. Z. Rygor-Słowikowski, *W tajnej służbie (In Secret Service). Polski wkład do*

zwycięstwa w drugiej wojnie światowej (*The Polish Contribution to Victory in the Second World War*), London 1977, passim.

82 TNA(PRO), HW 25/16, study about Enigma by S. A. Mayer, London 31 May 1974. Bertrand supposedly expressed his dissatisfaction over the fact that the Poles presented a replica of Enigma also to the British in the summer of 1939 and not only to the French. At the turn of 1939/1940 he opposed the British suggestion to create a joint cryptologic group in France. When in 1942 the British stopped delivering German radiograms Bertrand wanted to sever all contacts and even threatened that he would 'sell' Enigma. He was persuaded from doing that by Lt-Col. Langer. See also: PRO, HW 25/15, study by Hugh Alexander 'Polish Liaison'.

83 G. Bertrand, *Enigma*, op. cit., pp. 36–41.

84 W. Kozaczuk, *W kręgu*, op. cit., pp. 231–233, 238, 308–309 and IPMS, A.9.VI.10/1, 'Wykaz obywateli polskich w więzieniach hiszpańskich' (List of Polish citizens in Spanish prisons), London 27 April 1943.

85 IPMS, A XII 24/65, letter from Maj. Gaweł (?) to Cmdr. Dunderdale, 20 October 1944, and W. Kozaczuk, *W kręgu*, op. cit., pp. 310–311, 314. Facing serious difficulties with reconstructing a cryptologic cell for German ciphers Polish intelligence asked the French General Staff to return the replica of Enigma, the documentation of Station '300' and German radiograms intercepted on a day-to-day basis (IPMS, A XII 24/63, Col. S. Gano, Chief of the II Bureau of the Polish General Staff, to Lt-Col. Jan Leśniak, chairman of the Commission for the Disbandment of Station F. II in Paris, November 1944). Those efforts failed, too.

86 IPMS, A XII 24/63, M. Rejewski, 'Kilka uwag na temat trudności w jakich znajduje się w chwili obecnej Dział szyfrów niemieckich' (Some comments on current difficult situation of the German Cipher Subsection), 1 October 1944. See also: vol. 2.

87 TNA(PRO), HW 25/16, J. E. S. Cooper, study about Bertrand's book, 15 July 1974.

88 Ibid., study about Enigma by S. A. Mayer, London 31 May 1974.

47

Polish Radio Intelligence Service and Sigint

Eugenia Maresch

Even before the outbreak of the war, the British Admiralty suggested that the Director of the Government Code & Cypher School (GC&CS) should co-operate with Polish Intelligence, primarily to exchange signals intelligence from the Baltic region.[1] The unexpected course of the war made this co-operation more inclusive and more permanent.[2] In February 1940 Capt. (Navy) Tadeusz Podjazd-Morgerstern, the Naval Attaché at the Polish Legation in Stockholm, asked the Chief of the Polish Navy in London, Rear Admiral Jerzy Świrski, for permission to install listening equipment on the Polish submarines 'Żbik' and 'Ryś' (interned in Sweden), to which the Admiral had consented before the war.[3] An RSS document from November 1944 stated that until recently the Poles had managed to obtain excellent sigint material, which was picked up by Polish submarines. This confirmed that such equipment was, indeed, installed.[4]

Naval sigint was only a small part of the many and varied activities of Polish signals intelligence during the war. Important organisational and institutional support for these activities was provided by the British, with their extensive experience in this area.

British Signals Intelligence (the term 'Sigint' was used from October 1943), encompassed all the processes of interception and decryption as well as analysis and interpretation of intelligence material for which this service was responsible. Organisationally, this was manifested in the establishment of the Y Committee, later renamed the Y Board, whose membership consisted of the Chief of SIS, called 'C', the Director of GC&CS, the chiefs of Naval Intelligence Directorate (NID 9), Military Intelligence (MI1(b)), Air Intelligence (AI1(e)), and included communications officers, representatives of various government agencies and technical advisers. The results of their work depended on the close collaboration between operational and planning staffs.[5]

Unlike the Poles, this robust British organization had few limitations in terms of obtaining personnel or financial resources, especially for the purchase of technical equipment. When the war broke out, Polish Sigint suffered from numerous deficiencies. The Poles relied on telephone and courier communication, which reduced the effectiveness of their work. Their radios were unable to recode and transmit the material obtained. The operational detachments, whose task it was to quickly pass the most important information to the Centre and to the relevant military units, were underdeveloped. These deficiencies became clear in September 1939, when the three western-most radio stations, situated in Starogard, Poznań and Krzesławice, failed in the face of hostilities – though they were prepared for easy transportation, installation and operation in new positions. Not provided with their own means of transport, their commanders improvised by moving equipment first, with their ciphers following.[6] This led to some disarray, which was repeated during the evacuation from France. A negative opinion on the communications aspect of Polish Intelligence was thus created.[7]

The real co-operation between British and Polish Intelligence services began during the so-called French period, from November 1939 to June 1940. At this time, four mobile British W/T (Wireless-Telegraphy) stations, types 'B' and 'WGI' (Wireless Group Intelligence), were operating in France, working with French communications units. Among the latter was Cell P.C. Bruno, where the Polish team 'Z', led by Lt-Col. Gwidon Langer and the Polish cryptological group, were working (for more on this, see Chapter 46 on Enigma). Team 'Z' dealt with monitoring illegal radio stations, signals intelligence and transposition, but most of all with codes. It was sub-divided into the Russian (Capt. Graliński and 2nd Lt. Szachno) and German (Maj. Ciężki) Sections.

Information gathered in this way was exchanged with the British GC&CS. This procedure adopted in France was in force between December 1940 and October 1942, when the Polish Ciphers Office in France was closed.[8] At first, the communication between Paris (Dunderdale's office at Avenue Charles Floquet) and London was by daily courier. 'Air' and 'Meteo' cryptography, material including weather reports, was returned by teleprinter.[9]

The Polish team in France did not consider its decoding work to be very fruitful or educational. The team was small and had at its disposal only three Enigma machines. This caused Lt-Col. Langer to complain to the London Headquarters of Polish Intelligence of the II Bureau. He questioned whether his team's continued presence in France made much sense. Langer, who was not a signatory to any agreements with the French, suggested that the unit should undertake analytical work – thinking of Britain, of course.[10]

Langer describing the position within Station '300' following the fall of France maintained that the organisation of radio intelligence still left much to be desired. The exchange of information with GC&CS was at first stopped, and later restricted. The French clearly favoured certain areas of work, while considering others, for example on police codes, to be less useful, leaving these to ad hoc efforts.[11] This meant that the Polish team dealing with mechanical codes was falling behind in relation to leading cryptological centres and was unable to participate in the exchange of ideas and experiences with GC&CS, which by 1942 was forging achief, having at its disposal hundreds, and later thousands, of employees.[12]

The work carried out in France, however, did deliver measurable results, especially in identifying the codes used by German intelligence networks. By listening to four independent German Intelligence networks in Switzerland and to a Soviet agent who passed on to the Germans the original encrypted dispatches from an official USRR radio net, the German network in Marseilles (six radio stations and all their personnel) was compromised. All Sigint reports (including those on the western Mediterranean basin and Spain, from where the movements of Allied convoys were monitored) were sent to II Bureau in London. Langer's report for 1942 (for the period up to October) contained the information that 308 new and subsidiary keys (2, 3, and 4-digit), as well as 63 transpositional keys, were cracked.[13]

After the fall of France, it was necessary to establish a well-functioning radio communication with Poland and with Polish networks abroad. At the beginning of August 1940, a radio station called 'Marta' was set up at PGS in London, manned by four operators and two cryptologists. At first it operated without formal agreement from the British. The status of this station was settled when the Poles passed on to the British (MI8) the intelligence report by Lt-Col. Ignacy Kazimierz Banach, who was Chief of the Studies Department, the II Bureau.[14] This report, made public in full in April 2002, illustrated the scope of technical information obtained and the product of Polish radio intelligence aimed at the USSR.[15] This information was of interest to the head of the Russian Section, Lt-Col. John Tiltman, who ordered the immediate employment of a number of Poles.[16] Having examined Banach's report, GC&CS Director, Commander Alistair Denniston, suggested to his superior, SIS Col. Stewart Menzies, that contacts with the Poles should be established, provided that the direction of their work would be made dependent on the requirements of the British side.[17]

Any agreement on co-operation required official acceptance. Since it involved the Polish Army, the agreement had to operate through MI8. Writing to the Chief of PGS, Gen. Tadeusz Klimecki, Col. D. Arcedeckne-Butler expressed his willingness to participate in the reorganisation of the Polish Section, and offered a good working environment at the northern reaches of London, in Stanmore. The proximity to GC&CS's cryptological centre was an advantage. Butler also asked for 10 or 20 Polish operators with excellent Russian language.[18] Such a direction of Polish efforts was preferred by the British, a fact confirmed in a note to the Poles of 23 November 1940, by the Chief of Russian Section, Lt-Col. Tiltman. His note indicated that the entire product of interception was to be made available to the British, and delivered daily by messenger to Bletchley Park. The Polish cryptologists were only to retain copies for their own use.[19]

The usefulness of Polish Sigint experts in Soviet matters was clear,[20] since the British section dealing with Russian material before the war was not well developed. The occasional British surveillance of Soviet traffic was not sufficient in volume for new Soviet codes to be broken. Basically, they lacked high range stations, trained technical staff and linguists to meet the mounting demand. A note from Capt. Grant of GC&CS perfectly justified the need to employ the Polish team.[21]

The British unit, which monitored the Soviet traffic (M.S.Rs – Military Section, Russian), started its independent work in March 1940. It had a station in Flowerdown, which listened mainly to the Soviet Navy, and another in Cheadle, monitoring the Air Force. There was also the station in Sarafanda, located in Palestine since 1923, which monitored the Soviet Black Sea Fleet. Material coming in from the various stations was analysed at GC&CS, and then passed on to the interested parties, such as the Navy Department, the War Office (Russian Section and MI8) and the Air Ministry. This changed in early 1941, when the Chief of the Imperial General Staff – CIGS) decided to reorganize his Signals Intelligence. Sigint was detached from VIII Department, MI8, and joined with Section V of SIS, at first under Col. Valentine Vivian, and later under Col. Philip Cowgill. Its operations centre was located in St Albans. It would appear that these changes did not influence the functioning of the Polish Section in Stanmore, which started work on 8 December 1940 with two radio monitoring stations and five operators. The British report of 7 January 1941 expressed satisfaction with its progress and with the quality of monitored material, from the Lwów, Tarnopol and Czerniowce regions. Expecting the Polish team to expand, monitoring of the border between the Soviet Union and Romania was awaited.[22]

The work of Polish radio intelligence was carefully monitored by the RSS (Radio Security Service), as was evident from a note to Lt-Col. Vivian of 18 April 1944. This note informed him of a secret dossier which contained copies of all the radio dispatches which were kept, especially those of the Polish diplomatic contacts, mainly with Stockholm, Berne and the Middle East.[23] The British were suspicious of Polish contacts, based chiefly on alleged dealings with Abwehr's agents, which might have compromised the Polish Service and in turn, would affect the work of SIS.

From September 1941 Soviet monitoring was left exclusively in Polish hands, as can be seen from the note by the Chief of the Russian Section, A.C. Stuart-Smith, to Maj. Franciszek Sobecki of 16 October 1941, also a note to Commander Travis, asking for the issue of continuing Soviet monitoring by the Poles at Stanmore to be raised at the Y Board meeting.[24] These decisions were influenced by the USSR joining the anti-German coalition after 22 June 1941.

In this period, the Polish side had at its disposal a significantly strengthened ability to conduct monitoring. This was due to the Radio Centre of PGS, established in November 1940. Renamed later as Radio Bureau, PGS, it consisted of four sections, which served as radio intelligence and radiotelegraphy units. The Bureau was served by its own

Ciphers Section and Foreign Ciphers Section. The Centre, later Bureau, worked to the Chief of Communications, PGS, Col. Heliodor Cepa.[25] The co-operation with the British transcended the formal requirements and was friendly.[26] Formally speaking, the purpose was to enable the Poles to maintain communications with Poland, which in turn allowed the Polish Foreign Ministry to stay in touch with its diplomatic and political missions, without any control over Polish codes.

The centre in Stanmore had a different purpose. The task given to the Poles proved difficult, especially in the early stages, as the Soviet-German front moved rapidly eastwards, and because the Soviet radio stations improved their discipline. There were also severe personnel limitations on the Polish side: until August 1943, the monitored material was read by one cryptologist only, Private Czesław Kuraś, who, without sufficient theoretical grounding, managed nevertheless very well, thanks to his hard work and ambition. But the multi-digit and secondary codes were sent to GC&CS Centre.

Among others employed at Stanmore were Private Zbigniew Gaca, a cryptologist in the German Section, and Petty Officer Antoni Mateja, who experimentally attempted to listen in to the German submarines.[27] The materials of the German police from July 1941 also proved important, since in addition to technical information, they contained reports on the operational SS battalions active in the Wilno and border regions. These included detailed information on the extermination of the local population, called 'pacification in the woods', up to 7 August 1941, the number of dead was estimated at over thirty thousand.[28]

One of the most revealing documents, which confirmed that the Polish Section at Stanmore took over the monitoring of Soviet stations, was the daily register of dispatches from France.[29] The Soviet material was passed to the British on average 2 or 3 times a week and this flow ceased completely as late as 30 November 1941. The dates correspond to the decision taken by GC&CS to entrust all monitoring and decoding to the Polish Section at Stanmore. Within the following 7 months the Polish Section registered some 60 items.

When 'Station 300' in France was closed, it was hoped to transfer a group of eminent Polish cryptologists to Britain. Some arrests caused a delay, and the plan was put into practice only in the second half of 1943, when the Poles from France joined the new monitoring and decoding facilities in Felden near Hemel Hempstead 16 miles from Stanmore, led by Maj. Kazimierz Zieliński.

Their arrival in Great Britain led to further reorganization of the Radio Bureau, PGS, which became the Utilisation Platoon divided into 3 sections. Its Chief was Lt. Stanisław Szachno, who together with his deputy, Private Kuraś, was tasked with working on the Russian Section ('R') ciphers. The German Section ('N') was led by 2nd Lt. Marian Rejewski, and 2nd Lt Henryk Zygalski headed the General Section. The reorganisation brought the desired results. On average, the daily product was 61 Soviet and 37 German dispatches.[30] According to later assessments, some of the material was of little interest, only 18 dispatches from each category were of use.[31] In a letter to the Chief of the Intelligence Department, Maj. Żychoń, Cmdr. Dunderdale thanked the Poles for their excellent work. The SIS liaison officer stressed the importance of Polish monitoring as the only source of information on Russia.[32] In particular, Dunderdale praised Rejewski and his 'N' Section. How the Polish team's experience was used is shown in a note from GC&CS Hut 6. It suggested that the Poles be given the 6-digit Enigma codes used by the Gestapo and transmitted from Berlin, Oslo and Warsaw. These communications were not decrypted for some time, and the Poles had just begun listening to them.[33]

The tasks carried out by the Polish cryptologists of the Utilisation Platoon in Britain were not very demanding. They themselves described it as 'a low-level skill', which reduced them to the role of decoders. What they were hoping for was more conceptual, theoretical work, such as that carried out at GC&CS. For example, disillusioned Rejewski, demanded direct access to his British colleagues. He wanted to discuss the problems resulting from a complete change of the German police ciphers and asked for the Enigma to be returned to them.[34]

Polish-British radio intelligence co-operation took place also in other places, where the British interests coincided with the Polish presence, as in the case, for example, in the Middle East. An important monitoring, analysis and cryptology centre was situated in Heliopolis, some 15 kilometres from Cairo. A significant role was played by the training centres in Sarafand near Tel Aviv and in Habosh Camp, which had a cell in Mosul, near Baghdad, where the British Special Wireless Section 'F' was stationed, under the command of Capt. Sheppard. Towards the end of 1942, over 100 Polish soldiers were trained there in radiotelegraphy.[35] The Polish Monitoring Detachment, organised on the British pattern, had a number of Radio Intelligence Platoons. Two of those deserve special mention: no. 11, under Capt. Antoni Ziółkowski, and no. 12, under Capt. Józef Miński. These units had particular successes during the Tobruk and Monte Cassino battles. At Tobruk, the 12th Platoon, then under the command of Lt. Roman Pawłowicz and with the participation of three British officers, identified the broadcasts of 87 German stations and provided 70% of all monitored transmissions. The remaining 30% were dispatches from 59 Italian stations. A document preserved from 1943 shows one of the many important items of information obtained at Tobruk, by a radio station of 3. Carpathian Division: the German radio traffic rules.[36] At Monte Cassino, 12th Platoon worked closely with the British 105th. Section of SWS, exchanging equipment, personnel and experiences. The most spectacular success of the Polish unit was to obtain intelligence on the signal to abandon the monastery by the German parachutists. This information was used by General Władysław Anders when renewing his attack on the Abbey, which eventually ended in victory.[37]

The contribution of Polish signals intelligence, in the broad meaning of the term, can be seen partially by the incomplete statistical data below, which allows an opinion to be formed on the work of the Poles. They show that, even with a low level of staff, the number of intercepted dispatches reached almost hundred thousand, of which the Poles on their own managed to read over 25%. The number of intercepted and broken codes was 2,322. Regrettably, the archival material available does not reveal the contents of these dispatches. Therefore we cannot come to any conclusions as to how effectively this information was used.

A full assessment of the role played by this small team of very talented people is still to be expected. Not all the documents which were preserved and which might have been helpful to form a judgement are in the public domain. Certainly some of these documents are still in MI6 archives. This is the prime reason why this fragmentatary description of work undertaken by the Polish Radio Intelligence Services should be considered,, merely as a starting point for further historical work.

Table 7: Statistical data[38]

Date	Telegraphers	Cryptologists	Radio receivers	Monitored dispatches	Read dispatches	Utilised dispatches	Codes/keys	No. Of stations monitored daily
Aug–Dec 1940	–	1	–	1486	970	135	–	–
1941	–	1	–	8012	6022	932		
1942	18	2	7	12959	4588	734	132/84	67
Total Aug 1940– Dec 1942	18	2	2–7	22457	11580	1801	211/478	80
1943	17	3–6	7–9	24518	6942	738	802/718	87
List for				22937 R	6403 R			
Oct 1943– Oct 1944	–	–	–	12676 N	3047 N	–	–	–
1944	17–24	6	3–8	28111	7498	–	–	70 R
						–	–	11 N
Jan–Nov. 1945	22	3	9	112935	5086	–	–	77

Notes

1   TNA (PRO), HW 25/15, Hugh Alexander's notes of 1949 entitled *Polish Liaison*, which were intended as raw material for a history of Enigma. The notes refer to a document no. 88 of 2 August 1939, which stated that further development of sigint should provide for co-operation with the Poles, especially in the Baltic region.

2   TNA (PRO), HW 25/10, Nigel de Grey's notes, hand-written, with remarks by J.E.S. Cooper, of 1949, with the information that in 1937–1938 the British found out from the French (Scarlet Pimpernels) that on 8 May 1937 the Poles used the information provided to them without stating what these contained. According to Hugh Alexander, these were the keys for 3 months, which enabled the discovery of the cable connection.

3   IPMS, MAR.A V/31, ref. 20/M/tjn./40, a report by Capt. Morgenstern of the Polish Legation in Stockholm to Rear Admiral Świrski in London, 13 February 1940.

4   TNA (PRO), HW 34/14, ref. S1/P, S1/Q, a report of Maj. S. J. Till to Lt-Col. E.F.

Maltby [RSS] of 17 November 1944, criticizing Lt-Col. W. Langenfeld (Chief of Intelligence Department, II Bureau) for passing on inaccurate information. Till's report pertained to the situation in Felden, where the Poles operated 13 radio stations, plus 2 in Scotland (Kinross). In view of the excellent results achieved by the Polish team, which especially pleased 'C' (Chief of SIS), it was planned to install another 20 stations. As for Stockholm, Till said that until recently the British received valuable information from Polish submarines, which by then have sailed [which was not the case]. The radio personnel, however, stayed behind and awaited orders from Col. S. Gano (Chief of the II Bureau, PGS) and from Commander W.Dunderdale (SIS's liaison officer with the II Bureau).

5 *British Intelligence in the Second World War*, by F.H. Hinsley with E.E. Thomas, C.F.G. Ransom, R.C. Knight, vol. 1, London 1979.

6 IJPL, Kol. 133, the Langer collection, copy of a letter by Lt-Col G. Langer, Chief of Cipher Unit, to Chief of II Bureau. In this letter Langer explained why the results of the work undertaken by team 'Z' for the period from 1 September 1939 to 24 June 1940 did not reach the Polish authorities in London. The letter contained a detailed description of the events of the 1939 Polish and the 1940 French campaigns, quoting the specific cryptological achievements made in this period.

7 Ibid.

8 Ibid.

9 TNA(PRO), HW 14/4, Note of GC&CS's Director, Commander A. Denniston, to Col. L. Rivet, Chief of French Intelligence (II Bureau), of 2 March 1940, on cryptological intelligence. It contained instructions on how the product was to be exchanged between Paris and London.

10 IJPL, Kol. 134, the Langer collection, Langer's note of 25 February 1941 to Chief, II Bureau, with information on the hopeless position of his unit and the difficulties faced by it. In it, Langer asked for transfer to a different field of work. L.dz. 10/41.

11 IJPL, Kol. 134, the Langer Collection, fragments of a list of dispatches from 19 to 28 January 1942, sent to the Centre by Chief of Station '300' (Langer ['Wicher']. The dispatches dealt with current issues, working conditions, attitudes towards the French hosts and financial matters. They also contained statistics on the material gathered.

12 IPMS, Kol. 242/69, report of August 1943 on the activities of Station '300' from 1st January 1942 to 6 November 1942. This general report by Deputy Chief of the Station in France, Maj. Wiktor Michałowski, was sent to the Centre after Langer and Ciężki were arrested.

13 IJPL, Kol. 134. The report on the G-3 material for 1942 (until mid-October) contains the number of dispatches, broken keys and transpositions and a list of Soviet formations.

14 TNA(PRO), WO 208/5092, Note of Col. D. Arcedeckne-Butler (MI8) to Deputy Chief of Military Intelligence, War Office [Brig. Stawell] of 9 October 1940. It stated that Commander A. Denniston of GC&CS agreed to the establishment of a sigint centre near Bletchley Park, to facilitate the daily supply of information and that Denniston approved the technical requirements.

15 TNA(PRO), HW 47/1, ref. A.4/5632, Lt-Col. I.K. Banach's report of 16 August 1940, on the types of Soviet radio stations, based on information obtained between 1930 and 1940. The report recommended to the British that independent Sigint co-operation be established. It also appended some current dispatches.

16 Ibid., Note of 5 September 1940.

17 TNA(PRO), HW 14/7, ref. 2572, A D's [A. Denniston] note to CSS [Col. S. Menzies] of 5 October 1940.

18 TNA(PRO), HW 14/16, draft of undated letter of D. Arcedeckne-Butler to Maj. Gen. Tadeusz Klimecki on Polish operators for monitoring Soviet military and air force traffic.

19 TNA(PRO), HW 14/8, note of Capt. A. C. Stuart-Smith, Russian Section, to Lt-Col.

J.H. Tiltman, of 23d November 1940, with guidelines for Polish-British co-operation on radio monitoring (a part of the original, coded war-time documents originating at Stanmore, was found in 2001 in Bletchley and passed on to NDAP in Warsaw).

20 TNA(PRO), HW 74/1, 9 January 1941, part of a working report on Soviet monitoring by Private Kuraś, with annotations in Russian. Certified as accurate by the Chief of the Russian Section, Capt. A.C. Stuart-Smith.

21 TNA(PRO), HW 47/1 ref., RO/368, Capt. Grant's note to the Polish cryptological team of 19th November 1940, expressing satisfaction with their work. It contains further instructions on Soviet monitoring.

22 TNA(PRO), HW 14/10, Capt. A.C. Stuart-Smith's note to Lt-Col. J.H. Tiltman, of 7 January 1941. The writer complained that a year after his Section was established, he had only 4 monitoring sets and 7 operators at his disposal.

23 TNA(PRO), HW 34/0, Note of Col. E.F. Maltby, Deputy Chief of RSS, to NN (copied to Col. Vivian, Chief of Section V, SIS), of 7 May 1941. It informs the addressee that a secret file was kept with all the Polish radio correspondence, especially on the secret contacts of the Polish Government with its posts abroad. The idea was to ascertain whether the contacts with Abwehr, of which Lt-Col. Jan Kowalewski was suspected, would not compromise Polish Intelligence and affect the work of SIS.

24 TNA(PRO), HW 14/21, note of Capt. A.C. Stuart-Smith, Chief of the Russian Section, to Maj. F. Sobecki of 16 October 1941, and ibid., HW 14/19, note to Commander Travis of 22 September 1941 with a request for Y Board to consider the matter of Polish monitoring at Stanmore of Soviet traffic.

25 IPMS, Kol. 242/7, a paper prepared by Col. H. Cepa for Chief of II Bureau, Lt-Col. S. Gano, of 17 March 1941, for a conference with the British authorities.

26 IPMS, Kol. 242/7, note with Wilski's signature [Wilski was a codename of Commander W. Dunderdale] to Janio [Maj. Jan Żychoń] of 19 March 1941. It refers to a joint conference at which the principles of co-operation in radio communications and radio intelligence were discussed. These were to be based on the British structure and provided working in parallel, which delivered excellent results.

27 TNA (PRO), HW 14/15, ref. A4/8961 and S-2160/41, note of Commander Dunderdale of 7 May 1941 to GC&CS Director, Commander Travis, as an addendum to the report from Janio [Maj. Zychoń]. Janio informed that the U-Boat dispatches were read by Petty Officer Mateja. His report also contained an analysis of communications, listed new sending procedures, their frequencies and timings.

28 TNA(PRO), HW 14/18, ref. ZIP/MSGP 27, of 24 August 1941. The summary of the German police reports from Russia and Germany contained a general description of their activities, some characteristics of persons involved, the areas in which they were active and their radio communications. There was also detailed information on the escapes of POW's and on genocide, in particular that committed by SS Gruppenführer Prutzmann and Gruppenführer von dem Bach-Zelewski, on battles with the Soviets and the liquidation of partisans and Jewish communists by the Reit-Brigade.

29 IJPL, Kol. 100/11/1, Mayer's collection, correspondence register listing all dispatches and intelligence reports for Cmdr. Dunderdale. The register contained 1481 items for the period from 6 May 1941 to 1 June 1942.

30 IPMS Kol. 241/54, monthly report on the activities of radio intelligence for August 1943, provided to his superiors by the officer commanding the Radio Intelligence Company, Capt. K. Zieliński. The report contained a list of Soviet (and some German) stations monitored on behalf of British signals intelligence, a description of the conditions in which this work was carried out and its results, a list of material obtained, of cracked codes and ciphers, information on confirmed Soviet radio networks and some technical and personnel issues. l.dz. 132/Tjn R.W./43.

31 SPP, BII/218, *Historia Batalionu Łączności* (*History of the Communications Battalion*), mps, p. 81, written between 1946 and 1949 by Capt.s K. Zieliński and

K. Głazowski, was the basis on which the publication *Dziękuję wam rodacy* (*Thank you, Countrymen*), London 1973, was written.

32 IPMS, Kol. 242/55, official note of Maj. W. Gaweł of 23 July 1943 to Maj. Żychoń, informing the latter of recent developments and conversations with the British. It mentions a Polish platoon in the East (8 operators with 6 sets), which was at the disposal of the British side. It also quotes Dunderdale as saying that he is particularly interested in intelligence on Russia, since the Sigint company in Felden is the only source of information on the Soviets for the British.

33 TNA(PRO), HW 14/85, ref. Q/2007, Note of 23 August 1943, J.S. Colman (RSS) to Maj. Sawdon (GC&CS), suggesting that the Poles should be given the job of monitoring the German TGD network. In the first two years of the war, both teams were reading the German Ordnungspolizei ciphers. The Gestapo, on the other hand, was using an Enigma key called TGD, the name being taken from the Berlin station. In spite of significant efforts, and perhaps because their work was not co-ordinated, neither the British nor the Poles managed to break TGD.

34 IPMS, AXII/24, copy of Rejewski's memo entitled 'Some remarks on the difficulties currently facing the German Codes Unit', 20 October 1944 r., typescript. It is not known if it was passed onto the British authorities.

35 H. Skillen, *Spies of the Airwaves. A History of Y Section during the Second World War*, London 1989, chapter 23, p. 362. The book is dedicated 'to the Poles who gave so much and received so little'. It is based on the literature on the subject, on wartime eyewitness accounts and on British documents.

36 IPMS, Kol. 242/55, S-188/42, material on German monitoring from 1942. It contains call signs, frequency changes, the method of dispatch transmission, an assessment of such dispatches and the chiefers of German and Italian dispatches.

37 H. Skillen, *Spies of the Airwaves*, op. cit., p. 367.

38 IPMS, Kol. 245/54. These are the incomplete records containing average statistical data on the Polish radio intelligence, a compilation of documents: AXII.24.37. There are also annual reports on the intelligence work: Kol. 242/48, Intelligence Department, Communications Section: Reports on the work of the Section for 1944, part II, Radio Intelligence. The above-mentioned report does not contain information on the Italian period. R signifies the Russian Section, N – German Section. Daily monitoring covered 72 Russian and 11 German stations; TNA(PRO), WO 315/18, General Polish Report on the activities of the Radio Centre at Stanmore for 1942.

48
Polish Intelligence and the German 'Secret Weapons': V-1 and V-2*

Rafał Wnuk

The first serious research on the construction of rockets was undertaken in Germany between 1929 and 1930 by a group of enthusiasts, members of the Association for Space Travel (Verein für Raumschiffahrt – VfR). The German Army began its own research into this subject in the early 1930s. In June 1932 at the Kummersdorf testing ground it conducted a trial of the rocket constructed by Rudolf Nebel,[1] and by the mid-1934 the Army finally took control over the VfR scientists and the Association's achievements. Thanks to a vast injection of State funds, the research project was soon accelerated. By December 1934, the first successful trial of a liquid-fuelled rocket took place on the island of Borkum.

In 1936, the Luftwaffe and the Army of the Third Reich began the construction of a highly secret rocket research facility on the island of Usedom (Uznam), near Peenemünde. A year later the research team, directed by Werner von Braun and Walter Dornberger, was moved there from Berlin. The experimental A-5 rocket, with a mass of 1,300 kg., was built in Peenemünde in 1938, and during its trials in 1939, it reached the height of 13,000 metres. On 16 August 1942, the prototype of a 13-tonne A-4 (V-2) rocket took to the air. On 3 October 1942, the 19 in this series flew ballistically, reaching the height of 83 kilometres, and after 193 km in the air, came down only 5 km from its designated target. On 10 December 1942, the pilot-less flying bomb, the Fieseler Fi-103, later known as the V-1, was successfully tested.[2]

From 1939, the Allied intelligence services were obtaining scraps of information concerning the German trials of long-range rocket weapons. These were treated as gossip. According to the American Intelligence officer responsible for the assessment of the veracity of such reports, Commander E.G.N. Rushbrooke, all the information on such wonder weapons and 'similar alarmist reports were not treated seriously. It is well

* Technical consultation: Andrzej Glass

known that one element of the German policy was to play on our fears and to make us maintain large forces in this country'.[3]

At the turn of 1942 and 1943, SIS and OSS were getting numerous reports from Poland, Sweden and Denmark on the German rockets, their amazing capabilities and about the trials in the Peenemünde area. Such reports alarmed the British and American analysts,[4] even more so, since in March 1943 a German prisoner of war said under interrogation that he had overheard a conversation between two captured German Generals, Wilhelm von Thoma and Ludwig von Crüwel. It appeared that, having witnessed rocket trials in the region of Kummersdorf (?), one of them (and Field Marshal Walter von Brauchitsch) was approached by a Maj. from the facility, who said: 'Let us wait until next year – this is when the fun will begin'.[5] But the Allies still lacked reports containing any verifiable technical parameters of the weapons.

The first report containing such data was obtained by the Allies on 2 December 1942. The source was Home Army Intelligence. In early November 1942, in the Czech steel mill at Witkowice, one of its agents observed that the Germans were conducting experiments concerning 'the production of special shells [...] made from steel blocks rolled by Mannesman method',[6] which were then spot drilled to 2/3 of their length and then rolled. This was done under armed guard. The resulting semi-finished products were then sent to the 'Reinmetall Borsig-Berlin Tegel'[7] works. This was investigated further and the report of 18 January 1943 noted that some 80% of the iron ore used at Witkowice originated from Swedish mines at Kiruna and Gellivare. From there, the ore was shipped to Szczecin, and hence by river barges to Raciborz and by rail to Witkowice.[8]

The most important information originated at the Peenemünde testing facility itself. Contrary to the findings of Michel J. Neufeld or Dennis Piszkiewicz, their sources were not 'some unknown foreign forced labourers',[9] but agents of Home Army's 'Lombard' Offensive Intelligence Network, and specifically of its 'Bałtyk' cell, set up and run by Bernard Kaczmarek ('Wrzos', 'Jur'), and later by the parachutist, 'Cichociemny' from London Lt. Stefan Ignaszak ('Nordyk').

As far back as the beginning of 1943, Jan Szreder 'Furman' reported that the island of Uznam, where the testing ground was located, was subject to strict secrecy. The island was sub-divided into zones, and access to each required a special pass. A concentration camp, a POW camp and a labour camp were located there. Together, these employed thousands of people. Numerous deliveries of machinery and industrial materials were directed to the island. Szreder reported that Peenemünde was said to be 'an island of German brainpower', where in all likelihood the trials of 'aerial torpedoes' were being conducted.[10]

The most valuable information was provided by one of the three 'Bałtyk' cells, known as 'Bałtyk 303', led by Augustyn Träger ('Tragarz', 'Sęk', 'T-1'),[11] who managed to penetrate Peenemünde directly, since his son, Roman Träger ('T2-As') served in the Wehrmacht on the island of Uznam, in a unit which installed telephone links at the research facility.

Being allowed to move around with relative freedom, in February 1943 the younger Träger was able to confirm that the trials of the 'torpedoes', in the shape of a pilotless plane taking off from a special launch pad made of steel elements. He reported that in flight the plane made a sound 'as if an empty iron barrel was being rolled on a hard surface', and that there were exhaust flames coming at its rear.[12]

On the basis of such information, Home Army's Industrial Intelligence informed London in its monthly reports for February and March 1943, that in Peenemünde on the Baltic coast 'a construction and research center for rocket airplanes is centered', and that their propulsion enables such planes to reach the speed of up to 800 km/h in seconds. In addition the island houses a factory employing some 8,000 persons, laboratories and an experimental airfield. All the roads are closed within a distance of some kilometers from the Peenemünde station, and access is possible with special passes only'.[13]

The Chief of the VI Bureau, PGS, at the time, Lt-Col. Michał Protasewicz, was responsible for the inflow of information from Poland, wrote about these events:

> At the end of the winter of 1942–1943 we had information from Poland, that in a special centre situated on the Baltic the Germans were conducting some experiments with new weapons, which were to ensure their victory and speed up the end of the war. This information was of interest to PGS and to the British. We asked Poland for further details. By the spring of 1943, we had confirmation of the previous dispatch with the additional information, that the experiments were conducted in a highly protected area. This was the first time I have encountered the name Peenemünde [...]. The area of Peenemünde was of much interest to the British. What they asked for was the plan of the area (or camp). A bit of a tall order...
>
> Amazingly, a few weeks later, the plan of the camp arrived, via Vienna or possibly Sweden [...], with the buildings where the alleged research was conducted marked with penciled dots. The plan was accompanied by a brief description of the camp. I do not remember whether it contained any mention of the trials.

This was a Maj. success, since the facility was shrouded in secrecy. Congratulations for a job well done were sent to Poland, as well as a request for more information'.[14] These reports were of such interest to British Intelligence, that on 22 April and again on 14 May, 21 and 23 June 1943, a series of reconnaissance flights over the area were conducted. These confirmed the existence of V-1 and V-2 weapons. Col. Sandys prepared a report, entitled 'German Long-Range Rocket Development', which was accepted by Winston Churchill on 27 June 1943. In consequence, the decision to bomb the facility was taken. The air raid, carried out by 597 British bombers on the night of 17/18 August 1943, partially destroyed the research centre, the production facilities, the housing estate and the camp for forced labourers. There were 735 victims, including 178 among the German research and management personnel. Among the dead was the commander of the centre, Wolfgang von Chmier Glyczinski, and two of von Braun's closest collaborators, dr. Walter Thiel and engineer Helmut Walther.[15] Though the raid did not cause the abandonment of the German rocket programme, it was temporarily disorganised and delayed. This was important. As General Dwight Eisenhower recounted:

> Were the Germans able to perfect these new weapons six months earlier and to introduce them onto the battle field at the right moment, it was likely that our invasion of Europe would have encountered enormous difficulties and in certain circumstances would not have been possible. I am certain that after six months of such activity [Operation Overlord], that is the attack on Europe from England, would have been a washout'.[16]

This success would have been impossible without the information provided by Home Army Intelligence, which also delivered a damage report to London following the raid.[17] Interestingly, the agents' reports on the German rockets for the period February–August 1943, held at the National Archive near Washington, have lost their earlier designations, such as 'Polish Intelligence' or 'Danish sources'. Instead, they are now marked 'source Z', a description that has not been decoded. This was the source from which, for example, on 24 June 1943, the Americans supposedly received information on the testing of missiles with the range of some 200 kilometres, being launched along the Baltic coast in the direction of Gdynia. These weapons were apparently to be mass-produced from September or October. In reality the larger rockets were still at an experimental stage, and their bodies were to be produced in the Deutscher Oehrwerke Muehlheim works in the Ruhr. Some of their parts were to be manufactured at Witkowice.[18] The next report from 'source Z' was from the second half of August 1943, that is immediately after Peenemünde was bombed. It contained the specific geographical co-ordinates of the research facility on Uznam and the descriptions of two types of 'radio-controlled rockets': a smaller one, with the range of 250 km, and larger, capable of 450 km.[19] It also claimed that some parts for these weapons were being manufactured at Oświęcim, in the factory employing the prisoners of the concentration camp there (Auschwitz).[20]

A detailed analysis of the American and British intelligence documents held at NARA, though they were 'sanitized' to obscure their origin – which, clearly, was to prevent the uncovering of such sources – nevertheless permits the identification of their source, and therefore allows full confirmation of their Polish provenance.

First, let us examine the American Military Intelligence document prepared immediately following the raid on Peenemünde, and containing extracts from earlier reports. The first part of this document has many general, and usually incorrect, items of information, obtained from four

German POWs. The second part contains extracts from two reports from intelligence networks. Among reliable information on the Peenemünde facility and its satellite plants co-operating in the production of rockets, we find the following sentence: 'The confidential file reference of this scheme is [Program A-4]'.[21] The term 'Program A-4' was used to describe the research project on the V-2 ballistic rocket, but also, in the terminology used by the German scientists, the rocket itself. The usage of this term clearly indicates that the source of the report was to be found either within the research centre on the island of Uznam, or among the very limited circle of the highest-ranking officers and officials of the Third Reich, entrusted with the details of this secret project. The report uses the word 'Program', which could not have originated in the German language, since German knows no such word. In English the term 'Project' would have been used. The author of the report used this term in quotation marks. This means that it was a quotation from the original – that is, borrowed from a report from Home Army Intelligence!

The reports which reached the Washington office of OSS from the mysterious 'source Z', already mentioned above, were of equal importance. The analysis of their content indicates that in numerous instances this source used the information obtained from Polish Intelligence. This is evident, as some of the reports were basically slightly modified copies of the Polish materials found in archives. For example, almost all repeat the information about Witkowice and Oświęcim, that is, about places systematically observed exclusively by Home Army Intelligence.

The bombing of Peenemünde on the night of 17/18 August 1943 caused the production of V-2 rockets to be moved to the underground 'Dora Mittelwerk' works in the Harz Mountains, near Nordhausen. But the raid did not impact on the production of V-1 'flying bombs', since these were being manufactured in Kassel. The Germans also decided to move any further rocket trials to an area so removed from Allied bomber bases as to be beyond their flying range. This is why in September 1943 a large group of Peenemünde scientists were moved to the wooded area of Blizna near Mielec, called 'Heidelager Blizna' (cryptonym 'Frieda').[22] On 5th November 1943 the first trial of the V-2 rocket took place there.[23]

An intelligence network run by the Home Army Inspectorate for Dębica Area was operating in the Blizna region. Moreover, most of the local employees of the Forestry Commission were Home Army members. This is why, even before the first rocket trial took place, Home Army GHQ received reports that a large research centre was being constructed in the area. When the first test was reported, orders were given for the region to be kept under close observation. Among the many reports received by HQ, the one from 'Jur' (who was a Home Army Intelligence officer in Rzeszów), dated 11 December 1943, deserves particular attention. In addition to the typical descriptions of the launch of V-1 and V-2, 'Jur' mentioned what had to be a reference to liquid oxygen being used in the propulsion system, though the report's author was obviously not aware of this at the time:

A projectile resembling a rocket was observed. There was a flash and a small explosion in the air, followed by a powerful flash on the ground. Peculiar telephone conversations indicate that such occurrences will be frequent and that the Army was forewarned about this. It is characteristic that where these plane-resembling projectiles crashed to the ground – two did so near Blizna and one in the vicinity of the Sędziszów Industrial Plant – no parts of these projectiles were found (such as parts of the body, or the engines). All that was found were craters and bits of metal plate, strewn over a wide area.

Supplies for Blizna are being delivered in cisterns. As discovered from soldiers and other informants, the cisterns are filled with air frozen to –200°C, which is highly explosive. This is why the cisterns and armoured cars used for transport have outlets covered with a thick layer of hoarfrost. The outlets discharge small quantities of something resembling fog, which spreads on the ground.[24]

Home Army Intelligence network reported on all the trials. From 25 November 1943 a register was kept of every test firing, which included the time and the direction of flight! Whenever the location of the landing site could be established, the agents were ordered to attempt to reach it achief of the Germans and to collect any parts, which remained after the explosion. The first trials resulted in the rockets falling some 5–15 kilometres from the range. But from January 1944 the distances increased to 50 km, (Sandomierz), later to 150–170 km (the region of Częstochowa, Końskie, Kozienice and Rejowiec), and even to 250–300 km (Sochaczew and Sarnaki near Siedlce).[25]

Such close monitoring enabled Home Army to pass many details about the projectiles fired from Blizna to London via radio, in reports on 7th and 23 March 1944. By April, the reports mentioned plane projectiles, which came down in the vicinity of Rejowiec. There were also reports from the production works, for example from 'Dora' (intelligence reports 130/396 of 25 February 1944; 243/769 of 17 April 1944).[26] Attempts were made to obtain projectile fragments, to ascertain their design, the operation of individual mechanisms (including steering), to discover what fuel was used. The agents, who managed to reach the locations where the rockets came down immediately after they exploded, reported a strong smell of alcohol.[27]

These efforts were soon to bring unexpected benefits. On 24 April 1944 the gyro-compass of a V-2 rocket, which fell into the courtyard of Daniel Łopatiuk in the village of Klimczyce near Sarnaki, was obtained. In addition some liquid was collected from the remains of that particular rocket. The liquid was examined by Professor Marceli Struszuński of The Warsaw Polytechnic. It turned out to be concentrated, 80% perhydrol (hydrogen peroxide), something the Allies did not suspect at all.[28] But the biggest achievement was the acquisition of a complete rocket, which on 20 May 1944 fell into some muddy shrubs on the banks of the river Bug, not far from the village of Mężenin near Klimczyce. The soldiers from Tadeusz Jakubski's ('Czarny') platoon, 8th Company of Home Army's 22nd Regiment, camouflaged it so well with bullrushes and osier bed, that in spite of a search on foot and by plane, that lasted several days, the Germans were unable to find it. Almost a week later parts of the rocket were extracted from the mud and transported 8 kilometres, to Hołowczyce, where they were hidden in a barn. After several days, a group of experts arrived from Warsaw for preliminary examination of the find. They photographed the most important parts, some taken apart and transported to Warsaw.

Antoni Kocjan and Stefan Waciórski worked out the construction and operation of the rocket. They found out that the engine was propelled by liquid fuel, consisting of the fuel itself and oxidizer. Steering was through steering surfaces operated via servo-mechanism guided by gyro-compass or radio, and the device was also equipped with graphite steering surfaces placed in exhaust gasses. The British were very keen to know whether the rocket was directed to its target by radio and whether its flight could be altered by radio waves. Professor Janusz Groszkowski determined that the radio set inside the rocket was placed there merely to transmit information on its flight path and that it was also linked to the steering. The range of the radio indicated, however, that it could be used for steering in the first few kilometres of flight only.

The first more specific data on the rocket were passed on to London in a radio report no. 366 of 12 June 1944. Further information, with descriptions of individual parts, followed on 3 July 1944, in report no. 403/1327.[29]

The V-1 attack on London on 12 June 1944 significantly increased the British interest in the weapon. The British side suggested that a plane be despatched to Poland to collect the drawings and the most important parts of the rocket. On 8 July 1944, the VI Bureau, PGS sent the following dispatch to the Home Army Commander-in-Chief, General Tadeusz Bór-Komorowski:

> Your projectiles may be an improved type of a flying bomb, currently used against London. We are very keen to reconstruct the weapon you have, and our friends are organising the pick-up of all the documents, data and parts, most importantly the radio and fuel samples, by a two-way flight. The friends consider this to be of the highest priority.[30]

This made it necessary to decide which of the V-2 parts were to be despatched, and to prepare a final report with the Polish observations on the construction of the rocket and the trials held at the Blizna testing ground. The British Douglas C-47 Dakota put down at night of 25/26 July 1944 at a Home Army secret landing strip in the vicinity of Wał Ruda near Tarnów, as part of Operation 'Wildhorn III'. In addition to the rocket parts and Home Army Intelligence officer, Capt. Jerzy Chmielewski, the plane took back also the 'Special Report 1/R no. 242. Rocket Projectiles'.[31] The 'List of Reports to HQ with Information on Rocket Projectiles' was also enclosed. The List showed that in 1943 there were four such radio reports and two monthly ones. In 1944 there were fifteen radio reports and five monthly ones.[32]

On 26 July the precious cargo reached Italy, and on the 28 arrived in London. In the second half of July, the British managed to obtain some more parts of a V-2, which did not follow its course and crashed in Sweden. The parts and reports brought from Poland, and the remains of the 'Swedish' rocket, provided the British experts with invaluable information, which they attempted to use to come up with effective counter-measures for these projectiles, the first of which hit London on 8 September 1944.[33] In addition, the analysis of the material supplied enabled the Allies to select and bomb those German industrial centres, which had the technologies necessary to build the complex rocket – and hence to limit their manufacture. On the other hand attempts by the British scientists to construct a device which would change the rocket's flight-path, were not successful.

It is worth noting that Polish Intelligence provided the Allies with much important information on V-1 and V-2 from other parts of Europe. For example, Home Army Intelligence delivered information on the construction of a vast underground rocket factory in the region of Buchenwald, near Weimar, as early as in the summer of 1944.[34] When the bombing of London was at its most intense, the Poles provided 173 reports from France on the location of V-1 launch pads, five on the location of V-2 rocket launchers and two on where the launch crews were accommodated. The detailed map references were sent to London via radio. This allowed the Allied bombers to precisely destroy many German rocket installations.[35]

Perusal of Polish Intelligence archives showed that intelligence networks operating under the German occupation also provided the Western Allies with significant amounts of valuable information on other German inventions and improvements, used for example in tanks and in submarines. Among the thousands of reports there are some, as this one, from early 1944, which stated that 'in the last days of October (1943) at an industrial conference in Berlin, the matter of invading Great Britain was discussed. The invasion was to take place when the weather turned misty. The principal weapons were to be smoke-making machinery and [atom] devices'.[36] It may well be that the V-2 rockets were the designated carriers of German atomic weapons: the design of a fail-safe steering mechanism for them was certainly only a matter of time.

Notes

1   Z. Moszumański, *Artyleria rakietowa Wehrmachtu* (*Wehrmacht Rocket Artillery*), Warsaw 1995, p. 6.
2   Research on the rocket-propelled aircraft was also conducted there: on the He 112 in the autumn of 1938, the He 176 (which had its maiden flight on 10 June 1939) and the Me 163, on which (production number V-3) Heini Dittmar achieved the speed of 1004 km/h on 2 October 1941. (D. Hölsken, *V-Missiles of the Third Reich the V-1 and V-2*, Sturbridge 1994, pp. 16–42, 56–58; D. Piszkiewicz, *Przez zbrodnie do gwiazd* (*Through Crime to the Stars*), Polish edition Warsaw 2000, pp. 12–44; M. Murawski, *Samoloty Luftwaffe 1933–1945* (*The Planes of the Luftwaffe 1933–1945*), vol. 2, ed. 2, Warsaw 1997, pp. 49, 203–204).

3 NARA, RG 165, MID, Germany, Box 1231, File 6535, Naval Attaché (Capt. Callan) dispatch to Opnav 021627, dated March 2, 1943, Source British, Evaluation A-1. Also see Himsley Vol. I appx. 5 'Oslo' Report of November 1939 stated that Hitler developed rockets – which went innoticed by the British.

4 TNA (PRO), ref. CAB.121/211, German Long-Range Rocket Development. JIC/492/43, 21 April 1943, Most Secret, signed Denis Capel-Dunn, pp. 1–6; idem, Reports on long Range Rockets, M.I.10. 26 March 1943, signed Lt-Col. G.S., pp. 1-3.

5 NARA, RG 165, MID, Germany, Box 1229, File 6535, Secret, New Secret Weapon, P/Ws in England, March 10–1, 1943.

6 The dimensions of these blocks were: diameter 70 mm, length 1200 mm, and after rolling: outside diameter 1760 mm, internal diameter 600 mm, total length 1600 mm, undrilled length 600 mm. Chemical composition of the steel was: carbon 0.55–0.60%, manganese 1.00–1.20%, silicon 0.80–0.90%.

7 NARA, RG 165, MID, Germany, Box 1231, File 6535, Extract from Polish Intelligence Report, December 2, 1942, For the Chief of the Military Intelligence Service – Col. T.E. Roderick, General Staff Corps, Executive Officer, MIS for the Chief of the Military Intelligence Service.

8 Ibid., Box 180, File 4810, Polish Intelligence Report, No 213/43, 1/18/43.

9 M.J. Neufeld, *The Rocket and the Reich. Pennemünde and the Coming of the Ballistic Missile Era*, Harvard 1996, p. 199; D. Paszkiewicz, *Przez zbrodnie* (*Through Crime*), op. cit., p. 111 states, that these were Poles who perished during the bombing of the facility on 17 August 1943.

10 M. Wojewódzki, *Akcja V-1, V-2* (*Action V-1, V-2*), 4th edition, Warsaw 1984, pp. 11–28, 108; A. Glass, S. Kordaczuk, D. Stępniewska, *Wywiad Armii Krajowej w walce z V-1 i V-2* (*Home Army Intelligence in the Fight against V-1 and V-2*), Warsaw 2000, pp. 17–18.

11 Before the war, the Träger family lived in Bydgoszcz and considered themselves to be Poles of Austrian origin. To avoid deportation to General-gouvernement, they took German citizenship. See *Słowink biograficzny konspiracji pomorskiej 1939–1945*, pp. 168–174, also AAN KGm/2375/3.

12 Roman Träger was describing the V-1 trials. Their pulsejet engines made similar sounds.

13 *Meldunki miesięczne wywiadu przemysłowego KG ZWZ/AK 1941–1944* (*Monthly Reports of Home Army GHQ Industrial Intelligence 1941–1944*). Facsimile, part 2, prepared for publication by A. Glass, Warsaw 2000, p. 647.

14 IPMS, Kol. 177/5, Memoirs of Col. Protasewicz, pp. 242–243.

15 M. Wojewódzki, *Akcja* (*Action*), op. cit., pp. 129–142; M. Middlebrook, *Nalot na Peenemünde* (*Raid on Peenemünde*), Warsaw 1987; A. Glass, S. Kordaczuk, D. Stępniewska, *Wywiad* (*Intelligence*), op. cit., p. 20; D. Hölsken, *V-Missiles*, op. cit., p. 90; J. Garliński, *Ostatnia broń Hitlera*, London 1977, pp. 62–63 (English edition: *Hitler's Last Weapon V-1 – V-2*, London 1978).

16 D. Eisenhower, *Crusade in Europe*, New York 1952.

17 M. Wojewódzki, *Akcja* (*Action*), op. cit., pp. 20–28.

18 NARA, RG 165, MID, Germany, Box. 1215, File 6505, Rocket Weapon, Source Z, Date of Origin June 24, 1943.

19 This would indicate the V-1 and V-2 weapons.

20 NARA, RG 165, MID, Germany, Box 1229, File 6535, Secret Office of Strategic Services US Army Forces in the Middle East, No 7693, Date of info: August, Source: from Stock.

21 'Secret documents on this project are marked 'Program A-4''.

22 D. Hölsken, *V-Missiles*, op. cit., p. 101; A. Glass, S. Kordaczuk, D. Stępniewska, *Wywiad* (*Intelligence*), op. cit., p. 21.

23 D. Piszkiewicz, *Przez zbrodnie* (*Through Crime*), op. cit., pp. 134–137.

24 A WIH, III/35/10 – OPL on the relevant territory; M. Wojewódzki, *Akcja* (*Action*), op. cit., pp. 162–164; A. Glass, S. Kordaczuk, D. Stępniewska. *Wywiad* (*Intelligence*), op. cit., p. 23.

25 See AAN, Armia Krajowa. Komenda Główna. Oddział II (the Home Army GHQ, II Bureau), 203/III-15; AWIH, sign III/22/97, vol. II, k. 180-325; AWIH, sign III/26/7; M. Wiśniewski, *Polacy w walce z niemiecką bronią V* (*The Poles in the Fight Against the German V-weapons*), 'Wojskowy Przegląd Historyczny', 1966, no. 2, pp. 59–87.

26 AWIH, sign III/22/97; *Meldunki* (*Reports*), op. cit., pp. 1182, 1237.

27 M. Wojewódzki, *Akcja* (*Action*), op. cit., pp. 165–175, 188–193; A. Glass, S. Kordaczuk, D. Stępniewska, *Wywiad* (*Intelligence*), op. cit., p. 24.

28 M. Wojewódzki, *Akcja* (*Action*), op. cit., pp. 232, 238–240, 323; A. Glass, S. Kordaczuk, D. Stępniewska, *Wywiad* (*Intelligence*), op. cit., pp. 24, 30.

29 *Meldunki* (*Intelligence*), op. cit., part 2, III/22/97, k. 295.

30 *Armia Krajowa w dokumentach 1939–1945* (the *Home Army in Documents 1939–1945*), vol. 3, London 1985, pp. 509–510 (Dispatch no. 598).

31 The report consisted of 18 pages of the basic typescript, with 12 pages of appendices, a list of 7 original parts, 65 photographs with their descriptions and 12 schematic drawings of equipment: radio, steering, pomp, engine and so on. The second part was the description of the construction and operation of the rocket, and the third the description of the Blizna testing ground with maps, together with a description of the launcher, and a list of 118 starts and impacts observed, with the relevant dates. The report ended with a list of factories making V-2 parts. The appendices contained technical information, notes on the flight-paths and a description of the effects of their explosion (craters of 27–30 m diameter, 11 m deep. Some were 60 m and 15 m respectively, though the warchief did not carry the full explosive load) and a list of signs and markings found on exploded fragments. The report indicated also that two types of projectiles were found: smaller, 5–6 m long and with a maximum diameter of 1.5 m, and larger, 12 m long and with a diameter of 2 m. There were also two types of launch pads: angled obliquely and vertically. In other words, the description corresponded exactly to V-1 and V-2 (*Meldunki* [*Reports*], op. cit., pp. 1337–1378).

32 Ibid., p. 1351.

33 After the Red Army seized the testing ground in Blizna, in early August 1944, Stalin agreed to Churchill's request and permitted a visit by a group of British experts. They reached the site on 3 September and confirmed that V-2's were fuelled by liquid oxygen and alcohol.

34 AWIH, III/22/97, vol. 2, k. 201, Intelligence Report of 25 February 1944.

35 T. Szumowski, *Polska Organizacja Wojskowa we francuskim Ruchu Oporu w latach 1943–1944* (*Polish Military Organisation in the French Resistance, 1943–1944*), 'Wojskowy Przegląd Historyczny', 1959, no. 3, p. 246.

36 NARA, RG 165, MID, Germany, Box 1237, File 6540, Report No 1051, 1944, Germany, Industrial, Rumors concerning new Technical inventions.

49

Polish Intelligence on Key Military Operations in the West

Andrzej Suchcitz

As seen from previous chapters, Polish Intelligence operated widely on all fronts. It had organised cells throughout Europe, in the Mediterranean and in both Americas. The II Bureau, PGS, located first in France and later in London, received thousands of dispatches and reports from these sources. Many of these reports were relatively insignificant. Some, however, when put together with information from other sources, turned out to be of immense operational – and sometimes strategic – value. To a large degree, II Bureau was a 'post box' of sorts: it relayed requests and questions from SIS, and later also from American Intelligence, in one direction; the responses obtained from its own agents went the other way. The information considered important for Polish interests was analysed within II Bureau, and reports on wider issues were transmitted to the British and the Americans without any deeper analysis.[1] When combined with other available information, such reports often enabled a broader picture to be formed. To what degree the information provided by Polish Intelligence was used and what conclusions based on it were drawn, was an altogether different issue.

The Allies often stressed the decisive importance of the role of Polish Intelligence within occupied Poland and in the immediate vicinity of the Eastern Front. From the first months of the war the fast emerging Polish Intelligence networks were able to provide reliable and precise information whose importance went beyond the Eastern Front. One example of information of such wider importance is provided not by a classical intelligence activity, but by the achievement of one of the Polish submarines, ORP 'Orzeł'. In the early afternoon of 8 April 1940, this submarine sank the German transport ship 'Rio de Janeiro', carrying 400 Wehrmacht soldiers in preparation for the invasion of Norway. The survivors saved by the Norwegians confirmed that their destination was Bergen, which was to be taken by force.[2] Regrettably, the Norwegian Government and the Admiralty in London did not conclude that an imminent invasion was threatening yet another European country. The lost time may have allowed the Norwegians to prepare their defences. The achievement of ORP 'Orzeł' might have helped to eliminate the element of surprise.

In the spring of 1940, the II Bureau was tracing the movements of German military transports, which were systematically moved to the West, primarily to strengthen 'the Scandinavian Expeditionary Force and to provide reinforcements to the units stationed on the Belgian and Dutch borders'.[3] This meant that along the western border the Germans had 110 large units at their disposal. Polish Intelligence reported rumours that 'there is a possibility of an offensive being mounted soon in the West, with the main thrust on the northern flank'.[4]

Almost immediately following the conclusion of hostilities in Poland, the French and British intelligence services were being informed of the imminent offensive and of its anticipated thrust. The strategic plan, which was to be put into practice with some modifications, was in their hands in January 1940 – but its veracity was questioned. One of the most interesting episodes, related to the work of Polish Intelligence and concerning the planned attack on France, took place when Home Army Intelligence managed to obtain a document with the details of this plan. A courier dispatched by Col. Stefan Rowecki on 23 February 1940 arrived in Paris on 14 March. The source of the information was the brother of an aide-de-camp of Gen. Wilhelm Keitlel, Wehrmacht's Chief of Staff. Both the Commander-in-Chief of the Home Army, Gen. Kazimierz Sosnkowski, and the Chief of the II Bureau, Lt-Col. Tadeusz Wasilewski, thought that it might have been a German provocation. Nevertheless, the document was subjected to an analysis, 'if only because a falsified document always contains some grains of truth'.[5]

The purported plan of attack had provision for by-passing the Maginot Line from the north, sweeping aside the sovereignty of Belgium and Luxembourg, and from the south, ignoring Swiss neutrality; an attack on the centre of the French armies: the destruction of the French secondary line of defence; and the conquest of northern France. The idea of the main thrust going through Luxembourg and southern Belgium might have been of interest[6] to the French High Command. Unfortunately, it was not.

With the fall of France, the main weight of the German offensive was turned against Great Britain. As before and using various sources, the II Bureau obtained much information on the timetable of the attack on Britain and its execution. On its own, such information was of limited use. Combined with the reports of other intelligence services, however, the ability to form a fuller picture and to draw conclusions was there.

In a despatch of 1 July 1940 the Chief of II Bureau's Station in Bern, Maj. Szczęsny Choynacki, informed the Center of the forthcoming German offensive against England. The source of the information, placed near the headquarters of Swiss Intelligence, maintained that mass air raids on England were planned from airfields in northern France. The primary targets were to be ports, RN bases, war industry and communications centres. Invasion troops were to attack and hold the most important airfields and ports. The next step was to be an invasion from the sea in the Hull–Newcastle region.[7] II Bureau cell in Hungary provided the information that 12,000 assorted boats were being gathered for the mass transport of the first wave of the invasion, to follow the bombing raids.[8] More information was obtained on the planned invasion from early August, for example that it was to take place between 16 and 22 August, with all of the Luftwaffe being pressed into action.[9] Confirmation of some of this came in mid-August, when there was an intensification of air raids.

Whilst these successes of Polish Intelligence only supported the information obtained from other sources, the activities of Station 'Afr.', set up by the II Bureau, PGS, in North Africa, had a direct bearing on the conduct of the war. Led by Maj. Mieczysław Słowikowski 'Rygor', this Station was a permanent source of intelligence from occupied Africa. This intelligence was fundamental for the preparations for, and the conduct of, Operation 'Torch', the first counter-offensive assault mounted by the Allies.

The Allied Staffs recognised the impact of Station 'Afr.', stating for example that 'it contributed significantly to the success of operations in French Africa'. The American Brig. Gen. Hayes A. Krone said that 'the Polish Army has the best intelligence in the world. Its value for us is beyond price. Unfortunately, there is little we can give in return'.[10]

Polish agents of Station 'F', the II Bureau, working in France as well as exponents of the Polish Ministry of Defence, ensured a steady flow of information on the German troop movement there, on the building of fortifications and new construction works in the western ports, including submarine pens. They also supplied especially valuable intelligence on the location of V-1 launching pads.[11] This was the subject of 25 reports, containing data on 82 pads. On this basis it was possible to plan their destruction. This constituted a significant input of Polish Intelligence into the Allied war effort.

Station '300', operating within the 'Cadix' centre, continued its pre-war work of deciphering German codes, mainly 'Enigma'. The team lead by Lt-Col. Gwidon K. Langer and Maj. Maksymilian Ciężki provided the British with intelligence on German troop movements throughout the continent, on German submarines in French ports and on the extermination of the Jews.[12]

The significance of these achievements rested not only on the information gathered by the agents, but also on the means employed to obtain it – and this depended on the calibre of the individuals involved. It is worth recalling Halina Szymańska, who throughout the war maintained secret contacts with the Chief of Abwehr, Adm. Wilhelm Canaris, and later with his emissary, Hans-Bernd Gisevius, the German Deputy Consul in Zurich. She did so with the agreement of Polish Intelligence and with the knowledge of the British. Asked to carry on this work by SIS, she was aided by the local cell of the Polish Intelligence Station in Switzerland. Among the intelligence obtained through this route there was the warning of an imminent offensive in the West (information gathered in April 1940) and on the 'Barbarossa' plan. Confirmed by the information from a German diplomat in Lisbon, obtained by Lt-Col. Jan Kowalewski, Polish resident intelligence officer there. The British were also supplied with information on the activities of anti-Hitlerite opposition in Germany.[13]

Of equally important service was Capt. Roman Czerniawski, in the context of Operation 'Fortitude', which was a large-scale disinformation campaign attempting to confuse the Germans as to where on the French coast the invasion of Europe would begin.

These examples of the achievements of the II Bureau outside Poland (where intelligence-gathering was largely in the hands of II Bureau, the Home Army GHQ), for years forgotten and diminished by Western historians, demonstrate how extensive and effective was Polish Intelligence. What use was made of such intelligence by the politicians and the strategists is, of course, another matter.

Notes

1 M. Rygor-Słowikowski, *In the Secret Service. The Lighting of the Torch*, London 1988, pp. 233–234.
2 J. Pertek, *Dzieje ORP 'Orzeł' (The History of ORP 'Orzeł')*, Gdańsk 1998, pp. 188–193.
3 IPMS, A.XII.24/41, *Ogólna sytuacja wojskowa Niemiec (General Military Situation of Germany)*, the II Bureau, PGS, 23 April 1940.
4 Ibid.
5 IPMS, A.XII.24/46, Letter of Chief of the II Bureau to Gen. K. Sosnkowski, 21 March 1940.
6 Ibid., Map with main thrust of German attack.
7 IPMS, A.XII.30/17, coded despatch from Maj. S. Choynacki from Bern, 1 July 1940.
8 IPMS, A.XII.24/45, German preparations for the invasion of England, the II Bureau, PGS, London, 5 July 1940 and further information on the invasion.
9 IPMS, A.XII.24/45, German preparations for the invasion of England, the II Bureau, PGS, London, 15 August 1940.
10 IPMS, A.XII.24/37, Report on the Operations of II Bureau, PGS, for the period 1st July 1942–30 June 1943, pp. 3–4; J. Herman, *Agency Africa: Rygor's Franco-Polish Network and Operation Torch*, 'Journal of Contemporary History', Vol. 22, 1987, pp. 690–699.
11 IPMS, A.XII.24/37, List of V-1 Flying Bombs as reported by Polish agents in northern France and as assessed by the II Bureau, PGS, as valuable and of importance to the British.
12 A. Pepłoński, *Wywiad Polskich Sił Zbrojnych na Zachodzie 1939–1945 (Intelligence Service of the Polish Armed Forces in the West 1939–1945)*, Warsaw 1995, pp. 114–115; F.H. Hinsley, *British Intelligence in the Second World War*, London 1993, p. 51.
13 J. Garliński, *The Swiss Corridor*, London 1981, pp. 89–97; A. Pepłoński, *Wywiad (Intelligence)*, op.cit., pp. 191–192.

50
Summary of Home Army Intelligence Activity *

Andrzej Chmielarz

The product of Home Army Intelligence's activity was most fully utilised by British Intelligence. Often the information was obtained in response to a specific British request. The British side frequently stressed the high value of such information. Such acknowledgements on the part of British Intelligence were expressed not only in terms of praise, but also through financial contributions, which were of importance to Home Army's budget. The quarterly value of such grants was between 1 and 2 million US dollars. How significant was the amount, can be verified by the 1943 budget prepared by the VI Bureau, amounting to 10 million dollars. A number of Home Army Intelligence accomplishments were of particular value to the Allied war effort. Among them were:
- in 1940, the plans of the German attack on France;
- in 1940, a detailed analysis of the German military preparations in the Generalgouvernement, known as 'Plan Otto', with the conclusion that these were the preparations for a war with Russia; information on the German preparations for the African offensive was also delivered;
- in 1941, detailed information on the German concentration for the attack on Russia. More than 100 large military units were identified, and the date of the attack was correctly predicted as the 2nd half of June 1941; also a drawing of a miniature submarine;
- in the spring of 1942, Home Army Eastern Intelligence discovered that the target of the German offensive was not Moscow, but the Caucasus; information was submitted indicating the intention of occupying southern France; it was confirmed that the German battleship 'Tirpitz' was hidden in one of the fjords in Norway;
- in 1943, information was provided on the German experiments with rocket weapons, a number of factories producing

* This chapter contains the summary of the intelligence activities conducted by the II Bureau of the Home Army GHQ. For more on this subject, see Chapter 43.

components for these weapons were identified, as were all the plants producing synthetic fuel; the transfers of German units to Italy following the fall of Mussolini were described;

- in 1944, the German testing grounds at Blizna – Pustków, near Mielec, where experiments with V-weapons were conducted, were penetrated.
- Parts of a German V-2 rocket were collected and delivered, as were plans of the Atlantic Wall; detailed information on the German trials of a jet-powered aircraft were submitted.

The information on the Third Reich's armaments industry was of particular value. Home Army Intelligence penetrated all the Maj. industrial centres, shipyards and factories producing military equipment. Almost 1,200 industrial plants were under observation, which in many cases contributed to the bombing of strategically important objectives by Allied air forces. The detailed reports on the results of such raids allowed an assessment of their effectiveness to be made and decisions to be taken on the successive sets of targets.

The information submitted on the identity of German units was one of the key elements in recreating the full German Order of Battle such reports played a crucial role in the Allied planning of operations in Europe.

Following the signing of the military agreement with the Soviets on 14 August 1941, the Polish side was in a position to directly deliver intelligence information to the USSR. The Poles treated this ability as one of their bargaining counters with the Soviets, hoping in return to obtain Moscow's permission to establish a supply base on Soviet territory for the resistance movement in Poland. The Soviets were provided with information on the German units at the Eastern Front, on their supplies, on preparations for the various offensives and so on. Such information was obtained by Eastern intelligence, whose teams followed the German units. The direct intelligence co-operation, which provided much valuable information, including some gathered in response to direct Soviet requests, lasted 3 months. On 29 July 1942 NKVD General Georgij Zukov (not to be confused with his more famous namesake) told the Polish side that any further activities of the Station 'Wisła' would not serve any useful purpose. Many of the Home Army Intelligence successes were truly spectacular. Its activities were characterised by their vast scope, allowing it to reach deep into the territory held by the enemy. Home Army Intelligence invested vast efforts and much detailed work in this, which often ended with a martyr's death for its operatives.

But the most important achievement of Home Army Intelligence was the creation of very modern working methods. It regularly and systematically supplied military, economic and industrial reports not only from Poland, but also from the immediate rear of the Eastern Front and indeed from German territory.

This was accomplished through a combination of traditional ways of obtaining intelligence, that is, through agents on the ground, with a system of gathering and evaluating information on the enemy. Under that system every Home Army soldier acted as an agent. Thanks to this, Home Army Intelligence, though very ill-equipped with modern technical means, established a model, which became widely adopted only after the Second World War. Under this model the analytical work of intelligence units, relying on the collection and collation of vast amounts of information, not necessarily of a secret nature, produced valuable and reliable data. This modern system combined with a well-organised analysis and study department provided for the unprecedented effectiveness of Home Army Intelligence. The management of Home Army Intelligence put all actions at the forefront. Its basic aim was to observe regularly selected objects lke transports. This was combined with the practice of placing agents directly within selected targets and objects, not necessarily at high level.

In his introduction to a selection of accounts by the intelligence operatives of the resistance, Władysław Kozaczuk wrote: 'The struggles conducted by the intelligence services were in their essence a long-lasting and severe test of common sense, of organizational efficiency and of the ability to draw conclusions'.[1] The Intelligence Service of the Home Army have passed this test with flying colours. A comparison of the achievements of Home Army Intelligence with the effectiveness of other organisations operating in occupied Europe demonstrates, that Home Army Intelligence was significantly more productive than its French, Yugoslav or Soviet equivalents. The real value of the intelligence from Poland was determined by its topicality, reliability and precision.

How serious a threat Polish Intelligence was considered to be is well demonstrated by an official letter from the Oberkommando der Wehrmacht to the Gestapo cells in the Berlin Military District, dated 17 July 1943:

> Intelligence findings for the recent period allow us to state categorically that the Polish Intelligence Service is extremely active. It is already operating in a vast number of protected German factories, through the workers employed there. This creates threats to the production of military materiél. Such threats are multiplied, since Polish Intelligence, supported by the fanaticism of the Polish resistance, works with much skill and is difficult to contain.[2]

Notes

1 *Życie na krawędzi. Wspomnienia żołnierzy antyhitlerowskiego wywiadu* (*Life on the Edge. Accounts of the Soldiers of Anti-Hitler Intelligence*), Warsaw 1980, p. 7.
2 Quoted from J. Pollack, *Wywiad, sabotaż, dywersja. Polski ruch oporu w Berlinie 1939–1945* (*Intelligence, Sabotage, Diversion. Polish Resistance in Berlin 1939–1945*), Warsaw 1991, p. 99.

51
Naval Intelligence: Movements of Ships, Surveillance of Ports and Shipyards

Andrzej Pepłoński, Tadeusz Dubicki and Robert Majzner

From the first days of the war representatives of British and French intelligence services in Denmark and Lithuania intensified contacts with Polish intelligence cells. This stemmed from a rising need for information concerning the Navies and shipbuilding industries of the Axis countries. Although initially those contacts were basically limited to the network of Capt. Wacław Gilewicz, with time the II Bureau entrusted naval intelligence tasks to stations and cells functioning in southern France, Spain, Portugal, Greece, Turkey, North Africa and even Switzerland.[1] Reconnaissance encompassed the Mediterranean coast as well as the Atlantic, North Sea and Baltic coasts.[2] The first naval intelligence tasks came from London as early as November 1940. This involved determining the number of submarines built in the shipyards of Gdańsk and Piława (Pilau), their tonnage and date of readiness for service; the construction of other types of ships; the exact location of the shipyards in Gdańsk, Piława and Königsberg and the distribution of ships in the port of Gdynia.[3]

A week later, on 27 November 1940, Lt-Col. Stanisław Gano, Chief of the II (Intelligence) Bureau of the Polish General Staff, conveyed through the VI Bureau successive tasks prepared by British Intelligence. They pertained mainly to Gdańsk, since the British expected information about the functioning of the docks in the 'Danzig Schichau' shipyard, as well as the date of stay in Gdańsk of the battleship 'Bismarck', the aircraft carrier 'Graf Zeppelin', heavy battle cruisers 'Prinz Eugen' and 'Admiral Scheer'[4] and the light battle cruiser 'Leipzig'.[5]

At the beginning of June 1941 the Home Army GHQ received another cable from London which stated, inter alia that: 'The surveillance of the

German Navy and ports is of utmost significance for our friends [the British] who attach great importance to these issues. It is necessary for our joint effort and winning the war. Therefore, tight surveillance must be organised that would encompass the ports of Gdynia, Hel and Gdańsk as well as the ports in eastern Prussia and possibly Szczecin. The friends urgently request the quickest possible installation of W/T stations and daily cables to assure continuous information'.[6]

It was impossible to carry out such a task since in the second half of 1940 intelligence presence was only in Gdynia – a single independent intelligence cell, composed of several persons headed by Lt. Antoni Wilniewski. As a result, the Home Army GHQ rarely received information from the Baltic ports and the whole coast.

The Home Army Pomeranian District Intelligence was created in the summer of 1941, partially under the pressure of the General Staff, to improve naval intelligence. It was probably headed by Scoutmaster Bernard Myśliwek 'Konrad', commander of the Pomeranian Szare Szeregi Scout detachment. He was succeeded by Capt. Józef Olszewski. Nonetheless, the intelligence activity of the Coast Inspectorate was of fundamental significance. It was headed by Second Lt. J. Belau, who controlled two intelligence networks, both bearing the joint cryptonym 'V Korpus'. The Chief of the First Intelligence Group was Edmund Welz 'O1-187', and of the Second 2nd Lt. Stanisław Kaczmarek '02-186'.[7] Independently of the intelligence structures of the Home Army Pomeranian region there were central networks of offensive intelligence: 'Stragan' and 'Lombard', headed by Maj. Edward Jetter ('Edward', 'Prezes'). The latter included the intelligence cell 'Bałtyk' of Lt. Stefan Ignaszak 'Nordyk'. It was composed of three cells: 'Bałtyk 301' headed by Edmund Czarnowski ('Kolski'), which embraced the region of Toruń, Tczew, Gdynia and Gdańsk; 'Bałtyk 302' run by Apolinary Łaniewski ('Apollo'), active in Bydgoszcz, Łęgnów and Rostock; and 'Bałtyk 303' headed by Augustyn Träger ('Tragarz', 'T-1', 'Sęk') in the region of Bydgoszcz, Szczecin and Police. The entire work was co-ordinated by the Intelligence Section of the Naval Department of the Home Army GHQ ('Alfa', 'Ostryga'). The creation of a central structure of Naval Intelligence was the domain of several Navy officers: Cmdr. Rafał Czeczott, Capt. (Navy) A. Potyrała and Lt. Cmdr. Antoni Gniewecki.[8]

The information obtained through the reconnaissance of heavy industry in the Reich was extremely valuable for Naval Intelligence. Information about the production of semi-finished products and parts for the Kriegsmarine was acquired during the surveillance of steel mills, weapons factories and even small works, such as 'Huta Hulczyński' in Sosnowiec (monthly production of 160–180 tons of semi-finished products used in the construction of submarines); 'Telefunken' in Poznań (surveillance equipment and draught gauges); 'Famo' in Wrocław ('Diesel-Man' 1200 HP submarine engines); 'Wośniak' in Sosnowiec (casts of engines and torpedo equipment); 'John' in Łódź (monitoring apparatus); 'Akumulatorenfabrik A. G.' in Hannover-Stocken (150 large and 800–1,000 small batteries a month); 'Conze-Motor' near Hamburg (electrical units for submarines), or 'Zieleniewski' in Kraków (hulls for moor mines, mine-sweepers, steel pipes for periscopes).[9]

Intelligence reports included sketches of shipyards, factories working for the Kriegsmarine, technical drawings of products, commercial correspondence and even more important reports by informants.

Perceiving the difficulties encountered by Home Army intelligence cells in gathering information, and in order to systematise the obtained information and adapt them to their requirements, the British sent a long questionnaire at the beginning of June which specified the most important Polish intelligence task, namely the conduct intelligence assessments of the 'Danziger Werft', 'Schichau Werft' and 'Deutsche Werft Kiel-Werk Gotenhafen' shipyards in Gdynia, with particular attention paid to the number of shipways, their sizes and modernisation, as well as the details relating to all the ships built there, including submarines. Apart from construction information the British required essential information about the number of employed workers, work time and the number of shifts, the work rate and sources of raw materials acquisition. Moreover, they recommended that surveillance of the shipyard be conducted during air raids in order to determine the effectiveness of the fire brigades and the anti-aircraft defence.[10]

Following those directives, the Home Army GHQ in its monthly report no. 11/41 of November 1941 described the shipyards in Gdańsk, Gdynia and Elbląg, and informed that the 'Schichau' shipyard had four shipways for constructing submarines, which in the course of six months were used for launching 12–15 of 250–200-ton vessels, and two shipways for the construction and repair of other ships. The production capacity of the 'Danziger Werft' shipyard, which also had four shipways for building submarines and an additional three shipways and two floating graving docks, was assessed as twenty 250-ton ships in 6 months; whereas 'Schichau Werft' in Elbląg produced three 250-ton vessels in three months.[11]

In mid-1942 a monthly report M.M. 8/43 informed London that the annual submarine production of all the shipyards in Gdańsk could have reached the level of 46 vessels. It was estimated that the 'Danziger Werft' shipyard was capable of launching 18–20 submarines a year, and 'Schichau' 23–26 average tonnage ships. Such extensive production showed that the Gdańsk shipyards could be regarded as 'the most productive of all the shipyards at the disposal of the Germans'.[12]

That fact was the reason why particular attention was focused on the situation in Gdańsk. An extensive report sent to London in May 1942 contained a description of the port and local works, especially the 'Danziger Werft' shipyard. The information was supplemented by a sketch of that part of the shipyard where submarines were built.[13]

Much information about the scale of German shipyard production often mentioned symptoms of a crisis of the shipbuilding industry. For example, in March 1942 the 'Stragan' offensive intelligence network disclosed considerable problems with supplies, chiefly of steel and bronze 'reserved exclusively for submarines' in the 'Deutsche Werft Kiel-Werk Gotenhafen' shipyard in Gdynia, making it necessary to reduce the work day to 8.5 hours.[14]

In mid-1943 the British conveyed to the II Bureau of the Polish General Staff new questionnaires proposing an 'inspection' of seventeen ports – from Rendsburg and Rostock, Stralsund, Gdynia and Gdańsk to Königsberg and Libawa (Libau), focusing on naval training, the distribution of submarine bases, and the localisation of barracks and fuel depots as well as detailed descriptions of enemy ships, indicating the location and number of guns and the date a given vessel was discovered. In the case of merchant ships it was advised to pay attention to their names, tonnage and possibly length, type of cargo and route. Successive groups of questions related to enemy losses – warships and merchant ships, as well as the distribution of mine fields, the way of laying mines and the types of mines used, the organisation of coastal defence and the location of important targets to be bombed.[15]

Home Army intelligence reports show that information concerning the shipbuilding industry constituted an essential part of reconnaissance along the coast. Realisation of those 'orders' brought information about the construction of warships and merchant ships. For example, in March 1943 information came from the 'Schichau' shipyard in Gdańsk about a ship with a deadweight capacity of 9,000 BRT; three huge merchant ships in the Hamburg 'Blohm u. Voss' shipyard, as well as a ship with a deadweight capacity of 9 000 BRT and several tankers from the Bremen 'Vulcan' shipyard.[16]

A telegram of 31 August 1941 informed that a branch of 'Deutsche Werft Kiel', installed in the docks of the Gdynia shipyard, had been entrusted with redesigning six long-range ships into the so-called 'U-Boat-Jägers' as well as with repairing smaller vessels, such as motor torpedo boats and submarines. It was learned that the workshops on Oksywie conducted small repairs of sea vessels, and that the 'Schichau' and 'Danziger Werft' shipyards continued to produce submarines. On the other hand, a branch of the 'Schichau' shipyard in Elbląg built small vessels which were then floated to the sea *via* a water canal.[17]

The intelligence acquired from the shipbuilding industry indicated that the Germans had introduced new construction designs. In February 1943 it was established that 'Huta Katarzyna' in Sosnowiec had assembled three Diesel engines for submarines, each with 6,000–7,000 horse-power. Two of them were sent to Gdańsk. Moreover, the steel plant had received a set of parts necessary for assembling five new engines. It was underlined in the comments that the German submarines had to be able to reach the speed much exceeding 20 knots.

Details concerning technical solutions were systematically recorded. Numerous construction drawings were provided (for example, of the bow section and frame of the VIIc class U-boat), focusing on the thickness of the hull (16 mm), welding instead of riveting, and the use of aluminium alloys.[18] A thorough note was made of all repairs and modernisation of submarines, information of essential importance for the Allies since it indicated how deep the German submarines could submerge, indicate the resilience of their hulls, maximum underwater and surface speed, and finally, their armament. That was the reason why much attention was devoted to the operation of strengthening anti-aircraft armament, conducted from September 1943 to March 1944.[19] Information was provided that in the course of two months of redesigning, fifty submarines were additionally equipped with two single 20 mm guns (the so-called 'e' type) or one quadruple and one single gun (the 'f' type) or even one quadruple and one single 20 mm gun and one 37 mm gun (in case of the U-345 – U-362). That information was supplemented with detailed construction drawings of redesigned battle platforms. The reports drew attention to all sorts of untypical adaptations, e.g. at the turn of September and October 1943 the navigation platform of the U-390 was covered with a special resin substance in Gdańsk shipyard; or a 4 mm layer of rubber coating was noticed on the entire hull of the U-480 when it arrived in Gdynia shipyard in November 1943.[20]

In mid-1943 it was unambiguously concluded that German shipyards concentrated almost exclusively on submarine production.[21] In an attempt to establish the level of the yearly production in all the shipyards under surveillance, a monthly report no. 5/43 estimated that it could not exceed 261 ships. The assessed production capacity of the 'Blohm u. Voss' shipyard in Hamburg was about 96 ships, the 'Deutsche Werft' in Hamburg – 30, the 'Stulcken-Sohn' in Hamburg – 10, the 'Germania Werft' in Kiel – 48, the 'Deutsche Werke' in Kiel – 6, the 'Neptunwerke' in Rostock – 2, the 'Stettiner Oderwerke – 6, the 'Stettiner Vulcan' – 6, the 'Stocznia Gdańska' – 22, and the 'Schichau' in Gdańsk – 35. Since other shipyards, not penetrated by Home Army Intelligence, were capable of producing 52 ships, and the shipyards in Denmark, The Netherlands, Belgium and France – another 107, the annual production totalled around 420 ships, excluding the 'Hovaldswerke' shipyard in Hamburg,[22] which abandoned the production, and shipyards in Yugoslavia, Romania and Bulgaria, no precise information on production output available.[23] The employment level in German shipyards, excluding those in the occupied countries and allied states, was estimated at about 200,000 workers.[24]

Continuous surveillance of shipyard centres provided new information, e.g. from the Gdynia-based 'Deutsche Werke Kiel-Werk Gotenhafen', where following the reconstruction of the former Polish Navy shipyard along an industrial canal, nine building sites were organised, amassing at the same time about 300 Diesel engines. The assembly of medium type ships was launched at the beginning of March 1944;[25] those were probably 500-ton ships, totally welded, 75-metres long and equipped with six torpedo launchers.

Polish intelligence managed to register the introduction of new ships into service, e. g. on 10 January 1943 – the U-741; 5 February 1943 – the U-743; March 1943 – the U-428; April 1943 – the U-429, the U-430, the U-238, the U-280, the U-417, the U-424 and the U-564 (all medium type), as well as the U-538 (large type, 750–1,000 tons); May 1943 – the U-742 and the U-743, and on 5 June 1943 – the U-744.[26]

The priorities of searching for information changed after the first symptoms of the decrease in production of the German shipyards were observed at the beginning of 1944 – including the Gdańsk shipyard which launched only two submarines in two weeks. One of the most important tasks for Home Army Intelligence in the first half of 1944 was gathering all available information concerning modern types of German submarines, about which the British side had practically no knowledge.[27] The description of type XXIII – some 50 metres long and armed with two torpedo launchers,[28] as well as type XXI – about 100 metres long and armed with six torpedo launchers.[29] Furthermore, the Poles also provided details of the type of steel used for the construction (St 42), the thickness of the plating and ribs, the type of electrodes used for welding, construction techniques and even the technical drawings showing a cross section of the pressure hull (type XXIII). In mid-1944 information was provided on the construction of the so-called 'Einhullenboote', whose pressure hull was made of very thick, 25 mm plate, while a light tower structure and keel constituted the outer hull.[30]

In response to the questions put by the London Headquarters in May 1944 Home Army Intelligence confirmed that none of the workers questioned had ever heard about the construction of German submarines with a displacement smaller than 250 tons,[31] although, earlier, in January, it had informed about plans of building small vessels each with a crew of eight, and before that, in November 1943, about the alleged production of 25-metre long U-Boats, each with a displacement of about 100 tons.[32] The questions at the same time expressed anxiety of the Allies about the fate of the invasion fleet, which could be threatened by small and miniature submarines, thus more difficult to detect.[33]

The range of information from the Baltic region sent to London included also the commencement of building ocean-going ships: in February 1944 – submarine battle cruisers ('U-Kreuzer'), constructed in segment technology in Gdynia, among others; and in March 1944 a series of new 'American' type ships with a displacement of 1,800 tons, 140 meters long, with a 150-strong crew and equipped with six torpedo launchers on the bow and four on the stern; the ships were to be launched in the 'Schichau' shipyard in Gdańsk on 1 May 1944.[34]

Although it was stated in a monthly report of January 1943 that 'the whole effort of the German shipbuilding industry is aimed at the largest possible production of submarines at the cost of [...] other categories', therefore 'it is obvious that the Germans have totally resigned from planning a more serious naval campaign in which heavy battleships would play a fundamental role', those ships were not quite forgotten. Before 1943, the information about surface ships was provided relatively frequently, which is understandable, whereas much less was said about their construction, e.g. the finishing work on an aircraft carrier in the Szczecin 'Oderwerke A. G.',[35] three light battle cruisers in the 'Blohm u.

Voss' shipyard in Hamburg or five torpedo-boat destroyers in 'Schichau' in Elbląg.[36] The information mentioned, first of all, the repairs of: the battleship 'Tirpitz' (30 January 1942) and the heavy cruiser 'Admiral Scheer' (15 December 1941–February 1942) in the Gdańsk 'Schichau' shipyard.[37] The battleship 'Schleswig-Holstein' (6–23 April 1942), the heavy cruiser 'Admiral Hipper' (from 26 April 1942) and the light cruiser 'Leipzig' were, in turn, repaired in the Gdynia 'Deutsche Werft' shipyard;[38] and destroyers 'Hans Ludeman', 'Theodor Riedel', 'Herman Schoeman', 'Karl Galster' and 'Z 24' in the 'Blohm u. Voss' shipyard in Hamburg, and 'Bruno Heineman' – in the Kiel 'Deutsche Werk' shipyard.[39] Note was also taken of the adaptation of two Polish merchant ships: 'Rzeszów' and 'Bielsko' into auxiliary cruisers ('Hilfskreuzer').[40]

Maj. repair of the battleship 'Gneisenau'[41] was also thoroughly reported. The ship was hauled into Gdynia on 6 April 1942 and initially moored opposite the 'Warta' warehouses and then near a grain silo on 25 April, protected with a double anti-torpedo net. Specially arranged surveillance found out that the ship's port side was damaged, turret 'A' with three 280 mm calibre guns was gone, the front deck was totally ruined, two upper armoured decks were pierced and the third one was damaged. Commenting on the demands made by OKM that the ship be ready in three weeks, it was stated that considering the shallow waterway to Elbląg, Gdynia could be the only place where such repairs could be made. The six months of repairs, as initially assumed, were likely to be extended to 8–9 months, since bringing the ship into a new floating dock (20 thousand tons) would require not only taking maximum load off but also dredging the canal to make it 22 metres deep. That required bringing over a special dredger from Denmark. A description of the course of the repair mentioned that it was started with placing new armoured plates and putting the ruined interior, decks and rudder side into order. According to the information conveyed in August the repair would entail the removal of the damaged bow part (hull and armour), the repair of the main engine, damaged by the impact of the air raids, making the stern longer by eight metres, replacing the main armament by installing 380 calibre guns as well as providing aeroplanes, making it similar to the 'Bismarck'. On 15 October 1942, three days before the expected launching of 'Gneisenau' it was observed that the repair, which until then had exclusively consisted of dismantling the damaged parts, was frequently interrupted. Some of the precision devices were transferred to the sister ship 'Scharnhorst', while a part of the armament was dismantled and sent to Norway to reinforce local coastal defence.[42]

With the exception of intelligence of 15 March 1943 concerning the construction of the heavy cruiser 'Seydlitz',[43] from 1943 the conveyed information referred only to work on smaller vessels, so-called counter-torpedo boats, six of which were on the shipways of the Elbląg shipyard in May of that year, and torpedo boats, three of which were built in one year. According to one informant, because of a shortage of materials the construction time grew from two to two and a half years, and so did the costs – from 3.5 million to 8 million RM.[44] The most frequent subjects of the conveyed information were motor torpedo boats ('Schnellboote'), which were supposed to be built in Elbląg at a rate of six per month, mine sweepers, eight of which the 'Schichau' shipyard in Königsberg was to produce for the Kriegsmarine by 31 July 1942, and the so-called 'U-Jägers'; on 5 June 1943 three were being simultaneously built in the Elbląg shipyard. Sometimes, reports mentioned entirely new constructions of motor torpedo boats which attained the speed of 60, 49 and 47 knots and were armed with one or two torpedo launchers and a 37 mm gun.[45]

The last component of the reports sent to London, very important for the proposed targets of Allied air raids, was information coming from the surveillance of shipyards and co-operating factories.[46] For example, grave damage was inflicted in Hamburg in two floating docks with a counter-torpedo boat (1400 tons) and a submarine (800 tons), and a dry dock, damaged again on 26/27 October 1941 to such an extent that one of its 14-metre-high walls was ruined.[47]

Information about the effect of Allied air raids also took note of all cases of bombing of ships under construction, being repaired or simply stationed in the ports under surveillance, for instance, a light cruiser in the 'Blohm u. Voss' Hamburg shipyard was struck by one heavy bomb and three light ones causing the keel to break, which resulted in the ship being dismantled.[48] The battleship 'Gneisenau' in Kiel is another example or, finally, the submarine hunter 'UJ 1210', sunk on 9 October 1943 while moored in the 'Alte Werft' shipyard in Gdynia.[49]

Despite receiving a large number of reports the British were reserved in evaluating them, probably due to some mistakes, as in the case of the repairs of the 'Scharnhorst' and 'Gneisenau' battleships in June 1941 in the Kiel shipyard; both of them were actually moored in Brest.[50] Among the evaluations done by the Admiralty about the quality of the intelligence restrained opinions were rather predominant.[51] The British claimed: 'The information is improving but has not yet reached a suitable level', because it does not contain 'essential details': approximate sizes or tonnage, especially of submarines; the completion of work on the ships and the identification of the shipways, especially in view of the fact that 'the first two points should remain within the capabilities of every agent working in this field'.[52] It should be noted, on the other hand, that much of the acquired information was confirmed by British sources,[53] which used them to prepare, among others, the analysis of the level of production in particular shipyards and factories.[54]

Notes

1 Station 'S' was engaged in the surveillance of the ports in northern Italy.
2 IPMS, Kol. 242/63, Task for Stations 'P', 'F' and 'S'.
3 SPP, 2.3.6.2.2, Telegram from 'Godziemba' to 'Rakoń' of 20 November 1940.
4 This former 'pocket-size battle ship' as this class of ships was commonly called, was reclassified in February 1940 from a 'Panzerschiffe' to 'Schwere Kreuzer'.
5 SPP, call no. 2.3.6.2.2, Letter from Lt.Col. S. Gano to the chief of the VI Bureau of the Polish General Staff, 27 November 1940.

 6 SPP, 2.3.6.2.2, Telegram from 'Godziemba' to 'Kalina', l. dz. 1542/tj.41 of 8 June
    1942.
 7 A. Gąsiorowski, *Wywiad i dywersja w Okręgu Pomorskim ZWZ-AK (Intelligence
    and sabotage in the Home Army Pomeranian Region)* [in:] *Armia Krajowa na
    Pomorzu. Materiały z sesji naukowej w Toruniu 14–15 XI 1992 (The Home Army
    in Pomerania. Materials from a Scientific Session Held in Toruń on 14–15
    November 1992)*, ed. by E. Zawacka and M. Wojciechowski, Toruń 1993, pp. 88–90.
 8 B. Chrzanowski, A. Gąsiorowski, *Wydział Marynarki Wojennej 'Alfa' Komendy
    Gównej Armii Krajowej (The 'Alfa' Naval Section of the Home Army GHQ)*, Toruń
    2001, pp. 43–87. The 'Instruction for Homeland' of 21 June 1941, prepared by the
    General Staff, planned to create an Intelligence Department which was to become
    part of the II Bureau of the Home Army GHQ.
 9 *Meldunki miesięczne wywiadu przemysłowego KG ZWZ/AK 1941–1944. Faksimile,*
    (dalej: Meldunki), przygotował do wydania A. Glass, cz. 1-2, Warszawa 2000,
    (*Monthly Reports of the Industrial Intelligence of the Home Army GHQ, Facsimiles,*
    further as: *Meldunki*), prepared for publication by A. Glass, part 1-2, Warsaw 2000.
10 SPP, 2.3.6.2.2, Intelligence questionnaire 'The Naval Intelligence Network in
    Gdańsk and Gdynia on 27 May 1941'.
11 Meldunki , part 1, p. 20.
12 Ibid., p. 410 (M. M. 8/42).
13 NARA, RG 165, MID, Germany, Entry 77, Box 1173, File 4750, The Port of Danzig,
    N 227-739/42. Similar reports were written about the shipyards in Gdynia,
    Kołobrzeg, Elbląg, Hamburg and Emden.
14 *Meldunki*, part 1, p. 195.
15 SPP, 2.3.6.1, Questionnaire for particular ports, l. dz. 3255/N, of 15 June 1943.
16 *Meldunki*, part 2, p. 777, 1013, 1311 (M. M. 6/43, 11/43, 6/44).
17 AAN, KG AK, 203/III-8, Intelligence report of 31 August 1941.
18 *Meldunki,* part 2, p. 737, 762-764 (M. M. 5/43).
19 This was a response to Allied superiority in the air since from 1 May to 2 August
    1943 Allied planes sunk in the Bay of Biscay 28 U-Boats and damaged another 22
    (J. Lipiński, *Druga wojna światowa na morzu (The Second World War at Sea)*,
    fourth ed., Gdańsk 1976, p. 364). Consequently, Admiral Karl Dönitz ordered
    additional armament for all ships so that they could escort ships going out for
    patrol. The ones armed best, the so-called 'Flak-Falle', were to provoke Allied
    aeroplanes and to inflict maximum losses upon them (C. Blair, *Hitler's U-Boat War,
    1939–1942* vol. 2, Polish edition Warszawa 1998, p. 348.)
20 *Meldunki*, part 2, p. 896, 1013, 1119, 1188, 1281 (M. M. 8/43, 11/43, 3/44, 5/44). In
    both cases the informants probably noticed the special rubber coating on the
    'Alberich', whose task was to absorb and disperse the ray beams emitted by Allied
    radars. It is possible that so-called snorts were installed in the course of rebuilding
    – this is partially suggested by the description of the U-390; in June 1944 such
    'snorts' were also part of the U-480 (see: C. Blair, *Hitler,* op. cit., p. 607).
21 Besides, on 30 January 1943 Great Admiral Erich Raeder, Navy Commander-in-
    Chief, was replaced by Admiral Karl Dönitz, the commander of the U-Boat Fleet.
22 Soon afterwards M. M. [Monthly Report] 7/43, based on the materials obtained from
    two sources at the end of June 1943, informed about the construction of 500-ton
    and 750-ton ships with two or one gun, at the rate of one ship every fifteen days.
    Meanwhile, according to the information of 18 January 1943 (M. M. 10/42), at the
    end of August 1942, before the production was stopped, shipways had contained
    six submarines and on 29 October 1942 – five submarines (M. M. 11/42),
    (*Meldunki*, part 1, p. 464, 493; ibid., part. 2, p. 607, 825.)
23 One of the reports (M. M. 6/43) discussed the construction of submarines in
    Romania, although in reality this undertaking consisted of assembling six small II
    D-type ships in Galaţi, disassembled in Germany and transported by rail or 18 axle

trailers to Ingolstadt; from there they were floated on the Danube to the Black Sea, where they became part of the 30th submarine flotilla , operating from the port in Constanţa (J. Lipiński, *Druga wojna*, op. cit., p. 194; J. Pertek, *Na Bałtyku, w Arktyce i na Morzu Czarnym* (*On the Baltic, in the Arctic and on the Black Sea*), Poznań 1989, p. 50; see also: J. Meister, *Der Seekrieg in den Osteuropeischen Gewassern 1941–1945*, München 1958).

24 *Meldunki*, part 2, p. 738.
25 Ibid., p. 1242, 1281 (M. M. 4/44, 5/44).
26 Ibid., p. 650, 776, 825 (M. M. 3/43, 6/43, 7/43).
27 F. H. Hinsley, *British Intelligence in the Second World War*, vol. 3, part 1, London 1984, p. 49.
28 *Meldunki*, part 2, p. 1242 (M. M. 4/44). The first ship of this type, the U-2321, was launched in the 'Deutsche Werft' shipyard in Hamburg on 12 June 1944 (C. Blair, *Hitler*, op. cit., p. 600).
29 *Meldunki*, p. 1243 (M. M. 4/44). According to an informant this programme planned the construction of 140 such ships. The first ship of this type – the U-2501, was launched in the 'Blohm u. Voss' shipyard on 27 June 1944 (C. Blair, *Hitler*, op. cit., p. 600).
30 Ibid., p. 1312.
31 *Meldunki*, part 2, p. 1281. In reality, the Germans planned the construction of submarines of the XXII type, with a surface displacement of 155 tons (the underwater displacement remained unknown). Nonetheless, they introduced only type XXIII vessels (234 tons of surface displacement and 258 tons of underwater displacement) and miniature submarines : the 'Seehund'and the 'Hecht' (two-man crew) and the 'Biber' and the 'Molch' (one-man crew), as well as single-person vessels with electric propulsion – the 'Marder'/'Neger' (J. Lipiński, *Druga wojna*, op. cit., pp. 422–423, 450–452, 723–724).
32 Ibid., p. 1013, 1074 (M. M. 11/43, 1/44).
33 Those fears were additionally augmented by a telegram from a representative of the Japanese Navy in Berlin, who on 1 May 1944 informed Tokyo about a breakdown of the German programme of building 'fast U-Boats' and by the testimonies of POWs, according to which the 'Walters' were to be transported to France by rail and used to fight against the invasion forces. In this situation the Allies concluded that they would have to tackle 90 German submarines, including 50 fast ones, with a 250-ton displacement and a speed of 40-50 knots (C. Blair, *Hitler*, op. cit., p. 601).
34 Ibid., p. 1281.
35 Ibid., part 1, p. 447 (M. M. 9/42). Probably the 'Graf Zeppelin' aircraft carrier.
36 Ibid., p. 20, 74, 494 (M. M. 11/41, 1/42). At the same time, according to the intelligence, work on the light cruisers made very slow progress as the shortages of rivets, armour steel and specialists persist; furthermore, air raids damaged a hall containing plate cutters and two cranes. Report M. M. 1/42 informed that an air raid destroyed one of the cruisers (struck by four bombs, including a heavy one) and, as a result, all the finishing work was totally suspended and the dismantling the ship began (ibid., p. 70). The cruisers were probably the improved 'Nürnberg' type, initially known as: M, N and R (T. Wywerka-Prekurat, *Wykaz stanu flot wojennych państw uczestniczących w drugiej wojnie światowej* (*A Survey of the State of the Naval Fleets of the Belligerents in the Second World War*) [in:] J. Lipiński, *Druga wojna*, op. cit., p. 701).
37 *Meldunki*, part 1, p. 128, 215. (M. M. 2/42, 4/42). According to the informant (Stragan 33) this could have been the heavy cruiser 'Lutzow' as indicated by the characteristic armament (a single three-gun artillery turret on the bow and stern); today, we know that at the time it was being repaired in the Kiel 'Deutsche Werk' shipyard (C. Szoszkiewicz, *Pancerniki II wojny światowej* (*Battleships during the*

Second World War), vol. 1, Warszawa 1993, p. 158).

38 Ibid., p. 337, 413 (M. M. 6/42, 8/42). According to the informant (Stragan 52) the 'Schleswig-Holstein' was damaged in Norwegian waters (a 3x9 m hole in the stern and several smaller ones).

39 Ibid., p. 70, 71 (M. M /1/42), p. 280 (M. M. 5/42).

40 Ibidem, p. 261. 'Rzeszów', also known as 'Pelikan' (no. 26), was actually only an armed auxiliary ship ('Hilfsschiffe'), while the 'Bielsko', introduced into service on 17 September 1941, was an auxiliary cruiser which, bearing the name 'Michel' and the marking 'Schiff IX 'HS 28', sank 17 Allied ships in two trips (9 March 1942–2 March 1943, 4 April–17 October 1943).

41 The 'Gneisenau' was damaged first while moored in the port of Brest (struck by five bombs) and then during the 'Cerberus' operation on 11–13 February 1942 (one mine) and docked in Kiel 'Deutsche Werke'; subsequently it was bombed by the British Air Force on 26/27 February 1942 when the front ammunition room exploded and the whole bow of the ship was destroyed. (C. Szoszkiewicz, op. cit., p. 171).

42 *Meldunki*, part 1, p. 337, 411, 413, 494 (M. M. 6/42, 8/42 and 11/42.)

43 Ibidem, part 2, p. 694. This was a 'Prinz Eugen'-type ship, although the report incorrectly classified it as a light cruiser.

44 Ibidem, p. 1188, 1312 (M. M. 3/44, 6/44). At the same time the informer noted that the counter-torpedo boats and torpedo boats built in Elbląg (in the Kriegsmarine terminology they appeared as 'Flotten-Torpedoboote') had a displacement of up to 2,000 tons and armament composed of 2–4 guns, several anti-aircraft guns and two triple torpedo launchers.

45 Ibidem, part 1, p. 447; part 2, p. 609, 825, 874, 1121, 1188, 1283 (M. M. 9/42, 2/43, 8/43, 2/44, 3/44, 5/44). The 'U-Jäger' were 830-ton ships – actually known as 'Kriegs-Ujager', escort vessels and underwater defence ships (T. Wywerka-Prekurat, op. cit., p. 726).

46 Confirming, e.g., damage incurred in the 'Deutsche Werft' and 'Blohm u. Voss' shipyards in Hamburg (October and November 1941, July 1943, 29 September 1943), in Lübeck (30 March 1942), in Flensburg and Rostock (April and May 1942, 16–17 May 1943), the 'Vulcan Werft' shipyard in Bremen-Blumenthal (20 March 1943), the Kiel shipyard (16 May 1943), and the Gdynia shipyards (October and November 1942, 9 October 1943); minimal or no damage in the Szczecin shipyards (20 April 1943) or the Kiel 'Deutsche Werke' (9–10 October 1942).

47 *Meldunki*, part 1, pp. 20-21 (M. M. 11/41).

48 Ibidem, p. 70 (M .M. 1/42).

49 AAN, KG AK, 203/II-8, Annex to the Intelligence report 'Lombard', no. 9/44, source 1. 129, of 15 March 1944.

50 See: telegram from the VI Bureau, l. dz. 2231/41 of 2 July 1941; Questions and remarks relating to Dispatch no. 41 (*Armia Krajowa w dokumentach 1939–1945* (*The Home Army in Documents 1939–1945*), vol. VI, Wrocław-Kraków 1991, p. 194).

51 AAN, call no. 203/III-5, Microfilm 2375/2.

52 *Armia Krajowa*, op. cit., p. 230 (The II Bureau of the PGS to the VI Bureau, l. dz. 3137/II Wyw./42 of 1 April 1942).

53 NARA, RG 165, MID Germany, Box 1172, The Port of Danzig, Information dated May, 1942.

54 TNA (PRO), HS 4/280, Report of 31 October 1941, Part I – Industry.

52

Air Force Intelligence: the Construction of Aeroplanes and Airfields and the Effects of Air Raids

Tadeusz Dubicki, Robert Majzner and Krzysztof Spruch

'Instruction no. 2 for Citizen Rakoń', signed on 16 January 1940 by Gen. Kazimierz Sosnkowski, Commander-in-Chief of the Union of Armed Struggle (for simplicity it will be referred to in future as the Home Army), recognised the need for regularly provided intelligence information to be the tasks of prime importance.[1] An order issued by the General Headquarters of the Home Army (l. dz. 1134/tjn.40) at the beginning of January 1940 specified both the 'principles for the organisation of intelligence service' and the scope of tasks, inter alia in the form of so-called questionnaires.[2] Those decisions – conveyed to Poland in March 1940 as 'guidelines for the organisation of homeland intelligence service'[3] – became the basis for the functioning of the II Bureau of the Home Army GHQ.

Despite the fall of France in June 1940 and temporary chaos caused by the transfer of supreme military authorities to London, work in this area became clearly accelerated, especially that in contrast to France, Great Britain displayed much greater interest in intelligence co-operation. Upon his departure for Poland on 12 October 1940 Lt-Col. Kazimierz Iranek-Osmecki received many instructions and guidelines that included detailed directives for organising intelligence of the Home Army GHQ.[4] During the talks with Lt-Col. Wacław Berka 'Brodowicz', Chief of the II Bureau of the the Home Army GHQ, and his deputy Lt-Col. Marian Drobik 'Dzięcioł', it was agreed to create an intelligence cell centrally steered by the Chief of the II Bureau of the the Home Army GHQ. Its tasks would be to conduct surveillance of the German armament industry, in accordance with the 'requirements' of the British. Furthermore, in order to make this work more systematic it was decided to establish a Studies Department which would analyse the industrial, air force and naval issues.

A planned expansion of intelligence structures and the co-operation with other clandestine organisations, in response to the request issued by the II Bureau of the Polish General Staff on 28 July 1940 (l. dz.150/A),[5] brought about three types of reports sent to London in the spring of 1941: immediate, weekly and, from October, monthly.[6] In accordance with the instructions and directives prepared with the co-operation of British Intelligence Maj. parts of those reports related to the air force,[7] providing information about the level of production, construction solutions, Luftwaffe units, airfields, anti-aircraft defence and the assessments on the air raids effects.

An analysis of the aircraft industry in the Third Reich primarily supplied extremely detailed descriptions of factories producing for the needs of the Luftwaffe. Among particularly thoroughly examined targets, a campaign which led to numerous arrests,[8] were the 'Flugzeugwerke' works in Mielec,[9] the former PZL WP 2. According to the report M. M. 11/41 the works produced 120 sets of control surfaces and cockpits for the Heinkel 111 in one month. From November 1942 (M. M.1/43) it switched almost exclusively to control surfaces, elevators and rudders for Heinkel He 177 bombers. In connection with that, the production plans for the coming year envisaged 783 sets for 'Heinkelwerke' in Oranienburg, 237 sets for the 'Arado' works, and 445 sets of tail planes, 610 sets of elevators, 420 fins and 660 rudders for Gesellschaft für Luftfahrtbedarf G.m.b.H. Nonetheless, although it was categorically stated that the production of parts for He 111 and the repair of Ju 52 had been completely halted, in June, then in July and in September 1943 it was confirmed that the factory was once again designated to conduct the final assembly of the He 111. For that purpose it went into the co-operation with the works in Budzyń and Baranów. Next, the assembly of Heinkel He 219 was begun with a monthly production of 75 planes planned for 1945.[10]

The Mielec works was of course not the only one targeted by Polish intelligence for a thorough assessment. Much attention was devoted to the Rzeszów 'Flugmotorenwerke' – the producer of parts for the Daimler Benz DB 601, 603, 605 and 608 engines (about 200 sets a month). The same held true for the Poznań-based 'Focke Wulf' works which produced fuselages, wings and control surfaces for Fw 190, with the output 10-15 sets a month. Polish intelligence did not neglect also the Warsaw 'Mechanische Werke Neubrandenburg'- formerly 'Avia' – which supplied various types of parts and equipment, like 'Antriebe 30 and 31', or the 'Schloss 50/XB' bomb launcher (monthly planned production of about 9,000). One of the targets was also Bydgoszcz 'Fema-Metallfabrik A. G.', which produced mainly precision instruments, such as air-speed indicators, compasses and remote indication compasses.[11]

Another site of interest were the 'Flugzeugwerke' works in Grudziądz, which assembled 'Focke-Wulf 58' planes (10-15 per month) and later on Messerschmitt Bf 109.[12] Much attention was paid to repair works in Okęcie which, as it was established, conducted repairs of damaged and wrecked planes (also engines). From 3 August to 4 September 1943 they repaired 13 He 111s, 16 Me 109s, 10 Me 110s, 18 Ju 88s, 19 Ju 87s, 9 Ju 52s, 14 Fw 190s, 1 Ju 86s, 10 Ar 96s and 8 'Storch' type planes, and from 27 March to 22 April 1944 39 Fw 190s, 5 Fw 189s, 38 Me 109s, 2 Me 110s, 64 He 111s,

20 Ju 52s, 67 Ju 87s, 27 Ju 88s, 2 Ju 90s, 1 Si 204, 12 Fieseler 156s, 4 Ar 232s and 4 W 34s.[13] These figures reflected increasing productivity, on one hand, and growing losses suffered by the Luftwaffe, on the other.[14]

The reports mentioned the following co-operating factories: the 'Beru Werke' works in Kielce, which produced up to 70,000 spark plugs a month, 'Neuer Kühler' in Zabłocin near Kraków (about 60 radiators a month, another 550 repaired); 'Müller and Seidel' from Łódź (approximately 230 undercarriages for 'Stuka' airplanes a month); 'Polnische Philips Werke A.G.' in Warsaw (including Polish aircraft W/T stations, type VL 27 D (100 watt) – about 60 per month); 'Filter und Mann' in Łódź (approximately 1,000 fuel tanks for Focke Wulf planes per month); 'Maschinenfabrik Hans Müller' in Zawiercie (which in June 1943 alone supplied 240 petroleum tanks and 60 oxygen container stands for Me 109 as well as 180 air flaps and four gunner cockpit for the Me 110) and 'Erge Motor' in Poznań, whose monthly production totalled 1,200–2,000 sets of control devices for Heinkel He 111.[15]

The listed factories located in the Reich included 'Flugzeugwerke' in Haganov, which reportedly produced three twin-engine planes per day;[16] 'Henschel' in Schönefeld; 'Junkers Werke' in Dessau with a weekly production of 30 Ju 88 machines;[17] 'Weser Flugzeugbau G.m.b.H. Bremen', 'Hartmann und Braun' in Frankfurt-on-the-Main, 'J. Fimak' in Finsterwalde, 'Aradowerke' in Babelsberg, 'Dornierwerke' in Wismar and Friedrichshafen, 'Mitteldeutschewerke' in Tauch near Leipzig and 'Heinkelwerke' in Rostock.

Furthermore, this information was supplemented by getting access to the original documents from 'Wirtschaftsgruppe-Luftfahrtindustrie from Reichsverband der Deutschen Luftfahrtindustrie'. On the basis of that, London was provided with figures concerning the monthly production of German aircraft concerns which, for example, in April 1942 produced a total of 1,878 machines (Arado – 118, Dornier – 280, Focke Wulf – 382, Heinkel – 214, Henschel – 138, Junkers -412, Messerschmitt – 138, others about 200), and in May 1942 1,977 planes (Arado – 105, Dornier – 242, Focke Wulf – 391, Heinkel – 262, Henschel – 291, Junkers – 401, Messerschmitt – 205, others – 180). Commenting on these figures, which were supplemented by the number of repairs (406 in March, 611 in April, and 510 in May 1942),[18] it was noted that although initially German industry experienced a general production decline, explained by the lack of specialists and delays on the part of sub-contractors, it soon revealed a 5% growth. That was visible especially in case of Heinkel (98 machines), Messerschmitt (67) and Henschel (53). At the same time, emphasis was put on achieving the most far reaching saving of materials[19] and clear symptoms of transferring production to Austria, the Protectorate and the German-occupied Poland.[20]

Analyses of the production potential of the aircraft industry in the Third Reich, sent to London, mentioned all possible symptoms of raw material shortages, mainly alloy steel, tool steel, constructional steel, chromium-vanadium steel, manganese steel, manganese-vanadium steel and carbon steel.[21]

In characterising the production of particular works[22] Home Army Intelligence frequently provided information about their location in the form of descriptions and situation sketches, as in the case of 'Weser-Flugzeugbau G.m.b.H' in Bremen, 'Focke Wulf' in Poznań, Krzesiny and Sorau, 'Henschel Flugmotorenbau' near Kassel, 'Frontrepersturbetrieb G. L. für Daimler-Benz, Reichshof' in Rzeszów, 'Wiener Neustädter Flugzeugwerke' in Wiener Neustadt, 'Arado Werke' in Babelsberg, 'Krupp Nord-Kurbelwellenwerk Glinde', 'B.M.W.' in Eisenach, 'Heinkelwerke' in Rostock, Warnemünde and Düsseldorf, 'Weser Flugzeugwerke GmBH' in Berlin-Tempelhof, 'Henschel Flugzeugwerke' in Berlin and Rengershausen, 'Avia A. G.Ó' in Prague-Letov, 'Gothaer Wagonfabrik' in Gotha and Türingen, 'Junkers' in Dessau, Magdeburg and Aschersleben, or 'Heinkel Flugzeugwerke G. m. b. H' in Mielec and Budzyń near Kraśnik.

The structures of German aircraft consortiums were additionally identified when information was sent to London that the Arado consortium was composed of works in Anklam and Tutow near Szczecin, Babelsberg near Potsdam, Brandenburg-Havel, Malchin (Mecklenburg-Schwerin), Neudorf, Rathenow and Wittenberg near Leipzig; 'Messerschmitt' had works in Augsburg, Regensburg, Gabelin and Leibahn, and 'Focke-Wulf' in Cottbus, Bremen, Sorau, Poznań, Krzesiny, Gdynia and Malbork.[23]

Since the descriptions were presumably to include all factors that could influence the effectiveness of Allied air raids, forms of masking were also described[24] as well as the anti-aircraft defence structure in, e.g. the 'Arado' works in Neudorf (six anti-aircraft guns), 'Mitteldeutsche Motoren Werke' in Tauch near Leipzig (four batteries of anti-aircraft guns and a 105 mm gun railway battery) or 'Heinkel Werke' in Rostock ('densely positioned gun batteries and anti-aircraft machine-guns well as 60 barrage balloons').[25]

An equally important task entrusted to the Home Army Intelligence was gathering information about particular aeroplane constructions. At times, London received very detailed descriptions of all the planes produced or the designs under development, e.g. the unsymmetrical, reconnaissance Blohm u. Voss BV 141,[26] Heinkel He 219 heavy fighter, equipped with six guns or four guns and four machine guns;[27] Henschel Hs 129 – twin-engine, heavily armoured and powerfully equipped attack aircraft;[28] Messerschmitt Me 210 – much swifter than the heavy fighter Me 110;[29] transport Messerschmitt Me 323 which carried 100–120 soldiers;[30] Junkers Ju 188 an advanced version of the Ju 88, with a rounded cockpit, more powerful engines and shorter wings, and armed with two 7.9 mm machine guns for the rear gunner and a single 13 mm machine gun in the upper turret, as well as its advanced version: Junkers Ju 288 fast bomber with Jumo 211/222 engines and armament in the upper 'revolving gunner turret' and two machine guns in the tail part;[31] the new six-engine Junkers;[32] three-engine transport Junkers Ju 252 (60 soldiers) and its advanced version Ju 352;[33] Heinkel He 274 – a four-engine bomber, and Heinkel He 177 twin-engine bomber with armament reinforced in January 1944 with seven 13 mm machine guns and 20 mm guns;[34] four-engine

Junkers Ju 290 with three gunners and three turrets with machine guns, produced in Dessau (3–4 machines a month);[35] fast twin-engine bomber or 'destroyer' – Arado Ar 240[36] and, in May 1944, Fw 154 (Ta 154) two-engine fighter.

Intelligence informed also about successive versions and types of machines universally used by the Luftwaffe: Messerschmitt Bf 109,[37] Junkers Ju 87,[38] Junkers Ju 88 – the night fighter version and a torpedo plane,[39] Focke Wulf Fw 190,[40] Dornier Do 17 and the Do 217 – redesigned into night fighters[41] and even Junkers Ju 52, with additionally installed bomb torque boxes or mysterious rings.[42]

The reports often mentioned technical problems with certain constructions, such as He 177, in which it was decided to conduct 35 modifications as early as November 1942, after which machine guns were replaced, four-bladed propellers were replaced with three-bladed ones, the armour of the cockpit and the main undercarriage were strengthened and so were the elevator and the ends and central part of the wings.[43] The basic weakness of Messerschmitt Bf 109 was supposed to be its considerable vulnerability to landing abeam when its narrowly spaced and too delicate undercarriage leg had broken on a number of instances and the engine together with the cradle became partially detached from the fuselage. Four accidents at the Dęblin airfield also showed that the rear part of the fuselage, some 1.5 metres from the tail, broke off together with the control surfaces![44] Other information indicated problems with particular armament systems, for example, 'Schloss 50/X B-2' bomb release gear which broke off together with the bomb during a dive![45]

Information concerning German planes was sometimes supplemented by very detailed descriptions of aircraft engines, including Daimler-Benz DB 600-610, Junkers Jumo 211 and BMW 801. Besides maintenance details, like braking reports, they also contained examples of their application in constructions,[46] as well as instruction manuals, construction drawings and diagrams of the aeroplanes.[47]

From among the reports reaching London, obviously the most essential information related to the most modern and at the same time, most secret German or even Italian constructions. Already in March 1942 the British were told that the 'Caproni' works 'supposedly' 'produced a plane without a propeller' – probably a jet aeroplane – which achieved the speed of 1,000 km/h.[48] In February 1942 intelligence reports informed about the test flights of an aeroplane with a rocket tube above the fuselage. In October 1943 an analysis of the 'Arado' production programme noted that work was being conducted on Ar 234, a rocket fighter which was supposed to reach the speed of 800 km/h, while a model with two such engines and gaining the speed of approximately 1 000 km/h, was tested at the Havel airfield.[49] A report of November 1943 informed about He 280 reactive fighter. According to the monthly report no. 2/44 which dwelt on 'unconfirmed information dated 18 January 1944', two new 'types of Messerschmitt' were tested at the beginning of December 1943 at an experimental airfield in Lechweld, 25 km to the

506 INTELLIGENCE CO-OPERATION BETWEEN POLAND AND GREAT BRITAIN

north-east of Augsburg. One was a rocket fighter with a wing span and the length of fuselage of about 6 metres and a triangular wing shape. The other was one-seat 'Turbinenjäger'. Thanks to its two turbo Jumo engines the speed of 1,000 km/h was supposedly achieved, despite unsatisfactory construction durability. In a truly spectacular operation Polish intelligence got a diagram of this engine which was sent to London in December 1943 together with report M. M. 11/43.[50]

In response to the 'requirements' expressed by London, Polish intelligence conveyed all information about the most modern equipment, for example bombing,[51] navigation or even radio location.

For example, the monthly dispatch from March 1942 included a detailed description of the so-called automatic pilot, composed of two combined radio-goniometric receivers which made it possible to obtain very precise targeting, as well as an electro-hydraulic servo-stabilizer. The report conveyed in May 1942 referred to the so-called 'Kurstenerung', an automatic pilot supposedly installed in all machines of the type Bf 110, Ju 88, Do 17, He 111 type as well as in some Ju 52 planes.[52]

On the basis of 'unconfirmed information from 25 July, from the region of Okęcie', attention was drawn to a special 'television installation for night-time combat' in the form of metal nets on outriggers, assembled in Bf 110, Do 215 and Ju 88 aeroplanes. This information was soon supplemented with the confirmation that an element of this 'installation' was a screen on which enemy presence was marked with a lit sign, and that the whole design was known as 'Würzburg-Lichtenstein'. With time, reports included a description and a diagram of the 'FuSe 62 Würzburg Dora measuring device'.[53]

One of the components of the reports sent to London was made up of the following information: the location of airfields,[54] identification of Luftwaffe units[55] and the effects of Allied air raids. The reports contained information about the considerable damage inflicted by Allied bombing to the following: 'Heinkelwerke' in Rostock on the night of 8-9 May and on 25 October 1942, the 'Focke Wulf' works in Bremen in March 1943 which caused a decline in the production to only four planes per day, and eventually a halt. The list included also 'Henschel Flugzeugbau', which was totally destroyed according to information from December 1943. Other reports mentioned unsuccessful air raids against the 'VDM' works in Hamburg or 'Mitteldeutsche Motoren Werke' in Tauch near Leipzig. In the latter case, the closest bomb dropped on 30 August 1943 landed two kilometres away.[56] At least in one instance information was forwarded concerning the bombing of an airfield in the region of Halberstadt – on 21 May 1944 a 'Mustang' came over the airstrip and set a Focke Wulf Fw 190 on fire.[57]

The usefulness of the information about aircraft factories was confirmed by Allied air raids. The examples are Malbork (bombed on 9 October 1943), Szczecin-Arnimswalde (11 April 1944), Żary (Sorau), Poznań and Krzesiny near Poznań (29 May 1944),[58] to mention only those now located within the Polish territory.

Apart from the above discussed aircraft industry intelligence whose reports were prepared by the Economic Studies Department of the II Bureau of the Home Army General Headquarters, similar work was carried out by the Air Force Intelligence Section of the Records and Studies Department of the II Bureau (headed by Maj. Władysław Prohaska 'Sojka', and from 1 April 1943 by Lt. Jan Jokiel 'Ligota'). It dealt with Air Force intelligence used for preparing monthly military reports on:

- Luftwaffe units, their commanders, composition, marking, distribution, movements, organisation, etc.,
- airfields, their equipment and buildings as well as any changes, closing down, the creation of new airfields, fuel and bomb reserves, military subordination, stationing units,
- air traffic and aeroplane markings (which facilitated the identification of its unit),
- aviation schools, their organisation, number of trainees, the mood of the air force personnel,
- the effects of Allied air raids.

In 1942 Home Army Intelligence had at its disposal more than 40 plans of airfields. In the spring of 1944 the number of listed German airfields in Polish lands exceeded 300 (each airfield was given a special number). That figure did not include those in Germany and in Soviet territories under German occupation. The average monthly number of military reports in the first half of 1944 exceeded 40.[59]

Within the co-operation with British special services, established in 1940, Home Army offensive Intelligence cells organised an extremely efficient Air Force intelligence network which worked exclusively for the needs of the British. It collected and subsequently forwarded to London a lot of materials concerning the aircraft industry in the Third Reich, including its structure, location of factories and production potential. It also characterised in detail particular aviation constructions. Thanks to the commitment of many people it was possible to obtain information which not only facilitated air raids against German weapons factories but also contributed to learning such secrets as the construction of Me 163 'Komet', Me 262 'Schwalbe' and Ar 234, as well as combat and radio location equipment, and also the location of airports, and the identification of certain Luftwaffe units, a task for which British Intelligence frequently expressed its appreciation.[60]

Notes

1   *Armia Krajowa w dokumentach 1939–1945* (*The Home Army in Documents*) (further as: *Armia Krajowa*), vol. 1, London 1970, p. 75.
2   Ibid, vol. 6, pp. 118-120.
3   *Polskie Siły Zbrojne*, vol. 3, *Armia Krajowa* (*Home Army*), London 1950, p. 298.
4   Including 'Instruction no. 5 for Citizen Rakoń'.
5   In the order 'Godziemba' instructed 'Rakoń': 'The situational-intelligence cables are to be sent by radio once a week. The urgent ones are to be sent immediately' (*Armia Krajowa*, vol. 1, p. 273) . The instruction of 4 January 1941 (l. dz. 1309/40) obligated 'Rakoń' to send a radio cable at least once a week and a written report

– once a month (ibid., p. 445.)

6 A. Pepłoński, *Wywiad Polskich Sił Zbrojnych na Zachodzie 1939–1945* (*The Intelligence Service of the Polish Armed Forces in the West 1939–1945*), Warszawa 1995, p. 303; *Wywiad lotniczy Oddziału II KG ZWZ-AK* (*The Air Force Intelligence of the II Bureau of the Home Army GHQ*) [in:] H. Szołdrska, *Lotnictwo Armii Krajowej* (*The Air Force of the Home Army*) , Poznań 1998, pp. 175–198.

7 The order of 28 July 1940 (l. dz.150/A) indicated as 'priority tasks' the air force Order of Battle and 'war industry, armament, bases and the air force'. (*Armia Krajowa*, vol. 1, p. 273).

8 Monthly report no. 2/43 stated that 'owing to numerous arrests in the works and in town current information has not been received in the reporting period'. This situation must have lasted more or less until April 1943, since the report from May mentions that 'only loose information had been received from the factory', while the report for June 1943 described the production in great detail.

9 Especially that – as Col. Smoleński mentioned in his report l. dz. 2964/tjn./41 of 10 September 1941 – the British Intelligence Service inquired about the 'sort of planes that the parts produced by Mielec are intended for' (*Armia Krajowa*, vol. 2, London 1973, p. 59)

10 *Meldunki miesięczne wywiadu przemysłowego KG ZWZ/AK 1941–1944. Faksymile* (*Monthly Reports of the Industrial Intelligence of the Home Army GHQ 1941–1944. Facsimiles*, further as: *Meldunki*), prepared for publication by A. Glass, part 1, Warszawa 2000, p. 22; part 2, Warszawa 2000, p. 546, 817, 1007.

11 Ibid., part 2, p. 548, 549, 645, 691, 733, 774, 1117, 1118.

12 Ibid., part 1, p. 42, 277. The assembly of Bf 109 was mentioned first in a report from May 1942.

13 Ibid., part 2, p. 911, 1277. In the report the marking of 'Fieseler 186', which, by the way, never existed, was mistakenly ascribed to the popular 'Storch'.

14 Reports from January 1942 claimed that about 400 damaged planes were in specially built halls in the Henschel works (ibid., part 1, p.72).

15 Ibid., part 1, p. 22, 488; vol. 2, p. 603, 604, 871, 912, 1118.

16 Ibid., part 2, p. 1072.

17 Ibid., part 1, p. 389.

18 Such information was highly appreciated by the British; in a telegram of 19 October 1942 (l. dz. 4369/42) 'Rawa' sent 'Kalina' a translation of the evaluation made by the British Air Ministry concerning the list of planes repaired in the Junkers workshops (M. M. 7/42). The following statement was included : 'We consider the two reports as the most valuable among those recently received. They are extremely precise and contain new information worthy of further studies. Congratulations [...] We would be grateful if you could convey to the authors of the reports our appreciation and gratitude for providing such useful information' (*Armia Krajowa*, vol. 6, Wrocław-Kraków 1991, p. 263.)

19 For example, Dornier, Junkers and Heinkel were to apply a single layer of external protective paint.

20 *Meldunki*, part 1, p. 353, 405, 408, 435 (M. M. 5/42, 8/42, 9/42)

21 Ibid., part 2, p. 547, 600, 910. A 'list of missing materials for the production of He 177' was sent to London as the annex to the report M. M. 4/43.

22 Supplemented in the form of annexes to reports, such as 'the production programme and the producers of Fw 190' (M. M. 10/43), 'the production programme of He 177 and He 219' (M. M. 2/44), or 'a list of various types of the He 111 as well as produced planes' (M. M. 1/44).

23 Report no. 2/44 informed that Messerschmitt works are located also in Horthy Liget (Csepel) near Budapest (*Meldunki*, part 2, p. 646, 773, 1009, 1119.).

24 For example, roofs painted green and dense bushes around factory halls.

25 *Meldunki*, part 2, p. 603.

26 *Meldunki*, part 1, p. 352. According to the report, which claimed that the tests failed, the plane was never produced and was replaced by Focke Wulf Fw 189 – the so-called 'Fliegende Auge'.

27 Ibid., part 2, pp. 1010–1011, 1186.

28 Those three various types of weapons were: two machine guns and two guns; four machine guns and two guns as well as two machine guns and three guns – including a larger calibre one installed below the fuselage. All directed to the front, and a maximum of six bombs 25 kg each (ibid., p. 549). In reality, the bomb load reached a maximum of 250 kg and the gun below the fuselage could be a 37 mm calibre (version B2/R3), 50 mm, or even 75 mm calibre (B-3), which was the reason why it was named 'Buchsenoffner' (M. Murawski, *Samoloty Luftwaffe 1933–1945* (*Luftwaffe Aeroplanes 1933–1945*), vol. 2, Warszawa 1999, pp. 80–84.)

29 *Meldunki*, part 2, p. 604, 912. The information referred to armament composed of four guns in nose of the fuselage, two guns of the gunner (observer) and 250-300 kg of bombs. In reality, they achieved a maximum speed almost identical as Me 110 (563 km/h), but carried not 300 kg but a maximum of 1,000 kg of bombs and their standard equipment included two 20 mm guns and two 7.92 mm machine guns in the nose of the fuselage, and two 13 mm machine guns along the side of the fuselage in the FDL 131 remote control posts (M. Murawski, *Samoloty*, op. cit., pp. 212–217.).

30 *Meldunki*, part 2, p. 604. Actually, this was not 'Gigantik' but 'Giant'. M. M. 8/43 described the D-1 version (factory no. 323-1220) and the DT-IT registration, repaired in Luftwaffe workshops in Lwów (ibid., p. 872.). In reality, it could carry as many as 130 equipped soldiers or a FLAK 36 gun with a tractor, or a lorry with a trailer, or 52 250-litre barrels of fuel (M. Murawski, *Samoloty*, op. cit., pp. 238-242.)

31 *Meldunki*, part 2, p. 604, 1058, 1120. However, Ju 288 never went beyond the stage of a prototype.

32 Ibid., p. 604. Most likely, the information referred to the strategic bomber Ju 390, of which there were only two prototypes (M. Murawski, *Samoloty*, op. cit., pp. 153-154).

33 *Meldunki*, part 2, p .735, 1240.

34 Ibid., p. 822, 871, 1011, 1120. Information about He 274 comes from M.M. 11/43 although the plane was not tested until 1945. The version of the 'Greif' with the best armament (A6/R2) was equipped with a total of ten machine guns and guns. M.M. 1/43 warned that a 'high-altitude bomber' was under development (A7), but only six planes were built (M. Murawski, *Samoloty*, op. cit., pp. 50–55.). ZWZ-AK intelligence informed London that 'there has been no information that would allow to assume that He 177 is designed as a stratospheric aeroplane' (*Meldunki*, part 2, p. 547).

35 *Meldunki*, part 2, p. 1389. Despite the fact that a bomb version had been designed they were mainly used as reconnaissance (transport and naval) planes because they were capable of reaching Manchuria in a non-stop flight from Mielec or Odessa (M. Murawski, *Samoloty*, op. cit., pp. 145–147).

36 *Meldunki*, part 2, p. 961.

37 Its new version was 'Gustaw' – G2.

38 At first it was said that its new variant – observed on 9 March 1943 in Okęcie – was equipped with two 'small-calibre guns with long barrels, placed in a special casing underneath the wings'. Then, in a correction it was said that the 20 mm. guns were built inside the wings (ibid., p. 692, 912). Meanwhile, these were simply two different versions: first G1 – armed with a special 37 mm gun which, as was rightly noted, was used for combating tanks (the so-called 'Panzerknalker'), and then D5 (M. Murawski, *Samoloty*, op. cit., pp. 108–117).

39 *Meldunki*, part 2, p. 872, 1241.

40 Ibid., s. 1279. The armament was supposed to be composed of four 20 mm guns in the wings and two machine guns shooting through the propeller. On the other hand, aeroplanes operating in the east were adapted to carry two 250 kg bombs. In other words, the described plane was the 'F' combat version.

41 Ibid., p. 1120.

42 Ibid., s. 735, 775. Three such 'torque boxes' were installed in 15 Ju 52s between 11 and 17 April 1943. As suspected, each one was used for carrying small (possibly gas) bombs or a single bomb with a circumference of 40 cm, or for dropping 'supply containers'. The mysterious rings observed on 24 and 29 May 1943 in the area of Lwów, which were thought to be an element of a radio equipment, in reality were used for destroying mines with a strong radio-magnetic field produced by a 150 KW generator, with the current passing through the ring, or simply a coil (M. Murawski, *Samoloty*, op. cit., vol. 2, p. 94).

43 *Meldunki*, part 2, p. 547. He 177 'Greif' aeroplanes were of dangerous repute in the Luftwaffe as the so-called 'Luftwaffenfeuerzeug' (M. Murawski, *Samoloty*, op. cit., p. 50).

44 *Meldunki*, part 2, p. 648. According to the author of the report this 'fault' was to occur in the 'Emil' version, while problems with the excessively weak undercarriage appeared among all 109 models; while the tail broke off only in the 'Friedrich' version (M. Murawski, *Samoloty*, op. cit., p. 173–174).

45 *Meldunki*, part 2, p. 645. An annex to report M.M. 5/43 sent to London contained the original technical documentation of this bomb lock.

46 *Meldunki*, part 2, pp. 600–603, 1009.

47 London was supplied, among others, with instruction manuals for Ju 88 A-4 (M.M. 2/43) and Ju 88 D-1 (M. M. 10/43); plans for loading Bf 109 G-2 (M. M. 2/43) and Bf 110 G-3 (M. M. 1/44); diagrams of oxygen installations in He 177 (M. M. 7/43) and the fuel installation in Fw 190 (M. M. 9/43); photographs of Me 323 (M. M. 11/43); drawings of Ar 232 (M. M. 8/43, 11/43), Si 204 (M. M. 9/43), He 219 (M. M. 11/43), Ju 188 F-1 (M. M. 1/44); an extract from the factory manual of He 177 A-1 (M. M. 11/43); characteristics of the engines of DB 605 AS and BMW 801 (M. M. 11/43); the deck chart of Bf 110 G-2 (M. M. 2/44); the armament manual for Me 410 (M. M. 2/44); the fuel installation instruction for He 111 H-20 (M. M. 4/44), and the original full version of 'Flugzeug-Handbuch Ju 87 D-1 trop, teil 12c, Sonderwaffenanlage' of July 1942 (M.M. 10/43) and 'Vorlaufige Fluggenehmigung Fw 190 A-5' (M. M. 10/43).

48 *Meldunki*, part 1, p. 161. In reality, the 'Caproni-Campini N.1 (C. C . 2)' was a jet aeroplane, besides all tests with this construction (inaugurated on 27 August 1940) were stopped as early as August 1942. It was considered as 'not promising' (for example, the maximum speed was barely 360 km/h), (W. Bączkowski, *Włoskie samoloty wojskowe 1936–1945 (Italian Military Aeroplanes 1936–1945)*, Warszawa 1999, pp. 75–76).

49 *Meldunki*, part 2, p. 605 and 960. Do 217E with a ramjet engine was an aeroplane with 'a rocket tube'. Actually, Ar 234 was not a fighter but a reconnaissance bomber equipped with two jet engines thanks to which it reached 820 km/h during test flights, the first of which took place on 30 July 1943 (M. Murawski, *Samoloty* , op. cit., vol. 1, pp. 33–39).

50 *Meldunki*, part 2, p. 1119. In reality, these were prototypes: Me 163 'Komet', in which the pilot Heini Dittmar achieved the speed of 1004 km/h on 2 October 1941, and Me 262 'Schwalbe', which reached the speed of 800 km/h (M. Murawski, *Samoloty*, op. cit., vol. 2, pp. 203–204, 219–220).

51 Information was provided about the production of bombs for 'Henschel Gerät 293' and 'Henschel Gerät 294', described as 'sea torpedoes'. The production was begun in the 'Huta Bankowa' works (Dąbrowa Górnicza). Further information referred to 'Presswerk Labend' (Łabędy) near Gliwice which produced eight bombs weighing

1,800 kg each and the planned serial production (*Meldunki*, part 1, p. 271, 439, 487).
52 Ibid., p. 184, 276.
53 Ibid., part 2, p. 872, 1186, 962.
54 Apart from airfields located near industrial works or experimental airfields, such as Lechfeld or Peenemünde, new airfields were built in Baranowicze, Kołomyja and Rumia near Gdynia (*Meldukni* 2/44).
55 Part of this assignment involved sending to London an annex (to M.M. 2/44) with a table containing a hundred emblems of German aeroplanes, describing their colour, and informing about the place and time of spotting as well as the type of plane.
56 *Meldunki*, part 1, p. 352, 492; part 2, p. 603, 691, 912, 959, 1008, 1071.
57 Ibid., part 2, p. 1390.
58 PRO: Air Photo-Reconnaissance Reports, AIR: 40/462. 40/630,40/639, concerning the bombing of K 1776, K 2011, K 2293, K 2298, K 2514, K 2893.
59 AWIH, Meldunki wywiadowcze Oddziału II KG AK 1944 (Intelligence reports of the II Bureau of the Home Army GHQ in 1944) – call no. III/22/97.
60 This fact was also confirmed by a telegram sent by the Second Department of the Polish General Staff on 1 April 1942 (l. dz. 3137/II Wyw./42) to the VI Bureau. It mentioned that the British Staff wished to 'express [...] profound appreciation for the extraordinarily valuable work of the VI Bureau which won due admiration and the whole-hearted recognition of all the Departments' for supplying in 1941 'a certain number of first-rate reports containing [...] military, political, industrial and naval information' (*Armia Krajowa*, vol. 6, p. 230). In turn, a telegram sent by Col. Protasewicz to 'Kalina' on 5 August 1942 (l. dz. 3139/42), containing an evaluation passed by Secret Intelligent Service of the reports provided by Home Army intelligence during the first six months of 1942, reads : 'Polish Intelligence constitutes, as a rule, one of the best sources of information. It is undoubtedly fully appreciated by our authorities' (ibid., vol. 2, p. 294.).

53
Home Army Industrial and Economic Intelligence

Andrzej Glass

I. General characteristics of accomplishments

The powers engaged in the Second World War appreciated the role of information about the economic situation of the adversaries, their industrial production, technological progress and infrastructure. Apart from classical military intelligence the Home Army also conducted economic, industrial and technical intelligence.

The territorial range of this activity can be delineated quite well on the basis of a preserved set of monthly reports that the Home Army GHQ sent to London from October 1941 to July 1944.[1] Almost half of the information pertained to Polish lands together with Silesia, the Poznań region and Pomerania; the rest concerned Germany.[2]

Domains of intelligence

Since the whole economy of the Third Reich and the occupied countries worked to support the war effort, the industrial-economic reports encompassed weapons production, the chemical and power industry, the textile industry and agriculture. The intelligence reports included the following topics:

- metallurgical-mechanical (metal) production, arms and ammunition production as well as production for the needs of transport, including the railway;
- the production of explosives;
- the aircraft industry;
- the production of armour;
- the shipbuilding industry;
- the chemical and artificial fuel industry;
- the petroleum industry;
- the energy industry and the grid;
- the textile industry;
- agriculture;

- the communication infrastructure (the railway network, land and water routes), communication difficulties;
- industry organisation and finances;
- labour, employment, the demand for labour force;
- raw material shortages and scarcity of provisions.

As the war progressed the priorities of British Intelligence changed; hence in different periods there were requests for emphasising various domains of industry and economy. By way of example, increasing fuel problems in the German army stimulated interest in the production of petroleum, artificial fuel and electrical power. The positive effects of damage inflicted to German railway communication by Allied air raids increased interest in the production of steam locomotives.

Some of the trends of the gathered information indicate that the British wanted to obtain them for the Soviet Union. They wanted plans of the ports in Odessa and Mikolayev, the plans of Brześć-on-the-Bug or Smolensk, and partially of Königsberg, as well as railway, land and water routes or the power grid on Polish territories.

Types of information obtained

The reports devote greatest attention to industrial information describing:
1. industrial works, and in particular their:
   - location (information about sites, situation maps, distribution of buildings, their use, the positions of anti-aircraft defence);
   - production (goods, quantity of production, production plans, employment, suppliers and recipients);
2. construction of military equipment, armaments and means of transport (construction drawings or schemes of construction designs);
3. technical descriptions and military equipment instruction manuals;
4. summary specifications of production plans and production output;
5. organisation of the German war industry.

Reports covering the years in question contain information about several thousand industrial works and their production. The annexes include plans of about 140 war industry plants and drawings of approximately a hundred examples of military equipment; occasionally one product was depicted on more than ten drawings.

Usefulness of industrial-economic and technical intelligence information

Industrial, economic and technical reports made it possible to:
1. assess the situation of the war economy of the Third Reich, shortages and difficulties;
2. evaluate the production potential of the German war industry (aircraft, shipbuilding, armoured vehicles, ammunition and armament) – both as a whole and divided into particular domains and products;

3. learning the trends of the technological development of German armament and its new types and varieties;
4. use information about industrial plants to select air raid targets,
5. estimate the effects of air raids.

All these aspects were important for the Allies in the war against the Germans. It was the great accomplishment of Polish Intelligence to provide a wide spectrum of information which made it possible to evaluate the economic situation both in particular domains of the war economy and the economy as a whole.

II. Main achievements of Home Army industrial intelligence

The survey presented below does not include the achievements concerning the aircraft, rocket and shipbuilding industry as well as aircraft, rocket and naval technology – all are discussed in separate chapters.

The most spectacular are the successes of industrial intelligence concerning new types of weapons and constructions. Nonetheless, the main achievement of Polish Intelligence was to submit information, as complete as possible, about the potential of particular branches of the industry, current and planned production as well as emerging difficulties and shortages. Intelligence about production plants representing particular branches of industry and their production constituted a valuable guide for selecting air raid targets.

Home Army industrial intelligence worked predominantly on the Polish territory (Generalgouvernement, Silesia, the Poznań region and Pomerania), and subsequently in areas bordering with Poland (German Upper and Lower Silesia and the Czech Silesia). The other area of intelligence operation was the Third Reich. Much information came from Wrocław, and slightly less from Königsberg and Szczecin. There was a lot of information relating to the industry further inland coming from Berlin, Brandenburg, Schleswig-Holstein, Rostock, Köln, Lübeck, Bremen, Hamburg, Hanover, Duisburg, Eisenach, Frankfurt-on-the-Main, Munich, as well as Vienna, Vienna-Neustadt and Linz.

Thanks to the Home Army Intelligence agents and information obtained from Polish workers taken to the Reich for compulsory labour in works, it was possible to collect a lot of information about the German arms industry.

Technical intelligence

Apart from the information about the V weapons, planes and ships, discussed in this book, the most valuable achievements of technical intelligence included information concerning:

- the construction of artillery and anti-aircraft missiles;[3]
- the construction and types of bombs;
- the construction of tank units;
- the Fu Se 62 Würzburg Dora radar;[4]

- the documentation of R50 steam locomotive (renamed R52);[5]
- the composition of missile steel;
- types of radio lamps produced.

As an example, from among the intelligence information about armaments one can mention the technical documentation of the artillery missiles calibre 20 mm, 30 mm, 75 mm, 88 mm, F 88 mm, B1 105 mm, G1 105 mm, C1 150 mm, E1 150 mm, and H1 150 mm,[6] as well as the Minengranat 75 mm with pockets, the Sprenggranate DOK 21 cm,[7] the Panzerfaust 2, steering nose of the aerial torpedo,[8] the LFH Pz2 and Panther tank hulls,[9] and the armoured anti-aircraft defence carriage.[10]

Particular branches of industry

The armament and ammunition industry, including the metallurgical-mechanical industry

The production of weapons, ammunition and bombs was based on the output of steel plants, rolling mills and mechanical works. During the Second World War many steel plants produced armaments, ammunition and bombs, although regular production of weapons was simultaneously carried out by specialised factories.

Home Army intelligence described the following steel mills and armament works as well as their production on Polish territories: Stalowa Wola, Skarżysko-Kamienna, the Ostrowiec Works, Steyr (FK) Warsaw, Steyr (PWU) Radom, and Cegielski-Poznań; Silesian steel mills included: Baildon, Bankowa, Batory (Bismarckhutte), Hubertus (Łagiewniki), Hulczyński (Sosnowiec), Pokój, Zgoda (Świętochłowice) Hahn (Oderberg-Bogumin), Oberhutten (Gliwice), and Renard. In Czech Silesia the following works were examined Trzyniec and Witkowitzer Bergbau u. Hutten (Morawska Ostrava), while in the Reich they were: Steyr (Steyr), Hirtenberg, Krupp (Essen and Glinde near Hamburg), Höhenschöping near Berlin, Chemnitz, Salzgitter, Liezen, Kopfenberg, and others.

The following ammunition works were described: Starachowice, Hasag-Skarżysko Kamienna, Hasag Kielce, Schneider (Łódź), Zellgarn (Łódź), Luftmuna-Osowa Góra (near Bydgoszcz), Muna-Werke Krapitz (near Strzelęc), Schneider-Lipsk, Muna-Moditten, Muna-Moldenau, Muna-Ludwigsort, Marianfelde (near Berlin), DAG Krummel and Düneberg (near Hamburg), Hannover, Westhausen, and Torgelow near Jatznick.

The armour industry

Home Army Intelligence informed about the following armour industry works: Wawerma Ursus (Warsaw) and steels mills: Bankowa, Batory, Laura, Pokój, Famo-Wrocław, Linkę Hoffmann-Wrocław, Schichau-Elbląg, Alkett-Borsigwalde near Berlin, Maybach-Berlin, Niderschönefelde-Berlin, Zwickau, Miag-Brandenburg, Henschel-Kassel, Hannover, Hermann-Göring Werke-Linz and other plants, a well as enterprises producing Panther tanks.

The synthetic petrol industry

Apart from descriptions of the petroleum industry in Little Poland (Drohobycz and Borysław) and the Sub-Carpathian region (Limanowa), much information was obtained about synthetic petrol production plants (including maps of their location and buildings): IG Farben-Dwory near Oświęcim, Blechhammer, Reigersfeid-Heyderbreck, Oderthal, Matildenhöhe-Waldenburg, Failhammer-Waldenburg, Freiberg, Ditterbach, Altwasser, Pölitz-Stettin, Odermunde-Stettin, Forst near Cottbus, Espenheim near Leipzig, Tauchen near Leipzig, Leunawerke Düsseldorf, Wesselink near Bonn, Gelsenkirchen, Brabag-Ruhland, Heimstadt, Theigen near Zeitz, Zeitz and Ferse (Saxony), Ehrenforst, Holtau near Oberhausen, Brux, Hirschfelde, Huls near Krefeld, Altenburg (Thuringia), Ehingen near Ulm, and others.

The above-mentioned works representing three branches of the war industry exemplify the amplitude of intelligence material and its range. No mention is made of other branches of the industry, such as electro-technical, radio and optical production, etc., as well as agriculture, since an excess of information and names would distort a general picture. There was no lack of valuable information in those domains, either, such as the information about the main producer of submarine batteries in Hannover-Stöcken.

An holistic look at particular domains.

Intelligence materials contained plenty of information offering a holistic view of particular domains of the industry, production or the economy, such as:

- a list of works participating in the production of submarines (MM 11/41);
- a list of iron and steel industry works in Upper Silesia (MM 11/42);
- a list of works producing train engines, together with their production plans (the whole of Germany) (MM 11/42);
- a list of works co-operating in the production of train engines (the whole of Germany) (MM 11/42);
- a map of industrial works in Upper Silesia (MM 1/43);
- a list of iron and steel industry works in the Reich (MM 1/44);
- production in the Little Poland (Małopolska region) crude oil basin (since 1941);
- a list of armament enterprises in the Generalgouvernement (MM 2/42);
- a list of the Hermann Göring Werke steel mills in the Reich and occupied countries (MM 2/42);
- a list of factories in the Generalgouvernement working for the armour and aircraft industries (MM 3/44);
- a programme of the R50/R52 railway engine production.

Evaluation of the material

The most accurate evaluation could be performed by the recipients of the reports. It is known from the wartime information that about three-fourths of the materials received was actually used, and it was assessed as very valuable. How the information was used can be additionally seen by comparing the dates of receiving the information about particular industrial sites and the dates of Allied bombing. For example, the factories producing synthetic fuel in Police near Szczecin and in Silesia as well as the chemical works in Dwory-Oświęcim were bombed after maps of the sites and buildings were provided.

Notes

1 *Meldunki miesięczne wywiadu przemysłowego KG ZWZ/AK 1941–1944. Faksymile* (*Monthly Reports of the Home Army GHQ Industrial Intelligence 1941–1944. Facsimiles*), part 1-2, prep. for publication by A. Glass, Warszawa 2000. The reports total 2,800 pages of typescript and drawings.
2 Ibid., p. X.
3 Ibid., e.g. reports MM 1/42 W 7/42.
4 Ibid., report MM 4/44.
5 Ibid., reports MM 1/43 W 5/43.
6 Ibid., reports MM1/42 – 4/42.
7 Ibid., reports MM 5/43, 9/43, 1/44.
8 Ibid., reports MM 4/44, 5/44.
9 Ibid., reports MM 7/43,1/44.
10 Ibid., report MM 6/43.

54
Lt-Col. Jan Kowalewski's Mission in Portugal

Jan Stanisław Ciechanowski

Col. Jan Kowalewski was an outstanding Polish Intelligence Officer during the Second World War. Between 1928–1933 he was the Polish military attaché in Moscow, and from 1933 to 1937 in Bucharest. In September he was Director of the state-owned 'Tissa' enterprise which purchased strategic raw materials[1] for the Polish armaments industry, and which was linked to the II Bureau of the Polish General Staff. He was evacuated to Romania, and after the fall of France managed to reach Portugal, where he became a member of a committee dealing with refugees, at first in Figueira da Foz and later in Lisbon.[2]

On his arrival in the Portuguese capital, he reported to the Polish Legation. His first outside contact was with his old acquaintance, Jean (Ioan) Pangal, the Romanian Envoy, 'always full of great political plans',[3] who had the financial means and the contacts to pursue his principal objective: to persuade Romania, Hungary and Italy to join the Allies. The Romanian diplomat managed to persuade the Polish officer to stay in Lisbon; this was approved by Gen. Władysław Sikorski. On 15th January 1941 Kowalewski was appointed the Polish Interior Ministry's 'correspondent' and chief of a subordinate Lisbon 'Cell for Communications with the Continent and Continental Intelligence',[4] a part of the so-called Continental Action. The idea behind this was developed by Prof. Stanisław Kot, and Kowalewski had a significant impact on its final shape, having written (in November 1940) an aide-mémoire on the need to organise resistance against German political and military domination. In the Balkans General Sikorski incorporated some of Kowalewski's thoughts into his plan, presented to Prime Minister Winston Churchill. After some further debate, a project was worked out chiefly by Jan Librach, Secretary to the Polish Embassy in Paris, under the name 'Continental Action'. In November 1940 the Interior Ministry was asked to take charge of it.[5]

Kowalewski suggested that the 'centre of action' of the Continental Action be placed in Lisbon. Its various elements came together in the villa

'Ginalda', in Monte Estoril outside Lisbon, where Kowalewski, codename 'Piotr' and later 'Nart', had his radio communications equipment. All the communications linked to the work carried out by the Polish Interior Ministry (in co-ordination with the British Ministry of Economic Warfare) on the territories occupied by the Germans were in Kowalewski's hands. Kowalewski was first asked to establish contact with the Polish resistance in France, and did so, both with France and with Poland. Lisbon became an important link between London and France, used for the transit of people, technical resources and funds.[6] Within the Polish-British agreement, Kowalewski was also asked to observe political developments within the Axis powers in Europe and to conduct political diversion among German satellite countries. Kowalewski supplied information from France, obtained from new arrivals from there, and later also military information. This raised the standing of the Polish Interior Ministry and of its Lisbon post with the British. In addition Kowalewski prepared reviews of the press from occupied countries and from Portugal for his Ministry.[7]

From May 1941, Kowalewski maintained regular working contacts with the British, who valued the information he obtained. In early 1941, for example, he managed to lead British Intelligence to the secret German radio station, located between Cascais and Cabo Raso, probably used to maintain contact with German U-boats.[8] 'Piotr' very quickly established extensive political contacts in Lisbon, 'which was a very busy transit point into Europe'. Thanks to good organisation of work and the variety of material obtained mainly from foreign sources, he provided a good information service. His cell was designed to be 'a distant aerial for maintaining political contacts'. Kowalewski, 'despite his unusual discretion, was an extremely important political agent, also in the eyes of the British'. Brig. Colin McVean Gubbins of SOE agreed with Jan Librach that 'there is nobody else in place on the spot, who could use the skills and political activity of Piotr for the benefit of the British'.[9] In the assessment of the American Intelligence, the Polish intelligence missions in Portugal (those of the II Bureau and of the Continental Action) were 'probably the best offensive intelligence system in Lisbon'. A representative of the American Intelligence stressed that the Chiefs of both Polish cells, that is Kowalewski for the Interior Ministry and Lt-Col. Stanisław Kara for the II Bureau, were 'extremely able men'.[10]

Kowalewski needed to create a cover for his activities, which would stand up to German scrutiny. In a city as small as Lisbon, where the Germans had a significant presence, and where the so-called international police (PVDE) was well informed about the foreigners, this was no simple task. He constructed an elaborate, four-fold camouflage system consisting of extensive political contacts, an official press-cuttings service, a foreign trade enterprise and a fishing boat. The fishing boat, unfortunately, was soon destroyed by a cyclone in the port of Cascais and a 'normal' boat took its place. Kowalewski also had four secret hide-outs,[11] the most important being the villa in Monte Estoril. This was used for meeting his various contacts from the satellite countries of the Axis powers. In time, this was to be his main political task. Kowalewski himself, with his wife and daughter, resided in a small hotel in central Lisbon.

Col. Kowalewski's idée fixe was to pull Italy, Hungary, Romania, Bulgaria and Finland away from Germany. He attempted to do this by showing their representatives various ways in which their countries might join the other side, and by building up their scepticism as to the possibility of the final victory by the Third Reich.[12] The careful manoeuvrings of the Polish officer, supported by the Polish authorities in London, began in the winter of 1940/41. This is when Kowalewski presented himself as a possible honest broker. The Hungarians responded positively. The Hungarian envoy in Lisbon, Andor Wodianer de Maglód, a close friend of Pangal's, was not in favour of his country's alliance with the Germans. To begin with, the Hungarian diplomat was very cautious, though this changed following Kowalewski's letter to Prime Minister Bárdossy. The Hungarian politician reacted favourably and asked Wodianer to continue the contact, considering it potentially valuable for the future. As for the Romanians, in his reports to his government, Pangal expressed such an enthusiasm for the idea of Romania skilfully leaving the Axis orbit (the fact that Kowalewski was respected in Romania helped), that Marshal Ion Antonescu recalled him as ambassador. The first conversations with the Italian ambassador, Renato Bova Scoppa, who did not believe in German victory, also went well. Kowalewski established contact with the Italian in early June 1941, thanks to Pangal.[13] Kowalewski's tactic was to reach the key political figures in Italy, Hungary and Romania, to prepare the ground for the future exchange of alliances. The Italians, at least, needed no explanation as to the wisdom of such a manoeuvre, used by them in the First World War. Defeatism and pro-Allied propaganda, combined with encouraging some military circles to prepare themselves for taking over the responsibility for their countries when the time was right, were the main arguments.

Until the first German military defeats in 1942, Kowalewski was working on building up his contacts and on gentle probing. Early results were not expected, especially in view of the Wehrmacht's successes to that point, and since Romania and Hungary joined the war against the USSR, though not enthusiastically. Since the first contacts brought some positive results, at the beginning of 1943 the Polish authorities in London decided to provide Kowalewski with written instructions to continue, as part of Operation 'Trójnóg' (Tripod), aimed at concentrating their efforts on Hungary, Italy and Romania.[14] Most such contacts were maintained through high-ranking couriers from these countries, who had direct or indirect conversations with Kowalewski in Lisbon. In addition the Polish officer was sometimes informed, mainly by Hungarian or Romanian diplomats, of details of some German military plans.

Kowalewski also attempted to run a 'negative action' against the Germans. As it was not possible to persuade the three German satellites to withdraw completely and immediately from the war, the idea was to reduce their participation to a minimum. The condition was that they did not participate in any crimes against humanity, first of all in the mass extermination of the Jews. Attempts were also made to persuade them not to fight on the Eastern Front, to cease supplying the Germans and to aid allied refugees and officials in Hungary, Italy and Romania.

The next step was 'positive action', an attempt to persuade these countries to switch sides. This became impossible when at their meeting in Casablanca in January 1943, Churchill and Roosevelt demanded the 'unconditional surrender' of the Axis powers, and even more so following the Tehran conference, which decided, that all of central and eastern Europe was to find itself within the Soviet sphere of influence. But Kowalewski was not aware of the Tehran decisions, and continued with his far-reaching plans.[15] He was trying to steer information, so that the Allies would arrive at what he considered to be the best decision – to open a second front in the Balkans. He thought that this might allow the Hungarian and Romanian armies to attack the Germans at the side of the Western Allies. At the same time it would have prevented the Soviet occupation of these countries, which was considered to be the biggest threat.[16]

Thanks to the Colonel, it was quickly realised that the Italians were nervously looking for a compromise with the Allies.[17] But the British side did not allow the Poles as much freedom of manoeuvre with the Italians, as with the Romanians and Hungarians.[18] This precluded any independent Polish initiatives and required Polish diplomacy to attempt to soften the impression, created by a Polish officer conducting serious negotiations with the Italians. This is why Kowalewski's efforts were supported by Count Jan Szembek, the former Polish envoy in Budapest and Bucharest and a former Deputy Foreign Minister. Szembek resided in Estoril[19] outside Lisbon, where he conducted his activities. In January 1942 he established contact with the Polish Foreign Minister Count Edward Raczyński, and informed him of the possibility of conducting observation from Lisbon, as 'a window on the world'.[20] From May, Szembek begun to provide his interesting reports. The Polish Minister informed his British colleague, Anthony Eden, that the Italians, Hungarians and Romanians might be thinking of switching sides, and that such indications had been received by the Poles in Portugal. The British government was not prepared to continue such contacts. Asked to do so by the British, Raczyński had to order that such contacts, especially with the Italians, were to be reduced. Later, the Polish Foreign Minister discovered, that in general Stalin 'was against any such talks' with these three countries.[21]

In terms of Kowalewski's activities, the Italians were the most important of the three potential partners.[22] Were this strongest European ally of the Third Reich to withdraw from the war, this would have opened the road to the heart of the continent for the Allies.[23] The Polish officer decided to seek contact with a large group of important Italians who were against Il Duce's co-operation with Hitler. In Italy, this group was led by Dino Grandi, the former Foreign Minister and ambassador to London. Grandi was in touch with a number of Italian generals, who were waiting for some encouragement from the Allies. The fact that the Italians were not doing well militarily was also an important factor. They also hoped that there might be peace between the Germans and the British following the attack on the USSR. The Italian opposition had to proceed very carefully, as there existed a strong party wishing to continue the war together with Hitler. In the second half of 1942 the attempts to capitulate with honour, and/or for Italy to switch sides, were intensified. The Italians attached some importance to the possibility of Poland playing a role of a broker.[24]

However, following his promising contacts with Bova Scoppa, who soon left for a new posting in Bucharest, Kowalewski continued his talks with the trustworthy first secretary of the Italian embassy, Renato Giardini (who was aware of the antecedents) and with the military attaché Terragni and the commercial attaché Ovidio Lefevbre. They were all convinced that Germany would soon be defeated. Both Kowalewski and Pangal were telling the Italians that Il Duce and his Fascists would have to be removed, which was a condition sine qua non for the western Allies. And, if the collapse of the monarchy was to be avoided, it was the King, Vittorio Emanuelle III, who would need to be instrumental in depriving Mussolini of power.

At the end of 1942, defeatist attitudes in Italy were on the increase. In mid-December the Italian diplomats in Lisbon received instructions to intensify the talks which might have led to a separate peace. Also in December the Italian ambassador, Francesco Fransoni, told Pangal that the Italians were ready to talk about peace with the Allies, preferably with the Americans, and that they would be pleased with Gen. Sikorski's mediation. Kowalewski immediately passed this on to London. The Western Allies were not, however, prepared to abandon the condition of unconditional surrender, which in the opinion of the Italian diplomats, was 'lunacy', almost preventing any action on the part of the group, which wanted Italy out of the war.[25] In any case, in December 1942, following the policy proposed by Eden, who was very hostile towards Italy, the British adopted the tactics of not allowing any fast switch by the Italians, believing this country to be unnecessary ballast for the Allies.

Not aware of this policy, the Italians did not give up trying, partly because the military position of the Third Reich, especially at the Eastern Front, was deteriorating. In February 1943 Mussolini, believing he had little to lose, hit the anti-Axis group hard, dismissing its leaders. Interestingly, when one of them, Dino Grandi, left Italy for Portugal, he attempted to establish contact with Kowalewski, whom he met many times, as they were neighbours, in Monte Estoril, in 'Ginalda'.[26] At the same time Italy strengthened its links with Hitler, which for Mussolini appeared to be the only salvation. Il Duce did not give up his attempts to establish a channel, or perhaps even constructive dialogue, with the Allies. In March he entrusted such attempts to, amongst others, his envoy in Lisbon. By the end of April, however, these attempts were weakened, as Fransoni and Giardini were recalled. Their role was taken over by the secretary to the embassy, Raimondo Manzini, who facilitated the talks between

Kowalewski and the emissaries from Rome.[27] In September 1943 the Italians finally signed their unconditional surrender, though its form meant that the western Allies breached the initial agreement with Marshal Pietro Badoglio. The opportunity for Italy to join the Allies earlier was lost. Had it happened, the bloody Italian campaign might not have been necessary.

For the Poles, the Romanian angle was one of the most important issues within Continental Action. The main activities were concentrated in Lisbon. This was in part because the régime of António de Oliveira Salazar did not maintain relations with the USSR, and consequently Soviet agents in Portugal were not active there in any significant way. This allowed the Romanians to by-pass Moscow in the semi-formal talks with the British and the Americans, which took place in Lisbon. The most important factor, however, was that Kowalewski, a former military attaché there, knew Romania very well.

Kowalewski's first serious Romanian contact was his letter to Marshal Antonescu, with whom the Pole had remained in touch since his Bucharest days.[28] The letter stressed common political interests and expressed a willingness to maintain bilateral contacts. The Romanian politician responded positively, with a verbal message sent via a trusted intermediary. Permanent contact was thus established between the Polish post in Lisbon and the official Romanians (called 'the Cypresses' in the terminology adapted by the Polish Interior Ministry). These links survived even Kowalewski's recall to London in 1944, though they became much weaker. Antonescu even ordered that some of his emissaries were to contact the Pole.

Thanks to the Romanians, the post of the Polish Ministry of Internal Affairs in Lisbon was soon able to use the Romanian diplomatic mail, as well as the separate courier service used by the Bank of Romania and the Romanian Agricultural Institute. In the most sensitive cases the services of the most trusted Romanians were used, to pass verbal messages to the young King Michael I, to Deputy Prime Minister Mihai 'Ica' Antonescu, to the writer and politician Pamfil Şeicaru and to the leaders of the opposition, mainly those linked to the peasant activist, Iuliu Maniu. Romanian envoys would frequently travel to Lisbon. They either wanted to talk to Kowalewski, or were easily persuaded to do so by persons co-operating with him.

As already stated, Kowalewski's most important contact was the Romanian Ambassador, Jean Pangal, who resided in the luxurious 'Avenida Palace' hotel, frequented by many agents. Pangal was a well-known centre-right politician, a pre-war Deputy Foreign Minister and Romanian envoy to the Nationals in Burgos during the Spanish civil war.[29] During the Second World War he was appointed Romanian Envoy in Lisbon. At the end of 1941 Conducător Antonescu dismissed him for his pro-Allied stand – but Pangal remained in the Portuguese capital as a private citizen. He was – not quite correctly – considered to be loyal to the former King Carol II, who managed to leave Spain with the help of Polish Intelligence, among others Lt-Col. Jan Kowalewski, and settled in

Mexico. Pangal's activities were 'subsidised' by the Polish Foreign Ministry, the Interior Ministry and possibly also by Polish Intelligence.[30] In Lisbon, he was very active politically, with his relationship with Kowalewski as the base of this activity. Pangal was very loyal to the Polish Colonel, and was of valuable service to him on many occasions.[31]

Kowalewski maintained close links with the post-January 1942 Romanian Minister in Lisbon, Victor Cădere, who between 1932 and 1935 represented his country in Warsaw. Cădere was a cautious diplomat, and the Polish Interior Ministry thought that he was close to Marshal Antonescu. Kowalewski did not consider Cădere to be the best possible intermediary and, separately, remained in touch with more pro-Allied diplomats at the Romanian Legation in Lisbon.

In the spring of 1942 Deputy Prime Minister Mihai 'Ica' Antonescu informed the Romanian Minister that Bucharest would be delighted if the contacts with the British could be maintained via Kowalewski. He added that both he and the Conducător had very high regard for the Pole and would be glad to receive further suggestions from Kowalewski. The Polish officer did so some time later, and continued to receive numerous emissaries from Bucharest. On 22 April the Romanian envoy informed 'Nart' that he was in receipt of instructions to establish contact with the Allies and that this should be in absolute secrecy in view of the activities of German Intelligence in Lisbon. London remained unconvinced and made any such talks contingent on a common position agreed with the other Allies.[32] This reduced the chances of Romania switching its alliances at that juncture.

From the summer of 1943, and especially following Gen. Sikorski's death, the Polish-Romanian contact became clearly weaker. In parallel, the international position of Poland took a turn for the worse, even more so when its relationship with the USSR became increasingly difficult. Meantime in Romania the dominant thinking was that the only realistic policy would be to seek direct agreement with the Soviets. This was caused by the growing Soviet military might. Seen from Bucharest, the worsening position of Poland made its mediation less valuable. The example of Italy was also worrying. But it soon transpired that the idea of direct talks with Moscow was impossible. Against this background, in the late autumn more contacts took place, some via Kowalewski, with the idea of tying themselves to the western Allies. Through the intermediary of Poland, exploratory talks were held on the conditions and tactics of capitulation. The most important of these talks took place in Lisbon.

Kowalewski, armed with his government's instructions, tried to persuade the Romanians of the necessity to orient themselves towards Great Britain and America. He also pointed out the Soviet desire to occupy the German satellite countries, a view which was supported by President Edvard Beneš. For a time, the Romanians placed some hopes in the services of the Czechoslovak politician as a possible intermediary. Beneš attempted to pull Bucharest away from Poland and came back to the idea of the Balkan block, partly returning to the concept of the Little Entente.

The Romanians quickly discovered, however, that the Czechoslovak ideas, especially on Transylvania, were not realistic. For a time, they returned to talks with the Poles, especially with the still trusted Kowalewski. But on 17 September Cădere informed the Polish Col. that the Romanian policy towards Poland has changed. Poland became an inconvenient partner, as it had little bargaining power and was in conflict with the USSR. The Poles were also charged with pro-Hungarian sympathies, though Bucharest admitted, that Polish attitudes to Romania were friendly. The Polish Government in London was seen as temporary, since the influence of the communist Union of Polish Patriots was growing. All this meant that Bucharest could no longer accept Polish mediation efforts with the British and the Americans. The British did not much like 'the Polish intrigues on the question of Romania'.[33] In practice, this was the end of close co-operation between Poland and Romania. For understandable reasons, the Romanians were seeking ways of not antagonising Moscow. They were hoping that this might improve their standing with the Allies and hence reduce the Soviet threat. When the Red Army entered Poland, the Romanians lost any of their remaining illusions. The coup d'état, advocated earlier by Kowalewski among others, finally took place in August 1944. It was successful, in part because the German military were engaged in Hungary at the time. But by then the decisions were made, and Romania found itself within the Soviet sphere of influence. Moscow's attempt to prevent an earlier accord between the western Allies and Bucharest, and indeed Allied landings in the Balkans, were finally successful.

In the Polish-Romanian talks, conducted mainly through Col. Kowalewski, a frequent theme was the possibility of creating a central European federation, between the Baltic and the Black Sea. This was the mainly Polish concept of a 'Central Union', based on a historical idea of Międzymorze (Inter-Sea, meaning the area between the Baltic and the Black Sea). This was one of the reasons why the Poles worked for the improvement of relations between Budapest and Bucharest. In their talks, the issue of the Polish-Romanian border was also raised: it was clear that its lack would push Romania towards the Balkans.

The third issue for Kowalewski was the Hungarians ('Topazowicze' or 'Topazy'), the most pro-Polish of the three, and enthusiastically willing to co-operate. Once the pro-Allied Miklós Kállay von Nagy-Kálló became Prime Minister, Kowalewski's Hungarian contacts became more dynamic. His links with Wodianer were fruitful, though the Pole thought him a typical product of the old, Austro-Hungarian school of diplomacy. The Col. also worked with András Tamás, a Hungarian from Moldavia, who was the Lisbon representative of the Hungarian Revisionist League. The main task entrusted to him by Kowalewski was to help organise communications with Poland via Hungary. Thanks to this, the resistance in Poland was able to quickly send 'Nart' reports destined for London. The Hungarian diplomatic post was often used for this purpose.

In November 1942 Wodianer returned from Budapest with what appeared to be a Hungarian decision to withdraw from the war. The

Regent, Miklós Horthy de Nagybánya, the Prime Minister, Miklós Kállay, and the influential Count István Bethlen were awaiting the Allied instructions. For Budapest, the principal objective was to switch sides without risking the German occupation of Hungary. In this case, too, the Allies demanded an unconditional surrender – a decision which was beneficial only for the Soviets. On 11 September the Hungarian Foreign Minister, Jenő Ghiczy, empowered Wodianer to maintain official – and not unofficial, as was the case thus far – contacts with the Poles. In addition to Kowalewski, the other interlocutor was Count Jan Szembek.[34]

The German occupation, which begun in March 1944, was especially tragic for the Hungarians. It was introduced to safeguard Hungary as a communications route for the German army and as a base for the control of the Carpathian Mountains. The Hungarian attempt to avoid Soviet and German invasion did not work. The action undertaken by Kowalewski, Szembek and Pangal failed, because of the Allied demand for unconditional surrender, and because the idea of an Allied invasion of the Balkans was abandoned. In parallel, the decision was taken that Hungary was to become a part of the Soviet sphere of influence. The formula applied to the German satellites turned out to be shortsighted. The western Allies had no concept of how to involve these countries in an anti-Hitler coalition. A more flexible policy towards Italy, Romania, Hungary, Bulgaria and Finland might have shortened the war. Lack of such a policy meant that Kowalewski's mission was doomed to failure. The Poles were not the only ones who thought that this mission was worth undertaking: it is clear that many of Kowalewski's well-placed interlocutors in neutral Lisbon believed in it, too. Many years later Count Raczyński wrote, that the talks led by Kowalewski and Szembek were one of 'underused opportunities during the Second World War'.[35]

The British thought highly of the role the Polish officer played in Lisbon.[36] But in late January 1944 Frank K. Roberts of the Foreign Office wrote to Maj-Gen. Gubbins, who since September 1943 headed SOE, to draw attention to what he considered to be Kowalewski's damaging activity in Lisbon. Apparently during 1943 evidence emerged that the Col. had frequent contacts with 'enemy nationals' and that he acted on behalf of a Polish-Hungarian-Romanian-Italian block. Roberts feared that this block was aimed not only against Hitler's Germany, but also against the USSR.[37] The British diplomat drew attention to the anti-Soviet stance of the Polish officer. This, together with his contacts with the Germans, meant that his further stay in Lisbon, one of the most important theatres in the spying game, was not welcome.[38] The British Diplomatic Service became the principal source of pressure for the recall of Kowalewski from Lisbon. SOE, which was more pro-Polish, and incidentally was the best-informed concerning the real intentions of the Soviets among the British secret services, had more understanding for the Colonel. SOE advocated caution and indicated that the time for Kowalewski's recall was not right. In fact SOE believed that he was irreplaceable in Portugal.[39] Despite this, on 6 March Sir Alexander Cadogan, the Foreign Office's Permanent Under-secretary of State, in a conversation with Ambassador Raczyński, requested the recall of the Colonel. Cadogan stated that Kowalewski was not suspected of disloyalty – but that he maintained contact with the Germans in Lisbon. Such contacts were not leading anywhere but might have been dangerous for the Polish Government and for Kowalewski himself. At their next meeting, on 10 March 1944, Raczyński asked for specific accusations – but also informed his interlocutor that a decision to recall Kowalewski from Lisbon had been made. On 10 April Cadogan responded in writing and said that the British had nothing against Kowalewski personally and that the only issue was his contacts with the Germans. Cadogan was unable to provide further details. Documents on this case clearly indicate that it was the British special services which refused to inform the Polish side of Kowalewski's alleged contacts with the Germans.[40] The Polish Interior Ministry attempted to defend the Colonel, pointing to his valuable services to the Allies while in Lisbon, and to his abilities. His recall from Portugal would be 'a very severe and irreparable blow', it said. Nevertheless, the Polish side indicated its willingness to accede to the British 'request', in order to 'retain full harmony in all the fields of British-Polish co-operation'.[41] The Ministry of Internal Affairs continued:

> The British Government raised the issue of the recall of Col. Kowalewski in a form acceptable to us, that is without making any specific allegations against him or against the work he carried out. The stated motive relates solely to our political security. It would be a mistake for us to require the British to specify the reasons and to support such reasons with detailed allegations, since it would force the British to mention specific charges, which they did not specify thus far. Were they to do so, Col. Kowalewski might have become compromised and we would be deprived of the opportunity of working with him again. It would, moreover, question the political work already carried out in Lisbon.[42]

This is a very good indication of the degree to which the Polish Government was already incapacitated and ceased to be a partner for the British authorities.

It is true that, whilst in Portugal, the Col. met the Germans on several occasions. Each such event was reported in detail to the Polish authorities, and each was preceded by a specific permission to meet Hans Lazar, the press counsellor to the German Embassy in Madrid, and with Capt. Fritz Kramer of Abwehr. Lazar informed Kowalewski about the German plans to attack the USSR, and with other material. These meetings were of an exploratory nature – and the Polish authorities in London did not hide the meetings from the British. Why, then, the insistence on the recall of the Colonel, following the talks which took place at the end of 1943, and which did not lead to any positive conclusions? In the internal correspondence within the Foreign Office, Frank K. Roberts wrote that as far as Polish 'ill-advised' contacts were concerned, the most important were those between Kowalewski and the Germans. When asking for his recall, the British stated that they 'did not suspect his motives', except for his lack of discretion – perhaps meaning 'without our permission'. Roberts stated: 'In fact we know that Col. K listened to German emissaries who said that the German General Staff would try to introduce a more moderate regime in Poland. There is nothing to show that he did more than listen.' The internal exchange of views within the Foreign Office indicates, that the main worry concerning the uncontrolled (by the British) talks conducted by the Poles was the possibility that the Soviets might have objected.[43] There were fears that Kowalewski might have done something to make the emerging Soviet-British agreement on the future of Poland more difficult. And the only party which benefited from this agreement were the Soviets. Hence for the western Allies Kowalewski became a person who, in a minor but destructive way, might have done something to make the Soviet domination in Central and Eastern Europe more difficult. The demand for the Colonel's recall, interestingly made by the Foreign Office, coincided with the implementation of the decisions taken in Tehran by western diplomatic services. It is not surprising, therefore, that after Kowalewski's recall, the Foreign Office expressed its satisfaction, that his next posting would be within Great Britain.[44]

Kowalewski left Lisbon on 5 April 1944 by plane, bound for Britain. The departure of the most prominent agent in Portugal weakened any attempt at co-ordination between the countries of Central and Eastern Europe, increasingly aware of the Soviet threat. Lt-Col. Kowalewski became the Chief of the Polish Special Operations Office attached to SFHQ (Special Forces Headquarters), that is the representative of the Polish Ministries of Defence and of Internal Affairs within the body responsible for D-Day. The Col. co-ordinated the preparation of Polish sabotage and diversionary units for Operation 'Overlord', that is, the invasion in Normandy. With this in mind, he maintained regular communication with the Poles in France, using the contacts of the Polish Organisation of Struggle for Independence 'Monika',[45] which co-operated closely with SOE.

After the war, Kowalewski became a journalist. For ten years, he published the 'East Europe' periodical in London[46] and was an expert on East European issues. Following his death in London on 31 October 1965, Gen. Kazimierz Glabisz wrote that Kowalewski was one of the most eminent Polish staff officers.[47]

Notes

1   Zob. The Countess of Listowel, *Crusader in the Secret War*, London b.d. [1952], pp. 21–39; 'Dziennik Polski' (The Polish Diary) of 18th December 1967; T. Pełczyński, *Pułkownik Jan Kowalewski* (*Col. Jan Kowalewski*), 'Tydzień Polski', 4th December 1965; K. Glabisz, *Ś.P. Pułkownik Jan Kowalewski* (*Col. Jan Kowalewski RIP*), 'Orzeł Biały', January 1966, p. 22; A. Adamczyk, *Bogusław Miedziński (1891–1972). Biografia polityczna* (*Bogusław Miedziński [1891–1972]. A Political Biography*), Toruń 2000, pp. 259–261.

2   J. Kowalewski, *Cykl rumuński* (*The Romanian Cycle*), 'Zeszyty Historyczne' no. 6,

Paris 1964, pp. 117–145; T. Dubicki, *Wojsko polskie w Rumunii w latach 1939–1941* (*Polish Soldiers in Romania, 1939–1941*), Warsaw 1994, pp. 224–225; S. Schimitzek, *Na krawędzi Europy. Wspomnienia portugalskie 1939–1946* (*At the Edge of Europe. Memoirs from Portugal, 1939–1946*), Warsaw 1970, pp. 67, 212, 240, 287, 306; The Countess of Listowel, op.cit., p. 90; IPMS, B. 798, J. Kowalewski's Report from Portugal. On the war-time activities of this Polish officer see more in: The Countess of Listowel, op. cit. There is no doubt whatsoever that this book, written at the beginning of 1950s by the Colonel's co-worker, Judith Márffy-Mantuano Hare, Countess of Listowel, who was Hungarian by birth, was based on documents and/or detailed notes made by Kowalewski. In this book he is represented by the character 'Peter Nart', the name being based on his two codenames. The author is grateful to Dr. Krzysztof Strzałka for drawing his attention to this book. In any case Kowalewski himself provided a reference to this book in his article in 'Zeszyty Historyczne' (J. Kowalewski, *Cykl rumuński [The Romanian Cycle]*, op. cit.).

3 The Countess of Listowel, op. cit., p. 75.

4 IPMS, A.9.VI.17/2, S. Kot, Interior Minister, to Lt-Col. J. Kowalewski, b.m., 28th January 1941. The Chief of the Lisbon Post for Communication with Poland (the 'correspondent' of the Interior Ministry) was Stefan Murek ('Rogoziński'), with whom Kowalewski worked well, as well as with Tadeusz Cieplak 'Nowak', who replaced Murek in November 1943. (ibid., S. Kot to Lt-Col. J. Kowalewski, b.m. 3rd January 1941).

5 More in: J. Librach, *Nota o 'Akcji Kontynentalnej'* (*Note on the Continental Action*), 'Zeszyty Historyczne' no. 23, Paris 1973; The Countess of Listowel, op. cit., p. 90, T. Panecki, *Polonia zachodnioeuropejska w planach Rządu RP na emigracji (1940–1944) – Akcja Kontynentalna* (*Polish West European Emigrés in the Plans of the Polish Government-in-Exile [1940–1944] – Continental Action*), Warsaw 1986, passim, and S. Kot, *Listy z Rosji do gen. Sikorskiego* (*Letters from Russia to General Sikorski*), London 1955, p. 88.

6 The Countess of Listowel, op. cit., pp. 75–78, and IPMS, A.9, The list of codenames used by the Polish Interior Ministry.

7 Ibid., A.9.VI.17/2, J. Librach to Lt-Col. J. Kowalewski, 16 April 1941, and S. Schimitzek, *Na krawędzi* (*At the Edge*), op. cit., p. 369.

8 Ibid., pp. 332, 486, 575, and IPMS, A.9.VI.17/3, 'Arwa' to 'Piotr', London, 7th May 1941.

9 Ibid, J. Librach, note on my stay in Lisbon, b.m.d.

10 NARA, RG 165, MID, Portugal, Box 2847, Col. R.A. Solborg, US Mailitary and Air Attaché in Lisbon, to Chief of Military Intelligence Service, 16 November 1943.

11 In this context, meeting places.

12 To date most attention has been paid to the activities of Polish diplomacy in this field. See T. Piszczkowski, *Między Lizboną a Londynem. Z sekretów dyplomacji polskiej w czasie drugiej wojny światowej* (*Between Lisbon and London. Secrets of Polish Diplomacy in WW II*), London 1979 (whilst the author mentions Kowalewski only at the margin and does not quote the book by Countess of Listowel, he admits that a Polish officer, 'as chief of a secret cell, the so-called Continental Action', was spiritus movens of Jan Szembek's contacts. Szembek remained in direct contact with the Polish Foreign Ministry, ibid., p. 201; more in: Szembek's correspondence from Lisbon in 1941–1945 in: IPMS, Kol. 85), and W. Materski, *Zerwanie stosunków polsko-sowieckich* (*The Break-Up of Polish-Soviet Relations*), [in:] *Historia dyplomacji polskiej* (*History of Polish Diplomacy*), vol.5, 1939–1945, ed. by W. Michowicz, Warsaw 1999, pp. 344–347. In April 1943 the Polish Foreign Minister, Raczyński, instructed Szembek that the main thrust of contacts with the Italians, Hungarians and Romanians is to be left to Lt-Col. Kowalewski (IPMS, Kol. 85, 3/22, E. Raczyński to J. Szembek, London, 21 April 1943).

13 The Countess of Listowel, op.cit., pp. 90–96.
14 According to T. Piszczkowski, the term 'Trójnóg' was coined by Jan Count Szembek. The exclusion of Germany from this initiative was to cost the Germans dearly (T. Piszczkowski, *Między Lizboną (Between Lisbon)*, op. cit., p. 14); also T. Dubicki, *Rumuńskie aspekty Akcji Kontynentalnej (1940–1944) (The Romanian Aspects of Continental Action)*, [in:] *Kontakty polsko-rumuńskie na przestrzeni wieków (Polish-Romanian Contacts Through the Centuries)*, Suceava 2001, pp. 11–13.
15 Ibid., s.107–109. The leitmotif of Countess of Listowel's book is that the demand for 'unconditional surrender' was ill-considered and very harmful.
16 Ibid., pp. 104–105.
17 IPMS, A.9.VI.17/2, MSW, J. Librach to Lt-Col. J. Kowalewski, 30 October 1942.
18 See. T. Piszczkowski, *Między Lizboną (Between Lisbon)*, op. cit., pp. 38–41.
19 In a report for Salazar in July 1942, a diplomat from the Portugese Foreign Ministry, Henrique da Guerra Quaresma Vianna, summarized his conversation with Pangal. The Romanian told the Portuguese diplomat of his talks with the German Minister, who asked about the possibility of initiating peace talks with the British. The German also wanted to know the Polish position on this. Pangal sugested that the German should ask the Polish ambassador, or Szembek. In all probability, such a conversation (between the German and the Poles) never took place (Instituto dos Arquivos Nacionais/Torre do Tombo, Lisboa, Portugal – further: IAN/TT, Arquivo Salazar, AOS/CO/NE-2, Pt.41).
20 T. Piszczkowski, *Między Lizboną (Between Lisbon)*, op.cit., p. 13.
21 Ibid., pp. 39–42 (Szembek was irritated by the British meddling in Polish sovereign affairs), and E. Raczyński, *W sojuszniczym Londynie. Dziennik ambasadora Edwarda Raczyńskiego 1939–1945 (In Allied London. The Diary of Ambassador Edward Raczyński, 1939–1945)*, London 1997, p. 154.
22 For more on the talks between Kowalewski and Szembek with the Italians, see: T. Piszczkowski, *Między Lizboną (Between Lisbon)*, op. cit., pp. 31–58, and K. Strzałka, *Między przyjaźnią a wrogością. Z dziejów stosunków polsko-włoskich (1939–1945) (Between Friendship and Enmity. On the History of Polish-Italian Relations, 1939–1945)*, Kraków 2001, pp. 232–246.
23 J. Librach, *Nota*, op. cit., p. 166.
24 K. Strzałka, *Między przyjaźnią (Between Friendship)*, op. cit., p. 234.
25 The Countess of Listowel, op. cit., pp.116–118.
26 S. Schimitzek, *Na krawędzi (At the Edge)*, op. cit., pp. 486 i 575. When in Portugal, Grandi also had meetings with Szembek (T. Piszczkowski, *Między Lizboną (Between Lisbon)*, op. cit., p. 158).
27 The Countess of Listowel, op. cit., pp. 124–127, and S. Schimitzek, *Na krawędzi (At the Edge)*, op. cit., p. 575.
28 The Countess of Listowel, op. cit., p. 59. Kowalewski knew Antonescu when he was Polish military attaché in Romania. For example, they went skiing together in Predeal in the Carpathians.
29 M. Eiroa, *Las relaciones de Franco con Europa Centro-Oriental (1939–1955)*, Barcelona 2001, p. 24.
30 IPMS, A.9.VI.17/2, MSW, J. Librach to Lt-Col. Kowalewski, 31 October 1941, and IAN/TT, *Arquivo Salazar*, AOS/CO/NE-2F1. In the Salazar Archive in Lisbon there are numerous indications of the very forthcoming and pro-Allies activity of the former Romanian Minister.
31 As far as the Romanian and Russian angles are concerned, Kowalewski co-operated with ' Wasia', the Russian Bohomolec *vel* Bogomolec, a former British agent acting against the USSR. In Lisbon, this agent worked for the Romanian special services.
32 The Countess of Listowel, op. cit., pp.144-145; T. Dubicki, *Rumuński (Romanian)*, op. cit., pp. 16–19.

33 TNA(PRO), HS 4/235, MPO [R.H. Hazell] do D.H.109, 23 December 1943. See correspondence on Kowalewski's activity in: ibid., HS 4/261 and 235.

34 More in: The Countess of Listowel, op. cit., pp. 162–195.

35 T. Piszczkowski, *Między Lizboną* (Between Lisbon), op. cit., p. 5.

36 IPMS, A.9.VI.17/2, MSW, J. Librach to Lt-Col. J. Kowalewski, 27 September 1941.

37 The British were fully aware of Kowalewski's activities, and not only from Polish sources. They were secretly reading Polish correspondence, most of which passed through their hands. In April 1941, for example, 'Arwa' informed 'Piotr' that some packages sent by courier arrived very late, and formally protested this (IPMS, MSW, A.9.VI.17/2, 'Arwa' to 'Piotr', 22 April 1941). In November 1942 one package from Kowalewski was delivered by the British whilst open. The Polish Interior Ministry officially protested to the 'Hosts' (ibid, J. Librach to Lt-Col. J. Kowalewski, London, 3 November 1942). The fact that British Intelligence were regularly and secretly opening diplomatic packages and post crossing British territory (this included the Polish diplomatic mail) was confirmed after the war by 'Kim' Philby (K. Philby, *My Silent War*, New York 1968, pp. 63–64, Barcelona 1969, pp. 69–70).

38 TNA (PRO), HS 4/274, F.K. Roberts to Gubbins, London 23 January 1944.

39 See. ibid., HS 4/233, EU/P (SOE's liaison with the Polish Interior Ministry) to Maj. Mortimer, 3 March 1944, ibid. HS 4/144, D/F to V/OD, 3 February 1944.

40 IPMS, MSW, A.9.VI.17/3, A. Cadogan to E. Raczyński, London, 10 April 1944, and E. Raczyński, Note on conversation with Permanent Under-secretary of State A. Cadogan at Foreign Office, 10 March 1944.

41 Ibid., W. Banaczyk, Internal Affairs Minister, to the Earl of Selborne, Minister for Economic Warfare, London 13 March 1944; ibid., F.K. Roberts to Sporborg, London 13 March 1944.

42 Ibid., Note on the Kowalewski case, London 9th March 1944.

43 TNA (PRO), FO 371/39422, Note of F.K. Roberts, 23 March 1944; 'C' (S. Menzies, SIS Chief) to P.N. Loxley, London 9 March 1944, and A. Cadogan to D. Petrie, 29 March 1944.

44 Ibid., HS 4/233, F.K. Roberts to H.N. Sporborg Deputy Chief of SOE, London 22 March 1944.

45 More in: The Countess of Listowel, op. cit., pp. 240–241; correspondence in IPMS, MSW, A.9.VI.10/1 and 2, and A.9.VI.17; TNA (PRO), HS 4/227, Lt-Col. J. Kowalewski, Chief of Polish Operations Office at SFHQ, note on 'Monika' and the Polish presence in France, London 24 August 1944.

46 More in: The Countess of Listowel, op. cit., pp. 265–268. From July 1950 the name of this periodical was 'East Europe and Soviet Russia'.

47 K. Glabisz, *Ś.P. Pułkownik Jan Kowalewski (Col. Jan Kowalewski RIP)*, op. cit., p. 22.

55

Information on the Morale of the German Forces and the Civilian Population in Germany

Adam Grzegorz Dabrowski

Information on the current morale of the German army and the civilian population of the Third Reich was analysed and collated by the Studies and Propaganda Department. From mid-1941, such material was then presented in the monthly intelligence report summary (as Part 3, in addition to the chapters on the military and economic situation). At first, this was a short, uniform text, but by the end of 1941 it contained three sections on the military, devoted in turn to the front-line troops, rear echelons and the Reich. By the beginning of 1942, the document was given its final form, and consisted of four chapters: Propaganda, the Army, Civilian Society and General Remarks. Two of these were broken into sections: 'the Army into General Characteristics', 'At the Front', 'At the Rear', 'the German Allies', 'On the Road to the Front' (though this last one appeared only for a time) and the Navy (this appeared in one report only), and the chapter on the Civilian Society was sub-divided into 'General Characteristics', 'Occupied Territories' and 'In the Reich'.

When selecting material for inclusion in the reports, much attention was paid to the analysis of private letters of German soldiers at the Eastern Front to their families in the Reich. The numbers of analysed letters, which were intercepted and subjected to a preliminary screening by the counter-intelligence unit of the Warsaw Region, the Home Army), was normally some 3–3.5 thousand per month,[1] though on occasions it was as high as 4–5 thousand.[2] The results were presented in weekly reports, containing selected quotes or summaries of letters, and either field post office numbers or the destination addresses. The reports ended with general remarks on the content of intercepted letters (which included the percentages of objective letters, pessimistic letters and an assessment of the work of German censors).

Special attention was paid to remarks concerning the factors which might have influenced the German ability to fight and the general state of morale of the German army. This was getting worse mainly because of growing supply deficiencies ('When a horse dies, we throw ourselves on its carcass and devour even its innards',[3] or 'Without warm grub, only the horrible tinned rations, [and] there were the two days when I had nothing to eat at all. No cigarettes for ten days...')[4] or adverse climate ('...at minus fifteen degrees [Celsius], we speak of clement weather',[5] 'As soon as the ground froze, the beasts [Red Army] began their attacks'),[6] retreat and panic caused by the pressure by the Red Army ('I have never run back as fast as at that point')[7] or troop losses related to it ('All that is left of our Division are a few fighting groups').[8] Such material formed the basis for general assessment of the morale in the German army, since 1943 characterised by '...complete lack of any hope linked to this year's campaign in the East, to say nothing about enthusiasm. Nobody speaks about the interrupted campaign. Everybody fears the forthcoming winter, the third at the Russian front. Nobody can see any positive outcome to the war'.[9] One of the intercepted letters spoke thus about the mood of the army in 1944: '90% of the German Army does not believe in victory – but wants peace at any price. Discouragement shows itself in suicides, in internal depression, in trying to avoid being sent to the front. External discipline [is] still very carefully pretended, and insubordination meets with severe punishment'.[10]

In the chapters of the reports on civilian morale, much attention was being paid to the results of Allied air raids on Germany. The analysts from the the Studies and Propaganda Department reported that '...air raids are the main source of depression for soldiers [at the front], they sap his resistance. On learning of the impact of the raids, the soldier realizes the spiritual weakening of the country'.[11] On the other hand each successive '...reduction in the number of large-scale bombing raids on Germany contributed to the significant relaxation of his mood, since the primary personal consideration for each soldier is the fate of his family [left behind in Germany]'.[12] News of the damage caused by the raids were reaching the front-line soldiers in letters from families at home, which were also regularly inspected by the counter-intelligence of the Home Army Warsaw region. These letters from home contained many descriptions of air raids ('They dropped mainly two- and four-tonne bombs, and [following this raid] other planes came and dropped phosphorus bombs. At this moment, the whole town [Wuppertal] erupted in flames')[13] and of their impact on the morale of the German society ('As for the outcome, apart from the housing situation, the forced evacuation of children was most difficult',[14] 'Increasing numbers of dead, all we get now are funeral masses – though very beautiful ones, with music and singing – but this will not do much good to the [dead] poor wretches, nor will it bring them back to life').[15]

Before the systematic work on monthly reports began, short mentions of the morale of the army and the civilian population were included in the situation and intelligence reports, transmitted via couriers ('Desertions and arrests among the troops. In the Austrian units in Małopolska [the region of Poland with Kraków as its capital] the mood is depressed')[16] or by radio ('[The troops] are getting tired of the war, especially the older ones.

Among the Austrians and the Bavarians the morale is poorest')[17] to PGS.

The Studies Section of 'Lombard', the central intelligence network run by the Intelligence Department of the II Bureau, the Home Army GHQ, also undertook some small-scale investigations into the morale of the German society. The research was based on the German daily press and on some periodical publications. Their press reviews, prepared every two weeks as an attachment to 'Lombard's' intelligence report, contained reviews of economic and military issues, and in addition short, separate sections summarising the issues under the chiefings of 'Food', 'Legal Chronicle', 'Air Raids'. Press reports were considered to be potentially helpful in the context of a fuller report on the current mood in the Army and among the civilian population.

Notes

1 AAN, Armia Krajowa [1939–1941] 1942–1945 (the Home Army), 203/III/70, p. 128, Monthly Report no. 3/42.
2 Ibid., 203/III/71, p. 40, Monthly Report no. 2/42; sygn. 203/III/75, p. 313, Monthly Report no. 9/43.
3 Ibid., 203/I/17, p. 115, Monthly Report no. 4/42.
4 Ibid., 203/III/98, s. 75, Monthly Report on field correspondence intercepts for the period from 4 to 11 September 1942.
5 Ibid., 203/I/17, p. 116, Monthly Report no. 4/42.
6 Ibid., 203/III/73, p. 299, Monthly Report no. 12/42.
7 Ibid., 203/I/19, p. 605, Monthly Report no. 11/43.
8 Ibid., p. 606.
9 Ibid., 203/III/75, p. 314, Monthly Report no. 9/43.
10 *Meldunki miesięczne wywiadu przemysłowego KG ZWZ/AK* (*Monthly Reports of the Home Army GHQ Industrial Intelligence*), ed. A. Glass, Warsaw 2000, p. 1255, Monthly Report no. 4/44.
11 Ibid., 203/III/75, p. 316, Monthly Report no. 9/43.
12 Ibid., 203/III/73, s. 302, Monthly Report no. 12/42.
13 Ibid., 203/III/75, p. 107, Monthly Report no. 7/43.
14 Ibid., 203/I/19, p. 618, Monthly Report no. 11 / 43.
15 Ibid., p. 517, Monthly Report no. 10 / 43.
16 *Armia Krajowa w dokumentach 1939–1945* (*Documents on the Home Army 1939–1945*), vol. 1, Wrocław–Warsaw–Kraków 1990, p. 102, Situation and Intelligence Report of 22 February 1940.
17 AAN, AK, 203/I/15, p. 123, Situation Report no. 45 for December 1940.

56
Reports on the Holocaust

Jan Ciechanowski

One of the Maj. tasks facing both the Office of the Government Plenipotentiary for Poland known as 'Delegatura' and the Commander-in-Chief of the Home Army, and of their emissaries, was to regularly and in detail inform the Polish authorities in London and our Western Allies on the tragic position, persecution and genocide of Polish Jews by the Germans. This is evident in the numerous reports sent by the Government Plenipotentiary and the Home Army Commander-in-Chief, by radio and via couriers.[1] The emissaries, such as Jan Karski (1914-2000)[2] and Jan Nowak-Jeziorański, themselves witnessed the German persecution of Jews in Poland. The reports were prepared primarily on the basis of information obtained by Home Army Intelligence, by the Office of the Government Plenipotentiary for Poland and their special units dealing with Jewish affairs, including 'Żegota',[3] and by the representatives of the Jewish Resistance.[4]

The first emissary of the Government Plenipotentiary for Poland, who presented an extensive report on the position and genocide of Polish Jewry to the representatives of Polish and Allied governments, was Jan Karski, who personally reported to General Władysław Sikorski, President Franklin D. Roosevelt and the British Foreign Secretary Anthony Eden, among others, reached London via Germany, Belgium, France, Spain and Gibraltar at the end of November 1942. The second emissary was Jan Nowak-Jeziorański, who arrived in London via Sweden a year after Karski, on 9 December 1943.[5]

Before leaving Poland, on the orders of the Home Army Commander-in-Chief and the Government Plenipotentiary, Karski held a number of meetings with the representatives of the emerging Jewish Resistance: with Leon Feiner, who represented the socialist BUND party, Adolf Berman and Menachem Kirschenbaum, the leader of Zionists.[6] Both were aware that Karski was to travel to London in the immediate future, in part to present to the Polish and Allied authorities the tragic position of Polish Jews, who were being systematically murdered in large numbers by the Germans throughout Poland since the beginning of 1942.[7] 'The first thing I began to understand when talking to them' – wrote Karski – 'was the utter hopelessness of their position', as without significant help from the outside, by the Western Allies, they were condemned to total annihilation. 'You, the non-Jewish Poles, are lucky', said Feiner. 'You are suffering too, of course. Many of you shall die, but your nation lives and shall continue living. After the war, Poland shall rise from the dead. You shall rebuild your towns, and with time your wounds shall heal [...] your country shall be reborn, but there shall be no Polish Jews any more. We shall perish. Hitler shall lose the war against those who are humane, just and good, but he shall win his war against the Polish Jews. [...] The Jewish nation shall be no more'.[8]

Both representatives of the Jewish resistance were of the opinion that only external help was capable of saving Polish Jews from total annihilation. 'Please tell Allied governments' – they asked Karski – 'that, if they want to help us, they should publicly and officially notify the German government and the people of the Reich, that further persecution will cause mass reprisals and the systematic destruction of the whole German nation'.[9]

The Jewish leaders wanted Karski to tell 'the Polish Government, and the governments of the Allies and their great leaders [Churchill and Roosevelt – JC], that we are hopeless when faced with the German criminals. We cannot defend ourselves and nobody in Poland is in a position to defend us. The Resistance authorities may be able to save some of us, but they cannot save the nation [...] Perhaps a handful shall survive, but 3 million Polish Jews are condemned to die. Here, in Poland, there is no power able to prevent this: not the Polish Resistance, not the Jewish Resistance. Please, sir, make certain that no leader of the United Nations may be able to say in the future that he did not know that we are being murdered and that help may only come from the outside'.[10]

Karski asked the Jewish representatives to state what they demanded and expected from the Allied leaders:

The Germans can be influenced only by force and might [said the Zionist]. The German towns should be bombed without mercy, and each time leaflets should be dropped informing the Germans in full of the fate of Polish Jews. We should threaten the German nation with the same fate during the war and once it is over. We are not in favour of slaughter of the German nation, nor do we seek it. But such a threat is the only possible means to stop the German atrocities. Such a threat, when backed by force, might scare the German population sufficiently so that they will put pressure on their leaders to change their behaviour. Nothing else will help.[11]

The Jewish representatives also asked Karski to describe their situation and their views to the Jewish communities in the West, to wake them up and to convince the world that the methods being used by the Germans against the Jews 'have no precedent in history of the world'.[12]

Before departing for London, Karski was provided with intelligence reports, which showed that by September 1942 the Germans had already murdered some one million Polish citizens of Jewish origin.[13] In addition, to gain eyewitness knowledge of the living, and dying, conditions of the Polish Jewry, Karski was twice smuggled into the Warsaw Ghetto. In July 1942, the Germans began to transport its inmates to the Treblinka extermination camp,[14] and on one occasion to a death camp, probably the one in Izbica Lubelska, and not to Belżec, as is often mistakenly maintained.[15] What he saw there shook Karski to the core and stayed with him throughout his long life.[16]

Karski flew to London from Gibraltar on 25 November 1942. The first three days in Britain he spent at the Royal Victoria Patriotic School in Wandsworth,[17] (S. London) an MI5 establishment in which new arrivals from German-occupied Europe were interrogated.[18] There, in the presence of two Polish Intelligence officers, Karski delivered his testimony on his mission and his work for the Polish Resistance.[19] Meantime his dispatches, which contained also a wide-ranging report on the tragic position of the Polish Jews, were delivered to Great Britain achief of his own arrival.[20] Moreover Karski's report on the situation of the Jews,[21] summarised on two pages, was delivered to the British authorities, including Eden, prior to the Foreign Secretary's meeting with the Polish emissary.[22]

In his account to the Polish, British, American and Jewish leaders, in London and Washington, Karski stressed that without wide-ranging and immediate assistance of the Western Allies, the Jews under the German occupation would be condemned to death. Wherever he went and whoever he met, in his meetings with British and American leaders Karski in effect encountered the same substantive reaction: that the only effective help for the Jews rested on the Allied victory over the Third Reich and that their suffering, though most horrible, could not affect the Allied strategy.

Foreign Secretary Eden, who spoke to Karski twice in February 1943, was more interested in the Polish-Soviet relations and in the future borders between Poland and the USSR, than in any Allied action on behalf of murdered Jews – though he was convinced that the reports of the Polish emissary were true.[23] On 7 December 1942 Eden wrote to Lord Halifax, the British Ambassador in Washington, that as was clear from the reports recently received by the Polish Government, there could be no doubt that the German authorities in Poland 'conduct a policy of gradual extermination of all Jews, with the exception of highly qualified workers'.[24]

Eden stressed that the reports 'read convincingly'.[25] The first meeting between Eden and Karski took place on 4 February 1943. Eden listened attentively to the Pole's account of the fate and tragedy of Polish Jews, but when Karski suggested mass air-raids on German cities in retaliation for their extermination, the chief of British diplomacy stopped the emissary and said: 'The Polish reports on the atrocities had already reached us: the matter will take its proper course'.[26] In fact, that was the end of 'the matter'. Eden did not even agree that Karski should present his report personally to Churchill, since, as he put it, it was his duty to protect the elderly and overworked Prime Minister from too many petitioners. He promised, though, to pass the report to the chairman of the War Cabinet – and did so, on 17 February 1943.[27] Regrettably, Eden's note to Churchill on his meeting with Karski contained only one small reference to the Jews. The Minister reported that according to the Polish emissary, 'the entire population of Warsaw, including the remnants of the Jews, is united in their hatred for, and resistance to, the Germans'.[28]

The next of Karski's high-ranking British interlocutors, Lord Selborne, the chief of SOE, showed lively interest in the needs, operations and plans of the Home Army and in its co-operation with the Soviet partisans. As for the Jewish 'matter' this was secondary, quite as for Eden. Selborne categorically refused Karski's request for SOE to aid the Jews financially, in hard currency and in gold, in return for which some might have been able to purchase their lives from the Germans. This, he said, would not be acceptable to any Allied leader, since such funds could have been used by the Germans to buy raw materials and arms to fight the Allies with.[29] This, opined Lord Selborne, would amount to the Allied subsidy for the Reich's war effort.[30] On the other hand Selborne encouraged Karski to publicise his story of the German persecution of the Jews, since, he said, this would be helpful in maintaining anti-German feelings among the population. Personally, Selborne found it difficult to believe that the German atrocities were in fact on such a large scale.[31]

Karski's report and his entreaties were received better by the Polish authorities and persuaded them to seek assistance for the Jews in the shape of Allied declarations condemning the German persecution of the Jews, threats of reprisals against those Germans who participated in such acts, and punishing air raids on Germany. The Poles sought such declarations both in London and in Washington.[32]

In June 1943 the Polish Government dispatched Karski to the US, to carry out his mission on behalf of Poland and of the Polish Jewry. There, he was assisted by the Polish Ambassador in Washington, Jan Ciechanowski. Once in America, on 5 July 1943 Karski and Ciechanowski had a long meeting with Felix Frankfurter, the US Supreme Court Justice and a close adviser to President Franklin D. Roosevelt. Frankfurter was a scion of a Jewish family from Austria, which settled in the States when Felix was a child. Responding to a request from Frankfurter, Karski reported in detail on the German atrocities against the Jews in Poland, on his trip to the Ghetto and to a camp where the Germans murdered the Jews.[33] Frankfurter listened reluctantly and was inclined not to believe the report. His attitude was similar to that of many British and American personalities at the time. For many of them, the unvarnished truth about the scale of German atrocities against the Jews was beyond their comprehension.[34] Having listened to Karski, Frankfurter stated categorically: 'I am unable to believe you'.[35] Later he added: 'Ambassador, I am not saying that this young man [Karski] is lying; I am saying that I cannot believe him. There is a difference'.[36]

On 27 July 1943 Karski and Ciechanowski were received by Roosevelt.

As was the case with Eden and Selborne, the President was more interested in Polish than in Jewish affairs. He wanted to know about the organisation and activities of the Polish underground state, its contacts and communications with the Polish Government in London, the morale of the German troops, the corruption among the Germans and the relationships between the Soviet partisans and the Home Army. He asked Karski about the contacts between the Polish Resistance and those Poles who were deported for forced labour in Germany.[37] He promised assistance to the Home Army and praised its organisation. He also mentioned that Stalin would insist on the changes to the eastern borders of Poland.

In reality, Roosevelt was more interested in the Polish Resistance than in any immediate and effective assistance for the dying Jews, though Karski assured the President that the Polish reports on the tragic situation of the Jewry were not exaggerated.[38] Karski stressed that the Polish Resistance authorities were certain that the Germans intended to annihilate all the Jews throughout Europe. He reported to the American leader that, according to reliable estimates made by Polish Intelligence, up to September 1942 the Germans had murdered some 1,800,000 Polish citizens of Jewish extraction. The Polish emissary said that the leaders of Polish and Jewish Resistance asked him to inform the British and American military authorities that only direct reprisals against the Germans, such as mass air raids on German towns by the Allies, combined with dropped leaflets informing their inhabitants as to the reasons for it, might force Berlin to abandon its plans to exterminate the Jews, or at least reduce the scale of the genocide.

Having listened to the report and to Karski's pleas, Roosevelt immediately moved to another topic.[39] The long conversation between Karski and the President showed that the American leader was interested in everything which might have influenced the war effort of all the Allies, including Poland. But he was not thinking about immediate and direct assistance to the Jews. His position was that only a swift and complete Allied victory over the Third Reich would save the Jews and prevent their complete annihilation. This echoed the position of the British leaders.

When briefing Allied leaders, Karski stressed that the Germans intended to murder all the Jews before the war was over and whatever its outcome – and that this intention was not based on any military considerations. This, he maintained, must not be ignored. He also informed his interlocutors that the Jews in Poland were powerless and that while the Polish Resistance was able to save some, it was not capable of preventing mass extermination. Only the Great Powers were in a position to do that. In the name of Jewish leaders he demanded that the Allies take extraordinary but necessary reprisals to force the Germans to cease mass murder of the Jews. He also said that, should the Allies refuse to take such steps, the historical responsibility for this failure would rest on their governments. He kept repeating that the Jews want the Allies to state plainly and in public that one of the objectives of the war was to stop the Germans from exterminating the Jews.[40]

Thus ended Jan Karski's (Kozielewski) intervention with the top Allied authorities on behalf of the dying Jews. The mission of Jan Nowak-Jeziorański, who arrived in London on 9 December 1943, after the tragic end of the uprising in the Warsaw Ghetto, was about to begin. How the information brought by Nowak-Jeziorański was received in London is best shown by a report of the Chairman of the Joint Intelligence Committee, William Cavendish-Bentinck (who later became the 9th Duke of Portland) to Sir Alexander Cadogan, Permanent Under-Secretary at the Foreign Office, who was directly responsible for British Intelligence. This account is based on the statement by Nowak-Jeziorański, provided to the British (MI19)[41] on 29 December 1943.

Cavendish-Bentinck knew Poland and the Poles well: his diplomatic career began as Third Secretary of the British Legation in Warsaw in 1919, and ended in Warsaw in February 1947, where he was Ambassador. Sending Nowak-Jeziorański's testimony to Cadogan, Cavendish-Bentinck wrote on 6 January 1944 as follows:

> As a matter of principle, I try not to burden you with such reports from foreigners arriving in this country from enemy or occupied countries On this occasion I think that the accompanying report is worthy of your attention. This official [Jan Nowak-Jeziorański – J.C.] is not a Jew [underlined in the original – J.C.], but an intelligent, middle-class Pole. He escaped from Poland via Gdynia, smuggled in the coalbunker of a Swedish ship [...]. I am aware that the Poles consider this report to be very interesting, but they find it difficult to believe that the number of murdered Jews is as stated [...]. This Pole stated that when he was travelling through Gdynia on 1st November [1943 – J.C.] he noticed that the 'Admiral Hipper', 'Gneisenau' and 'Cup Arkona' were there at the time. The 'Prinz Eugen', was also there, though it cannot be differentiated from 'Admiral Hipper' at first glance.[42]

The part of Nowak-Jeziorański's statement concerning the German warships convinced Cavendish-Bentinck that the Home Army GHQ emissary's report was worthy of being sent to Cadogan, the FO Permanent Under-secretary.

The remainder of the document, and its implications, were deeply worrying. It demonstrated beyond any doubt that the reports on the persecution and genocide of the Jews from Axis countries and from German-occupied Europe were in the main completely ignored by the chiefs of the British Intelligence, especially if they came from Jewish or Polish sources, and that in consequence such reports were not reaching the British decision-makers. On the contrary, they were considered to be exaggerated, they were destroyed. Cavendish-Bentinck, the co-ordinator of British Intelligence, was of the opinion that Polish, and especially Jewish, reports on the German atrocities, were not credible. In August 1943 Cavendish-Bentinck stated that the Poles, and even more so the Jews, exaggerated the German atrocities, and did so to 'to stiffen our resolve'.[43]

After the war Cavendish-Bentinck, by then Duke of Portland, admitted
that this lack of faith in the Polish and Jewish reports on the atrocities was
a mistake. Another high-ranking Foreign Office official, Roger Allen, who
worked closely with Cavendish-Bentinck during the war, also had little
trust in the reports from Poland. In particular he refused to believe that the
Germans used gas chambers in Poland to murder people. At the end of
August 1943, Allen said that he 'could never understand what the
advantage of a gas chamber over a simple machine gun or over starving
people [to death – J.C.] would be'. He added that the recurring mentions
of gas chambers in various reports were very general and tended to come
from Jewish sources.[44]

It may be worth stating that, as Chairman of the Joint Intelligence
Committee and thanks to Enigma, Cavendish-Bentinck had access to the
decrypted German police and SS reports, which also mentioned the
persecution and genocide of the Jews on the territories held by the
Germans. This was a clear validation of Polish and Jewish information. It
is therefore clear that Cavendish-Bentinck was more interested in military
intelligence on the German Navy than in the fate of dying Polish Jews,
whose genocide was also described in Nowak-Jeziorański's report. As was
the case with his political master, Anthony Eden, who as Foreign Secretary
was politically responsible for SIS, Cavendish-Bentinck believed that only
the swiftest possible end to the war could save the Jews of occupied
Europe from complete annihilation.

The fate and the tragedy of Polish Jewry occupied the principal place
in Nowak-Jeziorański's report – though neither his name nor codename
was revealed. The emissary was described as 'a Polish official born on 15
May 1913, who left Poland on 1 November 1943 and reached Great Britain
via Stockholm on 10 December 1943'. It was also stated that he 'worked
for the Warsaw municipality in the office dealing with the real estate of
absentee owners. His particular task was the management of property
owned by Jewish citizens'. This confirmed that emissary was the famous
courier from Warsaw, Jan Nowak-Jeziorański.[45] His account of the Jewish
matters was very detailed and its impact horrifying:

> Ghetto. 23. Informant [Jan Nowak-Jeziorański – J.C.] confirmed the
> news that the Germans used troops, tanks and artillery to liquidate the
> ghetto in Warsaw. The informant showed photographs of buildings
> destroyed by the Germans during this 'battle' [the quotation marks as
> in the original – J.C.].
> 24. Some 40,000 Jews killed at this time. Only a few have survived,
> hiding in cellars, sewers etc.
> 25. Captured Jews, those who managed to survive, were taken to
> 'Transferstelle' at Żelazna Street 109(?), where they were tortured to
> make them tell where other hiding places might be, and then killed.
> 26. The centre of the ghetto was made into barracks capable of
> housing 10,000 and a gas chamber was placed there. The gas chamber
> is currently not in use and is empty.

Concentration Camps

27. The informant provided the following list of concentration camps in the Generalgouvernement:

a/ Bełżec

Treblinka

Sobibór: all are death camps, that is places where people are exterminated

b/ Majdanek, Oświęcim – the largest camp holds 50,000 people

c/ Wilno – 12,000 people (men, women, children), currently being liquidated

d/ Białystok 20,000 people (men, women, children)

e/ Poniatowa near Lublin

f/ Trawniki with 14,000 people in one camp and 8,000 in the other. It is uncertain which is which; these are reserved for workers only

g/ Lublin (four camps), 500 workers

h/ Kraśnik 4,000 workers

i/ Bodzentyn 1,000 workers

j/ Kraków Płaszów 8,000 workers (now under liquidation)

k/ Bochnia 8,000 workers (now under liquidation)

l/ Tarnów 5,000 reserved for tailors making military uniforms

m/ Dąbrowa and Będzin (in Wadowice) 5,000 people.

28. In addition there are special camps:

a/ Częstochowa 1,000 people sewing furs

b/ Łódź 35,000 Jews transported from other places

29. The children of Jews brought to Łódź are being murdered by injection immediately following birth.

Jewish Population

30. Before the war, the Jewish community in Poland had 3.5 million people. The informant calculates that by 1 August 1943, the total number of Jews remaining in Poland was some 200,000, including 10,000 in hiding in Warsaw.

31. In addition to those survivors, there were also the Jews who were in hiding and those who had Polish papers. The estimated numbers of those were:

in Warsaw	15,000
in southern Poland	25,000
in the remainder of Poland	90,000
Total	130,000.[46]

Jan Nowak-Jeziorański stressed that some 3,300,000 Polish Jews were murdered by the Germans between the beginning of the war and until 1 August 1943. He also provided the British with terrifying examples of German atrocities against the Jews and the Poles.

43. In Warsaw a Jewish lady sought shelter in an entrance to an apartment block to breast-feed her baby. She apparently did not see the two German policemen marching in step along the pavement. On

noticing the lady, one grabbed her by her neck and the other shot her on the spot, though [...] she begged them to spare her on her knees. The child fell from her grasp and loudly landed on the pavement. The baby was shot, too. The two Germans left, unperturbed and quietly conversing, as if nothing happened.

44. One afternoon in July [19]43 the informant saw how two German civilians stopped a woman and a boy at the corner of Nowy Świat and Warecka Street in Warsaw. The captives were taken to the 5th floor of the building at Warecka, number 8 or 9, and were forced to jump out of the window. The boy jumped first, but did not suffer any serious injuries, having landed on another boy who was passing by. The woman was killed. A Bible was found on her body – it transpired that she was not Jewish. The Polish police took the boy to the police station at Szpitalna Street. They were ordered by the Gestapo to kill him instantly. The Polish policemen refused. The Gestapo took him to Transferstelle where he was murdered.[47]

It is difficult to ascertain what impact such examples of German behaviour made on the high-ranking British officials. Nowak-Jeziorański said that all his 'comments' and suggestions were removed from his account, but all the information was faithfully reproduced. The courier from Warsaw told his British interlocutors, including Foreign Secretary Eden, that there were actions that could be taken to intervene on behalf of 'the dying remnants of Polish Jewry', for example by bombing the rail tracks leading to Auschwitz. The response he received was that this was no time for gestures, that the repairs to the damaged tracks would take the Germans just several hours, that the losses in air crew and planes might be large, and than only a swift end to the war might save the Jews. Nowak-Jeziorański is still bewildered by the length of the period his account was kept classified and secret. He believes that the reason might be that

> ... the UK and US officialdom for a long time preferred to pretend that they were not aware of the scale of the Holocaust. This is why in all the internal reports based on the testimony of Jan Karski, and a year later based on my account, the information provided by us on the genocide of the Jews was removed. The Allies were afraid that the Jewish diaspora would demand that operations be mounted which were not justified from a strictly military point of view. So, for example, when I read the minutes of the War Cabinet deliberations concerning the testimony of Jan Karski, all the references to the Jews were deleted from his account. But Karski stated clearly that the genocide of the Jews was one of two principal topics in his testimony. Similarly, when Eden wrote to Churchill on the subject of my account, he removed everything which pertained to the Jews.[48]

The account of Nowak-Jeziorański survived – but it did not reach the principal leaders of the Allies, Churchill and Roosevelt. The attitude of the higher echelons of the Foreign Office to the Polish reports on the German persecution of the Jews, or more precisely of Polish citizens of Jewish origin, was somewhat cynical. In December 1942 Frank K. Roberts, who between 1937 and 1945 dealt with Polish affairs, wrote: 'The Polish Government always gladly used every opportunity [...] to demonstrate that it is not anti-Semitic'. Roberts added: 'it is certain that there is persecution, but we have no reliable evidence for this'. In addition we cannot be certain 'whether all of the world Jewry wishes us to publicly draw attention to what is happening'. Roberts also stressed that this was not the best time to irritate Hitler more than was necessary, especially as far as Jewish affairs were concerned.[49]

Notes

1 *Armia Krajowa w dokumentach 1939–1945* (*Documents on the Home Army 1939–1945*), vol. 1–6, London 1970–1989; D. Stola, *Dyplomacja polska wobec zagłady Żydów* (*Polish Diplomacy and the Genocide of the Jews*) [in:] *Historia dyplomacji polskiej* (*History of Polish Diplomacy*), vol. 5, 1939–1945 (ed. by W. Michowicz), Warsaw 1999.

2 His real name was Jan Kozielewski.

3 Rada Pomocy Żydom (The Council for the Assistance to the Jews, [RPZ] 'Żegota' was set up in 1942 as a body subordinated to the Office of the Government Plenipotentiary for Poland. It replaced the earlier Konrad Żegota (this was a fictional character) Temporary Committee for the Assistance to the Jews, established on the initiative of the well-known writer, Zofia Kossak-Szczucka. 'Żegota' provided shelter, documents and financial assistance to Jews in hiding. Both Polish and Jewish political parties participated in its work. It had had branches in Kraków and Lwów since 1943. 'Żegota' was the only such organisation throughout occupied Europe and was financed mainly by the Office of the Government Plenipotentiary for Poland. For more, see: K. Iranek-Osmecki, *He who saves one life*, New York 1971, p. 50 and following, and T. Prekerowa, *Konspiracyjna Rada Pomocy Żydom w Warszawie 1942–45* (*The Underground Council for the Assistance to the Jews in Warsaw, 1942–1945*), Warsaw 1982.

4 K. Iranek-Osmecki, *He who saves*, op. cit., p. 170, and W. Laequer, *The Terrible Secret*, London 1980; J. Karski, *Story of a Secret State*, Boston 1944; S. Korboński, *The Polish Underground State*, New York 1978, pp. 120–140.

5 This was Karski's third journey as a courier to the Polish Government-in-Exile. The first took place in January 1940, when the Government was in Angers, in France; the second in early June 1940. Karski was arrested and tortured by the Gestapo in Slovakia, en route to Hungary. Being a courier, Karski was a depository of a number of Resistance secrets. Afraid that he might talk, Karski attempted suicide in prison. His life was, however, saved, and Karski was transported to the prison in Nowy Sącz, from where the Home Army managed to free him. For details see: J. Karski, *Story*, op. cit., pp. 135–190; E.T. Wood, S. Jankowski, *Karski, How one man tried to stop the Holocaust*, New York 1994, pp. 73–90; T. Bór-Komorowski, *Armia podziemna* (*Underground Army*), London 1950, pp. 46–47.

6 E.T. Wood, S. Jankowski, *Karski*, op. cit., p. 117.

7 M. Gilbert, *Auschwitz and the Allies: How the Allies responded to the News of Hitler's Final Solution*, London 1981, p. 52 and following.

8 J. Karski, *Story*, pp. 321–322.

9 Ibid., p. 326.

10 Ibid., p. 323.

11 Ibid., pp. 325–326.

12 Ibid., pp. 327–328.

13 Ibid., pp. 327–328.

14 Ibid., pp. 327–328.

15 More in: E.T. Wood, S. Jankowski, *Karski*, pp. 128–129.

16 Ibid., p. 234 and following.

17 In south-west London.

18 More on Karski's stay at the Royal Victoria Patriotic School in PRO,FO, 371/32231.

19 This first report delivered by Karski on his arrival in Great Britain can probably be found in the War Office papers, in folder WO208/3689 – Royal Victoria Patriotic School, November 1942. Unfortunately, this particular folder is closed until 2018. E.T. Wood, S. Jankowski, *Karski*, p. 143. The WO 208/3689 folder, at present in TNA (PRO), regretfully does not contain Jan Karski's narrative.

20 L.dz. 3735/Ti/42, 3.8.3.11/50, SPP. Chief of the VI Bureau, PGS, to the Home Army Commander-in-Chief, 17th November 1942.

21 This report was used by *Karski* when he wrote his *Story of a Secret State.*

22 TNA (PRO), FO 371/3092, News is reaching the Polish Government.

23 E.T. Wood, S. Jankowski, *Karski*, op. cit., p. 168 and following. The first Eden-Karski meeting took place on 4 February 1943. At the second, on the 17, Eden interrogated Karski on the attitudes of the leaders of Polish Resistance to the possible territorial concessions towards Moscow, which were demanded by Stalin and encouraged by the British Government. Ibid., pp. 169–170; E.T. Wood, S. Jankowski, *Karski*, op. cit., p. 170; also J. Ciechanowski, *The Warsaw Rising of 1944*, Cambridge 1974, p. 169.

24 Ibid., p. 152.

25 Ibid.

26 E.T. Wood, S. Jankowski, *Karski*, p. 168.

27 Ibid., p. 169.

28 TNA (PRO), FO 371/34550 (E1943/34/c). Memo, A. Eden to War Cabinet, 17 February 1943. This memo contains a single mention of the Jews, quoted in the text above.

29 E.T. Wood, S. Jankowski, *Karski*, op. cit., p. 171.

30 Ibid.

31 Ibid., pp. 171–172.

32 More in, for example: K. Iranek-Osmecki, *He who saves*, op. cit., p. 179 and following; J. Ciechanowski, *Defeat in Victory*, London 1948, p. 191 and following; W. Laquer, *The Terrible*, op. cit., pp. 101–122, 219–238; R. Breitman, *Official Secret*, London 2000, pp. 100, 116, 118–9, 140, 153–4, 207; M. Gilbert, *Auschwitz*, op. cit.; B. Wasserstein, *Britain and the Jews of Europe 1939–1945*, Oxford 1988; D.S. Wyman, *Pozostawieni swojemu losowi. Ameryka wobec Holocaustu* (*Left to Their Own Fate: America and the Holocaust*) 1941–1945, Warsaw 1994.

33 E.T. Wood, S. Jankowski, *Karski*, p. 186 and following, and J. Ciechanowski, *Defeat*, op. cit., p. 192.

34 E.T. Wood, S. Jankowski, *Karski*, p. 188.

35 Ibid.

36 Ibid. (for Karski this must have been a very heavy blow, especially since it was completely unjustified).

37 Roosevelt must have been aware that Polish Intelligence networks operating in the Third Reich and in countries occupied by the Germans were largely reliant on Polish forced labourers.

38 E.T. Wood, S. Jankowski, *Karski*, p. 199, and J. Ciechanowski, *Defeat*, op. cit., p. 194 and following.

39 J. Ciechanowski, *Defeat*, op. cit., p. 195 and following.

40 W. Laquer, *The Terrible*, pp. 232–235.

41 MI19 was a part of Military Intelligence. Its task was to gather information from

new arrivals from German-occupied Europe. TNA (PRO), FO 371/39449.
42 TNA (PRO), V. Cavendish-Bentinck to Sir Alexander Cadogan, 6 January 1944. TFO 371/39449.
43 TNA (PRO), FO, 1371/34551.
44 TNA (PRO), FO, 371/34551
45 For details of his trip to Stockholm and hence to London in 1943, see: J. Nowak-Jeziorański, *Kurier z Warszawy* (*Courier from Warsaw*), London 1978, p. 178 and following.
46 Jan Nowak-Jeziorański's account provided to MI19, 1936, 29 November 1943. TNA (PRO), FO 371/39449.
47 Ibid.
48 A letter by J. Nowak-Jeziorański to A. Suchcitz, 28 August 2001, a copy of which is in the hands of the author.
49 M. Gilbert, Auschwitz, op. cit., p. 96.

57
Summary

Daria Nałęcz

Together, the Polish and British historians undertook a very difficult task: to reconstruct the activities of Polish Intelligence Services in World War II, their co-operation with the Allies, in particular with the British, and to determine the influence of this activity on the outcome of the war. The Polish part of the Committee was also full of hope to find the documents passed on by Polish Intelligence to SIS between 1940–1945. These hopes, however, were dashed. Hence the task required the unification of source material dispersed throughout the archives of many countries. We needed to reach archival material hitherto unknown to historians and to incorporate the knowledge so far available only locally into the international academic thinking. This collective task produced some unexpectedly interesting results. We have managed not only to re-create the general picture of the work of individual networks and the central intelligence structures, but also to describe the activities of specific intelligence stations and cells, including some on which the literature available to date remained altogether, or mainly, silent – for example, those in the Americas, in the Iberian Peninsula or in Switzerland.

The conquest of Polish territory by the German and Soviet armies, the large-scale human losses resulting from the hostilities, the emigration of the principal organs of the State first to Romania, later to France and finally to Great Britain, the significant political changes among the ruling élites – all these factors provided significant challenges for the intelligence services. As luck would have it, the intelligence apparatus was not completely destroyed, though during the war it was those not connected to it before who played the most important part in intelligence gathering. Luckily, the organizational structures and a part of their professional personnel had managed to survive. This made it easier to re-create and enlarge the intelligence networks attuned to new tasks required of them by both Polish and Allied authorities. From the very beginning the Allies realized the role which Polish Intelligence and cryptographers could play – and the latter were among the first to be evacuated from Romania to France. In return for this contribution, the Polish side was expecting political benefits, first of all in the reconstruction of their independent state.

Throughout the hostilities Polish Intelligence was not centralised into a single structure. In addition to the units working to the PGS, the Ministries of Internal Affairs and National Defence had their own intelligence organisations. Acting upon a request from SIS, worried by the multiplicity of structures and of information channels, the means of communication with the Allies were unified. the II Bureau of the PGS[1] became the only official intermediary in the exchanges of reports and information. Unlike on other territories, the II Bureau did not have its own network in occupied Poland, which was the exclusive province of the structures working for the Home Army GHQ. But these structures, too, were subject to the II Bureau authority, though it was the VI Bureau of the PGS which was mainly responsible for their mutual contacts. the II Bureau's own network of stations and cells was systematically broadened, which was not always synonymous with numerical growth. The number of stations in existence reflected both current needs in terms of obtaining information and the ability of the station in a given territory and at a specific moment in time. At its wartime peak, in May 1944, there were 8 stations, 2 independent intelligence cells and 33 intelligence cells. This total included 2 stations and 8 cells located in enemy territory. The others were placed in neutral and allied countries. This structure was supplemented by the radio monitoring service, the Intelligence School, the A and B Liaison Missions attached to the British Supreme Command (War Office) and by 29 offices of military, air and naval attachés. These intelligence resources covered all of Europe, North and South America, Near, Far and Middle East, North Africa. Regular reports were received from Poland, Germany, Austria, Czechoslovakia, France, Belgium, Spain, Holland, Portugal, Romania, Sweden, Switzerland, Hungary, and occupied parts of the USSR and from both Americas. The 'Polish specialty', that is the territories where no other alternative allied intelligence networks were active, was, apart from Poland, Germany, Zaolzie (the territory immediately beyond the Olza river on the Polish-Czechoslovak border), Austria and the occupied parts of the USSR. The Polish intelligence-gathering, like the British one, was among the few active also beyond their own national territory.

It is much more difficult to assess the numerical strength of the Polish intelligence effort. This is due primarily to the requirements of operational security, which meant that no complete lists were made. In addition allowances would have to be made for frequent exchanges of personnel, to differentiate between occasional and permanent agents and informants not listed in any registers and of co-operation with the armed underground. Every underground soldier (and the structures of the Home Army alone consisted of approximately 350,000 persons) was obliged to pass on to his/her superiors all information concerning the occupiers. Each of them moved in some family, friendship and employment circles –

therefore the number of potential informants would have probably been even larger. In practice, however, not all had access to interesting information and not everybody had the right psychological predispositions. On the basis of partial lists, which still exist, it is possible to say that within the territory occupied by the Germans each of the local, district intelligence networks had some 100 permanent agents.[2] In the active and well-organised Kielce-Radom District, in 1944 the network consisted of some 2,000 persons, of whom 750 were women.[3] On this basis it is possible to assume that altogether the number of people co-operating with intelligence within all the local, district networks of the Home Army was some dozen times higher. This is merely an approximation, possibly requiring a revision downwards due to the low qualifications on the part of local personnel, and upwards because of co-operation with the civilian resistance structures working for the Office of the Government Delegate for the Homeland.[4] The size of the networks active outside Poland varied. The most numerous was created in France, where over 2,500 people co-operated with the F II structures. 739 of these can be considered to have been permanent agents. Other networks tended to be smaller. The number of agents working with the Vienna station was estimated at 600. The one in Hamburg had some 100. Whilst it is not possible to provide precise numbers of agents, it is worth stressing that not all were of equal value. On the other hand there are suggestions concerning unpaid informants whose input into the collection of interesting information has been greater than that of whole networks.

The number of submitted reports and their assessment by the Allies might be a better indication of quality of information than sheer numbers of agents. In 1944 alone Polish intelligence provided the British with 37,894 reports, the Americans with 12,068, the French with 793. Radio (signals) intelligence received 29,510 coded reports and managed to decipher 13,047. According to British ranking 25% of reports were assessed as of very high quality, 60% of high quality, 12% were considered valuable, 2% of little value and 1% of no value.[5] Altogether it is estimated that throughout the war Polish stations provided the British with some 80,000 reports.

The roots of the co-operation of Polish intelligence with its British and French counterparts can be traced to the pre-war years, and it became much more lively in the period immediately preceding the outbreak of hostilities. The British Military Mission arrived in Poland. The Western Allies were especially interested in the work of Polish cryptanalysts. In addition the British, wisely anticipating future developments, had high expectations concerning the information gathered by Polish agents on Soviet and German territory. The other ally, the US, emerged only during the war and contacts with the Americans strengthened and became regular following the signing of the agreement in 1941.

The principal financial burden of maintaining the Polish intelligence effort fell upon the British government. The sums allocated to specific tasks demonstrate its interests and preferences. Most resources were provided to the II Bureau of the Home Army GHQ, responsible for the provision of information from the Eastern Front and areas to its rear and from the USSR and the Third Reich. This was the source of the main reports warning about the German attack on the Soviets. As early as autumn of 1939 there were signals on the repairs to roads and bridges leading east. From spring of 1940 there were reports on fortification works and from the autumn of the same year, on the improvements to air bases and landing strips to the west of the Vistula, on the gradual build-up of Luftwaffe staff and the communications and technical personnel reinforcements. From May 1941 there were further reports on the movement of large military units from the West and from the Balkans. The composition of Panzer, Luftwaffe and quartermaster transports was provided. Since all lines of communication were under close observation, precise knowledge in this regard could be obtained. Full use was made of the fact that nine main railway lines, which carried some 75–80% of all transports, crossed Polish territory. An analysis of information obtained, especially on where these transports were off-loaded and on the areas of troop concentration, provided an indication of offensive directions. Following 22 June 1941, when the USSR joined the states at war with the Third Reich, such knowledge proved to be very useful and was the only means to verify the information obtained from the British cryptography centre at Bletchley Park. It became the basis on which the correct assessment was made as to the direction of the German summer offensive in 1942 upon the Southern part of the Eastern Front (and not on Moscow, which was what was really anticipated) and of the further direction of the Eastern campaign, including the halt of the attack on Leningrad and the defeat of Gen. Friedrich von Paulus at Stalingrad. The Allies passed this information to the Soviet General Staff. Subsequent intelligence on the developments in the East was of significant importance for the decisions concerning the Western Front, and in particular on the planned invasion of France. The developments in the East were also monitored by the stations in Scandinavia, in the Baltic States, in Hungary and Romania and in Yugoslavia and Turkey.

The establishment of the network in North Africa had a significant impact on the developments at the front. This was the only Allied network in the region. The intelligence gathered by this network helped in carrying out Operation 'Torch', the landings in Africa, and to minimise human losses. Maj. Słowikowski, who ran the network, received high British and American decorations for their achievements.

The North African network was built up on the basis of personnel of the earliest network, F, operating in France. This was not only the first, but also the longest-lasting Polish intelligence network operating during the war. Its successes impacted on the conduct of operations in Africa and in Western Europe. It is this network which provided the warning about the attack on France, Belgium and Luxembourg; it predicted the German intention to by-pass the Maginot Line. Later this network provided reports on the German army supplies coming from French ports. It also provided the information on the disposition of the German army in France and the

German coastal fortifications in Normandy, Brittany, in the Calais region and further inland. Cells linked to this network worked in Belgium, Holland, Luxembourg and Northern Italy. In March of 1943 a map of German defensive lines in Holland, Belgium and France was prepared. Capt. Roman Czerniawski, who originally co-operated with this network, found himself in German hands. After moving to England, he became one of the most important pillars of the Double Cross system, used to misinform the enemy. Thanks to him, the Germans were initially misled as to the accuracy of V-1 and V-2 weapons, and later made the wrong assumptions concerning the location and timing of Allied landings in France.

In accordance with British suggestions, the II Bureau broadened the scope of information supplied to include naval and air intelligence. The most penetrated area of activity of Polish networks, pre-dating the war, was the Baltic region, and in particular the surveillance of sea transport between Germany and the USSR. Responding to wartime requirements, the II Bureau had built up its station in Stockholm, which also ran cells in Lithuania, Latvia, Estonia and Denmark. It also placed its agents in the ports on the North Sea, the Mediterranean and the Atlantic. In all, 17 ports were put under surveillance. All the networks were involved in fulfilling naval intelligence tasks. They observed the movements of ships-of-the-line and other warships. The information gathered helped to sink the 'Bismarck'; warnings were given concerning the preparations for the German invasion of Norway. These reports, especially on the strength of Kriegsmarine, distribution of warships and their sea readiness and cargoes, were useful during the Battle of the Atlantic. Especially important, and not only in this particular period, was information concerning U-boats: on their production, maintenance, equipment, construction changes, the positioning of fuel stores and spare parts. Information on the location of anti-aircraft batteries was also collected to increase the effectiveness of aerial bombardment.

Air intelligence concentrated on information on aerial production: of complete planes, their sub-assemblies and individual parts, on the design characteristics and especially prototypes and on instruction manuals. Information on co-production was also gathered. Monthly statements of air production of individual manufacturers were prepared and aircraft maintenance was monitored. Plans and drawings of specific factories were supplied, as were data on the positioning and camouflage of anti-aircraft batteries – to facilitate precision attacks on these objectives. Similar information was provided on the descriptions and location of aircraft bases. Stores, and in time also the scope of savings introduced and raw material shortages were also of interest to Intelligence. Information on bases, transport and fuel supplies, on distribution and identification of Luftwaffe units was collected. The collection of information on the effectiveness of aerial bombardment was of importance.

One of the Maj. successes of Intelligence was the gathering of information on the construction of V-1 and V-2 weapons and on the location of their research centres and production facilities, as well as on their launching pads. The German high command was hoping that these weapons would determine the fate of the war. V-2's were to subjugate Great Britain. Station Lombard first encountered a trace of the Peenemünde research facility towards the end of 1942. The first technical data were conveyed to the British and the Americans in December of the same year. In March 1943 the Peenemünde facility was penetrated in detail. The information dispatched on this helped in making the decision to obliterate this facility. Aerial bombardment, though it did not destroy all the targets, was sufficiently successful to make the Germans move the testing range to Blizna near Tarnów. All the trials held there were observed by Home Army's Intelligence. This permitted the collection of important rocket sub-assemblies, which were not destroyed on impact. Their descriptions reached London first – and in July 1944 the British decided to transport the parts to Britain.

The information on V-weapons was not the only special success in terms of gathering intelligence on new weaponry, though undoubtedly it belongs to those achievements which helped to decide the conduct of the war. An important role, though with less direct consequences, was played by the technical data on the new Panther tank, on the miniature submarines, on anti-aircraft guns produced in Stalowa Wola and on new battlefield gasses.

One success, the impact of which on the outcome of the Second World War cannot be overestimated, was the deciphering of the German encoding system by three mathematicians and cryptographers. Marian Rejewski, Henryk Zygalski and Jerzy Różycki, from 1932 employed by the Cipher Section of the Polish Intelligence, managed to break the German 'Enigma' coding system and reconstructed the machine used in the process as well as the coding process. Not long before the outbreak of hostilities Polish Intelligence supplied their Western allies with both the machine and the decoding methodology, which enabled the allies to intercept a large proportion of German orders. The secrecy surrounding the possession of this secret weapon was preserved throughout the war, which determined its great potency. The deciphering of the Enigma codes was the most significant Polish contribution in the struggle against the Third Reich.

Polish Intelligence collected information concerning many areas, from the organisational structure of German military units and their staffing to the names of commanding officers. Gathering data on war transports, regrouping and various forms of military preparations, it was able to predict the areas or directions of some planned military operations. The identification of German military units was very often carried out at the request of the British allies. According to American sources, as early as in 1941 Polish II Bureau supplied documents precisely describing the total structure of German land and air forces.[6] It later re-created and regularly updated the German order of battle on the Eastern front. The value of information on the effectiveness of aerial bombardment increased when the Allies took the decision to bomb targets inside Germany, and the number of reports containing such data increased systematically.

This information was supplemented with data from industrial and economic intelligence, concerned with both in the production potential of plants working for the Third Reich and the products themselves: their characteristics, technology and the innovations being introduced. The agents obtained their information and materials mainly from persons employed in various plants and factories. Original German documents were also obtained, including technical plans and reports. This is how information was obtained on steel, oil, rubber and leather industries. In most cases the agents themselves provided drawings and situation plans. Since production capacity was dependent on the supply of raw materials, the co-production and supply systems in factories, as well as various changes and movements, were under observation. For obvious reasons most attention was paid to production and purchases of armaments. Where a particular product did not originate in any factory subjugated to the Germans, attempts were made to identify its origin and to obtain its technical specification. This was done, for example, in the case of weapons purchases made in Switzerland.

Knowledge about the political and social life, and in particular about the morale and mood in the armed forces and among the civilian population was an important constituent of wartime intelligence. The British and the Americans collected such information primarily through interrogating prisoners of war and refugees from occupied territories. Polish Intelligence was the only one to conduct daily observations near the battlefronts. As other organizations, it, too, monitored the private correspondence of soldiers. So many reports were prepared on this basis that to this day within the set entitled 'Morale' and kept at NARA, more than half are from Polish sources.

The most untypical role among all the agents of Polish intelligence was played by Lt-Col. Jan Kowalewski, active in Lisbon from 1941 to 1944. With the permission of the Prime Minister, he remained in contact with the highest diplomatic circles of Italy, Hungary and Romania, attempting to influence the reversal of alliances and persuading them to join the Allied side. Had he been successful, the war might well have been shortened. There were numerous indications that his interlocutors were prepared to begin negotiations with their hitherto enemies. The Allies, as was the case with the anti-Hitler opposition within the Third Reich, did not wish to enter into any complicated deals. Unconditional surrender was required. In these circumstances Kowalewski's mission lost any sense.

The reports prepared by Polish Intelligence grosso modo and through the office of Cmdr. Dunderdale were reaching the proper recipients within the British intelligence and Service departments. Subject to assessment and analysis, which led to many supplementary questions, such reports then played their role in the war-time Allied decision-making. Thus Polish Intelligence, with Polish soldiers fighting side-by-side with their Allies and with Polish resistance units fighting in occupied territories, became one of the three important factors impacting on the fate of the war. Their skill and their sometimes unprecedented heroism would not have been sufficient were they not to be accompanied by military and financial might. In war, the alliance with Great Britain proved to be of mutual benefit. British armed forces needed intelligence information to meet their military objectives. Polish intelligence proved equal to the task – but without its own resources needed financial and technical support. The principles of co-operation between the two were defined in an agreement, and the ebb and flow of war together with the need to fulfill specific tasks influenced the practicalities of its operation. Under these pressures new intelligence networks were established in places and in areas not previously covered by the II Bureau. The map of interdependencies between the war requirements and the efforts invested by territorial stations and networks was determined by the system of requests and questionnaires aimed at specific addressees. Full co-operation was also achieved in the field of counter-intelligence and in relation to sabotage and diversion. The purpose was common and fundamental: the defeat of the enemy, as swiftly as possible. The realization of this purpose extracted far heavier a toll, in victims, damages, resources and time, than originally expected. After more than five years the purpose was achieved – though victory in war did not bring victory in peace for all, and particularly not for the Poles.

Notes

1   IPMS, A.XII.24/46, Report of the Chief of the II Bureau to the Chief of Staff at Polish General Headquarters, 27 September 1940; ibidem, Official aide-memoire on the conference of 1 October 1940
2   P.M. Lisiewicz, *Bezimienni. Z dziejów wywiadu Armii Krajowej* (*Anonymous. A Partial History of the Home Army Intelligence*), Warsaw 1987, pp. 61–61
3   A. Ropelewski, *W służbie wywiadu Polski Walczącej* (*In the Service of Fighting Poland's Intelligence*), Gdańsk 1994, p. 39
4   W. Grabowski, *Delegatura Rządu Rzeczypospolitej Polskiej na Kraj 1940–1945* (*Office of the Government Delegate for the Homeland 1940–1945*), Warsaw 1995, p. 39 and other.
5   IPMS, A.XII.24/37, Sprawozdanie z pracy Wydziału Wywiadowczego za rok 1944 (Report on the Work of the Intelligence Department for 1944)
6   NARA, RG 165, MID Germany, Box 1202, file 6170, German Army Composition of Army Units, Army Headquarters, March 1941, pp. 1–36

58
Summary

Gill Bennett

The task of the British historians working on the Anglo-Polish Historical Committee was to search for information concerning the Polish contribution to Allied victory in the Second World War in the closed archives of the British Intelligence Agencies. The principal source was the archive of the Secret Intelligence Service (SIS, sometimes known as MI6), since SIS, as the agency concerned with foreign intelligence, was most closely involved with the wartime Polish Intelligence Services. The Committee had unprecedented access to SIS records, which are not released into the public domain, through the Chief Historian of the Foreign & Commonwealth Office.

The other sections of British Intelligence most closely involved with Polish wartime Intelligence were: the Government Code and Cypher School, (GC&CS, later Government Communications Headquarters, GCHQ), concerned with British and foreign cypher communications; the Radio Security Service (RSS), the intercept service involved in liaison with Polish cryptologists; and the Special Operations Executive (SOE), responsible for sabotage activities overseas. The majority of the relevant records originating in these agencies, and in Britain's domestic security agency, the Security Service (MI5), were already in the public domain, and some have been made public during the course of the Committee's work.

Much information on Polish wartime Intelligence and its contribution to the Allied war effort is contained in the official history by F.H. Hinsley et al, *British Intelligence in the Second World War*, published in five volumes between 1979 and 1990. This comprehensive work is based on British Intelligence records and there was inevitably some overlap with the research being carried out under the auspices of the Anglo-Polish Historical Committee. Nevertheless, the information contained in the British contribution to Parts IV, V, VI and VII of the joint Report is based almost entirely on material that is not available in the public domain.

On the outbreak of war in 1939 a close relationship already existed between British and Polish Intelligence. Before the invasion of Poland SIS worked closely with the Polish authorities on the German and Soviet order of battle, and although the defeat of Poland led to a temporary interruption in this liaison, close contact was soon established when the Polish General Staff was established in France. Although the French II Bureau wished all liaison between SIS and the Poles to pass through their channels, the Polish General Staff maintained an independent link with London and a close relationship was established between Cmdr. Dunderdale, then in Paris, and Col. Gano, the officer responsible within the Polish II Bureau for clandestine activities.

After the fall of France the Polish authorities were forced to escape again, though a number of Polish Intelligence operatives remained in France and were to set up effective networks and channels of communication. Gen. Sikorski and what became known as the Polish Government in Exile were established with full British support in the United Kingdom, and were unique among the governments in exile in being permitted to maintain and run their Intelligence services independently, including receiving and despatching wireless communications, and maintaining their own communications base and training establishment. However, SIS provided funds, supplies and logistical support, and in return the Poles agreed that all information received through clandestine sources which did not directly affect internal Polish affairs should be passed to the British authorities.

This arrangement was complicated by the existence of a number of different and sometimes competing Polish agencies involved with clandestine Intelligence. In August 1940, an SIS minute listed five different Intelligence Services thought to be maintained by the Polish Government in London: a Foreign Office service under the Polish Foreign Minister; a political bureau under Professor Kot, working directly to Gen. Sikorski; a military Intelligence service, in touch with the War Office; a naval security service, in direct touch with the Admiralty; and a further organisation run by the Polish General Staff. If, as information from Polish sources indicated, some of these agencies were not always sure what the others were doing, it was even more difficult for British Intelligence to be sure that they were receiving all relevant information.

The situation was made more complex with the establishment in the summer of 1940 of the Special Operations Executive (SOE) with whom the Polish Intelligence authorities also had close relations and from whom they sought facilities and equipment. In September 1940, in an attempt to cut through the confusion, Maj. Desmond Morton, the Prime Minister's Intelligence adviser, arranged a meeting between Brig. Stewart Menzies, chief of SIS, and Col. Mitkiewicz, the Polish Director of Military Intelligence. No formal record of this meeting has been found, but it appears from Maj. Morton's account to the Prime Minister that agreement was reached between Menzies and Mitkiewicz regarding future channels of communication between British and Polish Intelligence services.

Although liaison with the British authorities did not always run smoothly, the underlying relationship between Polish Intelligence and SIS was a strong one, and the situation improved after January 1941 with the agreement that Col. Gano should be the sole channel through which intelligence should pass to SIS, with Cmdr. Dunderdale's section known as A4 (later known as P5, then SLC), as the liaison channel in SIS. Under this regime the mutual flow of intelligence improved, and the relationship between the Polish II Bureau and SIS remained close throughout the war.

In addition to information from Polish agents in occupied Europe and elsewhere, Col. Gano passed information to SIS from Poland, originating with the Polish Underground, which was run by the VI Bureau at PGS in London. This important source included detailed reports on German deployment in Poland prior to the opening of the Russian campaign in 1941, reports on movements of troops, equipment and weapons across Poland to the Russian front, and information on the German development of V-weapons. Such reports would have been passed on urgently to interested departments such as the War Office and Foreign Office.

British and Polish Intelligence authorities also worked closely together in more technical areas. Co-operation in the field of cryptography, most notably in respect of the German ENIGMA encyphering machine, was well established before the outbreak of war. During the war the Polish cryptographers, whom SIS helped to escape from Poland to Romania and thence to France, continued to play an important part through their work in the cypher department of the French Deuxième Bureau under Col. Bertrand until 1942–3 when, again with SIS help, they escaped over the Pyrenees to the UK. In the UK, the close relationship between Polish Intelligence and the Radio Security Service (which passed from MI5 to SIS control in May 1941) ensured that Polish wireless communications to their overseas stations were both maintained and expanded.

The Polish Government in Exile was unique among its fellow exiles in continuing to operate stations and independent Posts abroad for the collection of naval and military Intelligence. In 1940 the Polish II (Intelligence) Bureau of the General Staff was divided into two main branches, naval and military, and both were closely connected with SIS. Their programmes of work, and any special instructions, were based on requirements stipulated by SIS, whose own agents were instructed to liaise with their Polish colleagues abroad where possible. Very little evidence has been found concerning these requirements, as requests for information would usually have been destroyed after the information had been received and circulated. There are, however, a few isolated examples of questionnaires or specific requests for information. For example, a report on the allocation of responsibilities in Cmdr. Dunderdale's A4 section, drawn up in August 1940, indicates areas on which SIS sought information. These included USSR military reports, Orders of Battle, reports on their aircraft industry; USSR railway, geographical and factory reports; military and geographical surveys of countries adjoining the USSR; military aerodromes in the Baltic States and occupied Poland; and details of the air forces of Bulgaria, Czechoslovakia, Austria and other countries.

There were occasional complaints about the amount or the quality of information received in London, but in general the documentation indicates an evolutionary process on both sides: as Polish stations and agents were established more widely in Europe and globally, and grew both more efficient and proficient, so SIS, while appreciating the reports they received, hoped for more detail and greater penetration. The urgency of this demand reflected, naturally enough, the progress of the war, the Axis domination of Europe, and the complex situation, providing both opportunity and threat to the Allies, created by the German invasion of the Soviet Union. As fast as Polish Intelligence came in, it was followed swiftly by greater demands. The British Prime Minister, Winston Churchill, and those directing the UK war effort were hungry for accurate information about the strength and disposition of their enemies: Polish Intelligence was more than willing to feed that hunger where it could.

Evidence in British Intelligence archives shows that Polish agents and networks spread literally throughout the world, working with British and other countries' Intelligence services, setting up courier and escape lines, using considerable resource and ingenuity to evade and frustrate the enemy, and feeding valuable information back to London. Unfortunately, very little documentation on these activities has survived in British Intelligence archives. In some cases, such as that of France and North Africa, a good picture can be built up of Polish activities: in others, such as Portugal or Turkey, it is clear that there was a great deal of Polish activity, but only tantalising glimpses can be gleaned from the archive.

The clearest and most comprehensive picture can be gained of Polish Intelligence activities in France, where many Poles had escaped after the German invasion. A Polish network, Station F2, was set up in July 1940, immediately after the fall of France, and by the end of that year, with the help of a number of French recruits, had expanded to cover most of Occupied France. Many other networks were set up, such as MARINE, operating in Marseilles and Nice, all working closely with the French: a closeness reflected in the fact that within SIS, Dunderdale's section was responsible for liaison both with the Poles and with non-Gaullist French activities. These networks were able to provide a wide range of information that was passed to SIS, on military, industrial, political and technical subjects. Although they suffered Maj. setbacks when betrayed from within or penetrated by the enemy, they were remarkably resilient and often regrouped to carry on their important work.

'Equipe 300', or 'Equipe Z', a centre of radio interception which had worked for the Polish Division of the French Army since the defeat of Poland, passed important information from its base in the Midi to London including decrypts of German and Italian Army messages. The Equipe was run by Col. Bertrand, an inspirational figure who had been chief of the French II Bureau's department of cryptography, and contrived to continue his work under the Vichy authorities, pursuing his clandestine activities tirelessly until his arrest in 1944 (from which he escaped and was rescued by SIS). With SIS help, Bertrand had facilitated the escape of Polish cryptographers, including those who had worked on ENIGMA, to France in 1939, and later to North Africa (where some joined the Polish RYGOR network), or over the Pyrenees to Spain, and, in some cases, to the UK.

Information was also found in British Intelligence archives on Polish Intelligence activities in the Iberian Peninsula and Latin America, Southern Europe and the Balkans, Northern and Central Europe, Scandinavia and the Baltic States, the Middle and Far East. Though the quantity and quality of the extant documentation varies, it paints a picture of vigorous and wide-ranging, if sometimes confused, activity on the part of both professional Polish Intelligence agents and a network of contacts and informants. The Polish practice of setting up parallel networks within a country, supposedly not aware of each other, could and did lead to difficulties, particularly for SIS who tended to form the point of contact (and financial support) for all such networks. Nevertheless, the overall picture is a positive and impressive one, enabling a great deal of valuable information to be passed to London and made use of by the British Government.

The constant inflow of reports into SIS was dealt with as swiftly as possible in order to ensure that the information reached those who needed it most as quickly as possible. Reports received from Polish Intelligence were translated, sanitised and circulated to customer departments such as the Foreign Office, War Office and Ministry of Economic Warfare. Although the majority of these reports have been destroyed, there is no doubt that they constituted a substantial and important contribution to the wartime Intelligence on which the British Government relied.

It is clear from SIS archives that a continuous process of evaluation and statistical assessment of Polish Intelligence was carried on, although very few examples of such evaluation survive. One report notes that between 1 January and 28 February 1941 more than 900 papers were received in SIS from Polish sources (including correspondence and copies of telegrams to Polish representatives abroad). Of these, over 400 were circulated to SIS Sections for passing on to other departments, the remainder consisting mainly of replies to specific enquiries, etc. The figure of 900 did not include series of telegrams from certain related sources which were circulated directly to Sections. In any case, the total for the period 1 January to 28 February 1941 exceeded by nearly 100% the number received between July and December 1940.

Over a broader period, a half-yearly progress report on the Polish II Bureau for the period January–June 1944 notes that 3,973 reports were issued on the basis of Polish information during that period, an increase of 12% over the second half of 1943. Of these 1,283 were military reports, 709 naval, 741 air, 982 economic and industrial, 150 political and 108 special material. A particular improvement was noted in the quality of Air reports, with an unsolicited testimonial from a senior official in the Ministry of Aircraft Production remarking on the 'strikingly good' service received from Polish II Bureau sources.

The assessment was not uncritical. Sometimes Polish information was criticised for being out of date – often the result of delays in the lines of communication – or for lack of precision. But the more information poured in, the more the demand grew, and Polish Intelligence sources did their best to increase the supply. When, in May 1945, Dunderdale compiled for the Prime Minister a summary statistical analysis of reports produced by his section between 3 September 1939 and 8 May 1945, the total was 45,770 reports – 22,047 of which were received from Polish sources – supplied by 1500 'British' agents (i.e. French, employed by Dunderdale), and 600 Polish agents.

In an Annex to his analysis, Cmdr. Dunderdale drew particular attention to the quality of Polish information on rocket trials in Poland, and on plants manufacturing V-weapons and components inside Germany. Information on V-weapons, enabling the Allied Command to track their manufacture and testing and to target their sites for bombing, is one of the best known areas where Polish Intelligence made a Maj. contribution to Allied victory: the other is the work of Polish crypto-graphers on breaking the ENIGMA code. Although both are covered in Hinsley's Official History and very little new information was uncovered in British Intelligence archives during the course of the Committee's work, it is clear that the Polish contribution in these areas alone would have merited the praise given by Dunderdale in his report to Churchill:

> It will thus be seen that Polish agents have worked unceasingly and well in Europe during the last five years, and that they have provided, often at great danger to themselves and to their relatives, a vast amount of material of all kinds on a wide range of subjects. The Polish IS has made an invaluable contribution to the planning and the successful execution of the invasion of France, and to the ultimate victory of the Allied forces in Europe.

59
Executive Summary

Tessa Stirling and Daria Nałęcz

The Anglo-Polish Historical Committee was charged with identifying and evaluating surviving documents which shed light on the Polish Intelligence contribution to the Allied war effort in World War II so that this vital contribution can be given its proper recognition in history. We believe that this report – the fruit of the work of the Committee over three years – fulfils that remit. It provides a fascinating and informative picture of Polish intelligence activity and Anglo-Polish co-operation that was not only highly successful but was unique among the Allies. The close relationship between the Polish and British intelligence went beyond any other collaborative operations with other countries.

This report is made up of a collection of papers by individual Polish and British historians with each paper casting light on certain aspects of intelligence work and an attempted analysis of the use to which it was put for the purposes of the realisation of wartime goals. Each of the papers is valuable and interesting in its own right and each adds to the sum of our knowledge of this aspect of our shared history. Together this collection of papers represents a real and lasting achievement.

The individual papers within each chapter of this report provide rich detail and quantitative assessments of intelligence activity and they paint a much fuller picture than has hitherto been known. They cover a wide range of aspects of Polish intelligence history during World War II as well as Anglo-Polish co-operation.

The papers written by authors of the Polish chapters in the joint report document the wide geographic range of Polish intelligence activity, not only on the immediate war front in Europe but also in North and South America and elsewhere. Together the Polish texts provide a comprehensive picture of the development structures, problems and operations of Polish intelligence. The UK papers, based on material taken from closed British Intelligence archives, complement the Polish accounts not only by adding detail to accounts of Polish operations overseas, but by describing the use made of Polish intelligence material by those directing the Allied war effort in London. The unique contribution made to that war effort by Polish Intelligence Services, dedicated to Allied use, emerges strongly from the British chapters.

This report illustrates the vital contribution that the Poles made in terms of breaking Enigma. This has long been acknowledged by historians but it is a story that is so important to the World War II effort that it must have a place of its own in this report. The same is true of the intelligence information supplied by Poles on the V-1 and V-2 weapons. But what this report also does is to highlight the volume of intelligence activity across the whole range of wartime operations. It is clear that without Polish intelligence activity and involvement, the prosecution of the war by Britain and her Allies would have been more difficult and protracted.

Index

(Does not include names in the Notes)